UNDER THE INFLUENCE

THE DISINFORMATION GUIDE TO DRUGS EDITED BY PRESTON PEET

Published by The Disinformation Company Ltd.
163 Third Avenue, Suite 108
New York, NY 10003
Tel.: +1.212.691.1605
Fax: +1.212.473.8096
www.disinfo.com

Design & Layout: Anlända

Library of Congress Control Number: 2004108002

ISBN 1-932857-00-1

Printed in USA

10 9 8 7 6 5 4 3 2 1

Distributed in the USA and Canada by:
Consortium Book Sales and Distribution
1045 Westgate Drive, Suite 90
St Paul, MN 55114
Toll Free: +1.800.283.3572
Local: +1.651.221.9035
Fax: +1.651.221.0124
www.cbsd.com

Distributed in the United Kingdom and Eire by:
Turnaround Publisher Services Ltd.
Unit 3, Olympia Trading Estate
Coburg Road
London, N22 6TZ
Tel.: +44.(0)20.8829.3000
Fax: +44.(0)20.8881.5088
www.turnaround-uk.com

Attention colleges and universities, corporations and other organizations: Quantity discounts are available on bulk purchases of this book for educational training purposes, fundraising and gift-giving. Special books, booklets, or book excerpts can also be created to fit your specific needs. For information contact Marketing Department of The Disinformation Company Ltd.

Disinformation is a registered trademark of The Disinformation Company Ltd.

The opinions and statements made in this book are those of the authors concerned. The Disinformation Company Ltd. has not verified and neither confirms nor denies any of the foregoing and no warranty or fitness is implied. The reader is encouraged to keep an open mind and to independently judge the contents.

Acknowledgments

To Vanessa Cleary, my muse for better and worse, through thick and thin. Thank you.

—Preston Peet

Thanks to Gary and Richard for their patience and faith, and for Disinformation. A big thanks to Mickey Z. for his sharp eyes and ready assistance. Thanks go to my parents Don and Carolyn and my siblings Michael, Joanna, Jessica, and Brenda. My thanks to Brian and Maria. Thanks to Jim Hunniford, who was happy to hear I wasn't dead after all. Jeff gets a serious "thank you." Thanks to Dana, Dan, Epic, James, and the others who helped me out in times of need and to Chaim for taking my pain seriously. Thanks go to Trudi and Deborah, and Jennifer who is missing in action. Thanks go to Alex, Dean Latimer and the three Steves, to Dan Russell, to Lucky at the New York Waste, and to all the DrugWar.com email list subscribers for inspiring me and constantly reminding me why I write what I do. Thanks especially to all the contributors in this book and those who didn't make it in, who all obviously care very much. Thank you Maureen Hodgan for your diligence, understanding, and care. Thanks to everyone else at Disinformation and elsewhere who helped put this book together and to you, the readers.

Last but definitely not least, I want to thank with all my heart all the activists, explorers, junkies, addicts, rebels, victims of "oops, wrong house" drug raids, capricious prosecution and prejudice, the prisoners, the overdose victims, all the law enforcement and judicial figures who are speaking out for change, the murdered and the collateral damage on all sides of the War, the researchers, the writers, the smokers and shooters, the dealers and buyers and everyone else who in all ways are helping bring the War on Some Drugs and Users to a close, one step at a time. This book is for you all.

—Preston Peet

Contents

Introduction

Some people say we should write what we know. In my own case, it's excellent advice that has served me well.

In 1996, I reached a major intersection in my life when I decided I was tired of living the life of a street-bound junkie, and needed drastic change. After some initial stumbling and lurching, I finally got my act together, ending my decade and a half long love/hate relationship with hard, illegal street drugs.

Having seen and lived the using side of the equation (see Appendix A), coming into repeated contact with prohibitionist policies and the police who enforce them, I wanted to know what was driving the War on Some Drugs and Users and why, no matter how many times I and my drug using friends and the dealers we bought from were getting arrested, there were always others on the streets to whom I could go to buy the drugs I'd wanted and needed.

I began coming across disturbing stories about CIA-connected drug trafficking, first reading Alexander Cockburn's allegations in the *New York Press*, then Gary Webb's *Dark Alliance* series, first published in the *San Jose Mercury News* in 1996. I was appalled to discover that the joking around we would do while getting high—about how the low-level streets dealers were not the ones who owned the airplanes that brought the drugs into the country, or the corporations that ship precursor chemicals needed to produce the cocaine and heroin we were doing, or the banks that launder the billions of money made each year in the international illegal drug trade, that our government had to be involved in some way in the trafficking—was truer than I'd ever seriously imagined. Why was I getting arrested for buying and using the very drugs that my government and its allies were both producing and bringing across the border?

By 1998, I had begun to write about this and other drug war related topics, pitching articles to any and all publications I thought might be interested in helping expose the hypocrisy and propaganda I was finding everywhere I looked concerning the War on Drugs. I sold my first article to *High Times* magazine in 1999, and was soon contributing regularly to the magazine and its website.

To help me get through the stresses and joys of life without hard street drugs, I reaffirmed my love and respect for marijuana, which got me through the hardest days and nights. This lead me one day proudly to tell a friend who'd brought me an eighth of pot that I was now regularly writing and publishing articles about the War on Drugs for *High Times*. He asked me if I'd heard of Disinformation's website, Disinfo.com. He typed it up on my computer to see if any of my work was linked there, to no avail. After he left, I wrote the publisher of the Disinformation website an email, pitching a dossier about CIA-Drug running. I got a reply from co-founder and publisher Gary Baddeley within twenty minutes, saying it was a topic right up their alley and that they'd be glad to take a look.

Needless to say, they published the finished dossier, leading to my publishing more than 60 articles for Disinformation, on many diverse topics but mostly about drugs and prohibition. When Disinformation had the idea in 2003 of publishing a book about drugs, they turned to me, and I gladly accepted the challenge. You are holding the results in your hands.

This book covers many different views of many different drugs and the fashion in which society deals with those drugs. Some of these essays are scholarly examinations of the deep politics and covert actions behind and justifying the War. Some of the contributors dissect the overt politics and history of the War. Some examine enforcement policies and some focus on what happens when one ingests any number of drugs, legal and illegal both. You will find discussions about what exactly constitutes a drug, why society deals with drugs and those who use them the way we do, and where we might be going in terms of attitudes and policies.

Considering that there are thousands of substances that can be considered drugs and laws governing their use(s) today, you might not find your drug(s) of choice here, though I've tried to offer as wide an assortment as possible for your education and entertainment. The War itself influences a broad spectrum of society today, eating up tax money and lives, corrupting governments and police agencies, driving bloody wars and violent repression, while drugs themselves offer both enlightenment and despair.

One thing you won't find much of here is the prohibitionists' viewpoint, because I feel they have enjoyed wide exposure for decades without many counterarguments in the mainstream press, basically given free reign to promote their lies, blatant deceits which end up causing much more damage to lives and society than any drug use or abuse ever has. The prohibitionists have insured that real drug education does not take place in the US, and despite the obvious groundswell among the population at large for more rational and humane ways of dealing with drugs and users, they show few signs themselves of altering their views or their tactics.

Nine US states have legalized medical marijuana use since 1996, and ten states (Alaska, California, Colorado, Nebraska, New York, North Carolina, Maine, Minnesota, Ohio, and Oregon) that have decriminalized outright the possession of marijuana since the 1970s, but the federal government continues to crack down on users, patients and suppliers.

The Association of American Physicians and Surgeons put the number of US citizens who suffer excruciating, life-affecting pain at 48 million in October 2003, yet the federal government is enthusiastically prosecuting doctors who specialize in treating chronic pain by prescribing powerful opiate-based medications, the most effective treatments for pain known to humanity today, scaring many doctors away from the pain treatment field and leaving patients to suffer without respite.

Many cultures around the planet have used a huge variety of drugs for religious, medical, and recreational reasons for millennia, but US prohibitionists prefer to treat nearly all drug use as abuse, continuing to issue baseless scare stories while sending out armed enforcers to corral small time users and dealers at ever increasing rates, filling US prisons to the breaking point.

By 2004, many countries such as Belgium, England, Canada, and Switzerland to name but a few, were radically changing the way they legislate drugs and their use, in many cases decriminalizing and even legalizing personal possession and use of small quantities of drugs. In March, 2004, the World Health Organization listed the leading causes of death in the US, with tobacco and obesity coming in first. The WHO then listed in descending order: alcohol use, pneumonia and influenza, exposure to pollutants and other toxic agents, motor vehicle accidents, shootings, and sexual behaviors. Illicit drug use came in last. Yet the US government continues spending billions of tax dollars every year waging war on its own citizens over this drug use.

All these issues and many more are covered in detail inside this anthology. An informed populace is necessary for a healthy democracy, but when it comes to drugs, the majority of the US populace is woefully ignorant today, their elected political representatives even more so. Until fears and prejudices are put aside, instituting rational drug policies will continue to be an unattainable pipedream, an alternate reality just out of reach. Lives will continue to be destroyed, both by ignorant legislation and by a dangerous lack of knowledge about drugs themselves. Driving a car is a dangerous, even at times deadly activity, but we do not pretend that people cannot drive sanely and responsibly. We do not insist that all cars are killers nor that driving will lead inevitably to destruction and death. What we do is teach people to use their automobiles safely, teaching them the road rules to ensure they reach their destinations alive. This is what we should be doing when it comes to drugs as well.

As long as the mainstream media continues to air endless commercials for drugs to treat incontinence, indigestion, obesity, depression, sexual dysfunction, and any other assortment of conditions, people will continue to be confused by the anti-drug messages promoted by the government. If anything sends the wrong message to kids, it is that some drugs, usually pharmaceuticals, are ok and some, often the natural ones which can be grown from the Earth, are not. There is no rational policy determining which is which.

Yet another wrong message for the kids is the government continuing to fund year after year anti-drug policies that to any critical eye are obviously not working—if in fact ending drug abuse and drug trafficking really are the goals of prohibitionist politicians and law enforcers. The War is becoming so obviously indefensible that the federal government has gone so far as to ban drug war reform advertising on public transportation systems that take federal money, refusing to allow citizens to use their own money to advertise sane policies while simultaneously using tax money to pay for anti-drug messages in the same public systems.

Ninety years after the passage of the Harrison Narcotics Act, the first federal anti-drug law in the U.S, it is my hope in editing this anthology that people will read it and learn some of what is really going on, that not all drug use is drug abuse nor all users degenerate losers in need of incarceration or treatment. I want readers to see that rational, humanitarian alternatives to the current system are not only possible but are ultimately preferable—then demand that their elected representatives examine these alternatives and end the War on Some Drugs and Users.

—**Preston Peet,** New York City

Know You're Right

Imagining a Post-Prohibition World

Phil Smith

What would happen if drugs were legal? Proponents of the status quo triumphantly present that question to would-be reformers as if the answer were not only obvious but devastating: There would be a huge increase in drug abuse, with all its horrifying implications—the orgiastic lusts, the drug-crazed frenzies, the children turned from bright-eyed innocents to pot-befogged zombies, the sunken-eye junkies prowling the neighborhoods, the buck Negroes hopped up on cocaine raping our white women.

But while this puritanical prohibitionist imagery of a world run amok on drugs is widely held in a culture raised on anti-drug propaganda, and even appears commonsensical—more people would use drugs if they were legal, right?—there is little hard evidence to support it. More on that below, but what's more, by focusing solely on whether or how much drug use would increase if punitive laws were removed, prohibitionists encourage a blinkered view of social reality, one that blinds us to the myriad ways the current global drug prohibition regime affects our societies or what a change in that regime might really mean.

Driven by what is in the final analysis a deeply totalitarian impulse—to control what others do with their own consciousness—the effects of drug prohibition as a public policy are broad and deep, spreading inexorably across more and more aspects of social life, impacting more and more institutions. A change from our current prohibitionist model to "legalization" in any of its various forms—decriminalization, medicalization, regulation, or a full-blown, free market in currently illicit drugs—has tremendous implications at every level, from the lives of individuals to the structures of global political and economic power.

But after a century of drug prohibition, many people cannot even imagine that things could be any other way. And change is a scary thing. Those who flex their minds enough to consider the possibility of ending prohibition recoil in fright from the spectral horrors they think they glimpse. According to a Pew poll in 2001, 74% of Americans believe the war on drugs is a failure, but support for legalization remains infinitesimal, and even efforts to nibble at the edges of prohibition, such as decriminalizing pot possession or allowing for medical marijuana, are fiercely contested and hard-won, if they are won at all. "Prohibition may not work, but what's the alternative?" people ask, as if the consequences of ending prohibition were too grim to even imagine.

But let's do just that. First, just what is the problem? Why do we invest so many resources in attempting to prohibit drug use and the trade which supplies it? The answer is that some drug use has negative consequences, for drug users themselves, for their families and communities, and for society as a whole. Drug users can suffer physical ill-effects from their use, ranging from malnutrition to contracting diseases and, ultimately, death by accidental overdose. They can suffer mental health consequences. They can suffer moral consequences, especially if they become dependent on a drug, losing some degree of personal autonomy to the substance they crave.

Some drug users neglect their children or endanger them through drug-induced stupidity. They get fired from jobs because they're too busy getting high. They cause their families to split up. They diminish the quality of life for others in the community by lying around in pools of vomit or by behaving psychotically in the street. There is no denying that drug use can have a very nasty downside, nor that society has a legitimate interest in trying to minimize those adverse effects.

Drug prohibition is ostensibly aimed at doing just that. The logic is simple: Reducing drug use will reduce the

> "PROHIBITION MAY NOT WORK, BUT WHAT'S THE ALTERNATIVE?" PEOPLE ASK, AS IF THE CONSEQUENCES OF ENDING PROHIBITION WERE TOO GRIM TO EVEN IMAGINE.

harm associated with drug use. But it is also simplistic, because prohibition carries with it its own negative consequences, for which drug users are unfairly and unthinkingly blamed. For example, we hear often of "drug-related deaths," a phrase that is accurate if one is talking about an OD or a deranged tweaker who shoots his girlfriend in a fit of paranoid rage. But many of the most unsettling "drug-related deaths"—the chaotic street shootings as dealers engage in turf battles, the cop killed during a drug raid—are not "drug-related" but "drug law enforcement-related." Drugs didn't kill these people; the drug laws did.

There is harm related to drug use and there is harm related to the way we attempt to deal with drug use as a social problem. In order to tease out the consequences of a drug policy regime change, we must remember not to confuse the two.

There are a variety of alternatives to the current global prohibition regime:

• **Decriminalization**—the removal of criminal sanctions for the use or possession of small amounts of drugs—would remove the threat of jail from tens of millions, but would leave intact the global black market in illicit substances.

• **Medicalization**—making drugs available through prescription or by maintenance doses in a controlled fashion—would transfer power from the law enforcement establishment to the medical/psychiatric establishment.

• **Regulation**—making drugs available in roughly the same manner as currently licit drugs, such as alcohol and tobacco—would perhaps be nearest to what is commonly thought of as "legalization."

• **A free market approach**—with illicit substances being treated as coffee is today— would be true legalization, or perhaps, normalization of drug use.

The latter approach represents the far, utopian (some would say dystopian) end of the policy spectrum. And neither decriminalization nor medicalization addresses the problem of that black market. So, for comparison's sake, let us use the model of regulation. Under regulated legalization, the international production of and commerce in currently illicit substances is integrated into legal markets and those substances are available to buyers with only minimal restrictions. Such a model does not presuppose that all countries would "legalize drugs," but it does assume that hold-outs would be few and would shrink over time. More importantly, it assumes that the United Nations Single Convention on Narcotics and its fellow conventions have been effectively repealed, and that in the United States, the federal Controlled Substances Act has been repealed and the various states treat illicit drugs the way they treat alcohol and tobacco, with a patchwork of different restrictions and regulations, but within a framework where a legal commerce in drugs is the bottom line.

How would such a world differ from ours? To answer that question, we must first return to the question of whether and how much drug use would increase if it were legal. If drug use were to increase dramatically under legalization, the harms fairly associated with some drug use would also presumably increase. In that case, the argument for prohibition becomes stronger. On the other hand, if drug use were to stay level or rise only slightly or temporarily under legalization, prohibition becomes increasingly untenable.

Will drug use go up?

Despite the common sense notion that drug use would increase dramatically if drugs were more freely available, there is little hard evidence to either support or dispute that notion. Cross-national comparisons of drug use rates suggest that drug use patterns are not a function of drug policy (in fact, the opposite may be more true), but of broader, more complex social forces at work. In their comprehensive look at drug policy, *Drug War Heresies*, (Cambridge University Press, 2001) US academics Robert MacCoun and Peter Reuter reviewed studies of marijuana use in the US and Western Europe. While their findings are limited by a paucity of hard numbers and the less than perfect fit among different surveys, their results indicate that marijuana use levels have little relation with official stances toward the drug. Among the 16 studies compared by MacCoun and Reuter, the single highest lifetime usage figure (42%) came among seventeen–to–twenty-year-old Americans. Likewise, when looking at pot use among teens, prohibitionist Sweden reported the lowest prevalence (8% for thirteen–seventeen-year-olds), but pot-friendly Holland was next lowest (10% for thirteen–fifteen-year-olds), with teen use levels well below those of the prohibitionist United States (14% for twelve–eighteen-year-olds) and Denmark (17% for thirteen–seventeen-year-olds). From these findings, it appears that drug prohibition has little impact on marijuana use rates.

Likewise, MacCoun and Reuter analyzed marijuana use within the Netherlands to examine whether increased access to pot under the Dutch government's coffee shop policy led to increased pot use. While they found that use began to increase after the coffee shops opened, there was a lag of several years. It was not a change in the law that caused the increase, they suggested, but commercialization. "There is no evidence that the [coffee shop] policy per se increased levels of cannabis use," they wrote. "On the other hand, the later growth in commercial access to cannabis, following the de facto legalization, was accompanied by steep increases in use." This is an important point, and one that does not bode well for the United States, where commercial advertisers can wrap themselves in the First Amendment as they lure prospective customers.

But the larger point is that drug policies in general seem to have limited impact on drug use levels. A comparison of European "drug-related deaths," which in this instance means primarily injection drug overdoses and chronic illnesses from a lifetime of drug abuse, shows an upward trend since 1985 across the continent—regardless of whether drug policies were prohibitionist or user-friendly. Similarly, a comparison of heroin use in Italy since 1975 found little correlation between policies, which oscillated between prohibition and depenalization of drug use, and drug use levels. As the Italian social scientist Solivetti noted, "the intervention of the criminal law has a very limited effect on a phenomenon whose evolution can be linked with the far more powerful pressure exerted by structural forces that lie at the very heart of the way society is organized."

In other words, broader social and cultural processes are a much more critical force than the law in determining drug use levels. Which is not to say that a regime of regulated, legal access to drugs would have no impact on drug use levels. According to MacCoun and Reuter, the result of a legalization regime would be a "non-trivial" increase in drug use, and a corresponding increase in the negative consequences of drug use.

So, would drug use go up in a regime of regulation and legalization? The short answer is probably yes, but by less than the amount commonly assumed, and the degree of increase would depend not only on broader social forces at play, but also on the precise nature of the regulatory scheme and the degree of commercialization allowed.

But unless reducing drug usage is the sole measure of success for a drug policy, usage rates provide only a hint of the consequences of drug legalization.

What would a new regime bring in terms of other impacts, such as health and public health, public safety and criminal justice, and respect for freedom and human rights in the United States? Internationally, what would a system of legal, regulated commerce in currently illicit drugs mean in terms of corruption, the black market, and the millions of people who currently work in the drug business, from Afghan opium farmers and Andean cocaleros to Brooklyn crack-slingers and Oklahoma meth cooks?

Health and Public Health

Assuming that regulated legalization would lead to higher levels of drug use, we can anticipate corresponding higher levels of adverse drug-related personal and public health consequences. But the correlation is not so simple, because a regime of regulated legalization would also remove some of the barriers to proper health care imposed by prohibition.

More drug users implies more drug abusers, which in turn implies more demand for drug treatment and for other drug-related health care costs. The United States already suffers from an identified lack of adequate treatment capacity, so the nation would presumably have to increase expenditures for treatment and other health care. But current drug treatment programs are also "demand side," in that arrested drug users are forced into them by drug courts and similar programs that demand they go to treatment or else face prison time. As a result, we face the truly bizarre situation of marijuana smokers taking up

almost half the treatment slots in the US, a phenomenon that is certainly not justifiable on any medical basis. In a society where drug treatment has not been colonized by law enforcement and the courts, the treatment slots filled by casual potheads in court-ordered treatment could be filled by people who would actually benefit from them.

Thus, while legal, regulated drug sales would presumably lead to increases in use, abuse, and the demand for treatment, the removal of drug treatment as a tool of the criminal justice system would free up so many slots that an expansion in resources devoted to drug treatment may be minimal. (Such a regulatory regime could maintain a vestigial role for drug courts and court-ordered drug treatment: Such courts could be used, but only for people whose drug use has led them to commit other crimes, much as alcohol abusers today are not sent to treatment for drinking alcohol, but for committing the crime of driving while intoxicated. If someone does methamphetamine and neglects her children, she would be a candidate for drug court. If someone does cocaine and flies into a psychotic rage, attacking others, he would be a candidate for drug court. If someone smokes heroin and picks his nose all day, he may be a candidate for a slap in the face, but not for court-ordered drug treatment.)

The impact of regulated legalization on other health aspects of drug use, such as HIV and Hepatitis C infection rates or drug overdose deaths, is two-way. On the one hand, with some increase in overall drug use, there presumably would be some increase in infections and overdose deaths.

BUT UNLESS REDUCING DRUG USAGE IS THE SOLE MEASURE OF SUCCESS FOR A DRUG POLICY, USAGE RATES PROVIDE ONLY A HINT OF THE CONSEQUENCES OF DRUG LEGALIZATION.

On the other hand, a regime where drug use and sales were legal would presumably remove all barriers to harm reduction approaches that could minimize those negative effects. Under regulation, hard drug users would have access to clean needles. Similarly, the friends, families, and acquaintances of people suffering from drug overdoses would not have to fear arrest upon notifying authorities, thus leading to a much greater willingness to seek medical help when necessary.

One other health and public health consequence of regulated legalization would be the virtual disappearance of medical marijuana and chronic untreated pain as burning political issues. The 50 million people reporting chronic pain and the millions more who claim relief from an array of symptoms with marijuana would have the ability to medicate themselves as they or their doctors see fit.

Overall, then, we could expect some increase in negative personal and public health consequences of regulated legalization, given an anticipated increase in drug use.

But the impact of that increase would be mitigated by a social structure that worked with and for drug users to minimize harm instead of criminalizing drug users. Indeed, implicit with a regulated legalization model is the assumption that revenues from the drug trade will be taxed and that at least some portion of those proceeds will be dedicated for drug abuse prevention, education, and treatment programs.

Public Safety, Quality of Life, and the Criminal Justice System

But if regulated legalization would lead to some increase in drug use and therefore some increase in negative personal and public health consequences, when it comes to the impact of regime change on costs associated with public safety, quality of life, and the criminal justice system, the balance begins to swing dramatically to the plus side. Many of the harms and costs attributed to "drugs" are in fact the result of efforts to enforce their prohibition—and the costs are both monetary and social.

In the United States alone, the federal government and states and localities spend in excess of $50 billion per year on drug law enforcement. This figure does not include such downstream costs as paying to imprison half a million Americans for years at a time, nor does it include the economic costs of all those human-years of lost labor which come to additional billions each year. In short, the US spends about as much each year to enforce prohibition as it costs to occupy a mid-sized foreign country.

Under a system of regulated legalization, drug law enforcement would no longer be a significant line-item in anyone's budget. At a stroke, America could save itself a huge amount of money, year after year after year. And those savings would ripple downstream, as prison, probation and parole, and related criminal justice budgets shrank. Currently, drug arrests make up somewhere between one-quarter and one-third of all arrests. With the end of prohibition, the size of the criminal justice system should shrink dramatically.

Some unquantified but significant portion of common crime is "drug-related," or more accurately, prohibition-related. "Drug-related" crime can be broken down into three categories: 1) biopharmacological, 2) economic compulsive, and 3) structural. Biopharmacological crimes are those driven by the action of the drug on the user, as is the case with alcohol-fueled assaults or tweakers' paranoia leading to homicide. These are the crimes that build the stereotype of the dangerous psycho hopped up on drugs. Such crimes do occur, but as a team of researchers led by Paul Goldstein demonstrated in a study of crack and crime

in New York City, they actually make up a small percentage of "drug-related" crimes—and some of those are crimes actually perpetrated on the intoxicated drug user, as was the case of Goldstein's jabbering crackhead shot in the face because he wouldn't shut up.

But while biopharmacological crime is the stuff of tabloid wet dreams, it is economic compulsive and structural crime that really degrades the quality of life and public safety for non-drug users. Economic compulsive crime is crime committed by dependent drug users in order to obtain money to buy drugs at inflated black market prices, or, in other words, that fucking junkie who stole my car stereo. And structural crimes are those associated with dispute adjudication in illegal markets—the murder of one street-corner dealer by another in a turf dispute, the killings of witnesses by nervous drug gangs, and of course, the deaths of innocents cut down in a hail of bullets fired by reckless and desperate young men in an illegal enterprise.

> JUST AS THE PRECISE AMOUNT OF INCREASE IN DRUG USE-RELATED HARM UNDER LEGALIZATION IS IMPOSSIBLE TO QUANTIFY, SO IS THE AMOUNT OF DECREASE IN OVERALL CRIME RATES THAT WOULD RESULT FROM ENDING PROHIBITION. SUFFICE IT TO SAY IT WILL BE SIGNIFICANT.

Just as the precise amount of increase in drug use-related harm under legalization is impossible to quantify, so is the amount of decrease in overall crime rates that would result from ending prohibition. Suffice it to say it will be significant. Police commonly hold drug users accountable for a large amount of street crime. Let us conservatively assume they account for one-quarter of all property and personal crime. With legalization, we can reasonably assume that only biopharmacological crime—people acting crazy or dangerous on drugs—would increase along with increased drug use. (But even that increase could be attenuated by the provision of social services for such eventualities, as well as by the relaxing of an adversarial relationship with police.) But since biopharm crime is only a small amount of "drug-related" crime, and neither stealing to pay for expensive drugs nor shooting your competitor would be necessary under legalization, ending prohibition is likely to result in a decrease in common crimes—burglaries, robberies, assaults, murders—of around 20%.

Coupled with the fact that drug law enforcement alone accounts for one-third to one-quarter of all arrests—nearly 1.5 million in 2002—this suggests that replacing prohibition with regulated legalization could cut crime rates dramatically and reduce arrest rates by around half. The eventual impact on police staffing levels, prison budgets, and the like would be earthshaking. America has more than 600,000 cops of various stripes right now. Should we be contemplating a massive job retraining and rehabilitation program for the hundreds of thousands of surplus officers once prohibition ends?

The effects on quality of life, especially for people in neighborhoods hardest hit by the drug war, would be equally dramatic, if unquantifiable. How do you measure being able to send your kids to school without worrying that they'll be gunned down on the way? Or not having to view the police as an occupying force? Or not seeing more young men go to jail than to college?

Freedom and Human Rights

But there is another quality of life issue related to drug policy, and that is human liberty. Most of us share the baseline assumption that, all things being equal, more liberty is better than less. There are limits, of course, aptly expressed in the old chestnut about my freedom to swing my fist ending at your nose. But absent harm to others or their property, the presumption of the Western philosophical tradition—and indeed, the modern nation-state—is that one should be free to do as one chooses.

THE POINT IS IT IS NOT THE NATURE OF THE PRODUCT BUT THE EXISTENCE OF WINDFALL PROFITS FROM PROHIBITED SUBSTANCES THAT FORMS THE LINK BETWEEN DRUGS AND WAR OR DRUGS AND TERRORISM. DRUGS DON'T FUND TERRORISTS, BLACK MARKET DRUG PROFITS DO.

Dealing with drug use and the drug trade by prohibiting them does grave, profound harm to this notion of freedom. It is unsupportable within the philosophies by which we claim to live, for what drug prohibition does is punish the drug user not because he has harmed anyone but because society is afraid someone else will hurt himself by using illicit drugs. The drug user (and by extension, the producer and seller) is punished although he hurt no one, except arguably himself.

Arresting nearly a million and a half people each year and stuffing American prisons with about half-a-million drug law violators at any given time because we disapprove of their choice of intoxicants is highly corrosive for a society that claims to be based on "liberty and justice for all." The inexorable logic of drug prohibition militates toward an ever-increasing state intrusion into the lives of its citizens, one that runs in the face of all we profess to believe in. Want a job? Go piss in a cup first. Want to live in public housing? You must promise not to smoke a joint. Want to drive down the highway? Be prepared to be pulled over on a pretext and be subjected to a roadside criminal investigation. Want to use heroin to relax instead of alcohol? Be prepared to have your door kicked down by armed, ninja-masked thugs and be thrown in prison. You get the idea.

Drug prohibition has corroded our freedoms. The Fourth Amendment, which protects us from unreasonable police searches, is in tatters, thanks to Supreme Court rulings guided by the inexorable logic of prohibition. Likewise, Fifth Amendment protections from self-incrimination go by the wayside as courts approve the use of drug test results as evidence in criminal cases. Drug dogs sniff at us with no probable cause, police raid our schools as if they were Baathist guerrilla hangouts, pot-seeking choppers overfly our homes and properties to spy on us. They seize our homes and bank accounts, spy on our financial records, and teach our children to be the eyes and ears of the state.

The informer is exalted as a public hero. Such a transformation in the perception of informers—from rat to public servant—is necessary for the health of the drug war, but noxious for the health of a free society. Prohibition demands a culture of informers because the people involved in using and selling drugs do so freely. There is no one to file a complaint because no one perceives himself to be harmed. Thus, to enforce prohibition, law enforcement must resort to practices loathed by any freedom-loving society. Even uglier is the use by prosecutors of a chain of informants, each generated by the one before, each threatened with decades in prison (along with the inevitable threat of rape) if he does not betray his friends. Under regulated legalization, the snitch and the culture of snitching would recede into nightmarish memory.

The end of prohibition promises the beginning of an era of increased personal freedom and decreased state intrusion into the lives of citizens. This is not a benefit that can be measured in dollars and cents, but it may be the most important of all.

The Black Market

The global black market generated by drug prohibition is estimated by the United Nations Office on Drugs and Crime to constitute 8% of the global economy, putting it on a par with the oil industry in terms of global economic impact. While by the nature of the beast precise dollar figures are impossible to come by, we are talking about hundreds of billions of dollars in black market drug profits generated every year. Those dollars contribute to all sorts of social evils. Under a regime of regulated legalization, this black market would, with some bumps and dislocations, eventually wither to nothing.

We touched above on the role of illegal markets in generating street crime, both because of thefts and robberies committed by drug users to pay black market drug prices and because of the violence associated with conflict resolution in markets where the players have no

CORRUPTION CORRODES PUBLIC TRUST IN LAW ENFORCEMENT AND THE POLITICAL CLASS. ENDING DRUG PROHIBITION REMOVES A HUGE SOURCE OF POTENTIAL CORRUPTION.

recourse to the justice system. These effects are by no means limited to drug consuming countries, although in drug producing countries violence is more often associated with conflict among rival drug trafficking enterprises. In Mexico, for example, more than 70 people died in January 2004 alone in fighting for control of the lucrative cartels. Ending drug prohibition could not but result in a dramatic diminution of black market-related criminal violence.

But black market drug profits play an even more nefarious role in financing armed conflict. This has been the case historically, and it is the case today. And those black market

AS THINGS NOW STAND, TENS OF THOUSANDS OF YOUNG MEN AND WOMEN IN URBAN AMERICA MAKE A LIVING SELLING DRUGS.

drug profits know no ideology. In Vietnam, for example, the French colonists financed their administration with illicit opium revenues, while Vietnamese nationalists used opium revenues to build up their army to defeat the French. The US, in turn, trafficked in opium to gain the support of Montagnard tribesmen as allies against the North Vietnamese and Viet Cong.

It must be pointed out that there is nothing inherent in opium or coca or cannabis that militates toward financing wars. It is only that armies—state-operated or insurrectionary—take their financing where they can get it. Guerrillas, terrorists, and other armed political actors thrive on black market drug money because it is there. In other conflicts, it is not drug money but proceeds from black market diamonds, or oil, or looted treasures that pays for war. The point is it is not the nature of the product but the existence of windfall profits from prohibited substances that forms the link between drugs and war or drugs and terrorism. Drugs don't fund terrorists, black market drug profits do.

Whether in Colombia, where all sides finance their war chests with cocaine profits, or Afghanistan, where profits from the opium trade flow into the treasuries of US-allied warlords and al Qaeda alike, drug prohibition fuels war and terrorism. To replace drug prohibition with regulated legalization would suck the air out of armed movements worldwide. Similarly, integrating the fortunes earned in the drug markets into the global financial system— perhaps through an amnesty—would regularize those fortunes. The owners of these sums could then conduct their political influence campaigns openly, just like any other sector seeking advantage.

Speaking of corruption, black market drug profits also generate corruption on a huge scale. While the finger is usually (and correctly) pointed at countries like Mexico, which appears not to fight to suppress the drug trade

so much as manage it, prohibition-related corruption is endemic worldwide and pervades law enforcement from top to bottom. As editor of the *Drug War Chronicle*, I run a weekly feature called "This Week's Corrupt Cops Story." There is never a shortage of candidates. Corruption corrodes public trust in law enforcement and the political class. Ending drug prohibition removes a huge source of potential corruption.

Renovating the international drug business

Moving from a regime of global drug prohibition to one of legalized use, production, and distribution will be complicated, with many unintended consequences, especially when it comes to creating a legal industry out of what is now a black market economy supporting millions of people around the planet. From the coca crops of the Andes to the poppy fields of Afghanistan and Burma to cannabis farmers everywhere (to give just one example, the UN last year estimated that some 250,000 families in one region of Morocco alone were dependent on cannabis farming), millions of poor peasants depend on illicit drug crops as their primary source of income.

Drug trafficking organizations employ hundreds of thousands more around the globe, ranging from bankers, lawyers, and accountants to smugglers and transport workers, from the legions of street-corner retail dealers, touts, and scouts to the enforcers who bring a rough

THIS ESSAY SUGGESTS THAT LEGALIZATION WOULD RESULT IN GREAT SAVINGS OF SOCIAL RESOURCES, A DRAMATIC REDUCTION IN CRIMINAL AND POLITICAL VIOLENCE, AND AN INCREASE IN HUMAN DIGNITY AND FREEDOM. THAT MUST BE WEIGHED AGAINST HOW MUCH WE HATE PEOPLE GETTING HIGH ON DRUGS WE DON'T LIKE.

justice where the police are absent. (And let us not forget the hundreds of thousands employed worldwide in the non-productive work of trying to repress the business, or as is the case with the drug testing industry, profiting from that repression.)

Because most drug profits accrue after the crop gets into the hands of middle-men, peasant producers are likely to see only a small negative impact on farm-gate prices for their opium, coca, and marijuana crops. At the same time, their livelihoods will no longer be subject to violent disruption by prohibition-enforcing police or soldiers. Which is not to suggest that legalization would be the cure-all for the endemic poverty of the Third World. While drug producing countries could tax, regulate, and even establish state monopolies as revenue-producing measures and could nearly eliminate spending on drug law enforcement, increasing the amount of resources available to national governments for economic and social development, peasant drug producers and countries heavily dependent on income from newly legalized drugs are also likely to face periodic downward plunges in prices. As has occurred in recent years with a legal drug, coffee, competition in a newly opened global drug market will inevitably lead to periods of oversupply and plunging prices. Still, for the coca farmers of the Andes or the Afghan peasant tending his poppies or the hash-growers of Morocco, a legalized market in the crops would be a huge boon.

For others employed in the illegal drug trade, the outlook is less rosy. As things now stand, tens of thousands of young men and women in urban America make a living selling drugs. So do a cadre of pistoleros, sicarios, and various thugs worldwide. There is no place for these people in a world where drug sales are legal and take place in a clean, well-lit place, not the street-corner. The kids may not be selling crack on the street anymore, but without something to replace the economic opportunity presented by drug dealing, the kids will still be on the street, and with one less means of making a buck.

What would regulated legalization do?

It is impossible to do more than outline the ramifications of a shift from repression and prohibition to tolerance and regulated legalization in an essay of this size. Still, we can summarize some of the impacts we can anticipate:

• **Drug use levels**—Drug use will increase by some non-trivial percentage.

• **Health and public health**—Increased drug use will bring with it some increased health costs for individual drug users and for society as a whole. But that effect will be ameliorated by full implementation of harm reduction, prevention, education, and targeted treatment programs.

• **Public safety, quality of life, and the criminal justice system**—Arrests will decrease dramatically, perhaps by as much as half, with no drug laws. Additionally, arrests for "natural" crimes—those acts that directly harm another or his property—will decrease to the degree that such crimes are currently committed by drug users acting from economic compulsion or drug sellers attempting to resolve disputes. Criminal justice system costs will drop dramatically and public safety and quality of life will increase.

• **Freedom and human rights**— Legalizing drug use and markets will be a great advance for the notion of freedom and human rights. The possibility of potential metaphorical enslavement to drug addiction for some is far outweighed by not having half a million Americans behind bars for using or selling the wrong intoxicant or having the police state apparatus to enforce prohibition.

• **The black market**—Regulated legalization by definition eliminates the black market in drugs, and the huge profits that finance political violence and corruption around the globe.

• **Remaking the illicit drug industry**—Ending prohibition would cause a massive restructuring of the drug trade. Peasant drug farmers would see the least impact, but the hundreds of thousands of people involved in current middle-man, smuggling, and black market retail sales stand to see their jobs vanish.

Whether regulated legalization is better than drug prohibition is, to some degree, a matter of value judgments.

This essay suggests that legalization would result in great savings of social resources, a dramatic reduction in criminal and political violence, and an increase in human dignity and freedom. That must be weighed against how much we hate people getting high on drugs we don't like.

How would regulated legalization work?

This model foresees a regime where illicit drugs are as available as alcohol or cigarettes. For the United States, it assumes that while the states can regulate drug sales more or less stringently, the bottom line is that they cannot prohibit them. This model allows for some local variation, just as there is with the regulation of alcohol sales. Alaska, for instance, could make all drugs available for retail sale behind the counter of convenience stores anytime of day or night, while South Dakota might allow them to be sold only at state-owned stores during limited hours, and Alabama might require potential drug buyers to acquire a license to purchase drugs (such a license could be revoked for drug-related misbehavior), and New York might make marijuana available at coffee shops and retail outlets while placing greater restrictions on the sales of other drugs.

Internationally, regulated legalization will require a transition from underground organizations to globally recognized economic actors. Existing drug trafficking and producing organizations will have to be either bought out or integrated into the global marketplace. This transition will of course be uneven and bumpy, but there is no reason to believe it cannot occur.

Washington, DC, 14th Street and Park Road NW, 8 PM, July 1, 2014.

The shadows lengthen over the nation's capital as another hot summer day comes to an end. A young man and young women walk north up 14th, past the Salvadoran-Mexican restaurants and tienditas, past the CVS Pharmacy, and into Mind Candy, "your one-stop shop for all your consciousness-altering needs." Ambient music throbs softly through the small, well-lit shop, and a bored clerk sits behind the counter flipping through a magazine. The walls behind the clerk and the glass-fronted counters are packed with wares on display.

Consulting a hand-written list, the young man clears his throat, and the clerk looks up. "Can I help you?"

"Uh, yeah," says the young man, "I need a half-ounce of weed…let's try some of the local stuff, so I guess I want the Virginia Violet."

"It's organic," the clerks says approvingly, "and it really gets you baked." He smiles. "Anything else?"

"An eightball of cocaine," the young man says. "Hey, I've been hearing good things about that Indonesian coke—you got that?"

"Sure," says the clerk, reaching behind him and setting a glass vial full of powder on the counter. "This is the real thing, government-certified Sumatra brand Indonesian coke. Cheaper than Andean, but just as good.

"We'll take it," interrupts the young woman, her eyes glistening, "and what do you have for opiates?"

"That must be some party you're planning," says the clerk. When this elicits no response, he continues: "Well, what do you want? We've got some fine Warlord brand smack from the Opium Emirates; it's guaranteed 99.4% pure, and we've just begun carrying Mexican Meltdown. Same price, same purity, some people say they like it because it doesn't make them scratch that much, but what do I know?" the clerk muttered.

"What about opium to smoke?" the girl asks.

"Oh, sure," says the clerk, reaching down and pulling out a tray holding small, labeled packages of resiny brown poppy nectar. "We got your Nepalese, we got your Burmese, we got your Afghani—all proceeds guaranteed to support your local Islamic fundamentalist," he snickered. "Take your pick."

The couple consult briefly. "All right, I'll take a gram of the Warlord, and what the hell, gimme a half ounce each of Nepalese and the Burmese. That should do it."

"Let's see," says the clerk scanning in the purchases. A half-ounce of Virginia Violet, that's $50 plus $10 dope tax, an eightball of Sumatra coke; that's $49.95 plus the dope tax, $10 again. And there's a gram of Warlord—that'll put you in a nice, fuzzy place—for $29.95, plus $7, and last but not least, one ounce of opium, half Nepalese, half Burmese, same price either way, that's $15, plus $3 for the junkies. Your total comes to $174.90—are you members of our frequent buyers' club?"

"Nah," says the young man. "Here you go. Thanks and have a good night."

"You, too," the clerk smiles. "Looks like you're gonna try. Remember, we're only open until 4 AM…"

Phil Smith

Chemical Bigotry

Mary Jane Borden

I'd like to introduce a new term into drug policy vernacular: chemical bigotry. We've endured the War on Drugs for more than thirty years and seen various threads of injustice weave through it. Until now, no wording has existed to label this injustice. [**Editor's note**: If one counts from the first federal anti-drug law, the Harrison Narcotics Act of 1914, it could be considered a 90-year long War on Some Drugs and Users. Many people today prefer to begin their count with Richard Nixon, who in 1968 campaigned on a strong law enforcement platform. Nixon used drugs as a distraction from disastrous foreign policies and

> THE ROOTS OF BOTH RACIAL DISCRIMINATION AND CHEMICAL DISCRIMINATION ARE THE SAME: BIGOTRY THAT IS BORN OF STEREOTYPES AND MYTHS

domestic situations, and through his subsequent words and actions is credited by many with setting the US on its current course in terms of warring against some drugs and users. Hence the 30-year number cited here.]

Webster's Dictionary defines *bigot* as one who is "obstinately or intolerantly devoted to his or her own opinions and prejudices." *Bigotry* is a bigot in action.

What is chemical bigotry? It is the application of obstinate opinions, prejudices, and intolerance to those whose chemical profile appears one way versus those whose chemical profile appears another way. Essentially, drug testing is this chemical profile made physical.

Consider the parallels of chemical bigotry with bigotry based on race, sex, national origin, or sexual orientation. For example, great myths arose around those of different races, these myths transforming into stereotypes. These myths and stereotypes then influenced the passage of Jim Crow laws and segregation.

In a similar vein, great myths grew up surrounding the users of some drugs as if everyone would turn out like Cheech and Chong. Crack babies are a

> WHETHER UNDER THE INFLUENCE OF DRUGS, TOO LITTLE SLEEP, OR MANIC DEPRESSION, BAD BEHAVIOR IS SIMPLY BAD BEHAVIOR.

proven myth. Through these myths came stereotypes and from the stereotypes came bad policy. The roots of both racial discrimination and chemical discrimination are the same: bigotry that is born of stereotypes and myths.

Bigotry has a long and costly history. At its worst, bigotry produced slavery and the Nazis. Because of some outward factor, groups of people became stigmatized and stereotyped, resulting in disastrous social policy that begot war and death. In a similar vein, chemical bigotry as manifest through the War on Drugs has produced disastrous social policy: bloated prisons, crime, police brutality, civil war, loss of rights, and terrorism.

Some might say that chemical bigotry is different than other bigotry – and thus justifiable—because people chose to use drugs and thus alter their chemical profile. Remember, this same argument has been applied time and again to religion and sexual orientation in order to justify legal, social, and cultural sanctions.

Some might argue that a chemical-free human body is pure and virtuous, something worth striving for. The problem here is that we are all by our very nature a chemical composition. We can never be chemically-free. When we look at ourselves as a chemical spectrum, we can begin to see that we are making judgment calls of good or bad based simply on what we add

> SOME MIGHT ARGUE THAT A CHEMICAL-FREE HUMAN BODY IS PURE AND VIRTUOUS, SOMETHING WORTH STRIVING FOR. THE PROBLEM HERE IS THAT WE ARE ALL BY OUR VERY NATURE A CHEMICAL COMPOSITION. WE CAN NEVER BE CHEMICALLY-FREE.

to our baseline body chemistry. Someone who adds marijuana— bad. Someone who adds aspirin—good. It doesn't matter that, in terms of death rate, aspirin is more dangerous than marijuana. Chemical bigotry is at work.

Some might contend that chemical bigotry is justifiable because drugs themselves cause death and destruction. This might have a slight ring of truth if drug policies were evenly applied. But as a result of chemical bigotry, a substance like marijuana that is comparatively benign is banned while a substance like alcohol that is fairly dangerous is aggressively advertised. Further, since a regulated market approach to the distribution of what are now illegal drugs has never been tried, perhaps much of the death and destruction attributable to drugs actually finds its roots in drug prohibition. Bigotry will always try to prevent the introduction of new social policies.

Some might insist that eliminating chemical bigotry would induce social chaos. Everyone would be running around stoned conducting mayhem. Fearmongers said much the same about freeing the slaves or giving women the right to vote. Whether under the influence of drugs, too little sleep, or manic depression, bad behavior is simply bad behavior.

Violence is still violence regardless of whether the perpetrator is black, gay, or Irish. Truly bad behavior which hurts others certainly deserves sanction. But, taking that extra leap to suggest that ingesting certain chemicals and not others engenders terrorism reveals the spirit of a bigot. Bigotry itself introduces far more social chaos than does its elimination.

Lest one sit back and say chemical bigotry doesn't apply to me, at some level this bigotry applies to all of us. All of us can become its victim. Those who use cannabis

ESSENTIALLY, WE ARE NO LONGER DEFINED SOLELY BY THE CONTENT OF OUR CHARACTER AND WHAT WE ACCOMPLISH IN LIFE, BUT ALSO BY OUR CHEMICAL COMPOSITION AT ANY PARTICULAR TIME.

for whatever reason know chemical bigotry first hand. Likewise, patients who need more powerful pain relievers feel the stigma of chemical bigotry, as do those trying to kick opiates with methadone and hopes of heroin maintenance. Chemical bigotry extends outward beyond what are now illegal drugs. It demonizes the responsible social drinker and tobacco smoker. It isolates the problem drug or alcohol user forcing them to hide their problem and shun help. It compels users of legal drugs to reveal their private medical history, endure debilitating side effects, and even avoid helpful medications, lest chemical bigotry spotlight them. It touches all these individuals and their families and communities as well. Essentially, we are no longer defined solely by the content of our character and what we accomplish in life, but also by our chemical composition at any particular time.

How do we fight chemical bigotry? Organizations like DrugSense/MAP, the Simon Wiesenthal Center, or the Southern Poverty Law Center for example, fight bigotry by shedding light on it. DrugSense/MAP, in particular, does this by collecting articles on drug policy, identifying incidences of chemical bigotry, and promoting media activism to bring it out in the open. Essentially, DrugSense/MAP and other organizations focused on drug policy reform are to chemical bigotry what the Simon Wiesenthal Center is to anti-Semitism or the Southern Poverty Law Center is to racism.

Those who have been scarred by chemical bigotry along with those who believe that bigotry-based public policy is wrong form a vibrant and growing drug policy reform community. This community needs to understand that the great struggle in which it is engaged is not a war on the War on Drugs, but an age-old fight against bigotry. In doing so, better strategies and tactics can be developed to enable change. Reformers may also find that they share much in common with others who throughout history have fought in so many ways to remove bigotry's shackles.

Organizations cited in this article:

DrugSense/MAP—http://www.mapinc.org
Simon Wiesenthal Center—http://www.wiesenthal.com
Southern Poverty Law Center—http://www.splcenter.org

On Cognitive Liberty
Parts i,ii,iii

Richard Glen Boire, Esq.

On Cognitive Liberty (Part I)

Thoughts are free and are subject to no rule.
— Paracelsus[1]

As we frantically race into the third millennium, with micro-processors becoming faster, cheaper, and smaller, with surveillance cameras proliferating in public spaces, with the Human Genome Project issuing its "working draft" of the human DNA sequence, and with an out-of-control Frankensteinian machine named the War on Drugs, all awhirl in the ocean of modern day culture, it

> **CONSCIOUSNESS IS SO COMPLEX AND MULTIFACETED THAT IT MAY NEVER BE UNDERSTOOD.**

is imperative that we, as a society, expressly acknowledge the fundamental human right to cognitive liberty and immediately begin to define its contours.

Encroachments on cognitive liberty can take various forms. New technologies such as biogenetic modification, human-computer interfacing, brain-scanning, nanotechnology, neural-networking, so-called "neuro-therapy," and new pharmaceuticals, raise exciting possibilities for human "evolution." But, if not developed and used responsibly, they and the legislation they spawn could also pose new threats to cognitive freedom.[2] The trend of technology is to overcome the limitations of the human body. The Web has been characterized as a virtual collective consciousness and unconsciousness. What are the implications for mental autonomy when wearable computers become wet-wired to our own minds and memory is augmented by a high-speed wireless connection to the Web? Similarly, advances in biotechnology and drug-design increasingly raise legal and ethical questions related to cognitive liberty, including what rights people will have to access these and other technologies, and what rights we will have to avoid them.

Calibrating Cognitive Liberty

Part of elucidating a theory of cognitive liberty is simply recognizing when free cognition is being infringed. Restrictions on physical liberty, for all their pain and terror, at least have the benefit of being relatively easy to recognize and call attention to. During World War II,

the Nazi concentration camps for Jews and the American internment camps for Japanese Americans, were marked by the machinery of physical control: fences, barbed wire, and guard towers. Similarly, from 1961 to 1989, a concrete and barbwire wall overseen by 116 guard towers divided the city of Berlin. Anyone who tried to cross that wall without a "special authorization" risked a bullet in the back of his or her skull. In contrast to the usual visibility of government restraints on physical liberty, restraints on cognitive liberty are most often difficult to recognize, if not invisible.

Consciousness is so complex and multifaceted that it may never be understood. Unfortunately, the inability to understand consciousness does not equate to an inability for others to control it. How then can we recognize nefarious attempts to control consciousness? In one respect, absolute control of one's own consciousness is an impossibility. While each of us carries our own brain in our own skull, the process of consciousness itself is interactive. All our senses continuously feed data into our brains, producing a dance of cognition that perpetually swirls the exterior world with the interior world creating a seamless, edgeless, apperceptive feedback loop. Our minds are continually changing, continually interfacing with "the other." Cognitive liberty clearly cannot mean cognitive isolation.

Mind control, like most everything else, comes in degrees. A discussion with a friend may make you change your opinion on a topic, it may even change your life, but does that amount to "mind control?" Was your cognitive liberty violated? Over $200 billion in US currency is spent each year by companies unabashedly striving to manipulate our desires, to literally *make* us want their product. If you see an advertisement (or many) for a product and that advertisement, replete with imagery of the good life, causes you to purchase the product, have you been the victim of mind control? Has your cognitive liberty been violated?

> **MIND CONTROL, LIKE MOST EVERYTHING ELSE, COMES IN DEGREES.**

What if the advertisement is embedded with auditory or visual subliminal messages? What if the advertisement is embedded in prime-time television programs, passing as program content, rather than demarked as a "commercial?"[3] Or, suppose you are a 12-year-old placed on Prozac® or Ritalin® largely because your schoolteacher has "diagnosed" you as depressed or suffering from Attention Deficit Disorder. Has your cognitive liberty been violated?

The answers to the above questions depend upon how finely one calibrates cognitive liberty. But some scenarios, some infringements on mental autonomy, are crystal clear and *ought* to present limit cases where general policies and specific rules emerge in high-definition clarity. Yet even in so-called limit cases, the US government, including its legal system, has often acted inconsistently.

A (Very) Brief History of US Government Mind Control

In 1969, Justice Marshall wrote, without mincing words, "Our whole constitutional heritage rebels at the thought of giving government the power to control

...SOME OF THE GOVERNMENT'S OFFENSES SEEM TO COME DIRECTLY FROM THE PAGES OF A DYSTOPIAN NOVEL LIKE GEORGE ORWELL'S *1984*.

men's minds."[4] Yet, contrary to Justice Marshall's strong pronouncement, the US government has not consistently respected or protected cognitive liberty. Indeed, some of the government's offenses seem to come directly from the pages of a dystopian novel like George Orwell's *1984*.[5]

Imagine, for example, if the government passed a law mandating that all citizens receive monthly injections of time-release sedatives, justifying the law on the "public health" grounds that sedated people are more productive at routine repetitive tasks, are less violent, and are less of a drain on public resources. What if those who did not voluntarily report at the time and place appointed

WHILE THE MKULTRA PROGRAM BEGAN WITH TESTS IN THE LABORATORY ON WILLING VOLUNTEERS, THE CIA QUICKLY SAW THE NEED TO EXPAND THE TESTING TO DETERMINE WHAT THE EFFECTS OF DRUGS SUCH AS LSD WOULD BE ON *UNSUSPECTING* PEOPLE.

for their injection were rounded up by the police and forcefully lobotomized? Would anyone doubt that such a law infringed not just on one's *physical* freedom but also on one's *cognitive* freedom? It's not exactly an unthinkable scenario. From the 1920s through 1970, pursuant to the laws of at least 32 states, more than 60,000 people were deemed "eugenically unfit." Many of these people were involuntarily sterilized, in part because of low scores on intelligence tests.[6] When one of these laws was challenged, and the case reached the United States Supreme Court, it was *upheld*—with Justice Oliver Wendell Holmes smugly proclaiming, "Three generations of imbeciles are enough."[7]

Until 1973, "homosexuality" was listed as a psychiatric disorder in the *Diagnostic and Statistical Manual of Mental Disorders* (DSM). People who admitted being homosexual, or who were "accused" of being gay or lesbian, were subject to involuntary confinement under mental health laws and subjected to "reparative therapy" or "conversion therapy" designed to convert them into heterosexuals. "Treatment," in addition to counseling, included penile plesthysmograph (electronic shock triggered by penile erection), drugging, and hypnosis. Even though homosexuality was deleted from the DSM in 1973, it was not until December 1998 that the American Psychiatric Association finally disapproved of "reparative" or "conversion" therapy.[8]

In the 1950s, 60s, and early 70s, the US government illegally and unethically drugged unwitting US citizens with psychoactive substances, including LSD, as part of projects BLUEBIRD, ARTICHOKE, and MKULTRA, all in an attempt to develop techniques of mind control. Richard Helms, the chief planner of MKULTRA, wrote in a planning memorandum that the program was designed in part to:

Investigate the development of chemical material which causes a reversible non-toxic aberrant mental state, the specific nature of which can be reasonably well predicted for each individual. This material could potentially aid in discrediting individuals, eliciting information, and implanting suggestions and other forms of mental control.[9]

While the MKULTRA program began with tests in the laboratory on willing volunteers, the CIA quickly saw the need to expand the testing to determine what the effects of drugs such as LSD would be on *unsuspecting* people. Thus, in 1953, the CIA moved its mind control program into the streets of America and began the "covert testing of materials on unwitting US citizens."[10]

In subsequent installments of this essay, we will see how the US Government continues to promulgate certain policies that, while cloaked in "public health" or "public safety" justifications, amount to an impermissible government action aimed at policing thought and interfering with the mental processes of citizens.

Freedom's Invisible Landscape

The right to control one's own consciousness is the quintessence of freedom. If freedom is to mean anything, it must mean that each person has an inviolable right to think for him- or herself. It must mean, at a minimum, that each person is free to direct one's own consciousness; one's own underlying mental processes, and one's beliefs, opinions, and worldview. This is self-evident and axiomatic.

In assessing what rights are fundamental and thus entitled to the most stringent legal protection, the US Supreme Court has stated that fundamental liberties are those "implicit in the concept of ordered liberty," such that "neither liberty nor justice would exist if [they] were sacrificed."[11] Under another test, fundamental liberties were characterized by the Court as those liberties that are "deeply rooted in this Nation's history and tradition."[12]

Slightly over seventy years ago, Justice Brandeis acknowledged in a landmark privacy case that cognitive freedom was one of the principal protections designed into the Constitution:

> The makers of our Constitution undertook to secure conditions favorable to the pursuit of happiness. They recognized the significance of man's spiritual nature, of his feelings and of his intellect. They knew that only a part of the pain, pleasure and satisfactions of life are to be found in material things. They sought to protect Americans in their beliefs, their thoughts, their emotions and their sensations. They conferred, as against the Government, the right to be let alone—the most comprehensive of rights and the right most valued by civilized man.[13]

But, while certain justices have, at times, pointedly acknowledged the fundamental nature of cognitive freedom and the nefarious nature of government (or other "outside") interference with the intellect, this important freedom remains only obliquely defined within the US legal system. Ironically, the lack of a comprehensive treatment may be because cognitive freedom is *so* self-evidently a basic human right. Whatever the reason, without a coherent cognitive liberty jurisprudence, present and future infringements on cognitive liberty risk passing unnoticed or unremedied.

On Cognitive Liberty (Part 2)

…without freedom of thought there can be no free society. — US Supreme Court Justice Felix Frankfurter[14]

An Introductory Note on Banned Books and other Controlled Substances

As you read this sentence you are receiving information. Words are carriers of thoughts, whether spoken from mouth to ear, digitized and passed electronically, or downloaded into ink and passed on paper across time and space. Because words are vehicles for thoughts, words can change your opinion, give you new ideas, reform your worldview, or foment a revolution.

Attempts to control the written word date from at least AD 325 when the Council of Nicaea ruled that Christ was 100% divine and forbade the dissemination of contrary beliefs. Since the invention of the printing press in 1452, governments have struggled to control the printed word. Presses were initially licensed and registered. Only certain people were permitted to own or control a printing press and only certain things could be printed or copied. (This was the origin of today's copyright rules.) Works printed without prior authorization were gathered up and destroyed, the authors and printers imprisoned.

Scholars disagree as to the exact date, but some time around 1560 Pope Paul IV published the *Index Librorum Prohibitorum*, a list of forbidden books (i.e., controlled substances) enforced by the Roman government. When the *Index* was (finally) abandoned in 1966, it listed over 4,000 forbidden books, including works by such people as Galileo, Kant, Pascal, Spinoza and John Locke.[15] The history of censorship has been extensively recorded by others. My point is simply the obvious one that efforts to prohibit heterodox texts and to make criminals out of those who "manufactured" such texts, were not so much interested in controlling ink patterns on paper, as in controlling the *ideas* encoded in printed words.

I submit that in the same way, the so-called "war on drugs" is not a war on pills, powder, plants, and potions, it is war on mental states—a war on consciousness itself—how much, what sort we are permitted to experience, and who gets to control it. More than an unintentional misnomer, the government-termed "war on drugs" is a strategic decoy label; a slight-of-hand move by the government to redirect attention away from what lies at ground zero of the war—each individual's fundamental right to control his or her own consciousness.

Entheogenic Oldspeak v. Drug War Newspeak

In George Orwell's dystopian novel *1984*, the Oceania government diligently worked to establish "Newspeak" a carefully crafted language designed by the government

> SINCE THE INVENTION OF THE PRINTING PRESS IN 1452, GOVERNMENTS HAVE STRUGGLED TO CONTROL THE PRINTED WORD.

> I SUBMIT THAT IN THE SAME WAY, THE SO-CALLED "WAR ON DRUGS" IS NOT A WAR ON PILLS, POWDER, PLANTS, AND POTIONS, IT IS WAR ON MENTAL STATES—A WAR ON CONSCIOUSNESS ITSELF—HOW MUCH, WHAT SORT WE ARE PERMITTED TO EXPERIENCE, AND WHO GETS TO CONTROL IT.

for the purpose of making unapproved "modes of thought impossible."[16] Prior to Newspeak, the people of Oceania communicated with "Oldspeak," an autonomous natural language capable of expressing nuanced emotions and multiple points of view. By controlling language through the imposition of Newspeak—by "eliminating undesirable words"—the government of Oceania was able to control and, in some cases, completely extinguish certain thoughts. As a character in *1984* explained to Winston Smith "Don't you see that the whole aim of Newspeak is to narrow the range of thought?...Every year fewer and fewer words, and the range of consciousness always a little smaller."[17] Those people raised with Newspeak, having never known the wider-range of Oldspeak, might fail to notice, indeed, might be unable to even perceive, that the Government was limiting consciousness.

In 1970, just four years after the Catholic Church finally abandoned the *Index Librorum Prohibitorum*, the United States government produced its own index of forbidden

| JUST AS NEWSPEAK WAS INTENDED TO MAKE CERTAIN OLD(SPEAK) THOUGHTS LITERALLY UNTHINKABLE, SO THE WAR ON ENTHEOGENS MAKES CERTAIN SORTS OF COGNITION AND AWARENESS ALL BUT INACCESSIBLE.

thought catalysts: the federal schedule of controlled substances. Included on the initial list of Schedule I substances were seventeen substances denoted as "hallucinogens," and declared to have "a high potential for abuse," "no currently accepted medical use" in the USA, and "a lack of accepted safety" even under medical supervision. Among the list of outlawed "hallucinogens" were psilocybin and psilocin, the active principles of *Psilocybe* mushrooms; dimethyltryptamine (DMT), the active principle in ayahuasca and many visionary snuffs; ibogaine, mescaline, peyote, and LSD.[18] The experience elicited by these substances in their chemical or natural plant forms is the *par excellence* of "Oldspeak"—a cognitive modality dating from pre-history.

| THOSE WHO HAVE NEVER EXPERIENCED THE MENTAL STATES THAT ARE NOW PROHIBITED DO NOT REALIZE WHAT THE LAWS ARE DENYING THEM. IT IS AS IF NOTHING IS BEING TAKEN AWAY, AT LEAST NOTHING NOTICEABLE, NOTHING THAT IS MISSED.

Archeological evidence suggests that humans have communed with visionary plants and potions for thousands of years. Peyote, for example, has been used for over 10,000 years. Lysergic acid diethylamide (LSD) was created by Dr. Albert Hofmann, a chemist employed by Sandoz Laboratories in Basel, Switzerland. In 1938, Dr. Hofmann synthesized LSD from a fungus commonly found in rye seeds. Its effect on consciousness remained undiscovered until April 16, 1943, when Dr. Hofmann accidentally ingested a minute amount of the substance and experienced a strange inebriation in which "the external world became changed as in a dream." Several years later, Hofmann discovered that the chemical structure

of LSD is nearly identical to that of the sacred entheogen *ololiuhqui*, prepared from morning glory seeds and used ritually by the Aztecs for thousands of years.

Mushrooms, of the genus *Psilocybe*, were used to produce visionary states at least as early as 4000 B.C. The *Psilocybe* mushroom was used in religious ceremonies long before the Aztec civilization. It was named *teonanácatl*, meaning "sacred mushroom." In 1957, working with mushrooms obtained by R. Gordon Wasson from the now famous curandera Maria Sabina, Dr. Hofmann isolated and later synthesized two active substances derived from the *Psilocybe* mushroom. He named these substances psilocybin and psilocin. In 1962, Dr. Hofmann traveled to Mexico and met with Maria Sabina. During a night ceremony, she ingested 30 milligrams of the synthetic psilocybin and later said the effect was indistinguishable from that elicited with the sacred mushrooms themselves.

Another substance placed on the government's 1970 list of criminalized "hallucinogens" was *N,N*-dimethyltryptamine (DMT). This substance was first synthesized in 1931, but its entheogenic properties were not discovered until 1956. It was subsequently learned that DMT is the principal active ingredient in numerous snuffs and brews long-used by various South American Indians during religious ceremonies. The DMT containing plant *Psychotria viridis* is a well-known admixture to the entheogenic brew known as ayahuasca or yajé, which archeological evidence suggests dates back as many as five thousand years.[19]

Some who ingest visionary plants believe that the plants talk to them and open up channels of communication with animals and other entities. Mazatec eaters of *Psilocybe* mushrooms, for example, are adamant that the mushrooms speak to them:

> The Mazatecs say that the mushrooms speak. If you ask a shaman where his imagery comes from, he is likely to reply: "I didn't say it, the mushrooms did." ...he who eats these mushrooms, if he is a man of language, becomes endowed with an inspired capacity to speak...The spontaneity they liberate is not only perceptual, but linguistic, the spontaneity of speech, of fervent, lucid discourse, of the logos in activity. For the shaman it is as if existence were uttering itself through him...words are materializations of consciousness; language is a privileged vehicle of our relation to reality.[20]

Just as Newspeak was intended to make certain Old(speak) thoughts literally unthinkable, so the War on Entheogens makes certain sorts of cognition and awareness all but inaccessible. Religious scholar Peter Lamborn Wilson has aptly framed the War on Entheogens as a battle over the nature of thought itself:

The War on Drugs is a war on cognition itself, about thought itself as the human condition. Is thought this dualist Cartesian reason? Or is cognition this mysterious, complex, organic, magical thing with little mushroom elves dancing around. Which is it to be?[21]

In Orwell's vision of *1984*, Newspeak's power to control and limit thought depended, in part, upon the passing of time and the birth of new generations that never knew Oldspeak. As explained by Orwell in the Appendix to *1984*, "It was intended that when Newspeak had been adopted once and for all and Oldspeak forgotten, a heretical thought—that is a thought diverging from the principles of Ingsoc—should be literally unthinkable, at least so far as thought is dependant on words."[22]

Just as Newspeak depended in part upon time eradicating knowledge of Oldspeak, today's War on Entheogens is sustainable, in part, because the current generation of young adults (those twenty-one to thirty years old) have never known a time when most entheogens were *not* illicit.

Those who have never experienced the mental states that are now prohibited do not realize what the laws are denying them. It is as if nothing is being taken away, at least nothing noticeable, nothing that is missed. As pointed out by the authors of a law review article on how mandatory schooling raises issues of mass-consciousness control: "[t]he more the government regulates formation of beliefs so as to interfere with personal consciousness,… the fewer people can conceive dissenting ideas or perceive contradictions between self-interest and government sustained ideological orthodoxy."[23]

Because of the personal experiential nature of entheogen-elicited cognition, only those who have been initiated into the modern day Mysteries—those who have tasted the forbidden fruit from the visionary plants of knowledge and have not fallen victim to the stigmatizing psycho-impact of "being a drug user"—are acutely aware of the gravity of what is being prohibited: powerful modalities for thinking, perceiving, and experiencing.

The very best argument for the potential value of entheogen-elicited mind states is in the entheogenic experience itself; an experience that has, in almost every case, been outlawed. That is the dilemma of entheogen policy reformation. The advocate for entheogenic-consciousness is left in an even worse position than the proverbial sighted man who must describe colors to a blind person. With regard to entheogen policy, the position is worse because the "blind" are in power and have declared it a crime to see colors.

Left with the impossible task of saying the unsayable, of describing the indescribable, those who have tasted the forbidden fruit must plead their case on the fundamental philosophical and political level of what it means to be truly free. They must state their appeal on the ground that, with respect to the inner-workings of each person's mind, the values of tolerance and respect are far weightier and far more conducive to the basic principles of democracy, than is the chillingly named "zero-tolerance" policy that is currently in vogue. This brings us, once again, to cognitive liberty as an essential substrate of freedom.

Free Thought and the First Amendment

Benjamin Cardozo, one of the most respected and influential American legal scholars of the last century and a former Justice of the US Supreme Court, affirmed cognitive liberty as central to most every other freedom:

> …freedom of thought…one may say…is the matrix, the indispensable condition, of nearly every other form of freedom. With rare aberrations a pervasive recognition of that truth can be traced in our history, political and legal.[24]

Cognitive liberty jurisprudence must begin, then, with an effort to distill the legal principles that support some of our most cherished and well-established freedoms, and then, over time, crystallize these principles into the foundation for a coherent legal scheme governing issues related to an individual's right to control his or her own consciousness.

Given the importance of the First Amendment to US and even international law, we will begin by examining how courts have construed the First Amendment—searching for evidence that the right of each person to autonomy over his or her own mind and thought processes is central to First Amendment jurisprudence.

> Congress shall make no law respecting an establishment of religion, or prohibiting the free exercise thereof; or abridging the freedom of speech, or of the press; or the right of the people peaceably to assemble, and to petition the Government for a redress of grievances. (The First Amendment.)[25]

The First Amendment's guarantees were designed to bar the government from controlling or prohibiting the dissemination of unpopular or dissenting ideas. Central to all five guarantees is the acknowledgement that people must be treated by the government as ends not means; each person free to develop his or her mind and own belief system, and encouraged to express his or her thoughts in the so-called "marketplace of ideas." As US Supreme Court Justice Felix Frankfurter emphasized in 1949, the freedom of expression guaranteed by the First Amendment guards against "thought becom[ing] checked and atrophied."[26]

Free speech, free exercise, free association, a free press and the right to assemble, are all moot if the thought that underlies these actions has already been constrained by the government. If the government is permitted to prohibit the experiencing of certain thought processes, or otherwise manipulate consciousness at its very roots—via drug prohibitions, religious indoctrination, monopolizing media, or any number of methods—it need not even worry about controlling the expression of such thoughts. By prohibiting the very formation of mind states—by strangling the free mind itself—free expression is made meaningless.

Thus, in order to prevent the erosion of the First Amendment's protection of expression, the Amendment must also provide at least as strong a protection for the underlying consciousness that forms the ideas that are later expressed. Indeed, the First Amendment was infused with the principle that each individual—not the government—ought to have control over his or her own mind, to think what he or she wants to think, and to freely form and express opinions and beliefs based on all the information at his or her disposal. The First Amendment, in other words, embraces cognitive liberty not simply as

> PROHIBITING AN OTHERWISE LAW-ABIDING PERSON FROM USING ENTHEOGENS IS MORE THAN MERELY AN "OBLIQUE INTRUSION" ON THE RIGHT TO CONTROL ONE'S OWN MENTAL PROCESSES, OR A SLIGHT TRESPASS ON THE "PROTECTED CAPACITY TO PRODUCE IDEAS"—IT IS A DIRECT FRONTAL ATTACK.

the desired outcome of the articulated guarantees (i.e., a right to express one's ideas), but also as a necessary precondition to those guaranteed freedoms (i.e., a right to form one's own ideas).

Mother May I Control My Own Consciousness?

In (the apropos year of) 1984, the Tenth Circuit Court of Appeal issued an opinion in a case involving a man who was involuntarily drugged with the "antipsychotic drug" thorazine while he was being held for trial on murder charges. The threshold issue was whether pretrial detainees have a fundamental right to refuse treatment with anti-psychotic drugs. To answer this question, the Tenth Circuit analogized to a 1982 case in which the US Supreme Court held that "'[l]iberty from bodily restraint always has been recognized as the core of the liberty protected by the Due Process Clause from arbitrary governmental action.'"[27] The Tenth Circuit reasoned that if freedom from *bodily* restraints is a fundamental right, then individuals must also have a liberty interest in freedom from "mental restraint of the kind potentially imposed by antipsychotic drugs."[28]

Thus, the Tenth Circuit found that freedom from government imposed mental restraints was just as fundamental as freedom from government imposed physical restraints—both were protected by the Due Process Clause. Furthermore, the Tenth Circuit found that the First Amendment was also implicated when the

government attempts to involuntarily psycho-medicate a person awaiting trial. In unequivocal language, the Tenth Circuit explained "[t]he First Amendment protects communication of ideas, which itself implies protection of the capacity to produce ideas."[29]

As Professor Laurence Tribe of Harvard Law School has cautioned:

> In a society whose "whole constitutional heritage rebels at the thought of giving government the power to control men's own minds," the governing institutions, and especially the courts, must not only reject direct attempts to exercise forbidden domination over mental processes; they must strictly examine as well oblique intrusions likely to produce or designed to produce, the same result.[30]

Prohibiting an otherwise law-abiding person from using entheogens is more than merely an "oblique intrusion" on the right to control one's own mental processes, or a slight trespass on the "protected capacity to produce ideas"—it is a direct frontal attack. Under the recently released *National Drug Control Strategy 2000*, the federal government will spend just shy of $20 billion ($20,000,000,000) on an all out attempt to keep people from evoking alternative states of consciousness by the use of controlled substances.[31]

On Cognitive Liberty (Part III)

In the last decade, new computer-based methods for storing, searching, and sharing data about individuals have proliferated. With the commercialization of the Internet, the tracking of individuals and their databodies has become big business, one in which governments increasingly participate. In a similar vein, optical devices have become smaller and cheaper, leading to an expansion of government and corporate surveillance cameras, which continuously monitor an ever-increasing number of private and public spaces. These technologically-facilitated developments have revitalized the ongoing debate about privacy. At issue is what form privacy will take—both as a principle, as well as a legal protection—in the so-called Information Age.

While it is commonly thought of as a fundamental right, privacy is not expressly protected by the US Constitution. In the United States, the law of privacy has developed in a hodge-podge manner, largely by Supreme Court decisions in which the Court was presented with a specific factual scenario and determined whether or not a privacy right existed in *that* specific instance. This development pattern has led some legal scholars to declare that rather than an overarching "right to privacy," citizens of the United States enjoy only particularized "rights" to privacy—those that the US Supreme Court has established in various cases, or that the US Congress has enacted as specific statutory protections.

The US Supreme Court, for example, has found a fundamental right to privacy in the following basic areas: (1) reproduction, (2) marriage, (3) activities inside the home, (4) the right to refuse medical treatment, and (5) raising children. Similarly, Congress has passed federal laws or regulations that grant (to a greater or lesser degree) privacy protection in a host of areas, including the contents of first-class mail, information concerning which videotapes you rent, and information about your bank records.

Although these protections were created by particular court decisions or by specific statutory enactments, they share an underlying reasoning and common principles, revealing that a *general* concept of privacy does indeed exist.

The legal concept of privacy has developed in fits and starts, often in union with technological developments. Up until the late 1800s, "privacy" was by-and-large limited to providing a remedy when someone physically interfered with your (private) property or with your physical body. A hundred years ago, the right to privacy was not much more than a right to be free from physical battery and a right to repel invaders from your land. A major development occurred in 1890, when Samuel Warren and Louis Brandeis penned an influential law review article titled "The Right to Privacy."[32] Warren and Brandeis wrote at the time when portable cameras and audio recording devices were—for the first time—available to common people, and newspaper reporters aggressively embraced these new devices. It was the genesis of the paparazzi.

In their article, Warren and Brandeis articulated a legal principle, based on general concepts of privacy, which would provide people with protection against reporters' efforts to publicize personal information. As Warren and Brandeis wrote:

> Instantaneous photographs and newspaper enterprises have invaded the sacred precinct of private and domestic life; and numerous mechanical devices threaten to make good the [biblical] prediction that "what is whispered in the closet shall be proclaimed from the housetops."[33]

With their focus on the events of their time, Warren and Brandeis sketched out a theory of privacy that was an extension of the common law protection of (private) property—a new theory designed to encompass and protect the public disclosure by reporters of private or personal information. This broader right they succinctly termed "the right to be let alone."

Over 100 years later, this basic phrase remains the touchstone of what is commonly meant by the "right to privacy."

Cognitive Liberty and the Right to Privacy

Just as Warren and Brandeis called for a revisioning of "privacy" in the then-new age of portable cameras and audio recorders, as we enter into the third millennium, with ongoing developments in drug creation, nano-technology, genetic engineering, and mind-machine interfacing, it is again time to explore the meaning of privacy and the scope of what is to receive legal protection as "private" in this (post)modern age. As the US Supreme Court noted in 1910:

> Legislation, both statutory and constitutional, is enacted, it is true, from an experience of evils but its general language should not, therefore, be necessarily confined to the form that evil had theretofore taken. Time works changes, brings into existence new conditions and purposes. Therefore a principle to be vital must be capable of wider application than the mischief which gave it birth. This is peculiarly true of Constitutions. They are not ephemeral enactments, designed to meet passing occasions. They are, to use the words of Chief Justice Marshall, "designed to approach immortality as nearly as human institutions can approach it.[34]

Thus, while the current privacy debate has centered on new computer surveillance technology with the power to capture and control more and more data about each of us, it is time for the privacy debate to acknowledge, and make explicit, that a person's mind and mental processes must be protected as private. "[T]he concept of privacy embodies the 'moral fact that a person belongs to himself and not others nor to society as a whole.'"[35] Certainly, a person's thoughts and thought processes belong to himself or herself, and not to society, the government, or any other meddlesome external force.

Inasmuch as a right to privacy entails the right to be let alone, and centers on the interior and intimate aspects of a person's life, cognitive freedom and autonomy should become a central touchstone for how we conceive of, and apply, a modern right to privacy. The areas in which the Supreme Court or Congress has expressly declared a right to privacy all center on interior spaces as opposed to exterior spaces, and serve to strengthen and protect the autonomy of the personal, or individual self. There is nothing more interior, and nothing more important and central to individual autonomy than one's consciousness. Indeed, without independent consciousness, no sense of self is even possible.

Despite its self-evident importance to us today, the idea that a person is entitled to privacy over his or her own thoughts and thought processes is actually a fairly recent concept. For most of history, the inner workings of the mind have been perceived as a threat to the Church-State.

Richard Glen Boire, Esq.

Broad expanses of the US legal system are premised on an Aristotelian-Thomistic world view. Both Aristotle and Thomas Aquinas viewed God as a "Supreme Being" who exists *outside of* and above humankind. In contrast to God, evil was located *within* the individual. The concept of privacy that developed under the Aristotelian-Thomistic belief system was one inherently skeptical of the human interior and sought to essentially force into private—to shield behind closed doors—such things as death, birth, and personal hygienic matters. Under the Aristolian-Thomistic tradition, the privacy protections that did exist were limited to those that would benefit the community and ultimately promote the pleasure of God. Privacy, then, to the extent that it exists under a Aristotelian-Thomistic paradigm is there to serve and promote the "general will" rather than to advance individual autonomy and self-actualization.

A Platonic or Buddhist belief system is just one among a host of other ways to view the world. In these systems of thought (and many other "religions," and/or "philosophies"), god(s) exists both inside and outside of each person. Thus, a person's interior thoughts and thought processes are not feared, but are instead cultivated, revered, and protected.

...THE STATE HAS NO BUSINESS TELLING A MAN OR WOMAN SITTING IN HIS OR HER OWN HOME, WHAT STATES OF CONSCIOUSNESS ARE ACCEPTABLE AND WHAT STATES OF CONSCIOUSNESS ARE NOT.

Today, however, the US prides itself on being a secular, pluralist country, free from the shackles of a dominating Church power. As such, it is no longer appropriate to limit the concept of privacy to centuries-old models; indeed, just as Brandeis and Warren did over a century ago, it is imperative that we continue to update our concept of privacy to fit current circumstances.

A modern conception of privacy must shed the long-standing allegiance to a single way of conceiving of Reality, and recognize that privacy is rooted in furthering human dignity and autonomy and in protecting each person's right to conceive of the world in his or her own way. Describing the contours of a modern right to privacy, Robert Ellis Smith, attorney and publisher of the *Privacy Journal*, aptly included "a sense of autonomy, a right to develop a unique personality and living space, and a right to distinguish one's own persona from everyone else's."[36]

As noted earlier, the US Supreme Court has a spotty record with regard to upholding individual privacy. The Court has found a narrow range of situations in which a protected privacy right exists and a host of situations in which it does not. In 1928, for example, the Supreme Court ruled that the police could tap a person's telephone so long as they did not enter the person's home in order to place the tap.[37] Not until 1967 did the Court rule that the content of telephone conversations was protected as private regardless of whether the line was tapped from inside or outside of the home.[38] In 1984, the Supreme Court held that people have no legitimate privacy right

with respect to garbage cans that they have placed on the curb for pickup. Such garbage, held the Court, may be examined by a police officer without any need to obtain a warrant.[39] In 1989, the Court held that the police did not violate the privacy right of an individual when they flew over his home in a helicopter and peered through a hole in his roof in a search for marijuana plants.[40] The latter two cases grew out of the War on (certain) Drugs, but their holdings extend far beyond drug cases, significantly reducing the right of privacy for all Americans.

In cases raising issues that directly concern the privacy of a person's *body* in the face of government intrusion, the decisional trend has been more in favor of individual autonomy. For example, in 1965 the Supreme Court held that the decision of whether to use birth control was a private issue for married couples (a ruling later extended to unmarried couples).[41] That case involved a Connecticut law prohibiting the use of "any drug, medicinal article or instrument for the purpose of preventing conception." Such a law, held the Court, infringed upon a constitutionally protected "zone of privacy" reserved to individuals—the right to make their own decisions about reproduction. The Court struck down the Connecticut law based on what it called "the familiar principle, so often applied by this Court, that a 'governmental purpose to control or prevent activities constitutionally subject to state regulation may not be achieved by means which sweep unnecessarily broadly and thereby invade the area of protected freedoms.'"[42]

In *Roe v. Wade*, the court held that the "zone of privacy" encompasses and protects a woman's decision to terminate her pregnancy.[43]

The principles underlying the Supreme Court's privacy rulings, especially those invoked in cases concerning an individual's right to make decisions about the interior of his or her body, support the proposition that personal decisions about how to manage one's interior *thought processes and consciousness* fall within a protected zone of privacy reserved for individuals, and protected against governmental invasion or usurpation. Just as the Connecticut law that banned all use of contraceptives was struck down as "unnecessarily broad," today's drug prohibition laws, which outlaw all use of certain plants and psychoactive chemicals, trespass upon the zone of privacy that protects an adult's right to make decisions about how to manage his or her own consciousness.

Society recognizes cognitive privacy as reasonable. What goes on exclusively inside a person's mind has traditionally been a private affair. The specter of Orwell's "mind police" is universally chilling, as is the idea of a government employing mind control or thought-manipulation techniques on its citizenry. It is, indeed, a conservative position to state that if freedom is to mean anything, it must mean that what goes on inside a person's skull is a private matter and something which *that person*—not the government—has the right to control.

Just about the only time this cognitive privacy principle is questioned is when it is applied to "drugs." For example, in 1968, the US Supreme Court held that "the mere private possession of obscene matter cannot be made a crime."[44] In this case, a Mr. Stanley was found in possession (in his own home) of some pornographic films. He was prosecuted under a Georgia law that made possession of "obscene matter" a crime. The US Supreme Court struck down the Georgia law, finding that the law violated the First Amendment. The Court distinguished laws that regulate the public *distribution* of "obscene material" from the Georgia law, which unlawfully targeted *mere private possession* of such matter. Hidden away in a footnote, however, the Court remarked that the same reasoning did not apply to drugs:

> What we have said in no way infringes upon the power of the State or Federal Government to make possession of other items, such as narcotics, firearms, or stolen goods, a crime. Our holding in the present case turns upon the Georgia statute's infringement of fundamental liberties protected by the First and Fourteenth Amendments. No First Amendment rights are involved in most statutes making mere possession criminal.[45]

This was non-binding dictum (commentary that is superfluous to the actual holding in the case). The Supreme Court has never been squarely presented with the argument that cognitive liberty is a fundamental right, or that outlawing mere possession or use of psychoactive drugs infringes on that fundamental right.

Aside from the comment in the footnote, the reasoning that pervades the Court's opinion in *Stanley* supports the fundamental principle that what goes on inside a person's head, the processing and information therein, is entitled to privacy. The Court emphasized that the Constitution "protects the right to receive information and ideas," and that this right holds irrespective of an idea's "social worth."[46] The Court also accepted Mr. Stanley's argument that he had a constitutional right to control his own intellect—to determine for himself what to read or watch in the privacy of his own home:

> [Mr. Stanley] is asserting the right to read or observe what he pleases—the right to satisfy his intellectual and emotional needs in the privacy of his own home. He is asserting the right to be free from state inquiry into the contents of his library. Georgia contends that appellant does not have these rights, that there are certain types of materials that the individual may not read or even possess. Georgia justifies this assertion by arguing that the films in the present case are obscene. But we think that mere categorization of these films as "obscene" is insufficient justification for such a drastic invasion of personal liberties guaranteed by the First and Fourteenth Amendments. Whatever may be the justifications for other statutes regulating obscenity, we do not think they reach into the privacy of one's own home. If the First Amendment means anything, it means that a State has no business telling a man, sitting alone in his own home, what books he may read or what films he may watch. Our whole constitutional heritage rebels at the thought of giving government the power to control men's minds.[47]

When Georgia countered that its law was necessary to protect people from the detrimental effects of obscenity, the US Supreme Court recoiled, noting that Georgia's argument was an inappropriate attempt "to control the moral content of a person's thoughts... an action wholly inconsistent with the philosophy of the First Amendment."[48] The government, explained the Court, "cannot constitutionally premise legislation on the desirability of controlling a person's private thoughts."[49]

In the end, the Court in *Stanley* concluded that the government may regulate obscenity, but "that power simply does not extend to mere possession by an individual in the privacy of his own home."[50]

The same principles ought to apply with regard to psychoactive drugs that are used by adults in the privacy of their own homes. If, as Justice Marshall wrote in *Stanley*, "[o]ur whole constitutional heritage rebels at the thought of giving government the power to control men's minds," the State has no business telling a man or woman sitting in his or her own home, what states of consciousness are acceptable and what states of consciousness are not.

While the US Supreme Court has never considered a case in which the issue was framed as "cognitive privacy," several

SOME PEOPLE CONSIDER THEIR MARIJUANA USE AT LEAST AS IMPORTANT AS THEIR CHOICE OF HAIRSTYLE

state courts have examined the issue of whether drug use falls within a protected privacy right.[51] In all but one case, these state courts have stacked the deck against cognitive privacy, by narrowly framing the issue as whether or not there is a fundamental right to use *drug x,* rather than whether or not there is a fundamental right to *control one's own consciousness*—a fundamental right upon which drug prohibition laws substantially infringe.

One interesting case was decided in 1975 by the Alaska Supreme Court. In *Ravin v. State*,[52] the Alaska Supreme Court held that the possession and use of marijuana within one's own home was included within the scope of the privacy protection guaranteed by the Alaska Constitution. The case centered on Irwin Ravin, a man arrested and charged with possession of marijuana. Mr. Ravin filed a motion to dismiss, arguing that Alaska's laws prohibiting marijuana use unconstitutionally infringed upon his right to privacy as guaranteed by both the US and Alaska Constitutions.

The Alaska court examined US Supreme Court precedent and concluded that the opinions by the high court do not support a privacy right to possess marijuana, because "the federal right to privacy only arises in connection with other fundamental rights." The Alaska court then went on to examine whether the privacy protection of the Alaska Constitution protects an adult's possession of marijuana *in his or her home*.[53] The court noted that in a previous case,[54] it struck down a public school rule that prohibited long hair, finding that the school's rule was prohibited by the Alaska Constitution's privacy protection. In that case, the Alaska Supreme Court explained that "the right 'to be let alone'—including the right to determine one's own hairstyle in accordance with individual preferences and without interference of governmental officials and agents—is a fundamental right under the constitution of Alaska."

The court then revealed an anti-marijuana bias, stating "few would believe they have been deprived of something of critical importance if deprived of marijuana, though they would if stripped of control over their personal appearance." Here, the court was making an assumption without evidentiary support, and was also incorrectly framing the issue. Some people consider their marijuana use at least as important as their choice of hairstyle. Further, the court drew a false comparison: comparing a broad principle: "to control one's appearance;" with a narrower principle: "to smoke marijuana." The correct analogy would have been to compare the two actions *at the same level of generality*; thus, the right to control one's *outward appearance* ought to have been compared to the right to control one's *inner cognition*.

Based on its faulty comparison, the *Ravin* court refused to find that marijuana smoking was within the Alaska constitution's privacy protection. Instead, the court relied on the well-established privacy protections surrounding *the home*. The court explained, "if there is any area of human activity to which a right to privacy pertains more than any other, it is the home."[55] The right to privacy within the home, held the court, "encompass[es] the possession and ingestion of substances such as marijuana in a purely non-commercial context in the home, unless the state can [show that outlawing possession of marijuana in the home is necessary to achieve a legitimate state interest.]" More specifically, the court noted that the government had the "burden of showing a close and substantial relationship between the public welfare and control of ingestion or possession of marijuana in the home for personal use."[56]

Having shifted the burden to the government, the court then examined whether the government had met its burden. At trial, the government claimed that the use of marijuana caused a host of health problems to the marijuana user, including damage to the immune system and chromosomal structure, extreme panic reactions, long-term psychological problems, loss of motivation, and occasional violent behavior.

Before addressing these assertions, the Alaska Supreme Court questioned whether the government has a legitimate interest in "protecting" a person from him or herself. While the court was able to conceive of some circumstances in which the government may have a legitimate interest in protecting a person from him or herself, such government paternalism was the exception rather than the rule:

> ...the authority of the state to exert control over the individual extends only to activities of the individual which affect others or the public at large as it relates to matters of public health or safety, or to provide for the general welfare. We believe this tenet to be basic to a free society. The state cannot impose its own notions of morality, propriety, or fashion on individuals when the public has no legitimate interest in the affairs of those individuals. The right of the individual to do as he pleases is not absolute, of course: it can be made to yield when it begins to infringe on the rights and welfare of others.[57]

Having stressed that the government should not be in the business of protecting people from themselves, the court nevertheless examined the government's claims that marijuana was dangerous to its users, finding the evidence of serious harm unpersuasive. The court explained:

> It appears that the effects of marijuana on the individual are not serious enough to justify widespread concern, at least as compared with the far more dangerous effects of alcohol, barbiturates and amphetamines.[58]

Ultimately, the Alaska Supreme Court concluded "no adequate justification for the state's intrusion into the citizen's right to privacy by its prohibition of possession of marijuana by an adult for personal consumption in the home has been shown."[59]

While the *Ravin* case was a clear victory for marijuana users, and for privacy advocates in general, it was more about the privacy of the home, than about cognitive freedom and privacy.[60] As mentioned earlier, the court did not consider whether cognitive liberty was protected by the United States Constitution or by the Alaska constitution. Instead, the decision simply underscored the longstanding and socially accepted principle that a "man's home is his castle." The case has yet to be forcefully made that our minds, as much as our homes, are a private inward domain entitled to protection against unwanted governmental intrusions and prohibitions.

Endnotes

1 J. Jacobi, ed., *Selected Writings* (New York: Pantheon Books, 1951).

2 One example of fiction-like technology looming just over the horizon was recently discussed by MIT-educated futurist Ray Kurzweil, who has forecasted the coming of nanobot brain scanners. These nanobots would be blood-cell-sized robots that travel through capillaries in the brain and take high-resolution scans of the neural features. These bots would be tied together on a wireless LAN, and comprise a distributed parallel computer with the same power as the brain that was scanned. ("The Story of the 21st Century" in *Technology Review* Jan./Feb. 2000, 82-83.)

   Kurzweil says that every aspect of this scenario is feasible today "except for size and cost." For more of Kurzweil's ideas, see his book *The Age of Spiritual Machines: When Computers Exceed Human Intelligence* (New York: Viking, 1999).

3 See "Big Brother Puts a New Twist on the Telescreen," *infra*, 60.

4 *Stanley v. Georgia* (1969) 394 US 557, 565.

5 G. Orwell, *1984* (New York: Harcourt, Brace & Co., Inc., 1949).

6 J. Robitscher, ed., *Eugenic Sterilization* (Springfield, Il: Charles C. Thomas, 1973), 118-119 [listing sterilization data for most states]; E. Brantlinger, *Sterilization of People with Mental Disabilities: Issues, Perspectives, and Cases* (Westport, Con.: Auburn House, 1995) 25; E.J. Larson & L. Nelson III, "Involuntary Sexual Sterilization of Incompetents in Alabama: Past, Present, and Future," 43 *Alabama L. Rev.* 399 (1992), 407.

7 *Buck v. Bell* (1927) 274 US 200, 207. Eugenic sterilization, including the Norplant contraceptive device, will be further discussed in subsequent installments of this essay.

8 "American Psychiatric Association Rebukes Reparative Therapy," Press Release No. 98-56, December 14, 1998. Viewable online at http://www.psych.org/news_stand/rep_therapy.html. [Accessed: 23 January 2000.]

   Alan Turing, one of the founding fathers of artificial intelligence theory, was arrested for violation of British homosexuality statutes in 1952 after he admitted having a homosexual affair. Believing that his sexual orientation was a personal matter, neither a sin nor a crime, he presented no defense at his trial, which occurred on 31 March 1952. In lieu of prison, he was ordered to submit to estrogen injections for a year. Following a period of depression, likely the result of the injections, he committed suicide on June 7, 1954.

9 "Memorandum from ADDP items to DCI Dulles, 4/3/53" quoted in *The Mind Manipulators* (Paddington Press, 1978), 132.

10 *Inspector General's Report on MKULTRA*, (August 14, 1963), 7, quoted in *The Mind Manipulators*, *supra*, 133.

   For more details on the government's BLUEBIRD, ARTCICHOKE, and MKULTRA programs (at least those details not lost forever when Richard Helms ordered the destruction of all records related to the projects in January 1973) see A. Scheflin & E. Opton, "Tampering With The Mind (l) & (ll)," in *The Mind Manipulators*, *supra*, (1978), 106-212.

11 In *Palko v. Connecticut* (1937) 302 US 319, 325, 326.

12 *Moore v. East Cleveland* (1977) 431 US 494, 503 (opinion of Powell, J.).

13 *Olmstead v. United States* (1928) 277 US 438, 478 (Brandeis, J., dissenting).

14 *Kovacs v. Cooper* (1949) 336 US 77, 97 (concurring opinion of J. Frankfurter).

15 For a fascinating survey of suppressed literature, see the multi-volume set *Banned Books*, published by Facts on File, which covers literature suppressed on religious, social, sexual, and political grounds.

16 George Orwell, *Nineteen Eighty-Four* (New York: Harcourt, Brace & Co., Inc., 1949), Appendix "The Principles of Newspeak" 246.

17 ibid., 46.

18 The substances initially listed in Schedule I as "hallucinogenic substances" were: (1) 3,4-methylenedioxy amphetamine; (2) 5-methoxy-3,4-methylenedioxy amphetamine; (3) 3,4,5-trimethoxy amphetamine; (4) Bufotenine; (5) Diethyltryptamine; (6) Dimethyltryptamine; (7) 4-methyl-2,5-dimethoxyamphetamine; (8) Ibogaine; (9) Lysergic acid diethylamide; (10) Marihuana; (11) Mescaline; (12) Peyote; (13) N-ethyl-3-piperidyl nezilate; (14) N-methyl-3-piperidyl benzilate; (15) Psilocybin; (16) Psilocyn; (17) Tetrahydrocannabinols. (PL 91-513, Oct. 27, 1970; 21 USC. sec. 812, subd. (b) (1970).)

   The list of Schedule I "hallucinogenic substances" now numbers 31 items. (21 CFR § 1308.11(d) (April 1999)).

19 For more on the historic and pre-historic use of entheogens, see Peter Furst, *Hallucinogens and Culture* (Novato, CA: Chandler & Sharp Publishers, Inc., 1976); R.E. Schultes, and A. Hofmann, *The Botany and Chemistry of Hallucinogenic Plants* (Springfield, IL: Charles C. Thomas, 1973).
7 H. Munn, in, *Hallucinogens and Shamanism*, ed. M. Harner (New York: Oxford University Press, 1973), 88-89.

   Philosopher and ethnobotanist Terence McKenna suggested that early man's ingestion of visionary plants may have been the very catalyst that led to the sudden expansion of human brain size between three and six million years ago, and the event which spawned the subsequent emergence of language itself. (See Terence McKenna, *Food of the Gods* (New York: Bantam Books, 1993), 25.)

20 Peter Lamborn Wilson, "Neurospace," in *21-C* (Newark, NJ: Gordon and Breach Publishers, 1996), (3)32.

21 Stephen Arons and Charles Lawrence, "The Manipulation of Consciousness: A First Amendment Critique of Schooling" in 15(2) *Harvard Civil Rights-Civil Liberties Law Review* 309-361 (Fall 1980), 312.

22 *Palko v. Connecticut* (1937) 302 US 319, 326-327.

23 Although the First Amendment only mentions "Congress," the US Supreme Court has held that the Fourteenth Amendment's Due Process Clause incorporates the First Amendment guarantees and thus makes those guarantees applicable to State governments as well as Congress. (See *Gitlow v. New York* (1925) 268 US 652, 666; *Board of Education v. Pico* (1981) 457 US 853, 855, fn. 1.)

24 The concept of a laissez faire marketplace where ideas compete for buyers appears to date from 1919 when US Supreme Court Justice Holmes wrote in *Abrams v. United States* (1919) 250 US 616, 630 "[T]he ultimate good desired is better reached by free trade in ideas ... the best test of truth is the power of the thought to get itself accepted in the competition of the market") (Holmes, J., dissenting).

   Using a "marketplace" analogy for the interaction and acceptance or rejection of ideas is problematic. Using market mechanisms to determine the logic or merit of ideas reduces ideas to commodities. When this happens the circulation of ideas is determined by their sales profiles. The 'consumer' is described as voting for the products of the *Consciousness Industry* [a term coined by Hans Magnus Enzensberger in his 1974 collection of essays of the same name] with his or her dollars (consumer sovereignty). Such metaphors suggest democracy and freedom of choice. They deflect attention away from the tightly controlled decision-making process that actually determine what ideas will gain entry into the commodity system. That is, they render the control system of the capitalistic consciousness industry invisible and thereby permit subterranean censorship based upon both market and political considerations. In sum, they permit elites to rule but preserve the semiotics of democracy. (Sue Curry Jansen, *Censorship: The Knot that Binds Power and Knowledge* (New York; Oxford: Oxford University Press, 1988), 134.)

[25] *Kovacs v. Cooper, supra*, at p. 95.

[26] *Bee v. Greaves* (10th Cir. 1984) 744 F.2d 1387, 1393 , cert. denied, (1985) 469 US 1214 .

[27] *Youngberg v. Romeo* (1982) 457 US 307, 316.

[28] *Bee v. Greaves, supra*, at p. 1393.

[29] ibid., 1393-1394; Accord, *Rogers v. Okin* (D.Mass. 1979) 478 F.Supp. 1342, 1366-1367. Other courts have held that inmates in mental hospitals have a constitutional "liberty interest" in maintaining the autonomy over their own minds in the face of doctors who want to involuntarily medicate them. (See, e.g., *United States v. Charters* (4th Cir.1988) (en banc) 863 F.2d 302, 305 (antipsychotic drugs intrude sufficiently upon "bodily security" to implicate a "protectable liberty interest"); And, still other courts have held that there is a constitutional "privacy protection" that encompasses "the right to protect one's mental processes from governmental interference." See, e.g., *Rennie v. Klein* (D.N.J. 1978) 462 F. Supp. 1131, 1144 ("the right of privacy is broad enough to include the right to protect one's mental processes from governmental interference").

For a comprehensive survey of forced mental treatment cases, see Bruce J. Winick, "The Right to Refuse Mental Health Treatment: A First Amendment Perspective," *University of Miami Law Review* (September 1989), 44(1) 1-103.

[30] L. Tribe, *American Constitutional Law* Sec. 15-5, at p. 889 (1978) (quoting *Stanley v. Georgia* (1969) 394 US 557, 565.)

[31] The *National Drug Control Strategy 2000* can be read online via the Alchemind Society's Drug Law Library at www. cognitiveliberty.org/links.htm [Accessed: May 17, 2000.]

[32] L.D. Brandeis and S. Warren, "The Right to Privacy. The Implicit Made Explicit," in *Harvard L.R.*, 4; (1890) 193-220.

[33] ibid., 82.

[34] *Weems v. United States* (1910) 217 US 349, 373.

[35] *Thornburgh v. American College of Obstetricians & Gynecologists* (1986) 476 US 747, 777, n. 5 (Stevens, J., concurring), quoting Fried, Correspondence, 6 *Phil. & Pub. Affairs* (1977) 288-289.

[36] Quoted in D. Brin, *The Transparent Society* (Reading, Mass.: Addison-Wesley, 1998) 77.

[37] *Olmstead v. United States* (1928) 227 US 438.

[38] *Katz v. United States* (1967) 389 US 347.

[39] *California v. Greenwood* (1988) 486 US 35.

[40] *Florida v. Riley* (1989) 488 US 445.

[41] *Griswold v. Connecticut* (1965) 381 US 479.

[42] ibid., 485, quoting, *NAACP v. Alabama* (1964) 377 US 288, 307.

[43] *Roe v. Wade* (1973) 410 US 113.

[44] *Stanley v. Georgia* (1968) 394 US 557, 559.

[45] ibid., 568, fn. 11.

[46] ibid., 564.

[47] ibid., 565.

[48] ibid., 565-566.

[49] ibid., 566.

[50] ibid., 568.

[51] *State v. Murphy*, 570 P.2d 1070, 1073 (Ariz. 1977); *Kreisher v. State*, 319 A.2d 31, 32 (Del. Super. Ct. 1974); *Laird v. State*, 342 So.2d 962, 963 (Fla. 1977); *Borras v. State*, 229 So.2d 244, 246 (Fla. 1969); *Blincoe v. State*, 204 S.E.2d 597, 599 (Ga. 1974); *State v. Renfro*, 542 P.2d 366, 368-69 (Haw. 1975); *State v. Baker*, 535 P.2d 1394, 1399 (Haw. 1975); *State v. Kincaid*, 566 P.2d 763, 765 (Idaho 1977); *State v. O'Bryan*, 531 P.2d 1193, 1198 (Idaho 1975); *NORML v. Scott*, 383 N.E.2d 1330, 1332-33 (Ill. App. Ct. 1978); *State v. Chrisman*, 364 So.2d 906, 907 (La. 1978); *Marcoux v. Attorney Gen.*, 375 N.E.2d 688, 691 (Mass. 1978); *Commonwealth v. Leis*, 243 N.E.2d 898, 903-04 (Mass. 1969); *People v. Alexander*, 223 N.W.2d 750, 752 (Mich. App. 1974); *State v. Kells*, 259 N.W.2d 19, 24 (Neb. 1977); *State v. Nugent*, 312 A.2d 158, 162 (N.J. Super. Ct. App. Div. 1973); *Miller v. State*, 458 S.W.2d 680, 684 (Tex. Crim. App. 1970); *State v. Anderson*, 558 P.2d 307, 309 (Wash. Ct. App. 1976); *State ex rel. Scott v. Conaty*, 187 S.E.2d 119, 123 (W.Va. 1972).

Some of these cases, as well as others not listed here, have compelling dissenting opinions in which judges elaborated certain aspects of cognitive liberty. For example, in *State v. Kramer* (Hawaii 1972) 493 P.2d 306, a case upholding the defendant's conviction for marijuana possession, Justice Levinson filed a dissenting opinion in which he argued that the experiences generated by the use of marijuana are mental in nature, and thus among the most personal and private experiences possible. (*Id.* at p. 315.)

[52] *Ravin v. State* (1975) 537 P.2d 494.

[53] Unlike the US Constitution, the Alaska constitution expressly provides for a right to privacy. Article I, Sec. 22 of the Alaska constitution states: "The right of the people to privacy is recognized and shall not be infringed."

[54] *Breese v. Smith* (Alaska 1972) 501 P.2d 159.

[55] *Ravin, supra*, 537 P.2d at p. 503.

[56] ibid., 504.

[57] ibid., 509.

[58] ibid., 509-510.

[59] ibid., 511.

[60] In 1982, the Alaska legislature codified *Ravin* in the state's criminal code by legalizing possession of up to four ounces of marijuana in a private place. (See 1982 Alaska Sess. Laws 2 ch. 45.) In 1990, Alaska voters adopted a Voter Initiative that amended Alaska Statutes section 11.71.060 so as to again make possession of marijuana in a private place illegal. The (state) constitutional validity of this initiative is dubious because the initiative merely altered the general Alaska Criminal Code, not the Alaska Constitution itself, upon which *Ravin* was based. (See, e.g., *State v. McNeil*, No. 1KE-93-947 (D. Alaska Oct. 29, 1993).

In the DEA's Line of Fire—
Ayahuasca: Visionary Vine of the Amazon

Peter Gorman

An ancient Amazonian ritual has gained popularity in the US, and with it, the attention of the Drug Enforcement Administration.

Overhead the night sky is pitch black. No sound comes from the nearby river. On the balsa-bark floor of the raised-platform hut five people sit in a circle in the darkness, lit only by the glow of a small kerosene lamp. One of them, an old man named Julio Jerena, blows smoke from his *mapacho*, a cigarette made with black jungle tobacco, into a cup then pours a small amount of thick brown liquid into it. As he does he mutters a few prayers in Spanish, blessing it before passing it to the woman at his immediate left. She drinks, struggles to keep the dank, acrid liquid down, then hands the cup back. Julio blows smoke into the cup again, pours more of the liquid into it while blessing it with prayers then passes it to the young man to the woman's left. His reaction on drinking the brew is similar to the woman's and he fights to keep the liquid down.

Julio repeats the ritual until everyone in the circle has been served with ayahuasca, the visionary healing tea of the Amazon, then puts the kerosene lamp out. Before long, the participants in the ceremony will begin the ayahuasca purge, a physical cleansing that frequently involves bouts of violent vomiting and diarrhea.

Shortly after they have purged themselves they will fall into what is called the ayahuasca dream, an altered state of consciousness in which they will lose awareness of themselves and be open to the brew's spiritual curative powers and visionary properties. During the course of their dreams, some of the participants might find themselves associating with animals or spirits, or visiting fantastic ethereal places; others might find themselves coping with deep-seated personal issues. Some of what they see will be hallucinations; some of it will be genuinely visionary—in either case, their dreams will probably be demanding and difficult, pushing them to explore their deepest wishes and darkest fears. Julio, the *curandero*, or doctor, on the river, will share their altered states to try to "see" the causes of his patients' physical, emotional or spiritual maladies and what is needed to be done to effect their cures on the physical plane.

The use of ayahuasca—which means "vine of the soul" in the Quechua language and is also called yage, hoasca and natem among other names—in Amazonia is probably thousands of years old.

It is still utilized by most of the region's inhabitants, but it took centuries to gain a foothold into the consciousness of Westerners. While a few Europeans became aware of it with the arrival of the Conquistadors, and Franciscan monks wrote about it as early as the 17th Century, it wasn't until William Burroughs and Allen Ginsberg published *The Yage Letters* in 1963 about their experiences with the vine that ayahuasca began to come to the attention of intellectual hipsters. Ten years later, adventurous baby boomers, whose interest in mind-expansion, spirituality and psychedelics had been piqued by LSD, Leary and Castaneda, began making the trek to the Amazon to experience for themselves ayahuasca's mystical properties. The late Terence McKenna also frequently talked about it during his lectures, spreading awareness of the vine among a new generation of spiritual seekers during the eighties and early 1990s.

Also during the early 1990s, two Brazilian religions that had been born in the 1920s, the Uñiao de Vegetal (UDV) and the Santo Daime, both mixes of Catholicism and ayahuasca use, gained popularity in Brazil's larger cities, eventually opening branches here in the US as well as in Europe. At the same time, Amazon tour agencies, particularly in Ecuador and Peru, found that adding an optional ayahuasca ceremony to their itinerary boosted participation on their tours significantly. Websites devoted to the discussion of ayahuasca use began to crop up as well, and exotic plant suppliers began to carry the plants needed to make ayahuasca for those who wished to use it in ceremonies outside the established religions in the US and Europe.

DEA Enters the Fray

The increased popularity of ayahuasca, though still limited to a small group of spiritual seekers willing to undergo a difficult experience, didn't go unnoticed by the authorities.

> THE USE OF AYAHUASCA—WHICH MEANS "VINE OF THE SOUL" IN THE QUECHUA LANGUAGE AND IS ALSO CALLED YAGE, HOASCA AND NATEM AMONG OTHER NAMES—IN AMAZONIA IS PROBABLY THOUSANDS OF YEARS OLD.

In the late '90s, the Santo Daime church in Amsterdam was raided by Dutch authorities—which resulted in a January, 2000 ruling permitting the church to use ayahuasca—and several raids of ayahuasca ceremonies in the US were carried out by the Drug Enforcement Administration and US Customs. Their justification was that one of the active alkaloids in the brew was dimethyltryptamine (DMT), a Schedule 1 drug on the Controlled Substances List, a classification that includes heroin, marijuana and LSD among other drugs. None of the raids included arrests, however, because while the alkaloid was classified, ayahuasca was not.

The most notable raid in the US didn't occur during a ceremony, however. It occurred on March 21, 1999 at the Santa Fe, N.M., offices of Jeffrey Bronfman, a member of the Canadian family that founded Seagram's and President of the Uñiao de Vegetal church in the United States. Federal agents, including the US Customs Bureau, seized 30 gallons of ayahuasca that had been shipped from Brazil for sacramental use in UDV ceremonies. Typical of the other raids, there were no arrests. This reporter inquired of the DEA in Washington, D.C., at that time why they were raiding homes and businesses for ayahuasca if they

NONE OF THE RAIDS INCLUDED ARRESTS, HOWEVER, BECAUSE WHILE THE ALKALOID WAS CLASSIFIED, AYAHUASCA WAS NOT.

were not intending to arrest anyone. An agent for the DEA who would not give his name suggested that "the higher-ups are probably looking for a test case before they go that route."

The Uñiao de Vegetal was not that case. Shortly after the seizure Bronfman filed suit against the US Department of Justice for the return of the ayahuasca that had been confiscated. His attorney, Nancy Hollander, additionally asked for a ruling permitting the UDV to legally use *hoasca*—as it's known among members of the UDV—as its sacrament as it was integral to the church's beliefs. Essentially, the suit asked for a similar exemption as the one earlier granted to the Native American Church permitting their use of peyote, also on Schedule 1 of the Controlled substances list.

The hearing was held before Judge James Parker of the United States District Court for the District of New Mexico, who handed down a 61-page ruling on the case on Aug. 12, 2002. In it Judge Parker dismissed several UDV motions but found for the church on the Religious Freedom Restoration Act. Based on that Act he defended the UDV's right to use *hoasca*, and ordered a temporary injunction against the further government interference with the UDV. In his ruling, Judge Parker noted that the government had failed in its attempt to show "a compelling...interest in protecting the health of UDV members using hoasca or in preventing the diversion of

hoasca to illicit use" [by prohibiting it]. He additionally noted that the United Nations' "...1971 Convention on Psychotropic Substances does not apply to the hoasca tea used by the UDV. Therefore, the United States' interest in adhering to the Convention does not, in this case, represent a compelling reason for extending the CSR's ban on DMT to the UDV's ceremonial hoasca use."

The government almost immediately appealed, and was granted a stay of Judge Parker's injunction pending the outcome of that appeal. The initial briefs in the appeal were filed by the government in January 2003.

Neither Attorney Nancy Hollander nor Jeffrey Bronfman would comment on the seizure or any aspect of the lawsuit due to "the sensitive nature of the ongoing case."

By the time Judge Parker issued his ruling regarding the UN's 1971 Convention on Psychotropic Substances, the UN had already clarified the issue in relation to the case against the use of ayahuasca by the Santo Daime religion in Amsterdam. In connection with that case, on January 17, 2001, Herbert Schaepe, Secretary of the United Nations International Narcotics Control Board in Vienna, Austria, wrote to the chief of the Inspectorate for Health care of the Dutch Ministry of Public Health. The letter notes, in part, that "No plants (natural materials) containing DMT are at present controlled under the 1971 Convention on Psychotropic Substances. Consequently, preparations (i.e. decoctions) made of these plants, including ayahuasca are not under international control and, therefore, not subject to any of the articles of the 1971 Convention."

A Different Tack: Going After the Plants Themselves

Despite the letter from the UN's Secretary of the International Narcotics Control Board, 12 days after it was written, another seizure was made, this one resulting in the "test case" the DEA had been looking for all along. But instead of going after ayahuasca in tea form, the US government took another tack and went after the plant material used to make it.

The case involves Alan Shoemaker, a US citizen who has been living in the jungle city of Iquitos, Peru since 1993. Prior to moving to Peru, Shoemaker spent nearly a year studying San Pedro and ayahuasca curing in Ecuador, and his study of ayahuasca continued when he moved to Iquitos. There he met and married Mariella Noriega, a Peruvian national who, in 1998, started a company called Chinchelejo (Dragonfly) that shipped medicinal plants from Peru to the US and Europe. Some of them, like *Uña de Gato* and *Sacha Jergon*, were non-psychotropic medicinal plants. Others, like *Banisteriopsis caapi* (ayahuasca vine) and *Diplopterys cabrerana* (Huambisa) and *Psychotria viridis* (chacruna), are the plants used to make ayahuasca.

Chinchelejo was not the first company to secure a plant-export license from Peru, and not the only one that shipped the plants necessary to make ayahuasca. Nonetheless, on January 29, 2000, it became the first and only Peruvian plant-exporter to have a shipment of plants seized by the DEA. The seizure was made after delivery of the shipment was completed to Alan's son Jesse Brock, who was starting a plant wholesale business just outside of Atlanta. The plants, 660 pounds of ayahuasca vine and 220 pounds of *huambisa* leaves—400 kilos altogether—were seized on the grounds that the leaves contained DMT.

The seizure was extremely unusual as the plants themselves were legal and the shipment had been exported with all the necessary Peruvian and international paperwork completed. Moreover, Chinchilejo had made similar shipments in the past. It seemed to make no sense. A call by

WHEN ASKED WHY THE SEIZURE HAD BEEN MADE AS THE PLANTS WERE LEGAL, MCCRACKEN RESPONDED: "I KNOW THEY'RE LEGAL, BUT I DON'T CARE. I THINK AYAHUASCA SHOULD BE ILLEGAL AND I SEIZED THE PLANTS. IT WILL COST $50 GRAND FOR A LAWYER TO FIGHT THE SEIZURE AND THAT'S MORE THAN ANYONE WILL MAKE SELLING THEM. SO EITHER WAY I WIN."

this reporter to the DEA agent who had made the seizure, a fellow named McCracken, did not clarify matters. When asked why the seizure had been made as the plants were legal, McCracken responded: "I know they're legal, but I don't care. I think ayahuasca should be illegal and I seized the plants. It will cost $50 grand for a lawyer to fight the seizure and that's more than anyone will make selling them. So either way I win."

It was an astonishingly honest, if confusing reply, but because of the way forfeiture law works, with the seized items guilty until proven innocent, McCracken was right. And everyone, from Alan Shoemaker and his wife, to his son Jesse, who'd received the shipment in Atlanta, to this reporter, thought that was the end of it. The seizure would bankrupt Chinchilejo, McCracken would have his pound of flesh and that would be that.

That didn't turn out to be the case. On April 1, 2002, when Alan Shoemaker flew from Iquitos, Peru to Miami en route to see his dying mother in Elizabethtown, Kentucky, he was picked up at Miami International Airport and told a sealed grand jury indictment had been handed down against him on January 24, 2002. Alan was charged with intent to distribute a Schedule 1 substance, DMT, along with a number of lesser charges. The charge carries 15 years in federal prison. His son Jesse, was also arrested at that time, though with a lesser charge.

Shoemaker was released on a $50,000 cash bond with the stipulation that he wear an ankle bracelet and remain at his late mother's home in Tennessee until the case was concluded. Prosecutors suggested he bring his wife and children to the US to keep his family intact, but he couldn't do that for fear that she would be arrested as well.

A spokesperson for the prosecutor's office in Atlanta refused to comment on the case except to note that "DMT is illegal and we will prosecute those who attempt to distribute it."

When reminded that virtually all DMT found on the streets is synthetic and that even the Controlled Substances Act list makes exclusive reference to synthetic DMT, the spokesperson commented that "it is the government's contention that all forms of DMT are illegal."

But while the prosecutor's office was close to mum, Shoemaker's attorney, Mark Sallee of Atlanta was more than willing to comment. "You have to look at the whole picture here," Sallee says. "Both the Santa Fe UDV case and Alan Shoemaker's case are closely related, because both are examples of the government's unwillingness to admit any loss of ground in its war on drugs. Any inroads into that will have negative impact on their overall attack on what they consider to be dangerous drugs.

"The government simply doesn't want to have their people making critical decisions about what's medicine, what's a religious sacrament and what is illegal street use. They want their people to be able to make arrests, not have to make distinctions. The government doesn't even like having to separate out peyote use or the Native American Church from non-church peyote use."

Asked why he thought the Chinchilejo shipment was seized rather than any of the thousands of other shipments that have legally entered the country both before and after the Chinchilejo seizure, Sallee echoed the statement made earlier by the DEA spokesman. "They were looking for a test case and because of its size, and perhaps because my client is well known for having written about ayahuasca use, this one was chosen as that test case.

"It's critical to remember that in the government's thinking they look at whether a drug is marketable, whether it will or could find its way to the streets. With the size of this shipment, they will make the case that it could have been marketable on the streets. In other words, the government is going after the leaves because they contain DMT, and even though they are not marketable as leaves, they are interpreting the law to include the possibility that they could have become marketable. This is a very elastic interpretation of the laws. Particularly because DMT occurs in so many common plants."

Dennis McKenna, a botanist and Senior Lecturer at the University of Minnesota who worked extensively with psychotropics with his late brother Terence, agrees. "There are at least 150 species of plants that are known to contain DMT; there is likely a much larger number but no one has bothered to look and to report it. Many of them are freely available in nurseries, or indeed, simply growing in fields and by the roadsides."

Asked what he thought the viability was of extracting DMT from those plants commercially, McKenna answered: "No one in their right mind who wanted to produce commercial quantities of the substance would extract it from a plant, when chemical synthesis is so much easier. For the same time and effort it would take to extract a few grams of DMT from a plant, one could synthesize a few kilos of the pure compound!"

David E. Nichols, Ph.D. of the Department of Medicinal Chemistry and Molecular Pharmacology at Perdue University made a similar statement on behalf of the UDV during its trial when discussing the possibility of extracting DMT from *hoasca* tea. The process, he noted, "would be expensive and time consuming and would completely eliminate any economic advantage that might be seen in the ready availability of an organic solvent for the extraction....Separation of the alkaloids to obtain pure, or nearly pure DMT is not likely to be applied on a useful scale [commercially] because it is simply uneconomical."

The Ayahuasca Hunt Continues: Colorado and Canada

Many spiritual seekers who had made their way to Amazonia to use ayahuasca with curanderos there had come back home with the idea that the medicine should be shared with their friends, but only in the context of a traditional ceremony. As not many people can afford either the time or money to make the expedition to South America, during the 1990s, experienced ayahuasca practitioners began to bring their curanderos north to hold ceremonies in the US, Canada and Europe. Word of such ceremonies traveled underground, making its way to those who were interested while not reaching the attention of those who were not.

But the DEA, with its interest peaked, began to take notice of such ceremonies and in several instances raided homes where they were to take place, confiscating the medicine. In some cases, agents barged in during the ceremonies themselves, when participants were at their most vulnerable, in their dream states.

Fortunately, no serious harm came to participants from those raids, either psychologically or as a result of legal action against them. There were, in fact, no arrests of participants during the course of several raids over a number of years.

But with the UDV and Shoemaker cases in the legal pipeline, the DEA wanted to up its ante and attack the use of ayahuasca from a third position. They got their chance on June 25, 2002, when Naomi Lake and her husband James Roderick stopped by the Post Office in Crestone, CO., to pick up a package containing ayahuasca tea. The medicine was for use by Lake's Peruvian teacher, who had come to the US to perform several ceremonies at Lake's request.

Naomi Lake, who holds a degree in anthropology, was not a novice at healing work: she has presented alternative medicine theory at Harvard Medical School, taught for the Holistic Nurse Association and at universities around the US and Mexico. She had made several trips to Peru to study ayahuasca and its healing properties. It is, in fact, unlikely that the DEA would have bothered with her if they hadn't been contacted by the Peruvian National Police, who said they had intercepted two packages containing narcotics addressed to Lake on June 6th and 7th, 2002. The DEA began surveillance of Lake and Roderick on the 21st of June, and picked them up not long after they'd retrieved one of the packages on the afternoon of the 25th.

> ...DURING THE SEARCH SEVERAL OF THE AGENTS TAUNTED HER BY ASKING HOW LONG SHE COULD HOLD HER PEE, AND TERRORIZED HER BY TELLING HER SHE WOULD BE GOING TO JAIL FOREVER.

The bust was a terrifying ordeal for Lake: she'd gone with her husband to a lake to join her two adult sons for a swim after the stop at the Post Office. Shortly after they arrived, half-a-dozen or so cars pulled up to where they were talking and more than a dozen federal agents wearing helmets and bulletproof vests and armed with automatic weapons leapt from the cars, told them all they were under arrest and ordered Lake and her family to lie face down on the ground. "The memory of the cold will be with me for, I think, a very long time," Lake said, shortly afterward.

The agents separated the family and brought Lake to her home where more than two-dozen other agents were already going through things. Lake would later say she was forced to lie on the ground for several hours while the home was searched, and that agents ignored her pleas to use the bathroom. Moreover, she told this reporter, during the search several of the agents taunted her by asking how long she could hold her pee, and terrorized her by telling her she would be going to jail forever.

To her surprise, when the agents finally left they didn't bring her to the station to be charged with any crime. They didn't charge her husband either, just told both of them they would be in touch.

Lake and Roderick called friends all over the country, looking for a lawyer who had dealt with cases in any way similar, and finally found Jeffrey Denner of Boston. Denner had represented alternative healers in a number of high-profile cases and was interested in theirs. Moreover, he was willing to work despite their not being able to raise his full retainer. They hired him.

Denner proved to be a good choice: within several weeks of signing on to the case he had convinced the Federal

District Attorney's office to drop the case, leaving it to the State of Colorado to choose to prosecute or not.

On April 23, 2003, nearly 10 months to the day of the raid, Lake and Roderick were re-arrested in connection with the ayahuasca they had received, this time by the State of Colorado. They were charged with possession and intent to distribute a Schedule 1 substance, DMT. Under state law they faced between 4-24 years in prison.

During the same period of time that the US DEA was pushing to attack ayahuasca use from three separate angles, a fourth case, this one in Canada, fell into their lap. If the DEA was hoping that something disastrous would happen in connection with ayahuasca use, the Canadian case, at least for a little while, looked to be the answer to their prayers.

> ...FOR THE DEA, DESPITE THE EVENT OCCURRING OUTSIDE OF THE US, THE DEATH WAS TRAGIC BUT EXHILARATING. IT MEANT THEY FINALLY HAD PROOF THAT AYAHUASCA COULD KILL. IT WAS ALL THEY WOULD NEED TO SEW UP THE OTHER CASES THEY HAD ON THE LEGAL FIRE AND MAKE AYAHUASCA ILLEGAL FOREVER.

The story began in May of 2001, when two traditional indigenous Shuar healers from Ecuador, Juan Uyunkar and his son Edgar Uyunkar, were invited by the Wilwemikong Health Centre of the First Nation of Manitoulin Island, in Ontario, Canada to do traditional Shuar healings with band members from the Ojibwe and Odawa tribes there.

Juan Uyunkar, 50, was well-known for his work with medicinal plants, including natem—ayahuasca in the Shuar language. He had already done healing ceremonies in Colombia, Spain, Egypt and the United States, and his 23-year-old son Edgar had traveled extensively with him. The invitation to go to Canada was a joyous opportunity to work in a new place.

The Uyunkars accepted the invitation and were flown by the Wilwemikong band council to Ontario in September of 2001. They held several ceremonies, treating more than 300 people. The healings were so successful that after two weeks, the director of the Health Centre, Mr. Roland Peltier, asked Juan Uyunkar to return to Ecuador for more medicine so that he could continue the ceremonies.

Unfortunately, after a healing held on October 19, 2001, an elderly Ojibwe woman, Mrs. Jane Maiangowi, 71, died. In the US, word of her death immediately hit the bulletin boards and chat rooms visited by those interested in ayahuasca, sending a ripple of panic through the small community. But for the DEA, despite the event occurring outside of the US, the death was tragic but exhilarating. It meant they finally had proof that ayahuasca could kill. It was all they would need to sew up the other cases they

had on the legal fire and make ayahuasca illegal forever. Their exhilaration didn't last long: an autopsy showed the cause of Maiangowi's death to be acute nicotine poisoning, not ayahuasca. The nicotine was administered at the end of the ayahuasca ceremony, an extract from wild Amazonian tobacco, meant to cleanse the nasal passages, throat and stomach of all remaining traces of ayahuasca. The elderly Maiangowi, for some reason, had not purged the extract from her stomach. Allowed to pass into her system, it killed her.

The Uyunkars were initially cleared of any criminal wrongdoing in the case and were told they were free to return to Ecuador. Confident that their actions had had no impact on the woman's death, however, they chose to stay. Three weeks later both Juan and Edgar Uyunkar, along with their interpreter Maria Ventura, were arrested. They were charged with criminal negligence in the administering of a noxious substance (nicotine) which caused a death, and also, at the urging of the US DEA, with importation, possession and administration of a controlled substance.

The Uyunkars were freed on bail, but their passports were confiscated by the police so they were unable to return to Ecuador. They were also unable to work, as they had tourist visas, during the 17 months it took before a preliminary hearing in their case was begun at the end of March, 2003.

Disposition of the Cases

The Uyunkars' case was decided on April 24, 2003, when both Juan and Edgar Uyunkar pleaded guilty in the Ontario Court of Justice to one count each of administering a noxious substance and one count of trafficking in a controlled substance.

The judge in the case, the Honorable Mr. Justice Gerald E. Michel noted at the time that "These two persons are not before the court for having administered sacred medicine... . They are before the court because the ingredients...contained substances prohibited in Canada and the combination of substances, which made the potion toxic."

Judge Michel freed Edgar but sentenced his father, Juan, to a twelve-month conditional sentence, followed by twelve- months probation. In his sentencing Judge Michel noted that "it is necessary...to bring home to all natural healers that they have to be careful with reference to substances and consequences." As we go to press, both Uyunkars have returned to Ecuador.

In the Colorado case of Naomi Lake and James Roderick, all charges were dropped by the State on December 3, 2003, when the Prosecutors admitted that the ayahuasca had disappeared. Without it there was no case. Lake and Roderick are currently working to have the record in the case against them sealed.

In the Shoemaker case, in March, 2003, just under a year from the date he was charged, Lisa Tarvin, the Asst. Federal Prosecutor handling the case, ordered the DEA to return Shoemaker's effects, which included his passport. Through his attorney, Mark Sallee, he was told he was free to travel, and his ankle-bracelet was removed. After several weeks at the Texas home of this journalist, he returned—with the blessing of the court—to Iquitos, Peru and his family there.

Immediately on his return to Peru, however, Tarvin asked the court that he be charged with Flight to Avoid Prosecution. Though Tarvin herself would not comment on the charge, her assistants claimed that she denied asking for or ordering the return of Shoemaker's passport to him. In conversation with his attorney, Tarvin suggested that Shoemaker must have slipped out of the US via Mexico. It was on that theory that she hung her hat when asking that the Flight charge be initiated. Sallee, in turn, explained to the judge what had really happened, and the judge told Shoemaker, via his attorney and this reporter, that if and when Shoemaker decided to return to the US he would be picked up on the charge, but that the charge would be dropped when he appeared in court.

The Flight to Avoid Prosecution charge puts Alan Shoemaker in an awkward position: if he returns to defend himself on the more serious charges of importation with intent to distribute a Schedule 1 substance, he opens himself up to doing several years if found guilty on the Flight charge—despite the promise by the judge to drop the charge on his return. If, on the other hand, he does not return when the more serious charges come up for trial, he can be tried in absentia, and would subsequently be tried on the Flight charge as well.

For his part, Shoemaker has taken Peruvian citizenship and will await a trial date before determining whether he will return to the US. At the moment, there is no extradition treaty between the US and Peru regarding ayahuasca, so he is not facing an imminent threat of being returned to the US.

In the case of the Uñiao de Vegetal, on September 5, 2003, a three-judge panel of the 10th US Circuit Court of Appeals in Denver upheld the preliminary injunction against the US attorney general, the DEA and other agencies that attempted to prohibit the use of ayahuasca by the UDV.

By a 2-1 ruling, the panel agreed with the US District Court in New Mexico that the UDV had "demonstrated a substantial likelihood of success" of winning the exemption they seek for sacramental use of ayahuasca. The ruling permits the continued use of the sacred medicine by the UDV at least until the suit filed by Jeffrey Bronfman is heard.

Already Tainted: The Sacred Tea

The fact that ayahuasca has never been a street drug, and there is little chance it will ever be one in the future—public purging wouldn't be likely to impress a date—is not evidently a factor in the government's thinking on this issue. Neither is the concept that extracting DMT from plant material is so much more expensive than simply making synthetic DMT that it wouldn't be commercially viable. As Alan Shoemaker's attorney Mark Sallee has noted: "In the government's opinion, and for their purposes, all drugs are dangerous, period." But, he adds, "the government is going to find it is its own worst enemy in this case. Here is something that is used by a very small segment of the public strictly for religious and sacramental purposes. By bringing these cases they are making a much larger segment of the population aware that certain plants could, in other forms, be used to produce something that could be used recreationally. Of course with huambisa leaves the process of extracting DMT into a smokeable form is so complex and involves such a refined knowledge of chemistry, as well as the use of dangerous and explosive solvents that the actuality of diverting these leaves to recreational use is nil. Nothing. Wouldn't happen."

Nonetheless, the government is proceeding with both the UDV case and the Shoemaker prosecution. And if they lose one or both, there are several other cases around the country where seizures have been made but no arrest warrants issued as yet that they might decide to prosecute.

As tragic as it would be, the issue is larger than whether Alan Shoemaker's life is ruined by not being able to return to the US, or, if he does, by spending 15 pointless years in a Federal lockup. The issue is also larger than the question of whether the Uñiao de Vegetal is finally given the right to drink hoasca without fear of government agents bursting through their church doors. Regardless of the outcome of these and any future cases, the government's war on drugs has already, through the three US cases and the Canadian case as well, tainted the sacramental use of the tea made from plants considered sacred for hundreds, possibly thousands of years.

Is All Use Abuse?

Craig Morris

In considering whether all use is abuse, the origins of the terms "use" and "abuse" will be examined to see how they have developed as ideas. It will be argued that they are the product of a number of historical developments and that they must be understood with reference to a particular view of language. This view is one in which language is not simply seen as a means of communication, but one in which it is language itself that often heavily influences the way that we understand both the physical and social worlds.

Humans, language, and power

Human beings are born into a world as creatures for whom everything (other people, objects, behavior, and events) is meaningful. In human society, meaning is communicated and understood primarily by the use of language. Language is what allows us to understand one another and language makes it possible for us to have a shared reality (common understandings, shared goals, etc.) and therefore for human society to exist at all (or at least in the complex ways that we know it to be).

> IN HUMAN SOCIETY, MEANING IS COMMUNICATED AND UNDERSTOOD PRIMARILY BY THE USE OF LANGUAGE.

Language allows the world to be a meaningful place for us and it facilitates human behavior, as we act on the basis of how we perceive things to be.

Let us look at an example. I woke up this morning and switched on the television. The issue being discussed was the continuing occupation of Iraq by the US and forces from other nations. The very act of watching the television is quite obviously dependent on language. I speak English, so do the people on the television. Through shared meanings of words I understand *what* "Iraq" is (it is a country) and I understand what is going on there (or at least a version of events). Earlier in the conflict I understood through shared language that as the US and British forces moved deeper into Iraq, towns were being "liberated." But let us just think about this—it could have been said that these towns were being slowly "occupied" or "invaded"—but no, they were being "liberated." Why this particular word? It would seem to be the case that the invasion of Iraq was being discussed in terms of "freedom," i.e. freeing Iraq from the rule of Saddam. Importantly

then, language not only allowed me to understand the television show (and more fundamentally to know what that box in the corner of my living room actually does), *but the meanings inherent in the language actually act upon us, through influencing how we perceive other people, objects, behavior, or events in our day to day lives.*

The point is that language and meaning are rarely socially, politically or culturally neutral. Language is often a political realm, in which meanings are contested (such as the contestation between "liberation" and "invasion") and may be intricately connected with issues of power (such as attempting to justify invading another country on the basis of *liberating* it, rather than simply *occupying* it). There are different ways of seeing all sorts of things in our day to day existence, but sometimes different understandings of things have implications as regards issues of power.

Let us look at another example. Many people today understand democracy, freedom, and the democratic political process to be progressive, libertarian, and central social and political principles to our existence. However, other people have come to see democracy as it is practiced as something of an ideological illusion, in which elected leaders (or even leaders whose election was not wholly convincing) defy the will of the U.N. and of a sizable proportion (if not a majority) of its citizens by waging war in the name of "freedom" or a "war on terrorism." For some people, democracy is not very democratic in practice. So democracy is about different things to different people. To some it remains a torch held high for humanity, for others it is, to a degree, a deception conducted by a powerful minority who exercise political power but have an interest in everyone else *believing* that they have a say in how society is run.

Clearly certain interests of power are contingent upon the former view of democracy being accepted by a majority of people rather than the latter. Power can be exercised by force, but it is a smoother process to exercise it by ideological means. I hope that this example does, however, demonstrate that language (i.e. the words we use to communicate and to represent ideas) is not simply a medium for communication but that it is also a political realm, in which the very understandings of things may be pre-packaged.

Of course the meanings of things also change over time, so to understand how and why some social phenomena is how it is, we must situate it within an historical context. To return to our example about democracy, if we suspect its practice to be somewhat *un*democratic at times then recourse to history may illuminate this matter. In Ancient Greece, democracy (or the rule of the people) was practiced on the basis of citizens (male non-slaves) proposing and voting on issues whilst publicly gathering together. There was no election of a class of people to "represent" them for four years. In Britain, parliament did not first originate

...IT WOULD SEEM THAT THE PRACTICE OF DEMOCRACY TODAY HAS NOTHING TO DO WITH THE ORIGINAL IDEA AND THAT THE SYSTEM OF POLITICAL REPRESENTATION DID NOT ACTUALLY ORIGINATE TO REPRESENT THE MAJORITY OF SOCIETY.

in order to represent the wishes of the populace, as the majority of the people did not have the vote at this point. So it would seem that the practice of democracy today has nothing to do with the original idea and that the system of political representation did not actually originate to represent the majority of society.

Again, the interests of certain social groups are contingent upon democracy not being perceived in such a way and hopefully this example shows how language and meaning is as much a political realm as any other.

"Use" and "abuse"

So far, we have seen how the meanings of everyday ideas are formulated at the level of language and may be part of highly political processes. We have seen how something as fundamental as democracy—surely an organizing principle in our day to day lives—can be seen in such radically different ways and how the acceptance of one meaning over another involves significant issues of power. We have also seen how the meanings of things change over time. So how does this relate to the question of whether all use is abuse? Let's look at this in another way – let's consider the terms "use" and "abuse" a little more.

First of all, the terms "use" and "abuse" clearly imply that there are clear "uses" and "abuses" of certain things such as objects (like drugs for example). However, we then need to ask ourselves where these ideas come from. Are there clear uses and abuses of objects inherent within them? Are the uses and abuses of objects properties of the objects themselves? The answer is no. How could there be? It is human beings that make sense of objects, events, other people and behavior. So when it comes to drugs, somewhere and at some point, someone decided on what these substances were to be appropriately used for (use) and were not to be used for (abuse). Some people got into the position of being able to tell the other people what to do with certain "objects."

It would seem then that as regards the question "is all use abuse," we need to understand who was able to construct the notions of "use" and "abuse" and how this happened historically.

The rise of scientific medicine, pharmacists, and the control of drugs

How did the idea of appropriate "uses" and inappropriate "abuses" of drugs come to exist (for they have not always existed and the emergence of this distinction can be chronologically pinpointed fairly accurately)? The question of who made the decisions about drugs and legislated on them is relatively simple. This involved the rising professions of the scientific-medical profession and of course government. The more involved question is, how did this happen?

Between the middle and the end of the nineteenth century much was to change as regards the use, control, and conception of drugs. At the beginning of this period, the distinction between drug "use" and drug "abuse" had hardly appeared (Blanchard and Atha, 1998). However, by the end of this period, the previous lack of distinction between medical and other uses, and the fear of addiction were clearly now seen as problematic. The solution to this "problem" was the growing trend towards

...AS LATE AS THE EIGHTEENTH CENTURY MOST PEOPLE SELF-MEDICATED, OR SIMPLY CHANGED THEIR LIFESTYLE WHEN ILL, BUT DID NOT SEEK THE HELP OF MEDICAL PRACTITIONERS

clear and enforceable categories (Grinspoon and Bakalar, 1993). This centralization and restriction was a part of the growing power and control being exerted by the rising scientific-medical profession.

In the United Kingdom, the scientific-medical profession rose to a near monopoly of the field of healthcare in the latter part of the nineteenth century and the early part of the twentieth century and is, as such, a comparatively recent development. If we look at health in England in the middle ages, we find two systems—folk practitioners who treated the majority of the populace, and those with the university conferred title of doctor, who treated the social elite. At this point the first source of distinction between those involved in healing emerges (Freidson, 1970), and this patronage, by the wealthy and powerful, of one of the many competing groups within the area of healthcare would prove to be a crucial factor in that group's rise to a position of near monopoly, familiar to us today.

Public healthcare arose in England as a response to the concerns around rapid industrialization (Fee and Porter, 1994), and it is the case thatas late as the eighteenth century most people self-medicated, or simply changed their lifestyle when ill, but did not seek the help of medical practitioners (Porter, 1992; cited in Lypton, 1995).

Blanchard and Atha (1998) comment that most people could not afford the services of a doctor and that they were not particularly well trusted by the populace anyway. So what factors might explain the rise to near monopoly of the scientific-medical profession? Clearly any such explanation will involve numerous factors, and will be open to argument, but there would seem to be certain factors that may credibly be employed here. These will be discussed below, and are:

(a) the relationship between the state and the medical profession,

(b) the medical profession's own occupational structure,

(c) the medical profession's scientific basis.

It will be argued that these are the main factors that explain the rise to dominance of one group of healers within what was a competitive social arena.

(a) the relationship between the state and the medical profession

It has been argued by many (Freidson, 1970; Lypton, 1995; Porter, 1997) that the relationship between the state (a social institution of growing significance itself at this point in British history), and the medical profession is one of the major factors in an explanation of its rise to the near monopolization of health.

As has already been discussed above, the medical profession had been patronized by the social elite from the time of the middle ages (Freidson, 1970), and with the rise of the state in the seventeenth and eighteenth centuries, medicine's influence began to grow (Lypton, 1995). This influence grew because of concerns around rapid industrialization and the accompanying social changes (Fee and Porter, 1994), the belief among the social elite and the state that the medical profession was the most skilled of the competing groups (Freidson, 1970), and legislation around who may practice within the area of health which effectively enshrined in law the near monopoly that we see today (Freidson, 1970).

It has already been noted that the medical profession had to attain the position of near monopoly against competition, and that this was effectively done through legislation made by the state. The two questions of relevance would seem to be who were the competition, and why were they legislated out of the sphere of health?

During the middle ages, as noted above, the university educated doctors treated the social elite who were

therefore a minority. Peasants and those who lived in the urban slums were treated by those practicing folk-medicine, part-time practitioners, and itinerant irregulars (Freidson, 1970). By the nineteenth century the medical profession faced competition from untrained chemists, druggists, and "quacks" (irregulars again) (Porter, 1997). It has been argued that the challenge from dispensing druggists, who before 1780 had largely only supplied medical practitioners, brought matters to a head in terms of the growing view that legislation was needed. After 1780, druggists began to open shops and sell preparations directly to the public, drastically undercutting practitioners. Worst of all, they even began to visit the sick (Loudon, 1994).

State legislation is most likely to be imposed around services in which it is feared that the public are unqualified to make a judgment about who can, and who can not, provide a safe and effective service. The state is likely to feel that legislation is required to protect the interests of the public (Freidson, 1970). This was the case in the sphere of health. Concerns around safety and unscrupulous practice led to the state legislating in favor of the group that it had clearly believed to be the most qualified and scrupulous for some period of time (having patronized them since the middle ages). The legislation that effectively gave the medical profession this monopoly did not occur in Europe and North America until the twentieth century (Freidson, 1970).

(b) the medical profession's own occupational structure

In the nineteenth century, national professional associations of the medical profession were established in England and in other countries (Freidson, 1970). In England, The Provincial Medical and Surgical Association was founded in 1832, and in 1855 this organization became the British Medical Association (Porter, 1997)—the organization that presides over the medical profession to this day in the UK Such representative bodies were of great importance within the process through which the medical profession came to obtain a monopoly over the sphere of health.

Although it was the state that passed the legislation making the medical profession dominant within its sphere, the profession was in no sense passive within this process. It was within interaction between the state and the representative body of the medical profession that the occupation's control over its work was established and shaped (Freidson, 1970). Central to this was the growing belief that the profession was uniquely qualified in the area of health. This belief served not only as a reason why the profession should be given the near monopoly over health in the first place, but also why it should then be granted autonomy over its own practices—which is

> ALTHOUGH IT WAS THE STATE THAT PASSED THE LEGISLATION MAKING THE MEDICAL PROFESSION DOMINANT WITHIN ITS SPHERE, THE PROFESSION WAS IN NO SENSE PASSIVE WITHIN THIS PROCESS.

one of the primary distinguishing factors of a *profession* (Freidson, 1970). Having obtained this monopoly over the sphere of health, and autonomy over its own practices, the medical profession was finally in a position from which it would develop to the proportions familiar to contemporary society.

(c) the medical profession's scientific basis

However, whilst state legislation gave the medical profession its monopoly, and the occupation's representative body played an active role in this, if the medical profession were not seen as not just scrupulous

> SCIENTIFIC MEDICINE COULD NOW OFFER EVIDENCE, OR MAKE THE ARGUMENT, THAT IT WAS SUPERIOR TO ITS COMPETITORS.

but also as effective within the area of healthcare then one might reasonably wonder how their position was obtained. It has been argued above that the medical profession was patronized by social elite since the middle-ages, but this does not explain why, even with a monopoly, they would suddenly become patronized by the population in general—as if they were not believed to be effective then, alternative choices or not, why would people have consulted them?

The answer to this question is to be found in the medical profession's increasingly scientific basis over the nineteenth century and since. Medicine became vastly more effective in treating illness when it "discovered" that diseases have specific causes which can be treated. Changes in the way that the body was seen, and accompanying medical practices were to revolutionize healthcare. Examples of such changes are the discovery of the cellular structure of plant and animals life in 1838, by Schleider and Schwann, the origins of antiseptic surgery in the 1860s, and of bacteriology in the 1870s (Weindling, 1994). During this period, illness and the body were

> TO BELIEVE THAT DRUGS ARE SOLELY CONTROLLED (AND THEREFORE SEEN WITHIN THE "USE" OR "ABUSE" PARADIGM) ON THE BASIS OF PROFESSIONAL INTEREST AND CONCERN FOR THE POPULACE'S WELL BEING WOULD BE TO IMPOSE A RATIONALITY ON THE HISTORY OF DRUG CONTROL WHICH IS SADLY LACKING!

reconceptualized. Symptomatic treatment was replaced by the knowledge and treatment of causes (Freidson, 1970). The doctor of 1800 could relieve the symptoms of some illnesses, but could not treat the causes of them, as at this point they were not known (Cartwright, 1977). With the invention of the microscope came the discovery of the causes of diseases such as cholera, tuberculosis and typhoid. Such discoveries, understandably, glorified the progress of scientific medicine (Rosenberg, 1988; cited in Lypton, 1995), and as Freidson comments, the:

> "...distinction between physician and so-called quack needed no longer to rest on the academic certification of the superiority of one superstition over another (1970: 16)."

Scientific medicine could now offer evidence, or make the argument, that it was superior to its competitors. The "unlocking" of the secrets of such causes of fear as typhoid, tuberculosis, and cholera, must surely have contributed to the belief that scientific-medicine was superior to its competition.

So over a relatively short period of time (and relatively recently), healthcare became professionalized, legislated and the province of a particular group of individuals. This, it has been argued, was the result of patronage by the powerful classes in society, professional organization of the profession and the success of scientific medicine in the fight against disease. I have argued this using the situation in the UK as an example, but a relatively similar process occurred across the Western, industrialized world.

This, however, only explains how a certain group was in the situation where it was capable of exerting control over certain substances. It does not explain *why* they did so. Now, it would seem a fair argument to say that the

> IN THE US, THE SMOKING OF CANNABIS WAS CREDITED WITH CAUSING ALL SORTS OF DANGEROUS ENCOUNTERS BETWEEN MEXICAN-AMERICANS AND WHITE SOCIETY AND THE USE OF COCAINE BY AFRICAN-AMERICANS WAS BELIEVED TO MAKE THEM BULLET-PROOF IN ENCOUNTERS WITH LAW

control of drugs by the group that came to dominate healthcare was done out of concern for the well-being of the populace and also because if you control health then you inherently control the use of drugs as "part and parcel" of this. Whilst these are both true, this is only a partial explanation as to why we have the legislation and practices of control seen today around drugs (legal and illicit). To believe that drugs are solely controlled (and therefore seen within the "use" or "abuse" paradigm) on the basis of professional interest and mconcern for the populace's well being would be to impose a rationality on the history of drug control which is sadly lacking! The fact is that the history of drug control is more political and irrational than these factors alone would suggest.

Drug control: Racism, sexuality, and irrationality

The main thrust of the next part of this argument will be that the control of drugs which was exercised by governments, with legal drugs being increasingly controlled (medical substances being prescribed by doctors and dispensed by licensed chemists, alcohol and tobacco being supplied in regulated ways) and illicit drugs being made so by legislation, is as much the outcome (if not more) of irrationality, social anxiety, and political expediency, as it is of rational social policy.

By the late 1800s, the availability of psychoactive and medicinally used substances was coming under legislation and control. It was increasingly believed that the general availability of these substances was a dangerous situation. But this belief was very much the result (to a degree) of the social anxieties of more powerful social groups about

WAR IS AN INCREDIBLY POWERFUL METAPHOR TO EMPLOY.

those less powerful than themselves, but often seen as "dangerous." In Victorian London, drunkenness among the working-class came to be seen more and more as a concern by the rising middle-class (including of course the medical profession) (Berridge, 1998). The smoking of opium came to be a great cause of social anxiety, as it was believed to facilitate the seduction of white women by Chinese men (Berridge, 1998), inter-racial sex being a huge taboo at this point. In the US, the smoking of cannabis was credited with causing all sorts of dangerous encounters between Mexican-Americans and white society and the use of cocaine by African-Americans was believed to make them bullet-proof in encounters with law (Coomber, 1997)!

Concerns about violence, social unrest, sexual behavior (and the list goes on) urged the growing control of substances.

IN FACT, SO MUCH MORE OF THE LANGUAGE AROUND DRUGS AND USERS IS SIMILARLY ALARMIST AND MORALISTIC IN TONE, FROM THE LABELS "JUNKIE" OR "CRACK-HEAD" THAT DEHUMANIZE THOSE THEY ARE APPLIED TO, TO THE DESCRIPTIONS OF SUBSTANCES AS "DEMON DRUGS," "DEADLY," AND "KILLERS."

Drugs came to symbolize a multitude of social anxieties in a changing world that was struggling (often unsuccessfully) to deal with those changes in a rational way (Kohn, 1992). Media-led scare-mongering facilitated the circulation of many of the above mentioned myths and harsh political solutions followed. Being seen to be "hard on drugs" became a vote-winner, a political currency, in societies that were paranoid about drugs. If you think that these myths sound ridiculous and that surely society must have moved on since accepting such ideas as fact, then just look at the comparatively recent paranoia over "crack" use, the myths (instant and inevitable addiction), the harsh penal solutions and the media frenzy, and you will realize that the drug

DISEASE IS THE OTHER POWERFUL METAPHOR EMPLOYED IN THE LANGUAGE OF THE "DRUG PROBLEM."

paranoia is as healthy as ever. See Reinarman and Levine (1997) for more on this. If the myth about cocaine making black males "bullet-proof" seems ridiculous then consider the contemporary myth about how many police officers are needed to subdue a PCP user.

The first half of the twentieth century featured moves towards the control of drugs on an international level.

By this stage, drug control had become more about international politics than the rise to power of the scientific medical profession (Mott and Bean 2000). It has been argued, however, that Britain's participation at the conventions and in attempts at control on an international level was sometimes more out of political expediency and international pressure than an attempt to address actual problems. For example, in the UK, cannabis became a banned substance at the 1925 Geneva International Convention on Narcotics Control, this decision being incorporated into the Dangerous Drugs Act in 1928 (Blanchard and Atha, 1997). However, prosecutions for cannabis related offences did not surpass those for opium and manufactured drugs, in the UK, until 1950 (Blanchard and Atha, 1997). Abel comments how at the 1925 convention, pressure principally emanating from the US, Egyptian, and South African delegates eventually resulted in the restriction of international trafficking in cannabis except for licensed medical or scientific purposes. Ironically not all the nations signed the final agreement, among them the US and Egypt (1980). At this point cannabis was rarely used in the UK and Europe and parliament passed the act more in the interest of controlling opiates and other drugs that it also covered than any real concern over cannabis (Gossop, 1993). Then, as now of course, alcohol and tobacco were still far more problematic substances to society than any of these illicit drugs.

So the complex social and historical route by which we arrive at the idea of appropriate "uses" and inappropriate "abuses" of substances is one of the rise of the scientific-medical establishment and a growing practice of control over the availability of substances, for a multitude of rational and irrational reasons.

Language and the "drug problem"

We have, then, arrived at a social and historical explanation of how societies in the Western and industrialized world came to control the use and availability of substances. The language used to speak about this and to think about it, reflects and actively plays a role in reproducing this state of affairs. This may be seen in the terms "use" and "abuse." In practice, unless we actively question it, this language quite simply dictates that drugs have uses and abuses and it is involved in the communication of what these are.

However, the whole language (not just "use" and "abuse") around drug consumption is value-laden (Coomber, 1995). Consistent with the argument above that drugs came to symbolize various social anxieties, it can be seen that the language used to speak about and to understand drugs and users is far from neutral and is in fact highly moralistic and anxiety-based. Let us consider a few examples.

"The War on Drugs" – War is an incredibly powerful metaphor to employ. It conveys the idea that society is beset by an enemy, that this is a desperate struggle for our survival and that only the most forceful of responses will suffice. It implores citizens to choose a side in the conflict (even if it means informing on your children to the authorities) and implies that it is an ongoing struggle which can be won, as opposed to it being a set of political responses to a perceived problem which in actuality is out of all proportion to reality. The reality is that cannabis, for example, is by far the most popular illegal drug and that most users are recreational and their use is only problematic because if they are arrested they may become criminalized.

"Drug Plague" – Disease is the other powerful metaphor employed in the language of the "drug problem." This time, society is portrayed metaphorically as a body, with a deadly disease spreading throughout. However, drug users are members of society, not bacteria from outside it! This metaphor again calls for urgent measures in the struggle for life. Consider the frequent description of "crack" use as an "epidemic," (Coomber, 1995) spreading through the body (society).

In fact, so much more of the language around drugs and users is similarly alarmist and moralistic in tone, from the labels "junkie" or "crack-head" that dehumanize those they are applied to, to the descriptions of substances as "demon drugs," "deadly," and "killers." Now of course, drug use *can* be a dangerous activity and for many people around the world, drug use *is* a source of many problems in their lives. However, the language around drug use frequently encourages us to marginalize them and to adopt the most draconian of measures in dealing with them. Much of this is achieved at the level of the language used to speak about and understand them. To repeat my argument, language is not a neutral realm, it is the very site at which meaning is formed.

Conclusion

It has been argued that "use" and "abuse" are historically produced *understandings* of what we should and should not do with drugs that have only become common cultural currency within the last two hundred years (at the most). It has also been argued that these *understandings* are the result of various socio-political changes and processes and that they have involved numerous factors. Underpinning this argument is a view of language that conceptualizes it not simply as a medium for the communication of our species, but also a as a key political site in the formation of the meaning of all sorts of things, including drugs…and notions about the appropriate "uses" or inappropriate "abuses" of them.

References

Abel, E.L., *Marihuana: The first twelve thousand years*, New York, Plenum Press, 1980.

Berridge, V. *Opium and the People*, London, Free Association Press, 1980.

Blanchard, S. and Atha, M. J., *Indian Hemp and the Dope Fiends of Old England: A socio-political history of cannabis and the British Empire 1840-1928*, 1998, http://quark.foobar.co.uk/users/ukcia/history/colonial.html (accessed January 1998).

Cartwright, F. F., *A Social History of Medicine*, London, Longman, 1977.

Coomber, R., "Drugs and the Media," in H. Shapiro and R. Coomber (eds.) *Drugs: Your Questions Answered*, London, ISDD, 1995.

Coomber, R., "Adulteration of Drugs—The discovery of a "myth,"" *Contemporary Drug Problems*, Vol. 24, No. 2, pp 239–271, 1997.

Freidson, E., *Profession of Medicine: A study of the sociology of applied knowledge*, New York, Dodd, Mead and Co, 1970.

Gossop, M. (1993), *Living with Drugs*, Aldershot, Ashgate.

Grinspoon, L. and Bakalar, J.B., *Marihuana, the Forbidden Medicine*, London, Yale University Press, 1993.

Loudon, I., "Medical practitioners 1750 – 1850 and the period of medical reform in Britain," in A. Wear (ed.) *Medicine in Society: Historical Essays*, Cambridge, Cambridge University Press, 1994. Lypton, D., *Medicine as Culture: Illness, disease and the body in Western Societies*, London, Sage Publications, 1995.

Mott, J. and Bean, P., "The Development of Drug Control in Britain," in R. Coomber (ed.) *The Control of Drugs and Users: Reason or Reaction,?* Amsterdam, Harwood Academic Publishers, 2000.

Porter, R., *The Greatest Benefit to Mankind: A medical history of humanity from antiquity to the present*, London, Fontana Press, 1997.

Weindling, P., "From Infections to Chronic Diseases: Changing patterns of sickness in the nineteenth and twentieth centuries," in A. Wear (ed.) *Medicine in Society: Historical Essays*, Cambridge, Cambridge University Press, 1994.

The Last Word on Drugs

Jules Siegel

"That's a funny thing; every one of the bastards that are out for legalizing marijuana is Jewish. What the Christ is the matter with the Jews, Bob, what is the matter with them? I suppose it's because most of them are psychiatrists, you know, there's so many, all the greatest psychiatrists are Jewish."

—Richard Nixon, Oval Office Tape, May 26, 1971.

Can we just stop and ask a simple question? What is this drug hysteria all about? Aren't drugs just silly? I took a *lot* of drugs, folks. Marijuana definitely turned me into a vegetable. I was grateful for that. I remember lying on the floor with Brian Wilson and the rest of the Beach Boys marijuana-consumption squad in a profoundly vegetabalized state laughing about the idea of going out and committing violent acts. "Ma-a-a-n, how could a *vegetable* be *violent*?" mused Michael Vosse. You've got to try to hear that old hippie doper drawl there. Now, imagine more loud giggles and different utterly stoned takes on being a vegetable, eventually inspiring the Vega-Tables song in *Smile*!

I never took heroin, but I used enough Percodan both recreationally and therapeutically to get a feeling for opiates. I smoked opium a couple of times in 1973. The

> CAN WE JUST STOP AND ASK A SIMPLE QUESTION? WHAT IS THIS DRUG HYSTERIA ALL ABOUT? AREN'T DRUGS JUST SILLY?

last time, I dreamed that I was Richard Nixon in the White House, which was a decrepit Southern mansion located in a dismal swamp filled with the wrong kind of graves. Pat Nixon (a perfectly costumed Southern belle) wrung her hands in terror. Although the visual style was pure Socialist Realism, it also looked like a scene from *Tales of the Crypt*. Watergate soon followed. I never smoked opium again. Seeing this was too scary.

I hated writing and took increasingly larger doses of Dexedrine to complete my assignments, often turning to LSD when this failed to produce the desired results. LSD (originally a vegetable product first isolated from ergot by

Albert Hofmann, I might add) eventually helped me see that I had to cut down on my drug use. When you have a bummer, you tend to make the connection that the habit of dropping any stuff that any head hands you conditions you to dropping substances that often produce a state best described by "Help. Let me out of here. I promise I will never do this again."

> CARY GRANT, ONCE A CONFIRMED BACHELOR, WAS ABLE TO SOLVE MANY EMOTIONAL PROBLEMS THROUGH LSD THERAPY, AND NOT ONLY MARRY A BEAUTIFUL WOMAN, BUT ALSO FATHER A CHILD.

This should be no surprise to those of us who first heard about LSD as a psychological wonder drug, not from well-meaning clown-geniuses like Timothy Leary, but from psychiatrists such as the late Humphrey Osmond. Dr. Osmond, creator of the term *psychedelic*, demonstrated that LSD combined with therapy could get alcoholics off booze for periods ranging from a several months to life. Cary Grant, once a confirmed bachelor, was able to solve many emotional problems through LSD therapy, and not only marry a beautiful woman, but also father a child.

Understandably, we approached taking LSD as an act of self-improvement. It worked for many, but not exactly in the way I personally expected. Does anyone else recall:

[1] The realization that human beings are devices that spin around eternity weaving self-important justifications for leaving the room and jerking off?

[2] The profound enlightenment that the sensation of oneness with the cosmos called "being God" was actually the ultimate form of masturbation?

[3] The recognition that the material universe and all it contains, including all living beings and the earth, the moon and the stars, is actually shit in various stages of activity?

[4] The appreciation that the forces of gravity and magnetism are merely larger manifestations of the same force of sexual attraction that we feel for the opposite sex?

[5] The absolutely side-splitting comprehension that the whole fucking thing—the agony and the ecstasy, the mud and the stars, the pride and the glory—is merely a really dumb joke whose punch line is that you fell for it yet another time?

When I took LSD, I often felt like a highly evolved amoeba. My pseudopods were so well articulated that they had bones and joints. I could see that my beloved wife and friends were all extensions or fragments of the same amoeba swimming in the same interconnected life soup. We were lumps in the soup but it was really all one soup filled with currents within currents *ad infinitum* that defined our existence(s). On my second trip, I saw the sky filled with massed angels and hearts and flowers and cherubs with bows and arrows arranged to spell out the words "Jerk Off!" This was awesome. It was a direct command. It was also so embarrassing that I cringe to write it.

How could these absurd visions justify putting people in prison? Well, start with the term absurd, from the Latin *absurdus*, "out of tune," figuratively "doesn't fit." All societies require that members fit in one slot or another. We must harmonize or go stand in the corner. Our society is a quasi-theological oligarchy trying to become a historical landmark totalitarian state. Its basic aim is control. There are masters (the rich and the super-rich) and there are slaves (the rest). In order for the master to truly feel masterful, the slaves must be spontaneously and fully servile. Human interaction, in this construction, will be a role-playing game called the *Law of the Boss*. The masters will be superheroes inside and out. The slaves will be programmed as hungry dogs jumping for gobbets of meat. Ideally, they will be suited up in sexually desirable perfect android bodies.

BY ALL STATISTICAL MEASURES, DRUGS SUCH AS OPIATES, MARIJUANA, THE PSYCHEDELICS AND COCAINE ARE MINOR PROBLEMS WHEN COMPARED TO THE GREATEST NUMBING DRUG OF ALL, ALCOHOL.

LSD lights up the tacky backstage of the game. Everyone's equal. We are all imbeciles jerking off in the mirror. LSD lets you see your life as a dream. Everyone in your dream is you. Why would you want to hurt yourselves? If you try to play the *Law of the Boss* with a silly grin on your face, the whole thing is just ruined. Although the feeling wears off, LSD insights are so intense that they install permanent doubts about the game. Some people drop out, but usually have to come back because not playing gets too much like solitary confinement. Back in the game, however, they have a renewed capacity for changing roles. John Lilly MD once told me that LSD came into American society labeled a peace drug, but it wasn't a peace drug. It was a problem-solving psychedelic, he said. A warrior who took it would not necessarily give up his trade, but could use it to become a better warrior. A slave might decide to become a master. Thus, LSD was a direct threat to the existing order. It also made people in power feel ridiculous. Does the executioner dress up in a clown costume?

By all statistical measures, drugs such as opiates, marijuana, the psychedelics and cocaine are minor problems when compared to the greatest numbing drug of all, alcohol. Different societies handle alcohol in different ways, but alcoholism has been a known negative condition since the earliest times. In the 1940s and 1950s, sociologists noticed that alcoholism was culturally defined, so much so that it was difficult to decide in a scientific way who was an alcoholic and who was just another drinker. One classic study defined alcoholism by cirrhosis of the liver, a physical marker that could be measured objectively. No matter what the measure, however, men drink more than women. Drinking declines as people get older, probably by attrition, as younger alcoholics die from accidents, cirrhosis, or other medical complications. Especially significant, Jews typically had very low rates of alcoholism, and other cultures that tolerated and integrated alcohol into their social rituals had lower rates, too. Cultures that insisted that alcohol was the Devil's work and therefore required total abstinence had the highest alcoholism rates. In the United States, states that tried to prohibit alcohol had the highest alcoholism rates.

Alcohol demonstrates the futility of drug prohibition. Dramatization or demonization of mind altering substances increases the possibilities that it will cause problems such as addiction, dependence or acting out of anti-social behavior. Drug criminalization is rather like making the common cold a crime. Not everyone has a cold at the same time, but everyone will eventually get one. The same goes for drug abuse. It's a human condition, not a vice. Making it a crime worse than murder glorifies drug abuse. It's a Hollywood circus of celebrity arrests, outrageous profits, millions of users, endless media feeding frenzy behavior. You know the drill: "Dealer slime busted with three grams of marijuana with a street value of umpteen million dollars!" That's the drug war in micro miniature. *Wow! That stuff must be potent! Look at all the commotion.* It's the psychological version of the DeBeers diamond scam. Without all the marketing and price control, what would the kind of diamond ring you buy in Sears go for? Why should flowers that you can grow in a window box be worth a prison term?

This becomes easier to understand when you look at life in modern industrial society as a vast prison, with many wards and dungeons. While you pretend that you are free, you remain a slave. You waste your power bouncing off invisible walls like a crazed fly banging against windows. It's a little easier to get out of a cage if you see the bars. The first step is to understand that the bars are invisible. You live in a mental cage of habits and attitudes installed in infancy when you were too little to doubt or even remember. In *The Rich and the Super-Rich*, Ferdinand Lundberg wrote:

> Instead of the rich being irresistible exploiters, then, as Marxists present them, the situation as a whole is much more like a sadomasochistic process with one small group internally programmed for command and the other, much larger, for submission. Freud looked upon all civilization as a process of necessary repression. Most of this repression is achieved by psychological means through the uptraining of children in certain ways by parents and parental substitutes.

James Clark Moloney, M.D., a U. S. Army psychiatrist, studied non-industrial childrearing techniques among the people of Okinawa in the preparations for the invasion of Japan during World War II. Continuing his research after the war, he concluded that in what we might call the normal family, based on the non-industrial model, there is an abundance of parental love and contact. Growth follows natural rhythms. Parents and children share small spaces, frequently sleeping in the same bed, and there is little secrecy. Sexual expression by children is usually considered amusing. Authority tends to be maternal rather than paternal. Children are spanked in all societies, but abusive punishment or denial is rare. Children compete for their parents' affection, but since there is an ever-flowing well of love, each child gets a fair share.

In our society, he told me, "After a pre-natal period in which the mother is in a state of growing fear and anxiety, the baby is born screaming in drugged confusion. The helpless infant is immediately separated from its mother. It is fed with a bottle, even though breast milk provides immunity from many childhood diseases. Then it is kept in a crib—a little cage—and fed not on demand when it is hungry but on a schedule. All forms of intimacy—from cuddling to nakedness—are either strictly rationed or forbidden. Pregnancy, infancy and childhood are treated as diseases. The child is not so much raised as cured of its afflictions."

Bottle nursing, cribs, and strict toilet training produce adults who are angry and depressed, unable to sustain satisfaction physically or emotionally, associate pleasure mostly with acquisition of objects, and are highly skilled in techniques of passive manipulation. The more overtly sadistic make excellent soldiers and police. Those adept at more subtle forms of aggression, such as pillage by propaganda, become managers. The totally beaten work on assembly lines. All consume. They pray to God (an all-powerful person in the sky) to give them money the way they once prayed to Mommy from the crib to give them bottles. Walled into the loneliness of their individual invisible chapels, society's prisoners soon learn to purchase their contacts with the outside world through artificial media such as the telephone, radio, postage stamps, books, television, movies whose characters take on life and populate the lonely prisoners' fantasy worlds. The inmates think they really know them. They buy perfume and blue jeans as communion.

Not they. We. Who are "they"? We are they.

This is painful stuff to take. We pacify ourselves with all kinds of toys, from automobiles to hypodermic needles. We look for mothering outside institutions to give our loyalty—the school, the state, the corporations. We do not allow ourselves direct personal contact with God—or nature—or each other—that divine feeling of connection to the whole. Those who do achieve this through mystical experiences or the use of drugs such as LSD become no longer fit. No one listens to them any more. They are suspect.

It's often said that drugs are a crutch. How true. They are also often the blind man's cane. We are psychological amputees. Parts of our souls are either missing or blocked. Much drug use is just normal human behavior, like kids spinning around to get dizzy for fun. But we also take drugs to break through the numbness, to meet the brutal economic demands of the prison workhouse, to sleep and to endure. People use cocaine in smog-filled cities for the same reason they use them in the Andes—to overcome oxygen deprivation. The media image of the killer drug dealer controlling his turf with a Glock misses the real point. To get the picture right, the drug dealer would have to be shown against a Ché Guevara poster. Dealers are often very compassionate, caring people. They don't see themselves as spreading death, but energy or happiness or relief from suffering. Do wine and liquor merchants consider themselves merchants of death because alcohol is so deadly?

Despite this, I don't advocate drugs. I condone them. I haven't taken Dexedrine or LSD in almost twenty-five years, nor have I taken a narcotic except as prescribed by a doctor for pain. No one had to force this abstinence on me. Drugs themselves taught me that we don't get out

THE MORE OVERTLY SADISTIC MAKE EXCELLENT SOLDIERS AND POLICE. THOSE ADEPT AT MORE SUBTLE FORMS OF AGGRESSION, SUCH AS PILLAGE BY PROPAGANDA, BECOME MANAGERS. THE TOTALLY BEATEN WORK ON ASSEMBLY LINES. ALL CONSUME.

of things ever; we get through them. The hardest part of living is to accept the bitter fact that life is loss. There is no escape from this. Nothing hurts worse than unrequited love. In industrial society, we begin with the loss of the mother. That pain never goes away. Eventually you lose everyone, including your precious self. In all the history of the world, no one has ever come up with an adequate antidote for this. Words don't suffice, nor do potions and spells. While you are still alive, the pain usually fades

IT'S OFTEN SAID THAT DRUGS ARE A CRUTCH. HOW TRUE. THEY ARE ALSO OFTEN THE BLIND MAN'S CANE.

on its own. It's self-limiting. You can only go on a given vibration for so long. But there are no short cuts. Drugs are, at best, temporary relief that can show us paths through the darkness, as if by flickering starlight; at worst, they can be suicide. They aren't an excuse for evading one's responsibilities to others. Most important of all, they are absolutely no excuse for yet another layer of tyranny and official terrorism.

The Incarceration of a Nation: Drug Enforcement and Prohibition

Nixon Tapes Pot Shocker

Mike Gray

WASHINGTON—The Watergate tapes from the Nixon White House are indeed the gift that keeps on giving.

The latest release of these secret recordings covers that period in 1971 when President Richard M. Nixon was preparing to crank up the war on marijuana. In his conversations with Chief of Staff Bob Haldeman and others, Nixon reveals, in his down-home, earthy style, that the whole thing was a fraud.

The president was in a box at this particular moment because a special drug commission that he had appointed was spinning out of control. "The National Commission on

> ...NIXON REVEALS, IN HIS DOWN-HOME, EARTHY STYLE, THAT THE WHOLE THING WAS A FRAUD.

Marijuana and Drug Abuse" was a creation of Congress, but Nixon had put his stamp on it by appointing a host of hard-liners. The headman was a former prosecutor, Gov. Ray Shafer of Pennsylvania, whose tough law-and-order reputation meshed with Nixon's vision.

Now there was word on the street that the so-called "Shafer Commission" was considering the legalization of marijuana.

The president had clearly expected Gov. Shafer to return with a damning indictment of the evil weed because he had already made up his mind to use the drug issue as a political axe in the upcoming election.

Unfortunately several of the commissioners were not in on the plan and they took the assignment seriously. They commissioned more than 50 scientific studies, surveyed

> [NIXON] RESPONDED CURTLY AT HIS NEXT PRESS CONFERENCE: "EVEN IF THE COMMISSION DOES RECOMMEND THAT IT BE LEGALIZED, I WILL NOT FOLLOW THAT RECOMMENDATION."

judges, probation officers, clinicians, and health experts, and they personally went all over the globe for a first-hand look at the situation. It was one of the most comprehensive examinations of marijuana in history.

One can imagine Nixon's surprise when rumors began circulating in early '71 that the "L-word" was on the table [Nixon] responded curtly at his next press conference: "Even if the Commission does recommend that it be legalized, I will not follow that recommendation."

This bold admission created a firestorm among the commissioners and several of them threatened to quit—or worse, to produce a dissenting minority report. Shafer, who was also angling for an appointment to the federal bench, was caught in the middle. He promised the insurrectionists he would meet with the President and try to straighten things out.

He was finally able to get an appointment in early September but it is clear that he knew this meeting was window dressing. Shafer told staffer Egil Krogh, Jr., "I know what the game is."

All Shafer wanted was a picture of himself with the President that he could take back to the Commission. "I'll tell them that we met, the President listened, was appreciative..."

> "I THINK THERE'S A NEED TO COME OUT WITH A REPORT THAT IS TOTALLY OBLIVIOUS TO SOME OBVIOUS DIFFERENCES BETWEEN MARIJUANA AND OTHER DRUGS."

Nixon let him have the picture but he was otherwise unrelenting. While admitting that there were significant differences between marijuana and other drugs, he wanted Shafer to cover up that fact. "I think there's a need to come out with a report that is totally oblivious to some obvious differences between marijuana and other drugs."

Throughout 1971 Nixon kept up the drumbeat. "I want a goddamn strong statement on marijuana," he told his high-level White House lieutenant Bob Haldeman, "I mean one that just tears the ass out of them." Somehow, it's not surprising to hear the President say, "You know, it's a funny thing, every one of the bastards that are out for legalizing marijuana is Jewish."

On March 21, 1972, the president told Haldeman, "We need—and I use the word—'all out war.'" The next day the Shafer Commission returned its report on marijuana and to the President's chagrin, not only did they refuse to declare war on marijuana, they recommended decriminalization.

Nixon declared his war on drugs anyway. Needless to say, Gov. Shafer did not get his judicial appointment and his voluminous report was swept under the rug.

"YOU KNOW, IT'S A FUNNY THING, EVERY ONE OF THE BASTARDS THAT ARE OUT FOR LEGALIZING MARIJUANA IS JEWISH."

For those who are curious about what this country might be like today if Richard Nixon had simply followed the advice of his own experts, we happen to have a comparative yardstick.

At the same moment that the Shafer Commission was hearing evidence in the United States, a Dutch commission was doing the same thing in The Netherlands and they came to the same conclusion. Unlike the Americans, they paid attention to their experts and decriminalized marijuana.

Today, per capita use of marijuana among teenagers in The Netherlands is half that of those in the United States. Meanwhile the people of this country were treated to a 30-year jihad that so far has resulted in the arrest of nearly 15 million citizens.

Prohibition is Treason

Dan Russell

The drug war is a neofascist protection racket, engineered by those heavily invested in the legal and illegal drug business, the legal and illegal arms trade, and the law enforcement and imprisonment business. It is not possible that those running the drug war don't know they are running a massive price support for illegal drugs—it's Economics 101—Republican economics no less, the pure physics of free enterprise.

Stifle the supply of a demanded commodity, and its price will rise to whatever level is necessary to overcome the

IT IS NOT POSSIBLE THAT THOSE RUNNING THE DRUG WAR DON'T KNOW THEY ARE RUNNING A MASSIVE PRICE SUPPORT FOR ILLEGAL DRUGS— IT'S ECONOMICS 101—REPUBLICAN ECONOMICS NO LESS, THE PURE PHYSICS OF FREE ENTERPRISE.

hurdle. That was well proven by alcohol Prohibition, and the lesson was not lost on disingenuous intelligence professionals.

The underground drug trade is worth in the neighborhood of 600 billion untaxable dollars a year. Many global centers of power would no more destroy that trade with controlled legalization than they would destroy the oil trade, or the arms trade.

The drug war is a fight for control of the multi-billion dollar street drug business. If eradication were the object, we would long ago have bankrupted the smugglers with medicalization and legalization.

Corruption on the Homefront

The first DEA, the Narcotics Division of the Prohibition Unit of the Treasury Department, was founded and funded by the Volstead Act of 1919, the enabling act of the 18th Amendment, Prohibition. The charter of the Narcotics Division, of course, was the State Department's Harrison Act of 1914, a device aimed at the opium-based British power in China, an original part of Prohibition's political package. Harrison had the full support of organized medicine, since the act gave it complete commercial control, through the prescription system, of the most valuable medicines.

"The Transfer": Ireland in Columbus *Dispatch*

The Harrison Narcotics Act was originally the responsibility of Treasury's Alcohol Tax Division, but went largely unenforced until the Volstead Act of 1919 funded the Prohibition Unit and its subdivision, the Narcotics Division.

The first chief of the Narcotics Division, Levi Nutt, held that job for ten years. But in 1930, Treasury Secretary Mellon appointed an Assistant Commissioner of Prohibition specializing in diplomacy, Harry Anslinger, to head Treasury's reorganized Bureau of Narcotics. Treasury's hopelessly corrupt Prohibition Unit was transferred to Justice.

One of the straws that forced this reorganization reveals the actual dynamics of the situation: the indictment of federal Narcotics Chief Levi Nutt and most of his New York division by a New York Grand Jury, for being on the Rothstein/Lansky/Luciano payroll.

THE DRUG WAR IS A FIGHT FOR CONTROL OF THE MULTI-BILLION DOLLAR STREET DRUG BUSINESS.

When the legendary gambler Arnold Rothstein was murdered by one of Dutch Schultz' hitters in 1928, his dying body was found with a small fortune in opium, morphine, heroin and cocaine—

and all his carefully kept legal books, including the history of his relationship with Nutt.

The rabid prohibitionist Nutt started his tenure as head of the Narcotics Division in 1920 with his son listed as Rothstein's attorney of record for tax matters with the Treasury Department, and his son-in-law operating as Rothstein's New York accountant and attorney.

It was Nutt's boss, Treasury Secretary Mellon, to the great benefit of DuPont, Hearst, and their Syndicate allies, who ordered Anslinger to engineer the "Reefer Madness" campaign that criminalized marijuana. Treasury Secretary Mellon, through the Mellon Bank, was the major financier of both defense contractor DuPont and the Red Menace's major media advocate, the Hearst yellow journals. DuPont looked forward to the replacement of the hemp industry with the synthetic fiber industry, the patents for which it owned. DuPont's 1937 *Annual Report* to its stockholders looked forward to "radical changes" due to "the revenue raising power of the government ...converted into an instrument for forcing acceptance of sudden new ideas of industrial and social reorganization."

The criminal-governmental symbiosis is a two-way street, of course. If gambling were legal, who'd need Annenberg's gambling wire? If marijuana were legalized, the hood monopoly would be broken and marijuana would lose 95% of its value. The great hoods, geniuses at organizing street muscle, were *for* Prohibition, and Assistant Commissioner of Prohibition Anslinger was one of their major allies, operating the side of the street they couldn't independently run.

Alcohol and Drug Prohibitionist Anslinger, like his soul-mate J. Edgar Hoover, was in bed with the Mellon-Hearst-Annenberg-Syndicate hoods from the beginning. Anslinger always regarded Drug Prohibition as a tool for "social reorganization," fearing "communist" unions far more than Syndicate heroin gangs, who were, after all, Mellon's, DuPont's, Hearst's and Annenberg's patriotic strike breakers. They were also J. Edgar Hoover's most dangerous COINTELPRO operatives—right from the murderous Palmer raids of 1919, which Hoover organized.

When the world's traditional inebriative herbs become illegal commodities, they become worth as much as precious metal, precious metal that can be *farmed*. That makes them, by definition, the preferred medium of exchange for armaments. Illegal drugs, solely because of the artificial value given them by Prohibition, have become the basis of military power anywhere they can be grown and delivered in quantity.

That's why Paul Helliwell, OSS chief of special intelligence in China during WWII, helped run Kuomintang opium and heroin. He was arming Chiang Kai-shek's KMT.

The "Soft" Underbelly of China

Claire Chennault, from 1937 to 1945, was Chiang Kai-shek's senior air force advisor. The CIA's proprietary airline, Civil Air Transport, had been founded in 1946 as an OSS-Kuomintang operation by Claire Chennault and Paul Helliwell. CAT was the peacetime version of Chennault's Flying Tigers, also cofounded with Helliwell. That grew into the CIA proprietary known as Air America, also a Helliwell operation.

During the war, the Flying Tigers and the OSS functioned in China through the Sino-American Cooperative Organization, SACO, under the directorship of General Tai Li. Tai Li headed Chiang's vast secret police, which ran as many as 300,000 operatives from China to San Francisco. It was this organization that was the inspiration for the KMT's dope-dealing World Anti-Communist League.

Chiang's Kuomintang used the Shanghai Green Gang, their Mafia, to organize its vast opium-for-arms trade. Green Gang death squads had helped Chiang and Tai Li put down the 1927 Communist uprising in Shanghai, and had been a key factor in Chiang's power structure ever since. Tu Yueh-sheng, the Green Gang leader, had been invested with the rank of major general by Chiang.

Wherever the Japanese conquered in north China after 1930, they immediately encouraged the planting of opium. Tu Yueh-sheng, on behalf of Chiang, worked out a plan whereby Japanese gunboats would ferry his and their Yangtze opium to his 24 heroin labs in Japanese-controlled north China. The heroin was then sold throughout all of China, in the north by the Japanese Army through its new chain of 6,900 pharmacies, and in the south by Chiang's KMT. In return, Tu, Chiang and Tai-Li were left in control of the Yangtze River opium trade and the export market for their surplus heroin. One of their more famous distributors was Lansky-Luciano partner Lepke Buchalter.

The OSS expected Chiang's opium traders to function as intelligence agents behind Japanese lines. Tai-Li and Tu, for instance, controlled all the dives and opium dens in

> THE PRACTICAL EFFECT OF THIS WAS TO TURN CHENNAULT'S VAUNTED FLYING TIGERS INTO FLYING DOPE PEDDLERS WHO, UNDER ORDERS, ASSIDUOUSLY AVOIDED DOING WHAT THEY HAD PROVEN THEY COULD DO VERY WELL—SHOOT DOWN JAPANESE PLANES.

Japanese-controlled Shanghai, as well as most of the labor unions and police. Thanks to Tai-Li, when the retreating Japanese decided to demolish the port, the OSS had the street muscle to prevent it. The inverse, of course, was also operative. Many of SACO's street fighters were Japanese agents, since the vast opium/heroin trade was sanctioned by both sides across the battle lines.

Assault: *New York Times*, 5/6/1952 and VA *Daily Sun*, 3/19/1955

General "Vinegar Joe" Stilwell, commander of American forces in the China-Burma-India theater, protested that the alliance with "the little peanut" Chiang was a de facto alliance with the Japanese, since Tai-Li, whom he called "the Chinese Himmler," was trading dope and arms on a massive scale with the enemy. The practical effect of this was to turn Chennault's vaunted Flying Tigers into Flying Dope Peddlers who, under orders, assiduously avoided doing what they had proven they could do very well—shoot down Japanese planes.

OSS agents who moved independently against SACO's pro-Japanese dope smugglers were murdered. Mao's Yenan-based force, which had to face SACO's KMT dope smugglers as well as the Japanese, was implacably hostile to all aspects of the opium trade, perceiving it as a security threat on all levels. Mao's troops, if they valued their lives, did not smoke opium. Stilwell, a great field general, insisted that Mao's force was "battle-hardened, disciplined, well trained in guerrilla war and fired by a bitter hatred of the Japanese." This from the commander of one of the greatest fighting units in the history of American arms, Merrill's Marauders.

The OSS Far Eastern chief, Capt. Milton Miles, was Tai-Li's first Deputy Director of SACO. Miles launched OSS operations throughout the opium-producing Golden Triangle of Burma, Laos and Thailand, closely coordinating his efforts with Tai-Li. Tai-Li's elite officer corps was trained by American agents on loan to the OSS from Hoover's FBI and Anslinger's FBN. At this time Tai-Li was the biggest opium and heroin smuggler in the world. That is, our operational high command considered the opium trade an inherent element of its power.

Helliwell founded SEA Supply of Bangkok in 1950 specifically to transport cargo, such as arms from Okinawa, to his Civil Air Transport for the Burma KMT operation. The 1950 idea was to use the Kuomintang troops in Burma to threaten "China's soft underbelly." But, since the underbelly didn't turn out to be so soft, the entrepreneurial KMT settled into the opium business instead, sending CAT's arms supply planes back to Bangkok and Taiwan loaded with opium or morphine from Burma's Shan states of Kokang, Wa and Kengtung.

In fact, with military control of the richest opium-producing area in the world, the KMT was no longer dependent on even the pretense of political legitimacy, since it now had the tactical support of the Thai and Taiwanese armies. The CIA's KMT operation, therefore, became self-sustaining, an enlightening object lesson for all intelligence professionals in achieving complete independence from civilian policy control. As DCI William Casey, who worked under Helliwell, later put it, "a completely self-funding, off-the-shelf operation."

Pursuant to this mandate, Harry Anslinger enlightened the United States Senate and the United Nations Narcotics Commission in 1951 about the Chinese Reds, holding up a bag of *Lions Globe* heroin he said they were shipping to our boys in Korea. This assertion was the basis of a major propaganda campaign that lasted for years.

Lions Globe was actually the brand manufactured by our own Kuomintang allies, Chiang's boys, and the more entrepreneurial of the natives, also our allies, in the Golden Triangle, as our boys in Nam discovered, and as our own Bureau of Narcotics confirmed in 1972.

In a famous 1959 case, Anslinger's top international agent, George White, an OSS/CIA operative, made a major heroin bust. It was Burmese Kuomintang heroin funneled through Hong Kong, bound for distribution by the American Syndicate. But by allowing the ringleader, a well-known member of San Francisco's KMT-organized Chinese Anti-Communist League to escape, White was enabled to claim that it was Red Chinese dope, "most of it from a vast poppy field near Chungking."

> THE FRENCH SECRET SERVICES, ALSO FINANCED BY AMERICAN MILITARY INTELLIGENCE, HAD BEEN USING CORSICAN OPIUM DEALERS THROUGHOUT INDOCHINA TO FINANCE THEIR OPERATION AGAINST THE VIETMINH.

Funding the Vietnam War...the French Way

The American Syndicate's allies, the world-straddling *Union Corse*, the French—and KMT-allied Corsicans, became important strategic assets. The CIA used the *Union Corse* to take Marseille away from the independent and communist unions, leaving the Corsican hoods in control of the most important port in France. The geopolitical rationale for this, from both the French and the American perspective, wasn't only the threat the leftists posed to control of France, but to the Indochina war. The Vietminh had considerable support among French leftists in 1947.

In an attempt to force the French government to negotiate with the our former wartime ally, the Vietminh, the communist dock worker unions, which were full of former *Maquis* fighters, refused to load American arms destined for Vietnam. The only outfits with enough muscle to challenge the communist unions for control of the docks, and the Marseille city council, were the union-busting Corsican hoods and their puppet-union goon squads. The 1947-48 street war for control of Marseille's docks, financed and coordinated by American military intelligence, was nasty, brutish and short.

The French secret services, also financed by American military intelligence, had been using Corsican opium dealers throughout Indochina to finance their operation against the Vietminh. Thus they had a system in place for the collection and distribution of opium and morphine base from all over the Golden Triangle of Laos, Burma and Thailand.

IS IT A COINCIDENCE THAT A HIGH-LEVEL CIA AGENT WHO HELPED RUN SANTOS TRAFFICANTE'S DOPE-DEALING ASSASSINS BECAME THE COUNTRY'S LEADING ANTIDRUG PROPAGANDIST? I DON'T THINK SO.

Morphine base is easily manufactured in makeshift jungle labs. Opium's major alkaloid is precipitated out of the raw sap by boiling it in water with lime. The white morphine floats to the top. That is drawn off and boiled with ammonia, filtered, boiled again, and then sun-dried. The resultant clay-like brown paste is morphine base.

That's where the Corsicans came in. Heroin is diacetylmorphine, morphine in combination with acetic acid, the naturally-occurring acid found in vinegar. Heroin is preferred by users because the acetic acid renders it highly soluble in blood, therefore quicker acting and more potent than unrefined morphine.

The combination process requires, firstly, the skillful use of acetic anhydride, chloroform, sodium carbonate, and alcohol. Then the last step, purification in the fourth stage, requires heating with ether and hydrochloric acid. Since the volatile ether had a habit of exploding, the *Union Corse* had to advertise for a few good chemists.

With huge protected surpluses of morphine base available, the Corsicans built a network of labs to refine not only the Indochinese, but also the Persian and Turkish product, shipping finished snow white #4 heroin out of a Marseille they now controlled. The *Union Corse* heroin was often shipped on the order of their Mafia partners, who controlled the great American retail market.

With that much leverage, the Corsican hoods became major CIA "assets" throughout the '50s. Anslinger's star international agents in the 50s, George White, Charles Siragusa and Sal Vizzini, actually brag in their memoirs about their operational CIA/*Deuxieme Bureau* connections. That is, as they themselves obliquely admit, their mission was essentially political, with the occasional cosmetic bust thrown in for credibility, or to destroy a competing "asset."

White is the man who pretended that Burmese-Kuomintang heroin came from the Reds. Siragusa is the man who caught Lucky Luciano with a half-ton of heroin being readied for shipment to Trafficante in Havana—and pursuant to Anslinger's orders, just let him go.

Both ends of this dealing structure had to be protected—not only the *Deuxieme Bureau* in Indochina, but the Syndicate in Havana. Different continents, same distribution apparatus.

Immediately after President Kennedy's assassination, the US Air Force's senior intelligence officer, Col. Fletcher Prouty, was Maj. Gen. Victor Krulak's lead officer on the Special Assistant for Counterinsurgency and Special Activities staff. SACSA was charged with coordinating the inexorable post-assassination escalation of the Vietnam conflict within the Department of Defense. "His contacts in this select circle in the Office of the Secretary of Defense," writes Prouty, "were such men as Major General Edward D. Lansdale, who was McNamara's special assistant for all matters involving the CIA and special operations; William Bundy, who appears throughout the Pentagon Papers as one of the key men of the Secret Team and was at that time a recent alumnus of the CIA, with ten years in that agency behind him; John T. McNaughton, another member of the ST and a McNamara favorite; Joseph Califano, who moved from the Office of the Secretary of Defense to the White House...and others."

We Are the Dealers, We Give You Everything You Need

Johnson terminated the counterproductive Cuba operation in April of 1964. This interrupted the efforts of Joe Califano. Califano was in charge of overall Defense Department liaison with the Cuban exiles, 1963-64, both before and after the assassination. Lt. Col. Alexander Haig worked under Califano.

"Califano and Haig worked hand in hand in keeping the nationalists from the Cuban Brigade happy," wrote Joe Trento in the *Wilmington News-Journal*, Jan. 10, 1981. "They even checked out potential members for the hit teams with older members of the Cuban Brigade." This was confirmed by both Ricardo Canette, a leading member of the hit teams, and a top official of the Defense Intelligence Agency who was Haig's Marine liaison in 1963-64.

Califano reported directly to Secretary of the Army Cyrus Vance. The "older members of the Cuban Brigade" Califano and Haig were so concerned to keep happy included the hard core of Santos Trafficante's Batistiano assassins, the former leaders of Castro-deposed Cuban dictator Fulgencio Batista's secret police. When the Cuba operation was discontinued, military intelligence sent Califano to the White House as Johnson's advisor.

Califano is a key to understanding the drug propaganda not only by virtue of an analysis of his intentional sophistry, but by virtue of his covert relationships. Is it a coincidence that a high-level CIA agent who helped run Santos Trafficante's dope-dealing assassins became the country's leading antidrug propagandist? I don't think so.

The centers of power responsible for dealing the drugs are the same centers of power disseminating the artificial hysteria necessary for their continued criminalization. That keeps illicit drug retail prices a hundred times higher than the natural value and the trade exclusively in the hands of *the muscle*. Another name for *the muscle* is *military intelligence*.

For American military intelligence, the Vietnam War was, to a very large extent, a drug war, and, just as in Cuba, *we* were the dealers. Oil and other mineral wealth, of course, played a major role, as did the great defense contractor boondoggle.

The Vietnam War was worth $240 billion to defense contractors in overt appropriations, and at least another $300 billion in covert and indirect appropriations. The artificial Prohibition-created value of the opium from Laos, Burma and Thailand became, therefore, a major factor in the Indochinese military equation—the means by which our clients could pay for our arms. Drug Prohibition has made the illegal drug trade the economic basis of military power throughout much of the world.

Califano's Vietnam era playmates, William Colby, Edward Lansdale, Ted Shackley, Thomas Clines, Edmund Wilson, Lucien Conein, Richard Secord, Richard Armitage, John Singlaub, Felix Rodriguez, Barry McCaffrey, and Oliver

> "THE 1990S WERE THE MOST PUNITIVE DECADE IN US HISTORY; MORE PEOPLE WERE INCARCERATED THAN IN ANY OTHER DECADE."

North, engineers of the Vang Pao-Laotian Opium connection, went on to engineer Reagan's Trafficante-supported Contra-Cocaine connection.

The "progressive" Califano, Carter's Secretary of Health, Education and Welfare, is now founder and chairman of The National Center on Addiction and Substance Abuse at Columbia University. Califano helps to channel a torrent of public money into 1930s-style politicized research, and coercive "treatment." Califano's CASA is one of the DEA's major tools for coordinating national propaganda.

For Califano all drug use is a "disease," an "epidemic," to use his words, which not so coincidentally, are the same as those used by the Pope in 1484 in *The Malleus Maleficarum* about "witches' medicines." Like so many

> ...INSTITUTIONALIZED DRUG WAR WILDLY PROFITABLE TO THE POLICE, THEIR DEFENSE CONTRACTOR SUPPLIERS, THE PRISON INDUSTRY AND THE PHARMACEUTICAL INDUSTRY.

Roman lawyers before him, the man is a genuine anthropological ignoramus. Not once in his pseudo-scientific *Radical Surgery* (1994) does he mention the origins of human inebriative behavior, tribal culture, or a single significant pharmacologist, anthropologist, ethnobotanist, or psychoanalyst, although he insists that "substance abuse and addiction...is the most devastating health pandemic threatening our people." Apparently it's uniquely contemporary, like computer fraud. There's not a single scholarly annotation in the whole book, which is written on a tenth-grade sound-bite level. In fact, he quotes prosecuting attorneys as anecdotal medical authorities.

Pharmacology Has Nothing To Do With It.

According to Califano, the absurd artificial value Prohibition gives inebriants, and the criminalization of people for simply trying to medicate themselves, in the absence of any sympathetic *curanderismo*, isn't the cause of today's street war. It's the act of self-medication *per se*, despite the fact that the leading sociologists insist, and can prove, that safe herbal inebriants, in cultures which teach their traditional uses, cause no social problems whatever, and are, in fact, highly beneficial.

Marijuana, officially in the US Pharmacopeia from 1850 to 1942, is just about the safest medically effective herb known. Dr. Lester Grinspoon, associate professor of psychiatry at Harvard Medical School, began to write *Marihuana Reconsidered* after his 14 year-old boy started receiving chemotherapy for acute lymphoblastic leukemia. "Vomiting for 8 hours a day was so demoralizing for this beautiful child."

Grinspoon found that marijuana was the only thing that could control the violent nausea. "When I began to study marijuana in 1967, I had no doubt that it was a very harmful drug....as I reviewed the scientific, medical and lay literature....I came to understand that I, like so many other people in this country, had been brainwashed."

"The greatest advantage of cannabis as a medicine is its unusual safety. The ratio of lethal dose to effective dose is estimated on the basis of extrapolation from animal data to be about 20,000:1 (compared to 350:1 for secobarbital and 4-10:1 for alcohol). Huge doses have been given to dogs without causing death, and there is no reliable evidence of death caused by cannabis in a human being. Cannabis also has the advantage of not disturbing any physiological functions or damaging any body organ when used in therapeutic doses. It produces little physical dependence or tolerance; there is no evidence that medical use of cannabis has ever led to its habitual use as an intoxicant."

But it's a "stepping stone" say Califano, McCaffrey, Hutchinson and now Tandy. Karen P. Tandy, former head of the Justice Department's Organized Crime Drug Enforcement Task Force, the new chief of the DEA, is going to fight organized crime exactly the same way all her predecessors did—by running its major legal price support, by arming and financing it. And the result, of course, will be exactly the same as it always has been, an institutionalized drug war wildly profitable to the police, their defense contractor suppliers, the prison industry and the pharmaceutical industry.

> "WHEN YOU'RE TELLING COPS THAT THEY'RE SOLDIERS IN A DRUG WAR, YOU'RE DESTROYING THE WHOLE CONCEPT OF THE CITIZEN PEACE OFFICER, A PEACE OFFICER WHOSE FUNDAMENTAL DUTY IS TO PROTECT LIFE AND BE A COMMUNITY SERVANT,"...

But urban police departments are local institutions, and many are quite honest about the real drug war. Even if they won't mention the tension they bring to the situation, they stress that it's the economics of Prohibition, the artificial underground economy, combined with the lack of opportunity, that is responsible for the gang warfare, not pharmacology *per se*.

"Drug traffickers kill to protect or seize drug turf, and addicts commit crimes to get money for drugs," says former Baltimore Mayor Kurt Schmoke, also a former police officer. "Almost half the murders in Baltimore in 1992 were drug related."

"When we say drug-related," explains Deputy Raymond Kelly of the New York City Police Department, "we're essentially talking about territorial disputes or disputes over possession...We're not talking about where somebody is deranged because they're on a drug."

It is only the artificial price support known as Prohibition that makes illegal drugs valuable. And it is only that value that causes street crime – pharmacology has nothing to do with it.

Arresting Our Way to a Better Future for All

The Sentencing Project has identified the Drug War as "the largest single factor behind the rise in prison population during the past decade." That rise has seen the US imprison a higher percentage of its people than any other nation in the world.

"The 1990s were the most punitive decade in US history; more people were incarcerated than in any other decade," notes the Chicago Legal Aid To Incarcerated Mothers' *Women in Prison Fact Sheet*. "The total number of prisoners reached two million in February of 2000, giving the US a quarter of the eight million prisoners in the world." Nonviolent drug offenders make up 60% of all federal prisoners, and half of them are first-time offenders, kids.

"In recent years the percentage increase in women incarcerated has grown much faster than that of men. Women prisoners are usually convicted of non-violent offenses, and their absence has an immediate, dramatic impact on their children and families."

"About 81% of women incarcerated in Illinois are mothers, affecting at least 25,000 children annually. Nationally, more than a quarter of a million children have mothers in jail or prison. Most of these women lived with their children prior to their incarceration; many are single mothers who were their children's sole caretakers."

One-third of women in prison are there for drug crimes. Would all those women be in jail if they weren't in such intense pain that they needed to medicate it? Why is self-medication a crime? What's wrong with taking pain killers if you're in pain? Why aren't safe *pharmakons* available? Whose body is it anyway?

Many of America's best law enforcement officials and public health workers are asking the same questions. A Hoover Institute poll of over 500 law-enforcement leaders conducted at the 9th International Conference on Drug Policy Reform, in Santa Monica, back on October 19, 1995, by former Kansas City and San José police chief Joseph McNamara, found that 95% thought the war on drugs was lost and 98% thought drug use wasn't primarily a police problem.

"When you're telling cops that they're soldiers in a Drug War, you're destroying the whole concept of the citizen peace officer, a peace officer whose fundamental duty is to protect life and be a community servant,"says McNamara. "General Colin Powell told us during the Persian Gulf War what a soldier's duty is. It's to kill the enemy. And when we allowed our politicians to push cops into a war that they'll never win, they can't win, and let them begin to think of themselves as soldiers, the mentality comes that anything goes."

Baltimore's chief nark told the Drug Abuse Council in 1975 that Baltimore police were using 800 active drug dealers as informants, in effect licensing them to deal and rat on the competition. Of course, with that much close contact with the dealing, cops end up choosing, for a price, which dealers will survive and which won't. No big city police force can function any other way, and no big city police force has ever made a permanent dent in the availability of drugs on the street.

McNamara points out that there isn't a major urban police force in the country that isn't thoroughly infiltrated by drug money. Hundreds of narcs are indicted for extortion, murder or drug-dealing every year. And the newspaper stories of police brutality during drug raids could fill a 600-page book annually.

In 1989, Freeway Ricky Ross, the greatest crack dealer in history, had his sentence radically reduced because he was "a percipient witness in a case involving serious misconduct." That is, Ross could back up the evidence of the FBI's sting of L.A.'s premier narcotics squad, "the Majors," who had gone into the extortion and resale business. Those cops were driving Ferraris.

Great dealing structures, like the Gangster Disciples, can use their army of wholesalers to front ambitious twelve-year-olds a "sixty-pack" of ten-dollar crack vials. An outgoing hustler can sell-out in half an hour. The kid keeps a hundred, turns $500 over to the wholesaler, and gets another sixty-pack. The kid can make $1000 in a day, a mind-bending fortune to a twelve-year-old, and the wholesaler, running an army of little hustlers, makes many times that. The cops end up at war with the whole neighborhood.

Prohibition is simply a legislative price support of the prohibited commodity. It wasn't alcohol that drove the

SOLELY BECAUSE OF THE ARTIFICIAL ILLEGAL VALUE, COCAINE IS BOLIVIA'S NUMBER ONE INDUSTRIAL EXPORT, AS IT IS PERU'S.

Prohibition gangs—they were hoods, not drunks. In 1918 Wayne Wheeler, the head of the Anti-Saloon League, insisted that the "contagious disease of alcoholism" would be stopped by a $5 million appropriation to the Prohibition Unit. By 1927 the beleaguered sixth Commissioner of Prohibition told Congress $300 million couldn't do it. God knows how many hundreds of billions in today's money we incinerate every year. Prison spending alone was up to $40 billion in 1994, a 1000% increase in twenty years.

"Mayor Schmoke described a school visit during which children told him that most of the youngsters dropping out of school did so not because they were hooked on drugs, but because they were hooked on easy drug money." (*Searching for Alternatives*, p.314)

Califano, and his DEA clones, are careful to invert this, insisting, in classic reefer madness style, that by some

demonic magic, pharmacology is the reason kids are shooting each other over dealing territory. Collapse the price with legalization, and the violence will collapse instantly. By creating an underground economy and then demonizing the normal money-seeking and ecstatic behavior of the young, we instigate their murder. As Eddy Engelsman, the former Dutch Minister of Health, puts it, "The effects of heroin and cocaine use are too often confused with the effects of their illegality."

Holland has 15%, one-seventh, of our hard drug use, crime and imprisonment rates. Is pharmacology different in Holland? No, of course not, but public policy is. Here is part of the official end-of-year report from the Dutch Ministry of Welfare, Health and Cultural Affairs, 1995, signed by the Ministers of Health, Justice and Interior:

> Dutch policy on the use of cannabis is based on the assumption that people are more likely to make the transition from soft to hard drugs as a result of social factors than because of physiological ones. If young adults wish to use soft drugs—and experience has shown that many do—the Netherlands believes that it is better that they should do so in a setting in which they are not exposed to the criminal subculture surrounding hard drugs. Tolerating relatively easy access to quantities of soft drugs for personal use is intended to keep the consumer markets for soft and hard drugs separate, thus creating a social barrier to the transition from soft to hard drugs…The decriminalization which took place in the 1970s did not lead to an increase in the use of soft drugs then either.
>
> The view held by some that the use of cannabis products alone causes a physiological or psychological need to use hard drugs as well—what is known as the stepping stone theory—has been belied by actual developments in the Netherlands. Dutch young people who use soft drugs are perfectly well aware of the greater dangers of using hard drugs such as heroin and have no desire to experiment with them. In the Netherlands the percentage of soft drugs users who also go on to use hard drugs is relatively low. In light of these findings the stepping stone theory should be regarded as one of the many myths in circulation about the use of drugs, though one which under certain circumstances could become a self-fulfilling prophesy: by treating the use of cannabis products and hard drugs such as heroin and cocaine in the same way may in fact make it more likely that cannabis-smokers will come into contact with hard drugs. Moreover, equating the one with the other undermines the credibility of the information provided about drugs to young people.

That is, prohibition of the safe herbs popularizes the hard drugs. Holland, in effect a massive empirical experiment, has proven this conclusively.

Cocaine Politics

Because Prohibition artificially inflates the price, a pound of Bolivian coca is literally worth twice what a pound of Bolivian tin is worth. Bolivian coca and cocaine exports consistently exceed the multi-billion dollar value of Bolivian tin exports.

Solely because of the artificial illegal value, cocaine is Bolivia's number one industrial export, as it is Peru's. More people are employed in the illegal cocaine business in Bolivia and Peru—growing, processing, trucking, refining, protecting—than in all legal mining and manufacturing operations combined. *The Economist*, in 1991, estimated that 1 in every 3.4 economically active Bolivians was involved in the coca/cocaine economy. That can hardly be called a criminal aberration. The artificial illegal value creates an export-oriented monoculture that otherwise wouldn't exist.

"Crop substitution" is a transparent sham to highland smallholders for whom coca is worth twenty times the value of any substitute ($9000 for coca to $500 for citrus per hectare in 1984). Since coca leaf can be cultivated year-round, and is harvested three or four times a year, highland coca production means year-round access to food and a cash income independent of agribusiness technology and banking.

The DEA estimated that when it turned up the heat on coca production in the Tingo María area of Peru in 1972, the amount of acreage devoted to coca shot from 4,000 to 50,000 by 1978. Effective enforcement, since it increases the commodity's value, is a *stimulus* to production.

Intelligence professionals have always understood this. It is not possible that George W. Bush, Dick Cheney, Donald Rumsfeld, John Walters , and Karen Tandy do not understand the basic ABC's of supply and demand. They are running an industrial price support, and they know it.

"IN MY 30-YEAR HISTORY IN THE DRUG ENFORCEMENT ADMINISTRATION AND RELATED AGENCIES, THE MAJOR TARGETS OF MY INVESTIGATIONS ALMOST INVARIABLY TURNED OUT TO BE WORKING FOR THE CIA,"...

The increased value created by squeezing off local supply in, say, leftist held areas of Colombia, strengthens the coke, heroin and marijuana distribution apparatus throughout the rest of Amazonia, which runs vast jungle plantations and pays hundreds of thousands of campesinos ten times what they could make in equivalent legal work. Twenty years ago, Colombia grew almost no coca leaf; now it has overtaken both Peru and Bolivia as the world's largest grower, and most of that is grown in government-held areas, which are not bombed with herbicides.

Colombia is now also the world's fourth largest source of opium. Because of its artificial value, global opium production shot from 1,000 metric tons in 1971 to 4,300 tons in 1996. In 1988 the Colombian cocaine industry employed 300,000 Colombians, earning 20% of the country's foreign exchange, $1.5 billion, as much as the country's biggest legal export, coffee. Just two years later, Colombian cocaine earned at least twice as much as Colombian coffee. Good ol' Juan Valdez.

"Even if you eradicate every coca plant on Colombian soil, you will simply raise prices and push production deeper into Peru, Bolivia, and Ecuador," notes Colombian sociologist and author Alfredo Molano. "You will also bring misery and suffering to many thousands of people."

Since *ipadú*, the alkaloid-poor lowland variety of coca grown in Colombia, can be cultivated anywhere on the Amazonian jungle floor, even if it were possible to destroy coca production in the Peruvian and Bolivian highlands, *ipadú* would fill the gap. The use of *ipadú* is ancient in Amazonia. In fact the word *ipadú* can refer to the lowland variety of coca itself or to the traditional toasted mixture of coca and yarumo leaves. The rain forest is being sliced up everywhere—in Brazil, Ecuador, Bolivia—because of *ipadú's* new-found value. That is solely an effect of Prohibition.

That is, "supply side" militarization is *good* for the fascist dope peddlers—it has just the opposite effect of crushing the trade—it centralizes it. This was confirmed by Dr. K. Jack Riley in a 1996 RAND study. Riley demonstrated that a mere $700 worth of raw coca leaves, at local Bolivian prices, can be turned into $150,000 worth of cocaine, at US street retail prices. Small-scale eradication programs therefore have no effect on overall supply, since the bulk of the money goes to the final processors and exporters, who are few enough in number to fix their prices on both ends.

They can manipulate the basic leaf price they pay to the small growers, switch sources of supply at will, and then turn around and gouge their wholesale customers. "Eradication," therefore, simply serves to militarize the trade, to turn the remaining small-scale growers—and almost all highland coca cultivation is small-scale—into intimidated sharecroppers. The very few big processors and dealers remain not only unaffected, but strong enough to buy every whore in the army.

"Even if [highland] coca is somehow almost fully eradicated from Bolivia and Peru...Colombia, Venezuela, Brazil, and Ecuador stand ready as potential alternate suppliers," added Riley. That of course is a reference to lowland *ipadú*, the trade of which is controlled by the same militarized structure.

Dan Russell

"The Latin American drug cartels have stretched their tentacles much deeper into our lives than most people believe," as William Colby, the former Director of the CIA put it. "It's possible they are calling the shots at all levels of government."

Raymond Kendall, Secretary General of Interpol from 1985 to 2000, the world's top cop, fully understood what the CIA's Colby was saying. On June 8, 1994, Kendall called for the international decriminalization of drug possession. The former Scotland Yard detective told BBC radio that "I am in favor of decriminalization but not in favor of legalization...If someone is caught with drugs they should be treated, not convicted." Kendall timed his remarks to coincide with the annual drug conference of Britain's Association of Chief Police Officers, which also called for coordinated international decriminalization.

Kendall expanded on his reasoning at the annual congress of his 176-nation International Criminal Police Organization meeting in Beijing in October of 1995. "If you look at the real threat to our societies today, what you have is a combination of organized crime and drug trafficking." Decriminalization, since it would collapse the commodities' value, would bankrupt the traffickers. This tactic is necessary because "we're pretty overwhelmed." Traffickers "have the ability to corrupt our institutions at the highest level. If they can do that, then it means our democracies are in real danger.'"

"'The illegal trade in narcotics is increasingly interwoven with the regular economy, at a national as well as international level,' says Raymond Kendall...now head of Interpol. 'This interweaving makes the combating of the drug trade on the financial front all the more difficult. Countries now face the increasing globalization of crime and criminal organizations.'" This as reported by the *Scotsman* (UK), on April 21, 1999.

"In my 30-year history in the Drug Enforcement Administration and related agencies, the major targets of my investigations almost invariably turned out to be working for the CIA," noted a disgusted Dennis Dayle, the 1978-82 chief of DEA's Central Tactical Units (Centac). These were the DEA's elite international strike forces created to operate against the major cartels. But Dayle found his units repeatedly blocked by American military intelligence. Dayle turned to novelist and reporter James Mills to advertise this. The result was Mills' *The Underground Empire: Where Crime and Governments Embrace*.

Dayle spent years demonstrating the cooperation of US military intelligence with the drug cartels to Mills, while he was running the DEA's Centac. The FBI's Bud Mullen, who himself ended up questioning policy, took over the DEA in 1982, when it became a subdivision of the FBI. It was Mullen who led the destruction of Dayle's Centac under President Reagan.

Just prior to the FBI's acquisition of the DEA, Congress' investigative arm, the General Accounting Office, issued the results of its yearlong investigation of Centac. The GAO hatchetmen were amazed, issuing one of the few positive reports in their history. Centac was "an effective approach...that needs to be expanded...respond[ing] effectively to highly mobile national and international organizations." Under Dayle, Centac, in three years, racked up 731 indictments, 36% of which were "the highest-level violators." The DEA average at the time was 12%. While comprising only 3% of all DEA agents, Centac accounted for 12% of arrests of major violators.

Needless to say, this made the DEA's regional and "drug-specific" commanders look inefficient, and caused innumerable political problems "in-country"—where the major violators were pillars of the establishment. The FBI's Mullen simply disbanded Centac.

As Interpol chief Raymond Kendall says, the only way to stop the smugglers is to bankrupt them. The value of their commodity must be collapsed by decriminalization. Absent that, no high-level bureaucrat who doesn't go along will get along.

From Panama to Mexico to Peru to Colombia to....

During the post-Contra confrontation with Panamanian President Manuel Noriega, the Reagan administration stressed the interception of Noriega's bulky, easy to smell marijuana, contributing to an explosion in the popularity of concentrated, profitable to smuggle cocaine, and to the popularization of crack and concentrated heroin.

President Bush's replacement for Noriega, Guillermo Endara, was a director and secretary of Banco Interoceánico, targeted by both the FBI and DEA as a major money laundry for both the Cali and Medellín cocaine cartels. How is it possible that President Bush, the former Director of the CIA, and President Reagan's chief of the South Florida Anti-Drug Task Force, didn't know that? It was George Bush who had authorized Noriega's substantial 1976 CIA paychecks, and it was he who insisted on putting Noriega back on the payroll in 1980, after Carter had the good sense to take him off.

From Bush's perspective, this made sense. Noriega and his Mossad advisor Mike Harrari, who worked closely with Bush aide Donald Gregg, proved invaluable in arming the Contras. "Since the beginning of the supply of arms to the Contras, the same infrastructure that was used for arms was used for drugs. The same pilots, the same planes, the same airstrips, the same people," noted José Blandón, Noriega's former chief of political intelligence.

Just before the December 1989 Panama invasion, in which future US Drug Czar Gen. Barry McCaffrey was in charge of barrio incineration, Endara's business partner, Carlos Eleta, was arrested in Georgia for conspiring to import a half-ton of cocaine per month. The charges were dropped as soon as Bush installed Endara as Panamanian president and Eleta became an "asset." Bush then insisted that "The answer to the problem of drugs lies more in solving the demand side of the equation than it does the supply side, than it does in interdiction or sealing the borders." That'll keep the price up *and* justify turning the US into a police state.

Endara's attorney general, treasury minister, and chief justice of the supreme court were all former directors of First Interamericas Bank, a wholly-owned subsidiary of Colombia's Cali cartel, one of its major money laundries, according to Panama's National Banking Commission. "Take my word for it," intoned a determined George Bush at his inaugural, "this scourge will stop!"

Not quite. After yet another Mexican narco-scandal, Clinton's Drug Czar Barry McCaffrey was relieved in December of 1996 at the appointment of a career army officer, Gen. José de Jesús Gutiérrez Rebollo, rather than another corrupt politician, to head Mexico's National Institute for Combating Drugs, the INCD. Gen. Gutiérrez, said McCaffrey, "has a reputation of impeccable integrity, and he is known as an extremely forceful and focused commander."

On February 19, 1997, after less than three months on the job, Gen. Gutiérrez was relieved of his INCD command and formally charged with being on the payroll of Amado Carillo Fuentes, Mexico's "Lord of the Skies." Carillo, a relative of the Medellín cartel's Jorge Ochoa, had pioneered the use of low-flying jetliners to transport multi-ton loads of cocaine from his Colombian partners to Mexico.

A power for years under Salinas, Carillo did this from his position within Mexican military intelligence. He carried Mexican Federal Judicial Police Group Chief credentials for special investigations and an officer's gold card.

Lucindo Carillo, cousin of Amado, was also *un Jefe de Grupo de PJF*, in Agua Prieta, Sonora, a port. The Federal Judicial Police (PJF) Commandant in Agua Prieta, Luis Manuel Palofax-Juarez, was also a documented associate of Amado Carillo. Gen. Gutiérrez, one of the most powerful men in Mexican military intelligence, and his two top military aides, were also formally charged with stacking the INCD with Carillo's agents.

Before he was relieved of command, Gutiérrez had been given repeated top-secret briefings on all Mexican-American anti-smuggling efforts and intelligence, including definitive lists of the INCD/DEA's paid Mexican informants. "The Lord of the Skies" might as well have been personally briefed by Gen. McCaffrey himself. Then head of the DEA, Thomas Constantine, said Gen. Gutiérrez probably would prove more damaging to the DEA than Aldrich Ames had been to the CIA.

Aw shucks, said McCaffrey, I didn't know. DEA spokesman James McGivney backed McCaffrey up, glibly stating, "It's not our job to vet these people. We don't go around spooking military and government officials; we've got enough to do with the crooks." Pollyanna is running the DEA? Am I supposed to believe that the former premier counterinsurgency expert of the vast US Southern Command naval, air, radar and information system "just ain't too good at this intelligence stuff"?

Gen. Gutiérrez' narcotics trafficking was well-covered in the DEA's NADDIS (Narcotics and Dangerous Drugs Information System) database long before McCaffrey hailed him as Mexico's salvation at the head of the INCD.

On February 18, 1997, Mexican Defense Secretary Gen. Enrique Cervantes Aguirre announced that Gutiérrez had systematically supported the Carillo cartel for 7 years. As head of the US Southern Command, Gen. McCaffrey worked with Gen. Gutiérrez for most of those years.

Before he became Mexico's top nark, Gen. Gutiérrez was in charge of the coastline port state of Jalisco, the capitol of which is Guadalajara. Gutiérrez earned his reputation as a nark by helping the Guadalajara cartel deal with its competition, most notably with the June 1995 arrest of Hector "Whitey" Palma, a leader of the rival Sinaloa crew.

> "UNFORTUNATELY, VIRTUALLY EVERY INVESTIGATION DEA CONDUCTS AGAINST MAJOR TRAFFICKERS IN MEXICO UNCOVERS SIGNIFICANT CORRUPTION OF LAW-ENFORCEMENT [MILITARY] OFFICIALS."

Since three-quarters of South America's cocaine must pass through Mexico on its way to the US, we are talking about a very high stakes power game—*tens of billions of dollars in regular trade*—$30 billion annually according to the US Justice Department. That's fully 10% of Mexico's GDP. Mexican military intelligence is not about to let that kind of power slide. That's why Gutiérrez' two top military aides were also indicted—they were under *orders*. That kind of money buys armaments.

Gen. Gutiérrez blew his cover to both press and police when he moved into a posh Mexico City apartment owned by one of Amado Carillo's top lieutenants, with whom he was repeatedly seen. He was also sloppy enough to allow himself to be recorded talking money with Carillo himself on the phone. The General, whose INCD was directly financed by the DEA, must have felt very comfortable to have behaved so stupidly.

Gutiérrez was defended in court by Tomás Arturo Gonzalez Velazquez, a very tough 43 year-old former military colleague of Gutiérrez. Gonzalez repeatedly insisted that the general's arrest was part of a power struggle within Mexican military intelligence. Gonzalez got very specific about the collaboration of top commanders, including defense minister Gen. Cervantes, with the chief smuggling organizations. He even asserted that President Zedillo's brother-in-law had ties to a major methamphetamine trafficker. In a classified report given to Attorney General Reno in February of 1998, DEA officials confirmed many of Gonzalez' accusations. Tomás Gonzalez was shot dead on April 21, 1998.

On December 22, 1997, 45 unarmed Tzotzil campesinos, including fifteen children, were slaughtered in their highland Chiapas village of Acteal. "This is a situation that defies understanding, where there has been no official will to get the violence under control," protested Bishop Samuel Ruiz, the senior Catholic prelate in the Chiapas highlands.

Ruiz insisted that PRI death squads were behind the massacre, because the Tzotzils had been peacefully supporting Zapatista political demands. Enraged Tzotzil youngsters who march off into the highlands to join the guerrillas, after burying their little sisters, will then be accused of preferring bullets to ballots—and of being narcotraficantes.

In fact, Gen. Gomez, commander of the Chiapas military district, immediately accused Bishop Ruiz of San Cristóbal de las Casas of being a guerrilla operative, as if that somehow mitigated the horror of the massacre. Gomez was apparently referring to the Bishop's protest against the NAFTA-engineered collapse of the price of Chiapas produce. The flood of cheap agricultural imports, which forced campesinos further into the slave-labor cash economy, was the major reason the Zapatistas rebelled in the first place.

The Zapatista "International Encounter" statement of August, 1996 insisted that the Drug War "has converted narcotrafficking into one of the most successful clandestine means of obtaining extraordinary profits" and called for "channeling the resources destined for combating narcotrafficking into programs of development and social welfare."

Gen. Tito Valencia Ortiz replaced the busted Gen. Gutiérrez as Mexico's Drug Czar, and then the whole outfit was reshuffled, again. McCaffrey didn't miss a beat, shoveling weaponry at Valencia just as fast as he shoveled it at Gutiérrez. Like his predecessor, Gen. Valencia used McCaffrey's bullets to chop up impoverished Mayans in the southern highlands, as if they were the ones who had been flying Carillo's coked-up 727s.

Despite the fact that not one single major narcotraficante had been extradited to the US since the signing of a mutual extradition treaty in 1980, Drug Czar McCaffrey, on Feb. 26, 1998, called Mexican drug cooperation "absolutely superlative." He went on to trumpet the creation of new police units and more additions to the Mexican military's alphabet soup.

That same day, Thomas Constantine, the head of the DEA, in formal testimony before the Senate, adamantly disagreed with McCaffrey: "None of these changes have produced significant results...None have resulted in the arrest of the leadership or the dismantlement of any of the well-known organized criminal groups operating out of Mexico Unfortunately, virtually every investigation DEA conducts against major traffickers in Mexico uncovers significant corruption of law-enforcement [military] officials."

The fascist corruption, based on the artificial value Prohibition gives these demanded commodities, will remain the same—in Peru, Mexico, Colombia, Burma, or Afghanistan. Artificially inflated, cocaine accounts for more than 50% of Peru's foreign trade. In 1995, the United Nations Drug Control Program estimated that Peru produced more than 500,000 kilos of cocaine. That's more than 600 tons, with a wholesale value in New York of more than $30 billion. Absent the price support of prohibition, the legal value of that cocaine would be about $3 billion.

No one who doesn't support that trade, and cocaine's continued illegality, will rise to control of the Peruvian military, because without illegal cocaine the Peruvian Army couldn't pay for weapons. That would lead to widespread campesino control of the voting process, and, God forbid, a populist government in Lima. That's why native activists want to collapse the price of cocaine with controlled legalization. It would end the fight for Indian land.

A shipload of legal marijuana would be worth a few million dollars. A shipload of illegal marijuana is worth in the neighborhood of one hundred million dollars, at master distributor discount. Does less pot pass through Panama now that "kingpin" Noriega is in jail? Has there been a crash in the pot market?

"In a daunting new turn in the traffic of Colombian cocaine into the United States," reported the New York Times on January 10, 1995, "smugglers are buying old passenger jets, taking out the seats and using the planes to fly huge amounts of the drug into Mexico, American and Mexican officials say. Traveling at night with their lights off, the Boeing 727s and French-made Caravelle jets are believed to be carrying as much as six tons or more of cocaine in a single flight. The cocaine is then transported overland into the United States, where the wholesale value of such a load is about $120 million."

That's enough to buy a new plane for each load, as the innovative Amado Carillo, and his partners in Colombian and Mexican military intelligence, well understood. The *legal* value of such a load would be 10% of the *illegal* value, or less.

On June 8, 1998, the first day of the U.N. General Assembly's three-day Special Session on drug policy, the *New York Times* published the Lindesmith Center's open letter to Secretary General Kofi Annan. Hundreds of the world's most astute scientists, writers and political leaders insisted that "the global war on drugs is now causing more harm than drug abuse itself." The signers numbered among them Isabel Allende, Ariel Dorfman, Belisario Betancur, Oscar Arias, Gunter Grass, George Papandreou, Javier Perez de Cuellar, Alan Cranston, Milton Friedman, Stephen Jay Gould, Lester Grinspoon, Nicholas Katzenbach, George Schultz, George Soros, and Paul Volcker.

But we are dealing with power here, not good intentions. That is, with the understanding that drugs are, to some centers of power, worth far more illegal than legal. Holland has 15% of our imprisonment rate. Imagine the disaster to our law enforcement contractors should our imprisonment rate fall by 85%. Government by dope dealer is here.

Oiling the Drug Trade for Afghanistan's Terrorists and US Allies

I was delighted to see the Taliban overthrown – they were genocidal maniacs, and seriously threatening, as Benazir Bhutto stressed, a jihadist coup in Pakistan that almost certainly would have led to the catastrophe of full scale war between India and Pakistan.

Journalist Rob Schultheis, author of *Bone Games, Night Letters* and the award-winning film *Homage to Hazarastan*, has covered Afghanistan since 1984, spending years on the frontline with the mujahedin during the Russian war. He has reported for *Time*, CBS, NPR, *Mother Jones*, the *New York Times*, the *Washington Post*, etc. His book on the Soviet occupation, *Night Letters*, was published by Crown.

The 1 1/2 million Hazaras, Shi'ites in a Sunni country, Mongols among Indo-European tribes like the Pushtuns who make up 99% of Taliban's core membership, were the last bastion of women's rights in the country," wrote Schultheis on Jan. 4, 1999, in *Genders Online Journal*. "Among the Hazaras you found women officials, teachers, doctors, medics, even soldiers; totally unlike life for women in Taliban-ruled territory. US support for the Hazaras: nil.

I also visited Taliban-ruled territory, where the picture was completely different. In the capital of Kabul, women flitted like frightened ghosts in shroud like burkahs, constantly harassed by Taliban thugs. Women were forbidden to work, to study, to 'walk loudly,' in the words of one Taliban edict. A woman who dared to breastfeed her baby near the roadside east of Kabul was beaten till she died. Another woman who broke one of Taliban's myriad rules was flogged to death in front of a howling mob in a Kabul stadium.

Even worse, the United States lent and continues to lend its tacit blessing to the Taliban by doing nothing to stop them. In fact, American oil giant UNOCAL, closely tied to Saudi Arabia's Delta Oil, was hosting Taliban delegates to the US and praising them in Washington at the same time the Taliban were murdering and terrorizing women in Afghanistan. And at the same time Osama bin Laden, who bombed our embassies in Africa, was living as a welcome guest of the Taliban and helping finance their takeover of Afghanistan—a bit of incidental irony.

The reason for this moral myopia? A projected UNOCAL-Delta pipeline from Turkmenistan to Pakistan, across Afghanistan, in cooperation with the Taliban, that would bring huge profits for American businessmen. Afghanistan, which sacrificed over a million people fighting against the Soviet Empire, is now viewed as nothing more than a corporate feeding-ground by American policy-makers. Just last week, Clinton's National Security Council lauded a multi-hundred million dollar deal signed between Taliban and a giant New Jersey communications corporation.

Now, with the capture of the Hazarajat by Taliban, even more Afghans are dying. At least one male Afghan U.N. worker has reportedly been murdered; not coincidentally, he was working with an agency that focused on women's welfare and rights. There are reports that hundreds of Hazara civilians have been arrested and killed as well.

Fast forward to Friday, November 28, 2003, when Reuters newswire reported that:

Poppy cultivation in Afghanistan doubled between 2002 and 2003 to a level 36 times higher than in the last year of rule by the Taliban, according to White House figures released Friday.

The area planted with poppies, used to make heroin and morphine, was 152,000 acres in 2003, compared with 76,900 acres in 2002 and 4,210 acres in 2001, the White House Office of National Drug Control Policy said in a statement.

The Taliban was cracking down on poppy production in the year before the US military drove the movement out of office in late 2001 in response to its friendship and cooperation with the al Qaeda organization of Osama bin Laden.

The new Afghan government, led by President Hamid Karzai, has not been able to impose its will in many areas of the country, which remain under the control of warlords.

The White House statement said, "A challenging security situation...has complicated significantly the task of implementing counternarcotics assistance programs and will continue to do so for the immediate future."

"Poppy cultivation in Afghanistan is a major and growing problem. Drug cultivation and trafficking are undermining the rule of law and putting money in the pocket of terrorists," it added, quoting office director John Walters.

This is just incredible. The Director of the White House ONDCP just flatly admits that his policies are financing the Taliban!

Rather than crack the power of the terrorists, rather than bankrupting them by getting legislatively honest about the Stalinist economics of Prohibition, the Bush administration, quite like the Clinton administration before it, prefers to view the drug trade with exactly the same amoral venality with which it viewed the oil trade.

Afridi warriors in Pakistan's Northwest Frontier enjoy their traditional smoke. *Asia*, 1925

But oil is a legal commodity—its value is determined by a genuine market. Drug value is completely artificial, solely a result of artificial criminalization. Only Prohibition guarantees an endless street fight for control of the trade—our warlords versus their terrorists. Were we ever able to tell the difference?

It is obvious, of course, that ending Prohibition would not only collapse drug value, but the value of the enormous military and political edifice built upon it. Eliminate Prohibition and the Office of National Mind Control Policy would cease to exist. The warlords, therefore, become ONDCP partners, and the terrorists become as politically useful as a Reichstag fire.

"One of the things that the Americans 'fixed' is drug production," wrote Ramtanu Maitra in the *Asia Times*,

July 15, 2003. "During the Taliban days, opium production had reached a peak of 5,000-plus tons. In 2001, with the warehouses filled to the ceiling with raw opium, the Taliban wanted to show how 'good' they were, and stopped poppy cultivation in the territories they controlled—about 95% of the country. The opium price soared, and the Taliban regime and its Pakistani benefactors made huge profits. At the same time, the Taliban, citing their efforts to end the venal drug trade, sought recognition as the legitimate Afghan government."

"Following the American invasion of Afghanistan in October 2001 and subsequent removal of the Taliban from power, competing agencies within the US government set about to prove their worth (with some individuals

ELIMINATE PROHIBITION AND THE OFFICE OF NATIONAL MIND CONTROL POLICY WOULD CEASE TO EXIST. THE WARLORDS, THEREFORE, BECOME ONDCP PARTNERS, AND THE TERRORISTS BECOME AS POLITICALLY USEFUL AS A REICHSTAG FIRE.

intensely involved in lining their pockets with the drug money) by adopting policies to 'short-cut' the process of Afghan reconstruction. One of these short-cuts involved a deal with the warlords. The deal was to allow the warlords to grow poppy, so that these warlords could buy arms and recruit militia to strengthen their ranks. In return, they would not only provide the Americans with the intelligence on where the al Qaeda and the Taliban are hiding, but would also provide the Americans with fighters."

"What came of this approach? The first thing that happened is that poppy fields and the poppy growers took over Afghanistan. In the year 2002, about 3,750 tons of opium was harvested. In cold cash, this translates conservatively into anything between US $5-6 billion for the warlords."

"The second thing that the policy did was further weaken Karzai, who was running from pillar to post to get some cash to show some 'improvement' in living conditions in Kabul to justify his and the Americans' presence, and he was deprived of revenue. The warlords claimed—and the American operatives endorsed their claims—that they needed the money to bolster their anti-Taliban militia and help the Americans find al Qaeda members. As a result, the Afghan warlords, who were virtually eliminated by the Taliban, are now stronger than ever. In a few more years, these warlords will be strong enough to kick out their American benefactors and American puppets."

So the team that gave us the Contra war has deftly snatched defeat from the jaws of victory in Afghanistan.

Ex-DEA Agent Michael Levine wrote, "The drug war under President Clinton is bigger and healthier than ever. It seems like every department in the federal government has a part in it—DEA, FBI, CIA, NSA, IRS, DIA, ATF, State Department, Pentagon, Customs, Coast Guard, Army, Navy, Air Force, Marines—and each one is fighting for more turf and a bigger chunk of the drug war budget. When I started out in 1965 there were two federal agencies enforcing the drug laws, and the budget was less than $10 million. Today [1993] there are 54 agencies involved and the budget is $13 billion. Orchestrating the whole mess is a Drug Czar who is generally a political appointment with no special qualifications for the job."

That is, since Jimmy Carter, the last President to put a qualified person in that job, the ONDCP chief has been expert at nothing other than expanding the police mission of the military. A good short definition of a *fascist police state* would be *"a state in which publicly-funded military-police agencies drive policy."*

The Realities of a Fascist Police State

US policy has been driven by the biggest publicly-funded police-agency propaganda barrage in history. The overt 1997 federal Drug War appropriation was $15.1 billion. The 1998 federal bill was $16 billion, the 1999 bill was $18 billion, with two-thirds of that simply being pumped into domestic law enforcement, that is, into filling the prisons with vulnerable kids. Most of the rest goes into propaganda and "treatment," or "reeducation," in the Stalinist sense. By 2002 it was up to $20 billion.

These budgetary figures don't include the tens of billions expended by the military, by the federal judicial and penal systems, or the state judicial and penal systems. In 1991, the RAND Corp. estimated the total outlay of public funds at $30 billion. The 2003 figure must be many times that.

For fiscal 1998 Clinton and McCaffrey announced a billion-dollar ONDCP/Ad Council blitz: "There is every reason to believe that this absolutely will turn around drug abuse by youngsters," intoned Bombastic Barry. I doubt there was a serious expert in the RAND Corp. or anywhere else anywhere who expected this blowhard to have any strategic effect whatever. But McCaffrey knew that. His job was to keep the Drug War going, that's all.

The Drug War is *designed* to be endless. At the same time artificial hysteria is engineered with the most extensive propaganda campaign in history, the military structures that are actually dealing the drugs—Colombian, Peruvian, Mexican, Burmese, Thai, Pakistani, Afghan—are heavily supplied and financed. These are major customers of America's defense contractors, the biggest drug money launderers in the world.

US POLICY HAS BEEN DRIVEN BY THE BIGGEST PUBLICLY-FUNDED POLICE-AGENCY PROPAGANDA BARRAGE IN HISTORY.

John Walters' ONDCP continues McCaffrey's blitz of bullshit with their National Youth Anti-Drug Media Campaign. Walters was forced to admit that the five-year, $929 million ad campaign developed by the Partnership for a Drug Free America "isn't reducing drug use" after a devastating study released recently by the Westat research firm and the University of Pennsylvania. After showing the ads to a group of twelve to eighteen year-olds, researchers found no decline in the number who said they intend to try drugs in the next year.

Some kids who saw the TV ads, particularly girls aged twelve to thirteen who did not already use drugs, said they were slightly more likely to smoke marijuana after seeing the ads— prompting Walters to admit that some of the ads may "incite curiosity."

From 1989 to 1991, Walters was chief of staff for ONDCP chief William Bennett, and, from 1991 to 1993, had the hilarious title of Deputy Director for Supply Reduction. Obviously gross strategic failure is not a disqualification for this job.

"The path you propose of more police, of more jails, use of the military in foreign countries, harsh penalties for drug users, and a whole panoply of repressive measures can only make a bad situation worse," wrote Prof. Milton Friedman in an open letter to then-director of the ONDCP, Bill Bennett, published Sept. 7, 1989 in the *Wall Street Journal*. "The drug war cannot be won by those tactics

LEGALIZATION, OR CONTROLLED DECRIMINALIZATION, WOULD COLLAPSE THE VALUE OF THIS TRADE, AND THAT, AS THE WHITE HOUSE HAS JUST ADMITTED, WOULD COLLAPSE TERRORIST POWER.

without undermining the human liberty and individual freedom that you and I cherish....Illegality creates obscene profits that finance the murderous tactics of the drug lords; illegality leads to the corruption of law enforcement officials; illegality monopolizes the efforts of honest law forces so that they are starved for resources to fight the simpler crimes of robbery, theft, and assault. Drugs are a tragedy for addicts. But criminalizing their use converts that tragedy into a disaster for society, for users and non-users alike."

"Legalizing drugs would simultaneously reduce the amount of crime and improve law enforcement," Friedman points out "It is hard to conceive of any other single measure that would accomplish so much to promote law and order."

This Nobel Prize-winning macroeconomic thinker estimates that controlled drug legalization would free up 400,000 police officers, who could then get serious about serial, violent and organized crime. Of course, getting serious about organized crime has a political dimension that will appeal only to the truly antifascist.

Instead of real strategic honesty, painfully obvious to virtually every macroeconomic thinker, law enforcement field general and first-rate journalist on the planet, we get the same shopworn scenario, over and over again—another great bust filmed at sea from a hovering chopper, as the panicked outlaw crew shovels illicit bales of whatever overboard. We get George White's 1959 heroin bust, over and over again. Now the heroin, once transformed by Harry Anslinger into Red Chinese dope, is transformed by the current *apparatchik* into al Qaedadope, and the intrepid Geraldo, reporting live on Faux News while hanging out of the chopper itself, never mentions that the bust is just one more price support for which heroin dealers worldwide are sincerely grateful.

Legalization, or controlled decriminalization, would collapse the value of this trade, and that, as the White House has just admitted, would collapse terrorist power. Legalization or controlled decriminalization would render drugs useless as a source of arms finance and political control. It would demilitarize Afghanistan— and Colombia—and the United States. And that could ultimately break the grip of the ruling military and police structures on the global purse, freeing up billions for a concerted attack on terrorism's major structural support, structural poverty. The Drug War is a fascist protection racket.

Prohibition is Treason.

Where Has All the Acid Gone?

Ryan Grim

Russell Hoy leans back into his patched, third-hand couch and blows out a puff of smoke that lingers over his cluttered coffee table. "It's been, I don't know, maybe a year and a half since I've seen it anywhere," he says. "Maybe it was at the String Cheese [Incident] show in Philly back in 2000."

The "it" Mr. Hoy, a 23-year old recent college graduate, is referring to is lysergic acid diethylamide, commonly known as LSD. Rather quietly, a key symbol and perhaps driving force of the late sixties counter culture movement, it is fading like an ex-hippie's short-term memory.

Once a staple of American drug culture, acid has gone from ready availability to near oblivion. According to both Justice Department officials and former users of the drug, LSD availability is down significantly. The

| ONCE A STAPLE OF AMERICAN DRUG CULTURE, ACID HAS GONE FROM READY AVAILABILITY TO NEAR OBLIVION.

National Institute on Drug Abuse's (NIDA) *Monitoring for the Future*'s 2003 survey on national drug use trends has LSD use plummeting by unprecedented levels since 2001. Emergency room visits are down 78% in the same time, according to the Substance Abuse and Mental Health Services Administration's (SAMHSA) Drug Abuse Warning Network. No major illicit drug has ever seen such a sustained significant decline, prompting prominent drug policy expert Dr. Peter Reuter to remark, "This is an event."

Nobody can fully explain why LSD is no longer available, but the decline could be due to a number of coinciding factors: increased popularity of the synthetic drug MDMA, or ecstasy; the end of the road for the Grateful Dead as an institutional distribution network; and a lack of knowledgeable chemists resulting from the end of university-sponsored research when the drug was prohibited; but it is also attributable, as unlikely as it may seem, to one major bust near the end of 2000.

On Monday, November 6, 2000, Clyde Apperson, 47, was on a Kansas highway heading west in a Ryder truck packed with a lab capable of producing as many as 10 million hits of acid in a five-week period. He and his partner, William Leonard Pickard, 57, driving a silver Buick Le Sabre, were pulled over and searched as part of

| NO MAJOR ILLICIT DRUG HAS EVER SEEN SUCH A SUSTAINED SIGNIFICANT DECLINE, PROMPTING PROMINENT DRUG POLICY EXPERT DR. PETER REUTER TO REMARK, "THIS IS AN EVENT."

an ongoing sting operation. Pickard, who initially escaped on foot by eluding two officers half his age, then DEA helicopters and tracking dogs, was arrested the next day at a farm near Wamego, Kansas, according to published reports. A subsequent search turned up just under 91 pounds of LSD, an amount equivalent to more than 400 million doses, according to DEA calculations, representing the largest seizure in their history. This figure assumes 100 micrograms per dose, common in the late '60s. In reality, the current weight is closer to 20 micrograms, which would quintuple the number of seized doses.

Pickard, a legend in LSD culture, had also been involved in the only other seizures of complete LSD labs, in 1996 and in 1998, both involving stints in jail. But it wasn't until the Wamego bust that agents had significantly impacted the production and distribution of any major illegal recreational drug. That impact is still felt today.

"I haven't seen it since right around that time [of the Pickard and Apperson arrests]. A friend said he saw some at a Phish show but that had to be at least two years ago,"

| A SUBSEQUENT SEARCH TURNED UP JUST UNDER 91 POUNDS OF LSD, AN AMOUNT EQUIVALENT TO MORE THAN 400 MILLION DOSES, ACCORDING TO DEA CALCULATIONS, REPRESENTING THE LARGEST SEIZURE IN THEIR HISTORY.

says Brad (not his real name), who works with mentally ill and drug-addicted men for a mental health agency, and who himself is a former frequent user of LSD. "I've had my ear out for it, but it's been dry."

The production of LSD is widely believed to be highly centralized. Officials estimate that no more than a half-dozen producers are active at one time, possibly even fewer, though they hazard to make a more precise guess.

With such tight centralization, knocking one producer out of the business, as happened in 2000, can have a significant impact. Acid is also extremely difficult to produce because of its instability as a chemical compound. Oxidization renders it impotent, and so great care must be taken in both its production and distribution. Furthermore, until LSD was prohibited in October of 1966, productive research was done at the university level. Since prohibition, knowledge relating to productive methodology has been closely guarded, mostly by groups such as the legendary Brotherhood of Eternal Love. Without university support for research, knowledge had to be passed on underground. Such characteristics made the significant disruption of production possible. However, because such small amounts make so many doses, the job of disruption was not an easy one.

"The arrest of Pickard and Apperson significantly impacted the production of LSD," said Special Agent Richard Meyer at the DEA San Francisco Division office. While not evidence of a national trend, according to Meyer, LSD arrests in San Francisco, once the cultural capital of the counter-culture movement, have gone down from 20 in 2000 to two in 2001 and zero in 2002, the last year he had statistics. One DEA agent, William J. Renton, Jr., has testified that LSD production declined 95% as a result of the bust.

Traditional theory implies that as long as demand exists for a drug, the supply will eventually be met. In such a way the rise of the drug ecstasy may now be playing a role in the demise of LSD. If ecstasy is indeed a substitute good for acid, then the previous levels of demand for LSD may not return. "Ecstasy is the lazy man's drug," says Jeff, also a former user. "But it's easier to produce and you can get a lot more for it." A dose of LSD typically sells for $5, whereas doses of ecstasy can often fetch $25 to $30. Given such a price structure, it's easy to see why a chemist would rather produce ecstasy.

Special Agent Meyer, when asked about the trend, disagreed.

"No. LSD is on its own. It was in its heyday in the late '60s, then became gradually less popular in the '70s as other drugs became more popular, especially cocaine. MDMA is a more recent phenomenon, beginning sometime in the mid-'90s," which coincides with the death of the Grateful Dead's Jerry Garcia.

Russell Hoy, still planted in his patched couch, agrees with Meyer, perhaps for the first time ever. "There's some overlap, but generally you're talking about different experiences...besides, you can still get 'shrooms [a psychedelic drug with similar hallucinogenic properties to acid]."

When presented with the theory above, Peter Reuter, drug policy expert and author of the influential *Drug War Heresies,* was initially skeptical.

"I don't think so," Reuter said in his University of Maryland office, cluttered with shelves of books on drug policy and culture. "I don't think the statistics will bear out a real decrease." To demonstrate his point he pulled out the *Monitoring the Future* manual from 2002, widely accepted as the standard bearer of drug trend data. As he ran his finger across a table the look on his face turned to one of shock. "This is entirely unprecedented...way outside the historic range. If this holds up in 2003, you've really got something here." He added, however, that a rebound would most likely occur, given traditional theory regarding drug trends. When the 2003 survey came out, not only did the decrease hold the line, but reported use among 12th graders dropped another 46%, down to an historic low of 1.9%.

While hallucinogenic mushrooms are indeed still available at steady levels, those familiar with the drug culture claim that there has been a clear shift in focus from acid to ecstasy. The shift was most visible, many say, at the 2000 New Years' festival put on by the band Phish, called Big Cyprus. There, for the first time say concert goers, ecstasy had flooded the market, while acid was difficult to find. Since Big Cyprus, shows at which acid once seemed to be given away at the door have become centers for the sale of ecstasy.

UNIQUE IN ITS PRODUCTIVE DIFFICULTY AND CENTRALIZED DISTRIBUTION NETWORK, THE LSD MODEL OFFERS LITTLE OF VALUE IN THE PURSUIT OF GREATER VICTORIES IN THE "WAR ON DRUGS."

Unique in its productive difficulty and centralized distribution network, the LSD model offers little of value in the pursuit of greater victories in the "War on Drugs." Other synthetic drugs, easier to manufacture, are more widely produced in smaller amounts in basements and silos all over the country. And the most popular drugs, such as marijuana, heroin, and cocaine, have such high demand that international markets overwhelm national attempts at disruption and interception.

The most recent amateur chemist to try his luck in the acid business is soon set to join Pickard and Apperson. Glenn Slayden, 37, a Seattle jazz pianist, was arrested on February 5, 2004, and charged with attempted manufacture of LSD and attempted possession of Ergotamine Tartrate—the banned chemical needed to produce acid—in what may prove to be only the fourth seizure of a full lab. The Kansas duo can rest assured, however: Slayden could have produced no more than 20,000 doses with his nascent lab, which was seized before a single sheet was dipped. This, however, must be small solace to Pickard and Apperson, who in August of 2003 were sentenced to life and 30 years in prison respectively for their role in what may be the beginning of the end of a nation's love affair with breathing walls, melting colors, and five-dollar conversations with God.

The Gang That Couldn't Grow Straight

Michael Simmons

On June 14, 2000, Peter McWilliams had just drawn a bath at his home in the Hollywood Hills when he suddenly collapsed.

At the time of his death, the flamboyant and controversial 50-year-old best-selling author, publisher, and medical-marijuana activist, whose supporters crossed the political spectrum from William F. Buckley on the right to Paul Krassner on the left, was awaiting sentencing on 1998 federal charges that he'd financed several large-scale marijuana grows.

An AIDS patient and cancer survivor, he had been instructed by the judge who presided over his case, Federal District Court Judge George H. King, that if he smoked the marijuana that kept him from vomiting the multiple medications he needed to stay alive, he would forfeit his bond, and the homes that his mother and brother had put up for collateral would be seized.

> LIKE A HERO IN CLASSIC GREEK TRAGEDY, HE WAS AT ODDS WITH TWO FORMIDABLE ENEMIES—AND ONE OF THEM WAS HIMSELF.

McWilliams had complained publicly of the time-consuming ordeal of hot baths and bed rest that, with hit-and-miss accuracy, allowed him to hold down his multi-pilled cocktail, bolster his immune system and ward off the many opportunistic diseases that can kill an AIDS victim.

Reaction to his death was immediate and outraged. "Overdose by government!" screamed the e-mails and op-eds. "What was he doing when he died?" asked Buckley. "Vomiting. The vomiting hit him while in his bathtub, and he choked to death." Richard Brookhiser, another conservative pundit, noted in the *New York Observer*, "Here is a verifiable case of a choked innocent." "Peter McWilliams would not be dead today if not for the heartless, lethal War on Drugs," declared Steve Dasbach, national chairman of the Libertarian Party. "The federal government killed Peter McWilliams by denying him the medical marijuana he needed to stay alive as surely as if its drug warriors had put a gun to his head and pulled the trigger."

In the months that followed, McWilliams was proclaimed by many to be the most prominent martyr of the battle over medical marijuana. At Arianna Huffington's Shadow Convention in Los Angeles that August, the McWilliams name was invoked several times as a personification of all the victims of the War on Drugs.

But tracking the complexities of the slow death of Peter McWilliams is as circuitous as trying to follow a thought after having smoked some serious bud. One's mind can wander hither and thither and completely forget what that original thought was at all. The truth is that Peter McWilliams did not die from choking on his own vomit, and yet this is the commonly accepted version. Furthermore, McWilliams did indeed initiate and pay for a major marijuana-growing scheme that he was not prepared to take the consequences for. Like a hero in classic Greek tragedy, he was at odds with two formidable enemies— and one of them was himself.

Peter McWilliams had a shock of curly hair, a vivacious smile, and a manic energy explainable, at least partly, by his self-acknowledged manic depression, which he treated with Hypericum (St. John's Wort). Like many manic depressives, when he was "up," he'd spit out another book or magazine article, read voraciously, chat endlessly. I witnessed McWilliams's loquacious charm, as well as his vindictive streak and unrealistic worldview, during several interviews conducted from July 1997 through April 1998, and on one occasion was a lunch guest at his home. Many of his quotes in this article are culled from those interviews.

Born August 5, 1949, in Allen Park, Michigan, a suburb of Detroit, McWilliams came of age in the 1960s. Gay, literate, and rebellious, he idolized both Yippie co-founder Paul Krassner (who, having been founder/editor of *The Realist* in the '50s, was later dubbed "the father of the underground press") and fellow Michiganite and White Panther chairman John Sinclair (who in 1969 was dealt a nine-and-a-half to ten-year sentence for giving an undercover nark two joints). These counter-cultural legacies—iconoclastic self-publishing and pot-political POW—would resonate in the McWilliams story until the end.

In 1967, at the age of seventeen, McWilliams wrote a collection of poems titled *Come Love With Me & Be My Life*. He self-published it, as he would most of his prodigious output. It became a bestseller, and he was dubbed "the paperback Rod McKuen."

A restless polymath, McWilliams followed through on his initial success with such popular works as *The TM Book* (1975), on transcendental meditation (he'd become a devotee of the Maharishi Mahesh Yogi), and (with two co-authors) *How to Survive the Loss of a Love* (1976). Krassner explains McWilliams's motivation for the latter

> "IF, ON THE OTHER HAND, I CHOOSE TO BUY A FARM AND GROW MARIJUANA WITH THE INTENT OF SELLING IT FOR PROFIT, I WOULD BE A FELON, A CRIMINAL, A DRUG LORD, AND A DISGRACE. UNDER CURRENT FEDERAL LAW, I COULD BE PUT TO DEATH."

project: "He'd been hurt badly, and his instinct was to survive and then to share what he learned from his loss with others. Whatever he discovered, he wanted to share."

McWilliams later chose as his spiritual mentor California cult leader John-Roger, whose acolytes included Picasso biographer and then-conservative theorist Arianna Huffington. McWilliams and John-Roger co-wrote *Life 101: Everything We Wish We Had Learned About Life in School But Didn't* (1991) and six other books, though McWilliams would later claim he himself was sole author of all the books.

After McWilliams broke with John-Roger in 1994, he publicly criticized Huffington's involvement with that erstwhile mentor, making available a video of Huffington allegedly dressed in a white robe being baptized in the Ganges by the guru. According to Krassner, when arch drug-warrior Democrat Dianne Feinstein subsequently defeated Michael Huffington in the 1994 California senatorial campaign, McWilliams fretted that his outing of the Republican candidate's wife as a cult member had contributed to her husband's loss.

In 1979, McWilliams wrote and published *The Word Processing Book* (a.k.a. *The Personal Computer Book*), considered by many the first how-to book to explain to novices the nuts-and-bolts of the computer revolution. A huge seller, the work caught the attention of William F. Buckley, who wrote a column about it. "I was enormously impressed by it, partly because I had been psychologically resisting the whole theme," Buckley told me after McWilliams's death. The two authors began exchanging correspondence and became lifelong friends. "I thought he was a very charming guy...a bird of paradise," Buckley remembers.

All told, McWilliams produced nearly 40 books in areas ranging from self-help to medicine, poetry to photography. He became a regular both on the *New York Times* best-seller list and the talk-show circuit. But it was *Ain't Nobody's Business If You Do: The Absurdity of Consensual Crimes in Our Free Country* (1993) that became his most important work. An entertaining and simply written plea for government to stay out of the sex lives, gambling habits, and, interestingly, health care and drug intake of its citizens, *Ain't Nobody's Business*...appealed to many, including subscribers of Libertarian philosophy, which advocates unfettered personal freedoms as well as free markets. McWilliams, a self-avowed Libertarian, maintained that the book represented half of his beliefs, the other half being a completely laissez-faire economic system.

Although he was not a drug user when he wrote *Ain't Nobody's Business...*, it contains an eerily prescient passage that cites the perfectly legitimate business of a winemaker, and then adds: "If, on the other hand, I choose to buy a farm and grow marijuana with the intent of selling it for profit, I would be a felon, a criminal, a drug lord, and a disgrace. Under current federal law, I could be put to death."

In 1996, McWilliams was diagnosed with AIDS and non-Hodgkin's lymphoma. To quell the intense nausea from chemotherapy and multiple medications, he began using marijuana medicinally. He hadn't smoked pot in decades, but he took to it as enthusiastically as he had to the Maharishi and John-Roger. "The scales fell from my eyes, and I was like Paul on the road to Damascus," he told me. Later, he would publicly admit to smoking ten joints and popping ten Marinol pills (prescription synthetic tetrahydrocannabinol, or THC) daily, but insisted he no longer got high from this gargantuan habit, claiming that one builds up a tolerance.

> "THE SCALES FELL FROM MY EYES, AND I WAS LIKE PAUL ON THE ROAD TO DAMASCUS,"...

That same year, California voters passed Proposition 215, the initiative that legalized medical marijuana under state (though not federal) law. Those were heady days, and many med-mar proponents let the euphoria go to their heads. Peter had become a member of the fledgling Los Angeles Cannabis Buyers' Club, a group of patients organized by Scott Imler in October 1995 to pool their money to buy marijuana in order to treat their illnesses. (Disclosure: Imler is a close friend of mine and I'm a medical marijuana user as well as a former member of the L.A. club—though not during most of the events described in this article.) Imler had co-authored Prop 215 and had engineered a similarly successful med-mar initiative in Santa Cruz, California, in 1992. He also had rented the LACBC office space from Peter in the building that housed Prelude Press, McWilliams' publishing company, in West Hollywood. When the then-small LACBC was busted by the West Hollywood Sheriff's Department on September 16, 1996, less than two months before the passage of 215, McWilliams staged an impromptu press conference outside the jail where four volunteers were held, and, to the consternation of the LACBC staff, he misrepresented himself as a spokesman for the club.

After 215's passage, McWilliams saw something on television that changed the course of his life. He told me, "You had [Drug Enforcement Administration head Thomas] Constantine going in front of Congress saying, 'Marijuana is legal in California!' All the law-enforcement people...basically saying, 'We're throwing up our hands.' We interpreted this as being 'It's now all legal.'"

Sensing historic opportunity, McWilliams devised a plan for a medical marijuana advocacy, research, and distribution entity called the Medical Botanical Foundation. He got in touch with Jeffrey Farrington, the "farmacist" for the LACBC, and invited him to grow for him, telling him they'd be "millionaires in a year" and that he wanted to be "the R.J. Reynolds of medical marijuana."

THE CANNABIS-LOVING CELEBS AND CUTIES WEREN'T WHAT DISTINGUISHED LIBERTY CASTLE OR ATTRACTED THE ATTENTION OF THE LAW THOUGH; IT WAS THE ENORMOUS QUANTITY OF MARIJUANA BEING GROWN THERE.

Farrington declined to be involved. McWilliams then phoned his friend Buckley, who is a longtime foe of the War on Drugs. Buckley referred McWilliams to Richard Cowan, another conservative drug law reformer who in the early nineties had been a director of the National Organization for the Reform of Marijuana Laws, where his tenure was marked by controversy. As a pot-patriate in Amsterdam, Cowan had befriended fellow American hempster and avid—albeit non-credentialed—medical marijuana researcher Todd McCormick. Brimming with visions of becoming med-mar's first mogul, McWilliams got in touch with Cowan, who introduced him to Todd McCormick.

———————————————————

Twenty-six years old at the time he met McWilliams, Todd McCormick had suffered histiocytosis-X, a rare cancer, from the age of two to 15, and had undergone nine surgeries to remove tumors. As a result, the native Rhode Islander remains physically diminutive and is a chronic pain patient.

McCormick's first encounter with medical marijuana had been at the age of nine. His mother, Ann McCormick, who had read a magazine report on studies maintaining that cannabis could soften pain, reduce the nausea of chemotherapy and radiation, and restore one's appetite, gave Todd a joint and told him to smoke it like a cigarette. "It immediately removed my dizziness, my nausea, and gave me an appetite," McCormick stated to me in a 1997 interview. "My overall health increased." His cancer eventually went into remission, but because his left hip had failed to develop normally owing to repeated radiation treatments, as well as the fact that the first five vertebrae in his neck were fused, McCormick still endured intense pain. With his life radically improved by cannabis, he began researching and advocating medical marijuana, an endeavor in which he engaged with messianic fervor.

In the two years before he was introduced to McWilliams, McCormick had cut a swath through the cannabis culture. He founded a medical marijuana club in San Diego, and worked with Jack Herer, the father of the hem movement, on a failed initiative to legalize marijuana in California. US Customs had allowed McCormick to bring two pounds of cannabis into the country from Amsterdam in March 1995 after he showed an international prescription. He then got busted in Ohio that July for having more than 30 pounds of grass in his car allegedly destined for a cannabis club in Rhode Island. He would eventually beat the Ohio rap when a judge ruled the search-and-seizure illegal, but three days after the arrest, the DEA shut down the San Diego club.

In November 1995, McCormick split again for Amsterdam, the Shangri-la of over-the-counter cannabis coffee shops, and it was thus in Amsterdam that he met Cowan. Over the next year, McCormick experimented with different strains of weed to determine which were most efficacious for individual illnesses. Ironically, he found a strain low in THC and high in a less psychoactive cannabinoid called CBD to be most effective in controlling his neck pain. In the Netherlands he also edited one issue of a magazine called *HempLife*.

Upon hearing from McWilliams in December 1996, Todd flew to Los Angeles, where he and Peter struck a deal to write a book about medical marijuana—or perhaps create a video. (They were often vague when asked about their arrangement.) McWilliams immediately began writing checks—by his own estimate around $150,000 over a short time—to Todd, who had never written a book. A laughably slapdash volume called *How to Grow Medical Marijuana*—co-written by McCormick and a minutely credited co-author with a rambling 12-page foreword by McWilliams, a transcript of a TV interview and full-sized photos on virtually every other page—was eventually published in 1999.

In February 1997, using McWilliams's cash advances, McCormick rented a mammoth, turreted, moated, gang planked, five-story mansion on Stone Canyon Road in the tony Bel-Air section of Los Angeles, where his new neighbors included Ronald Reagan and Elizabeth Taylor. The mansion—"the ugliest house in Bel-Air" McWilliams would joke—was dubbed Liberty Castle, and instantly became a destination for Tinseltown's partying set. Indeed, stories of the brief reign of "the Pot Prince of Bel-Air" and the celebrity smokers and nubile hempie girls who gathered at Liberty Castle are legion in the marijuana movement.

The cannabis-loving celebs and cuties weren't what distinguished Liberty Castle or attracted the attention of the law though; it was the enormous quantity of marijuana being grown there. McCormick was continuing his botanical-cum-biochemical research into the medical efficacy of a variety of strains, and there were plants on the patio, plants visible through the windows, plants everywhere.

Clearly, more than a book and a video on medical marijuana were in the works. In interviews, both McCormick and McWilliams told me that they had drawn up plans to distribute the crop to one or more of the many cannabis clubs that had surfaced in California in the nineties. "Our agreement was that anything that got sold was for medical purposes," he said. In the spring of 1997, McWilliams invited Scott Imler, who was now director of the Los Angeles Cannabis Resource Center (the former LACBC), to his home in Laurel Canyon. At that meeting McWilliams asked for an exclusive contract to supply the club with marijuana. The exclusivity was a one-way deal in Peter's favor. There were alleged plans to distribute to other clubs and engage in interstate commerce by mailing plant clones to patients around the country. Imler has always advocated a by-Prop-215 approach to production and distribution ("personal medical use"), predicated on a specific amount of marijuana grown or procured per club member (one plant and one clone). He declined Peter's offer, believing the magnitude of it would put it outside 215.

(Another important event occurred that spring, when McWilliams was busted with seven joints at the Detroit Metro Airport. That case wound its way through several state courts, but was rendered moot when the feds were ultimately given overriding jurisdiction over McWilliams.)

Any plans to distribute McCormick's crop, whether to cannabis clubs or elsewhere, were snuffed on July 29, 1997, when 50 flak-jacketed, heavily armed L.A. County sheriff's deputies and DEA agents descended on Liberty Castle. McCormick was arrested along with four other people, including Renee Boje, a 28-year-old artist who the DEA claimed was observed "watering plants." (Boje is currently in Canada, fighting extradition and facing a

ten-year federal mandatory-minimum sentence in the United States. She has become a cause celebre, profiled in Glamour magazine and elsewhere. "Call me naive," she later stated to me. "Todd told me it was legal.")

Among the items seized was a newspaper interview with McCormick while he'd been incarcerated in Ohio. "When I get out of jail, I am going to go nuts and have plants growing in my front yard," McCormick boasted to a

...50 FLAK-JACKETED, HEAVILY ARMED L.A. COUNTY SHERIFF'S DEPUTIES AND DEA AGENTS DESCENDED ON LIBERTY CASTLE.

reporter. "If they want to come and get me, let them." The Liberty Castle bust became a media sensation because of the upscale location, flamboyant setting, but above all, the sheer number of plants: 4,116, as cited by law enforcement. While cop counts are often exaggerations, the photos that ran in the *Los Angeles Times* and elsewhere showed what looked like a sea of denuded pots. I visited the mansion two weeks after the raid, and saw the empty pots on the patio.

McCormick sat in jail for two weeks, until movie star and hemp activist Woody Harrelson posted the $500,000 bail. "I am helping Todd because he is a friend, but more importantly because he is working to help others in a way that California voters have declared perfectly legal, in spite of the fact that the DEA considers this legislation a threat to their somewhat questionable reason for being," Harrelson told the press.

Harrelson's well-meaning defense notwithstanding, McCormick's willful or woeful ignorance of 215 was immediately obvious. Even if one were to claim legality under Proposition 215, the California statute exempts marijuana

BEFORE BEING LED AWAY, HE VOMITED. "ISN'T THERE SOMETHING YOU CAN TAKE TO SETTLE YOUR STOMACH?" ASKED ONE OF THE AGENTS. THE NARK QUICKLY REALIZED THE ABSURDITY OF THE QUERY. "OH YEAH," HE SAID, ANSWERING HIS OWN QUESTION.

only for "personal medical use. "While McCormick maintained that the huge amount of pot he was growing was in fact for his own personal medical use, 215 does not exempt research projects, books, or videos. It was a muddled approach, demonstrating that McCormick and McWilliams had not given much forethought to what was a terribly risky endeavor.

Following the Liberty Castle bust, the DEA began conducting an investigation of McWilliams, interviewing friends, associates, med-mar activists, his electrician, and McWilliams himself. "The government says I'm the kingpin of the Medicine [pronounced like Medellin, Colombia] Cartel," he would joke. On December 17, 1997, nine DEA agents showed up at his house, handcuffed him, and proceeded to turn the place upside down. They found a relatively small amount of grass, but they also seized his computer. When it was returned some time later, the book he'd been working on was missing. They also installed a tracking device in his Lexus, then impounded it, causing the car's lease to be revoked.

Uncowed, McWilliams refused to lower his profile. He wrote and paid for a two-page ad in the entertainment-industry trade paper *Variety*, condemning DEA chief Constantine for his criticism of fictitious sitcom character Murphy Brown's use of med-mar, and accusing Hollywood of showing no spine in the face of governmental complaints about drug use in films and television. He also announced the formation of a publishing company devoted exclusively to the drug war, and on July 4, 1998, he gave a speech to the Libertarian Party National Convention in which he fulminated against both the Clinton administration and the DEA, and displayed his irreverent wit ("I'm one of those laissez fairies").

Then, on July 23, 1998, a year after the Bel-Air bust, McWilliams was arrested at his home by the DEA. Before being led away, he vomited. "Isn't there something you can take to settle your stomach?" asked one of the agents. The nark quickly realized the absurdity of the query. "Oh yeah," he said, answering his own question.

McWilliams's arrest wasn't as surprising as the 43-page conspiracy indictment, released the same day, which indicted McWilliams and three others as well as re-indicting McCormick and the four other defendants from the Bel-Air bust. The new indictment singled out four grow sites (including Bel-Air) and alluded to two others, with McWilliams as the kingpin who had allegedly cut the checks through Prelude Press to finance the operations. The checks and credit-card receipts showed that, despite McWilliams' earlier statement to this writer that "Todd's arrest got rid of any thoughts of doing any independent growing at once in one fell swoop," Peter indeed continued to pay people whose primary occupation appeared to be growing marijuana, even as he knew the feds were dogging him.

> YET MCCORMICK CLAIMED IMLER HAD DROPPED THE DIME ON HIS WHOLE OPERATION.

Most of the 182 "overt acts" of the indictment consisted of money advanced from McWilliams to the defendants, the use of his credit card by them, delivery of grow equipment to Prelude Press and Liberty Castle, set-ups for the grow ops, etc. Five items in the indictment were testimony to a federal grand jury by Imler, Farrington and Jeff Yablan of the LACRC, who were given limited immunity,

meaning they couldn't plead the Fifth Amendment to avoid testifying. The questions were based on an earlier interview by the DEA, before which McWilliams had told Imler to tell the truth. The three LACRC members—patients all—knew little about Liberty Castle and only slightly more about McWilliams' plans.

Imler testified about the exclusive grow contract McWilliams offered and repeated Peter's claim that he'd be the Bill Gates of medical marijuana—none of which was anything that the feds needed to make their case. They had the plants, the money trail and the plans to distribute

> BUT THIS VERY CONTROVERSY BEGGED A LARGER QUESTION: IF THEY WERE OPERATING UNDER STATE LAW AND HAD NOTHING TO HIDE—AS THEY CLAIMED—WHAT WAS THE BIG SECRET?

retrieved from computer files. McWilliams backpedaled from his commitment to the truth. He evidently wanted the three LACRC employees to lie; directly jeopardizing the health care of then-450 or so members of that center, 90% of whom had cancer or AIDS. He branded the testimony a betrayal. Soon, Imler began receiving death threats. "He did what he did and he's gonna get caught," a cryptic McWilliams told me. "Not by me, but word's gonna get out." (In an interview in the June 2001 issue of *High Times*, Todd echoed Peter's original advice, saying he'd told Renee Boje "...to cooperate because there was nothing I didn't admit to. It's not like I was hiding anything. She couldn't have told them anymore than I already had.")

Yet McCormick claimed Imler had dropped the dime on his whole operation. During the discovery process of his trial, McCormick had obtained the Liberty Castle search warrant written by a Sheriff's Department detective. The warrant was based on the revelations of a confidential informant who McCormick baselessly insisted was Imler. Dated the day of the Bel-Air bust, the document contains no indication that the CI was Imler, who, in any event, was in Atlanta at a Methodist conference the week the informant squawked. What's more, according to an affidavit from a DEA agent, the feds knew about the pot mansion seven days before the warrant was written when, on July 22, 1997, they'd busted a woman named Susan Korski in nearby Culver City on charges of cultivation of weed and possession of cocaine. She fingered McCormick and said he was growing marijuana in a "castle-type" house in Bel-Air. Furthermore, a DEA investigation report dated August 4 clearly states that the confidential informant from the Liberty Castle search warrant was the same person who'd been arrested in Culver City and who'd turned in McCormick—Susan Korski. Sources close to the case confirm that Korski was the informant. The US Attorney's office declined to prosecute her.

The attempt to malign Imler as a snitch was obvious payback for the LACRC director's public criticism of the outlaw style of the Bel-Air grow and for his honesty in front of the grand jury. For McCormick and McWilliams, the buck stopped everywhere but Liberty Castle, which had bustled with members of the hemp community: growers, dealers, celebrities, ganja groupies. The informant could have been any one of the human traffic that visited the Bel-Air mansion. But this very controversy begged a larger question: If they were operating under state law and had nothing to hide—as they claimed—what was the big secret? They neither practiced a stealth policy nor tried to work quietly with politicians and law enforcement, as have many major cannabis clubs in California with varying degrees of success.

McWilliams spent four weeks in jail. The government asked for and was granted a bond of $250,000, which McWilliams was unable to post. While in custody, he was denied his AIDS medicines for at least four days, a cessation of treatment that can cause the HIV virus to replicate into untreatable mutations. The American Civil Liberties Union had to petition US Attorney Nora Manella in order to ensure that McWilliams received his AIDS medications. He was also refused the Marinol that to a lesser degree could have helped him keep from vomiting his medications. Even when his jailers did get around to medicating him, the drugs were irregularly dispensed.

McWilliams's difficult side surfaced, not surprisingly, while he was in jail. When he couldn't make bail, he called his friend Steven Markoff, a wealthy businessman and civil libertarian, who says that McWilliams was "hysterical, in tears, very distraught, crying, 'You've gotta get me out!'" Markoff retained Bruce Margolin, a well-known California drug-defense lawyer. Two days after Margolin took the case, McWilliams called Markoff from jail, pleading for another lawyer. Markoff naturally inquired as to the whereabouts of Margolin. Peter had fired him in less than 48 hours over a strategy dispute. Markoff went back to Margolin, and, pleading that McWilliams was under enormous pressure, persuaded Margolin to take the case again. Two days later, McWilliams fired Margolin a second time. "This is a man languishing in jail, unmedicated," recalls Markoff. "It was a wonderful example of how self-destructive by being stubborn Peter could be."

Eventually, McWilliams's mother and brother put up their homes for bail while Markoff covered the rest in cash (he also loaned Peter $200,000). McWilliams was ordered to undergo random urine testing; if the tests came back positive for cannabis, his family's homes would be forfeited and he would be imprisoned for the duration of his trial.

McWilliams's health began to suffer demonstrably. He lost 30 pounds, his viral load (the measure of the active AIDS virus in the body) skyrocketed, and his T-cell count ("good" cells that bolster the immune system) plummeted. In spite of emergency pleas, neither Judge King nor a magistrate judge would allow McWilliams to use the most efficacious medication for his particular condition. Without marijuana to ward off the nausea and vomiting caused by his medications, McWilliams resorted to a regimen of Marinol, herbs, acupuncture, and bed rest to increase the amount of time that he was able to metabolize his medications.

After failing a urine test, Todd spent twelve days in jail. Arguing that his Marinol prescription was causing him to piss dirty, the feds came up with a test they claimed could distinguish between the pure THC of Marinol and another cannabinoid.

A judge ruled that the test was neither peer reviewed nor tested on live subjects and denied the government the right to use it. This meant that Peter and Todd's urine tests were useless as the test was designed to detect THC. Sources close to McWilliams believe that, out of fear, he refrained from cannabis use. As we shall see, McCormick may have been less strict.

In the meantime there were political developments. On March 17, 1999, the Institute of Medicine released a report, commissioned by White House Drug Czar Barry McCaffrey, that, with some caveats, validated the medical use of cannabis for people suffering from chronic conditions like AIDS wasting. And on September 13, 1999, the federal Ninth Circuit Court of Appeals in San Francisco ruled that the government ought to take into account medical necessity with cannabis use. Based on these, McWilliams' new attorney, Tom Ballanco, petitioned Judge King to ward off, as McWilliams called it, "my ongoing toboggan ride to death." King once again denied the motion.

McWilliams continued to write and give interviews. But Prelude Press had closed, he'd filed for bankruptcy, and he was about to lose his house. In photographs he appeared gaunt, his hair thinning, and was often in a wheelchair. On November 5, 1999, King ruled that neither McWilliams nor McCormick could use a medical necessity defense, mention Prop 215, or even discuss their respective physical conditions because it "is not available as a matter of law." All the talk of research, foundations, books, and videos was immaterial. McWilliams and McCormick were left with no choice. Facing ten-year

> ARGUING THAT HIS MARINOL PRESCRIPTION WAS CAUSING HIM TO PISS DIRTY, THE FEDS CAME UP WITH A TEST THEY CLAIMED COULD DISTINGUISH BETWEEN THE PURE THC OF MARINOL AND ANOTHER CANNABINOID.

federal mandatory-minimum sentences each, they negotiated a plea agreement. In exchange for a guilty plea entered on November 19, 1999, the prosecution dropped the manufacturing charges. Instead, McWilliams and McCormick were found guilty of "committing an offense against the United States government"—in this particular

| "THERE WAS NO VOMIT," HE TOLD ME LATER. "I
| DON'T KNOW WHO MADE THAT BULLSHIT UP."

case, the manufacture and distribution of marijuana. It was a legalistic technicality that lowered the maximum sentence to five years each.

McWilliams planned to ask for mercy from the court and request home detention because of his ill health. McCormick planned to appeal based on medical necessity while remaining free on bond. But McCormick would fuck up—big—one last time.

On November 21, 1999, a California Highway Patrol officer observed a black Nissan doing 90 miles an hour and began following it. After the cop turned on his overhead lights, the driver of the Nissan threw a small object from the window. The car then slowed down and pulled over. The cop did the same. He walked over to the driver's window, smelled marijuana, and noticed the driver was trembling and his voice was shaky. Asked if he'd been smoking

| "HE WAS TORTURED TO DEATH BY THE GOVERNMENT."

pot, the driver didn't answer. He had no registration, no insurance, no license, but he said he had a birth certificate. He reached into a backpack to retrieve it, then suddenly put the car in gear and took off.

The Nissan led two CHiPs vehicles on a high-speed, four-mile pursuit for approximately five minutes. Though no weed was found, a photocopy of a passport was, and Todd McCormick was placed under arrest.

According to Todd's attorney, David Michael, Federal Magistrate James McMahon reviewed the car chase and McCormick's having changed addresses without notifying his Supervision Officer. He revoked McCormick's bail on January 5th, 2000 and Todd was sent to prison. On March 27, 2000, he was sentenced to five years on the conspiracy charges and imprisoned at Terminal Island in Los Angeles.

Peter McWilliams began the new millennium with an undetectable viral load and the possibility of home detention. Mixed news, at best, but not without some

measure of hope. Meanwhile, his case was attracting attention. On Friday, June 9, 2000, TV journalist John Stossel profiled McWilliams on ABC's 20/20 during a segment called "Give Me a Break." And more than a thousand letters were sent by McWilliams' supporters to Judge King, asking for leniency when he was to be sentenced on August 15.

In the early evening of Sunday, June 11, a fire broke out in McWilliams' home. Billy Rader, a neighbor and friend, placed a ladder to the second-story window and helped McWilliams to the ground. Peter had suffered some smoke inhalation and scrapes and bruises, but was relatively unscathed and refused hospitalization. The house, however, was severely damaged, and the computer in which the manuscript of his latest book was stored was wrecked. The book, said to have been "the truth" about his case, was lost. Understandably, Peter was reported "upset and depressed."

A few days later, on the afternoon of Wednesday, June 14, McWilliams' housekeeper, Natalie Fisher, summoned Rader back to the house. McWilliams had gone into the bathroom earlier and was not responding to her calls. Unable to open the door, Rader was forced to break it in. In the bathroom he discovered McWilliams's body.

The claims that McWilliams had died from vomiting began circulating the next day. In an e-mail to supporters dated June 15, Ann McCormick, Todd's mother, wrote, "The preliminary cause of death is listed as asphyxiation. It appears that [McWilliams] was alone, vomited, and was unable, in his weakened state, to clear his airway." But the coroner's report, released on July 27, says McWilliams had 80% occlusion of the left main coronary artery and left anterior descending artery, and that he died of coronary artery disease—a heart attack. No foul play or trauma. Natural causes. No reference to vomiting. The only person to see Peter's body before the paramedics arrived was Billy Rader. "There was no vomit," he told me later. "I don't know who made that bullshit up."

Nonetheless, some activists shall not be swayed. "The government obviously got to the coroner," one prominent hempster told me. "It doesn't matter," said Kevin Zeese, the president of Common Sense for Drug Policy, when advised of the facts. "He was tortured to death by the government."

Todd McCormick's appeal was denied by the Ninth Circuit Court of Appeals in 2002. Disregarding the grand jury testimony, the court based its decision on McCormick's own plea agreement: "The facts to which McCormick stipulated as part of his plea proceedings established that there was a six-figure investment in the operation, annual earnings of $710,000 to $999,000 were anticipated, and he possessed 4,116 marijuana plants, far too much for one person to use." Todd was released from federal prison on December 10, 2003. He continues to insist that he was acting according to state law and, in spite of clear evidence to the contrary, continues to name Imler as the Liberty Castle informant. He plans to work on his organization AHEMP—Artists Helping End Marijuana Prohibition—and write a book helping others survive imprisonment.

The Bush Administration, with Attorney General John Ashcroft calling the shots, began raiding cannabis clubs and medical growers throughout California in 2001. On October 25th of that year, the DEA raided the LACRC and shut it down. Imler, Farrington and Yablan were charged with maintaining a drug house. The three men pled guilty in Judge Howard Matz's courtroom on November 24th, 2003. US Attorney Patrick Fitzgerald agreed to a downward sentencing departure based on their cooperation during the McWilliams case, but nonetheless requested that they be sentenced to prison. Taking into account their close

> IN A JUST NATION, NONE OF THIS WOULD BE
> OF CONCERN TO THE FEDERAL GOVERNMENT
> OR LAW ENFORCEMENT.

relationship with the City of West Hollywood, attempts to bring the feds to the table by applying for a growing license and other actions, and overall adherence to the truth and transparency—as well as Imler's recent cancer diagnosis—Matz ignored Fitzgerald's wishes and declined to imprison them. Calling Imler a "mensch," they received one-year probation, community service, and an order to refrain from cannabis use.

Peter McWilliams alternated between loyal friend and furious foe, articulate spokesman and royal screw-up. Despite their public solidarity, he bickered and broke with McCormick repeatedly. When his plans faltered, he'd blame everyone but himself, although he did once confess to me that he "was very foolish to give Todd a large amount of money."

It's within reason that the stress McWilliams endured in the last three years of his life contributed to his death. If he had settled for being the Michael Moore of medical marijuana instead of the R.J. Reynolds, he might be alive today. "The vomit remains as a metaphorical truth," suggests Paul Krassner. Unfortunately, the metaphor continues to be repeated as fact.

In spite of McWilliams being the financier of The Gang That Couldn't Grow Straight, it must be noted that we're discussing marijuana—and marijuana for sick people at that.In a just nation, none of this would be of concern to the federal government or law enforcement. What was

a barely thought out, poorly executed scheme became quite literally a federal case. Whatever Peter McWilliams' transgressions may have been, they don't even begin to approach the scope of the United States of America's 67-year old insane prohibition of a medically beneficial, moderately psychoactive plant.

Tales of a Recovering Drug Warrior

Eric E. Sterling

"Hello, my name is Eric and I am a recovering drug warrior."

"Hi, Eric."

Within a couple of days of becoming a lawyer in October, 1976, I was in court representing a man accused of possessing an illegal drug (PCP), and distributing it to another, a minor, if I recall correctly. I was an assistant public defender.

Three and a half years later, I was sitting on the dais of a Judiciary Committee hearing room in the Rayburn House Office Building at the US Capitol asking questions of Peter Bensinger, the Administrator of the US Drug Enforcement Administration, about DEA's anti-drug program.

For the next decade, I wrote speeches, questions, bills, reports, and amendments that became the "nuclear weapons" of the modern War on Drugs.

By my rough estimate, my work has helped to send over one hundred thousand men and women to federal prison for terms much longer than they deserve, as a result of the politically inspired and hastily considered mandatory minimum sentences of 1986. These laws, coupled with laws regarding informants, asset forfeitures, numerous gun laws, and other provisions have become, for many communities of the United States, "weapons of mass destruction." Sadly, the numerous bad laws that I helped to write are not likely to be changed in the foreseeable future.

> BY MY ROUGH ESTIMATE, MY WORK HAS HELPED TO SEND OVER ONE HUNDRED THOUSAND MEN AND WOMEN TO FEDERAL PRISON FOR TERMS MUCH LONGER THAN THEY DESERVE, AS A RESULT OF THE POLITICALLY INSPIRED AND HASTILY CONSIDERED MANDATORY MINIMUM SENTENCES OF 1986.

I left this work behind in January, 1989, and since then I have been working full-time to repeal those laws, to replace the War on Drugs with a system that will more effectively control the so-called "controlled substances." The oxymoron, "controlled substances," is just paradigmatic of a cultural blindness to the nature of drugs and their existence in that culture. Author and essayist Joshua Wolf Shenk insightfully compared our culture's frenzied condemnation of drug users to the lethal obsession of Dr. Jekyll to his evil self, Mr. Hyde.

One of the greatest challenges facing the American people is to abandon a punitive approach to drug use that is eating our young. A system of regulated, legalized control of drug use and distribution will protect the public from crime and violence. More importantly, if successful, it will restore control to an out of control criminal justice system, now rife with corruption and indifferent to the suffering it inflicts. And even more importantly, such control will significantly reduce the deaths and injuries to drug users from the use of drugs.

These pages are some of my stories.

As a young criminal defense lawyer representing accused burglars, thieves, drug dealers, robbers, etc., I used to flatter myself that I was the only participant in the courtroom required to be present by the US Constitution (pursuant to the Sixth Amendment guarantee of the enjoyment of the right ... "to have the assistance of counsel for his defense.")

I worked as zealously as I could for my clients—all of whom were poor and most of whom were poorly educated, socially maladjusted, and many of whom either had learning disabilities or were mentally ill.

I was poorly paid and was expected to supplement my income from fee-paying civil clients. Thus I was discouraged from focusing the development of my professional expertise in the criminal law.

My training, other than the courses I took in law school, was strictly on-the-job. There was no training program, and little formal collaboration. Our office of 25 or so attorneys had the minimal assistance of two investigators. We had no assistance to understand technical and scientific matters such as fingerprint testimony or forensic chemistry presented by the government against our clients. Our caseload was excessively large. Once, when three new cases were assigned to me, I asked that they be reassigned to another attorney because I felt I was at the limit of my ability to properly manage my cases. I was told that I would lose my job if I did not accept those cases. There was no dynamic leadership encouraging us to improve our skills and to do our best for our clients. Once the chief public defender referred to our clients as "those poor bastards."

Most of our cases were resolved by guilty pleas after we had negotiated a plea bargain with an assistant district attorney. Before a court can accept a plea of guilty, the court should be assured that the accused defendant has knowingly and intelligently waived his constitutionally protected rights under the Fourth, Fifth, and Sixth Amendments of the US Constitution. The process of providing this assurance is known as a guilty plea colloquy.

In my court, the defense attorney followed a script that posed various questions to the defendant. Do you know you are accused of the crime of blank and that it carries a maximum penalty of blank years imprisonment and a fine of blank dollars? Answer—"yes." Do you know that you are presumed by law to be innocent and that to be convicted, the government must prove that you are guilty by proof beyond a reasonable doubt, and that by pleading guilty you are giving up that right? Answer—"yes." Do you know that you are entitled to be represented by an attorney at every stage of the proceedings and that I am your attorney? Answer—"yes." Do you know that you have a right to a trial by a jury of your peers and that they must be unanimous in their agreement that you are guilty by proof beyond a reasonable doubt in order for you to be convicted, and that in pleading guilty you are giving up that right? Answer—"yes." Do you know that you have a right to hear all of the witnesses openly testify against you and to cross-examine them about their testimony? And so forth for all of the various rights that the Supreme Court had determined must be explicitly understood in order for them to be "knowingly and intelligently" waived. Because so many cases were resolved by guilty pleas, for most attorneys, the guilty plea colloquy of their client was the most extensive questioning they engaged in open court—and for almost all of us, it was utterly rote.

I prided myself on fighting hard for my clients. I was perfectly willing to take even a losing case to trial if my client wished since I was paid the same amount in any event, and I was eager for the experience. We might even win. Of course, when the facts suggested that the government had a strong case, I often recommended that my client consider a plea bargain to obtain a reduced sentence. I prided myself in never beginning a plea negotiation until I had met with my client and had an authorization to do so.

Once the plea bargain had been agreed to, I made a show in my guilty plea colloquy of taking a great deal of time and care to explain to my client the rights he was waiving and to show that my client appeared to fully understand those rights.

In retrospect, I was quite pathetic, for in carrying out this elaborate guilty plea colloquy—beyond the minimum required by the court—I was actually doing the work of the government and undermining my client's interest. In the event that my client would at some later time want to argue that my representation of him had been constitutionally inadequate or that he did not understand the plea bargain, my courtroom showmanship helped to foreclose his ability to make such a challenge. I was, in my inexperience and vanity, giving away more of my client's rights than were necessary to accomplish the plea bargain.

How I became a public defender is somewhat illustrative of the shoddiness of the public defender office. The day I was admitted to the bar, I signed up to have public defender cases assigned to me. All of the attorneys in the county who were struggling to make a living were on that list. But after two and a half months, a county home rule charter took effect, restructuring the county government. The public defender's office was transferred from the control of the court to the county's executive branch. The long-time public defender (a patronage employee of the court) was fired, and a new public defender was named, a man with less than two years of experience as a lawyer. His principal qualification was that he was the son of a very generous contributor to the county Republican party. His employment was a patronage pay-off.

I happened to know the new public defender somewhat well—I was his subtenant in a small law office. He was hiring full-time salaried assistants to create a public defender office, and I applied for one of the jobs. He frankly told me that he could not hire me because I was a Democrat and that without the approval of the township Republican chairman where I lived, he could not approve my job application.

A number of months later, the leading Democratic candidate for the county council charged that the new county government, dominated by the Republican incumbents, was not hiring any Democrats for the new public defender office. "How could it be that there is not a single qualified Democratic attorney seeking a position as an assistant public defender?" he asked. I got a call from the public defender asking me if I still wanted to

> IN RETROSPECT, I WAS QUITE PATHETIC, FOR IN CARRYING OUT THIS ELABORATE GUILTY PLEA COLLOQUY—BEYOND THE MINIMUM REQUIRED BY THE COURT—I WAS ACTUALLY DOING THE WORK OF THE GOVERNMENT AND UNDERMINING MY CLIENT'S INTEREST.

apply for a job—I could be hired now. Thus I was hired as the token Democrat in the public defenders office.

Each year all of the assistant public defenders were asked to buy a ticket to the county annual Republican dinner. The public defender had a quota of tickets he had to sell. As the token Democrat I was exempt from this obligation.

I was struggling to learn. The most valuable continuing legal education I received in those days were the legal programs offered by NORML, the National Organization for the Reform of Marijuana Laws, when I attended their annual conventions in Washington, DC, December of 1976, 1977, and 1978. I heard many of finest attorneys in the country—Gerald Goldstein, Michael Stepanian, Alan Silber, Alan Ellis, Michael Kennedy, Michael Tigar, Susan Jordan, Bruce Margolin, Ed Mallett, Robert Fogelnest, John Zwerling, Marvin Miller, Richard Atkins, Theodore Simon, William Moffitt, James Shellow, Keith Stroup, Frank Fioramonti, Bill Rittenberg, Charlie Daniels, Jim Jenkins, Al Horn, Reber Boult, Michael Pritzker, Buzzie Ware, Marc Kurzman, et al. I aspired to be like them.

I was a reasonably active member of my county bar association. Around the nation, bar associations sponsor programs on May 1st to educate the public and students about the legal system.

Our program one year was to demonstrate what goes on in court. The bar association program was to demonstrate a guilty plea colloquy. Pathetically, I was proud to demonstrate to high school students how to plead guilty—how to give up your constitutional rights in a constitutionally sufficient manner.

Thirty years ago, the government had an enormous advantage over the accused—who are innocent until proven guilty—in the trial of criminal cases. The overwhelming majority of those who were arrested were prosecuted and convicted. A substantial fraction of non-violent first offenders could get a special treatment in which their guilty plea was conditional—if they successfully completed a term of probation, the guilty plea would not be entered and they would escape conviction. This was never the case for serious offenders.

Yet the public mistakenly believed that the courts routinely released major criminals due to the exploitation of "loopholes" in the law by sneaky defense counsel abetted by liberal "let 'em loose" judges. That caricature was never accurate.

Nevertheless, there remained a sensitivity among some judges that the failure of the police and prosecution to stay within the bounds of the Constitution in the investigation and prosecution of cases required a sanction.

It was believed that the best way to deter the police or the prosecution from breaking the rules was to exclude evidence that had been obtained illegally and to dismiss the charges against the accused. The alternative would have been to impose fines against the agency which would have simply been paid by the taxpayers, not the rule-breaking public officials.

Today the police have vastly expanded authority to conduct investigations. The US Supreme Court and other courts have, for the last twenty-five years, almost invariably approved new tactics that were, at the time, seen as pushing the envelope of the Constitution, but which soon were seen as routine. The Congress and state legislatures have extended new powers in surveillance and

TODAY, THE BEST ANALOGY OF THE ROLE OF THE AVERAGE CRIMINAL DEFENSE LAWYER IS THAT OF THE US DEPARTMENT OF AGRICULTURE MEAT INSPECTOR AT A SLAUGHTERHOUSE.

investigation to law enforcement agencies. Wiretapping, for example, was considered such an invasive law enforcement technique, it was banned generally, and only permitted under very narrow circumstances for a limited number of crimes, after a showing that traditional investigative techniques were insufficient to gather the necessary evidence. Now Congress almost routinely, when it creates a new crime, provides authority for wiretapping. The privacy that existed in tax records, in banking records, in school records, in medical records, in records of transactions with the telephone company, with car rental companies or airlines or hotels has been substantially reduced if not eliminated.

The creation of numerous chemical and scientific tests has created the belief that there is a great ability to identify not only fingerprints, but hair, clothing, etc. If very carefully carried out, some such tests can be reliable, but reliability is not guaranteed. The ability of the accused to finance an independent examination of such tests is extremely rare.

Today, the best analogy of the role of the average criminal defense lawyer is that of the US Department of Agriculture meat inspector at a slaughterhouse. As the gruesome assembly-line of beef carcasses streams by to the packinghouse, the inspector is supposed to pick out the meat with evidence of disease. USDA inspection is an illusion of food safety. The presence of a handful of inspectors, inadequate to the task, perpetuates the illusion that meat is free of tumors, fecal matter, or disease carrying organisms such as salmonella and E. Coli.

In far too many instances, the presence of the criminal defense lawyer in the courtroom perpetuates the illusion—to the press and the public, at least—that there is a balanced system of justice that can be relied upon to produce fair trials before the accused are convicted and shipped off to prison.

Just as the provision of a public defender or a court appointed lawyer helps maintain the illusion of a balanced and fair system of justice, our two-party electoral system and the ostensibly open, public nature of the legislative process helps maintain the illusion that public policy results from a balanced debate between distinct political philosophies and an analysis of the facts.

For almost five years, from 1979 to 1984, I used to feel a thrill when I walked from my office in the House Office Buildings across Independence Avenue to the US Capitol. Here is the place where one of the great democracies of

> MANY CONSERVATIVE VOICES ARGUED THAT DECRIMINALIZING MARIJUANA WOULD SEND THE "WRONG MESSAGE" TO OUR NATION'S YOUTH.

the world is based. I sat in the seats on the Democratic side of the Chamber of the US House of Representatives and felt myself grounded in the history of a republic based on law, and the importance of a government selected by the people, dependent upon the people for its power and its legitimacy. When I let my mind wander from the debate on whatever legislation that I had helped to write (or amendments that I was helping to advance or defeat), I felt an awe of this chamber, this institution, this process as a triumph of representative democracy. But by my last four years on Capitol Hill, I was repeatedly reminded that critical decisions about public policy were more likely the result of the crassest political calculations than the flowering of wise deliberation.

Eager to leave the public defender office and the routine of representing petty criminals, I was hired in 1979 to help Rep. Robert F. Drinan (D-MA), a Jesuit priest and former law school dean and the new chairman of the House Subcommittee on Criminal Justice, in the major task of rewriting the entire Federal criminal code. The criminal code is arranged alphabetically, rather than conceptually as is the Model Penal Code. More importantly, it is a hodgepodge of inconsistent provisions enacted by Congress since 1789.

To my delight, I was assigned the sections on drugs. One provision we were debating was whether to decriminalize the possession of small amounts of marijuana, which had been the position of the Administration of President Jimmy Carter in 1977, and supported by a substantial number of Senators and Representatives. But teenage marijuana use had been steadily increasing during the 1970s. By 1979, one in ten high school seniors was reporting that they were getting high every day. Parents and teachers around the nation were alarmed that there was an epidemic of teenage marijuana use. Many conservative voices argued that decriminalizing marijuana would send the "wrong message" to our nation's youth. But the

Subcommittee recommended reducing the penalties for the possession of small amounts. This recommendation was eliminated by the full Committee in its deliberations "to avoid the time-consuming debate that this issue would create" (quoting H. Rept. 96-1396, p. 386, fn 2 (1980) to accompany H.R. 6915).

In the Spring of 1980, Father Drinan announced he would not seek re-election. When the 97th Congress convened, I was traded like a ballplayer to a new owner, US Rep. William J. Hughes (D-NJ), an excellent Member of Congress and the new Chairman of the Subcommittee on Crime. In part, I was traded because the Judiciary Committee's jurisdiction over drug issues and DEA was being transferred to the Crime Subcommittee. Thus began my career as a drug warrior, in a very new political environment. Ronald Reagan had defeated Jimmy Carter, and the Republicans took control of the US Senate for the first time since the early 1950s. At the same time, Rep. Hughes joined the House Select Committee on Narcotics Abuse and Control, chaired by Rep. Charles Rangel (D-NY), and I was charged with staffing Hughes' work on the Narcotics Committee, which meant attending as many of the Select Committee's hearings and meetings as I could.

Drug use has always been subject to the whims of fashion in the same, unpredictable manner as shoe design, hair length, facial hair, or the length of skirts and dresses, etc. However, legislators and law enforcement officers have always insisted that drug use is either going down because of tough laws (and we shouldn't let up now), or going up because the laws are not tough enough. This is *hubris*. Most folks don't make their everyday decisions by consulting the *Congressional Record* or the criminal code. Economists believe that drug use simply follows the price. But it isn't that simple. Culture plays a very big role in the styles and trends of drug use.

The amiable Presidents Jerry Ford and Jimmy Carter both brought some relief from the frenzied and heated domestic political conflicts of the Johnson and Nixon Administrations. The public was ready to chill. When the war on Vietnam ended, at last, a lot of the conflict around it wound down as well. President Carter pardoned thousands of men who had broken the draft laws. Military style haircuts were no longer *de rigueur* among men in authority. Such men could begin to wear their hair longer and not worry that it was a sign of disreputability. The drug that fit the national Zeitgeist was marijuana. People were willing to be cool now that everyone was not either marching in the streets or being exhorted one way or another.

> I IDENTIFIED THESE CUTS AND PREPARED TALKING POINTS FOR MY BOSS TO CRITICIZE THE WHITE HOUSE FOR CUTTING TREMENDOUSLY IMPORTANT ANTI-DRUG PROGRAMS. WE HAD A RHETORICAL FIELD DAY.

Through the 1970s the prevalence of marijuana use among adults and teenagers increased steadily. As noted, by 1979, 10% of high school seniors reported that they were getting stoned every day. Parents and teachers were becoming alarmed, and were being mobilized by a conservative movement that led to the nomination and election of Ronald Reagan.

Reagan arrived in Washington in January, 1981, in an armada of limousines, and to the chant, "We're Number One!" In the early 1980s, the drug of the man who wanted to feel like he was the top broker, the top salesman, the top basketball star, the drug that would add that ephemeral psychological edge of believing that one is the best, the drug of Hollywood and Wall Street, was cocaine. Reagan and company strode onto the world stage from the right bearing the banner, "America is Number One!" At training seminars around the nation, executives and athletes were being counseled to improve their performance through the use of affirmations around the theme, "I am the best." After a couple of lines of cocaine, almost everyone believed it.

With a Republican in the White House and a Democratic Congress, the drug issue was quickly re-politicized. Within a few months of the inauguration, the Office of Management and Budget (OMB) proposed cuts in many domestic programs. One proposed cut was something less than $1 million as I recall, from three DEA programs: overseas investigations and liaison; domestic state and local task forces, and investigation of the diversion of legal controlled substances from medical channels of distribution to the street markets. I identified these cuts and prepared talking points for my boss to criticize the White House for cutting tremendously important anti-drug programs. We had a rhetorical field day. I made up a number of arguments. Overseas investigations give us the most bang for the buck. Destroying drugs in other nations is much more efficient than trying to capture them in the US on the way to market. Federal funding of state and local task forces "leveraged" federal expenditures. A relatively small federal expenditure provided specialized assistance that supported officers who were paid by state and local agencies. This effort was an extremely efficient way to spend anti-drug funds we argued. And finally, the data from the Drug Abuse Warning Network (DAWN) from medical examiners and hospital emergency rooms told us that the drugs that produced the greatest numbers of deaths and injuries were the pharmaceuticals used in medicine that had been "diverted" to abuse. We moved from simply criticizing these small cuts as ill considered, to suggesting that these were the most important of all federal anti-drug programs, and that these reductions cut to the bone of drug enforcement. We repeatedly criticized the White House.

One anti-drug law required that the White House annually issue a document laying out an anti-drug strategy. These documents were usually profoundly superficial. But by the end of 1981 we attacked the Administration repeatedly for failing to issue an anti-drug strategy.

We mocked and attacked the White House for not creating a drug czar. Rep. Charles Rangel (D-NY) would ask witnesses with incomparable sarcasm, "Who is in charge? Don't tell me the President is in charge? He's not coordinating the departments and agencies on this!"

In October 1982, the Administration counter-attacked. After supporting the cuts in drug enforcement, three weeks before the election, they announced a war on drugs package. Associate Attorney General Rudy Giuliani summoned congressional staff to a conference room at the US Department of Justice to present the package of $175 million in initiatives. I asked him how they would measure the effectiveness of the program. First he answered that there would be increased arrests, etc., but I pressed him. How would they measure the effectiveness in terms of the drug markets? What were their objectives? Giuliani suggested that you can't measure the effectiveness of anti-crime programs. But I pressed him again. This is not about general anti-crime programs. What was it that they wanted to see happen in terms of the price or purity of drugs in the drug market? Did they have any objective or target that they were hoping to reach? What was the request for so many personnel and so much money designed to achieve? He got snippy with me and suggested that I didn't understand. My friends dubbed me the "Mad Questioner."

The first War on Drugs bill that I was involved with in the Subcommittee on Crime was developed in 1982. The authority of the Probation Division of the Administrative Office of the United States Courts to give urine tests to men and women on probation and parole, and to provide them with drug treatment, was expiring, and we wanted to extend it. In the office, we called this little bill the "pee in the bottle bill" even though we took it very seriously. We engaged in extensive oversight of the Probation Division's administration of the program and its effectiveness. In the lame duck session after the 1982 election, six other much more important crime bills were packaged together with the "pee in the bottle bill," quickly passed by the House and the Senate and sent to the President. The package included an expansion of the forfeiture powers in drug cases, the creation of a crime of tampering with food and drugs (after the national panic associated with the tampering with Tylenol and similar copycat crimes), a revision of the US procedures for applying international extraditions, the re-creation of a program of federal assistance to state and local law enforcement, a law to combat terrorism (in particular, aircraft hijacking), and a law to create a federal drug "czar" that was offered by Senator Joseph Biden (D-DE), the ranking Democrat on the Senate Judiciary Committee. The entire bill was agreed to by the Chairman of the Senate Judiciary Committee, Strom

Thurmond (R-SC), which created the impression among all the Members of Congress that the bill was acceptable to the Republican Administration. But President Reagan vetoed the bill, objecting that the drug "czar" would have the power to interfere with the operations of the Attorney General.

Very disappointed that so much legislative work was lost, the leading members of the Judiciary Committees in the House and the Senate from both parties agreed in early 1983 that they would not move packages of crime legislation, but would move discrete bills separately. A few weeks later the President sent a very large crime

> THESE CORRUPT PERUVIAN LAW ENFORCEMENT OFFICERS (AND THEIR DEA ADVISORS) WERE SO BRAZEN THEY THOUGHT WE WERE EITHER AS CORRUPT AS THEY WERE, OR UNINFORMED, OR INDIFFERENT, AND WE WOULD NOT UNDERSTAND WHAT THEY WERE DOING.

package to Capitol Hill, the Comprehensive Crime Control Act. There is an old saying in Washington, "The President proposes and the Congress disposes."

In the House, the various titles and sections of this very large bill were referred to a variety of committees and subcommittees. There were seven subcommittees of the House Judiciary Committee. Provisions to curtail the right of bail were sent to one subcommittee. Provisions to reform sentencing by creating a US Sentencing Committee to establish sentencing guidelines were sent to another subcommittee. The provisions relating to drugs were referred to my subcommittee, as well as pornography and other matters.

Legislatively, there were all kinds of issues to explore. The concerns about drugs even applied to non-controlled substances that were represented to be illegal drugs. At one point, there was a media/law enforcement generated alarm about "look alike" drugs. Over the counter stimulants like pseudoephedrine, caffeine, and phenylpropanolamine were packaged in capsules that looked like prescription amphetamines. At the hearing we set up to take advantage of this media concern, we heard testimony about how lethal this drug combination could be. We amended the Controlled Substances Act to prosecute those who represented over-the-counter drugs to be controlled substances.

On another occasion, the Crime Subcommittee flew to El Paso, TX on a fact finding mission to tour the DEA's El Paso Intelligence Center (EPIC), and see the border. The DEA was eager for us to see their state-of-the-art intelligence analysis facility that involved participation from every Federal law enforcement agency, intelligence agency, and military branch. EPIC was to provide instant responses to inquiries by police around the country. For example, if a

cop on a stakeout saw a car drive up to the suspected drug house, he could call in the license plate and get immediate information on the owner and whether the vehicle was already connected to the drug trade.

We flew over the US-Mexico border in a Customs Service helicopter. As I looked down, it was obvious that we could not keep people from crossing the narrow stream called the Rio Grande, or hopping the simple fence that ran west from El Paso through the desert.

In August 1983, I accompanied the Select Committee on Narcotics Abuse and Control on a fact-finding mission to Mexico, Peru, Bolivia, Colombia, and Jamaica. I met all of the top American anti-drug officials, and the top law enforcement and anti-drug officials in each nation, as well as Presidents, Attorneys General and members of the national legislatures. These meetings were remarkably similar in their artificiality. We commended the foreign leaders for the good work they were doing, lamented the problems they had, and encouraged them to do much more to fight the scourge of drugs.

In Peru, a small group of us flew over the Andes to the Upper Huallaga Valley, where the Sendero Luminoso guerillas profited from the cultivation of coca. We toured little farms where peasants grew coca. We saw a raided coca paste "laboratory" in the jungle. This was a pit in ground about the size of a septic tank, lined with plastic and filled with chemicals. The recently arrested laboratory worker seemed astonishingly relaxed in explaining in Spanish to the North Americans exactly how he extracted coca paste from coca leaf. At another location we saw a factory that was supposed to process an alternative crop, I think it was cacao, into what I thought was cocoa powder. Unfortunately this place was utterly isolated from any roads or water routes that could economically transport the produce to any market. This alternative crop approach was a pipe dream.

Later we saw workers engaged in what was said to be the eradication of coca. In our research into coca eradication, we knew that to be effective, the plant had to be cut down and the herbicide applied directly to the root stock. What we saw was the pruning of very old bushes, covered in moss, and the spraying of the herbicide on the ground around the bush. What we were witnessing was in fact the improvement of an old coca field, not a genuine effort at eradication. These corrupt Peruvian law enforcement officers (and their DEA advisors) were so brazen they thought we were either as corrupt as they were, or uninformed, or indifferent, and we would not understand what they were doing. My boss leaned over to me and said, "Now I understand the meaning of the phrase, 'pissing into the wind.'"

The capital of Bolivia is La Paz, elevation about 13,000 feet. This great height often causes altitude sickness in visitors. The national beverage is *mate de coca*, a tea made of coca leaves, containing a small amount of cocaine, that is illegal to import or possess in the United States. At our La Paz hotel in our hospitality suite, along with American beers, wines, and familiar liquors, and bottled American water, was a box of *mate de coca*. I tried the tea to prevent headache. When we met the Minister of the Interior in his offices, he cordially offered us *mate de coca* of course. Some Members of Congress accepted the drink and others declined.

In Colombia, I accompanied four Members of Congress to the La Guarija peninsula to see the efforts of the Colombian Army in eradicating marijuana. As we helicoptered in, we could see bright green fields of marijuana up and down the valley. Once again, the futility of the eradication operation was obvious.

In 1984, Rep Henry Waxman (D-CA) brought a courageous and far-sighted bill, H.R. 5290, the Compassionate Pain Relief Act, out of the Health and Environment Subcommittee of the Committee on Energy and Commerce, to create a temporary program (for five years) to permit heroin to be prescribed for the relief of pain. Heroin has been officially legal to prescribe for pain relief in Great Britain since the Rolleston Committee's report of 1926. Canada legalized heroin for pain relief in the early 1980s. I helped my boss, Rep. William J. Hughes (D-NJ), develop amendments (H. Amdt.1109) to strengthen the Waxman bill against charges that it might lead to diversion of legal heroin to the criminal market. They were defeated, 178-232. The bill was defeated on September 19, 1984, 55-355, in a wave of frenzied objections that the measure would send the wrong message. "The National Federation of Parents for Drug Free Youth was quoted during the floor debate. . . 'to falsely legitimize heroin sends the wrong message about this devastating and illegal drug to our youth.' Rep. Hamilton Fish, Jr. (R-NY, Ranking Minority Member of the Judiciary Committee) proclaimed, 'This bill will send a signal to the youth of this nation that *heroin is ok*.'" It was clear that meaning of the term "heroin" was a concept utterly disconnected from the compound itself and its actual effect upon human physiology.

For as long as I can remember, opponents of humane drug law reforms have objected that any such changes "send the wrong message." Implicitly, this objection is not that the policy itself is wrong, but that there would be unintended, grave consequences attached to the *meaning* of the change in policy. The same objection is made to permitting the use of marijuana for medical purposes.

In 1992, the first President Bush closed the federal compassionate use program for seriously ill persons to obtain federally-grown marijuana grown—because the existence of the program "sent the wrong message."

Today, opponents of drug policy reform, such as ONDCP Director John Walters, insist that there are few persons in prison for the simple possession of drugs. The purpose of the assertion is to defuse the widespread and legitimate concern that imprisonment is an excessively harsh punishment for using drugs. Implicit in the assertion is a concession that imprisonment for simple possession is a poor policy (after all, they are not arguing that an insufficient number of simple possessors are incarcerated). In the next breath the opponents of reform argue that this unjust punishment should not be reduced on "wrong message" grounds. To change the law (namely, to end the admitted injustice) would tell young people, the argument goes, that recreational drug use is "okay."

Of course that "wrong message" is only one lesson that might be taken from the change in policy. Those who use this argument are asserting either their belief in the inherent stupidity and irrationality of young people, or their own incompetence as educators. (Essentially they confess themselves incapable of explaining subtleties, i.e. it is excessive to imprison drug users, but to not imprison them is not a blessing of drug use by such persons.)

To allow heroin or marijuana to be used in medicine, like cocaine, morphine, or amphetamines, demonstrates to everyone that heroin or marijuana are "okay" to use to treat pain and disease in a medical setting—and that is always okay. Those spluttering about the wrong "message" never quite express how the wrong message might actually be framed or who might actually be expressing it.

> THOSE WHO USE THIS ARGUMENT ARE ASSERTING EITHER THEIR BELIEF IN THE INHERENT STUPIDITY AND IRRATIONALITY OF YOUNG PEOPLE, OR THEIR OWN INCOMPETENCE AS EDUCATORS.

It must be understood that the policy world is a political world, and is intensely partisan. All readers are aware of the quadrennial conflict between the parties for control of the White House. For the Congress however, the quarter century between 1955 and 1980, was a time of remarkable stability. The Democrats dominated the House and the Senate, and the Republicans were in the minority. That perception of the natural order of things (certainly from the Democratic perspective) was destroyed in November 1980, when the Republicans won control of the Senate.

This change intensified the partisan struggle. The Democrats were eager to displace the Republican "usurpers." The Republicans were eager to use their control of the White House and the Senate to expand their power. While the Democrats hoped that former Vice President Walter Mondale would defeat Ronald Reagan for re-election, more realistically they plotted to gain seats in the House and to regain control of the Senate.

On February 2, 1984, the Republican-controlled Senate passed the Comprehensive Crime Control Act (S. 1762, Senate Report 98-225). The President and the Republicans began attacking the Democrats as soft on crime for failing to pass his bill in the House. The intensity of the attack increased during the summer and as the November elections approached.

The Constitution forbids any federal expenditure not appropriated by an Act of Congress. Every fall the Congress is supposed to pass each of the thirteen spending bills—the Appropriations—that together fund all of the expenditures by the Federal government. This should be done so they can be signed by the President before the start of the new fiscal year on October 1. There are

> "IN THE DRUG WARRIOR FRAMING OF THE PROBLEM, THE DASTARDLY DISTRIBUTORS OF DRUGS WERE FIENDISHLY SYNTHESIZING AND SELLING NEW, MIND-ALTERING CHEMICALS THAT HAD NOT YET BEEN EXPLICITLY FORBIDDEN BECAUSE THEY WANTED TO DO SOMETHING WRONG WITHOUT ACTUALLY VIOLATING THE LAW."

also supplemental appropriations bills which are often considered to fund unanticipated contingencies. During the election campaign and after inauguration, the Reagan Administration had been attacking and attempting to slash domestic spending, characterized as wasteful social programs, especially in the debate on appropriations bills.

One feature of the parliamentary procedure that the House follows is a protective device for the minority known as the motion to recommit with instructions. At the end of all debate and amendment on a bill, before the final vote on passage of a bill, the floor manager for the minority may be recognized to offer a motion to recommit the bill with instructions. This motion essentially allows any kind of amendment to the bill—it is the last opportunity for the minority to score political points. Debate is typically limited to a total of ten minutes, five minutes for each side.

In the early 1980s, in the battle over federal spending during consideration of Appropriations bills, the ranking minority member of the Appropriations Committee would offer a motion to recommit that commonly moved to strike out every dollar amount and reduce it by some amount, such as 2% or 3%.

In late September, if it is clear that some of the Appropriations bills won't pass both Houses before the start of the new fiscal year, there is a procedure to pass a special, limited bill to temporarily fund the federal government until the proper Appropriations bills are passed. This bill is called a continuing resolution.

In the consideration of the continuing resolution on September 25, 1984, the Republicans had a surprise. The Ranking Minority Member of Appropriations, when recognized to offer the motion to recommit, yielded to Rep. Dan Lungren (D-CA) who offered the entire text of the Comprehensive Crime Control Act as it had passed the Senate.

Once the President's crime bill amendment was on the House floor, being debated for a few minutes, the quickly assembled arguments of the Democratic leadership in the five minutes of debate were insufficient to assure many Democrats that they would soon have the opportunity to cast clear anti-crime votes that they could report to their constituents. The Democratic members were justifiably afraid that they would be attacked for the next six weeks until election day for having voted against the President's anti-crime package. Many Democrats were unpersuaded that they would be able to campaign as having voted for tough anti-crime provisions if they only waited a few weeks for the bills that were about to be reported by the House Judiciary Committee—especially since the committee was justifiably seen by Members of both parties as a bastion of liberalism in the House. Appeals to party loyalty were equally unpersuasive. Ultimately, eighty-nine Democrats voted for the Republican motion to recommit, and it passed.

This meant that the House and Senate were going to an informal conference on an Appropriations bill with a gigantic amendment on the House appropriation—a House and Senate passed crime bill—and no crime bill amendment on the Senate appropriation. Obviously the Senate would accept that amendment. But the irony was that the "House crime bill" did not reflect the policy or language of the anti-crime provisions that had been developed in the House Judiciary subcommittees over the past year. Formally, it would be a conference on two identical texts between conferees who held dramatically different views of the policies involved. The House conferees would be trying to get the Senate to agree to change the bill to reflect the approaches they had developed in their subcommittee consideration, without any leverage.

Since this was a continuing resolution, those of us on the Judiciary committee staff were told by the Appropriations committee staff that we had less than 24 hours to complete action on the bill. A few hours later, at about 10pm, I joined a dozen or so other key staffers in the private office of the President Pro Tempore of the Senate, Strom Thurmond (R-SC). This was the site of the conference, and it was being co-chaired by Sen. Warren Rudman (R-NH) and Rep. Neal Smith (D-IA), the respective co-chairs of the Appropriations subcommittee for the Departments of Justice, State, Commerce, and the Judiciary. They had a list of about ten major issues—in a bill that was hundreds of pages long. Senators Kennedy, Metzenbaum, Simon,

Hatch, Specter, and others were there along with Reps. Rodino, Fish, Hughes. Senators Rudman and Smith were driving the process to get compromise and agreement, in the practice typical of the Appropriations committee, and they wanted the deal done quickly. After about one and half hours, Rudman and Smith had gone through the list and obtained the outlines of an agreement.

Staff were directed to begin writing and explaining the text, and it soon became clear that this would be an all-night venture. This was most likely the last big anti-crime bill that was finished by physically cutting and pasting text. Without word processors we actually used scissors and tape. This was a hasty, mistake prone procedure. For example, one provision that was agreed to, permitted DEA to deputize local law enforcement officers in task forces so that local police officers who were undercover could travel out-of-state to make undercover drug deals without losing their powers as law enforcement officers. The piece of paper with this amendment came loose from the rest of the bill, was mislaid, and was never included in the document later signed by the Speaker and the Vice President.

I FOUND IT STRANGE THAT AT ONE POINT MEMBERS OF CONGRESS WERE VYING FOR THE DUBIOUS TITLE AS "CONGRESSMAN FROM THE METHAMPHETAMINE CAPITAL OF THE NATION."

However, instead of being rushed to floor immediately after our cut and paste job, another short term continuing resolution was passed. With more time we could have fixed some of the mistakes that our hasty all-nighter made—both accidentally and in terms of policy, but Judiciary was cut out of the process.

The continuing appropriation with the Crime bill attached was signed by President Reagan on October 12, 1984. It didn't hurt his re-election blowout against Walter Mondale. What were some of the provisions in this bill?

In the mid-1980s, we began to see the problem of so-called "designer drugs." In the drug warrior framing of the problem, the dastardly distributors of drugs were fiendishly synthesizing and selling new, mind-altering chemicals that had not yet been explicitly forbidden because they wanted to do something wrong without actually violating the law. No one in the Congress or the law enforcement community could conceive in a million years that there might be an effort to find better drugs—drugs that might produce more desirable highs with less likelihood of unwanted side effects.

Synthetic opiates were being synthesized illegally, and were given street names, the most exciting of which was, "china white." This term was supposedly used to describe especially pure heroin, reputedly imported from China (in contrast to Mexican "brown" heroin, aka "Mexican mud." Often it was not heroin at all. One common active ingredient of "china white" was MPPP, an analog of meperidine. But MPPP, if not synthesized properly, was easily contaminated with MPTP. MPTP when ingested, it was tragically discovered, fairly quickly mimicked the paralysis of end stage Parkinson's disease, and these effects were not reversible. Of course, the handfuls of such cases were characterized as an epidemic, and it was then reported that "designer drugs cause Parkinson's disease!"

Other versions of "china white" contained variations on the powerful narcotic used in surgery, Fentanyl. Fentanyl was reported to be 10 to 100 times more potent than heroin, and its analogues, sufentanil, and alfentanil were even thousands of times more potent than heroin.

The Controlled Substances Act of 1970 gave the DEA the authority to schedule new drugs, and the DEA routinely did so, frequently at the urging of pharmaceutical companies that were developing a new, patented medication to market. There were seven criteria that the DEA had to study, and the DEA needed to get the opinion of the Secretary of Health and Human Services (i.e., the Food and Drug Administration) about the drug. The DEA argued that this regulatory fact finding approach was too slow to enable it to schedule quickly the newly created "designer" drugs so that they could prosecute the manufacturers and distributors. As part of the House consideration of the Comprehensive Crime Control Act 1984, I drafted language to give the DEA the power to schedule drugs on an emergency but temporary basis.

Before this legislation was passed, the DEA had published in the Federal Register its intention to schedule a largely unknown drug, MDMA (now known around the world as Ecstasy) in Schedule I, which would ban its legal use. A number of psychotherapists who were using MDMA in their practice filed a petition with the DEA, pursuant to the law, proposing that MDMA be placed in Schedule III where it would be controlled, but would not be outlawed. Such placement would require all manufacturers to be licensed, and would forbid any distribution outside that prescribed by a medical practitioner registered with the DEA. While that administrative regulatory process was underway, with fact-finding and argument by the parties, Congress passed the emergency scheduling legislation that I had crafted as part of the Comprehensive Crime Control Act of 1984. The DEA's first use of that power was in May, 1985, to place MDMA in Schedule I on a temporary basis, short-circuiting the administrative process that was underway. But the DEA's fact finder recommended that MDMA be placed in Schedule III. The DEA Administrator over-ruled that recommendation. In fact, the DEA botched its use of the emergency scheduling power we gave it, and its action was blocked by a lawsuit brought by Lester Grinspoon, M.D. and others (*Grinspoon v. DEA* (1st Cir. 1987) 828 F.2d 881). But finally DEA got it right, and Ecstasy was banned.

I found it strange that at one point Members of Congress were vying for the dubious title as "Congressman from the methamphetamine capital of the nation." The Philadelphia congressmen claimed that the Philadelphia-area was the crank capital—the nickname for methamphetamine used by the outlaw Warlock Motorcycle Club. The House Majority Leader, Jim Wright (D-TX) claimed that Fort Worth, Texas, was the methamphetamine capital of the nation. Rep. Ron Wyden (D-OR) claimed that Portland, OR was the nation's speed capital. Rep. Duncan Hunter (R-CA) claimed his city, San Diego was the speed capital.

The DEA was not satisfied with the power to ban new drugs on a quick, emergency but temporary basis, pending a thorough review. It wanted to avoid the responsibility of actually identifying a drug abuse problem before it could ban a drug. It didn't want to have to provide public notice or participation in the banning process, as was the case with MDMA. The DEA argued that anything that was made that might have an effect like a controlled substance or that chemically resembled a controlled substance ought to be banned like a controlled substance. DEA wanted a stripped down test. They didn't want a regulatory fact-finding approach with cumulative evaluation of the evidence: if the bird looked, walked, *and* quacked like a duck, then it would be considered a duck. They wanted a single factor test: if any single duck-like attributes were found, then it would be treated like a duck, or in the case of a chemical, banned like a Schedule I drug.

I raised the question, how could we ban something that had not yet been identified or named? Did such a prohibition comply with the requirement of due process that the public must be given clear notice of what was actually prohibited? In the summer of 1986, this issue was being debated among members of the Subcommittee on Crime. Rep. Bruce Morrison (D-CT) had a background as a chemist and argued for the multiple factor approach. Rep. Dan Lungren (R-CA), one of the leading Republican drug warriors in the Congress, argued for the single factor approach, which is what was enacted. (Lungren went on to gain national notoriety as the California Attorney General who went after cannabis clubs in 1996 and was satirized in Gary Trudeau's comic strip *Doonesbury.*)

We felt the Reagan Administration was not doing enough to fight money laundering by organized crime and large-scale drug traffickers. It was clear the penalties of the Bank Secrecy Act of 1970 (also known as the Currency and Foreign Transaction Reporting Act) were inadequate

to deter large scale money launderers. The BSA required that reports be filed with the Treasury Department when a person deposited a large sum of cash at a bank or other financial institution, but the penalties were light. The Treasury Department had used its regulatory power to define a variety of types of businesses as "financial institutions," but it did not include gambling casinos in the list.

Drug traffickers and other criminals were using gambling casinos to launder their money. A drug dealer could show up at the cashier's cage of casino with a sack of $50,000 in cash from drug sales, and deposit them to begin a session of gambling. After gambling for a day and losing some sum, let's say $5000, they would ask the cashier to send the balance of the deposit to their off-shore bank account by wire. Laundering completed at a cost of 10%.

The major reason why the Treasury Department was not including gambling casinos in the list of "financial institutions" was political. The senior Senator from Nevada was Paul Laxalt (R-NV). Laxalt was a senior member of the Senate Judiciary Committee. More importantly, he chaired the Senate Appropriations Subcommittee on the Treasury and other agencies. He was also the US Senator considered the closest personal friend of President Reagan.

DRUG TRAFFICKERS AND OTHER CRIMINALS WERE USING GAMBLING CASINOS TO LAUNDER THEIR MONEY.

The Crime Subcommittee encouraged the Treasury Department to amend the regulations defining "financial institution" under the Bank Secrecy Act to include gambling casinos. I set up a hearing for the Crime Subcommittee to expose the problem of money laundering in gambling casinos to put pressure on Treasury. We arranged to hold the hearing in Atlantic City, NJ. Holding this hearing in Atlantic City is an example of the tremendous integrity and political courage of my boss, Rep. William J. Hughes (D-NJ), because Atlantic City was the biggest city in his congressional district, and the gambling industry and tourism were the largest industries. Our hearing was successful in creating the pressure on Treasury to act.

In 1984, the drug components of the Comprehensive Crime Control Act had been assigned to me. The DEA was seeking more power—as usual—this time to stop physicians from improperly writing prescriptions for controlled substances. It was said that most of these physicians were senile, alcoholic, or drug addicted themselves, i.e., "impaired." DEA claimed these "impaired" physicians were a major source of the diversion of controlled substances like tranquilizers, depressants, and amphetamines from medical distribution to illegal distribution and abuse. DEA sought the authority to revoke or suspend the prescribing power of doctors if DEA found that the suspension would be in the public interest, and it was passed. Indeed, my revision of the Administration's draft of these provisions were actually preferred by DEA to the version approved by the Republican-controlled Senate and my language was agreed to by the Senate in the all-night paste-up.

Today these provisions regarding physicians are being misused by the DEA in one of the newest fronts in the war on drugs: the war on doctors who specialize in the treatment of pain and who must prescribe large doses of powerful pain killers to effectively treat their pain patients.

Members of Congress are always competing to get the attention of journalists and television cameras. Policy issues were frequently picked on the basis that the press is likely to be covering the issue. A hearing about a drug abuse crisis was as likely as any to get television coverage and newspaper reportage.

By 1985 and 1986 there was evidence that middle class cocaine use was diminishing as it dropped out of fashion. People stopped wearing silver coke spoons as jewelry. Cautionary tales of cocaine burn outs were increasingly in circulation.

The US Navy and Coast Guard, supported by Marine Corps AWACS aircraft strangled the slow maritime marijuana trade. The shipment of tons of cannabis in bales in the holds of slow moving fishing boats from the coast of Colombia no longer seemed to be such a lucrative gamble. The price of commercial grade Colombian marijuana rose, and as domestically cultivated marijuana was increasingly high end, the average price of pot climbed in the 1980s. In the early 1970s, one could buy an ounce of marijuana for $10 or $15. The "dime bag" ($10 worth) was a hefty quantity. By 1986, the "dime bag" was scarce.

If you were going to invest $100,000 into a shipment of drugs at a time when the government had begun using the military and the CIA to detect when and where that shipment was moving across the Caribbean Sea, then the decision to switch to a less easily detected and speedier means of shipment, i.e. by airplane, was elementary. This was a great time to be an adventure seeking pilot willing to fly a twin engine plane in and out of a crude, dirt airstrip in Colombia or Central America and low over the Caribbean and the Gulf of Mexico to Florida, Georgia, Tennessee, Arkansas, etc.

As the Reagan Administration's effort to undermine the leftist Sandinista government in Nicaragua was kept underground to evade the Boland Amendment, the federal government was legally flying "humanitarian assistance" to the Contras (and illegally, weapons, and ammunition) in these locations in Central America.

At the same time, cocaine was going down market. Cocaine hydrochloride, which is what the alkaloid of the coca plant is processed into for export, is water soluble. It dissolves in the mucous of the nose and can be absorbed by the blood vessels in the nose which made snorting feasible—cocaine could get to the brain relatively quickly this way.

But if the salt (cocaine hydrochloride) was mixed with a base, like baking soda, cocaine was converted to base. Cocaine base (the alkaloid) can be vaporized at a temperature much lower than cocaine hydrochloride—a cigarette lighter is hot enough, and inhaled like smoke. Inhaling drugs is an extremely efficient and rapid way to get drugs to the brain because the circulatory system is designed to direct blood from the lungs, enriched with oxygen, directly to the brain.

Smoking crack quickly became a popular way to achieve a cocaine rush. Crack is not a pure form of cocaine, as was said ad nauseam. Indeed, crack usually contained the impurities that were in the cut cocaine that was used to make the crack. But heating crack made the inhalation of cocaine vapor easy, and that made getting high on cocaine easy.

With the government's marijuana interdiction program in full swing, the price for cannabis actually started going up. Americans increasingly tried their hand at growing cannabis and used the techniques of plant breeding popularized by Luther Burbank and others to improve the psychoactive quality of cannabis. Pyraponics Industries and other companies made a wide variety of light boxes to enable growers to grow their own high-grade marijuana in their bedroom or living room. As the quality of cannabis improved, that further drove up the price.

By the mid-1980s, the "nickel" and "dime" bags of marijuana became much less common in the street drug markets. A market niche for cheap drugs opened up. That niche was filled by the "nickel" and "dime" vial of a few chips of crack cocaine—good for a high of twenty or thirty minutes.

One popular saying of the 1970s and 1980s was that cocaine makes you feel like a new man—and the first thing the new man wants to do is have another line of cocaine. For crack users, the same experience was true.

In the mid-1980s, reports about the smoking of cocaine base (crack, rock) were heard by street epidemiologists in Miami and other cities. By 1986 crack use was becoming popular in many cities, including New York, where crack use was associated with the smashing of car windows and the theft of car radios and electronics. The sound of car alarms going off in the night was common. In the early Spring, two or three New York Members of Congress introduced bills to provide for mandatory sentences for selling small quantities of crack cocaine.

On June 18, 1986, Len Bias, the star basketball player for the championship Maryland Terrapins signed a contract to play for the NBA champion Boston Celtics. That night, back home in the dormitory in College Park, M.D., he died—drinking alcohol and snorting cocaine. Bias, whose highlights had been seen on Washington, DC television stations almost nightly during four basketball seasons, was well known to Members of Congress. Members of Congress have a basketball court in the House gym, and as keen competitors themselves, pay close attention to the sport. It is also a subject that any Member of Congress can talk about with almost any constituent. Members soon went home for the district work period over the Fourth of July. The Speaker of the House, Tip O'Neill, was from Cambridge, MA, across the Charles River from Boston. He heard an earful about the Bias tragedy.

He realized the Democrats could use the public attention to drugs to take the mantle of toughness from President Reagan and the Republicans, use it to gain seats in November, even perhaps to take the Senate back for the Democrats. Upon his return to Washington, he convened the Democratic Steering and Policy Committee and directed that all House committees begin at once to assemble the components of a grand anti-drug bill. We were given four weeks to hold hearings and write the legislation, so that all the committee work would be finished before the August recess began. This would enable Democratic members to campaign in their districts about their anti-drug activities. The staff would assemble the parts and it would be voted on soon after Labor Day.

Almost immediately, Capitol Hill became a political anti-drug circus. Every committee began holding hearings on some anti-drug proposal or another. Every member was issuing press releases about their anti-drug initiative. I was busy on two fronts. First, the Crime Subcommittee

FOR THE ONLY TIME IN MY EXPERIENCE OF OVER NINE YEARS ON THE STAFF OF THE HOUSE JUDICIARY COMMITTEE, WE BEGAN OUR PROCESS OF MARKING-UP A BILL IN SUBCOMMITTEE WITHOUT A HEARING, INDEED, WITHOUT EVEN HAVING A BILL, OR A DRAFT OF A BILL, THAT HAD BEEN PRINTED AND CIRCULATED TO THE PUBLIC, OR TO THE INTERESTED FEDERAL AGENCIES. WE WERE RACING THE CLOCK AND MAKING IT UP AS WE WENT ALONG.

had its complex legislative projects to conclude before the end of the session, and second, as the expert on drug law, I was attending the meetings in the Speaker's conference room at which all the top Committee staff were reporting on their anti-drug legislating.

The Crime Subcommittee finished developing the new crime of money laundering. This was complex because the act was typically a legal act: opening a bank account, making a deposit, making a withdrawal. What made it

illegal were the circumstances and the intent, and those had to be defined very carefully to comply with the Constitutional requirement of due process that a law be clear so a citizen can know exactly what is prohibited and what is legal.

The crime of money laundering involves the intent to conceal the criminal origin of the funds; the intent to use the funds to facilitate or carry out a criminal act; or the intent to conceal one's true identity or participation in a financial transaction that involves funds criminally derived or destined.

THE CRIME SUBCOMMITTEE FINISHED DEVELOPING THE NEW CRIME OF MONEY LAUNDERING.

But concealment of identity in a transaction, by itself, should not make out the offense. For example, assume that you want to build a large office tower in New York City covering an entire block. The particular block that you are interested in may be divided into 80 separate lots. If the current property owners learn that the neighboring lots are being purchased by the same person, or for the purpose of building such a tower, they will hold out selling, knowing that as the block is assembled, the holdouts will receive offers to sell that are far above the usual market price because they are holding up the start and completion of the project. To successfully assemble this block of properties, the developer must arrange for the properties to be purchased by seemingly unrelated parties. It is critical that you, the developer (that is the true party in interest) conceal your identity until all the properties have been purchased. The circumstance of concealment of one's identity in a financial transaction should not be enough to create the crime of money laundering.

Another bill that our subcommittee was racing to complete was a bill to ban "designer drugs," that is, all of the various potential chemical analogues of all of the controlled substances. Congress was trying to prohibit the manufacture and sale of compounds that had not yet been invented. Again, how do we comply with the requirement of due process in defining the crime? I argued that the prohibited new substances should be both chemically substantially the same as a controlled substance and have an effect on the brain that is substantially similar to that of a controlled substance. However, the DEA and US Rep. Dan Lungren argued that only one of those elements needs to be satisfied. Their approach was tougher, and it prevailed.

We held hearings on various administrative problems that DEA had that needed to be fixed.

In the last week before the adjournment for the August recess, the Republicans insisted that we report a new bill to increase the punishment for drug traffickers. The Comprehensive Crime Control Act of 1984 had included the Sentencing Reform Act of 1984 that created a US Sentencing Commission to study the appropriate sentences for federal crimes. The commission was deeply engaged in the challenge of determining the circumstances that warranted long sentences up to the maximum penalty of twenty years for a first offense, and the maximum of forty years that existed for a second offense. Their report was not due until the spring of 1987. But politically, members of Congress wanted to be tough. They wanted to be able to say that they were "throwing the book" at high-level drug traffickers. They wanted mandatory minimum sentences.

For the only time in my experience of over nine years on the staff of the House Judiciary Committee, we began our process of marking-up a bill in subcommittee without a hearing, indeed, without even having a bill, or a draft of a bill, that had been printed and circulated to the public, or to the interested federal agencies. We were racing the clock and making it up as we went along.

The general idea was that we would establish two classes of mandatory minimum sentences: one for the highest level traffickers, and a lesser level for the mid-level traffickers. Our challenge was to identify such traffickers in the law. The Controlled Substances Act already had a king-pin provision, called continuing criminal enterprise. If you supervised as few as five other persons, and served as the manager of a drug distribution enterprise that committed at least two violations of the drug law, and you made substantial income from this enterprise, you faced, since 1970, a mandatory minimum sentence of twenty years, up to life imprisonment. It would seem that we had the high-level traffickers—and a lot of lesser traffickers—already facing long sentences.

I was asked to find quantities that would be indicative of high level traffickers. At one point, I suggested using DEA's class 1 trafficker classification from its G-DEP program. A class 1 trafficker might be responsible for distributing one hundred thousand doses of some serious controlled substance each month. But Rep. Romano Mazzoli (D-KY) objected. There were no drug traffickers in his home town of Louisville, KY, he suggested, who were trafficking at that levels. Such a level would end up not being useful there.

Back to the drawing board. I approached Jehru ("Johnnie") St. Valentine Brown, the most experienced drug investigator with the Metropolitan Police Department of Washington, D.C. who had been detailed to the US House Select Committee on Narcotics Abuse and Control to advise it about drugs. Brown was considered not only one of the most experienced narcotics detectives around, but a genuine drug expert. He outlined to me various quantities of drugs that would indicate that one was either a high-level or mid-level drug trafficker. These were quantities substantially lower than DEA's class 1 trafficker.

Aside from the obviousness of the mistakes we made as the law was applied, my reliance on Brown's experience, authority and qualifications were a mistake that only became clear in recent years. Brown's expertise was utterly unchallenged until 1999. Two civil attorneys had been appointed to represent two drug defendants in the D.C. court. Peter Grenier and Saul Singer did what they always did when facing an expert witness, they did the investigation to checkout his credentials. Unlike hundreds of criminal defense lawyers who had prepared to cross examine Brown, these attorneys discovered that Brown was not, as he usually testified, a graduate of the Howard University School of Pharmacy. Brown was not, as he usually testified, a licensed pharmacist. He had not served as a homicide detective, as he usually testified. [DC DRUG investigator] brown had testified in something like 4000 narcotics cases, and possibly lied in every one of them.

Did Brown lie to me about the quantities of drugs that were indicative of high-level or mid-level drug traffickers? Perhaps, but it probably didn't matter. Members of Congress were intent on using their own judgments about drugs, even though they lacked any real knowledge of the drug market or any fluency with the metric system of measurement. Certainly the quantities that Congress used as the basis to trigger long mandatories were not indicative of high level trafficking.

The language we were developing provided that distribution of some quantity of a substance containing a "detectable" amount of a controlled substance would trigger the mandatory sentence of five or ten years. I knew that this would mean that accumulating the weight of a number of small packages of impure, frequently "cut" street-level drugs could get someone a longer sentence than lesser weight of a package of pure drugs that had just been imported—when the actual amount of the controlled substance in the first instance was much smaller than the amount of the drug in the second instance. The further down the distribution chain, the more frequently the drugs are cut and the less pure they are. The purity of the drug never increases as importers deliver to brokers

> [DC DRUG INVESTIGATOR] BROWN HAD TESTIFIED IN SOMETHING LIKE 4000 NARCOTICS CASES, AND POSSIBLY LIED IN EVERY ONE OF THEM.

> BUT BECAUSE OF THE LACK OF HEARINGS AND INORDINATE HASTE WITH WHICH THIS BILL WAS DEVELOPED, THIS CRITICAL ERROR WAS NEVER DETECTED OR CORRECTED. THOUSANDS OF INJUSTICES HAVE FOLLOWED, ESPECIALLY IN LSD CASES.

who deliver to wholesalers who deliver to packagers who deliver to street dealers. I knew that this term, "a detectable amount" would lead to many injustices in which higher level offenders would actually receive shorter sentences than many lower level offenders.

In subcommittee meetings and hearings, when I had an idea like this and had to communicate it to the Chairman for whom I worked, I usually had to write it down and pass it to him. I could see that given the speed of this debate, I would not have the time to write down this point and get the chairman to read it and act on it before it was too late. Therefore I did something that I had never done before in a meeting of the Subcommittee— I raised my hand and sought recognition to speak. In our Subcommittee meetings, my speaking role was limited to calling the roll in a recorded vote, and announcing the result. Chairman Hughes was surprised but recognized me. I explained that the quantity of drugs that triggered the mandatory minimums ought to be the quantity of pure drugs, and not the weight of the adulterants that are included. The Chairman turned to ask the DEA's representative who was sitting a few rows away for DEA's opinion. Frank Shults was the long-time DEA legislative specialist assigned to us. We had worked with him for six years, and we all liked and respected him. Frank, however, had not been an agent. Would it be feasible for DEA to determine the purity of a drug sample and compute the amount of pure drugs in a sample? No, Frank replied, it would involve new, expensive laboratory procedures. This was not a good idea. Unfortunately Frank was wrong. The DEA labs routinely reported the purity of every drug sample they analyzed. Every DEA lab report that an agent receives states the weight and the purity of the evidence. It would have involved no change and no additional cost to make this determination. Frank was simply doing his job, protecting his agency against potential problems.

But because of the lack of hearings and inordinate haste with which this bill was developed, this critical error was never detected or corrected. Thousands of injustices have followed, especially in LSD cases.

At least DEA had an observer we could consult, or rather, a dishonest undercover police officer. We were moving so quickly, we never heard directly or indirectly from the Judicial Conference, the Sentencing Commission, the Parole Commission, the rank and file narcotics officers, or the Narcotics and Dangerous Drug Section of the Criminal Division of the Justice Department. We didn't hear from any of the law professors or scholars who had studied mandatory minimums at the state level, or during the 1950s and 1960s. We didn't hear from any of the officials of any of the states with mandatory minimums about their experiences.

We finished our subcommittee markup on Thursday, we rushed the bill to the full Committee on Friday, and the House soon adjourned for recess.

The House bill provided for a 10 year mandatory minimum (up to 30 years) for trafficking (or possessing with intent to distribute) at least: 1 kilo of a mixture containing "a detectable amount of heroin"; 5 kilos of "a detectable amount" of cocaine (other than cocaine freebase); 2.5 kilos (or 6000 tablets) of a narcotic drug in schedule I or II; 100 grams of cocaine freebase (crack); 100 grams of a controlled substance analogue (a "designer drug"); 100 grams of a fentanyl analogue; 946 milliliters (1 quart) of PCP or 34 grams of pure phencyclidine, or 1 gram of LSD.

The 5-year mandatory minimum (up to 20 years) was triggered by 125 grams of heroin, 1 kilo of cocaine, 125 grams (or 300 tablets) of a schedule I or II narcotic; 20 grams of crack; 10 grams of a designer drug; 10 grams of a fentanyl analogue; 28 milliliters of liquid PCP; 10 grams of pure PCP; or 500 milligrams of LSD.

After Labor Day, as the House took up the enormous package of bills from all the various committees, the Democrats could not stop Republicans from flanking them to recapture the mantle of toughness. For example, the Republicans were eager to compel Democrats to vote on floor amendments to end the "Exclusionary Rule." This would change criminal procedure to require federal courts to admit illegally obtained evidence—that is evidence that was obtained in violation of the rulings of the Supreme Court interpreting the limits of the Fourth Amendment to the Constitution—if the mistake was made by a police officer who was acting in a good faith belief that the prohibited conduct did not violate the Fourth Amendment. Later, this provision was ultimately blocked by Senator Warren Rudman (R-NH), who as a former state attorney general credibly argued that a "good faith belief" exception would swallow the rule. Every police officer, he argued, would be able to argue that they had a good faith belief that their conduct was actually legal.

After the bill passed the House on September 11, the Republicans in the Senate took their swing at it. They rewrote the money laundering bill to make it easier to convict someone.

On the mandatory minimums, they raised the maximum penalties and changed the drug triggering quantities. The 10 year mandatory minimum now carried a maximum of life in prison instead of a maximum of 30 years. The 5-year minimum now carried a maximum of 40 years instead of 20 years. The 10 year crack trigger was reduced from 100 grams to 50 grams. The 5-year crack trigger was reduced from 20 grams to 5 grams. But the Senate raised the 10 year trigger for LSD from 1 gram to 10 grams, and the 5-year trigger from a half-gram to 1 gram.

The Senate raised the quantity triggers for PCP and the analogues of fentanyl. They eliminated a number of drugs from the mandatory minimums, such as the designer drugs and the other narcotics on Schedule I and

II, and they created mandatory minimums for marijuana: 5 years for 100 kilos or more and 10 years for 1000 kilos or more. (Congress has since added a mandatory minimum of 5 years for 100 marijuana plants, and 10 years for 1000 marijuana plants, and mandatory minimums for methamphetamine.)

The House and Senate finally finished with the Anti-Drug Abuse Act of 1986 on October 17 and raced out of town for the final three weeks of the election campaign.

In the summer of 1988, the House Democratic leadership decided to do this again. This time, the sense of urgency and genuine concern due to the death of Len Bias was altogether missing. This was purely a partisan political exercise. The other congressional staffers no longer had any sense that this legislation was about the drug problem, and the cynicism about the process was intense.

In 1989, I left the House Judiciary Committee and started the Criminal Justice Policy Foundation. We saw the war on drugs as a major problem of the criminal justice system.

IT WAS CLEAR EVEN THEN THAT THE NATION'S NEWS MEDIA CRAVED HONEST, ALTERNATIVE VOICES TO THE PARTISAN RHETORIC THEY HAD BEEN GETTING.

In the 1980s, whenever there was an announcement of drug strategy from the White House, the news media always sought reaction from the Democrats. This was "balanced" journalism. The Democratic reaction was always, "it's not tough enough." The actual elements or premises of the White House announcement were never questioned.

I had helped write the legislation in the Anti-Drug Abuse Act of 1988 that created the Office of National Drug Control Policy (ONDCP), the "drug czar," and that required the issuance of an annual strategy. To provide an alternative response to the Democratic and Republican *faux* criticism of drug strategy proposal, I convened the National Drug Strategy Network, using my contacts in "establishment" Washington.

Knowing then-drug czar William Bennett was releasing a strategy, the National Drug Strategy Network organized a press conference with critics of the premises of the strategy: the leaders of the ACLU, the National Association of Criminal Defense Lawyers, the Drug Policy Foundation, Clergy Enlightened for Rational Drug Policy and NORML. We had great success by Washington standards. We had almost a dozen television cameras, and Ira Glasser from the ACLU was on national news (instead of the usual politician).

It was clear even then that the nation's news media craved honest, alternative voices to the partisan rhetoric they had been getting. Now, in 2004, the news media routinely contact the Drug Policy Alliance or the Marijuana Policy Project or other opponents to the war on drugs instead of sticking strictly to politicians from the other party.

Unfortunately, in the past fifteen years the highly politicized and irrational environment around drug policy has not been erased, yet the voices of reason are heard repeatedly, even on the floor of the House of Representatives.

The evil of the war on drugs will be ended. But it is impossible to predict when.

Kicking Out the Demons by Humanizing the Experience
—An Interview with Anthony Papa

Preston Peet

Editor's note- Anthony Papa is an accomplished artist and ardent activist from New York City, using his art to promote prison and Drug War reform. After being set up, then arrested in a drug sting operation in 1985, he received two concurrent sentences of fifteen years to life in New York State's Sing Sing prison for his first offense under the Rockefeller Drug Law's mandatory minimum sentencing guidelines. After gaining widespread attention through the harrowing and beautiful paintings he was creating from inside his prison cell, he received clemency after serving twelve years from New York Governor George Pataki in 1997. Papa graciously took time recently to sit down for a long and illuminating discussion with me, covering such topics as his art, the benefits of art for rehabilitation of prisoners, who the real targets of the War on Drugs really are and why the War continues, and some of the efforts he and friends are making to instigate positive changes in the system.

Anthony Papa,
Artist and Activist

P- You were arrested in 1985 for passing an envelope of cocaine to undercover narcotics officers. Was it a setup, or were you just unlucky?

AP- It was a sting operation. What had happened in 1984 was I was married, had a child and was self-employed with a radio business in

HE SAID I JUST HAD TO DELIVER THIS PACKAGE TO MT. VERNON. I DID, BROUGHT IT TO MT. VERNON, NY AND WALKED INTO A STING OPERATION. TWENTY NARCOTICS OFFICERS CAME OUT FROM EVERYWHERE.

the South Tremont section of the Bronx. I belonged to a bowling team in Westchester County. Business was slow, my car kept breaking down and I kept showing up late to the leagues. So one of my teammates asked me what was going on. I told him about my car, he asked why didn't I fix it, and I told him I couldn't, things were slow. He said, "Do you want to make some money? I know somebody." He introduced me to this guy who was a drug dealer, dealing in the bowling alleys in Westchester. So to make a long story short, the guy asked me if I wanted to deliver an envelope, to Mt. Vernon from New York City. He'd give me $500, and said it might become a steady thing. At first I said no, I'm not into that.

P- You pretty much knew it was drugs then?

AP- Yeah, I knew what it was about. A couple months went by, he came back around Christmas time and asked me again. Now things were really bad financially, so I asked him what I had to do. He said I just had to deliver this package to Mt. Vernon. I did, brought it to Mt. Vernon, New York and walked into a sting operation. Twenty narcotics officers came out from everywhere. The individual who actually set me up was working for the police. He had three sealed indictments against him, so what his thing was, the more people he got involved, the less time he was supposed to get. So he reached out for everybody he knew. For me it was a bad mistake and afterwards I did everything wrong. I got this shyster lawyer. They offered me a cop-out to three to life because they knew I wasn't dealing the drugs, that I was just the courier, a mule. I didn't take it because I was desperate, didn't want to leave my wife and kid and wound up listening to this attorney, going to trial, and ended up with two fifteen-year to life sentences.

P- You get a worse sentence if you fight it , right?

AP- Yeah, in New York State. The Rockefeller Drug Laws were enacted in 1973. The legislative intent was to catch the drug kingpins and curb the drug epidemic. They're a dismal failure. We're going to the 30-year anniversary on May 8th of 2002. The kingpins are still out there and the prisons are bursting at the seams. Of 72,000 in prison, 24,000 are incarcerated under the Rockefeller Drug laws. The prison population in 1973 was 12,500, now it's 72,000. Of those incarcerated under these Rockefeller Drug Laws, 94 percent are black and Latino. Marginalized, disenfranchised individuals, they come from seven inner city neighborhoods in New York City , 75 percent of those individuals are non-violent offenders.

I WAS IN PRISON FOR TWELVE YEARS UNDER THE ROCKEFELLER DRUG LAWS, SENTENCED FIFTEEN YEARS TO LIFE. THE ONLY WAY I SURVIVED IT WAS MY DISCOVERY OF MY ART.

P- Wait a minute. How many come from those 7 inner city neighborhoods?

AP- Seventy-five percent come from seven communities in NYC, and 94 percent of them are black and Latino. So there's definitely racism involved in these issues. From my perspective, I was in prison for twelve years under the Rockefeller Drug Laws, sentenced fifteen years to life. The only way I survived it was my discovery of my art. From there I transcended the negativity of the imprisonment through the art. It became for me meaning, gave me purpose in life and helped me maintain my humanity, my self-esteem, which is very essential in order to positively interact with society upon release. I met an individual who turned me onto painting, and it created this positive, crazy energy, but a crazy energy in a socially acceptable way.

P- Ok, let me come back to that. Did you use drugs personally at the time of your arrest?

AP- I did. I was a casual user, I never really used cocaine, I smoked pot and drank. Couldn't afford hard drugs, coke, stuff like that, but yeah, I was a drug user at the time.

IT'S A MAIN BELIEF OF MY LIBERATION THEOLOGY THAT YOU CAN TALK ABOUT THE BIBLE, YOU CAN TALK ABOUT TRADITION ALL YOU WANT, BUT IF THERE'S NO TANGIBLE CHANGE OR CHALLENGE TO THE PRINCIPALITIES, TO THE POWERS THAT BE, NOTHING IS GOING TO HAPPEN, NO CHANGE IS GOING TO OCCUR.

P- In your case, prison turned you onto creating art, which is obviously a positive result of your imprisonment. Are you the exception, or the rule?

AP- I say there's plenty of individuals in prison who experience what I experienced because of the existential nature of imprisonment. What I mean by that is there's something mystical about spending a lot of time in a 6 by 9 cell. You get to discover who you are. So for me, I pull this artist that lay dormant inside. There's plenty of individuals who do that. That's why in prison, I believe in a restorative approach of justice as opposed to a punitive approach. The punitive approach is a terrible approach because it sleeps in the shadows of life itself. The "lock them up" type of mentality doesn't think of the future of the incarcerated individual, whereas restorative justice maintains an individual yet allows him or her to hold onto their self-esteem which is very important.

IF PRISONS WERE MEANT TO REHABILITATE, EVERY STEP OF THE WAY WOULD BE REHABILITATIVE IN VALUE AND THERAPEUTIC.

P- That could lead to actual rehabilitation.

AP- Right. Rehabilitation exists only if you have the programs available to someone to take advantage of, to turn their lives around.

P- You earned two degrees, one in paralegal studies, and another Behavioral Sciences, as well as earning a graduate degree in ministry from the NY Theological Seminary while in prison. How does that education help you now in spreading your message?

AP- Oh, tremendously, because it gives me credibility when I speak. I'm a legal assistant for a patent trade firm, Fish and Neave. I've been here 5 years. The reason I got the job was because I was prepared. I had a college education and a graduate degree so it made things easier for me to be released and to interact with society. I think also that my education helped, especially in my theological background, because I studied liberation theology.

P- Which is?

AP- Which is a theology which was created in Third World countries as opposed to White Man theology. It's a main belief of my liberation theology that you can talk about the bible, you can talk about tradition all you want, but if there's no tangible change or challenge to the principalities, to the powers that be, nothing is going to happen, no change is going to occur. We believe in the hands on, the hermeneutical approach, the study of the nucleus of liberation theology. What it talks about is practical change, practical use of problems and challenges in a way that's tangible, not just talking about the issues, but reacting and taking care of business in a positive and tangible way. This has helped me with my art. What really turned me onto art was when I studied art at first, I got into the French Impressionists, then somebody told me art is nice, but there's more to art than pretty beach scenes and frilly white dresses. I said, what do you mean? I was into Manet, Monet, all these French impressionist artists, and he said art can be used for political purposes. He sent me a book about the Mexican muralist, Diego Rivera, who used art showing the oppressors against the oppressed, basically challenging the powers that be. So I took that and used my art. In prison I became a political artist. I saw the artist in his role as a social commentator.

P- What do think of current art, and in that I include music, film, literature, as well as fine arts. Do you find that those artists using their art to promote a serious social message, such as yourself, are not given as much attention, nor funding, as those artists who create the emptiest of art, art without any message whatsoever?

AP- You're exactly right. There's a body of art out there, a collection of artists who are political artists, who use art as a vehicle for social commentary, which is what I think art is for, yet because of the politics involved, they are not getting the grants from foundations, they're just not considered part of the elite like the handful of artists are who paint *diabetic art*. By that I mean sugar and spice, sweet stuff kind of art. I just went to the Whitney Museum Biennial, and I was amazed at the crap they showed there. I didn't see one political piece in the whole show. There is a problem of breaking out with your art and getting discovered if you are going to use your art in a political context. In society today, mainstream artists really don't do things that way.

Anthony Papa with ribbon for 1997 Best Donated Work at "Correction On Canvas" prison art show.

P- Yeah, my girlfriend overheard a conversation between two guys on the bus the other day, where one was telling the other how he hates it when a musician tries to "get all political, it's just a song." She was struggling not to light into this guy.

AP- That's what art is for, to use it as a vehicle to get that social message out. I think it is very important. You really interact with society that way. I think it's positive. Film makers, musicians, visual artists, performance artists, all can be positive in using their art to promote social change.

P- Do you feel that prisons are at all concerned with rehabilitation?

> I THINK BY WAGING THE WAR ON DRUGS, WHICH IS REALLY A WAR ON PEOPLE NOT ON DRUGS, IT'S CREATED A BIGGER PROBLEM, BECAUSE THE BLACK MARKET EXISTS. WHAT IT HAS BECOME NOW IS A VEHICLE TO FUEL THE PRISON-INDUSTRIAL COMPLEX.

AP- Not at this point. It used to be a concern, but all it is now is warehousing individuals. I was there, I know personally, and I speak from that viewpoint. If prisons were meant to rehabilitate, every step of the way would be rehabilitative in value and therapeutic.

P- You took your own initiative?

AP- Yeah, I took it upon myself to take advantage of what was available. In 1995 they cut out college education, they did away with Pell and Tap grants, because again, politicians used crime as a political issue, where first federal money was taken away, then state followed.

P- So prisoners in prison now are not getting an education?

AP- There's a small movement in New York State where there are volunteers, college students working at Bedford Hills for women, and at Sing Sing for men, instructors working on a volunteer basis and it is run strictly on private donations.

P- Which would you say is more damaging to individuals and society as a whole—drug use, or the War on Drugs?

AP- I would say the War on Drugs. We've been involved with drug use for thousands of years. It's nothing new, we've dealt with it, there's always going to be an inkling for an individual to escape reality, so we can't control it

in that capacity. But I think by waging the War on Drugs, which is really a War on People not on Drugs, it's created a bigger problem, because the black market exists. What it has become now is a vehicle to fuel the prison-industrial complex. Money is raised from State, local and federal level through people's misery. By creating this fictitious war it's caused all sorts of problems. Now we've become comfortable with locking up non-violent offenders. New York State for example, 90 percent of the prisons upstate are in Republican territory where they fight each other to build the next prison. Prisons have become a commodity. What happens is they keep them filled with non-violent offenders. In 1995, when Clinton's Crime Bill was passed it was a big mistake, because it gave millions of dollars to states to build prisons. Advocates spoke out against this, because when these prisons are built you're going to have to keep them filled. And what do you fill them with? Drug users. Drug users today are like communists in the McCarthy era. Drug use is a stigma, something they demonize.

P- Do you have a position on decriminalization or legalization?

AP- At this point if we tried legalization right now, we wouldn't do it, it wouldn't work. I think we should try out decriminalization first, as a society, see how that works, especially with marijuana. Hard drugs are always going to be a problem. Personally I think we have the right to self-medication. I believe in the harm reduction theory. Some people will always be addicted to drugs, but let's make it easy for them, let's give them treatment. Let's do it the right way.

P- You're talking about the option for treatment, not mandated treatment.

AP- Right. I don't believe in mandated treatment at all. But again, when you put it all together in the big picture, it

> WE HUMANIZE THE EXPERIENCE, WE DON'T DEMONIZE THE EXPERIENCE. WE TELL PEOPLE THAT THESE ARE HUMAN BEINGS THAT DESERVE SECOND CHANCES.

becomes part of the War on Drugs, which fuels the prison-industrial complex, because there's more money involved when you mandate. That's the whole story on that.

P- And they keep people in the system.

AP- It's a constant, vicious cycle that continues because of the monetary gain made into the whole issue.

P- Do you see any shift among police and politicians in how them themselves are perceiving the way drugs should be dealt with?

AP- My personal point of view is that five years ago, when I first got out of prison, there wasn't a lot going on in the form of politicians taking stances on drug policy reforms, because it was a sure fire way to look soft on crime, which is advocating for reduced sentencing or against the Rockefeller Drug Laws. But in the five years I've been out here working with my organization, the *William Kunstler Fund for Racial Justice*, and other groups, like the *Drug Policy Awareness Project*, teaching people about the war through art and education. Through the efforts of groups

THEY WANT TO DO AWAY WITH PAROLE, THEY WANT TO INCREASE PENALTIES FOR MARIJUANA. POLITICIANS NEVER WANT TO GIVE UP ANYTHING FOR FREE.

like these, politicians and people in general are beginning to understand there's a significant problem. Why? Because we humanize the experience, we don't demonize the experience. We tell people that these are human beings that deserve second chances. Then we have the issue of mandatory minimum sentencing, which was really enacted with the Rockefeller Drug Laws in 1973, and they in turn became the catalyst for the federal government to make the mandatory minimum sentencing the laws in the federal government, and went to all 50 states where there's now some form of mandatory minimum sentencing. It really got out of hand. It took the judges' ability to look at the totality of the facts of each case, where everybody is just pigeonholed by the weight itself. My case for instance, the judge didn't want to sentence me to fifteen years to life, but he had no choice because I went to trial and lost. Under mandatory sentencing he could give me in my case fifteen years to life, and could have sentenced me to 25 years to life, but he sentenced me to two fifteen years to life sentences because it was my first offence.

I THINK IT'S A UNIVERSAL ISSUE THAT EVERYONE SHOULD BE INVOLVED WITH BECAUSE THE WAR ON DRUGS, ALTHOUGH CLEARLY RACIST IN MANY WAYS, HAS NO CLASS BARRIERS, NO COLOR BARRIERS. IT AFFECTS EVERYBODY.

P- Fifteen years to life for your first offence?

AP- Right, first offence, non-violent, no criminal record at all.

P- Not even a smudge on your record?

AP- I had a violation, but that's not a criminal record. I had a stolen license plate on my car I'd borrowed from my boss. Five years earlier he's forgotten he put it in his trunk and called the police to report it stolen. Five years later he found it and gave it to me. I got a $25 fine for that. I'd also actually gotten another violation for a joint back in 1973, again not a criminal offence, but a violation.

P- You were arrested for selling cocaine to the cops in 1985?

AP- I was arrested in 1985.

P- You did twelve years? Then Gov. Pataki gave you clemency in 1997?

AP- Yeah. I painted my way out of prison I like to say. In 1988, while sitting in my cell one night, I painted my self-portrait. I'd looked in the mirror and saw this individual who was going to be spending the most productive years of his life in a cage.

P- How old were you?

AP- I was 30 years old when I went into prison. I picked up this canvas and painted this self-portrait titled *Fifteen years to life*, where seven years later it wound up in a show at the Whitney Museum of American Art as part of a retrospective of Mike Kelly's work.

P- So again I ask you, do you see any shift in how politicians and police perceive and/or wage the War on Drugs?

AP- I do see a shift especially among the black and Latino caucus in the New York State Assembly, but not in the Senate and not among the Republicans. Well, maybe some but not a lot of moderate Republicans. I lobby a lot in Albany, and there's a different opinion behind closed doors as to these drug laws as opposed to what is said and done in the public arena. "Yeah, these are terrible laws, I don't support them," they might say privately, but they can't go out and overtly support changes because they'd loose their constituency. Behind closed doors they all know it doesn't work right. But now there's a lot of black and Latino caucuses especially that support a change in the Rockefeller Drug Laws. For the first time in 30 years, we have the Governor, the Senate, and the Assembly that all want change, but at the end of the last session they couldn't come to an agreement, so at this point there's a stalemate on it, which is why it is so important for activists and advocates to go out and protest, to raise out voices and make a lot of noise to let them know we're still involved in this issue.

P- Now aren't they on the one hand moving towards small reforms and on the other trying to increase penalties for things like marijuana?

AP- It's always about that. The governor wants to change the Rockefeller Drug Laws in some ways, but in really watered down fashion. I'd rather have no changes at all. They want to do away with parole, they want to increase penalties for marijuana. Politicians never want to give up anything for free. They always something for something.

P- Do you really think that it would be political suicide even today if a politician stood up and said flat out, "these laws are fucked up, let make some changes"? I mean amongst their voters. Their financial backers are probably going to be upset at this kind of stance, but there does seem to be a lot of groundswell among the common people that the War is wrong.

AP- It depends on their constituency and where you live. If you live in redneck Republican territory where everybody is conservative, if a politician came out suddenly, like say Dale Volker, a staunch Republican who is all for the Rockefeller Drug Laws, who has nine prisons in his district, the 59th New York Senate District, he'd loose his job. This is why he supports the Rockefeller Drug Laws. If he came out opposed to the Rockefeller Drug Laws, his constituency wouldn't be too happy.

P- Because he's got all those prisons in his district.

AP- Right, He would probably lose his office. But let's say someone from the South Bronx, from an area like that, where drugs are prevalent so people know about the issue, it's not going to hurt the politician that much to advocate for changing the drug laws.

P- Plus people in those areas see a lot of families broken apart by the War.

AP- Exactly. I think it's different than it was 5 years ago when no one wanted change. I think then it would have been total political death. Right now I think it's really not, it's a smart issue to get involved with, but politics are politics. Some people are just not going to do it because of their politics.

P- Do you yourself hold any political affiliation?

AP- I'm a registered democrat. I was actually registered for five years but couldn't vote because I was on parole. I just got off parole in February, so this November [2002] is the first time I'm going to be able to vote, so I'm definitely going to exercise that right.

P- I know that Bush and his ilk are talking about ratcheting up the War on Drugs, and already have in many ways. But under Clinton we also had this huge explosion in the prison population and in the Drug Laws. Do you see much of a difference between the Democrats and the Republicans on the Drug War issue?

AP- On the federal level? I think basically there's not too much difference, because we're talking about politics across the board, so politicians are afraid of supporting change at that level. There are some Democrats who support some change in mandatory minimum sentencing laws, but at the federal level I don't think there's much difference.

P- Do you have any ideas on how to build more and stronger ties between the different ethnic communities on this issue? I know that in New York, well actually at most all of the conferences and events about the Drug War, with the notable exception of the Drug War Awareness Project's recent party on 4-20, that there are almost all white faces in the audience, and almost all white faces up on stage speaking and presenting. Very rarely do I see blacks and Latinos at these events. Do you have any ideas

on how to bridge the cultural divides, or whatever it is that's keep the communities apart?

AP- In my experience, in the places that I've gone to conferences, I've seen a majority of black and Latinos, along with a few whites, so I don't know the audiences you're talking about.

P- That's precisely what I'm talking about. The places I'm going to, as a white guy, I see mainly white folk, but you, a Latino, see mainly blacks and Latinos. How do we get these groups together, to work together?

AP- I really can't answer that.

P- No ideas?

AP- I think it's a universal issue that everyone should be involved with because the War on Drugs, although clearly racist in many ways, has no class barriers, no color barriers. It affects everybody. The prosecutorial tools were created to curb the drug epidemic, then in turn those laws are used against average citizens who doesn't even use drugs, like exclusionary rules, the 4th Amendment, search and seizure…

P- Asset Forfeiture.

AP- Yeah, asset forfeiture laws, these are all tools that prosecutors use. They use them beyond their intended purposes. They go to the average citizen, where you can even loose your home for something like a marijuana cigarette.

P- Do you focus your efforts mainly in NY State, or do you also work on national efforts for reform?

AP- I work with the Kunstler Fund for Racial Justice mainly on the Rockefeller Drug Laws, and at the federal level I work with groups like Families Against Mandatory Minimum Sentencing (FAMM) and The November Coalition. I've been to Washington DC and lobbied on Capital Hill. Because the Rockefeller Drug Laws really touched me on a personal level, that's my main area of concentration.

P- Does being an ex-con hinder you in any way, say in your work as a legal assistant?

AP- Oh, a lot. For instance, let's say in this community here, this job. there's a lot of people here with PhD's, attorneys, people from sort of the higher echelons of society, who went to the best schools. What I've calmed down is promoting what I'm about here at the firm. At first people used to hear about me and knew I was an artist. But they really didn't know what kind of artist, so when I exposed myself and they saw the art and heard the story that I was in prison, it created a stigma.

P- Just like that?

AP- Just like that. It's a stigma I'll live with all my life. They look at me differently, maybe they won't even say hi to me. That's some people. Not all people, but a majority of people in this firm. My next door neighbor doesn't know I'm an ex-prisoner. I'm always paranoid. I've been living there in a private house, with a little Italian couple who love me, yet they don't know my past. I remember when people would be coming over to do interviews, with all their production equipment, and I used to freak out because I have a small apartment and all this stuff would be out in the hall, and there's a knock on the door. Who is it but my landlord. She asked what was going on and I told her they were making a film about my art. She said, "ooh, can I see it when it's done?" I said sure, but I never showed it to her. I always live with this stigma, carrying a Scarlet Letter as I call it. It's universal the stigma I carry, it tainted me, but it also gives me courage and strength to go on in a positive way. I use it as a tool now. Because what happens when you do an extraordinary amount of time, many people want to put it aside and go on with their life. But with me, I use it as a vehicle to become who I am, this activist involved in change, positive change and transformation to make things better for people still inside and people outside, yet still wear this Scarlet Letter, that label as a convicted felon.

> IT'S A STIGMA I'LL LIVE WITH ALL MY LIFE. THEY LOOK AT ME DIFFERENTLY, MAYBE THEY WON'T EVEN SAY HI TO ME.

P- One last question. Do you find it a bit ironic that you served 12 years in prison under the Rockefeller Drug laws, and now you work in the Rockefeller Center?

AP- I work at Rockefeller Center. I think it's very appropriate that I help stage rallies at 50th and 5th at the Rockefeller Center. Everything has evolved around the Rockefeller Center, so this is the place for me to be.

Anthony Papa's art work can be seen at www.15yearstolife.com, where you can also read and sign the petition demanding that New York State reinstate the Corrections on Canvas art show, and the rights of prisoners to arts and education.

Frying Pans and Fires: Forcible Medication, Medical Marijuana and the Logic of Control

Heidi Lypps

"Over himself, over his own body and mind, the individual is sovereign."
—John Stuart Mill, "On Liberty," 1859

"Force and fraud are in war the two cardinal virtues."—Thomas Hobbes

Drugs and Social Control

There is a paradox in modern thinking about drugs. "Wonder drugs" promise to improve our lives, even to save them. Yet illegal drugs are considered a social scourge: dangerous, disordering, the ruin of the model citizen, their users enemies of the state. We perceive this threat to stem from the alleged disorderly states of

> THE MODERN STATE, HERE THE US GOVERNMENT, WANTS DESPERATELY TO CONTROL THE ENORMOUS POWER OF SUBSTANCES THAT ALTER OUR BODIES AND OUR CONSCIOUSNESS.

mind drugs cause, the moral decay, and the destructive behavior resulting from drug use. Yet our culture is ever more pharmaceutically obsessed: from Ritalin to Thorazine to Viagra, we find our solace and our cures in a pill. Small wonder, then, that the concept of "better living through chemistry" has a dark side—the ubiquitous use of illicit drugs, addiction, and craving that leads to crime.

The modern state, here the US government, wants desperately to control the enormous power of substances that alter our bodies and our consciousness. The power of drugs, so the thinking goes, must be mediated by authority; only science and the law can mediate the power and the danger drugs pose. The state, therefore, has an interest in gaining the power to define good and useful drugs from bad and dangerous ones. The inconsistency of these definitions is shown by the fact that many substances dangerous to health, such as tobacco and alcohol, remain legal while less dangerous substances such as cannabis are strictly banned.

Some, like civil liberties attorney Julie Ruiz-Sierra, argue that the modern phenomenon of drug criminalization is a symptom of "an attempt by the majority to enforce a

> LIKE THE "ETERNAL" WAR BETWEEN OCEANIA AND EURASIA IN ORWELL'S 1984, THE DRUG WAR CAN SEEM UNENDING, THE GOVERNMENT'S DRUG POLICIES UNASSAILABLE.

moral code on the whole of society through the police power of the state."[1] This occurs despite the value placed on personal liberty in the US Constitution, justified by a paternalistic government that seeks to protect us from the

> PREVIOUSLY PROTECTED PERSONAL RIGHTS, WE ARE TOLD, MUST GIVE WAY BEFORE THE DEMANDS OF SECURITY AND SAFETY.

dangers of drugs through criminalization, and to protect us from madness, through the use of drugs.

Since 2001, The US Department of Justice and The Drug Enforcement Administration have carried out a crackdown on medical marijuana in California. One of nine states to pass laws legalizing the medical use of marijuana, California has been targeted for a large number of raids and arrests. This "war on the sick" has targeted medical cannabis suppliers, many of whom happen to be vocal activists.

In ironic contrast, recent years have also seen a pair of high-profile cases in which forcible drugging of defendants in the legal system led to battles decided by the US Supreme Court. Respected British medical journal The Lancet reported that in 2003 alone, 59 mentally ill prisoners in the US legal system were drugged against their will.[2]

Though the government's policies on forcible medication and medical marijuana seem maddeningly irrational and mutually opposed, there is an underlying logic and consistency to these two positions. It's about control, about imposing a moral code and a standard of behavior on the private thoughts and lives of ordinary citizens. The state encroaches ever more on the domain of our minds and liberties, with figures like Attorney General John Ashcroft leading the way. Previously protected personal rights, we are told, must give way before the demands of security and safety. To bolster this position, the state misuses science and law to back its position. The prolonged attack on California medical marijuana suppliers and activists, as well as the government's disturbing attempt to gain the right to forcibly medicate mentally ill prisoners, are examples of this policy of social control.

Charting the Course of the War on Drugs

Like the "eternal" war between Oceania and Eurasia in Orwell's *1984*, the drug war can seem unending, the government's drug policies unassailable. The rhetoric of the war is deeply culturally entrenched, and many believe that drugs have been traditionally banned in the US.

STRANGE TO THINK, BUT DRUG LAWS WERE UNIMAGINABLE UNDER PRE-MODERN LEGAL SYSTEMS. EVEN MUSLIM COUNTRIES WITH STRICT BANS ON ALCOHOL ALLOWED (AND MANY STILL ALLOW) THE USE OF HASHISH AND OPIUM.

Instead, anti-drug laws are a relatively new phenomenon of the last 80 years, as governments sought to extend their sphere of control over the private lives of its citizens. The modern "War on Drugs" as we know it dates from the Nixon era.

Strange to think, but drug laws were unimaginable under pre-modern legal systems. Even Muslim countries with strict bans on alcohol allowed (and many still allow) the use of hashish and opium. Under medieval common law, there were no victimless crimes; unless an accuser came forward, there was no basis for a trial—and thus no ban on the use of intoxicants. It is richly ironic, too, that medieval and renaissance systems of justice, best known for brutality, witch-hunts, and torture, involved a far lower percentage of the population than the modern judicial system. In modern-day America, those who have never been touched by the long arm of the law are few and far between. Who among us has never had at least a traffic ticket? A large and growing segment of the population is imprisoned as well; people of color disproportionately so.

Absinthe forms an early case study in media hype leading to drug proscription. French authorities mobilized citizens' fear and loathing of the green liquor to ban it. They charged the alcoholic beverage with causing "absinthism"—mania, hallucinations, violent behavior—

THE SHEER NUMBER OF LIVES AFFECTED BY DRUG PROSCRIPTION IS STAGGERING; THE WAR ON DRUGS, IS, AFTER ALL, A WAR ON OUR OWN PEOPLE.

do these charges sound familiar? Several gruesome murders were widely attributed to Absinthe (somehow other alcoholic beverages escaped suspicion) and a series of quack experiments "proved" that Absinthe was dangerous, lending the authority of science to the Absinthe hysteria, and the drink was banned in the US and almost all European countries by 1915.[3] The social-control basis for the Absinthe ban set the tone for future prohibitions and drug laws. Alcohol prohibition in the US soon followed, with all its speakeasies, corruption, and organized crime. After the failure of the alcohol ban,

marijuana was next on the block; after another fevered dose of propaganda (including the infamous 1936 film *Reefer Madness*), the Marijuana Tax stamp act of 1937 made the plant illegal.

In the late 1960s, Richard Nixon (known for his paranoia and desire to control dissent) declared a "War on Drugs," followed by the Controlled Substances Act in 1970. This new federal law was followed by the creation of a new law enforcement agency, the Drug Enforcement Administration, in 1972. Militarization of law enforcement (remember those tanks that demolished crack houses on TV in the 1980s?) and a skyrocketing prison population followed. In our own day, nearly 800,000 people are arrested every year on marijuana charges alone; 90% for simple possession.[4] By way of comparison, the number of active-duty soldiers in the US is 500,000 as of January 2004. The sheer number of lives affected by drug proscription is staggering; the War on Drugs, is, after all, a war on our own people.

The Needle and the Damage Done

In stark irony to the government's "just say no" hype is the increasing incidence of forcible drugging for some of these prisoners. The former Soviet Union caused an

IT IS RICHLY IRONIC, TOO, THAT MEDIEVAL AND RENAISSANCE SYSTEMS OF JUSTICE, BEST KNOWN FOR BRUTALITY, WITCH-HUNTS, AND TORTURE, INVOLVED A FAR LOWER PERCENTAGE OF THE POPULATION THAN THE MODERN JUDICIAL SYSTEM.

international human rights scandal by misusing psychiatry to silence dissidents. Those considered disruptive were sometimes declared insane and sentenced to psychiatric hospitals or prisons, where they were given high doses of psychotherapeutic drugs in a clear attempt to silence them. The comparison to recent cases in the US is unflattering, at best.[5]

A 1986 Supreme Court decision mercifully banned execution of the insane. Unfortunately, prosecutors have found a way around this ban—forcibly drugging defendants to restore sanity—in order to execute them constitutionally. The Supreme Court used this rationale to decide the case of Charles Singleton, an Arkansas death-row inmate, in 2003. Despite the fierce opposition of dissenting judges, the European Union, and human rights groups, Singleton was injected with psychotherapeutic drugs to render him "sane" for execution, then given a lethal injection on January 6, 2004.[6]

Singleton, who had been on death row since 1979 for the murder of an Arkansas woman, had been diagnosed with severe schizophrenia. The 1990 US Supreme Court ruling in *Washington v. Harper* gives state officials the right to "treat a prison inmate who has a serious mental illness with antipsychotic drugs against his will, if he is dangerous to himself or others and the treatment is in his medical interest."[7] It is exceedingly difficult to see how forcing medications on a prisoner in order to execute him is in his best interest. It is in the interest, however, of the state officials, who can now force chemical "sanity" on prisoners in order to bring them to the death chamber.

Another forcible drugging case was seen in 2003 as well—one that was less barbaric than Singleton's but may have broader implications. In June, the US Supreme Court ruled on the involuntary drugging case of Dr. Charles Thomas Sell. Charged with 63 counts of Medicaid fraud in 1997, Dr. Sell was diagnosed with "delusional disorder, persecutory type," and found incompetent to stand trial. The Missouri dentist was determined by a lower court not to pose a danger to himself or others, and competent to determine his own medical treatment. The question at the heart of the Sell case was whether the government can forcibly medicate mentally ill defendants in order to make them stand trial.[8]

> IT IS EXCEEDINGLY DIFFICULT TO SEE HOW FORCING MEDICATIONS ON A PRISONER IN ORDER TO EXECUTE HIM IS IN HIS BEST INTEREST.

Although anti-psychotic drugs have severe side effects and only suppress the symptoms of mental illness, the government claimed the authority to chemically compel Dr. Sell's mental competence by forcing medication on him.[9] Dr. Sell's attorneys argued in their brief to the Supreme Court that "The right to be free from unwanted physical and mental intrusions has long been recognized as an integral part of an individual's constitutional freedom."[10] A civil liberties group, the Center for Cognitive Liberty & Ethics, concentrated on Dr. Sell's freedom of thought. "On the one hand the government is bent on creating a 'Drug-Free America,' while on the other hand it forces a citizen to take mind-altering drugs despite his repeated objection," said Richard Glen Boire, a CCLE attorney. "The only thing consistent here is the government's astonishingly arrogant assertion that it has the power to determine which types of thinking are allowed and which it can prohibit or coerce."[11]

> PSYCHOTHERAPEUTIC DRUGS PRODUCE AN ARTIFICIAL SANITY, OR THE REPLACEMENT OF THE VISIBLE EFFECTS OF MADNESS WITH THE VISIBLE EFFECTS OF A DRUG.

Psychotherapeutic drugs produce an artificial sanity, or the replacement of the visible effects of madness with the visible effects of a drug. In the case of Mellaril, one of the psychotherapeutic drugs that prison officials wanted to administer to Sell, those effects are considerable. The high relapse rate of patients on psychotherapeutics like Mellaril argues against claims that they truly restore sanity: 75-95% of mental health patients relapse if their pharmaceutical therapy is terminated. Only an estimated15% can go back to "normalcy"; the rest must have their condition permanently managed with mind-altering drugs.[12]

The last few decades have seen the systematic clearing out of mental hospitals, as psychotherapeutic pharmaceuticals are used to replace institutionalization. In 1955, there were 680,000 mental health patients in institutions, with 350,000 admissions per year. In 1993, only 120,000 institutionalized patients remained, while a staggering 750,000 were admitted. These antipsychotics are used as tools to get patients out of expensive institutions while maintaining control over their behavior. Sadly, they are a very flawed success: many mental health patients end up in prison or homeless, despite treatment.[13]

In addition, many of these pharmaceuticals have dangerous side effects. Compare Mellaril, one of the drugs that prison officials sought to use on Dr. Sell, with the mild effects of marijuana, for example. The side effects of Mellaril include: tardive dyskinesia (uncontrolled movements of the tongue, mouth, arms and legs, which may be permanent and may come after stopping the drug), seizures, liver damage, serious brain and eye damage (with long-term use) and it can cause a serious and sometimes fatal reaction called neuroleptic malignant syndrome. It may cause rigid muscles coma, rapid heartbeat and breathing, sweating, shaking and seizures. The death rate is 20%. Finally, it may cause fatal heart arrhythmias.[14] Is it any wonder that Dr. Sell preferred trial to treatment with these drugs?

In the end, the court ruled that Dr. Sell cannot be forcibly drugged—but there are cases in which defendants might be. A four-part test will be applied to future cases, establishing strict legal standards for medicating defendants to ensure trial. Nonetheless, the Court failed to question whether forcible medication for trial competence is appropriate or ethical in any situation. Sell has already spent six years in prison, longer than he would have served had he simply been convicted of every fraud charge he faced. In a final irony, Sell is caught in a legal Catch-22: by refusing medication, he ensures that he will neither be brought to trial nor released from the institution where he is imprisoned.

The Sell case represents a violation of autonomy in favor of the government's interest. The standard measure of involuntary medication—whether the medication would be in the patient's "best interest," is clearly left aside here, overridden by the government's interest in bringing Dr. Sell to the stand. The resulting decision did set clear limits on government's ability to forcibly medicate, but failed to call the practice of forcible medication for legal rather than medical purposes into question. Also left out of the equation was much consideration for personal mental autonomy and integrity. There is a new and stringent legal test to pass, but nonetheless, the right to remain free of the government needle wasn't articulated. With an estimated 5% of the US population affected by some form of mental illness, the Sell and Singleton decisions will affect quite a few people.

The safety of patients is clearly considered less important than control over their behavior, even if, as in the case of Dr. Sell, that behavior has been deemed nonviolent and no danger to self or others. Drugging him or any defendant involuntarily would be a violation of cognitive liberty—a less concrete but no less important right to privacy and control over one's own mind.[15] Some drugs can get you thrown in jail, it seems; and given the right conditions, even more dangerous drugs can be legally shoved into your veins while you're there. It's all a matter of the government's interest.

Your Tax Dollars at Work: The DEA's War on the Sick

The state of California passed Proposition 215, known as the Compassionate Use Act, in 1996. The broadly-worded bill legalized the use of medical marijuana with a doctor's prescription, infuriating the federal authorities and setting off a trend. Though federal law claims to supersede state law, nine states (Alaska, California, Colorado, Hawaii, Maine, Maryland, Nevada, Oregon, and Washington) have now passed medical marijuana bills. Anxious to stop the trend and make an example of California, the DEA moved to shut down medical cannabis clubs, including the Los Angeles Cannabis Resource Center, the Market Street Cannabis Club, CHAMPS, the Oakland Cannabis Resource Center, and Santa Rosa's Aiko Compassion Club.[16]

With the advent of the Bush administration, the federal government moved to stop the growers of medical marijuana. The Wo/Men's Alliance for medical marijuana in Santa Cruz was one such victim. The Santa Cruz collective was one of the state's most carefully law-abiding operations, requiring doctors' prescriptions and issuing IDs for the group's patients; WAMM's collective garden was planted with full knowledge and sanction of county and state officials, who did not cooperate with the raid. Of the WAMM collective members, 80% are terminally ill. Notably, founder Valerie Corral is a longtime medical marijuana activist and was one of the authors of Proposition 215.

SOME DRUGS CAN GET YOU THROWN IN JAIL, IT SEEMS; AND GIVEN THE RIGHT CONDITIONS, EVEN MORE DANGEROUS DRUGS CAN BE LEGALLY SHOVED INTO YOUR VEINS WHILE YOU'RE THERE.

Nonetheless, the DEA raided the WAMM garden on September 5, 2002, destroying the crop of 150 plants shortly before harvest. Besides the WAMM raid, sixteen other medical marijuana providers have suffered federal raids and arrest since 2001.

Famous marijuana activist and author Ed Rosenthal was convicted of felony cultivation charges in January 2003. He was sentenced to one day in jail (the charges normally carry a five year sentence) for growing medical marijuana in Oakland, after a lengthy and contentious trial; the federal judge caused outcry when he forbade the jury from consideration of Proposition 215, or any medical marijuana defense.

The War on Drugs, particularly in the case of the California crackdown, is based neither on the safety nor the will of the people. Prop. 215 was passed by popular referendum, a fact that is ignored by the DEA as they kick down doors, tear up gardens, and terrorize the severely ill. The conservative Bush administration that champions "states' rights" in all other cases shows contempt for California law when it comes to medical marijuana.

The authority of science is often misused to bolster the paternalistic rationale for the War on Drugs. In 2003, Johns Hopkins University revealed that its two recent DEA-supported studies showing significant neurological damage from MDMA (Ecstasy) use were completely false. The drug used to produce the toxic test results was not MDMA at all, but methamphetamine. Is this evidence of scientific progress or scientific complicity?

But the safety of patients is not the government's main concern. As I've shown, many psychiatric drugs forced on the mentally ill in prison have far more dangerous side effects than cannabis. As a DEA judge wrote in 1988, "marijuana, in its natural form, is one of the safest therapeutically active substances known to man...." Its LD-50 ratio (the amount per kilogram that must be taken for a killing dose in 50% of the subjects) is an incredibly high 1:20,000 to 1:40,000. "In layman's terms... a smoker would theoretically have to consume 20,000 to 40,000 times as much marijuana as is contained in one marijuana cigarette...nearly 1500 pounds of marijuana within about fifteen minutes to induce a lethal response."[17]

Statistics show that between 65 and 95 million Americans have used marijuana at least once in their lifetime, and a January 30, 2004 Field poll showed that Californians support Prop. 215 and the use of medical marijuana at a rate of 74%, higher than the 56% who approved the law in 1996. A June 2003 study in *American Demographics* magazine showed that 80% of those polled favor legalization for medical purposes; 30% favor complete legalization of marijuana. "At the DEA, we feel that the public needs to be protected from marijuana and drug dealers," commented DEA spokesman Richard Meyer.[18] How, exactly, does targeting patients for arrest and imprisonment protect them from anything?

Despite (or perhaps because of) the large number of Americans who have tried pot and/ or support legalization, the demonization of drugs and drug users is intense. LA police chief Daryl Gates echoed a popular Reagan-era sentiment when he snapped, "casual drug users should be taken out and shot. Smoke a joint, lose your life," before a Senate Judiciary committee in 1990. With extremes like this voiced in official circles, it would be an admission of embarrassing wrong to admit that cannabis causes relatively little harm, is frequently used by cancer and AIDS patients, and seems to have medical benefit and no dangerous side effects.

Part of the problem, too, is that cannabis is not a corporate-created pharmaceutical, isn't patented, and won't produce huge profits for a pharmaceutical company. Marijuana is a grow-it-yourself medication, safe enough to remain unstandardized. However, its official status as a "forbidden" drug, no matter how wrongheaded, outdated and destructive the policy may be, makes the federal government redouble its efforts to control cannabis and punish all users.

There is a small exception. The debut of the anti-nausea drug Marinol (dronabinol), a synthetic form of THC, is an attempt to bring a form of marijuana under the umbrella of accepted treatment. A Schedule III drug used as an anti-nausea and analgesic drug, it is considered less effective than smoked whole cannabis by a large number of patients and oncologists.[19] The very existence and use of Marinol as a therapeutic agent gives the lie to DEA officials and others who claim that marijuana has no known health benefits; Marinol passed the stiff battery of safety and efficacy tests and gained FDA approval.

PROP. 215 WAS PASSED BY POPULAR REFERENDUM, A FACT THAT IS IGNORED BY THE DEA AS THEY KICK DOWN DOORS, TEAR UP GARDENS, AND TERRORIZE THE SEVERELY ILL.

But if Marinol is in use, why not wait for science to take the lead in developing more standardized, safe, cannabis-based pharmaceuticals? Cannabis and any derived substance are automatically placed in Schedule I of the Controlled Substances Act, effectively deterring further research, and a better drug in ten years does not help those who are sick at present.[20] Even the medical establishment chafes at being used by the federal government to justify repressive cannabis laws. The editor-in-chief of the *New England Journal of Medicine* noted that "that prohibiting physicians from helping their suffering patients by suggesting that they use marijuana is "misguided, heavy-handed, and inhumane."[21] He further recommended that marijuana be reclassified as a Schedule II drug and be made available by prescription without the usual requirement of controlled clinical trials. Studies show no increase in death rates among marijuana users,[22] while anecdotal, as well as scientific evidence of the effectiveness of smoked marijuana abounds.[23]

... IT IS A DANGEROUS FORM OF SYSTEMATIC MADNESS TO ATTEMPT TO CHEMICALLY FORCE SANITY ON THOSE ACCUSED OF CRIMES.

In cancer and AIDS patients, marijuana has been credited with counteracting such side effects of treatment as exhaustion, severe nausea, vomiting, and loss of appetite.[24] A centuries-old analgesic, marijuana was not removed from the US Pharmacopeia until 1941, several years after its ban in 1937. Nonetheless, in the face of much existing scientific evidence, cannabis remains a Schedule I controlled substance, officially designated as a highly dangerous drug with no medical value. DEA officials insist that "We will not turn a blind eye toward our responsibility to enforce federal law and to preserve the integrity of medical and scientific process to determine if drugs have medical value before allowing them to be used."[25] The DEA was attempting to use medical science as a source of authority; but doctors themselves took exception, filing suit against this unconvincing argument the same year.

Nonetheless, there are cracks in the façade. On December 16, 2003, the 9th US Circuit Court of Appeals created an exception to the federal ban that overrules Proposition 215. The Court ruled that federal criminal laws against marijuana are unconstitutional when applied to sick people who are using the drug with their doctor's approval in accordance with state law. The home of one defendant, Diane Monson was raided and her six marijuana plants confiscated in 2002.[26] Another decision by the same court supported the right of doctors to discuss medical marijuana with their patients, free of government interference. (*Conant v. Walters* (9th Cir 2002) 309 F.3d 629, cert denied Oct. 14, 2003) Undaunted by federal interference, California lawmakers recently passed SB 420 (terrible pun, it's true), a bill that extends legal protections for medical cannabis providers. The law sets up a voluntary ID card system to help protect patients from arrest, assures access to medical marijuana for the state's prisoners, and allows communities to set guidelines for allowable amounts in possession. Signed by former governor Gray Davis, the bill was scheduled to go into effect January 1, 2004—but is currently blocked by the Schwarzenegger administration.

Less directly, landmark *Lawrence v. Texas* case, decided by the Supreme Court in 2003, may hold hope for the concept of personal freedom. Overturning a previous decision, the privacy and personal liberty of two gay men was upheld, and state sodomy laws were rendered unconstitutional.[27] With this decision, the door may be opened for re-assessing the value of personal liberty vs. the dubious benefits of social control. Hopefully, the personal liberty interest over private behavior that was affirmed in the *Lawrence* decision will extend to areas of law beyond sexuality—to personal drug use, cognitive liberty, and beyond. Until then, it is a dangerous form of systematic madness to attempt to chemically force sanity on those accused of crimes. To simultaneously wage war on desperately ill people who want an "unapproved" but safe medicine is further evidence of an inhumane policy that values control over any benefit to the governed. The social costs of these policies are too great to justify, and the impact on individual freedom too great. Private, consensual, and victimless behavior of any kind should never be under government control.

Endnotes

1 Ruiz-Sierra, Julie, Private and Consensual Acts: Charting the Boundaries of Personal Freedom in America. Unpublished manuscript, 2004.

2 Ashrad, Haroon, US Supreme Court Limits Forced Drugging, *The Lancet*, Vol. 361 No. 9375, June 21, 2003.

3 Erowid.org, Absinthe Vault accessed online at: [http://www.erowid.org] Jan 28, 2004.

4 Ruiz-Sierra, Julie, Private and Consensual Acts: Charting the Boundaries of Personal Freedom in America. Unpublished manuscript, 2004.

5 Lypps, Heidi, Better Living Through Chemistry, *The Humanist*, September/October 2003.

6 "Randall, Kate, Mentally ill Inmate Put to Death after Medical 'Treatment' Prepares Execution, accessed online at: [http://www.wsws.org] January 8, 2004.

7 Boire, Richard Glen, Mind Matters, *Journal of Cognitive Liberties*, Vol.4 No.1, 2003.

8 Lypps, Heidi, Better Living Through Chemistry, *The Humanist*, September/October 2003. Also see: *Sell v. United States*, US Supreme Court 02-5664, June 16, 2003.

9 Center for Cognitive Liberty & Ethics press release: Supreme Court Upholds Right to Refuse Mind-Altering Drugs-CCLE Amicus Brief Argues Forced Medication Infringes Fundamental Liberty, June 16, 2003.

10 Eviatar, Daphne, If Sanity Is Forced on a Defendant, Who Is on Trial? *New York Times*, June 21, 2003.

11 CCLE Press Release, CCLE Argues Freedom of Thought in Landmark US Supreme Court Case, December 19, 2002.

12 Mosby, Ray and Ksir, *Drugs, Society, and Human Behavior*, 1993.

13 Goode, Erich, *Drugs in American Society*, 5th edition, Erich Goode, 1998.

14 Thioridazine (Brand name Mellaril) drug monograph, Accessed online at: [http://www.mentalhealth.com/] Jan 28, 2004. Also see FDA MedWatch, July 7, 2000, Accessed online at: [http://www.fda.gov]

15 For further definitions of "cognitive liberty," see the CCLE's Web site at: [www.cognitiveliberty.org]

16 Lypps, Heidi, The DEA's War on California: The Crackdown on Medical Marijuana, *CounterPunch News*, accessed online at:[http://www.counterpunch.org] Jan 30, 2004).

17 In the Matter of Marijuana Rescheduling Petition, US Dept. of Justice, DEA, Docket No. 86-22, Sept. 6, 1988 (Young, J.).

18 Egelko, Bob, Medical pot law gains acceptance: Prop. 215 polls better now than when it passed, *San Francisco Chronicle*, Jan. 30, 2003.

19 Doblin RE, Kleiman MA. Marijuana as antiemetic medicine: a survey of oncologists' experiences and attitudes, *Journal of Clinical Oncology* 1991; Vol.9:1314-9.

20 Joy, Janet E.; Stanley J. Watson, Jr.; John A. Benson, Jr., Eds. *Marijuana and Medicine: Assessing the Science Base*. 1999.

21 Kassirer, JP, Federal foolishness and marijuana. *New England Journal of Medicine* Vol. 336,1997.

22 Sidney S, Beck JE, Tekawa IS, Quesenberry CP Jr, Friedman GD. Marijuana use and mortality. *American Journal of Public Health* 1997; 87:585-90.

23 Grinspoon L, Bakalar JB. *Marihuana: the forbidden medicine*. New Haven, Conn.: Yale University Press, 1995.

24 Annas, George, Reefer Madness: The Federal Response to California's Medical Marijuana Law, *New England Journal of Medicine*, August 7, 1997.

25 Federal News Service. White House briefing news conference, December 30, 1996.

26 Boire, Richard Glen, Court Plants Red Cross in the War on Marijuana, *California Daily Journal*, Dec. 24, 2003. Also see: Harrison, Ann, A Victory for Medical Pot Patients, AlterNet, accessed online at: [http://www.alternet.org/story.html?StoryID=17419] December 18, 2003. Also see: Raich v. Ashcroft, 2003 US App. LEXIS 25317 (9th Cir. Dec. 16, 2003).

27 Ruiz-Sierra, Julie, Private and Consensual Acts: Charting the Boundaries of Personal Freedom in America. Unpublished manuscript, 2004.

End Prohibition Now!

Retired Narcotics Undercover Agent, Jack A. Cole

I represent LEAP (Law Enforcement Against Prohibition), an international nonprofit educational organization created to give voice to all the current and former members of law enforcement who believe the US war on drugs is a failed policy. These law enforcement professionals support alternative policies that will lower the incidence of death, disease, crime, and addiction—four categories of harm that are supposed to be alleviated by the war on drugs but which in truth are instead made infinitely worse.

The idea of an organization made up of former drug-warriors speaking out about the excesses and abuses of current drug policies and the utter failure of the war on drugs originated with Peter Christ, a retired police captain living in New York. Peter believed that an organization modeled after Vietnam Veterans Against the War would both catch the attention of the media and ring true to many other drug-warriors who were questioning current US drug policies. Vietnam Veterans Against the War played a very significant role in ending that costly and destructive war. When they spoke their credibility was unassailable. We believed LEAP would have the same credibility if we spoke out about the horrors created by the war on drugs. However, LEAP as an organization was a long time in coming.

> ...CURRENT AND FORMER DRUG-WARRIORS WOULD BE THE BEST PEOPLE TO CARRY THE MESSAGE OF ENDING DRUG PROHIBITION TO THE PUBLIC, THE MEDIA, AND THE POLICY-MAKERS.

An Interest in Changing Policy

In 1998, Peter worked with Mark Greer, director of the drug policy reform organization Drug Sense, to create a secure email listserv, called Drug Policy Forum for Law-Enforcement Officers, restricted to current and former police officers interested in changing US drug policy. I joined Peter in that endeavor and we soon collected a group of twenty-five other police officers interested in discussing the issue. Peter convinced me early on that current and former drug-warriors would be the best people to carry the message of ending drug prohibition to the public, the media, and the policy-makers. But at that time I was absorbed with my own issues; I was a doctoral candidate in the Public Policy Ph.D. Program at the University of Massachusetts and was finding it hard to find the time necessary for that schooling. I felt I was too busy to take up the challenge of creating an organization,

and of course, there was the money problem. Where would we ever get funding to start such an organization?

Then at the beginning of 2002 that changed. A number of police officers across the country who had been speaking out individually against the war on drugs were sent letters by the Marijuana Policy Project (MPP), a Washington, DC based drug-policy reform group. The letters suggested MPP would be willing to fund any group of police starting an organization that would call for decriminalizing marijuana. Peter and I enlisted the help of three other officers who'd also received those letters; two former police officers, Howard Wooldridge in Texas and Daniel Solano in Michigan; and a currently serving police officer, John Gayder in Ontario, Canada. Together we became the founding members and directors of LEAP. We sent a reply to MPP that not only would we call for decriminalizing marijuana we would call for the legalization of all drugs. We received our funding in August, 2002, and started our speakers' bureau by the end of September. In December 2002, we were joined by Board Member Edward Ellison, a retired Detective Chief Inspector in the London Metropolitan Police Department, who had been Scotland Yard's operational head of drug task forces for all of England. In May, 2003, Walter McKay, a retired Constable from the Vancouver Police Department, became a LEAP Board Member. Then in November, 2003, our board was graced by Eleanor Schockett, a Florida Circuit Court Judge who retired as she says, "to regain my civil rights—to be able to speak out about this terrible war."

LEAP went public in July of 2002 and has grown from the five founding members to over 1,000 participants. We have 55 speakers living in 30 of the United States and in 5 other countries. All LEAP speakers are current or former drug-warriors. We also have a powerful and respected Advisory Board, made up of a former US governor, four sitting Federal District Court judges, a county sheriff, four former police chiefs (including a former commissioner of New York City Police Department), the Mayor of Vancouver, British Colombia who is retired from the Royal Canadian Mounted Police, the former Attorney General of Colombia, South America and from the United Kingdom, a former Chief Constable of Police.[28]

In the eighteen months since the birth of our speakers' bureau we have given over 550 presentations to civic, professional, religious, educational, and political organizations, as well as at many public forums. Speakers have appeared on radio and television in Australia, Canada, Central America, Europe, New Zealand, and across the United States. In the coming year we hope to elevate

> **LEAP'S ULTIMATE GOAL IS TO REDUCE THE MULTITUDE OF HARMS RESULTING FROM FIGHTING THE WAR ON DRUGS AND TO LESSEN THE INCIDENCE OF DEATH, DISEASE, CRIME, AND ADDICTION BY ULTIMATELY ENDING DRUG PROHIBITION.**

that number to 1,500 presentations. LEAP is a grassroots educational movement that gains momentum and mass with each passing day, like the preverbal snowball rolling downhill. In eighteen months our speakers' bureau increased by 1100%. Each of those 55 speakers will go out and bring aboard more members and more speakers and those speakers…etc.

We believe LEAP must educate the public, the media, and the policy-makers to the failure of current drug policy by presenting a true picture of the history, causes and effects of drug abuse, and the crimes that should be related to drug prohibition, not drug pharmacology. We do that by explaining the impact of current drug policies on police/community relations; the safety of law enforcement officers and suspects; police corruption and misconduct; as well as the financial and human costs to our society. LEAP's ultimate goal is to reduce the multitude of harms resulting from fighting the war on drugs and to lessen the incidence of death, disease, crime, and addiction by ultimately ending drug prohibition.

At first I was pessimistic about the possibility for change in US drug policy. Then we launched our speakers' bureau and I began speaking to the public. Some 250 presentations later I am very optimistic about the possibility for change. The public is ready to end drug prohibition.

Of course the legislative bodies are far behind in the process of suggesting change to our US drug policies but we shouldn't blame them too much. Politicians are seldom leaders on issues such as this. They have to get reelected in order to make any changes so before they will call for an end to the war on drugs they must be convinced they will not loose one more vote then they will gain as a result of their actions. That is why LEAP believes we must educate the public and the media. Once the politicians see they are not vulnerable to attack by voting for logical alternatives to the attitude of a war on drugs they will support those alternatives.

> **THIS IS NOT A WAR ON DRUGS, THIS IS A WAR ON PEOPLE—OUR OWN PEOPLE—OUR CHILDREN, OUR PARENTS, OURSELVES.**

The public is solidly behind us in our goals though many don't yet realize that fact. LEAP tries to confront and educate those who are supporting the drug-warriors. We don't waste much of our energy preaching to the choir. In my presentations I talk mainly with groups where the majority of participants are on the side of the drug-warriors before my arrival. After a 30 minute to an hour discussion I feel sure that around 80% of those participants agree with the goals of LEAP. There are times when 100% of them agree with us. I have had standing ovations from Rotaries, even Pachyderm Clubs after standing in front of them and declaring, "We must legalize all drugs—legalize them so we can control and regulate them and keep them out of the hands of our children." What could convince those folks of the error of our policies? It is not the fact that I am a particularly good speaker but the fact that I tell them the truth—a truth few have ever heard. After learning of the costly and destructive affects prohibition has had on our society the logic of ending drug prohibition demands the audience endorse alternative policies which are more productive. What kind of talk can elicit such a reaction for the public? Below is the text of my presentations, which includes some suggestions for constructive policy changes.

A Total and Abject Failure

The first thing I need to tell you good people is that the US policy of a "war on drugs" has been, is, and forever will be, a total and abject failure. This is not a war on drugs, this is a war on people—our own people—our children, our parents, ourselves.

I joined the New Jersey State Police in 1964 and six years later joined their narcotic bureau. I started working in narcotics at the beginning of the war on drugs. The term

> **"WE MUST LEGALIZE ALL DRUGS—LEGALIZE THEM SO WE CAN CONTROL AND REGULATE THEM AND KEEP THEM OUT OF THE HANDS OF OUR CHILDREN."**

"war on drugs" was coined and created by Richard Milhous Nixon in 1968 when he was running for president. Nixon believed a "tough on crime" platform would garner a lot of votes. As we all know now, it worked. Mr. Nixon was elected President and by 1970 he had convinced Congress to pass legislation giving massive funding to any police department willing to hire officers to fight his war on drugs. To give you an idea of how large those grants were, in 1964 we had 1,700 officers and a seven man narcotics unit. That unit had always seemed adequate for the job we needed to do. Six years later, when I was trying to join the narcotics unit we still had the same numbers. Then overnight in October 1970 we went from a seven man narcotics unit to a 76 person narcotics bureau. All paid for by federal tax dollars. That program was replicated in police departments across the country.

One-third of the 76 new detectives were designated "undercover agents." I happened to fall in that one-third and that is how I spent most of the next fourteen years of my life. After two-weeks training we hit the streets, where we were supposed to start arresting drug dealers, not an easy job for a couple of reasons.

First, in 1970 we really didn't have much of a problem with drugs. What problems we did have were basically with soft drugs, marijuana, hashish, LSD, psilocybin (mushrooms), etc. Hard drugs such as methamphetamine, cocaine, and heroin were almost unheard of back then—certainly unheard of compared to today. Drugs were more a nuisance than a threat to our society. For instance, in 1970, people were less likely to die as a result of the drug culture than from falling down the stairs in their own homes or choking to death at their own dinner tables. Second, back then neither we nor our bosses had any idea how to fight a war on drugs. Our bosses did know one thing though; they knew how to keep that federal cash-cow being milked in their personal barnyard. To accomplish that they had to make the drug war appear an absolute necessity, so early on we were encouraged to lie about most of our statistics and lie we did. Because dealers were not on most street corners or in all our schools—as they are now—we targeted our undercover officers on small friendship groups of kids in college, in high school or in-between who were "dipping and dabbing" in drugs.

We arrested people who were basically drug-users and charged them as drug-dealers. We exaggerated the amount of drugs we seized by adding in the weight any cutting agents we found to the weight of the illegal drug (so we might seize one ounce of cocaine and four pounds of lactose or milk sugar—but somewhere between the location where we'd seized it and the police laboratory it all magically became cocaine). We also the inflated the worth of seized drugs by releasing the "estimated street value" of those drugs to the media, which vastly elevated their importance. For instance, in 1971 I was buying individual ounces of cocaine for fifteen hundred dollars each but when we released the estimated street value of one ounce of cocaine to the media it was closer to $20,000. Ratchet it up just a little and the drug war would appear absolutely essential. The federal dollars would keep flowing to our departments and our bosses would be happy. Who was to question our estimates, and if they did who would they come to with their questions? Us. We could always justify it in some way.

As the war on drugs ground on we soon no longer had to lie about it getting worse. With each passing year of the war, the "drug problem" became exponentially more dreadful—an unintended effect which I believe was caused by the war itself. The war publicized and aggrandized the use and sale of drugs and peaked the interest of a large portion of the youth of our country. In many cases, the drug culture portrayed in movies and on television seemed exciting and romantic to American teenagers. Many poor young people in the centers of our larger cities looked to the drug dealer as a role model—and the only way out of the poverty and misery of the ghetto. The dealer was the one person in their communities with the hot cars, hotter women, "money to burn," and leisure time in which to burn it.

> WE ARRESTED PEOPLE WHO WERE BASICALLY DRUG-USERS AND CHARGED THEM AS DRUG-DEALERS.

In the first years the vast majority of arrests we made were for using or transporting marijuana, the drug easiest to interdict due to its sheer bulk and the fact that police officers could actually detect the odor of pot if large amounts were being carried in the trunk of a vehicle they had stopped on the highway. At that time the media equated marijuana with heroin and cocaine; the majority of the public hardly knew the difference between one drug and another. Marijuana seizures were the first drug interdictions police could count in the thousands of pounds but to the public drugs were drugs and a thousand pounds was an awful lot of drugs—this also made the drug problem appear much more important that it actually was at the time.

Unintended Consequences

There have been many unintended consequences in the war on drugs. One unintended consequence of successfully interdicting large amounts of marijuana was that it caused many marijuana dealers to switch to what were, pound for pound, less detectable and far more profitable harder drugs, such as heroin and cocaine. Even worse was that in a few short years the price of marijuana increased by 2,500%, from $160 a pound to $4,000 a pound, causing many users to switch to harder drugs as well, which were easier to hide, more plentiful and were becoming ever cheaper. The effect was that the war on drugs actually increased hard drug usage.

> THE EFFECT WAS THAT THE WAR ON DRUGS ACTUALLY INCREASED HARD DRUG USAGE.

Political motivation has always been evident in many of the drug arrests made by police. Holdovers from the "turn-on and drop-out" flower children of the late 1960s, most of whom also protested the United States' involvement in the war in Vietnam, were among the first groups we concentrated on, but we quickly included activist groups from racial and ethnic minorities, such as the Black Panthers. After all, H.R. Haldemann, Nixon's Chief of Staff, recorded in his 1969 diary entry that Nixon emphasized, "You have to face the fact that the whole problem is really the blacks. The key is to devise a system that recognizes this all while not appearing to." The system they devised was the war on drugs and for Nixon's purposes he could have hardly hoped for more.[29] The war on drugs has spawned the most racist laws seen in the United States since the 1896 "separate but equal" ruling of the Supreme Court in *Plessy v. Ferguson*.[30]

By three years into the war, we were actually arresting some real mid-level dealers of other drugs, like the members of "The Breed" motorcycle gang who were selling methamphetamine out of the Philadelphia area.

In 1977, seven years into the drug war, I kicked down a door in the Corona section of Queens, New York and seized around $350,000 and what was touted by the newspapers as "the largest shipment of Mexican brown heroin ever confiscated in the United States." We were in the newspapers over a week on that case—the heroin seizure, which is a little embarrassing to mention today, amounted to nineteen pounds. By 1979, the "drug problem" had expanded to the point where I was working on billion dollar international cocaine and heroin trafficking rings.

WE ARE NOW ARRESTING 1.6 MILLION NONVIOLENT DRUG VIOLATORS EACH YEAR—FULLY HALF OF THOSE ARRESTS ARE FOR MARIJUANA VIOLATIONS AND 80% OF THE MARIJUANA ARRESTS FOR SIMPLE POSSESSION.

I was assigned in 1982 to a deep cover investigation, living nearly two years in Boston and New York City, posing as a fugitive drug dealer wanted for murder, while tracking members of a terrorist organization that robbed banks, planted bombs in corporate headquarters, courthouses, police stations, and airplanes, and who ultimately murdered a New Jersey State Trooper. When I returned to New Jersey in 1984, I never went back to working narcotics cases and was very happy about it. This is the reason why.

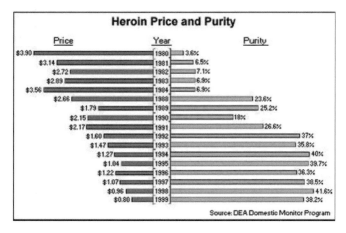

The "Heroin Price and Purity" chart was created by the federal Drug Enforcement Administration (DEA) and placed on their Internet web site in what they called the *DEA Briefing Book 2001*. The chart depicts the cost and purity of heroin—by year—from 1980 to 1999. The "price" they were talking about was the average cost for one heroin user to "get high" one time, and "purity" was the average purity of one dose of street level heroin. DEA started their chart in 1980 but I started buying heroin in 1970, so I can back this chart up ten years.

In 1970, we purchased "tre-bags" of heroin, so called because they cost $3 per bag. We bought them in multiples of two, because a heroin user needed to shoot two of these bags to get high. Two bags at $3 each, so in 1970 it cost $6 to get high. At that time the purity of the product was only about 1.5% (purity means how much of the white or brown powder contained in the small glassine envelopes was actually heroin). After ten years of fighting the "drug war," the purity had more than doubled and the cost to get high had dipped to $3.90. After thirty years of "drug war" the price to "get off" using heroin had plummeted to 80 cents because the purity of street heroin had increased by 20 times its original level, registering over 38% pure in street buys.[31]

Why are so many people overdosing on drugs today? Addicts do not consume increasingly more drugs each day until their bodies can no longer take the poison so they die. They quite often overdose because they get what is known in the trade as a "Hot-Shot." If for any reason the drug dealer is distracted while mixing the nearly pure heroin he gets from another country with the cutting agent he is using to dilute the drug before reselling it, he is left with a lumpy product. On that day, some of his clients are going to be very angry because they get the part that contains mostly cutting agent and think the dealer beat them out of their money. But another unlucky group of his clients will get the part of the mix that contains mostly pure heroin. When they cook up the powder they think is 10% heroin and it is really 80 or 90% heroin and inject it, they don't get angry, they get dead—there is no second chance for them, it is all over. That is why we are hearing of more and more cases where five, ten, even twenty people overdose in the same suburban town on the same day. That is due to a bad mix. Folks, these kids who are overdosing are somebody's children—they could be yours.

The worse the problem gets, the more police and money we throw into the mix. Local and state police were not the only ones benefiting from the influx of big bucks being offered to fight the war on drugs. The DEA had about

3,000 employees when it was created in 1973 to replace the old Bureau of Narcotics and Dangerous Drugs. By 2001, DEA had tripled its staff but its budget, the money we give it to fight a failed war, had increased to 20 times the original amount—from $75 million in 1973 to over $1.5 Billion in 2001.

Politicians told cops, "Just do your job better—arrest more people and we will pass such harsh laws (mandatory minimums and "three strikes, you're out" laws), cops will only have to deal with them once, then we'll lock them up and throw away the key and our problem will be solved." Well, lock them up we did—tripling our yearly arrest figures between 1980 and 2000. We are now arresting 1.6 million nonviolent drug violators each year—fully half of those arrests are for marijuana violations and 80% of the marijuana arrests for simple possession. I throw around a lot of numbers in this essay and numbers out of context are meaningless. How many are 1.6 million people? That number is the population of New Mexico, so just imagine that we arrest every man, woman, and child in New Mexico each year for nonviolent drug violations.

HOW CAN JOHN WALTERS SAY THIS STUDY SHOWS OUR DRUG PREVENTION EFFORTS ARE WORKING? COULD HE AND OTHER DRUG-WARRIORS POSSIBLY BE LYING TO US?

What have we accomplished with all our hard work and monetary investment? I have a photograph I cut out of the *New York Times* back on February 5, 1994. It caught my eye for several reasons. There was no accompanying article, just the picture. The picture was buried on page 23 of the newspaper, and the event portrayed occurred in the Corona section of Queens, New York, just down the street from where seventeen years earlier I had made the largest seizure ever of brown heroin—nineteen pounds. The police in this photo did a little better than I did. The caption relates, "police and federal authorities recovered 4,800 pounds of cocaine, with an estimated street value of $350 million...."

THE JOB OF ALL UNDERCOVER AGENTS IS TO BECOME THE BEST FRIEND AND CLOSEST CONFIDANT OF THE PERSONS THEY ARE TARGETED AGAINST—SO THEY CAN BETRAY THEM AND SEND THEM TO JAIL.

Nearly two and a half tons of cocaine and yet, to the *New York Times*, this didn't even rate a single article—let alone being in the paper every day for a week. "How could that be?" you might ask. How could we have degenerated to the point where the seizure of tons of cocaine hardly matters? It is because by 1994 the police were doing such a great job for us, regularly seizing tons of not just cocaine but heroin. They were seizing so much and so often that the *New York Times* apparently felt it couldn't keep up with us writing articles so they took to summarizing those multi-ton shipments.

How has the war on drugs aided our children? Has it reduced drug availability or use in our schools? When I give my public presentations, I always ask how many people know who John Walters is. Almost no one ever knows. I tell them John Walters is President George W. Bush's Drug Czar of the United States—the "Top Cop"—the one in charge of coordinating the US war on drugs. I also tell them there is no reason they should know his name since every year or so we throw out the old Czar and appoint a new one because the old one has never been capable of diminishing this country's "drug problem." However, I suggest to them, we shouldn't be too hard on the drug czars because we have given them an impossible task—we cannot arrest our way out of our drug problem. The only thing that changes from the old drug czar to the new drug czar is the new drug czar tends to lie a whole lot better than the old one. John Walters would have you believe we are winning this war. He pointed to *Monitoring the Future 2002*,[32] the largest government study ever done on the behaviors, attitudes, and values of American secondary school students, college students, and young adults, saying, "This survey confirms that our drug-prevention efforts are working...."[33] What did the report really say? The study asserted that over a ten-year period, between 1991 and 2002, marijuana use among students in all school grades across the United States increased. How

WHEN A POLICY HAS FAILED SO MISERABLY OVER SUCH A LONG PERIOD, IT IS TIME TO STOP DIGGING AND FIND ALTERNATIVE STRATEGIES.

much did it increase? Thirty percent for twelfth graders; 65% for tenth graders; and for eighth graders, an 88% increase. How can John Walters say this study shows our drug prevention efforts are working? Could he and other drug-warriors possibly be lying to us?

This same report revealed that schoolchildren across the country say it is easier for them to buy illegal drugs than it is to buy beer and cigarettes.[34] They do not say easier for them to buy marijuana, they say "easier to buy illegal drugs"—heroin, cocaine, LSD, PCP, you name it. How can that be?

The answer really isn't complicated. When I first worked undercover, I was hanging out with about 20 kids in front of a bowling alley at a strip-mall. They were not criminals. They didn't mistreat anyone, rob, or steal, and they were not drug dealers, at least not as I identify the term. In the words of one of the courageous Juvenile Court Judges that later threw out many of these types of cases, "They were not selling drugs, they were simply accommodating friends." What would happen was one night "person A" got a chance to use his parents' car so he could make the trip to New York to buy drugs for the whole group. The next night it might be "person B" or "person C" who made the trip to the city. Whoever made the run first went to all the friends, took orders for what each wanted and collected enough money from them to pay for the drugs they ordered. On returning from the city, the individual doses of drugs were handed out to those who had ordered them. No profit was made on the transactions. Most probably didn't even earn enough to pay for their gas.

Victimless and Consensual Crimes

Because I had befriended them, I could also buy drugs from them in that manner. That after all is the job of an undercover agent. It is not the romanticized work you see in the movies or on television. Every war must have a spy and in the war on drugs the spy is the undercover agent. You see, the drug culture may not involve victimless crimes but it does involve consensual crimes. Both the seller and the buyer get something they want from the transaction and neither is going to report the other party to the police. That is why it is necessary to infiltrate that world with an undercover agent who is willing to arrest any-and-all players, whether they are dealers or users. The job of all undercover agents is to become the best friend and closest confidant of the persons they are targeted against—so they can betray them and send them to jail. When they are through with each person, they are targeted against the next and the pattern repeats—friendship-betrayal-jail—over and over, hundreds of times. I caused the arrest of more than a thousand young people during my tour as an undercover officer. If you multiply that times all the police doing this job it is not hard to see how we can be arresting 1.6 million human beings every year.

I digress. Those kids in the parking lot, none of whom were 21 years old, could and did sell me any kind of illegal drugs you can name but they often came up to me and said, "Hey, Jack, we're thirsty—will you go into the liquor store and buy us some beer? We can't buy beer." They could get all the illegal drugs they wanted but couldn't buy beer. How can that be?

The answer is so simple that it has apparently never occurred to our drug czars. Beer and cigarettes are legal and the people who sell them are licensed to do that. Selling those drugs is the way they make their livelihood and they will do whatever they can to protect those licenses. I am not saying if drugs were legal that no children would be able to get drugs. Nothing works perfectly. But no illicit drug dealer is going to worry about checking your child's birth certificate to see if he or she is old enough to buy drugs. The street dealer only wants one thing—"Show me the money." Once they've seen the money it doesn't matter if the child is four years old, he or she will be given the drugs.

How much money am I talking about here? Enough money to bribe a cop, to buy off a judge, a politician, or a banker, and enough to buy whole countries. Over $400 billion each year is spent on illegal drugs—8% of the world's gross product, about the same amount as spent in the international textile trade.[35] One of the differences between the two trades is that folks in the textile industry only make a few percent profit on their investment—in the illegal drug industry nearly everything is profit. After all, what we are talking about here are simply weeds. It doesn't matter whether we are talking about marijuana from the cannabis plant, cocaine from the coca bush, or heroin from the opium poppy—all are just weeds. These weeds have zero value—until we make them illegal. Then their value becomes astronomical, nearly beyond belief. So much so that from the locations where they are grown, much of it in third-world countries such as Afghanistan and Colombia, to where they are sold in New York or Los Angeles, the increase in value can be up to 17,000%!

How would you business folks reading this like to work on a mere 17,000% increase in value of your product?

> HOW MUCH MONEY AM I TALKING ABOUT HERE? ENOUGH MONEY TO BRIBE A COP, TO BUY OFF A JUDGE, A POLITICIAN, OR A BANKER, AND ENOUGH TO BUY WHOLE COUNTRIES.

I realized long ago that when a uniformed officer arrested a robber or rapist the officer made our community safer for everyone, but when I arrested a drug pusher, I simply created a job opening for someone in a long line of people willing to take that individual's place. I would suggest to you that armies of police cannot stop drug trafficking when the profits are this immense.

Let me summarize what I have said. After three decades of fueling this war with over half-a-trillion dollars of our taxes and creating increasingly punitive policies toward drug users, what are the results? Our court system is choked with ever-increasing drug prosecutions and our quadrupled prison population has made building prisons this nation's fastest growing industry, with 2.2 million incarcerated today and another 1.6 million arrested every year for nonviolent drug violations, more per capita than any country in the world. The United States has 4.6% of the world's population and 22.5% of its prisoners[36]—in this land of freedom! Meanwhile, drug barons continue growing richer every year, terrorists make fortunes on the trade, and our citizens continue dying on the streets. The final outcome to this terrible story is, today, illicit drugs are cheaper, more potent, and easier to get than they were 33 years ago when I first started buying heroin on those streets. To me, this represents the very definition of a failed public policy. Will Rogers said, "If you find yourself in a hole, the first thing to do is stop digging." When a policy has failed so miserably over such a long period, it is time to stop digging and find alternative strategies.

This failure of US drug policy is the only thing I wish to convince you of. I am now going to make a couple suggestions that I hope will answer what I believe is your obvious question—"Is there anything that can be done to stop this scourge on our nation and the world?"

THE FIRST THING WE MUST DO IS ADMIT THAT MOST OF THE DEATH, DISEASE, CRIME, AND ADDICTION ATTRIBUTED TO DRUG USE IS ACTUALLY CAUSED BY DRUG PROHIBITION.

I believe there is. I am going to offer you a policy model I have been working on for some years. I am not presenting it to convince you of its worth so much as to open your mind to the fact that alternatives to these failed drug policies do exist. If you contact another LEAP speaker you may get an entirely different alternative policy. All LEAP requires of its speakers is that they believe the war on drugs is a failure and that the speaker support alternative policies that will lessen the incidence of death, disease, crime and addiction by ultimately ending drug prohibition. We speak to thousands of very intelligent people during our presentations and with the hope that once the public's minds are open to alternative solutions, they will think of workable policies that are much better than any we have yet considered.

This then is my suggested solution.

Alternative Drug Policy

The first thing we must do is admit that most of the death, disease, crime, and addiction attributed to drug use is actually caused by drug prohibition. Then we can stop the horrors associated with that prohibition by removing the profit motive generated within the drug culture.

IF DRUGS WERE LEGAL, WE COULD ALSO ALLEVIATE SOME OF THE MORE EGREGIOUS FORMS OF INSTITUTIONALIZED RACISM WITHIN OUR LEGAL SYSTEM.

How? We end drug prohibition! We legalize drugs!

"Ah..." I hear you saying, "But won't legalization cause everyone to use drugs? Won't we become a drugged-out zombie nation within a year?" The answer is NO! Drugs were not illegal in this country until 1914 and we seemed to get through the first 200 years without that occurring.

If we look around the world, we have many fine examples of policies we could try. Policies that show us drug use will not increase with legalization. Drugs are virtually legal in Holland because the police look the other way unless the user is causing some other kind of trouble. There you can go into a coffee shop and, *if you are an adult*, order from a menu that offers a wide variety of choices of marijuana and hashish. You make your choice, put your money on the counter and they sell you five grams of that product. You can smoke it there or put in a doggy bag and take with you—nobody cares. In Holland researchers surveyed all the tenth graders to see how many had ever tried marijuana: 28% had tried it. Then they conducted the same survey in the United States. Here, where people like me will not only arrest your sons and daughters for possessing so much as one joint but we will take away their driver's licenses, so if they live in the suburbs where there is no public transportation, they can no longer get to schools or hold gainful employment. If they reside in urban centers that have public transportation but happen to live in government-subsidized housing, we will not only throw them out of the house but their whole family will be put out of their home—and if they live with their grandparents they are also thrown out. Last year the Supreme Court of the United States ruled that this kind of massive punishment is OK. It is OK, according to them, because "We are fighting a war on drugs" and when you fight a war almost anything is acceptable.

When this punished child finally gets free from the lockup and off probation or parole and wants to go back to school to better their condition, the State tells him or her they can never again in their lifetime get a government educational grant or loan—but if they were simply a murder or a rapist the loan would be available to them.

In the US, 41% of tenth graders have used marijuana,[37] and 28% use marijuana where it is virtually legal and 41% use it where it's the devil's own weed—another paradox of the war on drugs. The researchers went to the Minister of Health in Amsterdam and asked, "How can this be?" The Minister replied, "Well, I think what we have done in Holland, is we have managed to make pot boring."[38] Young people are not as likely to act out by doing things they believe are boring. In fact, the per capita use of all drugs in the Netherlands is half or less the per capita use in the United States and their homicide rate is one quarter the per capita rate of the United States.

Jack A. Cole

Comparing Important Drug and Violence Indicators in the US and the Netherlands[39]

Social Indicator	Years	USA	Netherlands
Lifetime prevalence of marijuana use (ages 12+)	1998 vs. 1997	33%[A]	15.6%[B]
Past month prevalence of marijuana use (ages 12+)	1998 vs. 1997	5%[C]	2.5%[D]
Lifetime prevalence of heroin use (ages 12+)	1998 vs. 1997	1.1%[E]	0.3%[F]
Incarceration Rate per 100,000 population	1997 vs. 1996	645[G]	77.3[H]
Per capita spending on drug-related law enforcement	1997 vs. 1995	$81[I]	$27[J]
Homicide rate per 100,000 population	1995 vs. 1995	8[K]	1.8[L]

So what would the outcomes of drug legalization entail?

The first outcome would be that we wouldn't have to arrest 1.6 million fellow citizens every year for nonviolent drug violations.

IN BOTH SWITZERLAND AND HOLLAND HEROIN ADDICTED PEOPLE ARE TREATED BY GIVING THEM FREE HEROIN.

Not arresting those 1.6 million people would be monetarily important to every person in this country because each year our local, state, and federal government spends $69 billion to interdict drugs at our borders and beyond; to arrest the dealers and users of the 90% of those drugs that penetrate that sieve at the border; to prosecute those arrested; and to warehouse those convicted of nonviolent drug violations—many for the rest of their lives[40]—to the tune of $26,000 per person, per year, nationally. In my home state of Massachusetts this figure is even higher, totaling approximately $35,000 each.

If drugs were legal, we could also alleviate some of the more egregious forms of institutionalized racism within our legal system.

According to the 1998 Federal Household Survey:

- Whites constitute 72% of all drug users in the US

- Blacks constitute 13.5% of all drug users in the US

- But 37% of those arrested for drug violations are Black.

- Over 42% of those in federal prisons for drug violations are black.

- African-Americans comprise almost 60% of those in state prisons for drug felonies.[41]

According to US Bureau of Justice statistics:

- Of convicted defendants, 33% of whites received a prison sentence and 51% of African-Americans received prison sentences.

- In New York state prisons, nine out of ten of the 19,000 people serving mandatory sentences for drug offenses are black or Latino.

- A black male baby born today has a one-in-three chance of serving time in prison

- Disenfranchisement: Due to the fact that many state laws say no one convicted of a felony can vote and the fact that nearly all drug violations are felonies, 14% of the total voting population of black men in the US have lost their right to vote due to felony convictions—In Texas 31% have lost their voting rights.[42]

Step 2 would be to have the government produce the drugs and control them for quality, potency, and standardized measurement. This would virtually end overdoses. They don't have to happen! If we can keep those people who feel they must continue to use drugs from overdosing perhaps we can wean them off their addictions.

Step 3. This is the most important point, the one that actually removes the profit motive. Distribute free maintenance doses of drugs to any adult requesting them. This sounds radical but it isn't. We have been giving drugs to addicted people for years in what is called the methadone maintenance programs.

In both Switzerland and Holland heroin addicted people are treated by giving them free heroin. The outcomes of those policies are nothing short of amazing. Among those treated: Crime was slashed by 60%; cocaine use among addicts plummeted from 35 to 5%; unstable housing situations dropped by nearly two-thirds; homelessness fell from 12% to zero; drug-caused deaths dropped 34% between the years of 2001 and 2002,[43] and those countries now register the lowest per capita rate of AIDS and Hepatitis of any countries in Europe. Moreover, fulltime employment more than doubled to 42% of participants. Of those going back to full time employment, 22% decided to give up their addictions to heroin.

What are the outcomes of free governmental distribution?

1. No profit motive for drug distribution. (The drug market would no longer exist.)

2. No individuals selling drugs anywhere. (They couldn't make any money at it.)

3. No crimes committed to obtain drugs. (Those who still felt they must use drugs could get them free.)

4. No criminal association for drug users. (They will not have to go to criminals to obtain their drugs and will not end up in prison with violent criminals because they use them.)

5. No diseases passed by sharing needles. (AIDS and Hepatitis are terrible medical problems. In the US 50% of the new cases can be traced to intravenous-drug-users sharing needles.)

6. Users are able to stabilize their addictions. (A drug addicted person thinks of three things as soon as he or she wakes up in the morning and those thoughts are in the forefront of their thinking throughout the day: "Where do I get my fix? How do I pay for it? Am I going to get ripped off? Drug addicts are the most obvious victims of crime in our society. Who are they going to complain to if they are robbed or beaten? The police? Not likely.)

7. No shootings of dealers by other dealers. (When was the last time you heard of two Budweiser distributors shooting it out over who was going to supply this restaurant with beer? One would reach in his pocket and pull out a piece of paper and say, "I have a contract for this territory. I'll take you to court." Not so with the distributor of prohibited drugs. If you were to encroach on his territory he would reach in his other pocket, pull out a gun, and shoot you! Or he might miss you and hit some little child behind you.)

8. No kids caught in crossfire. (In Detroit, Michigan, United States of America—eleven children shot down in drug related crossfire in one year. It doesn't have to happen!)

9. No police killed fighting drug war. (This is a big one to me—three colleagues died while I was in the Narcotics Bureau.)

10. No one killed by police in the drug war. (This is also a big one to me: I will only cite two cases but I am sure you can think of similar episodes from where you live. Boston, 1999: A 78-year-old Black minister sat in an easy chair in his own living room reading his Bible, when suddenly his door was crushed down. A dozen police charged in, dressed in black from their booted feet to their helmeted heads, with ski masks over their faces, goggles over the ski masks, wearing knee pads, elbow pads, and flack jackets, carrying machineguns with laser beam type flashlights taped to their barrels, looking like storm troopers from a "Star Wars" movie. The minister ran for his life but his pursuers wrestled him to the floor in his own bedroom. After he lay face down on the floor, with his hands cuffed behind his back, and his heart stopped, the police discovered something. They discovered that they had hit the wrong apartment. New York City, May, 2003: 57 year-old Alberta Spruill, a respected participant in her church and

an employee of the city, was dressing to go to work when her apartment door was battered open by a SWAT team of NYPD Narcotics officers. Before entering, they threw in a concussion grenade because their informant had told them the occupants of the apartment were armed and dangerous. After charging in, subduing Ms. Spruill and placing her face down on the floor with her hands cuffed behind her back, those police also discovered they had hit the wrong apartment. They released her from her bindings, then finding her short of breath rushed her to a hospital. She died of a heart attack in the ambulance. There are too many WRONG houses hit! It does not need to happen!)

11. No advertisements to aggrandize or romanticize drug use. (The local drug dealer will no longer be a role model for young people trying to extricate themselves from the poverty of the slums of our cities.)

12. Nobody will solicit one more drug user for any reason! (Why should they? There is no money to be made by doing so. In fact, with this model the only way to profit from the drug culture would be as a social worker trying to help drug users stop their addictions.)

Step 4 is to take those $69 billion we save each year and redirect them in two ways. First, to programs that offer hope for the future. Over the 35 years I have worked in this field I have found that addicted people tend to have one thing in common—they have nearly no hope for the future. Give them hope and the vast majority will leave their addictions behind them. The drug use of US soldiers during and after the Vietnam War reinforces this theory. Many (perhaps the majority) of US soldiers used marijuana during the early part of the Vietnam War because they had been placed in an untenable position—one where hope for the future was close to nonexistent. When President Nixon heard about the marijuana use, he started a very strong enforcement program to track down users and force them to quit. The program was quite successful but had terrible unintended side effects—most of the US troops simply switched to the lower priced and easier concealed #4 grade heroin, which was available all over the country. That heroin was so potent that they could smoke it with tobacco or dip toothpicks in the liquid and chew them as they went about their business. Countless soldiers were thus exposed to regular use of heroin over a long period. At the end of their tours, when the soldiers expected to return to the United States, their bosses said they could not leave until they came up with clean urine. Talk about an incentive program! So they all cleaned up and returned home. Some years later the US media

Members of the Women's Organization for National Prohibition Reform pose for a photograph in 1932—courtesy of the Hagly Museum & Library, Wilmington, Delaware

bet it does! Again, we have a perfect example of a policy that did work: In 1965, 42% of the adult US population smoked tobacco, the most deadly and addictive drug known to us. Smoking tobacco kills 430,000 people in the US every year, while the use of all illicit drugs and the misuse of all prescription drugs combined kills less than 13,000 per year. After a strong drug-education policy in the early 1990s aimed at lowering tobacco use, by 1998 only 24% of the adult US population smoked. This is a policy that works and we didn't have to destroy a single life to make it work. Perhaps we should listen to some of our great thinkers in the United States as they expound on US drug policy. Albert Einstein had this to say about prohibition:

The prestige of government has undoubtedly been lowered considerably by the Prohibition law. For nothing is more destructive of respect for the government and the law of the land than passing laws which *cannot be enforced*. It is an open secret that the dangerous increase of crime in this country is closely connected with this.[45]

That was in 1921 and Einstein was talking about alcohol prohibition. There is little difference between alcohol prohibition and drug prohibition but what difference existed was better under alcohol prohibition. For instance, with alcohol prohibition we didn't arrest users, only sellers and distributors. The drive to arrest drug-users came with the Reagan Administration. So now we enforce a policy that says we have to arrest our children in order to save them.

When will we ever learn? That is all we are saying at LEAP, "Save our children—stamp out prohibition!"

lamented about the many soldiers who became addicted to heroin in Vietnam and continued their addictions after discharge from the service. Actually, only around 5% of the soldiers who were regular users of heroin in Vietnam ever returned to the drug once back in the US, and most who did return to heroin probably saw as little hope for their future here as they did in Vietnam.

Hope comes in the guise of available rehabilitation centers that offer a way out of the addictions. Two-thirds of those asking for help can't find it because we are spending so much money locking them up we don't have any left to help them end their addictions.

WE ARE THE RICHEST COUNTRY IN THE WORLD AND WE CHOOSE TO SPEND $69 BILLION EACH YEAR TO DESTROY LIVES RATHER THAN TO HELP PEOPLE PUT THEIR LIVES BACK TOGETHER.

Hope can also rise on the wings of guaranteed minimums. Minimums for: Housing; Health Care; Education; Job Training; Employment; Livable Wages. We are the richest country in the world and we choose to spend $69 billion each year to destroy lives rather than to help people put their lives back together. Give drug users hope for the future and they have less need to use drugs; less need to use drugs means less drug addicts. And isn't reducing the rate of drug addiction the reason we concocted the war on drugs?

The last half of step four is to redirect another part of those saved billions of dollars to programs that offer true education about drugs. I'm not talking about the failed policy of teaching D.A.R.E.[44] but real programs that tell the truth about drugs. Does drug education work? You

Sources

Baum, Dan. *Smoke and Mirrors: The War on Drugs and the Politics of Failure*. New York: Little, Brown and Company, 1996.

Beck, Allen J., Ph.D. and Christopher J. Mumola. US Department of Justice, Bureau of Justice Statistics. *Prisoners in 1998*. (Washington DC: US Department of Justice, Bureau of Justice Statistics, August 1999).

Brown, Justice Henry Billings. "Majority opinion in *Plessy v. Ferguson*," Desegregation and the Supreme Court , ed. Benjamin Munn Ziegler (Boston: D.C. Heath and Company, 1958) 50-51.

Levin, David J., Patrick A. Langan and Jodi M. Brown. US Department of Justice, Bureau of Justice Statistics. *State Court Sentencing of Convicted Felons, 1996*. (Washington DC: US Department of Justice, February 2000).

Lusane, Clarence *Pipe Dream Blues: Racism & the War on Drugs*, Boston: South End Press, 1991

McCoy, Alfred W. *The politics of heroin: CIA complicity in the global drug trade*, New York: Lawrenceville books, 1991.

Miller, Richard Lawrence. *Drug Warriors and Their Prey: From Police Power to Police State*. Westport, CT: Praeger Publishers, 1996.

National Household Survey on Drug Abuse: Summary Report 1998. (Rockville, M.D.: Substance Abuse and Mental Health Services Administration, 1999).

Prisoners and Jail Inmates at Midyear 1999. Bureau of Justice Statistics. (Washington DC: US Department of Justice, April 2000).

Sourcebook of Criminal Justice Statistics 1998 Bureau of Justice Statistics, (Washington DC: US Department of Justice, Bureau of Justice Statistics, August 1999)

Summary of Findings from the 1999 National Household Survey on Drug Abuse. (Rockville, M.D.: Substance Abuse and Mental Health Services Administration, August 2000).

Trebach, Arnold S. *"Can Prohibition Be Enforced in Washington?"* The Truth Seeker, Sept/Oct 1989.

Endnotes

[1] The LEAP Advisory Board is composed of the following esteemed and respected current and former members of law enforcement:

The Honorable Larry W. Campbell, Mayor of Vancouver, British Colombia and former member of the Royal Canadian Mounted Police

The Honorable Warren W. Eginton, Judge, US District Court, Bridgeport, Connecticut, USA.

The Honorable Gustavo de Greiff, former Attorney General of Colombia, and Ambassador to Mexico, Bogotá, Colombia

The Honorable Gary E. Johnson, former Governor of the State of New Mexico, USA.

The Honorable John L. Kane, Judge, US District Court, Denver, Colorado, USA.

The Honorable Whitman Knapp, Judge, US District Court, New York City, New York, USA.

Sheriff Bill Masters, Sheriff of San Miguel County, Telluride, Colorado, USA.

Dr. Joseph McNamara, former Chief of Kansas City, Missouri and San Jose, California Police Departments, USA.

Mr. Patrick V. Murphy, former Police Commissioner, New York City Police Department, USA.

Mr. Robert P. Owens, former Chief of San Fernando and Oxnard, California Police Departments, USA.

The Honorable Robert W. Sweet, Judge, US District Court, New York City, New York, USA.

Mr. Francis Wilkinson, Esq., former Chief Constable, Gwent Police Force, South Wales, UK

[2] Baum, Dan, *Smoke and Mirrors: The War on Drugs and the Politics of Failure*, New York: Little, Brown and Company, 1996, p 13.

[3] In 1896, the Supreme Court of the United States heard Plessy's case and found him guilty of sitting in the white's only car of a train traveling through Louisiana. Speaking for a seven-person majority, Justice Henry Brown wrote: "That [the Separate Car Act] does not conflict with the Thirteenth Amendment, which abolished slavery...is too clear for argument...A statute which implies merely a legal distinction between the white and colored races -- a distinction which is founded in the color of the two races, and which must always exist so long as white men are distinguished from the other race by color -- has no tendency to destroy the legal equality of the two races...The object of the [Fourteenth A]mendment was undoubtedly to enforce the absolute equality of the two races before the law, but in the nature of things it could not have been intended to abolish distinctions based upon color, or to enforce social, as distinguished from political equality, or a commingling of the two races upon terms unsatisfactory to either."

[4] DEA Chart indicates the cost to the user (Price) of getting high on heroin and the purity of the substance purchased (Purity) listed by year from 1980 through 1999.

According to a United Nations report, "US authorities reported the mean purity level of heroin to be around 6% in 1987 but about 37% in 1997, in which year levels were even reaching 60% in New York."
United Nations Office for Drug Control and Crime Prevention, Global Illicit Drug Trends 1999 (New York, NY: UNODCCP, 1999), p. 86.
With inflation, every other product has risen in price over the last 30 years but that is not so for illegal hard drugs. According to the economic law of supply and demand when a market becomes saturated with a given product the price of that product will drop as a direct correlation to the over supply.
According to a United Nations report, "Over the past decade, inflation-adjusted prices in Western Europe fell by 45% for cocaine and 60% for heroin. Comparative falls in the United States were about 50% for cocaine and 70% for heroin."
United Nations Office for Drug Control and Crime Prevention, Global Illicit Drug Trends 1999 (New York, NY: UNODCCP, 1999), p. 86.

[5] Monitoring the Future, a survey of 8th-, 10th- and 12th-graders done for the United States Department of Health and Human Services. Monitoring the Future is an ongoing study of the behaviors, attitudes, and values of American secondary school students, college students, and young adults. Each year, a total of some 50,000 8th, 10th and 12th grade students are surveyed (12th graders since 1975, and 8th and 10th graders since 1991.) In addition, annual follow-up questionnaires are mailed to a sample of each graduating class for a number of years after their initial participation. This 2002 annual survey was funded by the National Institute on Drug Abuse and tracked illicit drug use and attitudes among 44,000 students from 394 schools. http://www.monitoringthefuture.org/data/02data.html

[6] "Drug use on decline for US teens," Associated Press, Washington, December 16, 2002. http://www.jointogether.org/sa/news/summaries/reader/0%2C1854%2C555848%2C00.html

[7] Kranish, Michael, "More Students Say Schools Drug Free Yet Survey Finds Marijuana Easier To Get Than Beer" Globe Staff, August 21, 2002 , A2, Boston Globe.

[8] The international illicit drug business generates as much as $400 billion in trade annually according to the United Nations International Drug Control Program. That amounts to 8% of all international trade and is comparable to the annual turnover in textiles. Source: United Nations Office for Drug Control and Crime Prevention, Economic and Social Consequences of Drug Abuse and Illicit Trafficking (New York, NY: UNODCP, 1998), p. 3.

[9] "More than 8.75 million people are held in penal institutions throughout the world, mostly as pre-trial detainees (remand prisoners) or having been convicted and sentenced. About half of these are in the United States (1.96m), Russia (0.92m) or China (1.43m plus pre-trial detainees and prisoners in 'administrative detention')." According to the US Census Bureau, the population of the US represents 4.6% of the world's total population (291,450,886 out of a total 6,303,683,217). Walmsley, Roy, "World Prison Population List (Fourth Edition)" (London, England, UK: Home Office Research, Development and Statistics Directorate, 2003), p. 1, from the web at http://www.homeoffice.gov.uk/rds/pdfs2/r188.pdf last accessed April 29, 2003; and US Census Bureau, Population Division, from the web at http://www.census.gov/main/www/popclock.html accessed July 8, 2003.

[10] "The MTF study found that in 1999 41% of tenth grade students in the United States had used marijuana or cannabis ...." Source: Johnston, Lloyd D., Ph.D., Patrick M. O'Malley, Ph.D., and Jerald G. Bachman, Ph.D., "Monitoring The Future: National Survey Results on Drug Use, 1975-2000, Volume 1: Secondary School Students" (Bethesda, M.D.: National Institute on Drug Abuse, August 2001), p. 363. http://members.lycos.nl/medicalinfo/adolescents.html.

[11] "The Netherlands decriminalized possession and allowed small scale sales of marijuana beginning in 1976. Yet, marijuana use in Holland is half the rate of use in the USA." Source: [Center for Drug Research, "Licit and Illicit Drug Use in The Netherlands 1997" (University of Amsterdam, The Netherlands: CEDRO, 1999; Netherlands Ministry of Health, Welfare and Sport, "Drug Policy in the Netherlands: Progress Report Sept. 1997-Sept. 1999 (The Hague, The Netherlands: Ministry of Health, Welfare and Sport, Nov. 1999); US Dept. of Health and Human Services,

Substance Abuse and Mental Health Services Administration, National Household Survey on Drug Abuse 1998, 1999, and 2000 (Washington, DC: SAMHSA).
See: "Forbidden Fruit" Effect
A 1996 Washington Post article, "Marijuana Users' Air of Defiance," quoted several local students' opinions that marijuana is "cool" and that pot smokers get "respect." A National Council on Crime and Delinquency publication notes that children "are sometimes attracted to drugs because they are illegal."
Best-selling natural health author Andrew Weil, M.D., wrote in 1993, "Because drugs are so surrounded by taboos, they invite rebellious behavior....Unfortunately, our society's attempt to control drug-taking by making some substances illegal plays into the hands of rebellious children."
The Netherlands Institute of Mental Health and Addiction explains that in order to prevent alcohol and drug abuse, these substances must be "stripped of their taboo image and of the sensational and emotional tone of voice that did in fact act as an attraction."
http://www.mpp.org/adolescents.html

[12] Multiple sources A through L.
A: US Department of Health and Human Services, Substance Abuse and Mental Health Services Administration, National Household Survey on Drug Abuse: Main Findings 1998 (Washington, DC: US Department of Health and Human Services, March 2000), pp. 18, 24
B: Abraham, Manja D., Cohen, Peter D.A., van Til, Roelf-Jan, and de Winter, Marielle A.L., University of Amsterdam, Centre for Drug Research, Licit and Illicit Drug Use in the Netherlands, 1997 (Amsterdam: University of Amsterdam, September 1999), pp. 39, 45.
C: US Department of Health and Human Services, Substance Abuse and Mental Health Services Administration, National Household Survey on Drug Abuse: Main Findings 1998 (Washington, DC: US Department of Health and Human Services, March 2000), pp. 18, 24.
D: Abraham, Manja D., Cohen, Peter D.A., van Til, Roelf-Jan, and de Winter, Marielle A.L., University of Amsterdam, Centre for Drug Research, Licit and Illicit Drug Use in the Netherlands, 1997 (Amsterdam: University of Amsterdam, September 1999), pp. 39, 47.
E: US Department of Health and Human Services, Substance Abuse and Mental Health Services Administration, National Household Survey on Drug Abuse: Main Findings 1998 (Washington, DC: US Department of Health and Human Services, March 2000), pp. 24, 62.
F: Abraham, Manja D., Cohen, Peter D.A., van Til, Roelf-Jan, and de Winter, Marielle A.L., University of Amsterdam, Centre for Drug Research, Licit and Illicit Drug Use in the Netherlands, 1997 (Amsterdam: University of Amsterdam, September 1999), pp. 40, 45.
G: Bureau of Justice Statistics; Based on total US population in 1997 of 267,636,000 per the US Census Bureau.
H: According to the Dutch Bureau of Statistics, CBS Voorburg, as of September 30, 1996 the Netherlands had 11,931 prisoners with an approximate population of 15,424,122. This data was provided by a statistician at CBS Voorburg and obtained from Statistics Netherlands: Statistical Yearbook 1998, p. 434, table 53.

I: Office of National Drug Control Policy, National Drug Control Strategy, 1997: Budget Summary, Washington DC: US Government Printing Office (1997); MacCoun, R. & Reuter, P., "Interpreting Dutch Cannabis Policy: Reasoning by Analogy in the Legalization Debate," Science, 278: 47 (1997); Based on total US population in 1997 of 267,636,000 per US Census Bureau.
J: Drug-related law enforcement spending in the Netherlands in 1995 is estimated at 640 million Dutch gilders according to the Dutch Justice Department.
K: The FBI reported that the homicide rate in 1995 was 8 per 100,000 people, for a total of 21,597 homicides. (Uniform Crime Reports: Dept. of Justice Press Release, Oct. 13, 1996).
L: In both 1995 and 1996, the Netherlands recorded 273 homicides, which is a homicide rate of 1.8 persons per 100,000 inhabitants. (Registered Murders in the Netherlands, Press Release, CBS Voorburg - Statistics Netherlands, 7/14/98).

[13] "Every year drug abuse kills 14,000 Americans and costs taxpayers nearly $70 billion." Source: "A Police Chiefs Guide to the Legalization Issue," Federal Drug Enforcement Administration, http://www.dea.gov/demand/policechief.htm, June 29, 2003.

[14] Substance Abuse and Mental Health Services Administration, National Household Survey on Drug Abuse: Summary Report 1998 (Rockville, M.D.: Substance Abuse and Mental Health Services Administration, 1999), p. 13.

[15] US Department of Justice, Bureau of Justice Statistics, Sourcebook of Criminal Justice Statistics 1998 (Washington DC: US Department of Justice, Bureau of Justice Statistics, August 1999), p. 343, Table 4.10, p. 435, Table 5.48, and p. 505, Table 6.52; Beck, Allen J., Ph.D. and Mumola, Christopher J., US Department of Justice, Bureau of Justice Statistics, Prisoners in 1998 (Washington DC: US Department of Justice, Bureau of Justice Statistics, August 1999), p. 10, Table 16.

[16] Condon, Tom, Heroin Fight Needs New Approach, Hartford Courant, November 10, 2002.

[17] "The Education Issue," ReconsiDer Quarterly, Winter 2001-2002, Vol 1, No. 4, Syracuse, NY: ReconsiDer: Forum on Drug Policy, 2002, pp.30.

[18] Source: Einstein, Albert. Ideas and Opinions (based on Mein Weltbild, edited By Carl Seelig, and other sources) New translations and revisions by Sonja Bargmann, New York: Crown Publishers, 1982. p. 6. From My First Impressions of the USA (an interview for Nieuwe Rotterdamshe Courant, 1921; The interview appeared in Berliner Patageblatt on July 7, 1921.

Perceptions of Race, Class, and America's War on Drugs

Clifford Wallace Thornton

"If one doesn't understand racism—what it is—how it works—then everything else you do understand will only confuse you."—Dr. Francis Cress Welsing.

If one doesn't understand racism, white privilege, classism, terrorism, and the war on drugs—what these terms mean—how these concepts work—then everything else you do understand will only confuse you.

The war on drugs is the most fascinating subject I have ever encountered. The drug war is two degrees from almost everything. It dictates most of our international policy and all of our domestic policy. My argument is not about drug use per se; my argument is about a sound, logical, reasonable approach to the overall drug war. What a person chooses to put in their body is another argument entirely. This drug war affects almost all aspects of our lives and most people cannot even see it or choose not to see it.

> THE WAR ON DRUGS IS THE MOST FASCINATING SUBJECT I HAVE EVER ENCOUNTERED. THE DRUG WAR IS TWO DEGREES FROM ALMOST EVERYTHING. IT DICTATES MOST OF OUR INTERNATIONAL POLICY AND ALL OF OUR DOMESTIC POLICY.

In economic terms, our policy of drug prohibition has made illegal drugs worth more than gold. In health terms, we have seen AIDS and Hepatitis C spread through needle sharing, homosexual and heterosexual acts. Our educational system has perpetuated this lie to unprecedented proportions under the guise of protecting our children, white children for the most part. Despite the billions spent to prevent it, there is not a person in this country that doesn't know someone affected by illegal drugs.

Despite authorities who utter such declaratives as "drugs are bad, drugs cause crime and our children are at risk," the truth is that drugs cause crime like forks cause obesity.

The war on drugs is America's cash cow. Paraphrasing from a poem written in the 1930s about alcohol prohibition, *"prohibition doesn't prohibit worth a dime, it's filled with graft and crime, yet we seem to like it."* This is also true of drug prohibition. The strategy of drug prohibition creates the very problem that it claims to solve. The entire strategy is a hoax with the same effect as an air force which bombs its own cities instead of its enemies. The drug war has absolutely nothing to do with drugs. It's about power, control, coercion, and it's about money—plain and simple.

What can be done about it? Why are most people afraid to talk about it in the manner that it should be addressed? Are we incompetent, outright cowards or both?

The US Federal Government's *National Household Survey on Drug Abuse* is the most common set of statistics on the use of illegal drugs. According to the latest surveys, about 12.7 million US citizens used an illegal drug in the past month, and about 30-40 million have used an illegal drug in the past year. Among the 12.7 million who used an illegal drug in the past month, approximately 10 million are casual drug users and about 2.7 million are drug addicts. The figures produced by the *National Household Survey on Drug Abuse* are obtained over the phone. Therefore, they do not include those without phones and what about those who didn't answer their phones, refused to participate, or answered the questions dishonestly? Other surveys put the figures at least twice as high.

There are huge race and class discrepancies in enforcement, arrest, and incarceration for drug law violations. The drug war is well on its way to re-instituting the legal status that black Americans were saddled with in the dark days of the nation's past, that of non-persons. It is a tragic devolution, embarked upon in the name of protecting America's (mostly) white children. The truth is we will never arrest enough black kids to scare other kids away from drugs. If there were one in three white male youths in the "system" or if 13% of the white population were ineligible to vote, there would be armed insurrection in the street.

The drug war is definitely a race and class issue when it comes to legislation, enforcement and incarceration. In the 1930s, Harry Anslinger (a rabid drug policy maker) said Mexicans and Negroes would look to rape white women once intoxicated with marijuana. Later, the crack cocaine hysteria, which was viewed as mainly a black problem, produced mandatory minimum drug laws during the mid to late 1980s. Tip O'Neill was speaker of the house and an avid fan of the Boston Celtics, as were many in

Bean-Town. Boston had ruled professional basketball for many years, but was about to enter a period of decline. Boston had drafted Len Bias, a young and gifted black. An individual of his caliber comes along once in a lifetime. Unfortunately, Bias died of a cocaine poisoning/overdose just before the season started. This sent Tip O'Neill into a frenzy to enact legislation to stop the use of crack. This was the catalyst for mandatory minimums. Race and class discrimination played out here but few people recognize this.

Race and class played and still play a dominant role in legislation of laws, enforcement, arrest and incarceration, or at least that is what all the history, statistics and percentages point to. I feel very comfortable saying that when you have a social policy directed at a minority, a political minority that doesn't have the clout to force change in the political arena just by virtue of their numbers—blacks are only 12% of the population—then race and class are clearly playing a role. This is also compounded by economic and political factors.

Consider this: Connecticut has a population of 3.3 million people. Black and Latino males make up less than 6% of the population. The prison population as of 2003 was a little over 22,000 and almost 68% were black and Latino males. Almost 70% of these prisoners are there for drug related charges. These percentages are pretty constant in state after state. Race and class are the driving forces behind the enforcement of our drug laws, so how do we prove that to skeptics?

Dan Baum, in his book, *Smoke and Mirrors*, demonstrates how the race/class issue is most certainly the driving force in drug policy. In the diary of H.R. Haldeman, one of Nixon's key advisors, Baum quotes Nixon saying, "You have to face the fact that the whole problem is really the blacks. The key is to devise a system that recognizes this while not appearing to." Then, on January 17, 1971, Nixon declared the war on drugs.

Although nearly five times as many whites use illegal drugs on average as African Americans, nearly twice the number of black men and woman are being put behind bars for drug offenses. Among the charges made in *Punishment and Prejudice: Racial Disparities in the War on Drugs*, a 2001 Human Rights Watch study, is that the US war on drugs has been waged overwhelmingly against Black Americans. In the report, Human Rights Watch conducted a 37 state study of the role of race and drugs in convictions. All states that provided data were found to incarcerate African Americans at a far higher rate than whites. As American prisons approach a population of 2.3 million inmates, the highest in the world, many citizens are asking if justice is really served by locking up so many non-violent drug offenders, disproportionately from communities of color.

Nationwide, black men are sent to prison on drug charges at thirteen times the rate of white men. In at least fifteen states, black men are sent to prison at rates that go from 20 to 57 times the rate of white men. The federal government's own data shows there are twice as many whites using cocaine, both crack and powdered, than blacks.

ALTHOUGH NEARLY FIVE TIMES AS MANY WHITES USE ILLEGAL DRUGS ON AVERAGE AS AFRICAN AMERICANS, NEARLY TWICE THE NUMBER OF BLACK MEN AND WOMAN ARE BEING PUT BEHIND BARS FOR DRUG OFFENSES.

The complexity of the issue causes people to misidentify the cause of the problem as drugs, when it is truly the drug war that is the problem. Hence, earlier legislation on illegal drugs was accepted, though overt and callous, and passed with blatant racial overtones. The 1980s legislation was stealthy and coded, and with the approval of blacks who were in the legislature, passed because of shallow understanding from people of good will, which is more frustrating than absolute misunderstanding from people of ill will.

Because of legislation in the last century, the war on drugs is now the major legal mechanism for maintaining white privilege and stigmatizing people of color, especially blacks. Its effects have replaced legal segregation as the legal and social mechanism to maintain white privilege, yet most blacks can't see it, or those blacks in power don't want to see it. Racism takes the form of fear with many white people. They are not going to look at this issue because it maintains their white privilege and the illusion of protection. In their class and place, they don't see themselves as racist because they were taught to recognize racism only in individual acts of meanness by members of their group, never in invisible systems conferring unsought racial dominance on a group from birth. The risk of offending those living in profound ignorance by establishing that they are ignorant and that their belief system is built on false assumptions is not really a risk at all; it's an essential first step.

THE RISK OF OFFENDING THOSE LIVING IN PROFOUND IGNORANCE BY ESTABLISHING THAT THEY ARE IGNORANT AND THAT THEIR BELIEF SYSTEM IS BUILT ON FALSE ASSUMPTIONS IS NOT REALLY A RISK AT ALL; IT'S AN ESSENTIAL FIRST STEP.

The idea that we can tear down a metaphoric wall (drug prohibition, racism and classism) "one brick at a time" is very attractive, but nevertheless a delusion. When we agree with the "drugs are evil" premise upon which the false notion of prohibition is built, we agree with and implicitly strengthen our opponents' message. The drug war is predicated on several errors and those predicates not only can't be examined under present rules, they have never been examined historically.

Clifford Wallace Thornton

Gallup conducted one of the most expansive polls ever on race a couple of years ago, from which one can only deduce that white America is in a state of mass delusion. This poll stated that only 6% of white America viewed racism as still being a very serious problem. While larger percentages viewed racism to be somewhat of a problem, only this small share viewed it as a prominent issue.

But when twice that number—as many as 12%—said that Elvis Presley is still alive, then what can be said about the perception of white America? When one looks back to 1963, before civil rights legislation when racial discrimination was most blatant, 60% of whites said blacks were treated equally in their communities. More evidence indicates mass delusion with the *Brown vs. Board of Education* decision that in 1954 outlawed segregation in the nation's schools. By 1962, 84% of whites were convinced that blacks had equal educational opportunity, but this was well before schools actually moved to integrate their schools according to the law.

The facts don't seem to matter because whites tend to ignore them.

As long as we live in pockets of isolation we conjure up our own perceptions. These perceptions become our realities but are not necessarily the truth.

In one recent poll, 75% of whites said they have multiple close black friends. This gives the impression we are on the road to racial harmony until you realize that 75% represents 145 million people who say they have multiple close black friends, despite the fact that there only 35 million blacks in this country. So we are talking past each other, clinging desperately to our half-truths. We all are morally exhausted, while white Americans can't face the fact that racism is alive and well and black Americans, many in leadership roles, are the gatekeepers of racism.

In New York City, from 1997 to 1998, the NYPD's Street Crime Unit stopped and frisked 135,000 people, 85% people of color. Only 4500 persons were ultimately arrested and prosecuted, meaning that over 95% of those harassed were innocent. Interestingly, whites who were stopped were significantly more likely to be found with drugs or other contraband, indicating that not only was this policy of mainly racial stops and searches a biased one but it failed the test as valid crime control on its own merits as well.

One of the key reasons for this disparity is the area where police are conducting drug law enforcement. Arrests are primarily made in minority neighborhoods where drug dealing is more public and therefore arrests are easier to make. Whites are using and selling drugs in their houses, country clubs, bars or clubs, or places of work, but rarely on the street. Therefore, they are harder to arrest and are left alone.

Black politicians surely know this but do not deal with it. Black leaders and politicians are a disgrace to themselves, the community they represent at large and must be called "Uncle Toms." This is not rocket science. Those that do have a clue want to address poverty, crime and education but can't connect the dots that include the drug war for fear of losing their jobs. Blacks and whites alike have to realize that anyone who supports drug prohibition after decades of failure is directly responsible for its results.

The drug war has created a self-fulfilling prophecy. The stronger law enforcement becomes the worse the problem becomes and the more we expect the laws to work. We as a people keep electing the same people who helped create this atrocity. Carl Sagan said, "if we have been bamboozled long enough, we tend to reject any evidence of the bamboozled, we are no longer interested in finding the truth. The bamboozle has captured us. It's simply too painful to acknowledge, even to ourselves, that we have been taken. Once you give a charlatan power over you, you almost never get it back. So the old bamboozled tend to persist as new ones arise."

Do we as black people deserve what has ensued during this insane drug war? Why do we accept and tolerate it?

Insanity is doing the same thing over and over again and expecting a different result. Insanity is allowing the same people who created this mess in the first place to the table.

Insanity is the belief that the above ground economy can compete with the underground economy when illegal drugs are seven times more valuable than gold. Insanity is thinking that the war on drugs protects our children when they have unlimited access to these illegal drugs. Insanity is having more policemen in our communities who take away so many of our young and believing the community will somehow be better off. Blacks are as much of the problem as those who have enslaved us in the name of an unrealistic "drug free America." So yes, we deserve what has ensued.

Because Blacks are blinded by fear, they don't ask the basic questions. All drug policy reform begins with this question, "Are people ever going to stop using illegal drugs?" The overwhelmingly response is, "no." The next question becomes, "How do we create a society that does the least amount of harm to the people that use and secondly the least amount of harm to society as a whole?" We are acting like a dog chasing its tail. As the dog never catches its tail, we will never come to grips with the problem using the same old tactics.

WE ALL ARE MORALLY EXHAUSTED, WHILE WHITE AMERICANS CAN'T FACE THE FACT THAT RACISM IS ALIVE AND WELL AND BLACK AMERICANS, MANY IN LEADERSHIP ROLES, ARE THE GATEKEEPERS OF RACISM.

Those who are in the drug policy movement are always asking me, "Why aren't blacks up in arms over this issue and how can we get more blacks involved?" My answer is that black leaders, be they religious, political, or businessmen, are controlled by and depend upon the white establishment for their monetary existence. Most minority organizations are tied in some way to local, state or federal funding and those government organizations that fund inner city organizations forbid discussion of drug reform. "Follow the party line or face potential loss of funding" seems to be the rule.

In Cleveland, Ohio a year or so ago, a religious leader said to me, "The religious community is basically doing what the white establishment tells them to do and it is not to end the drug war. What we need is time to study this issue at length." But I ask, how much time does one need? We have had almost nine decades of drug prohibition and we have entered the fourth decade of the "war on drugs." It continues to be the most destructive force in black neighborhoods since slavery and segregation.

Another question is whether the drug policy reform movement is ready for an infusion of blacks. I would have to say no. Even though the drug policy reform movement, which is 98% white, believes we are ready for this, I have my reservations. Most people don't realize that most of us are very ethnocentric. We tend to judge people by terms set by our own culture. If we want more blacks in the movement we have to first validate issues of minority concern, such as affirmative action, education, housing, reparations and institutionalized racism. Reparations are an issue within the drug policy reform movement that reformers don't want to address because of a feared backlash by the white populace. The idea of reparations is tied to slavery in America and has been shunned by most drug policy reformers. When I speak of reparations for the drug war that word becomes ambiguous at best.

Human Rights Watch traditionally advocates reparations as part of the remedy for any serious human rights abuse. For example, under traditional human rights law and policy, we expect governments that practice or tolerate racial discrimination to acknowledge and end this human rights violation and compensate the victims.

I envision reparations for the drug war as follows: Taxes derived from the outright legalization of cannabis (Indica, Sativa, and Ruderalus) should be put back into those areas hardest hit by the drug war. Those communities are overwhelmingly communities of color. These taxes could and should be spent on the rebuilding of the infrastructure devastated by the drug war. It should be administered for a period of time no longer than the drug war has been in place. The government could accomplish this or community boards could be set up through the democratic process to administer these monies. Legalization without indemnification is insufficient to me and does not address the wrong that has been committed along race and class lines.

Reformers scramble to find words other than "reparations." This reminds me of two other words in American history that had the same impact. The first is "integration" when used in the civil rights movement and the second is "legalization" in the drug policy reform movement.

In my childhood, a gentleman visiting our house discussed integration. He explained that white and black society of that time frame viewed this word as white women and black men getting together and we should be talking about jobs, education and housing only. (Our house was a place where all sorts of issues were explored in great detail.) But integration was the word to use. This was in the early to mid-fifties.

Legalization is a word that many reformers have not embraced for a variety of excuses, and has reformers scrambling for other replacement words like regulation and control. The first excuse is "fear of rejection." The rest range from "ill-defined" to "an inappropriate message to

REFORMERS SCRAMBLE TO FIND WORDS OTHER THAN "REPARATIONS." THIS REMINDS ME OF TWO OTHER WORDS IN AMERICAN HISTORY THAT HAD THE SAME IMPACT. THE FIRST IS "INTEGRATION" WHEN USED IN THE CIVIL RIGHTS MOVEMENT AND THE SECOND IS "LEGALIZATION" IN THE DRUG POLICY REFORM MOVEMENT.

our children." I myself advocate legalization of cannabis, the medicalization of heroin, cocaine, methamphetamine and ecstasy, and decriminalization of all other illegal drugs for future debate and medicinal study.

I believe that if you do not mean what you say and say what you mean, you are doomed to be at the disposal of your opponents. I witnessed in the army that if you don't have a point man you and your company would eventually be destroyed. *Legalization of drugs means to bring under legal control.*

"American reformers need to understand that yes, the war on drugs is worse than the tolerant climate in Europe, but that tolerance came from left-wing governments and is not here to stay," said Marco Cappato, member of the European Parliament (Radicals, Italy) and coordinator of the Parliamentary activities of the International Anti-Prohibitionist League on December 5, 2003. Drug law reformers in the US should heed his message. "Stopping at tolerance is short sighted. Without legalization of some sort, being tolerant eventually gives an opening to the political opposition to attack you as soft on drugs or soft on crime. If you don't stand firm for legalization, sooner or later your are on the defensive. That is what is happening now in Italy, Holland and Spain."

Legalization explored in depth is actually a highly conservative policy in that it seeks to tremendously limit the access that our children have to these illegal drugs. Also, it will tax a $400 billion underground economy.

"Prohibition makes anything precious."—Mark Twain

There have been many horror stories about people addicted to drugs and how drugs have affected their lives. Again, this is a self-fulfilling prophecy. Let me now give the story of a person who has been addicted to drugs but in a different way, whose article further illustrates the plight of tens of thousands in Black America. This gentleman was first brought to my attention a few years ago where his writings were featured at a conference I spoke at in Canada. This man has been tragically robbed of opportunity to develop his talent, a gift, which I believe has the potential to be great. The following are his words, unedited.

Inner City Mayhem: the Lures, Causes, and Effects of Inner-City Drug Dealing Epidemic, or Government Plan?

I was born Reginald Alexander; the inner-city streets christened me "Cash." A nickname that in my younger, misguided years was flaunted and worn like a badge of honor, and one that stood testimonial to my reputation as a big money maker in the illegal drug trade. Now, years later and having been imprisoned for the past 2,603 days in a cold, drab cell, my street moniker is like an unwanted tattoo that covers my body and misrepresents my true character. One that hints of monetary success but belies the hard facts—the many interconnected tragedies that dwell underneath.

Perhaps more accurately descriptive of my years in the drug trade—even more than my moniker—are the gunshot wounds that tatter my body, or the many surgical skin grafts that were necessary to repair these wounds. These are permanent reminders of near-brushes with instant death that occurred while chasing that elusive all-American dream to become rich. A dream delusionally pursued, and encouraged by the almost indescribable lures of drug dealing; fast money, faster women, and inner-city street fame!

Foolishly, like too many of my people before me and after, I once thought it glamorous to be a drug dealer. A macabre philosophy I estimate is shared by 75% of inner-city youths and the majority of all the inner city's residents. An astronomical percentage,

yes. But unerringly reflective of the social maladies that pervades urban America. Understand that in the inner city—"the Hood" we call it—the drug dealer is more prominent than the college graduate, or the long-tenured working man. The barometer is money, and ghetto fame; the means by which either is acquired matters none. In the 'hood, it serves you better to be feared than respected, and the collective faith in any God is fast dwindling to no greater than a grown-up's faith in Santa Claus. Money has become omnipotent in place of the Supreme Being we were once taught to worship.

City officials have put up fences around the low-income housing projects, with armed security stationed at entrance and exit points. They claim it was done to keep "undesirables" out. But my people know it was done to keep us all trapped in. Hope has bowed out to desperation and, in the mad scramble to rise above poverty, my people have fallen victim to the intoxicating lures of drug dealing. It offers the quickest reprieve from nothingness, though it has been repeatedly proven that such a lifestyle will end in an early, tragic death or a lifetime behind bars.

With a bleak and fatalistic ending virtually assured, why do so many still choose to become drug dealers? What exactly is the lure and causes? Ultimately, what are the unpropagandized effects of drug dealing in the inner city? Who all share in the blame? Illicit drugs have been prevalent throughout the inner city for as long anyone can remember. Drugs and crime seem to go hand-in-hand with poverty, misery, oppression, desperation, and despair. When cocaine—particularly crack—hit the city's streets in the early 80s, like a mid-winter snowstorm, sparing no neighborhoods or class of people, it wreaked irrevocable havoc on the ghettos across the nation. The ghetto's inhabitants were easy prey for crack's euphoric high, its temporary escape from oppression and, of course, its "get rich quick" potential. Not long after crack's appearance on the scene, the inner city further deteriorated into an abysmal existence, as rival street gangs and dealers waged bloody war over the right to sell drugs on certain corners. Many young men lost their lives, and continue to die and kill over drug turf! Too many lost their freedom as a result of dealing drugs and succumbing to this insidious drug game, and today America's prisons overflow with the convicted; victims and casualties of these tumultuous times.

Yet the lure remains strong, in part because the local drug dealer who has thus far prevailed, or guilefully evaded such catastrophe has temporarily benefited from the huge demand for crack. He has become the neighborhood star! And is often praised and emulated. His luxury cars, wads of money, and perceived independence are often envied. He seems to represent what few of my people can match; financial security, and a station beyond oppression. That is a large part of the lure.

Tragedy, and painfully acquired wisdom, have changed who I am and how I think; yet I can relate to the inner-city's mindset and pulse because I've been there. My blood still stains the ground where I had lain, gunned down, crying, and praying to a God I'd abandoned. Begging Him to rescue me from the clutches of death and spare my children and wife the heartbreak of trying to survive in this unforgiving world without me.

Death did not claim me that night, but prison would a few years later. Make no mistake; prison is death too. Just very, very slow.

I must at this point say, while peer pressure and physical threats from local street gangs certainly share a small portion of the blame for luring some into dealing drugs, it is a vast media misconception that this takes place on a large scale. I suspect that the media is not thoroughly misled, rather it chooses to produce mass disinformation. Those who believe the media have little awareness of the true mechanisms that churn the wheels of inner-city illegal drug trade. Never forget that nothing motivates crime like prolonged poverty!

When discussing the lures and causes of drug dealing in the inner city, all discussions must start there! Webster's Dictionary defines poverty as "lack of money or possessions." Those of us born into poverty know that it is also a lack of hope!

Poverty breeds a feeling of inferiority that can suffocate a generation of people. Drug dealing misleadingly offers fast money and instantaneous elevation from a poverty-stricken existence. That bait—to my people—is like a hooked worm to a fish. I speak from first-hand experience, not presumption. Yet I often wish that wasn't so. I'd not hesitate to trade my grave experiences for the return of my freedom. Eight years of physical imprisonment and an everyday struggle to avoid a systemic mental shackling.

In the illegal drug trade, it has been proven, time and time again, that early death, or prison, is imminent. Still, one drive through any ghetto in America will expose you to drug dealers on every other corner.

Why? Because poverty is imprisoning too. It chokes like a hangman's noose! What would any of us not do to escape that fate?

The street creed dictates that the strong must feed, on any prey at hand. An unforgiving and dispassionate idealism, no doubt! Media disinformation campaigns accredit such idealism to my inner-city brethren. But "corporate America" ruthlessly practices the identical creed, in fact invented it.

Crack cocaine is a highly addictive drug; it has brought down politicians from lofty perches. It has turned mothers into five-dollar whores, husbands into vagabonds. No one familiar with the drug can deny its addictiveness. Yet I seriously state that the addictiveness to using crack pales in comparison to the hot addictiveness to dealing or selling the drug! I have first-hand knowledge of that type of addictiveness.

Once a person who was once penniless, hopeless, insecure, and degraded has used drug dealing as his tool to overcome that multiple psychological oppression, he will go to all extremes to prevent his return to it. Any type of freedom is a hard thing to willingly surrender. My ancestors died fighting for freedom. Prisoners have been gunned down attempting to scale razor wire fences, trying to return to freedom. Wealthy businessmen have cheated their partners, and have sometimes killed to preserve their financial freedom. So, then, although illegal and moralistically wrong, it becomes clearer why many of my people, including myself, resorted to drug dealing as a means to prosperity and maintaining it.

I've witnessed many of my people say they'd rather die young than live a long life in poverty. That message is reflected in today's music, which mirrors life. A New York rapper, DMX, says in a song: "Either let me fly or give me death / let my soul rest / take my breath / Cause if I can't fly I'm gonna die anyway / Ain't gonna' be long, I'll be gone any day."

To "fly" is to be free. Poverty imprisons him, as does lyrical censorship, and he is saying he'd rather die than remain impoverished and throttled.

Clifford Wallace Thornton

It is undeniable, the vast majority of fatalities and drug-related crimes are committed by the young, black, inner-city male. Because the system has made him the most susceptible. Go into any prison in America and you'll find the inmate population is predominantly African American. A drastic disproportionate ratio to society-at-large. Among this disproportionate amount of incarcerated black men, you'll find that an innumerable amount of them are imprisoned on drug-related offenses.

I suspect a not so unplanned phenomenon, which I explore in great detail in my full papers. It is my hope that you'll be provided with the full text at some point. But let me continue on for a short while, then I'll conclude.

From the slums of New York to the palatial estates in Hollywood, material possessions are more valued than moral virtues. This media and societal concept is what inducement turned me, Reginald Alexander, a high school honor student who dreamed of becoming a journalist and a Pulitzer prize winner, into "Cash" the drug dealer.

The media, large companies, advertisers, manufacturers and small businesses are to blame for the continued widespread dealing of drugs. Consider that many companies such as NIKE, and designers such as Tommy Hilfiger, create a lucrative line of products and apparel, and market their ads directly for the inner-city youths. They do this despite the staggering prices of their products and the reality that the inner-city family has the lowest average income of any class of people in America. You can bet that marketing staff at NIKE and these other companies are well aware of the numbers. Yet they continue to make and market $180 sneakers, and their target customer is not mainstream America. So-called mainstream Americans realize that $180 for a pair of shoes for a kid who will quickly outgrow them or wear them out, is not a sound investment. These products are aimed at inner-city drug money and help to perpetuate the continuous inner-city drug phenomenon.

I challenge you to explain away the wrongness of the thousands of neighborhood pawnshop owners, used car salesmen and proprietors, and jewelry flea market operators who specifically cater to and exploit the drug dealer, and silently encourage him to continue an ill-fated life of crime. For their business' success solely depends on the drug dealer's illegal acumen. Why else are their display cases stuffed with gaudy gold necklaces and pendants, items made for and directed at drug dealers? Who else in the ghetto will purchase fist-sized gold replicas of a .357 magnum? Or wear wrist-thick gold chains around their neck, with a gold pendant replicating a scale used to measure out cocaine?

These supposedly honorable businessmen have set up shop in the inner-city areas where they prey on the weak—me and my people!—then at night escape back to the suburbs.

All of these predatory companies and businesses have a collateral and negative effect in the inner city, and continue to play a substantial, but unblamed, role in promoting the illegal drug trade. The collective effect on the inner city and its inhabitants is monstrous! It is what fertilizes and allows for the cycle of my people's destruction to persist. Year after year. Tragedy after tragedy. Incarceration after incarceration. Death, pain, tears, regret, and on and on—nonstop!

The neighborhood that I'm from is not unlike any other poverty-ridden neighborhood in the US. It consists of worn-down houses, condemned buildings and lives. Rat and crime-infested projects, broken homes, shattered dreams, broken hearts and endless suffering. Delusion. Despair. Downright sociological misery. In every single home there's someone who has lost a loved one to this drug war, this insidious scheme. The inner-city drug dealer has been portrayed as the most despicable of the human race. But don't you believe that! We are mere pawns in a huge chess game, where the Super High devil creators and perpetrators of America's illegal drug trade continue to remain anonymous. We pawns have been sacrificed by the Kings!

A misinformed outsider may suggest that an easy alternative to poverty is to go to college and earn a degree, to improve our legitimate earning potential. To these I say: the trap is set long before we are the age to attend college. Then, too, try to comprehend that at no point in his or her life has the inner-city person been intimately exposed to a blueprint for legitimate success. While the "powers that be" make certain we are exposed to a drug dealer on every corner. Hence the fence around the projects.

Swallow this: I don't even know one college graduate—not personally!

At birth I was blessed with a mental faculty to house an impressive intellect, but in my 'hood it was useless—a non-commodity! No one advised me as to how to use it. So the 'hood beat my intellect into drug-dealing guile, then prison snatched me into its unrelenting vise.

Now what do I have? The inner city has changed my given name from Reginald to Cash. Prison erased both my street name and my moniker, and replaced them with a number. I am now inmate number 292215! The decimation of my name and of my existence is sad. Even sadder is that there are thousands and thousands of stories like mine. Some have said there are no words to describe the collective, well-disguised extermination of my people. I say there are too many words to describe it! I was allotted this time, at this forum, to try and personalize my story—my people's predicament. I've ventured, and I've tried, to scream out to you with my pen. My words are on behalf of myself and all others convicted of drug offenses and related crimes. I also speak for my brothers and sisters who are silenced, but not forgotten, in their graves.

As I conclude this message, this article of truth, I can feel the sting of tears pushing at the corner of my eyes. But I refuse to let them flow. I feel lost in coming up with a cure-all answer to my people's problems—our fight against this unseen, undisclosed juggernaut. But I do know that the answer is not tears. For like intelligence, compassion without direction is useless in this war.

By Reginald Alexander EF 292215
Georgia State Prison, Reidsville, GA 30499

P.S. The Parole Board recently denied my parole and won't reconsider again until 2007!

A colleague of mine, Mike Gray, wrote the book *Drug Crazy*. His account talks about many adventures of the police and drug dealers. The following excerpt takes place in the south side of Chicago with police and a drug dealer's car, describing the money that's being made in most cities of America.

> He checks the driver's side in front and spots a slight bulge in the carpet next to the rocker panel. It's a floor-mounted switch. Goff clicks it with his foot and the back of the rear seat falls forward. And there it is—bagged and ready for sale—seventeen pounds of powder cocaine, along with bundles of cash. Tens and twenties mostly. It takes a quarter of an hour to count it. It totals $53,000.

> Goff is impressed. "The day's receipts," he says. And a glance at De-De's ledger bears him out. The account book they found with the dope gives a glimpse of the incredible scale of the problem facing Frank Goff and his colleagues. In the first ten days of March, this mid-level deliveryman for the Gangster Disciples took in $451,000.

This is the main reason, along with the crime that ensues with drug prohibition, that economic investment in the inner city is so infrequent. Legitimate economic investment can never be more profitable than prohibition induced drug trafficking or cultivation. Hence the alternatives to this problem have to be as far-reaching and pervasive as the problem itself.

One might think, after reading the story and excerpt, that the authorities are making progress in eliminating drugs and drug dealers. But with this type of cash to be made, police accomplish only one thing. All they create is a job vacancies. Law enforcement is actually doing the job of rival drug dealers, in that they have eliminated a powerful competitor, thereby creating a vacuum that will be filled by another drug dealer immediately – and violently.

One must understand what happens with drug sweeps and arrests of drug dealers. In my birthplace of Hartford, Connecticut, drug sweeps and arrests have been going on for ages, as takes place all over the country. This is another aspect of that self-fulfilling prophecy. State and local police have joined forces to rid the city of known drug dealers and arrest people with outstanding warrants. The authorities are very good at this and get most of these people. Reformers have been saying that the police will succeed in this endeavor but what will ensue will be a record number of shooting and killings vying for drug selling turf. This always happens, but no one is accountable. This type of thinking and the people who administer such projects have to go. The authorities are part of the problem and can't see it or don't want to.

There are programs within the drug policy reform movement to address and educate minorities on the many issues of the war on drugs, which include the effects, the outcomes, and what can be done for communities of color. One of them is the forum, *Breaking the Chains,* which tours the country, with two at this writing conducted in predominately communities of color. More are planned and seem to be well received in these areas. However, the program does not explore alternatives in depth such as legalization, medicalization and decriminalization. I have explored and explained the reasons for legalization earlier in this essay.

In summation, drug prohibition has been going on for almost nine decades, yet there are more illegal drugs at cheaper prices on the streets of America that ever before. There are six and a half million people in our criminal justice system who are either on parole or probation, or in prison, jail, or half way houses. Almost two thirds of them are young black or Latino males. Almost 70% are there for drug related charges. Ten percent of the African American population is in the criminal justice system. We have spent almost a trillion dollars and are no closer to coming to grips with this problem, never mind solving it, than when prohibition began.

Economically we cannot continue with the drug war. Every state in America, except two, is in a budget crisis. At the core of this budgetary crisis are mandatory minimum drug sentencing, prison building, and law enforcement budgets.

Many of these drug offenders will be released in the coming months. Society has not prepared for their release. These prisoners are for the most part not skilled to compete in today's legitimate society, which means there are not enough jobs or training programs for these former inmates.

Their families can measure the humanitarian costs resulting from all the people in our criminal justice system, the loss of taxes in the respective communities, which lead to cuts in social programs and the inability to participate in civic life. Many of these prisoners can no longer vote. There are unending consequences that prevail with felons and eventually affect the community at large. This is the end product of that self-fulfilling prophecy.

We are just about at the end of the road. Until we decide to remove the profit motive and the race/class and white privilege issues from drug prohibition, it will only get worse.

Wake up America. Legalization, medicalization, decriminalization now, legalization, medicalization, decriminalization tomorrow, legalization medicalization, decriminalization forever.

An End to Marijuana Prohibition

Ethan A. Nadelmann

The Drive To Legalize Picks Up

Never before have so many Americans supported decriminalizing and even legalizing marijuana.

Seventy-two percent say that for simple marijuana possession, people should not be incarcerated but fined: the generally accepted definition of "decriminalization." Even more Americans support making marijuana legal for medical purposes.

Support for broader legalization ranges between 25 and 42 percent, depending on how one asks the question.

Two of every five Americans—according to a 2003 Zogby poll—say "the government should treat marijuana more or less the same way it treats alcohol: It should regulate it, control it, tax it, and only make it illegal for children."

Close to 100 million Americans—including more than half of those between the ages of 18 and 50—have tried marijuana at least once. Military and police recruiters often have no choice but to ignore past marijuana use

AL GORE, BILL BRADLEY, AND JOHN KERRY ALL SAY THEY SMOKED POT IN DAYS PAST. SO DID BILL CLINTON, WITH HIS NOTORIOUS CAVEAT.

by job seekers. The public apparently feels the same way about presidential and other political candidates. Al Gore, Bill Bradley, and John Kerry all say they smoked pot in days past. So did Bill Clinton, with his notorious caveat.

George W. Bush won't deny he did. And ever more political, business, religious, intellectual and other leaders plead guilty as well.

The debate over ending marijuana prohibition simmers just below the surface of mainstream politics, crossing ideological and partisan boundaries. Marijuana is no longer the symbol of Sixties rebellion and Seventies permissiveness, and it's not just liberals and libertarians who say it should be legal, as William F. Buckley Jr. has demonstrated better than anyone.

As director of the country's leading drug policy reform organization, the Drug Policy Alliance, I've had countless conversations with police and prosecutors, judges and politicians, and hundreds of others who quietly agree that the criminalization of marijuana is costly, foolish, and destructive. What's most needed now is principled conservative leadership. Buckley has led the way, and New Mexico's former governor, Gary Johnson, spoke out courageously while in office.

How about others?

A Systemic Overreaction

Marijuana prohibition is unique among American criminal laws. No other law is both enforced so widely and harshly and yet deemed unnecessary by such a substantial portion of the populace.

Police make about 700,000 arrests per year for marijuana offenses. That's almost the same number as are arrested each year for cocaine, heroin, methamphetamine, Ecstasy, and all other illicit drugs combined. Roughly 600,000, or 87 percent, of marijuana arrests are for nothing more than possession of small amounts.

Millions of Americans have never been arrested or convicted of any criminal offense except this. Enforcing marijuana laws costs an estimated $10-$15 billion in direct costs alone. Punishments range widely across the country, from modest fines to a few days in jail to many years in prison.

MARIJUANA PROHIBITION IS UNIQUE AMONG AMERICAN CRIMINAL LAWS. NO OTHER LAW IS BOTH ENFORCED SO WIDELY AND HARSHLY AND YET DEEMED UNNECESSARY BY SUCH A SUBSTANTIAL PORTION OF THE POPULACE.

Prosecutors often contend that no one goes to prison for simple possession—but tens, perhaps hundreds of thousands of people on probation and parole are locked up each year because their urine tested positive for marijuana or because they were picked up in possession of a joint. Alabama currently locks up people convicted three times of marijuana possession for 15 years to life. There are probably—no firm estimates exist—100,000 Americans behind bars tonight for one marijuana offense or another. And even for those who don't lose their freedom, simply being arrested can be traumatic and costly.

A parent's marijuana use can be the basis for taking away her children and putting them in foster care. Foreign-born residents of the US can be deported for a marijuana offense no matter how long they have lived in this country, no matter if their children are US citizens, and no matter how long they have been legally employed.

THE FEDERAL HIGHER EDUCATION ACT PROHIBITS STUDENT LOANS TO YOUNG PEOPLE CONVICTED OF ANY DRUG OFFENSE; ALL OTHER CRIMINAL OFFENDERS REMAIN ELIGIBLE.

More than half the states revoke or suspend driver's licenses of people arrested for marijuana possession even though they were not driving at the time of arrest.

The federal Higher Education Act prohibits student loans to young people convicted of any drug offense; all other criminal offenders remain eligible.

This is clearly an overreaction on the part of government. No drug is perfectly safe, and every psychoactive drug can be used in ways that are problematic. The federal government has spent billions of dollars on advertisements and anti-drug programs that preach the dangers of marijuana—that it's a gateway drug, and addictive in its own right, and dramatically more potent than it used to be, and responsible for all sorts of physical and social diseases as well as international terrorism.

But the government has yet to repudiate the 1988 finding of the Drug Enforcement Administration's own administrative law judge, Francis Young, who concluded after extensive testimony that "marijuana in its natural form is one of the safest therapeutically active substances known to man."

Is marijuana a gateway drug? Yes, insofar as most Americans try marijuana before they try other illicit drugs.

But no, insofar as the vast majority of Americans who have tried marijuana have never gone on to try other illegal drugs, much less get in trouble with them, and most have never even gone on to become regular or problem marijuana users.

Trying to reduce heroin addiction by preventing marijuana use, it's been said, is like trying to reduce motorcycle fatalities by cracking down on bicycle riding.

If marijuana did not exist, there's little reason to believe that there would be less drug abuse in the US; indeed, its role would most likely be filled by a more dangerous substance.

Is marijuana dramatically more potent today?

There's certainly a greater variety of high-quality marijuana available today than 30 years ago. But anyone who smoked marijuana in the 1970s and 1980s can recall smoking pot that was just as strong as anything available today.

What's more, one needs to take only a few puffs of higher-potency pot to get the desired effect, so there's less wear and tear on the lungs.

Is marijuana addictive?

Yes, it can be, in that some people use it to excess, in ways that are problematic for themselves and those around them, and find it hard to stop. But marijuana may well be the least addictive and least damaging of all commonly used psychoactive drugs, including many that are now legal.

Most people who smoke marijuana never become dependent.

FEWER THAN ONE IN FIVE PEOPLE ENTERING DRUG TREATMENT FOR MARIJUANA DO SO VOLUNTARILY. MORE THAN HALF WERE REFERRED BY THE CRIMINAL JUSTICE SYSTEM.

Withdrawal symptoms pale compared with those from other drugs.

No one has ever died from a marijuana overdose, which cannot be said of most other drugs.

Marijuana is not associated with violent behavior and only minimally with reckless sexual behavior. Even heavy marijuana smokers smoke only a fraction of what cigarette addicts smoke.

Lung cancers involving only marijuana are rare.

The government's most recent claim is that marijuana abuse accounts for more people entering treatment than any other illegal drug. That shouldn't be surprising, given that tens of millions of Americans smoke marijuana while only a few million use all other illicit drugs.

But the claim is spurious nonetheless. Few Americans who enter "treatment" for marijuana are addicted. Fewer than one in five people entering drug treatment for marijuana do so voluntarily. More than half were referred by the criminal justice system. They go because they got caught with a joint or failed a drug test at school or work (typically for having smoked marijuana days ago, not for being impaired), or because they were caught by a law-enforcement officer—and attending a marijuana "treatment" program is what's required to avoid expulsion, dismissal, or incarceration. Many traditional drug treatment programs shamelessly participate in this charade to preserve a profitable and captive client stream.

Even those who recoil at the "nanny state" telling adults what they can or cannot sell to one another often make an exception when it comes to marijuana—to "protect the kids." This is a bad joke, as any teenager will attest. The criminalization of marijuana for adults has not prevented young people from having better access to marijuana than anyone else. Even as marijuana's popularity has waxed and waned since the 1970s, one statistic has remained constant: More than 80 percent of high school students report it's easy to get. Meanwhile, the government's exaggerations and outright dishonesty easily backfire. For every teen who refrains from trying marijuana because it's illegal (for adults), another is tempted by its status as "forbidden fruit." Many respond to the lies about marijuana by disbelieving warnings about more dangerous drugs.

So much for protecting the kids by criminalizing the adults.

The Medical Dimension

The debate over medical marijuana obviously colors the broader debate over marijuana prohibition. Marijuana's medical efficacy is no longer in serious dispute.

Its use as a medicine dates back thousands of years. Pharmaceutical products containing marijuana's central ingredient, THC, are legally sold in the US, and more are emerging.

Some people find the pill form satisfactory, and others consume it in teas or baked products.

Most find smoking the easiest and most effective way to consume this unusual medicine, but non-smoking consumption methods, notably vaporizers, are emerging. Federal law still prohibits medical marijuana.

But every state ballot initiative to legalize medical marijuana has been approved, often by wide margins—in California, Washington, Oregon, Alaska, Colorado, Nevada, Maine, and Washington, D.C. State legislatures in Vermont, Hawaii, and Maryland have followed suit, and many others are now considering their own medical marijuana bills—including New York, Connecticut, Rhode Island, and Illinois. Support is often bipartisan, with Republican governors like Gary Johnson and Maryland's Bob Ehrlich taking the lead. In New York's 2002 gubernatorial campaign, the conservative candidate of the Independence party, Tom Golisano, surprised everyone by campaigning heavily on this issue.

The medical marijuana bill now before the New York legislature is backed not just by leading Republicans but even by some Conservative party leaders.

The political battleground increasingly pits the White House—first under Clinton and now Bush—against everyone else. Majorities in virtually every state in the country would vote, if given the chance, to legalize medical marijuana. Even Congress is beginning to turn; last summer [2003] about two-thirds of House Democrats and a dozen Republicans voted in favor of an amendment co-sponsored by Republican Dana Rohrabacher to prohibit federal funding of any Justice Department crackdowns on medical marijuana in the states that had legalized it. (Many more Republicans privately expressed support, but were directed to vote against.) And federal courts have imposed limits on federal aggression: first in Conant v. Walters, which now protects the First Amendment rights of doctors and patients to discuss medical marijuana, and more recently in Raich v. Ashcroft and Santa Cruz v. Ashcroft, which determined that the federal government's power to regulate interstate commerce does not provide a basis for prohibiting medical marijuana operations that are entirely local and non-commercial. (The Supreme Court let the Conant decision stand, but has yet to consider the others.)

State and local governments are increasingly involved in trying to regulate medical marijuana, notwithstanding the federal prohibition. California, Oregon, Hawaii, Alaska, Colorado, and Nevada have created confidential medical marijuana patient registries, which protect bona fide patients and caregivers from arrest or prosecution. Some municipal governments are now trying to figure out how to regulate production and distribution. In California, where dozens of medical marijuana programs now operate openly, with tacit approval by local authorities, some program directors are asking to be licensed and regulated.

MARIJUANA'S MEDICAL EFFICACY IS NO LONGER IN SERIOUS DISPUTE.

THE FEDERAL GOVERNMENT CURRENTLY PROVIDES MARIJUANA—FROM ITS OWN PRODUCTION SITE IN MISSISSIPPI—TO A FEW PATIENTS WHO YEARS AGO WERE RECOGNIZED BY THE COURTS AS BONA FIDE PATIENTS.

Many state and local authorities, including law enforcement, favor this but are intimidated by federal threats to arrest and prosecute them for violating federal law.

The drug czar and DEA spokespersons recite the mantra that "there is no such thing as medical marijuana," but the claim is so specious on its face that it clearly undermines federal credibility. The federal government currently provides marijuana—from its own production site in Mississippi—to a few patients who years ago were recognized by the courts as bona fide patients. No one wants to debate those who have used marijuana for medical purposes, be it Santa Cruz medical-marijuana hospice founder Valerie Corral or *National Review's* Richard Brookhiser. Even many federal officials quietly regret the assault on medical marijuana.

MILLIONS OF AMERICANS USE MARIJUANA NOT JUST "FOR FUN" BUT BECAUSE THEY FIND IT USEFUL FOR MANY OF THE SAME REASONS THAT PEOPLE DRINK ALCOHOL OR TAKE PHARMACEUTICAL DRUGS.

When the DEA raided Corral's hospice in September 2002, one agent was heard to say, "Maybe I'm going to think about getting another job sometime soon."

The Broader Movement

The bigger battle, of course, concerns whether marijuana prohibition will ultimately go the way of alcohol Prohibition, replaced by a variety of state and local tax and regulatory policies with modest federal involvement. Dedicated prohibitionists see medical marijuana as the first step down a slippery slope to full legalization. The voters who approved the medical-marijuana ballot initiatives (as well as the wealthy men who helped fund the campaigns) were roughly divided between those who support broader legalization and those who don't, but united in seeing the criminalization and persecution of medical marijuana patients as the most distasteful aspect of the war on marijuana. (This was a point that Buckley made forcefully in his columns about the plight of Peter McWilliams, who likely died because federal authorities effectively forbade him to use marijuana as medicine.)

The medical marijuana effort has probably aided the broader anti-prohibitionist campaign in three ways. It helped transform the face of marijuana in the media, from the stereotypical rebel with long hair and tie-dyed shirt to an ordinary middle-aged American struggling with MS or cancer or AIDS. By winning first Proposition 215, the 1996 medical-marijuana ballot initiative in California, and then a string of similar victories in other states, the nascent drug policy reform movement demonstrated that it could win in the big leagues of American politics.

And the emergence of successful models of medical marijuana control is likely to boost public confidence in the possibilities and virtue of regulating nonmedical use as well.

In this regard, the history of Dutch policy on cannabis (i.e., marijuana and hashish) is instructive. The "coffee shop" model in the Netherlands, where retail (but not wholesale) sale of cannabis is de facto legal, was not legislated into existence.

It evolved in fits and starts following the decriminalization of cannabis by Parliament in 1976, as consumers, growers, and entrepreneurs negotiated and collaborated with local police, prosecutors, and other authorities to find an acceptable middle-ground policy. "Coffee shops" now operate throughout the country, subject to local regulations. Troublesome shops are shut down, and most are well integrated into local city cultures. Cannabis is no more popular than in the US and other Western countries, notwithstanding the effective absence of criminal sanctions and controls. Parallel developments are now underway in other countries.

Like the Dutch decriminalization law in 1976, California's Prop. 215 in 1996 initiated a dialogue over how best to implement the new law. The variety of outlets that have emerged—ranging from pharmacy-like stores to medical "coffee shops" to hospices, all of which provide marijuana only to people with a patient ID card or doctor's recommendation—play a key role as the most public symbol and manifestation of this dialogue.

More such outlets will likely pop up around the country as other states legalize marijuana for medical purposes and then seek ways to regulate distribution and access.

And the question will inevitably arise: If the emerging system is successful in controlling production and distribution of marijuana for those with a medical need, can it not also expand to provide for those without medical need?

Millions of Americans use marijuana not just "for fun" but because they find it useful for many of the same reasons that people drink alcohol or take pharmaceutical drugs.

It's akin to the beer, glass of wine, or cocktail at the end of the workday, or the prescribed drug to alleviate depression or anxiety, or the sleeping pill, or the aid to sexual function and pleasure. More and more Americans are apt to describe some or all of their marijuana use as "medical" as the definition of that term evolves and broadens. Their anecdotal experiences are increasingly backed by new scientific research into marijuana's essential ingredients, the cannabinoids. Last year, a subsidiary of the *Lancet*, Britain's leading medical journal, speculated whether marijuana might soon emerge as the "aspirin of the 21st century," providing a wide array of medical benefits at low cost to diverse populations. Perhaps the expansion of the medical-control model provides the best answer—at least in the US—to the question of how best to reduce the substantial costs and harms of marijuana prohibition without inviting significant increases in real drug abuse.

It's analogous to the evolution of many pharmaceutical drugs from prescription to over-the-counter, but with stricter controls still in place.

It's also an incrementalist approach to reform that can provide both the control and the reassurance that cautious politicians and voters desire.

In 1931, with public support for alcohol Prohibition rapidly waning, President Hoover released the report of the Wickersham Commission. The report included a devastating critique of Prohibition's failures and costly consequences, but the commissioners, apparently fearful of getting out too far ahead of public opinion, opposed repeal.

Franklin P. Adams of the *New York World* neatly summed up their findings:

Prohibition is an awful flop.
We like it.
It can't stop what it's meant to stop.
We like it.
It's left a trail of graft and slime
It don't prohibit worth a dime
It's filled our land with vice and crime,
Nevertheless, we're for it.

Two years later, federal alcohol Prohibition was history.

What support there is for marijuana prohibition would likely end quickly absent the billions of dollars spent annually by federal and other governments to prop it up. All those anti-marijuana ads pretend to be about reducing drug abuse, but in fact their basic purpose is sustaining popular support for the war on marijuana. What's needed now are conservative politicians willing to say enough is enough: Tens of billions of taxpayer dollars down the drain each year. People losing their jobs, their property, and their freedom for nothing more than possessing a joint or growing a few marijuana plants. And all for what? To send a message?

To keep pretending that we're protecting our children? Alcohol Prohibition made a lot more sense than marijuana prohibition does today—and it, too, was a disaster.

Reform and Politics

Rainbow Farm and Beyond: The Green Panthers Prepare for Civil War

Cletus Nelson

Stoner Last Stand

On Friday, August 31, 2001, Grover "Tom" Crosslin shouldered a Ruger Mini-14 Assault Rifle and prepared to defend his way of life. After enduring five years of unrelenting harassment by narcotics agents and a fanatical local prosecutor, it seemed that the Midwestern hemp activist had reached the end of his rope.

Initially conceived in 1996 as a rural sanctuary for the nation's pot smokers, his 50-acre Michigan property, known to the faithful as Rainbow Farm, was facing imminent seizure under drug war asset forfeiture laws. Even worse, Crosslin and his longtime partner, 28-year-old Rolland "Rollie" Rohm, were looking at lengthy prison sentences after a recent raid on the property unearthed firearms and a marijuana cultivation operation.

Fearing the worst, the 46-year-old Crosslin spent the day giving away his possessions and setting fire to buildings and equipment lest these items fall victim to what he considered the legal theft of his property. Later that evening, it was alleged that shots were fired at a news helicopter circling the smoke-filled campground—a federal offense. Soon the roads surrounding Rainbow Farm began to fill with police and FBI. The die was cast.

Although attempts were made to initiate negotiations, by Labor Day morning, Crosslin's time was running out. As he returned back from a surreptitious trek to gather food and supplies at a neighbor's cabin, he inadvertently stumbled upon two FBI snipers monitoring the scene from behind some heavily-wooded brush. The two agents opened fire and the well-known local figure was killed instantly by a .308 round that shattered his skull. The next day, Rohm would be also be felled by police gunfire after a fire broke out in the main house.

> "ARE YOU PLANNING TO BURN US OUT LIKE THEY DID AT WACO, OR WILL YOU HAVE SNIPERS SHOOT US THROUGH WINDOWS LIKE THE WEAVERS AT RUBY RIDGE?"

The controversy surrounding the events at Rainbow Farm was largely overshadowed by the September terror bombings. Thus, few questioned what motivated two members of the marijuana counterculture to cross the line from peaceful opposition to violent resistance. Yet it is a question well worth asking. A letter Crosslin wrote in the days before his death speaks volumes about his state of mind prior to the siege. "How should we be prepared to die?" he asked provocatively. "Are you planning to burn us out like they did at Waco, or will you have snipers shoot us through windows like the Weavers at Ruby Ridge?"[1]

To Terry Mitchell, chief spokesman for the Green Panthers, a gun-toting legalization group, the tragedy at Rainbow Farm was far from surprising. "We predicted the very type of [armored] vehicle that was used," he says in reference to the LAV deployed by law enforcement to block the two men from escaping. "Eventually somebody was going to fight back. I think there will probably be more incidents like that," he adds.

War Against the Counterculture

It should come as little surprise that the first rumblings of gun-toting opposition to antiquated federal drug laws should emanate from the legions of America's embattled pot smokers. As the most visible demographic of illegal drug users, they have long borne the brunt of this well-funded campaign.

On any given day in America, a suspected marijuana offender is arrested and detained every 45 seconds. In 2002 alone, the FBI Uniform Crime Report indicates that nearly 700,000 individuals were taken into custody for marijuana-related offenses; a staggering number that far surpasses the total arrests for all violent crimes combined including murder, manslaughter, rape, robbery, and felonious assault.[2] Comprising nearly half of all drug arrests, those who posses or cultivate the illicit herb face life-threatening home invasion-type raids, jail time, asset forfeiture, loss of employment, and the very distinct possibility of spending years in a court-ordered community 12-step program.[3]

A well-orchestrated campaign by the Office of National Drug Control Policy (ONDCP) to implicate stoners as financial supporters of global terrorism indicates that the exigencies of the War on Terror will serve as yet another justification to clamp down on pot war dissidents. Indeed, the inexplicable raid of a Los Angeles dispensary of medical marijuana within weeks of the 9/11 attacks served as a less-than-subtle warning that federal officials were quite willing to endanger national security by allocating precious manpower to marijuana busts during a time of national crisis.

However, as any student of history knows, for every drastic action undertaken by the state, one can expect a swift and appropriate reaction—a countervailing show of defiance largely unimagined by those in power. In the realm of pot politics, this social phenomenon is exemplified by the Green Panthers.

An Armed Alternative

Headquartered in Cincinnati, Ohio, the Green Panthers are perhaps one of the nation's most controversial marijuana advocacy groups. These outspoken pot patriots perceive the largely one-sided "war" on pot in the most literal sense of the word. They represent the armed alternative to the many peaceful drug reform groups that checker the American landscape and have chosen to boldly move in a different direction. Indeed, they stand alone as one of the first paramilitary organizations to emerge in reaction to the prohibition of cannabis.

Although some of their detractors allege that the Panthers are either a band of gun-crazy cranks or a government-sponsored creation designed to discredit the global hemp movement, there is more to this phenomenon than meets the eye. As thousands of drug war MIAs languish in prison, the Panthers speak to a palpable outrage percolating within the movement. Indeed, Mitchell believes his organization is merely a natural evolution of earlier reform efforts. "When you are a borderline guerrilla group like the Green Panthers, there is only one way to evolve—to the armed struggle," he says. "You're not going to get people who, a month before, were blockading a prison, to start standing on street corners gathering signatures for some hopeless petition. There's no backing up."

Possessing a polite Southern drawl, a razor sharp wit, and a colorful turn of phrase, the native Texan expresses his opinions in a disarmingly pleasant tone that often belies his intense nature. Applying Orwell's dictum that political speech be as clear as a pane of glass, Mitchell is an effective propagandist and skilled journalist who rarely engages in polemics. Instead, he offers his unique insights in an understated tone that makes his alarming forecasts all the more disturbing.

Although he displays an encyclopedic knowledge of the drug war's hidden history, Mitchell's primary interest is what one might call the politics of chaos. Rejecting what he calls the "narrow focus" of the pot movement, Terry closely tracks global incidents of death-by-government, ethnic cleansing, terrorism, and religious wars. These disturbing explorations into the darker side of man's nature have left him with the firm belief that better times are behind us.

The Coming Storm

While it is tempting to liken the Panthers to other armed revolutionary groups that emerged from the nation's pot culture during the turbulent '60s, these armed insurgents have little in common with their historical predecessors. Instead of actively seeking to foment revolution through violence, their decision to arm themselves is a tactical one rooted in the belief that one day in the future they will be forced to defend themselves by force of arms. They urge fellow pot smokers to consider this option.

"Life in the United States has changed so much since 9/11 that everything must be reassessed," Mitchell observes. "We are all living under the national emergency that was declared following the attacks. This national emergency has never been rescinded, and there is no indication that it ever will be."

One might call him the dark prophet of the 21st century counterculture. In contrast to the rose-colored speculations of his fellow stoners, the Panther spokesman foresees a nightmarish future on the immediate horizon. Indeed, the former Navy serviceman and his associates remain convinced that a combination of external and internal pressures will soon send America teetering into civil war with various cultural and ethnic insurgents battling for survival—much like conditions in post-Soviet Yugoslavia.

"As racial violence spreads to small towns, martial law will spread to every corner of America, but it will be for naught," Terry explains, for, "Once paychecks for the police and military stop, the whole government mechanism will fall apart."

When this fateful day occurs, the battlefield strategist plans to be prepared. "We're the failsafe button for the whole culture," Mitchell asserts. Although the group allegedly possesses pockets of armed resistance throughout the nation, Terry is reticent to disclose how many covert partisans are carrying the Panther banner. "When a group gets 300 or more people they get raided. When we're asked nosey questions about how many members we have we just say 'those that know don't say and those that say don't know,'" he says. What are the demographics of Panther supporters? "Our group tends to attract Vietnam vets, post-Vietnam vets, Gulf War vets, and people just pissed off from being fucked over by the drug war in general."

> HOWEVER, AS ANY STUDENT OF HISTORY KNOWS, FOR EVERY DRASTIC ACTION UNDERTAKEN BY THE STATE, ONE CAN EXPECT A SWIFT AND APPROPRIATE REACTION—A COUNTERVAILING SHOW OF DEFIANCE LARGELY UNIMAGINED BY THOSE IN POWER.

A Journey to the Fringes

While many will dismiss Mitchell's ominous scenario as the product of a lively imagination and a few too many hits of the green stuff, his controversial views are the product of decades spent in the rough-and-tumble world of opposition politics. "I make no apology for having gone through a lengthy political evolution," Mitchell remarks. "In fact, that's supposedly what the founders intended; that we be able to experiment with politics until we find our political home."

Raised in a family of military veterans, Mitchell spent his entire childhood preparing to be a soldier. A native of Midland, Texas, the hometown of our current Commander-in-Chief, the future radical fondly remembers participating in the Cub Scouts, Boy Scouts, Explorers, and his high school ROTC. "I left high school a totally indoctrinated American," he recalls.

With the Vietnam War in full swing, he volunteered to serve in the Navy in 1969. The experience would prove to be a turning point in his early political development. In Basic Training, Mitchell fell under the leadership of a particularly sadistic commanding officer at a time when the limitations against the physical abuse of trainees had yet to be instituted. It was a brutal ordeal that led to the suicides of three men in his company. As his resentment grew, he began to rethink the patriotism of his youth.

A temporary assignment near Chicago to undergo training as a medical corpsman would lead to yet another life-changing event. The disillusioned sailor was given free admission to a performance of the anti-war musical "Hair"—an experience that would have a lasting impact. "I left that theater a communist. I didn't know much about it, but I knew I didn't want to get fed into the killing machine of Vietnam," Mitchell remembers. While still in the service, he began advocating against the war—a particularly dangerous practice at that time.

Undaunted, he began examining the structure of military life with a critical eye and was shocked at the injustice meted out to fellow sailors. "The abuse of women in the Navy at that time was monstrous," Mitchell states. "Many women sailors deliberately got pregnant, some by men they didn't even like, in order to escape being the sex slaves of men with higher rank." Meanwhile gay soldiers were subjected to beatings and administrative sanctions. "At Great Lakes, there was a special barracks for homosexuals awaiting discharge called the 'faggot shack,'" he remarks. "Those men felt truly betrayed by their country. They took their country at its word, that everyone was equal. Their trust and patriotism was rewarded with general discharge."

Although Terry had spent his entire life preparing for the ordeal of combat, his experiences in the Navy and subsequent disillusionment with the war in Vietnam left him with a profound sense of betrayal. However, he returned home with a clearly defined mission. "I began a search to find what politics were the most just—and hopefully a moral army," he says.

What followed was a period of political experimentation that would span the political spectrum. As a student of political theory, Mitchell's "leftist phase" would leave a lasting impression—particularly the writings of Mao. "I learned the lesson that stuck the hardest, 'political power flows from the barrel of a gun,'" Terry observes. "Whether Mao's phrase was articulated a little differently by Thomas Jefferson or others, the meaning remains the same," he adds.

Another insight he gleaned during this stage of his political life: the Watergate lesson—follow the money. As Woodward and Bernstein

HOWEVER, THE LATE 1980S SAW AN UNPRECEDENTED ESCALATION OF THE DRUG WAR WITH THE INTRODUCTION OF "HIGH-TECH MILITARY ASSETS," SURVEILLANCE EQUIPMENT, AND CRYPTO-SOVIET LEGAL MEASURES DESIGNED TO EMPOWER SNITCHES AND ALLOW THE STATE TO SEIZE ANYONE'S PROPERTY BASED UPON THE SMALLEST PRETEXT.

proved, tracking the flow of money can lead one to understand the underlying motivations and operational strategy behind government initiatives. As his political evolution continued, he would also learn from the far-right that culture and race are often key components in every conflict. This revelation would play a key role in his future worldview.

As the 1980s dawned, Terry became aware of libertarian politics and began moving in that direction. In 1985, he offered his services as a volunteer at the headquarters of the national Libertarian Party (which was then located in Houston). Although barely a decade in existence, the newly-formed third party would provide an invaluable learning experience for the dedicated activist who quickly rose to the position of Assistant National Director. However, he began to see the limitations of working outside the two-party system. "They [Republicans and Democrats] have a death grip on the electoral system in this country. The only thing a third party can do is hope and pray that one of the two major parties scoops an idea now and then," he remarks. By 1987, the seasoned activist was ready to move on.

In 1988, Terry began a two-year tenure in Washington with the National Organization for the Reform of Marijuana Laws (NORML). Initially impressed by what he calls the "NGO [non-governmental organization] approach," Mitchell started taking note of the powerful social forces arrayed against any type of reform. "While court challenges can whittle away at laws, those cases never seem to be completely settled," he observes. "Each victory faces another appeal, and the cycle is repeated over and over again. Look at Alaska, it's like an endless Moebius loop."

Green Panthers on the March

Nevertheless, it was an interesting time for a budding revolutionary to be in the nation's capital. As the gay community erupted in open warfare against perceived indifference toward the plight of AIDS patients, groundbreaking organizations like ACT-UP began utilizing highly confrontational "direct action" protest methods. Mitchell closely observed these innovative tactics. By the time he left NORML in 1990, Terry and a handful of trusted colleagues decided to strike out on their own and form a legalization organization unlike any other.

Mitchell concedes the Panthers would never have existed had marijuana prohibition not raised the probability of Waco-style raids on suspected pot offenders. However, the

WHILE THE MERE THOUGHT OF SEVERAL MICRO-NATIONS SPROUTING FROM THE CARCASS OF THE UNITED STATES SOUNDS UNTHINKABLE, THERE IS CERTAINLY NO LACK OF HISTORICAL PRECEDENT. ONE NEED ONLY EXAMINE THE RAPID DISINTEGRATION OF IMPERIAL ROME OR MORE RECENTLY, THE FALL OF THE ONCE MIGHTY SOVIET UNION FOR EXAMPLES.

late 1980s saw an unprecedented escalation of the drug war with the introduction of "high-tech military assets," surveillance equipment, and crypto-Soviet legal measures designed to empower snitches and allow the state to seize anyone's property based upon the smallest pretext. "Had things stayed on the policy level, the non-profits would have been left to fight the fight," he admits.

During the group's "direct action" phase in the early 1990s, the Panthers engaged in a whirlwind of well-orchestrated actions against perceived drug war proponents. For example, the Partnership for a Drug Free America, a consortium of advertising executives dedicated to producing highly tendentious ads decrying marijuana, found themselves under siege after a well-organized squad of protesters appeared at its Manhattan Headquarters. The Panthers would also resurface to protest a government property auction that involved the sale of assets seized by the state under the aegis of the drug war. Another action involved blockading the Merman S. Toulson prison in Jessup, Maryland. Known for its "boot camp" program for drug offenders, the demonstration brought prison activity to a screeching halt for several hours.

The organization also instituted a publication, the *Revolutionary Toker* (later renamed *Revolutionary Times*) that became a vital source in the ongoing information war between stoners and law enforcement. Gleaning insights from a variety of sources both within and outside the government, the periodical was often far ahead of the curve in predicting the use of military hardware in the enforcement of drug laws. Mitchell's discussion of the implementation of the Homelands Defense Force (HDF), penned some four years before 9/11, presciently foretold America's current imperial ambitions:

"It is obvious that the United States is a collapsing empire. As it garrisons more and more of its troops overseas in vain attempts to mold the world in its image, it must resort to stronger and stronger controls over its own population. Layers upon layers of laws enacted under the guise of controlling drug use, gun control, quelling school violence, gang suppression, and other lies, set the stage for the direct use of the military against the private citizen."[4]

The Panthers also began disseminating a "Diagram of the War on Drugs" which outlined the hierarchical structure of global prohibition efforts. Gleaned from an expensive publication catering to buyers of high-dollar defense stocks known as *Tactical Technology* and other sources, the diagram contradicts those who believe the War on Drugs is a uniquely American initiative. Instead, Panther researchers argued that the prohibition of marijuana is an international effort largely directed by the United States. While many within the reform community were skeptical of this assertion, attempts by the UN-backed International Narcotics Control Board (INCB) in 1998 to squelch public speech on the Internet pertaining to "discussions of the merits of alternatives to prohibition" seem to lend credence to this theory.[5]

However, by the mid-1990s, Mitchell and his associates were unconvinced they were making any headway. As the group states on its web page, "It didn't take long before we realized that just like the letters and petitions, our direct action and protests were having less and less effect—our enemy was learning to counter our ideas quickly. Buyers' Clubs across the country were being shut down—activists and patients arrested. Nothing was changing for the better."[6]

UNLIKE PRIOR BATTLES IN WHICH COMBAT WAS LARGELY INITIATED, CONTROLLED, AND DIRECTED BY GOVERNMENT OFFICIALS, THIS DECENTRALIZED FORM OF WAR WILL INVOLVE CIVILIAN-SOLDIERS.

Stoner Homeland

The Panthers then began to adopt a more radical perspective. As ethnic cleansing swept through the former Yugoslavia, and nationalist and religionist insurgents began to lay claim to various Soviet bloc nations, they started closely examining the internal dynamics of the US. As they watched the growth of separatist movements such as the Republic of Texas, Nation of Islam, Aztlan, and other groups vying for a slice of America, the organization then came upon what Mitchell called its "endgame strategy": secession.

By the late 1990s, the Panthers were convinced that the future survival of the counterculture rested in the creation of a separatist "Stoner Homeland." After extensive research, Mitchell and his colleagues determined that the highest percentage of both Libertarians and pot smokers resided in a strip of land along the Pacific Coast between San Francisco and Portland, Oregon.

Represented by a white flag bearing a large green marijuana leaf, a set of by-laws was drawn up for the new prospective country based on a compendium of landmark documents such as the US Constitution, Articles of Confederation, and Iroquois Confederacy. "Some of the best forward thinking minds came up with the by-laws," Mitchell says. Each "Autonomous Area" in the Homeland would provide a "Home Guard" of cannabis commandos prepared to repel any attempts at dislodging the new settlers from their hard-fought territory.

However, Mitchell's dreams of a Stoner Homeland have since been dashed. "The movement can't stay focused," he says. "If you look globally, pot heads can co-exist within other cultures but they're not a stand alone culture," he says. This is not to say that he doesn't consider the possibility of a new nation emerging within the former US that will allow the use and cultivation of marijuana. "If pot heads are lucky, one of the new emerging nations will have an open drug policy," he says.

Thinking the Unthinkable

While the mere thought of several micro-nations sprouting from the carcass of the United States sounds unthinkable, there is certainly no lack of historical precedent. One need only examine the rapid disintegration of Imperial Rome or more recently, the fall of the once mighty Soviet Union for examples. In both instances, these once mighty superpowers were torn apart by internal corruption, political infighting, and expansive imperial ambitions.

Terry's views can find validation in the writings of renowned military analyst William Lind. The former Congressional Aide and military scholar believes future military engagements will be waged in accordance with what he calls "Fourth Generation Warfare." Unlike prior battles in which combat was largely initiated, controlled, and directed by government officials, this decentralized form of war will involve civilian-soldiers. As Lind observes, "Many different entities, not just government or states will wage war. They will wage war for many different reasons, not just 'the extension of politics by other means.'"[7]

According to Lind, culture and/or ethnicity will provide the motivation for tomorrow's Fourth Generation Warriors. However, the preconditions for the growth of these insurgent forces are the irrelevancy of the state and existing tensions between divergent political, racial, and sociological groups. Lind believes that America's notoriously corrupt political system and simmering racial tensions leave it open to exploitation by fourth Generation Forces.

Terry is quick to point out that Lind's academic theories which are taught at respectable military academies are not dissimilar from his own. Indeed, Mitchell believes the 9/11 attacks will only escalate America's final collapse. As a preemptive measure, the Panthers have since gone "underground." Within weeks of the terrorist strikes, the organization pulled its web page off-line, ceased publication of *Revolutionary Times*, and suspended all activities within the pot movement. They urge fellow members of the counterculture to consider a similar strategy.

"Rule number one for the foreseeable future: Stay out of jail," Mitchell advises. "You have a choice to either participate in the coming revolution—to have a say in what sort of world lies on the other side—or to watch helplessly through the bars of a jail cell. Stay out of jail and be ready to relocate at any time. If you're not going to fight, you should at least be able to run."

Endnotes

[1] Peter Carlson, "Was Rainbow Farm Another Waco?" *Washington Post* (January 27, 2002).

[2] NORML News Release, "Pot Smokers Arrested in America at Rate of One Every 45 Seconds," October 28, 2003.

[3] Stanton Peele, Charles Bufe, Archie Brodsky, "Resisting 12-Step Coercion" (Tucson, AZ: See Sharp Press, 2000). This revealing book indicates that every year over 1 million Americans are coerced into some type of 12-step treatment by courts, employers, schools and other institutions. Since drug use is considered illegal, even the most casual pot smoker faces the prospect of being "automatically labeled an abuser or addict" and forced into treatment.

[4] Terry Mitchell, "The Homelands Defense Force: Government Preparing for Civil War," *Revolutionary Times* (Winter, 1999).

[5] Richard Cowen, "Freedom Has Nothing to Fear From the Truth," *MarijuanaNews* (March 21, 1998). See: http://www.marijuananews.com/

[6] "Gone Underground, You Should Too," GP website See: http://www.discgolfthenw.net/tm/

[7] William Lind, "Understanding Fourth Generation Warfare," On War #47 See: http://www.freecongress.org/

A War on Sanity

Paul Campos

The government doesn't even want you to have the right to protest its stupid war on drugs.

December is the season for giving, and no one gives more generous gifts than the US Congress. Of course, Congress has the advantage of doing its last-minute holiday shopping at someone else's expense, namely yours and mine.

For example, on December 8, 2003 the House of Representatives passed a bill that gives the White House drug czar's office $145,000,000 of taxpayer money to run anti-marijuana propaganda ads. My personal favorite in this genre is a television ad in which police rough up a high school student when arresting him in the school's marijuana-smoke-filled bathroom. This is followed by a caption reading, "Marijuana: Harmless? Think again." (And no, I did not make that up).

Yet this bill contains something far more obnoxious than pots of money for another round of clueless anti-marijuana propaganda. A section of the bill prohibits any local transit system that receives federal funding from running privately funded ads that call for marijuana policy reform.

In other words, at the same time that the federal government is forcing you to spend your money to publicize its willingness to engage in storm trooper tactics to persecute the tens of millions Americans who smoke or have smoked marijuana, it is trying to prohibit you from having the freedom to spend your money to protest these same tactics.

If this bill becomes law, it will be illegal for the average American to buy advertising space on a city bus or in a subway station, advocating that doctors be given the right to prescribe marijuana as a painkiller for their terminally ill patients.

Two words that are thrown around far too loosely in political debate are "fascism" and "unconstitutional." Nevertheless, this sort of thing has a distinctly fascist tinge. And if the First Amendment means anything, it ought to mean that the government cannot take away the right of citizens to engage in public political protest.

Anyone who has doubts that the drug war is wrong ought to consider what it tells us when our federal government tries to make it illegal to protest that war. Fence sitters might also want to view the video from the surveillance tape at a Goose Creek, S.C., high school, which on November 5, 2003 was raided by police looking for drugs. (A photo from the tape can be viewed at www.mpp.org).

> ANYONE WHO HAS DOUBTS THAT THE DRUG WAR IS WRONG OUGHT TO CONSIDER WHAT IT TELLS US WHEN OUR FEDERAL GOVERNMENT TRIES TO MAKE IT ILLEGAL TO PROTEST THAT WAR.

After an extensive search, the police found no drugs, but they did terrorize more than 100 students (two-thirds of whom were black, even though less than 25% of the school's student body is black). With guns pointed at their heads, students were handcuffed and forced to lie on the floor, or to kneel with their faces to the wall.

One student said he assumed the police "were trying to protect us, that it was like Columbine, that somebody got in the school that was crazy or dangerous. But then a police officer pointed a gun at me. It was really scary."

> WITH GUNS POINTED AT THEIR HEADS, STUDENTS WERE HANDCUFFED AND FORCED TO LIE ON THE FLOOR, OR TO KNEEL WITH THEIR FACES TO THE WALL.

What's really scary is that incidents such as this seem to stir so little outrage. What level of government persecution will put a dent in public apathy about the madness that is the war on drugs?

If the police at the Goose Creek high school had inadvertently shot a student or two in their zealous search for marijuana cigarettes, would that be enough to distract people from holiday shopping and channel surfing? Or would such an incident be shrugged off as another regrettable accident of the sort that is inevitable in wartime? Take a look at that photograph, and consider: This is your government on drugs.

Marijuana Will Never Be Legal as Long as Most Pot-Smokers Are Apathetic Airheads

Steven Wishnia

It was only one of the 735,000 pot busts in the United States in 2000, one of 66 that afternoon on Boston Common. The handcuffed kid, a scrawny, stringy-haired youth of about 17, struggled to walk down the hill, hustled and shoved by the undercover cop who'd caught him puffing a joint. A crowd of about 50 angry protesters followed, chanting "ass-hole, ass-hole" in singsong, like Fenway Park fans heckling a Yankee beanball pitcher, and throwing plastic bottles at the cop, a balding, beefy white guy unconvincingly disguised in a Baja surfer hoodie with a yellow headshop sticker over his gut. Police reinforcements rushed up to fend them off, and the kid was locked up in the makeshift holding tank at the edge of the park, along with the rest of the day's prisoners.

What is telling is what happened next, when two young men accosted a marijuana-magazine reporter. Did they want to know what the confrontation was about? This, after all, was the annual Boston Freedom Rally, the second-largest pot-legalization demonstration in the country. No. They wanted to find out "where anyone's selling any glass pieces, man?"

The laws against marijuana probably have less rational justification than any ordinance on the books, except for the recently invalidated sodomy proscriptions. Yet it is unlikely that pot will be legalized in the near future, despite recent gains on issues like medical use. Much of the blame for this has to be put on pot-smokers. When it comes to working to legalize marijuana, the vast majority of stoners live up to the apathetic-airhead stereotype. They are proud to defy the law by lighting up, but do absolutely nothing to change it.

> THE LAWS AGAINST MARIJUANA PROBABLY HAVE LESS RATIONAL JUSTIFICATION THAN ANY ORDINANCE ON THE BOOKS, EXCEPT FOR THE RECENTLY INVALIDATED SODOMY PROSCRIPTIONS.

This is amazing, considering how flimsy the most common arguments for marijuana prohibition are. One is the "gateway theory," the idea that marijuana leads to hard drugs. Second is the claim that the trees of today are so much more potent than the grass of Haight-Ashbury and the weed of Woodstock that it's essentially a different and deadly drug. And when all else fails, prohibitionists preach that "we have to send the right message to the children."

None of these arguments stand up to reality. The gateway theory—"marijuana users are 85 times as likely to become drug addicts as non-users"—is a half-truth; the overwhelming majority of heroin and cocaine addicts tried pot first, but the overwhelming majority of pot-smokers don't go on to other drugs. Similar claims about potheads in treatment and emergency-room visits are also the product of statistical misrepresentations; while there are people with genuine smoking problems, most of the ones in rehab for marijuana have been forced into it by an arrest or failed drug test.

The potency argument is also a half-truth. The supply of top-quality ganja has certainly become more consistent over the past 30 years, but there was spectacular stuff around in the 1960s too, and much of the country is still smoking commercial Mexican. In any case, it's as ridiculous as arguing that alcohol should be outlawed because cognac is more than ten times as potent as Coors Light. The main purpose of this argument is to cover the asses of baby-boomer politicians and parents who inhaled a bit in their time and don't want to look hypocritical.

As for "sending a message to the children," why should adults go to jail to prevent teenagers from using drugs? Aren't adults capable of telling their children, "I can drink, but you're not old enough"? This line is especially ridiculous when used to justify banning medical marijuana. How many people do heroin because their parents had a prescription for codeine?

If you ask prohibitionists why pot shouldn't be legal and regulated like alcohol—only sold to adults, only smoked in certain public places, driving while intoxicated banned, and limited home cultivation allowed—they'll usually spew that "legalizing drugs" means selling methamphetamine to eight-year-olds. If you ask them to make a sober comparison between marijuana and alcohol, or between marijuana and other drugs, they'll avoid a straight answer. In their 1996 book, *Body Count*, Bush II drug czar John Walters and his mentor, Bush I drug czar William Bennett, respond to the argument that few pot-smokers go on to heroin with a non sequitur about how most heroin users are addicts.

And if you ask prohibitionists point-blank why people should go to jail for smoking marijuana—the crux of the issue—they're reluctant to defend it. "I don't know enough to give you a subjective answer," House drug-policy subcommittee chair John Mica told me in 1998. The usual dodge—Mica had just delivered a version to his subcommittee, and I've also heard it from local prosecutors and a top Christian-right antidrug officials—that "nobody really goes to jail for marijuana possession," but "there has to be some sanction." (That no one goes to jail for herb would be news to the more than 600,000 people arrested for possession each year, or to the 200,000-odd New Yorkers who spent a night or a weekend in jail during former mayor Rudolph Giuliani's crackdown on pot-smokers.)

I believe the real reasons for pot prohibition have more to do with culture war and a kind of existential fascism, though you probably wouldn't get anyone other than William Bennett to make those arguments in public. (How much do you want to bet?) Marijuana prohibition's culture-war roots go deep into history, from the "black jazz musicians are going to seduce your daughter with the unholy pleasure of their enormous reefers" scare campaign of the '30s to the anti-hippie crusade of the Nixon era. These days, it's an excuse to lock up the unruly young, the unconventional, and the dark-skinned. Giuliani, considered by some to be the architect of the Reagan drug war during his tenure in the Justice Department, used it for ethnic cleansing in New York City: Of the 70,000 people a year arrested for pot—mainly for smoking in public—at the height of the Duce of Gotham's crackdown, 80% were black or Latino.

The "existential fascism" argument is that laws against mild vices or otherwise harmless behavior provide an easy filter for weeding out the defiant and disobedient. It's essentially the "broken-window theory" gone wild—if you grab 20 people for breaking small rules, no matter how arbitrary, you'll catch one who'll break the big ones, and you'll discourage others from stepping out of line. As such, it has very little to do with any actual harm caused by marijuana. It's the equivalent of the government passing a law against women dyeing their hair, based on the belief that all bleached blondes are sluts and that letting people break the law for such frivolous vanity would "send a message" that you can get away with any kind of immorality.

I suspect that this is the reason for the Bush junta's jihad against marijuana. Virtually all pot-smokers believe that they are defying a ridiculous and unjust law that doesn't deserve a roach of respect. Glass-pipe manufacturers, another Bush target, believe that they are selling functional and pleasurable works of art, not the equivalent of crack vials. (On the other hand, people who'll spend $350 on a bong but won't give $35 to NORML are part of the problem.) Medical-cannabis providers devoutly believe that they are not criminals, that they are performing a public service permitted by state law. Thus, they are all the moral equivalent of sociopaths and must be crushed mercilessly.

"I wish they'd legalize marijuana so we could get on to the really difficult drug problems," a Canadian drug-policy activist told me in the spring of 2003.

As feeble as the arguments for continuing marijuana prohibition are, the organized opposition to it is politically weak. There is only one current national-level elected official—senator, House member, governor, or big-city mayor—who has come out for legalizing marijuana under regulations similar to alcohol: Rep. Dennis Kucinich of Ohio, as a long shot candidate for the 2004 Democratic presidential nomination. In the past 20 years, there have been maybe three other politicians of any significance who endorsed legalization: former New Mexico governor Gary Johnson, former Baltimore mayor Kurt Schmoke, and former Congressmember Dan Hamburg, who represented California's sinsemilla belt in the early 1990s. Even the outspoken and acerbic Rep. Barney Frank, who has addressed NORML conferences and sponsored medical-marijuana legislation, has not publicly committed himself to anything stronger than decriminalization.

Why is this? For politicians, coming out for legalizing pot could get them as much flak as a gay Red Sox outfielder would get from the bleacher creatures at Yankee Stadium. If they weren't hammered as "soft on drugs," with their opponents preparing attack ads that scream "Senator Stonewell WANTS TO LET DRUG DEALERS OUT OF JAIL," they'd be ridiculed as spaced-out clowns, with cartoons depicting them floating several inches off the ground, a loopy grin on their face as their campaign-headquarters phone crackles, "That'll be 420 large mushroom pizzas and 100,000 Twinkies?"

> I BELIEVE THE REAL REASONS FOR POT PROHIBITION HAVE MORE TO DO WITH CULTURE WAR AND A KIND OF EXISTENTIAL FASCISM

> MARIJUANA PROHIBITION'S CULTURE-WAR ROOTS GO DEEP INTO HISTORY, FROM THE "BLACK JAZZ MUSICIANS ARE GOING TO SEDUCE YOUR DAUGHTER WITH THE UNHOLY PLEASURE OF THEIR ENORMOUS REEFERS" SCARE CAMPAIGN OF THE '30S TO THE ANTI-HIPPIE CRUSADE OF THE NIXON ERA.

> [IN THE EYES OF THE PROHIBITIONISTS] THEY ARE ALL THE MORAL EQUIVALENT OF SOCIOPATHS AND MUST BE CRUSHED MERCILESSLY.

> ...THE HYPOCRISY OF SECONDARY-VIRGIN PROHIBITIONISTS IS REPULSIVE.

Steven Wishnia

It's no wonder that in a time where virtually every American under 55 grew up around people who smoked pot, the only acceptable discourse for politicians who got high when they were younger is "I experimented with it, and I didn't like it." Still, the hypocrisy of secondary-virgin prohibitionists is repulsive. Bill Clinton, who allegedly enjoyed hash brownies—*didn't inhale*—as a young man, tried to get California doctors' licenses revoked for recommending medical marijuana. Clarence Thomas wrote the Supreme Court decision against allowing medical use of marijuana. Former House Speaker Newt Gingrich advocated the death penalty for pot smuggling. New York governor George Pataki proposed tougher penalties for selling herb (while ostensibly "reforming" the state's draconian Rockefeller drug laws). Most of all, convicted drunk driver George W. Bush, who has consistently ducked questions about his past use of cocaine, has made medical marijuana a top federal law-enforcement priority.

By that standard, Gary Johnson is the only honest pothead-turned-politician in the nation. "I didn't experiment with marijuana—I smoked it," he repeatedly declared. Johnson now is sober to the point of being puritanical, but he still got ridiculed for his eminently reasonable statements about pot. If you drink in a bar, Johnson contended, you're not committing a crime. If you drink too much, he'd continue, it's still legal. But the minute you go out to the parking lot and put your key in the ignition, then you've crossed the line. "Why shouldn't it be the same with marijuana?" he'd ask.

Another reason for the lack of political support is the general failure of American liberalism over the last 25 years. The far right is willing to advocate positions consistent with its principles, no matter how extreme, from abolishing the minimum wage to eliminating environmental regulations. Liberals are not. They are afraid of being tarred as futile losers, stoned-out socialists who'd give our children to Saddam Hussein as sex slaves. They have failed to shout against the Republican right's cancerous redistribution of wealth to the rich, its belief that outlawing gay sex is the government's job but regulating occupational safety is none of its business. They have also failed to say, "Why should the government arrest people for pot? Why shouldn't it be available like alcohol?" Most liberals will discreetly support decriminalization, realizing that the current laws are destructive and inhumane, but mouth the "there has to be some sanction" line, trying to avoid the soft-on-drugs stigma.

There is something to be said for not blowing your resources on hopeless causes, for not going out on a half-grown limb—Barney Frank, for instance, is relentlessly pragmatic—but ultimately, timid, piecemeal challenges to prohibition avoid the basic issue. If pot is not as evil as the

prohibitionists say it is, and prohibition does more harm than good, then people should be able to get it without having to go to or become felons. Mere decriminalization of pot possession would actually leave the laws stricter than alcohol Prohibition, which allowed possession of alcohol, medical use, and personal-quantity home-brewing.

Most politicians would change their ways if they were facing a strong grass-roots movement for legalization, and this is where pot-smokers' lack of political involvement does the most damage. As Malcolm X once said, if every black person in the country would contribute a small sum to an Afro-American lobbying group, "Washington's worst 'nigger-hater' would leap up: 'Well, how *are* you? Come on *in* here!'" According to federal drug surveys, about 11 million Americans smoke marijuana at least once a month—or are willing to tell a government pollster that they do—and over 4 million get high at least three times a week. About 150,000 to 200,000 are committed enough stoners to buy *High Times* or *Cannabis Culture* magazines.

Out of these people, NORML, the National Organization for the Reform of Marijuana Laws, had a little more than 10,000 members in late 2003. The Marijuana Policy Project had around 13,500. The Drug Policy Alliance had 10,500. The three groups did have 35,000 to 50,000 people on their e-mail lists, but the membership counts the people who write a check once a year. Fewer still will turn out for demonstrations, write letters to newspapers and legislators, or spend a Saturday handing out flyers.

In contrast, the National Rifle Association has 4 million members.

This is consistent with the general American lack of activism. Classic Jeffersonian democracy demands an informed citizenry, a body politic willing to follow issues and go to meetings. This is rare in a country where many people perceive political debate as talking heads yammering and bickering about incomprehensible details. Activism is often a specific subculture, and one that most people aren't willing to join, whether it's from lack of time, laziness, hopelessness, or because meetings are boring.

It is understandable that many stoners are too paranoid to come out in public. Dealers and growers have obvious reasons not to, and people with jobs can get hit with drug tests, or fired on the spot for moral turpitude. For parents, especially those with vindictive exes, pot use can be twisted into "using drugs in the presence of a minor."

On the other hand, there is nothing that stops these people from discreetly giving money. A 1997 NORML Foundation survey estimated that marijuana was the fourth largest cash crop in America—behind only corn, soybeans, and hay—worth about $15 billion wholesale

> MERE DECRIMINALIZATION OF POT POSSESSION WOULD ACTUALLY LEAVE THE LAWS STRICTER THAN ALCOHOL PROHIBITION, WHICH ALLOWED POSSESSION OF ALCOHOL, MEDICAL USE, AND PERSONAL-QUANTITY HOME-BREWING.

and $25 billion retail. Pot-growing is a major component of the economy in Northern California, the Pacific Northwest, and Appalachia. California NORML currently estimates retail reefer sales in that state at $3 to $5 billion a year, which would project to between $20 and $40 billion nationally. These figures could be inflated, but if there are 4 million people spending $20 a week on buds, that still works out to a $4-billion-a-year market.

Meanwhile, the vast majority of American pot-smokers can't even be bothered to cough up the price of an eighth-ounce of mediocre commercial weed once a year in order to support the cause of keeping themselves out of jail. The legalization movement depends on a handful of multimillionaires for most of its funding.

Apathy is probably a bigger reason for this than paranoia. As long as it's not their asses that are being thrown in jail, why should potheads bother doing anything to change the law? It's no accident that the people most likely to turn out for political pot protests are medical users and those who have already been busted (along with a handful of lawyers and libertarians). There is a hard core of a few thousand activists, including some who've been at it since the '70s, such as Keith Stroup of NORML and Kevin Zeese, and an encouraging generation of student activists. Medical-marijuana patients in particular show extraordinary courage: Cheryl Miller of New Jersey, who got arrested protesting the Congressional suppression of Washington, DC's medical-marijuana vote while she was dying of multiple sclerosis; Eddie Smith of Kentucky, ravaged by AIDS, who traveled to Michigan to sit vigil in the rain after the Rainbow Farm killings of 2001; Marcy Duda of Massachusetts, who picketed the local DEA office despite migraines of spike-in-the-head agony. In contrast,

BREAKING ARBITRARY AND AUTHORITARIAN RULES IS CERTAINLY FUN, BUT IT'S NOT A SUBSTITUTE FOR THE HARD WORK OF CONVERTING THE UNCONVERTED, FINDING WAYS TO SPEAK TO THEM IN LANGUAGE THEY CAN UNDERSTAND, AND DEVELOPING EFFECTIVE STRATEGIES FOR AFFECTING THE POWER STRUCTURE.

the average stoner might turn out for festival-style protests like the Boston Freedom Rally and the Seattle Hempfest, which draw tens of thousands of people every year, but strictly political rallies—that is, ones where you're there to make a point and can't smoke—are lucky to get 100.

Compare this to the "beer parades" of 1932, the anti-Prohibition rallies that drew 15,000 people in Detroit and over 100,000 in New York. They were not about getting drunk. They were relatively sober, if festive, affairs where people held up signs that read "We Want Beer and We Will Pay the Tax," and charts explained how a tax on alcohol could help get the country out of the Depression.

There has been significant "tie-dye vs. suits" debate in the legalization movement, argument over whether advocates with severely hippiefied appearances hinder the cause. This parallels the contretemps over whether drag queens and topless dykes on bikes hold back mainstream acceptance of gay rights. There are occasions when dressing soberly is definitely advisable, but ultimately, if marijuana, like homosexuality, is an issue of cultural warfare, victory requires winning acceptance of what was once deviant.

In my experience, what is often perceived as a problem of appearance is more often a question of clarity versus incoherence. I once witnessed the aforementioned Rep. John Mica listen reasonably respectfully to a green-

"WHY ARE WE DOING SO MANY STORIES ON TULIA?" A TOP EDITOR SNEERED WHEN 35 OF THE PEOPLE BUSTED IN THE TEXAS TOWN'S RACIST DRUG DRAGNET FINALLY WON IN COURT.

haired man in a black-lace dress who politely disputed his positions. Someone who calmly asks, "Why can't I smoke a joint as legally as you drink a beer?" is less likely to be dismissed as a nutcase than someone who delivers a muddled barrage of babble about the hemp conspiracy, "George Washington smoked weed," the religious significance of 420, and "all marijuana use is medical."

A related problem in reaching the unconverted is the "pot evangelism" of some people in the movement: the belief that cannabis is a miracle herb and therefore people who aren't stoned most of the time are somehow suspect. Some argue that the presence of THC receptors and endogenous cannabinoids in the brain indicates that not being high is an incomplete, inadequate state. Others spout Genesis 1:29—"Behold, I have given you every herb bearing seed"—as if it were a Biblical admonition to get blunted. At a New York pot rally a few years ago, the organizer demanded "one free ounce of marijuana per week for every man, woman, and child in the country." As a mock-serious demand like a five-hour workweek, this is entertaining. As a way to persuade non-stoners—whose biggest fears about legalizing pot are that their kids would become burnouts and it would lead to a nation of indolent wastoids—it's disastrous. As in "not only do these people want kids to smoke pot—they want the government to buy it for them!" Parallel to this are the people who think that merely acting out their weedhead cultural identity constitutes political action. An extreme case of this is the story I heard of a woman who insisted that her posing on a pot-porn Web site, buds adorning her shaven labia, was "activism." Giving stoner guys something to masturbate to may be a noble service—let him who is without the sin of Onan cast the first stone—but it's not going to change the law.

You cannot build a social movement around a commodity, where the more you consume the more "radical" you are, whether it's punk-rock records or black-power T-shirts. You especially cannot build a social movement around an intoxicating commodity, but many people in the marijuana world think you can. They believe that if someone is cool for smoking one joint, then someone who smokes 20 joints a day is 20 times cooler—and the one who only burns one is a "lightweight." This is a recipe for making baked couch potatoes, not social change.

Another subset is the people who propose absurdly effortless magic-bullet solutions. When I was news editor at *High Times*, I used to get around one e-mail a week arguing that all we had to do to legalize cannabis instantaneously was get everyone to just "plant their seeds," and the government would be overgrown by a surfeit of pot plants. (They were obviously completely ignorant of how much the DEA pads its marijuana-eradication figures with wild hemp uprooted from roadside ditches in Kentucky and Missouri.) Others argued that prohibition would evaporate if we'd only tell people that the Bible sanctifies herb, or get them to call it "cannabis" instead of "marijuana," which they believe is a reefer-madness slur coined and promoted by Harry Anslinger and William Randolph Hearst. (Malaysia imposes the death penalty for possession of seven ounces of "cannabis.")

High Times, the world's largest marijuana magazine, also deserves criticism. Its news department once published groundbreaking stories on medical marijuana and forfeiture abuses, but was gradually shrunk and finally eliminated (along with my job), replaced with a mixture of celebrity fluff and conspiracy-theory ravings. "Why are we doing so many stories on *Tulia*?" a top editor sneered when 35 of the people busted in the Texas town's racist drug dragnet finally won in court.

"There's a war on pot-smokers," a prominent young activist told me in 2002. "There are 700,000 of us busted every year. *High Times* should be in the forefront of the fight against that. Instead, you're writing about fucking UFOs." That may have changed since the magazine revamped its format. Still, the biggest problem with *High Times* is that its owners are limousine-leftist hypocrites who pretend to be "counterculture" while tossing out longtime workers as if they were used condoms and firing those who refuse to perform rites of submission like being fingerprinted for the office's biometric timeclock.

Many potheads also think that defying the law is enough, that all they have to do is blaze away as if prohibition were irrelevant. Breaking arbitrary and authoritarian rules is certainly fun, but it's not a substitute for the hard work of converting the unconverted, finding ways to speak to them in language they can understand, and developing effective strategies for affecting the power structure. If breaking the rules were all it took, gay men would have fucked and sucked homophobia out of existence in the 1970s.

This is not to denigrate the few thousand people out there who are smart, courageous, and dedicated activists for pot legalization. They are doing the best that they can with very limited resources, and with pathetically low support from their fellow stoners. But as long as their constituency can't be bothered to stick up for themselves, they're not likely to get very far.

Seeking Peace in the War on Drugs

Ethan A. Nadelmann

A new anti-war movement emerges, challenging the militarization of drug policy.

"So what you're saying is, you want to legalize drugs, right?"

That's the first question I'm typically asked when I start talking about drug policy reform. My short answer is, "No, that's not what I'm saying. Legalize marijuana? Yes, I think we need to head in that direction. But no, I'm not suggesting we make heroin and cocaine available the way we do alcohol and cigarettes."

"So what are you recommending?" is the second question. "And what do you mean by drug policy reform?"

Here's the longer answer.

There is no drug legalization movement in America. What there is, is a nascent political and social movement for drug policy reform. It consists of the growing number of citizens who have been victimized, in one way or another,

> THERE IS NO DRUG LEGALIZATION MOVEMENT IN AMERICA. WHAT THERE IS, IS A NASCENT POLITICAL AND SOCIAL MOVEMENT FOR DRUG POLICY REFORM.

by the drug war, and who now believe that our current drug policies, like alcohol prohibition in the 1920s, do more harm than good. Most members of this "movement" barely perceive themselves as part of any broader cause.

The movement might include the judge required by inflexible, mandatory minimum sentencing laws to send a drug addict, or petty dealer, or dealer's girlfriend, or Third World drug courier to prison for a longer time than many rapists and murderers serve.

Or the corrections officer who recalls the days when prisons housed "real" criminals, not the petty, nonviolent offenders who fill the cells these days.

Or the addict in recovery—employed, law abiding, a worthy citizen in every respect—who must travel a hundred miles each day to pick up her methadone, because current laws do not allow methadone prescriptions to be filled at a local pharmacy.

Or the nurse in the oncology or AIDS unit obliged to look the other way while a patient wracked with pain smokes her forbidden medicine, which works better than anything else.

Or the teacher or counselor warned by school authorities not to speak so frankly about drug use with his students lest he violate federal regulations prohibiting anything other than "just say no" bromides.

Or the doctor who's afraid to prescribe medically appropriate doses of opioid analgesics to a patient in pain because any variations from the norm bring unfriendly scrutiny from government agents and state medical boards.

Or the employee with an outstanding record who fails a drug test on Monday morning because she shared a joint with her husband over the weekend and is fired.

Or the struggling North Dakota farmer who wonders why farmers in Canada and dozens of other countries can plant hemp, but he cannot.

Or the conservative Republican who abhors the extraordinary powers of police and prosecutors to seize private property from citizens who have not been convicted of violating any laws, and who worries about the corruption inherent in sending forfeited proceeds directly to law enforcement agencies.

Or the upstanding African American citizen repeatedly stopped by police for "driving while black" or even "walking while black."

> A PUNITIVE APPROACH TO DRUG USE AND A TEMPERANCE IDEOLOGY ALMOST AS OLD AS THE NATION ITSELF ARE DEEPLY EMBEDDED IN AMERICAN LAWS, INSTITUTIONS, AND CULTURE.

The people who embrace the idea of drug policy reform are the ones who have connected the dots—the ones who understand how our prohibitionist drug policies are fueling serious social problems. We may not agree on what aspect of prohibition is most pernicious—the spread of violence, the corruption, the black market, the spread of disease, the loss of freedom, or simply the lies and hypocrisies—and we certainly don't agree on the optimal solutions, but we all regard the current drug policies as a fundamental mistake in American society.

Any effort to reform drug policies confront powerful obstacles. A punitive approach to drug use and a temperance ideology almost as old as the nation itself are deeply embedded in American laws, institutions, and culture. It amounts to a national hysteria, rejuvenated each time a new drug emerges, ripe for political posturing and media mania. But America's war on drugs is neither monolithic nor irreversible. Dissent is popping out all over. Most Americans have strong doubts about the drug war, according to opinion polls and recent referendum votes. They support treatment instead of incarceration for drug addicts. They think marijuana should be legally available for medical purposes. They don't want the government seizing money and property from people who have never been convicted of a crime. They're beginning to have doubts about the cost and meaning of incarcerating almost half a million of their fellow citizens for drug law violations.

DRUG PROHIBITION IS NOW BIG BUSINESS IN THE UNITED STATES.

So why does the drug war keep growing?

Part of the answer lies in what might best be described as a "drug prohibition complex" (taking off on President Eisenhower's warning about the military-industrial complex) composed of the hundreds of thousands of law enforcement officials, private prison corporations, anti-drug organizations, drug testing companies, and many others who benefit economically, politically, emotionally, and otherwise from continued crackdowns on use of marijuana and other drugs. Drug prohibition is now big business in the United States.

Nonetheless, signs of reform abound. Hardcore drug opponents may still be powerful, but they're gradually losing credibility. They look on marijuana with the same horror that anti-liquor crusaders like Carrie Nation viewed a mug of beer. Just as the temperance advocates became ever more shrill and silly as Prohibition stumbled along, so today's anti-drug extremists sound increasingly foolish to the average American parent of today, who probably knows a thing or two about marijuana.

The most powerful evidence of shifting views on drug reform occurred on Election Day last year, when voters in five states—California, Nevada, Colorado, Oregon, and Utah—approved drug policy reform ballot initiatives. In California, voters overwhelmingly endorsed Proposition 36, the "treatment instead of incarceration" ballot initiative that should result in tens of thousands of nonviolent drug possession offenders being diverted from jail and prison into programs that may help them get their lives together. Voters in Nevada and Colorado approved medical marijuana ballot initiatives. In Oregon and Utah, voters overwhelmingly approved (by margins of two to one) ballot initiatives requiring police and prosecutors to meet a reasonable burden of proof before

seizing money and other property from people they suspect of criminal activity. The measure also mandates that the proceeds from legal forfeitures be handed over not to the police and prosecuting agencies that had seized the property but rather to funds for public education or drug treatment. (The only setbacks were in Massachusetts, where voters narrowly defeated a combined forfeiture reform/diversion into treatment initiative, and in Alaska, where voters rejected a far-reaching marijuana legalization initiative.)

This followed up on other political victories. California's Proposition 36 was modeled on one Arizona passed four years earlier. Oregon voters, meanwhile, affirmed the state's marijuana decriminalization policies by a two-to-one margin in 1998. And voters in Mendocino, California, approved a ballot initiative last year to decriminalize cultivation of small amounts of cannabis. Clearly, more and more citizens realize that the drug war has failed and are looking for new approaches. The votes also suggest that there are limits to what people will accept in the name of fighting drugs. Parents don't want their teenagers to smoke marijuana, but they also don't want sick people who could benefit from the plant's pain relief properties to suffer because of the war on drugs. Americans don't

JUST AS THE TEMPERANCE ADVOCATES BECAME EVER MORE SHRILL AND SILLY AS PROHIBITION STUMBLED ALONG, SO TODAY'S ANTI-DRUG EXTREMISTS SOUND INCREASINGLY FOOLISH TO THE AVERAGE AMERICAN PARENT OF TODAY, WHO PROBABLY KNOWS A THING OR TWO ABOUT MARIJUANA.

approve of people using heroin or cocaine, but neither do they think it makes either economic or human sense to lock up drug addicts without first offering them a few opportunities to get their lives together outside prison walls.

The initiative victories demonstrated once again that the public is ahead of the politicians when it comes to embracing pragmatic drug policy reforms. But there is growing evidence that even some politicians are beginning to get it. Hawaii passed a medical marijuana law last year with the support of Governor Benjamin Cayetano. Three states—North Dakota, Minnesota, and Hawaii—enacted laws legalizing the cultivation of hemp (to the extent permitted by federal law), and hemp legalization bills are beginning to advance through other state legislatures as well. Vermont, one of eight states that prohibited methadone maintenance treatment, last year enacted a law that may ultimately lead to this treatment being made available not just in specialized clinics but also through public health clinics and private physicians. And, most significantly in terms of potential lives saved, three states—New York, New Hampshire, and Rhode Island—each enacted laws making it easier to purchase sterile syringes in pharmacies.

The governor of New Mexico, Republican Gary Johnson, is committed to far-reaching drug policy reform. And Salt Lake City's new mayor, Rocky Anderson, has abandoned the popular but demonstrably ineffective DARE program.

Perhaps it's too early to claim that all this adds up to a national vote of no confidence in the war on drugs. After all, drug war rhetoric still goes down easy in many parts of the country, and Congress has yet to demonstrate any reluctance to enact ever harsher and more far reaching drug war legislation. But the pendulum does seem to be reversing direction. The initiatives and recent state legislative victories, the reform bills making their way through legislative committees, the governors and mayors beginning to speak out, the rapidly rising anti-war sentiment among African American leaders—all these are beginning to add up to something new in American politics. Call it a new anti-war movement. Call it a nascent movement for common sense justice. Or simply call it a rising chorus of dissent from the war on drugs.

The D.A.R.E Generation vs. The H.E.A.

Abby Bair

In the early 1980s, President Reagan told the nation that a "War on Drugs" needed to be waged to "protect America's children." Throughout the 1980s and '90s, America witnessed the massive expansion of the so-called War on Drugs. Abstinence-based education programs like the Drug Abuse Resistance Education program, commonly known as D.A.R.E., were implemented. Zero-tolerance drug policies on campus were initiated. Billions of dollars were spent, and new government agencies were created.

Today, drugs are cheaper, easier to get, and more dangerous than ever before. According to the Manhattan Institute, a New York-based conservative think tank, more than 40% of 12th-graders in urban and suburban schools have used illegal drugs. The children Reagan was trying to protect are now grown, and many have begun to mobilize against the War on Drugs. Alternative solutions to the current War on Drugs are urgently needed.

Insightful members of the DARE generation formed an organization called Students for Sensible Drug Policy (SSDP) to provide education on harms caused by the War on Drugs. SSDP's mission is to involve youth in the political process, and to promote an open, honest and rational discussion of alternative solutions to our nation's drug problems.

I joined SSDP and the drug policy reform movement after realizing that the so-called War on Drugs should instead be called smoke and mirrors. The first time I read the Drug Reform Coordination Network's *Drug War Chronicle*, I thought that it was an *Onion* knock-off. It was so hysterical! I read the publication with disbelief. To make sure that my entire belief system was still intact, I fact-checked and cross-referenced the *Drug War Chronicle*. Finally, I understood that political dogma perpetuated the multi-billion dollar war. The next morning, I phoned DRCNet (http://stopthedrugwar.org) and asked to intern in their office. After interning with DRCNet in Washington, D.C., I returned to Ohio University to co-found an SSDP chapter. I wanted to continue learning and proliferating the truth about the War on Drugs.

More than 200 high school, college, and graduate chapters nationwide now work to bring attention to the issues that affect youth and other underrepresented communities most. SSDP leaders range from high school students to Rhodes scholars to tier I law students. SSDP's primary focus is to repeal the Higher Education Act (HEA) "drug provision."

The HEA drug provision blocks financial aid to students with drug convictions. More than 124,000 students have lost access to higher education since the law was enacted in 1998. The law applies to both current and past offenders. A student can get treatment in return for financial aid, but this is not an option for most students. There is usually a waiting-list for treatment, and it can cost up to $1000. If a student needs financial aid, then they probably cannot afford drug treatment.

The drug provision denies education to young people who have already been punished for their mistakes. Marisa Garcia was attending college in California when she paid a $400 fine after police found a pipe in her car. She was shocked when she found out that her educational future was jeopardized by this obscure law.

OHIO STATE SENATOR BOB HAGAN FIRMLY BELIEVES THAT THE HEA DRUG PROVISION SHOULD BE REPEALED, AND ARGUES THAT THE LAW SETS A DANGEROUS PRECEDENT FOR STATE GOVERNMENTS TO USE FINANCIAL AID AS A FORM OF BEHAVIOR CONTROL.

"When I got caught with a pipe, I did not even tell my mom. I paid the fine and went on with my life. I did not even know about this law until I filled out my financial aid forms," Garcia said. "It does not make sense. This law punishes students twice for the same crime and makes it harder for people to go to college. My family cannot afford college without school loans."

The provision is harmful because it has had the effect of disqualifying a large number of deserving, low to middle income students from receiving financial aid to attend college, often for misdemeanor drug offenses. According to The Sentencing Project (http://www.sentencingproject.org/), African-Americans comprise 13% of both the population and drug users, but 55% of convicted drug offenders. The War on Drugs, HEA drug provision included, disproportionately impacts racial minorities and members of the lower socio-economic classes.

Ohio state senator Bob Hagan firmly believes that the HEA drug provision should be repealed, and argues that the law sets a dangerous precedent for state governments to use financial aid as a form of behavior control.

"The Ohio General Assembly recently enacted a statute that will lead to the expulsion of students and denial of state financial aid for two years following conviction

MOST PEOPLE REALIZE THAT THERE IS A DIRECT CORRELATION BETWEEN EDUCATION AND A CITIZENS' PRODUCTIVENESS IN SOCIETY. EDUCATED PERSONS ARE FAR LESS LIKELY TO ENGAGE IN CRIMINAL ACTIVITY.

for rioting, aggravated rioting and failure to disperse. Although the statute was partially enacted to deal with raucous behavior following sporting events here in Columbus and throughout Ohio, the end result will be to convict, expel, and deny financial aid to students, many of whom are out in droves demonstrating against the war in Iraq, globalization and environmental degradation to name just a few," Senator Hagan said. "Congress has passed measures that prohibit students from receiving federal aid if convicted of petty drug offenses. In each instance government action and the means employed to combat 'youthful indiscretion' do not and never will justify the ends. When we strip our young people of their financial aid eligibility, we take away their opportunity to succeed."

The Colorado state legislature tried to enact a similar law for similar reasons, but Colorado student leaders successfully prevented the legislature from revoking state financial aid to students convicted of "rioting," on the basis that the law disproportionately affected minorities.

The DARE generation, SSDP, and the drug policy reform community have launched a major campaign to minimize the harmful consequences of the drug provision and to repeal the law. Most people realize that there is a direct correlation between education and a citizens' productiveness in society. Educated persons are far less likely to engage in criminal activity.

THE HIGHER EDUCATION ACT WAS DESIGNED TO MAKE IT EASIER TO OBTAIN EDUCATION, NOT TO CREATE OBSTACLES.

The John Perry Scholarship fund, Yale University, Hampshire University, Western Washington University and Amherst offer scholarships to help HEA victims afford tuition. SSDP activists actively lobby student governments and legislators for support for repeal. The campaign to repeal the HEA drug provision has garnered media

from almost every major TV and print source and from hundreds of local newspapers.

Legislators are starting to get the message that the "tough on drugs" era has passed. Progressive leaders are starting to feel comfortable about drug policy reform while regressive leaders experience backlash.

During the 2004 New Hampshire presidential primary, six presidential candidates announced their support for repeal. Presidential hopeful Howard Dean said "Get rid of it. Repeal it, period. It's a dumb idea…If you want people to go to college, you don't prevent them because they have a drug conviction. There's no possible sense in doing that." Dennis Kucinich, presidential hopeful and Congressman, takes a leadership role in repealing the HEA drug provision.

Efforts to repeal the drug provision have taken SSDP into the crux of congressional races. Rep. Souder almost lost the 2002 Republican primary, in large part because SSDP formed a political action committee to un-seat him. SSDP set up shop in Rep. Souder's home district, educating voters about the HEA Drug Provision and running advertisements in local papers. SSDP activists attended candidate nights, trying to address Rep. Souder about the HEA drug provision. The race was very close. Souder was the lone congressman to receive a presidential endorsement.

Souder has proposed an amendment to his ill-conceived bill to only revoke financial aid from current drug offenders. His proposal is similar to putting a band-aid on a hemorrhage. Sooner or later, Congress will have to

LEGISLATORS ARE STARTING TO GET THE MESSAGE THAT THE "TOUGH ON DRUGS" ERA HAS PASSED.

acknowledge that the law's very premise is flawed. The Higher Education Act was designed to make it easier to obtain education, not to create obstacles.

Rep. Souder's HEA Drug provision is ironic because it has motivated so many people, from every political ideology, to look closer at our nation's drug policies. More and more students are focusing on drug policy in their graduate and law programs. The drug provision is a catalyst for growth for organizations like the Marijuana Policy Project, the National Organization to Reform Marijuana Laws, DanceSafe and SSDP. I thank Souder for helping to shift the paradigm and for helping to launch the student movement to end the drug war.

The War on Drugs affects almost every area of our lives. As the DARE generation grows older, fills the ranks in the drug policy reform community, mainstream business, law firms, and judicial benches, our nation will have a better understanding of drugs and solutions to the problems our drug policies cause.

Medical Marijuana Mom: A Maryland Patient Tells Her Story

Erin Hildebrandt

It's a unique and humbling experience to stand with the leaders and policy makers of Maryland, to witness the birth of new ideals and new hope for the patients of our state. On May 22, 2003, with my baby daughter in my arms, we watched Governor Robert Ehrlich sign the Darrell Putman Compassionate Use Act, reducing the penalty for possession of medical marijuana to a $100 fine, into law. All I could think as I approached his desk was, "Please God, don't let me throw up on the governor!"

Having experienced the miracle of using medical marijuana to treat my Crohn's disease, migraines, and hyperemesis gravidarum, a dangerous complication of pregnancy which frequently leads to malnutrition, I was a firm believer in the necessity of making it legally available. I had also enjoyed many college experiences with this fine herb, saw the enormous difference between its effects and the effects of alcohol, and believed in full legalization, even though I had very few facts to back up my beliefs.

My personal experiences have greatly shaped my views. My days used to be spent between bed, toilet, and doctors' offices, with occasional trips to emergency and operating

> **THE MORE WE READ ABOUT GOOD PEOPLE WHO WERE LOSING THEIR LIVELIHOODS, POSSESSIONS, AND EVEN THEIR LIVES IN OUR NATION'S RIDICULOUS PURSUIT OF SELECTIVE SOBRIETY, THE MORE OUR OUTRAGE INCREASED.**

rooms for variety. Most of the time I was completely disabled by illness, unable to care for myself, let alone my family.

Cannabis changed all of this for me. After I'd exhausted what conventional medicine could offer and had been unable to eat for days, barely able to keep down water and nibbles of saltines, a friend suggested that marijuana could help. She offered me a few doses of the first medicine to provide me relief without devastating side effects. It just may have saved my life.

I became involved in marijuana-law reform very recently, in 2002. After reading online about a demonstration in Washington, my husband, Bill, and I packed up the minivan and our five kids, and hit the road—but, completely unfamiliar with the DC area, we couldn't find the protest.

I wrote to Hilary McQuie at Americans for Safe Access, who put me in touch with Kevin Zeese at Common Sense for Drug Policy, who warmly welcomed me into this wild world of activism. When he invited us to attend future

> **ALL I COULD THINK AS I APPROACHED HIS DESK WAS, "PLEASE GOD, DON'T LET ME THROW UP ON THE GOVERNOR!"**

demonstrations, I began to learn about Bryan Epis and the ten year federal prison sentence he's now serving for his humanitarian efforts to provide himself and other suffering patients with a safe source for their medicine. Late at night, Bill and I would discuss how this could be our family, and how we had to do more to stop this kind of injustice. The more we read about good people who were losing their livelihoods, possessions, and even their lives in our nation's ridiculous pursuit of selective sobriety, the more our outrage increased.

Finally, Bill agreed to sacrifice a small part of his own freedom in order to make a statement about the obscenity of Epis' sentencing. On Oct. 7, 2002, along with Chuck Thomas of Unitarian Universalists for Drug Policy Reform, Dave Guard of the Drug Reform Coordination Network, and Bruce Mirken of the Marijuana Policy Project, Bill was arrested in front of the White House for refusing to obey the police and leave when he was told to do so. They had hoped to garner some press attention, but CNN appeared to be more committed to covering a hot-dog eating contest that day.

While the 2002 elections and this lack of concern in the press for medical-marijuana issues were terribly disappointing, we went on undaunted. I started a small website, parentsendingprohibition.org. Though initially not very well organized, it was very helpful to

> **IT'S NOT TOO OFTEN THAT HOUSEWIVES FIND THEMSELVES STANDING BEFORE THE STATE SENATE JUDICIAL PROCEEDINGS COMMITTEE, IN FRONT OF NUMEROUS PEOPLE IN POLICE UNIFORMS, EXPLAINING HOW THEY BROKE THE LAW AND THAT THEY'RE VERY GLAD THEY DID!**

me in learning about the issues surrounding cannabis prohibition, and how to more effectively communicate my ideas.

In January, I began hearing that there would be a bill introduced in our state that could legalize medical marijuana. Intrigued with the possibility I could help somehow, right here at home, I contacted Bruce Mirken at MPP and asked what I could do. Soon after, his colleague Larry Sandell asked if I would consider testifying before the Maryland Senate about my experiences. I was excited, but terrified.

For weeks, they worked with me, answering my many questions and giving me pep talks when I would panic. They were indispensable resources in an area that was terribly foreign to me. After all, I was just an ordinary "soccer mom." It's not too often that housewives find themselves standing before the state Senate Judicial Proceedings Committee, in front of numerous people in police uniforms, explaining how they broke the law and that they're very glad they did!

I arrived in Annapolis on February 26, 2003 prepared to speak to the committee. It was eye-opening to watch people like Eric Sterling of the Criminal Justice Policy Foundation and State Senator Paula Hollinger present the bill to the committee and field their questions. One question posed involved the absurd tale of a woman whose baby had been "harmed" by "pot smoke drifting through an open window" from an apartment above. The senator demanded to know what provisions would be made to keep these newly legal medical users from being able to "poison" other people's kids.

It was very difficult to keep from standing up and stating my disgust. I had traveled there to talk about the need in Maryland to stop arresting sick people for taking medicine, and this man was so afraid of marijuana that he couldn't even recognize the absurdity of his question, nor could he comprehend the inhumanity of putting people like me in jail. His sole focus was his own reefer madness.

Nonplussed, Sterling took a deep breath and fired off statistics and studies showing that marijuana, in the example given, could not possibly harm a child. He went on to add that the bill before them would not make it legal to use marijuana in any public places nor in the presence of children; therefore, the point was moot. He then went back to discussing the real issues.

Considering that right now, an individual can legally chain-smoke cigarettes in a closed room with a child, the idea that we would prioritize a purely theoretical "danger" over basic human rights and dignities is pathetic. For every child who could be spared this sort of "risk," there are millions of patients who suffer real harms and real dangers created entirely by marijuana prohibition.

One glaring example of the desire of some of the committee members to remain blind to the real issues came while I was waiting for my turn to be heard. I noticed two of the senators ignoring the people speaking in favor of perusing a copy of *High Times*. This could have been a positive adjunct to their research into this issue. However, they missed vital testimony during their adolescent titillation with the magazine, and ultimately, both voted against the bill. This was a shameful display of childish arrogance and willful ignorance from two leaders from whom I would have expected better. When it came time for me to speak, I was completely overwhelmed and intimidated. The last time I had spoken in front of a group of people was a decade before, at my wedding. Shaking, I approached the podium. I decided all I had was the truth, and I'd emphasize both how disabling my diseases had been and the stark, cold terror I'd been forced to live with just to feel better. I can't remember much of what actually came out of my mouth, but I pleaded with them to pass this bill, so people like me and my family wouldn't be forced into this awful situation anymore.

Reporters started questioning me after I testified, and I realized I was supposed to come up with brief ways of saying why I was there. I hadn't really thought much about these quotes that seemed routine for everyone else. I had all of these personal epiphanies running through my mind, and opinions about every aspect of this odd war on some drugs. It was very difficult to try to put my outrage into a two-sentence sound bite.

With editorial assistance from Mirken, I began writing letters to editors, and had an op-ed article printed in the Baltimore Sun. My ordinary life has been turned upside down, with a little unexpected fame and a success with writing that's opened up new worlds to me.

However, the finest moment of all was watching Shaleen Murphy, Darrell Putman's widow, before the lights and cameras after the bill-signing, proclaiming victory in seeing the bill that bore her husband's name finally signed into law. Putman was a cancer patient who used medical marijuana and lost his battle with the disease in 1999. His dear friend, former Delegate Donald Murphy, introduced a version of this bill in 2000 in his honor. Shay Murphy and everyone else supporting it agonized for three years, trying to make the elected officials understand how despicable it is to lock up people like Darrell Putman, before finding a legislature compassionate and educated enough to pass this bill.

Now, as of October 1, 2003, when the bill went into effect, the patients in Maryland who benefit from the use of cannabis will no longer have to face state prison sentences for doing so, but could still face arrest and harassment. While far from an ideal situation, it's an improvement. I'm very grateful to Governor Ehrlich for having the courage

> I STILL HAVE TO LIVE WITH THE FEAR OF HAVING ARMED MEN RAID MY HOME, AND ALL THE DANGERS THAT ENTAILS, SHOULD I NEED MY MEDICINE AGAIN.

to do the right thing, in spite of pressure from the highest offices in the Bush administration to demand that he veto this bill. He stood by his campaign promises to protect the patients in his state, which gives me great hope he will do so again.

I still have to live with the fear of having armed men raid my home, and all the dangers that entails, should I need my medicine again. With seven people and a cat, what are the chances no one would make a sudden move while the raiders had their guns drawn? Still, I firmly believe our best chance to see an end to these unjust laws is by simply living honestly and being unabashedly open about our medicine. In order to change hearts, our collective outrage must exceed our collective trepidation. There is nothing inherently shameful about using marijuana. Cannabis is far safer than the dozens of drugs peddled to me by MDs, and one of the few medicines without any side effects that I mind experiencing. It quelled my nausea, reduced my pain, and made me want to eat and laugh again.

While they could arrest me, no judge or police officer can change the fact that locking me up, or others like me, doesn't mean we did anything wrong. It's time for our government to recognize that they're filling our prisons with people just like themselves and their loved ones. Just like you and me.

Strategizing to Beat State Drug-Reform Initiatives in the U.S. Capitol - Yeah, the One with the Dome

Daniel Forbes

Proponents of the drug war status quo rarely play nice, though they clutch all the publicly funded marbles. Consider the concerted, secret effort by Ohio Governor Bob Taft, his wife, and the highest reaches of his administration to subvert his state's electoral process and thus defeat a treatment rather than incarceration state ballot initiative in November, 2002. With overall control over budgets, jobs and sentencing policy at stake (Ohio spent $106 million on "community-based treatment" in FY 2000), the Taft administration organized a sophisticated, sub-rosa campaign that began some 18 months before the November election. It involved Gov. Taft himself, First Lady Hope Taft, his chief of staff, Brian Hicks, his top officials for criminal justice and substance abuse treatment as well as numerous senior and support staff.

> PROPONENTS OF THE DRUG WAR STATUS QUO RARELY PLAY NICE, THOUGH THEY CLUTCH ALL THE PUBLICLY FUNDED MARBLES.

This Republican effort in Ohio was aided by federal officials, including President Bush's publicly announced nominee to be deputy director of the White House drug czar's office (since confirmed) and a senior U.S. Senate staffer. The drug czars of Florida and Michigan, as well as a senior Drug Enforcement Administration agent participated in the scheme. Ohio officials consulted with and enlisted the aid of the wife of the finance chairman of the Republican National Committee from 1997 to 2000, as well as several taxpayer-supported, staunch anti-drug organizations, including the Partnership for a Drug-Free America. Though it ultimately bowed out, the Partnership was slated to produce TV ads to sway public opinion in favor of the Ohio drug-policy status quo. Additionally, the Taft administration proposed diverting U.S. Department of Justice crime-fighting grants to fund their campaign's polling, focus groups and any potential advertising.

> WHAT VOTERS READ AS THEY PONDERED WHICH LEVER TO PULL WAS THE LUDICROUS ASSERTION THAT THE MEASURE WOULD COST TAXPAYERS HUNDREDS OF MILLIONS OF DOLLARS. THIS DESPITE THE FACT—THINK ABOUT IT—THAT DRUG TREATMENT IS ALWAYS CHEAPER THAN INCARCERATION.

The effort entailed hundreds of man-hours of state-paid time, as well as state funds paying for out of town trips and overnight lodging. I detailed the first several months of this cloaked campaign in a report published by the venerable Washington think tank, the Institute for Policy Studies.[1]

Opposition to the proposed amendment, which was known as the *Ohio Constitutional Amendment for Treatment of Substance-Abusing Offenders*, was crafted during at least one formal Ohio cabinet meeting. Ohio's first lady and key members of the Taft administration, including senior staffers in the governor's office, attended weekly anti-amendment strategy sessions. Ohio officials also planned to create a state wide coalition stocked with wealthy and famous Ohioans including Ohio State's football coach. An entity to be sprung full-grown from the governor's office, the intent was for this coalition to be guided by the administration in both funding and eventually pursuing the counter-initiative campaign.

Modeled on a similar measure, Proposition 36, that voters passed overwhelmingly in California in 2000, the Ohio amendment proposed to offer treatment rather than prison solely to defendants charged with a first or second instance of simple drug possession. Almost invariably, any crime beyond possession would have precluded participation. The measure was backed by the same rich trio—billionaires George Soros and Peter Lewis, and multimillionaire John Sperling—who have financed state drug reform initiatives since 1996, including California's Prop. 36 and several successful medical marijuana measures.

Coupled with the Taft administration's official opposition, a wildly inaccurate official ballot summary proved the measure's death knell, and it was soundly defeated in November 2002. The official summary stated that the measure would cost $247 million over seven years. Indeed it would— it would also save at least that much and more by reducing the state's incarceration rates. What voters read as they pondered which lever to pull was the ludicrous assertion that the measure would cost taxpayers hundreds of millions of dollars. This despite the fact—think about it—that drug treatment is always cheaper than incarceration.

Of particular note, not least because its setting makes it worth reconsidering here, was the day-long strategy session convened for Mrs. Taft and crew on July 17, 2001 by a senior U.S. Senate staffer and held in the U.S. Capitol building itself, in the East Front 100 room. In attendance were Hope Taft, Lucielle Fleming, Director of the Ohio Department of Alcohol and Drug Addiction Services, Domingo Herraiz, Director of the Ohio Office of Criminal

> "LEGALIZATION," OF COURSE, IS THE SMEAR ATTACHED TO ANY ATTEMPT TO REIN IN THE WAR ON DRUGS—NOT THAT THE HIGHLY REGULATED TREATMENT REGIMEN, REPLETE WITH CRIMINAL SANCTIONS, THAT THE OHIO MEASURE WOULD HAVE INSTITUTED WAS ANYWHERE NEAR LEGALIZATION.

Justice Services, other Ohio officials as well as executives from the Partnership for a Drug-Free America and the Community Anti-Drug Coalitions of America.

The day-long session was hosted by William Olson, a well-connected federal drug warrior with an extensive background, someone with the stated belief that marijuana use impairs judgment for up to four days. Depending on which party controlled the Senate, for years Olson was either majority or minority staff director of the Senate Caucus on International Narcotics Control. While it's curious and perhaps illegal—certainly unethical—that such an unabashed political session occurred in the Capitol, equally curious is why it occurred under the auspices of the Senate Caucus on International Narcotics Control. After all, the caucus' declared focus is "international cooperation against drug abuse and narcotics trafficking." Additionally, says its web site, "As a formal organization of the Senate, the Caucus has the status of a standing committee," including subpoena power.

Established in 1985, the caucus was then chaired by Sen. Joseph Biden (D-Del.) and co-chaired by Sen. Charles E. Grassley (R-IA). By all accounts, Biden is more interested in his far more prestigious Judiciary committee assignments, including running the Crime and Drugs subcommittee. No matter which party held sway in the Senate and thus chaired committees, Grassley probably retained more interest in the caucus than any of his colleagues. And Grassley's man on the caucus, his point man on drug policy in general, was William Olson. Several weeks before the July meeting, Hope Taft had written two memos to her husband and his chief of staff, Brian Hicks, calling for the administration's opposition to the amendment. Prompted by a *Wall Street Journal* article on the initiative's trio of wealthy backers, in the second memo, Mrs. Taft stated, "the time might be ripe for working out a plan to pre-empt the Prop. 36-type [treatment] initiative." She included "an outline of a counter-strategy," written by Jeffrey Tauber, a retired judge and founder of the Drug Court Professionals Association.

Mrs. Taft also discussed Olson as a strategic asset, someone who could help grease the wheels for producing any television ads that would trumpet drug courts as an alternative to the amendment. She wrote, "Bill Olson is very knowledgeable on the ways of these propositions and is willing to advise and bring together a group of people to see how some of the national groups like Drug Court Professionals, PDFA, etc., can develop PSAs that highlight the best aspects of the current drug court system"—that is, the status quo. She added, "Bill would like to pull together a group of people for me to talk with on my next trip to D.C." (The PDFA refers to the Partnership for a Drug-Free America; PSAs are public service announcements.)

Judge Tauber also attended the D.C. strategy session. He told me Olson was "the person who got it together and led the discussion to some extent." Ohio criminal justice chief Domingo Herraiz told me Olson was a "facilitator" who gathered people together. Olson himself acknowledged that he held the reins; in a letter on Senate caucus letterhead, he informed Hope Taft, "I have laid out the day in three segments," and "I have kept the groups small," etc.

As Mrs. Taft anticipated, Olson did produce the top four executives of the Partnership for a Drug-Free America for a three-hour strategy session, including its President and CEO, Stephen J. Pasierb; Vice Chairman, Thomas A. Hedrick, Jr.; and Director of Public Affairs, Stephen D. Dnistrian. In his letter confirming his and the three others' participation, the PDFA's Director of Operations, Michael Y. Townsend addressed Olson as the senate drug caucus "Staff Director"—not some private expert—and said he looked forward to a productive "counter-legalization brainstorm session."

"Legalization," of course, is the smear attached to any attempt to rein in the war on drugs—not that the highly regulated treatment regimen, replete with criminal sanctions, that the Ohio measure would have instituted was anywhere near legalization.

The PDFA executives were accompanied by Peter Kerr, then responsible for communications at the New York-based treatment provider, Phoenix House. (Prior to the passage of treatment-not-jail Prop. 36 in California, the president of Phoenix House termed it "a dangerously deceptive measure," and also "a giant step toward decriminalization.") No doubt the Taft administration would have welcomed a similar high-profile endorsement from the treatment community.

Kerr and the PDFA foursome were the only non-Ohioans present that morning aside from their host, Olson. Therefore political advertising—Hope Taft's sanitized reference is to 'PSAs'—presumably dominated the discussion. Mrs. Taft's staffer, Marcie Seidel, generated one of three extant memos describing the day's events. Employing the frequent obfuscation, "educational," she phrased one of the consensus recommendations as: "PDFA can do educational PSAs starting now about success stories of people who were required to get treatment. They could start these educational PSAs before the political season begins."

Plugged In, Locked, and Loaded

Apart from getting the PDFA bigwigs there, what did Olson bring to the table? With a wealth of experience, he's well plugged in to Republican drug-war circles. Prior to the inaugural in 2001, for instance, Olson was on President-

THE SEMBLERS ARE KNOWN FOR HAVING RUN THE CONTROVERSIAL AND COERCIVE PRIVATE DRUG TREATMENT PROGRAM, STRAIGHT, INC., WHOSE AFFILIATES HAVE BEEN CLOSED DOWN BY SEVERAL STATE GOVERNMENTS.

select George W. Bush's transition team, focusing on drug policy. Back during Bush the First's administration, he was Deputy Assistant Secretary of State for International Narcotics Matters. According to the biographical squib accompanying one of his published articles, he was also an acting deputy assistant secretary of defense for "low intensity conflict."

Active long enough to know any fellow drug warrior worth knowing, Olson was able to invite Betty Sembler to the July meeting. Referring to opposition to past medical marijuana initiatives, a former Clinton administration observer said, "Betty Sembler [was] active and vocal, and Olson is close to that crowd. He spoke at one of Betty Sembler's conferences in Florida on medical marijuana."

Betty Sembler's husband Mel, a wealthy shopping center developer, was Finance Chairman for the Republican National Committee from 1997 to 2000, ambassador to Australia under Bush the First and current ambassador to Italy. The Semblers are known for having run the controversial and coercive private drug treatment program, Straight, Inc., whose affiliates have been closed down by several state governments. The last branch, according to Fox News, closed in 1993. Fox cited lawsuits resulting in Straight payments to plaintiffs of $220,000 and $721,000, and it referred to accusations from Straight critics of vicious physical and mental abuse "at Straight chapters all over the country." Betty Sembler, according to the Drug Free America Foundation website, has been a delegate to a White House drug policy conference, has served on the Governor's Drug Policy Task Force in Florida, and is vice-chair of something called Drug Abuse Resistance Education International.

Getting back to Olson, another Washington drug policy insider referred to him as "Grassley's point man." His most important connection, though, according to this source, is that, "Olson is good buddies with [Drug Czar] John Walters, dating back to when Walters headed supply interdiction at ONDCP during Bush I and Olson worked with him." Once Grassley appointed Olson to the Senate caucus, this source recalled that Olson worked with Walters "behind the scenes." John Carnevale worked in a senior analytical capacity at ONDCP throughout the '90s and ran Bush's drug policy transition effort; Olson was Carnevale's "number two" on the transition, this source said. This person figured that in 2001, Olson was "functioning at the behest of Walters, implementing Walters' ideas."

William D. McColl was then director of national affairs for the Drug Policy Alliance, which receives funding from the same wealthy financial backers pushing the Ohio amendment. Prior to joining the DPA, McColl represented a treatment-provider professional association and so had dealings with Olson in the Senate. Even by Republican, professional drug warrior standards, said McColl, Olson is "an extreme hardliner" who declared his belief that the government should focus almost entirely on law enforcement, interdiction and source country production. McColl said Olson made it clear that, "He had staked out the intellectual position that treatment is not effective."

Interviewed by the *Pittsburgh Post-Gazette* in March, 1999, Olson was asked about the "recreational" use of marijuana. He said, "What you're talking about here is people becoming addicted to a substance that disrupts their lives and makes them dangerous to be around. And the effects of marijuana last for two, three and four days in terms of impairment of judgment."

"WHAT YOU'RE TALKING ABOUT HERE IS PEOPLE BECOMING ADDICTED TO A SUBSTANCE THAT DISRUPTS THEIR LIVES AND MAKES THEM DANGEROUS TO BE AROUND. AND THE EFFECTS OF MARIJUANA LAST FOR TWO, THREE AND FOUR DAYS IN TERMS OF IMPAIRMENT OF JUDGMENT."

Never mind the supposed danger and disruption, consider that four days of impairment—a remarkable assertion.

Illegal - Or Just Unethical?

Some folks might question the impaired judgment of a senior U.S. Senate staffer who brought private anti-drug advocates together with top state officials under the Capitol dome itself to craft a strategy to defeat a state ballot initiative.

Queried on the propriety of Olson running a political strategy session in the Capitol building, Jill Kozeny, Sen. Grassley's press secretary, said, "It was official business related to public education."

In this case, however, the "public" consisted of the first lady of Ohio, two members of the governor's cabinet responsible for multi-million dollar public agencies, the PDFA's top leadership and the wife of the Republican National Committee's chief fund-raiser. As to the oft-repeated phrase "education," it refers here to changing voters' views, not imparting knowledge. Recall the PDFA's Michael Townsend telling Olson he looked forward to a productive "counter-legalization brainstorm session."

Pressed for an explanation, Kozeny said the meeting involved "talking with people with an interest in these referenda." Indeed. She reiterated, it was formal Senate caucus business: "a discussion of public policy." Kozeny subsequently said the meeting was "a policy debate." An odd debate, this, with only side of the issue represented. She added that it occurred "under Senate auspices." Rather than a debate's pros and cons, Olson's written summary of the day, which he soon sent to Hope Taft, yields an unmistakable political blueprint. He stressed such dictates as: "Take back the language," and, "This effort then needs a strong follow-up element to act as a focal point for implementing any plans and to be the point of contact for coordinating efforts."

> "THAT'S REALLY DIRTY. TO HAVE A MEETING FURTHERING A POLITICAL CONSPIRACY AGAINST OHIO VOTERS SPAWNED IN THE U.S. CAPITOL MAKES IT EVEN MORE DISGUSTING."

Kozeny said the skull session was organized by Olson on his own initiative and that Sen. Grassley "was not involved in the meeting." Asked if Grassley approved it, she said he had "by virtue of the fact that Bill works for him." Over a period of weeks, Olson did not return nearly a dozen phone calls. He has since left the Senate.

Marcia Lee, the Senate caucus's then majority staff director, works for Sen. Joe Biden. She knew nothing of the meeting and declined further comment.

Biden's press secretary, Margaret Aitken, said Olson "is a Republican staff person" who doesn't work for Biden. Aitken noted that Biden "thinks treatment has gotten the short end of the stick." Referring to Olson's meeting, she added, "It doesn't seem like something Sen. Biden would want his staff to do."

White House spokesperson Marcy Viana referred to the Office of National Drug Control Policy my questions on the propriety of Bush transition team member Olson leading a strategy session on quashing state ballot measures.

Despite the White House referral, ONDCP communications director Tom Riley refused to comment on the meeting. He said, "The transition is over. Mr. Walters has been confirmed, and his time is here and now."

Salute when ready

Alexander Robinson, a public policy consultant with the government relations firm Robinson & Foster, Inc., was less reticent: "Potential referenda becoming official Senate business is bogus and completely over-reaching, contrasting with the conservative politics that are supposed to protect states rights." Robinson, who does such work as helping to organize opposition to Attorney General John Ashcroft's confirmation, added, "I can't imagine under what circumstances the Senate might have a role to play. It's a state-based campaign, and that's where it should remain."

Dave Fratello was National Campaign Manager of the Ohio initiative's main proponent, the California-based Campaign for New Drug Policies. Fratello charged that Olson's meeting brought the idea of multi-state, anti-initiative cooperation to a reality. As to its Senate location, he said, "That's really dirty. To have a meeting furthering a political conspiracy against Ohio voters spawned in the U.S. Capitol makes it even more disgusting."

Not surprisingly, the Senate Ethics Manual has a long chapter entitled, "Political Activity." Cutting to the quick, its very first paragraph states that Title 31 of the U.S. Code "has been interpreted in Congress to mean that congressional employees receive publicly funded salaries for performance of official duties and, therefore, *campaign or other non-official activities should not take place on Senate time, using Senate equipment or facilities*." [Emphasis added.] That explains the game attempts by Grassley's spokesperson to characterize the meeting as official senate business.

Two paragraphs on, the ethics manual declares: "Senate employees are compensated from funds of the Treasury for regular performance of official duties. They are not paid to do campaign work." And the next page indicates that Senate employees can "engage in campaign activities on their own time … provided they do not do so in congressional offices or otherwise use official resources." Generally speaking, though, Olson's actions as a Senate staffer were of greater consequence than the use of the room, no matter the edifice.

One Capitol Hill pro told me the rules are usually interpreted in such fashion that, "I could see numerous circumstances where [the meeting] might be official Senate business…. It's an ethics call. It's for the member to defend." This source concluded that the whole thing "is Grassley's to defend. Official Senate business is not defined."

Dismissing Peter Kerr and the four PDFA executives, Olson and the Taftites broke for sandwiches in the room known as East Front 100. They were soon joined by Sue Thau, lobbyist for the Community Anti-Drug Coalitions of America, who remained for much of the afternoon session, according to Judge Tauber, the drug court proponent. CADCA's website boasts that Thau is "recognized for her advocacy and legislative accomplishments.... She was a driving force behind the passage and full funding of the Drug-Free Communities Act...."

Along with Thau, both Olson and his boss, Grassley, were prime architects of the original Drug-Free Communities Support Program. Sen. Grassley claimed paternity, stating

OLSON INDICATED THE MEETING PARTICIPANTS DISAGREED WHETHER AN INDIRECT APPROACH OR A "STRAIGHTFORWARD EFFORT TO KILL THE INITIATIVE" WAS PREFERABLE.

he "won passage by the U.S. Senate of his bill." (His attempt to name it after himself failed.) Reps. Sander Levin, a Michigan Democrat, and Rob Portman, a Republican of Ohio, were the chief House sponsors of both the original, 1997 bill and the subsequent reauthorization. Along with the PDFA's Steve Pasierb, they also serve on CADCA's board.

The Drug-Free Communities program has grown wildly since its June, 1997 enactment. Initially funded at $10 million a year, 2002's total of $50 million for just that year was a full 25% increase over the prior year, and the sky's the limit.

That is, the program's first five years were initially funded at a cumulative total of $144 million. Then in December, 2001 while attending CADCA's annual meeting, Bush signed its reauthorization bill. With $450 million guaranteed over the next five years, annual appropriations will increase steadily until maxing out at nearly $100 million in 2007.

AS A SUBSEQUENT MEMO GENERATED BY LUCILLE FLEMING'S TREATMENT OFFICE ADMITTED, "... THERE ARE MORE PEOPLE IN PRISON FOR DRUG OFFENSES ALONE THAN THERE NEEDS TO BE (APPROX. 3,000)."

Up to 20 percent of the money can be used for what is loosely termed "voter education"—the sort of education potentially found in anti-initiative media campaigns, for example.

The afternoon session in the Capitol featured the wealthy Mrs. Sembler, who Hope Taft had informed her husband "was the possible source of some funding for a counter-effort." As to Tauber, he had already sent to Mrs. Taft an

initiative "counter-strategy" that declared: "We need to co-opt the initiative proponents" by capturing "the allegiance" of treatment providers so as to "be seen as the real reformers." He also called for boosting drug courts, a PR effort, and "a substantial amount of money to stay in the game." Sue Rusche of National Families in Action, an active opponent of past drug reform ballot measures, rounded out the afternoon.

So, this July day in the Capitol was when Taft and company's 18-month effort took root. For further details, see the Institute for Policy Studies report referenced above.[2] Olson sent Hope Taft, Lucille Fleming, and Domingo Herraiz a summary of the discussion. Like Tauber, he emphasized being "proactive." He added, "Do not wait for the other side to define the debate and respond to their initiatives. It is important to take their arguments away from them.... *Frame the debate*." [Emphasis in original.] Olson indicated the meeting participants disagreed whether an indirect approach or a "straightforward effort to kill the initiative" was preferable. But they agreed on the importance of fund-raising: "If one theme predominated it was money."

Domingo Herraiz also summarized some of the recommendations generated in the People's House, as the Capitol is known to the fifth graders who visit: "Develop a positive campaign to counteract their amendment," and, "Review and update our drug policies in order to counteract this initiative," and a third, "If we are proactive and not defensive, we stand a good chance to defeat their efforts." Then there are these bullet points: "Pre-empt their message and their ability to steal the issue," and, "Fundraising is most important issue in defeating this initiative in Ohio." Finally, some outright misinformation wasn't deemed out of bounds: "Make it appear as if everyone is against it," and, "... build off the anti-tax theme as if this was taxation." This nugget was later reflected in the official ballot summary that ultimately sank the measure.

Taft staff chief Brian Hicks received a copy of Herraiz's notes. Referring to "potential strategies to be addressed or placed in a timeline," Herraiz lauded his two top aids' "assistance and dedication to this effort." He called on the governor's chief aide to, "Let me know how you would like to proceed and what additionally you may need, and I will move forward." He also attached his four-page, single-spaced document: Potential Strategies to Utilize in Ohio for a Proactive Approach to Prop 36.

If some surprising admissions are to be believed, there was a lot of room for improvement in Ohio. As Herraiz wrote of the Capitol session: "Recognize that incarceration without treatment makes no sense—they will exploit this and take the high ground if we do not." In such notes' truncated diction, he continued: "Takes us to places that we normally would not go, such as changing drug laws—felony to misdemeanor." Think of it! And, finally: "Need a comprehensive approach—treatment and prevention—some mandated minimums are too harsh."

Or, as a subsequent memo generated by Lucille Fleming's treatment office admitted, "… there are more people in prison for drug offenses alone than there needs to be (approx. 3,000)." In other words, what is the number of hapless addicts needed to fill Ohio's criminal justice complex? How "harsh" do the minimum sentences need to be?

Footnotes

[1] "The Governor's Sub-Rosa Plot to Subvert an Election in Ohio," http://www.ips-dc.org

[2] ibid.

War on Foreign Shores

Who Takes Responsibility for Thailand's Bloody Drug War "Victory"?

Preston Peet

Editor's note - American ex-patriot and human rights campaigner Matthew McDaniel, quoted in the following article, was arrested by Thai immigration officials at the Mae Sai immigration office when he went to renew his visa on April 15, 2004. As this book goes to press, it appears McDaniel will be thrown out of the country. What will happen to his pregnant Akha wife and four children, still at home in their remote village in Chiang Rai province, is still unsure, but what is known is that the Thai government and its military and police do not like nor want interference from pesky, outspoken foreigners who publicize the atrocities they are committing against certain segments of their society. McDaniel has been particularly derisive of the Thai government's War on Some Drugs and Users, as is apparent from his comments which follow.

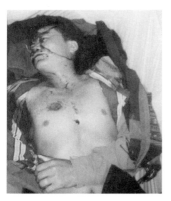

Akha man Leeh Huuh, murdered after police called him to the police station. He never made it.

Thailand's Prime Minister Thaksin Shinawatra inexplicably declared a victory in Thailand's recent all out War on Drugs campaign, on December 3, 2003 (simultaneously declaring a new War on Poverty), but there are still drugs, traffickers and users all over the country, despite the bodies of thousands of now-dead druggies, dealers, and smugglers strewn throughout Thailand's cities and villages.

The first three months of the campaign, launched by Prime Minister Thaksin on February 1, 2003, became a murder spree, with police committing thousands of what many human rights organizations are calling "extra-judicial killings" of suspected drug dealers and addicts. Police and government officials counter that most of the more than 2500 known killings, 1500 in the first five weeks alone, were carried out by other drug dealers turning on one another in gang warfare or while trying to silence potential snitches, or by police acting in self-defense. Police officials claim that only 46 of the

...THE POLICE SHOOTING TO DEATH DRUG DEALERS AND USERS IN THE STREETS WAS PROBABLY NOT WHAT AMNESTY INTERNATIONAL HAD IN MIND FOR REFORMS.

slayings were carried out by fellow officers. The slain include elderly people and children, some as young as sixteen months according to a recent report from Amnesty International titled "Thailand: Widespread abuses in the administration of justice."

There's no denying that widespread drug trafficking and sky-high addiction rates are a problem in Thailand. Over the last ten years, there has been a huge increase in the smuggling of methamphetamine pills, called "*ya ba*" by locals, becoming even more prevalent than the region's traditionally smuggled opium. Made extremely cheaply in neighboring Myanmar factories, the pills are then smuggled across Thailand's border. With the fifteen prisons across the country designed to hold just 90,000 currently overflowing with over 173,900 inmates, killing suspects rather than arresting and trying them in court would of course keep the prison population from further swelling. There were, as of May 31, 2002, a total 106,256 people in Thai prisons for drug offenses (77,970 men and 28,286 women), a whoping 66.46% of the total prison population, according to the Thailand Corrections Department website.

The human rights organization Amnesty International has for years voiced concerns with "the long-term problems of torture and ill-treatment, and by prison conditions amounting to cruel, inhuman or degrading treatment in

THE FIRST THREE MONTHS OF THE CAMPAIGN... BECAME A MURDER SPREE, WITH POLICE COMMITTING THOUSANDS OF WHAT MANY HUMAN RIGHTS ORGANIZATIONS ARE CALLING "EXTRA-JUDICIAL KILLINGS" OF SUSPECTED DRUG DEALERS AND ADDICTS.

Thailand." But the police shooting to death drug dealers and users in the streets was probably not what Amnesty International had in mind for reforms.

"The drug war was a smashing of people, targeting the local boys mostly, kids, the police informers, the mules the police used to make their job look good, people the police did not like," said Matthew McDaniel, founder and director of the Akha Heritage Foundation in Thailand,

"IT'S ALL WAR ON DRUGS BUT NO EMPHASIS ON HUMAN RIGHTS. THE PRISON POPULATION OF THE HILL TRIBES IS VERY HIGH. MANY PEOPLE KNOW THIS IS JUST ETHNIC CLEANSING...

(www.akha.org). "It was just violence without due process. Many people were murdered, many clearly with no drug connection." Living and working with the Akha hill tribe people for over twelve years, US ex-patriot McDaniel has seen firsthand the results of both drug addiction and the violent repression of the poverty-stricken Akha people by police and military forces. He concedes that one result of the latest campaign has been "less drug activity" but that "there never was any effort to work with the villages which would have worked as well, besides just killing everyone. In addition the economic situation is now worse, as drugs bridged the gap for farm land taken from the Akha, and now there is neither farm land or a drug economy" for the struggling Akha. McDaniel points out that Thailand's government waged their anti-drug campaign with support from the US, the DEA having an office there. The US takes part in joint military anti-drug training operations every year with Thai forces called Cobra Gold. The US supplies the Thai military equipment as well as training, and US Special Forces has a small contingent of "advisors" working with Thai anti-drug forces.

Although Prime Minister Thaksin's stated reason for declaring the War was to bring about a drug-free Thailand by Dec. 5, 2003, as a birthday present for Thailand's King Bhumibol Adulyadej, McDaniel doesn't believe that is the real reason for this bloody campaign. "It's all War

THE US REPORT DESCRIBED OFFICIAL BLACKLISTS OF SUSPECTED DRUG CRIMINALS, FROM WHICH POLICE WERE EXPECTED TO CULL A "PRESCRIBED PERCENTAGE," OR THEY'D BE FIRED.

on Drugs but no emphasis on human rights. The prison population of the hill tribes is very high. Many people know this is just ethnic cleansing. But the police are not included, nor businessmen and government people. None of them were killed." Hill tribe people in Thailand number just under one million, including the Akha, Lahu, Yao, Lisu, and Karen groups. They do not have citizenship, and according to Amnesty International "face discrimination with regard to education, health care, and other basic rights. At the same time they are exploited as a tourist

attraction while often being accused by the authorities and others of destroying the environment and using opium and other illegal drugs."

"I think the big operators wanted a consolidation," says McDaniel. "It also improved the control structure of the police and government, which is all central. Thai people tell me that because of the drug war killings they are now afraid to say anything at all about anything. So that was a success, now wasn't it. The US absolutely supported this. The killings with US-made equipment are in violation of the Leahy Amendment." The Leahy Amendment, first passed as part of the US Foreign Operations Appropriations Act in 1997, prohibits US military assistance to foreign military units that violate human rights with impunity, which aptly describes what has happened in Thailand.

Human rights workers and activists are not alone condemning the Thai anti-drug campaign. King Adulyadej himself stated in a 76th birthday speech that "The government reported about 2,500 people were killed. Some say more than 10,000 died. There must be some who were killed that we don't know about. In this country, who is going to take responsibility?" the king asked. "In the end, the prime minister must take responsibility."

Postscript: Despite "Victory" Yet Another War on Some Drugs and Users Declared in Thailand

Thailand's Prime Minister Thaksin Shinawatra declared yet another "new" War on Some Drugs and Users on Feb. 27, 2004, after declaring victory less than two months previously. Last year's 10 month "war on drugs," declared over December 3, 2003, left at least 2500, and possibly many more alleged druggies dead at police hands but did nothing to stop the flow of illegal drugs.

"Critics only focus on the death toll of bad people, rather than those officials who lost their lives for the public and the country. The criticisms are quite imbalanced," said Thaksin in response to the US government's annual *Country Reports on Human Rights Practices 2003* (released Feb. 25, 2004), which decried the Thai government's violent anti-drug campaign. But official Thai figures put the number of police and military troops killed during the campaign at approximately 31, compared to the thousands of suspects killed in the streets by police and military forces. The US report described official blacklists of suspected drug criminals, from which police were expected to cull a "prescribed percentage," or they'd be fired. "The [Thai] Government threatened retaliation against local officials who did not produce results," notes the US report.

"It's unacceptable to me the way the US came out with the report by citing media reports. What kind of friend are they?" said Thaksin, quoted in Thailand's *Nation* on Feb. 28. Considering previous and current US support of any and all anti-drug efforts around the world, one might understand Thaksin's frustration. "There were no human-rights violations during the 'war on drugs,'" said Rasamee Vistaveth, the deputy secretary general of Thailand's Narcotics Control Board, two days after Thaksin announced the resumption of the war.

"This operation is re-launched not because drugs are rampant again, but it is launched when enemies are retreating," said Thaksin when declaring the new campaign. "We must reinforce our attacks before they can recover and I am confident we will be able to contain them." A cynic might be forgiven for doubting this new War on Some Drugs and Users will be any more effective at ending drug use or abuse than the last.

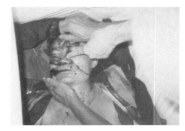

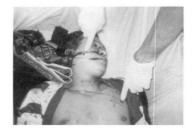

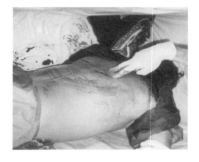

Loh Pah (looking to his left) and Leeh Huuh (looking to his right) were both murder after Phrao police of Chiangmai Province of Thailand called them both in for questioning. They never made it to the station.

Preface: Drugs, Oil, and War

Peter Dale Scott

This book, *Drugs, Oil, and War: The United States in Afghanistan, Colombia, and Indochina*, explores the underlying factors that have engendered a US strategy of indirect intervention in Third World countries through alliances with drug-trafficking proxies. This strategy was originally developed in the late 1940s to contain communist China; it has since been used to secure control over foreign petroleum resources. The result has been a staggering increase in the global drug traffic and the mafias assorted with it, a problem that will worsen until there is a change in policy.

The book also traces some of the processes by which covert interventions have escalated into war. Parts 1-2 of this book include an extensive introduction and lengthy new chapters on Afghanistan and Colombia. Part 3 consists of five updated chapters from my 1972 book *The War Conspiracy: The Secret Road to the Second Indochina War*.

This book explores ongoing causal patterns that have helped shape US foreign policy, sometimes at a deeper level than was recognized even by bureaucrats in high places. Under pressure from interested outsiders, decisions were made by the United States, after World War II in Burma and again in Laos in 1959-1965, to back armies and governments that were supporting themselves through the drug traffic. This has led to a linked succession of wars, from Vietnam to Afghanistan, which have suited the purposes of international oil corporations and US drug proxy allies, far more than those of either the US government or its people. Those decisions were also major causes for the dramatic increase in drug trafficking over the last half century.

Today drug networks are important factors in the politics of every continent. The United States returns repeatedly to the posture of fighting wars in areas of petroleum reserves with the aid of drug-trafficking allies (or what I call drug proxies) with which it has a penchant to become involved. Surprisingly, this is true even in Colombia, where we are nominally fighting a war on drugs; yet the chief drug-trafficking faction, the paramilitaries, are allies

> THE UNITED STATES RETURNS REPEATEDLY TO THE POSTURE OF FIGHTING WARS IN AREAS OF PETROLEUM RESERVES WITH THE AID OF DRUG-TRAFFICKING ALLIES (OR WHAT I CALL DRUG PROXIES) WITH WHICH IT HAS A PENCHANT TO BECOME INVOLVED.

of our allies, the Colombian army. Worse, they are the descendants of yet another clever CIA notion—to train terrorists to fight the left—which has once again come back to haunt us.

This is the situation that has recently engaged the United States in Afghanistan, a country through which until 1998 a US oil company, UNOCAL, hoped to build oil and gas pipelines. The drug-trafficking network of al Qaeda and Osama bin Laden, a former CIA ally operating out of caves designed and paid for by the CIA, has just been defeated with the help of another drug proxy, the Afghan Northern Alliance. In the pursuit of bin Laden, the United States defeated his allies the Taliban (which in 2000 had enforced a total ban on opium cultivation in its area), with the aid of the Northern Alliance (which in the same period had overseen a trebling of opium cultivation in its area).

As this book goes to press, (March, 2003) the new Afghan government has initiated a nominal ban on opium cultivation. But the United States has not given the Hamid Karzai regime enough financial support to make the ban work. Clearly the drug traffic itself is now a well-financed transnational power player in the region, and there are no serious current plans to reduce it. (There are only minimal plans to repair the devastation wrought by US bombing on an Afghan economy that was already in ruins after decades of international and civil war.)

Even if there were an effective ban on opium production and trafficking in Afghanistan, one could still predict with some confidence that it would increase in a neighboring area, such as Tajikistan or Kyrgyzstan. As the drug traffic grows in the new area, it will help destabilize the host states in the region, none of which is too secure to begin with. Without a change in policy, the United States, which has already sent troops into the region, will sooner or later be confronted with another crisis that calls for intervention.

These problems facing America are by no means entirely of its own making. But one recurring cause, commonly recognized, is US dependence on foreign oil and its need to control international oil markets. Past US support for drug proxies is another more covert and less recognized contributing factor, one that must be acknowledged if the root causes for these crises are to be addressed.

Conversely, the great resistance that still exists to acknowledging past US involvement in and responsibility for covert intrigues contributes to our present inability to bring true peace and security to the rest of the world. The agencies responsible for past errors are too concerned to preserve not only their reputations but their alliances and, above all, the corrupt social systems in which such alliances have thrived. Consequently an international drug traffic, which the United States helped enlarge, continues to thrive.

I shall argue in this book that covert operations, when they generate or reinforce autonomous political power, almost always outlast the specific purpose for which they were designed. Instead they enlarge and become part of the hostile forces the United States has to contend with. To put it in terms I find more precise, *parapolitics*, the exercise of power by covert means, tends to metastasize into *deep politics*, an interplay of unacknowledged forces over which the original parapolitical agent no longer has control. This is the heart of the analysis.

In my book *Deep Politics and the Death of JFK* (pp. 7-8), I give a seminal example of this process: US parapolitical use of Mafia figures like Vito Genovese in postwar Italy. This was a conscious operation that soon led to the deep political dominance of Italian party politics by a Mafia out of control. That example will serve in miniature for the history of all US interventions since then in Asia. In 1951 a decision was made to ship arms and supplies to the armies of the Kuomintang (KMT) drug network in Burma. This led to a fivefold increase in Burmese opium production in less than a decade, from eighty to four hundred tons. By 1999, the peak year before the ban imposed by the Taliban took effect, world opium production had reached 7,000 tons. Of this, 4,700 tons, or 70%, was being grown in Afghanistan and trafficked by heirs of the mujahedin who in the 1980s had been financed, armed, and supported by the CIA.

Again, the United States was not solely responsible for this growth. Some of it would have occurred anyway, possibly (as the US government used to contend) under the guidance of a hostile power such as China or the Soviet Union. The point is that the drug problem cannot be understood, let alone properly addressed, until the parapolitical consequences of CIA involvement have been acknowledged and corrected.

> ...COVERT OPERATIONS, WHEN THEY GENERATE OR REINFORCE AUTONOMOUS POLITICAL POWER, ALMOST ALWAYS OUTLAST THE SPECIFIC PURPOSE FOR WHICH THEY WERE DESIGNED. INSTEAD THEY ENLARGE AND BECOME PART OF THE HOSTILE FORCES THE UNITED STATES HAS TO CONTEND WITH.

Oil

The presence of drug trafficking in the background of these interventions is paralleled by considerations about oil. Here too decisions made freely after World War II have helped to enmesh the United States in a problematical situation—the risks from terrorism are continuously increasing and extrication will not now be easy.

Right after World War II, building on the so-called Quincy Agreements with Saudi Arabia in 1945, the United States moved to dominate a global system for the production and distribution of oil. Starting with the Truman Doctrine in 1946, US geostrategic thinking was oil based. What began as a strategy for containment of the Soviet Union has become more and more nakedly a determination to control the oil resources of the world. This pursuit has progressively deformed the domestic US economy, rendering it more and more unbalanced and dependent on heavy military expenditures in remote and ungovernable areas—most recently Afghanistan. It has also made the United States an increasingly belligerent power, fighting wars, especially in Asia, where it turns time after time to allies and assets prominent in the global drug traffic.

From the outset US strategy in Southeast Asia envisaged protecting what President Eisenhower once referred to as "the rich empire of Indonesia," whose primary export was oil.[8] In the 1970s, as opium production in Asia shifted west from the Golden Triangle to the Golden Crescent, so also US interventions, first covert and then overt, shifted from Indochina to Afghanistan.

I do not mean to suggest that domination of oil resources was the sole consideration on the minds of US policy

> IN SHORT THE ETIOLOGY OR ORIGIN OF GLOBAL TERRORISM IS ROOTED PARTLY IN THE HISTORICAL CONTEXT OF PREVIOUS US POLICY DECISIONS WITH RESPECT TO BOTH DRUGS AND OIL. I SAY THIS NOT TO CAST BLAME BUT TO SUGGEST THE PROPER DIRECTION TO SEARCH FOR SOLUTIONS

planners. On the contrary, they believed in their own rhetoric of defending the so-called free world from communist domination, whether Soviet or Chinese. But inasmuch as what they feared above all was communist control of oil resources, the result of their planning was continuously to strengthen US domination of an increasingly unified global oil system.

From Iran in 1953 to Indonesia in 1965 and Ghana in 1966 the CIA was involved in the covert overthrow of governments around the world that (as Michael Tanzer noted years ago) had threatened to nationalize their oil industries.[9] As US interventions overseas increased in the 1960s, so did US dependence on overseas oil to meet its growing demands. When this exposure led to the oil shocks of the 1970s, the United States was forced into a double policy of controlling the international flow of oil and petrodollars. As we shall see, it solved the latter problem by means of secret agreements that maintained the strength of the US dollar at the expense of the Third World.

The resulting impoverishment of the Third World has been accompanied by a disastrous increase in global terrorism, which has now become a major focus of US foreign policy. Yet, as Frank Viviano observed in the *San Francisco Chronicle* (September 26, 2001), "The hidden stakes in the war against terrorism can be summed up in a single word:

> WITH RESPECT TO DRUGS, I WILL ONLY SAY THAT THE UNITED STATES MUST END THOSE REPRESSIVE POLICIES WHOSE RESULT (AND OFTEN INTENTION) IS TO MAINTAIN THE HIGH DRUG PRICES THAT STRENGTHEN AND ENRICH THE INTERNATIONAL DRUG TRAFFIC.

oil. The map of terrorist sanctuaries and targets in the Middle East and Central Asia is also, to an extraordinary degree, a map of the world's principal energy sources in the 21st century. The defense of these energy resources—rather than a simple confrontation between Islam and the West—will be the primary flash point of global conflict for decades to come, say observers in the region."[10]

Although it was not part of his subject, Viviano's observations can be applied also to other regions of oil and terrorism, such as Indonesia, Colombia, Somalia, and (because of oil pipelines) Chechnya and even Kosovo.

In short the etiology or origin of global terrorism is rooted partly in the historical context of previous US policy decisions with respect to both drugs and oil. I say this not to cast blame but to suggest the proper direction to search for solutions. Decision makers of a half century ago cannot be faulted for lacking the foreknowledge that comes more easily in retrospect. It is, however, not too late to address the legacy they have left us—a suspect affluence grounded in part on the impoverishment of the rest of the world. As long as that legacy is not corrected, we can be sure that the problem of terrorism will remain with us.

What to Do

The problem will not be solved by putting more and more US troops abroad, from Colombia to Kyrgyzstan. (Both countries, as it happens, are in oil regions and are experiencing a rapid increase in drug trafficking.) The quintessential example of such a build-up of US arms and personnel was Iran in the 1970s—a major cause, as is now obvious, for the Iranian revolution against the US client Shah. Hundreds of millions of US dollars for the Somali dictator Siad Barre encouraged him to pursue increasingly oppressive policies, which led in 1991 to his overthrow.

With respect to drugs, I will only say that the United States must end those repressive policies whose result (and often intention) is to maintain the high drug prices that strengthen and enrich the international drug traffic. With respect to oil, we must intensify the search for technological ways to reduce consumption at home and move toward a more multilateral and equitable oil system abroad. Above all, the United States must return to the multilateral system of global regulation that it helped establish after World War II and renounce the fatal temptation to become a hegemon. We must not repeat the follies of Napoleon and Hitler in the heartlands of Eurasia.

This shift will require a different strategy to deal with the dollar and with petrodollars, particularly those from Saudi Arabia and its neighbors in the Persian Gulf. At present the United States balances its payments by secret agreements with Saudi Arabia to recycle petrodollars to the United States and to ensure that OPEC sales all over the world are denominated in US dollars. These arrangements to ease pressure on the US currency have helped, as an inevitable consequence, to create debt crises all over the Third World.

The same secret agreements are perhaps the prime example of how secret US policies, barely documented, can give rise to global conditions of misery and unrest. People's strategies of public opposition to official policies, such as the rallies that activists like Noam Chomsky indefatigably address, are in my opinion unlikely to succeed until they expose the unjust secret arrangements and deals on which these official policies are based. The US political establishment, seemingly unassailable on its surface, becomes more vulnerable when the private, covert, and sometimes conspiratorial origins of what passes for public policy are exposed. This book is dedicated to examining war policies at this deeper level.

Meanwhile, official strategies that enrich the United States by impoverishing the rest of the world diminish the possibilities of peace and progress for this country. And our security is put still more at risk by giving military aid to

> THE US POLITICAL ESTABLISHMENT, SEEMINGLY UNASSAILABLE ON ITS SURFACE, BECOMES MORE VULNERABLE WHEN THE PRIVATE, COVERT, AND SOMETIMES CONSPIRATORIAL ORIGINS OF WHAT PASSES FOR PUBLIC POLICY ARE EXPOSED.

unpopular dictators. The United States tried this strategy in Vietnam in the 1960s, Iran in the 1970s, and Somalia in the 1980s, to name a few. We are still suffering from the anti-American reactions these policies produced. Yet today, as if we had learned nothing, we are establishing bases and giving military aid to the dictator of Uzbekistan—an ex-Soviet apparatchik with no program for dealing with his extensive Muslim opposition except to imprison them.

We cannot expect a reversal of these strategies from America's present leaders of either party, constrained as they are by an increasingly oppressive global system that is in large part of those parties' own making. Recent revelations have shown the extent to which contributions from energy companies have constrained both parties in America as they have politicians abroad. What we hear instead from Washington, although not without opposition, are increasingly strident calls for unilateralist policies in an allegedly unipolar world. Triumphal unilateralism in the United States and terroristic Islamism abroad have become more and more similar to (and dependent on) each other, with each invoking its opposite to justify its excesses.

The future of American democracy rests on our ability to recognize and separate our nation from the causal factors that lie at the heart of US global policies—policies that have produced such harmful results, not only for those who have been victimized on a world scale but also for Americans.

It would be folly to suggest that this book can bring peace to the world. But I do believe that it suggests new ways in which to search for peace. Above all I hope that it may help Americans understand how they may love their country and still come to accept its share of responsibility for an international order that cries out for amendment.

Just as some in the US government demonize others as terrorists forming an "axis of evil," so others turn such epithets back on the US government itself. I myself see little value in depicting either the United States or its enemies as an intractable other, to be opposed by means that may well prove counterproductive. Just as Islamism needs to be understood in its complexity, so does US power, which is at least as complex. Above all we have to recognize that US influence is grounded not just in military and economic superiority but also in so-called soft power (an "ability... that shapes the preferences of others," that "tends to be associated with intangible power resources such as an attractive culture, ideology, and institutions").[11]

We need a "soft politics" of persuasion and nonviolence to address and modify this country's soft power. Such a proposal is not utopian: the soft politics of the antiwar movement helped, despite many key errors of strategy, to hasten US disengagement from Vietnam. As it becomes increasingly clear that that war "dealt a major blow to the United States' ability to remain the world's dominant economic power,"[12] even the exponents of America's hard power may come in time to express their gratitude to critics of the Vietnam War.

As this book goes to press, this country is facing yet another needless and disastrous intervention in Iraq. For our sake as well as for the sake of the rest of the world, we must continue to develop alternative soft processes of change.

Endnotes

[1] Dwight D. Eisenhower, speech, August 4, 1953; *The Pentagon Papers: The Defense Department History of United States Decision Making on Vietnam*, Senator Gravel ed. (Boston: Beacon, 1971-1972), 1:592.

[2] Michael Tanzer, *The Political Economy of International Oil and the Underdeveloped Countries* (Boston: Beacon, 1969).

[3] Frank Viviano, *San Francisco Chronicle*, September 26, 2001.

[4] Joseph S. Nye Jr., *The Paradox of American Power: Why the World's Only Superpower Can't Go It Alone* (Oxford: Oxford University Press, 2002), 9.

[5] Immanuel Wallerstein, "The Eagle Has Crash Landed," *Foreign Policy*, July-August 2002.

Hashish and the War on Terror—Drugs in Uniform

Ron Jacobs

In the late 1970s, I used to visit with a Lebanese fellow who lived next door to my friends in Anaheim, California. This man had been a member of the rightwing Phalangist militia and had escaped the guns of other Lebanese militias with the help of the Israelis.

Usually our conversations revolved around safe topics like his children, his wife, and his growing interest in baseball, but on those occasions when he joined my friends and I in draining a fifth or two of bourbon, darker stories would emerge from the recesses of his memory. I was always careful to never let him know of my sympathies for the Palestinian cause, given my understanding that the Phalangists were intimately involved in Israel's campaign to wipe that phenomenon from the earth.

It became apparent over the course of these conversations that my acquaintance was mostly involved with the fundraising side of things in the Phalange movement. His tales of bank robberies and other types of fund transfers made for good adventure stories no matter what the politics behind them were.

The last time I saw him was on Christmas Eve of 1979. The rest of my friends were already asleep on the couches and chairs that sat in their living room. The former Phalangist and I were finishing the second fifth of bourbon and waiting for Santa. I decided to dig into my backpack for a pipeful of weed that I had brought along. I didn't know if my drinking buddy smoked, but I was getting tired of the alcohol buzz and needed something to lift its fog from my brain.

As I lit the pipe, he looked at me and told me that I must put it out. I asked him why and he grabbed the pipe from my hand, put out the ember with his thumb, went to the window and threw the pipe into the street. I was a bit startled by his actions and also unwilling to find out how pathological he was about marijuana so I said nothing. He explained that he was trying to become a citizen and did not want to do anything illegal, so he took away my pipe. I nodded. He continued, telling me that he smoked "many kilos" of hashish in Lebanon, but had sworn it off when he moved to the US. In fact, he had been a hashish smuggler during his last two years in the Middle East. (As it turned out, the Israelis had also helped him escape the clutches of Interpol and the US Drug Enforcement Agency after he was busted in a smuggling operation.)

> AS IT TURNED OUT, THE ISRAELIS HAD ALSO HELPED HIM ESCAPE THE CLUTCHES OF INTERPOL AND THE US DRUG ENFORCEMENT AGENCY AFTER HE WAS BUSTED IN A SMUGGLING OPERATION.

I must have looked interested, because he proceeded to tell me a story of how the Phalangist militia had occupied a region of Lebanon where marijuana was grown and turned into hashish. The region had been under the control of another faction in the multi-sided war then going on in Lebanon, but when the Phalange took it over, the hashish makers began doing business with them—money was money to them. The profits went to the movement and the movement bought guns with them. In this part of the world, said my drinking buddy, everybody made money from the drugs: Christian, Jew, Moslem, Lebanese, Palestinian, Israeli, everyone.

As I write this there have been at least three publicized hashish seizures in the various bodies of water that the US patrols in the Middle East. According to the Pentagon and its shills, the drugs in these seizures are being sold to make money for al Qaeda and other non-state terror organizations. Now, I don't know about you, dear reader, but I find this just a little too convenient. How the hell does the Pentagon know who is buying and selling these drugs, unless it's a Pentagon/CIA operation? Nevertheless, let's assume that the Pentagon is telling the truth. In that case, one has to wonder who is making the money from the increased opium production in liberated Afghanistan? Is the situation like that in Latin America, where the armed peasant organizations pay a reasonable price and take their cut from coca growers in their zones while the government supported militias see the drug from cultivation to production and rarely suffer any consequence (while also turning a tidy profit)? Or, is it like it was in Laos and other parts of Southeast Asia during the war there, with the CIA providing deniable transport for drug shipments to those warlords who do

> IN THIS PART OF THE WORLD, SAID MY DRINKING BUDDY, EVERYBODY MADE MONEY FROM THE DRUGS: CHRISTIAN, JEW, MOSLEM, LEBANESE, PALESTINIAN, ISRAELI, EVERYONE.

the US's dirty work? If this is the case, then is the war in Afghanistan just another drug dealing operation and are the captured shipments owned by drug producers who won't work with the CIA for ideological or other reasons?

If one recalls the various US wars on Central American countries during the 1980s, he or she will certainly remember the so-called Iran-Contra affair. In essence, this was a US operation that was run out of the Vice President's office (Pappy Bush) that traded guns for cocaine to the CIA proxy army in Nicaragua (the Contras) and in turn traded weapons parts and technology via Israel to the Khomeini government in Iran for cash. This cash came from the sales of the contra cocaine to various drug dealers in the United States—some of whom were enterprising enough to turn the coca paste and powder into a substance that would turn many of our country's inner cities into cocaine-fueled war zones. The substance I am referring to became known as crack.

The tale related to me by my Lebanese acquaintance and the endless reports of secret US involvement in drug dealing prove only one thing: That is that there is probably no armed organization, local or international, that has not been involved in this business. It is a quick and sure way to make money that cannot be traced and does not need to be accounted for. When the US trumpets a drug seizure in the Gulf or in the deserts of Texas, remember to ask yourself how many others they let through, either because of individual corruption or because of those shipments' role in funding their national security.

Aha! Is this one more reason to keep drugs illegal? If so then, not only does the "war on drugs" provide an easy method to lock up unruly and potentially unruly elements of society as a means of maintaining internal security for the elites and their supporters, it also provides a rationale that can be used to wrongfully board and seize ships suspected of carrying illegal drugs in international waters. In a complementary manner, the pretext of potential terrorism as a reason to violate previously agreed to international laws and standards as to various human and sovereignty issues, when combining anti-drug with anti-terror laws, has created an authoritarian international military and intelligence apparatus composed of government and private military entities that is capable of investigating and incarcerating virtually any of the earth's citizens.

In an aside, one has to wonder how long it will be before US troops begin to use some of the drugs they are capturing. After all, in a war-torn land where they must celebrate New Year's with non-alcoholic beer, the desire of some soldiers for some kind of mood modification and stress release will eventually override any fear they have of the military's anti-drug regimen. Sure, it's not the 1960s or Vietnam, but many human psyches can take only so much of a life without the type of release afforded by alcohol and other mood altering substances. During the Soviet war in Afghanistan their military also suffered from a drug problem thanks to the easy availability of hashish and opium combined with troop morale as low as that of the American soldiers during the last few years of America's war in Vietnam.

...IS THE WAR IN AFGHANISTAN JUST ANOTHER DRUG DEALING OPERATION AND ARE THE CAPTURED SHIPMENTS OWNED BY DRUG PRODUCERS WHO WON'T WORK WITH THE CIA FOR IDEOLOGICAL OR OTHER REASONS?

IN AN ASIDE, ONE HAS TO WONDER HOW LONG IT WILL BE BEFORE US TROOPS BEGIN TO USE SOME OF THE DRUGS THEY ARE CAPTURING.

Afghanistan: Drug War Yields to Terror War as Rumsfeld Glad-Hands Drug Dealing Warlords

Phil Smith

Despite all its fulminations about wiping out the global drug trade, the US government is once again turning a blind eye to the trade when some of its key allies are the ones overseeing the drug running. The country in question is Afghanistan, by far the world's largest opium producer, and the allies with dirty hands are some of that violence-torn country's warlords. Despite longstanding allegations linking warlords including Abdul Rashid Dostum and Ustad Attas Mohammed to the opium trade, US Secretary of Defense Donald Rumsfeld publicly embraced the pair at a meeting in Afghanistan early in December, 2003.

The defense secretary was not congratulating the warlords for their role in supplying Western Europe with cheap heroin. Instead, he was thanking them for ending armed clashes between their supporters and allowing the Afghan government led by President Hamid Karzai to take possession of some of the tanks and other heavy military equipment they control.

Rumsfeld's interest in the warlords is all about realpolitik. Since the overthrow of the Taliban government as part of the US "war on terror" in December 2001, the US has tried desperately to cobble together a regime that can govern the fractious nation, and the Afghan warlords are a central component in that plan. In fact, warlords like Dostum and Mohammed are the face of the regime in the vast areas they control; the central government headed by Karzai effectively governs only Kabul and its outlying areas. Dostum has also been rewarded by being named Deputy Secretary of Defense for the Karzai government.

If Rumsfeld is interested in dalliances with men who do not allow scruples to get in the way of political necessity, he has certainly found his man in Dostum. An Uzbek from Mazar-i-Sharif in the Afghan north, Dostum rose to power as a Communist labor leader in the 1970s, forming militias to fight on the side of the Russians and then their Afghan puppet, Najibullah. But seeing that Najibullah was doomed, Dostum switched sides, joining the US-financed

> DESPITE LONGSTANDING ALLEGATIONS LINKING WARLORDS INCLUDING ABDUL RASHID DOSTUM AND USTAD ATTAS MOHAMMED TO THE OPIUM TRADE, US SECRETARY OF DEFENSE DONALD RUMSFELD PUBLICLY EMBRACED THE PAIR AT A MEETING IN AFGHANISTAN EARLY IN DECEMBER, 2003.

mujahedin in their jihad against the Communists. During the 1990s, Dostum's forces switched sides repeatedly, helping plunge Afghanistan into the chaos that led to the rise of the Taliban in 1995. He fled to Turkey with the rise of the Taliban, returning to rejoin the US-backed Northern Alliance as it drove the Taliban from power in late 2001.

Dostum has been described as a "war criminal" by groups such as Human Rights Watch and Amnesty International, which cite not only his role in the Afghan civil wars of the 1990s—particularly massive rocket attacks on Kabul in 1994 by his forces that killed thousands of civilians— but also his treatment of prisoners, including the deaths of hundreds who suffocated or froze to death in the shipping containers Dostum used to hold them in after the battle of Mazar-i-Sharif in December 2001. He is also notorious for his treatment of his own men: He is widely alleged to have punished troops by tying them to the treads of tanks and driving the tanks until nothing is left but pieces of flesh.

> IF RUMSFELD IS INTERESTED IN DALLIANCES WITH MEN WHO DO NOT ALLOW SCRUPLES TO GET IN THE WAY OF POLITICAL NECESSITY, HE HAS CERTAINLY FOUND HIS MAN IN DOSTUM.

> HE IS WIDELY ALLEGED TO HAVE PUNISHED TROOPS BY TYING THEM TO THE TREADS OF TANKS AND DRIVING THE TANKS UNTIL NOTHING IS LEFT BUT PIECES OF FLESH.

Dostum and the Northern Alliance, which now dominates the government in Kabul, have been linked repeatedly to the opium trade. According to the US State Department, after the Taliban ban on opium planting in 2001, almost all the opium in the country that year—77 tons—came from areas dominated by the Northern Alliance. And since the Alliance-dominated government came to power, opium production has gone through the roof, with the area under cultivation more than doubling over last year and increasing 36-fold from 2001.

The poppy crop is spreading rapidly, particularly in northeast Afghanistan, where the ethnic Tajik Northern Alliance is in control, said Christopher Langton of the London-based International Institute for Strategic Studies. Warlord Mohammed, one of the men with whom Rumsfeld shook hands, is the man in charge there. Some of the opium produced there is "leaking" south to Pakistan, Langston told the London *Guardian*, where the Taliban and al Qaeda could be benefiting, he added.

The opium crop is projected to generate a billion dollars in revenue inside Afghanistan this year, half of the country's Gross Domestic Product, and the fruits of that harvest are widely shared.

> THE OPIUM CROP IS PROJECTED TO GENERATE A BILLION DOLLARS IN REVENUE INSIDE AFGHANISTAN THIS YEAR, HALF OF THE COUNTRY'S GROSS DOMESTIC PRODUCT, AND THE FRUITS OF THAT HARVEST ARE WIDELY SHARED.

"They're all benefiting: the Taliban, al Qaeda, some former commanders, warlords who control their own territories," said Abdul Raheem Yaseer, assistant director of the Institute for Afghan Studies at the University of Nebraska-Omaha, one of the leading Afghan studies programs in the US "It is the higher up administrators and politicians who benefit more than the common people," he told DRCNet. "The warlords and commanders have used this to make money for years."

For the United Nations, US support of the warlords is doubly vexing. "Why is the international presence in Afghanistan not able to bring under control a phenomenon connected to international terrorism and organized crime?" asked Antonio Maria Costa, head of the UN drug office, in February. "Why is the central government in Kabul not able to enforce the ban on opium cultivation as effectively as the Taliban regime did in 2000-01?"

The answer is that the warlords control the opium trade, and the United States supports the warlords because it needs them to fend off a resurgent Taliban and its al Qaeda allies and to build a strong central government.

> WHILE WALTERS TALKS THE PROHIBITIONIST TALK, RUMSFELD WALKS THE REALPOLITIK WALK, AND THE US HOPS IN BED WITH SOME OF THE PLANET'S LARGEST DRUG DEALERS.

On December 9, the UN's top envoy to Afghanistan, Lakhdar Brahimi, again attacked the warlords. Many Afghans are angered by their corruption and prominent role in the government, said Brahimi in a discussion paper. "The perception that corruption exists... is coupled with the fear that the rapid expansion of the drug economy will undermine the nascent institutions of the state," he wrote. What is worse, Brahimi continued, is the disaffection, particularly in the Pashtun-dominated south, home of the Taliban and scene of increased fighting in recent weeks. "Now, a critical stage has been reached," wrote Brahimi. "The Taliban never accepted defeat... They and others are taking full advantage of the popular disaffection."

It is the threat of a resurgent Taliban that finally roused US drug warriors to at least pay lip service to their nominally prohibitionist policy. A few days before Rumsfeld met with Dostum and Mohammed, US drug czar John Walters launched a rhetorical broadside against the Afghan opium trade. "Poppy cultivation in Afghanistan is a major and growing problem," said Walters. "Drug cultivation and trafficking are undermining the rule of law and putting money in the pocket of terrorists. The drug trade is hindering the ability of the Afghan people to rebuild their country and rejoin the international community. It is in the interest of all nations, including our European partners, to help the Karzai government fight the drug trade."

A strong US anti-opium effort in Afghanistan would be welcome news to the US's European partners. Britain, where much of the Afghan opium will end up as heroin, has for the past two years tried a limited Afghan eradication campaign, but with little result. Britain has not succeeded in getting US assistance in its anti-opium campaign.

And what goes on with Afghani poppies has a huge impact on the global opium market. According to the United Nations Office on Drugs and Crime, when the Taliban ban on production went into effect in 2000, global opium production dropped by 19% to 4,700 tons. Since the end of the Taliban, Afghan production has spurred new growth in the global poppy crop, with the Afghans producing nearly 4,000 of the estimated 6,000 ton annual harvest this year. In its annual survey, *Global Illicit Drug Trends*, the UN reports that global production is increasing despite a shrinking number of acres devoted to the poppy. Poppy production is decreasing in Laos and Myanmar, but that crop is being replaced by more efficient Afghan production.

Walters also announced Operation Containment, designed to staunch the flow of opium from Afghanistan into Central Asia and on to Europe, but provided few details.

If recent history is any indication, however, Operation Containment will ignore the warlords allied to the US. More likely to be a real operation is Operation Avalanche, which with 2,000 US troops sweeping toward the Afghan-Pakistan border in the southeast, is designed to root out Taliban and al Qaeda fighters before the winter. It is the largest US military operation in Afghanistan since the fall of the Taliban. (As of December 10, Operation Avalanche has killed fifteen Afghan children and two peasant farmers, but no Taliban or al Qaeda.)

While Walters talks the prohibitionist talk, Rumsfeld walks the realpolitik walk, and the U.S. hops in bed with some of the planet's largest drug dealers. This is not new. In fact, it is not even new in Afghanistan. That country became the world's largest opium producer during the 1980s, when the US, through its intermediaries in Pakistan's intelligence services, sponsored the mujahedin fighters in their jihad against the Russian occupiers. Those opium fields helped overthrow the Russians, and the US turned a blind eye.

Similarly, the US turned a blind eye to cocaine trafficking among its Contra allies in Central America in the 1980s, opium and heroin trafficking among its Hmong and South Vietnamese government allies in Southeast Asia in the 1960s, and to heroin trafficking by French and Italian mobsters in Marseilles in the 1950s. (Better the mob than the Communist unions, went the argument.)

"This is not the first time we've had contradictory policies," concurred Ted Galen Carpenter, an international drug policy specialist at the Cato Institute in Washington, DC and author of *Bad Neighbor Policy: Washington's Futile War on Drugs in Latin America*. "The CIA, for example, at least looked the other way while its allies in Central America trafficked in drugs," he told DRCNet. "The need to eradicate drugs collides with the overall US policy of promoting stability in Afghanistan. I can't imagine the US doing anything that would promote political instability there, and trying to crack down on the drug trade would certainly carry that risk."

John Thompson, executive director of Canada's Mackenzie Institute, a free-market think-tank that studies political violence, largely agreed, telling DRCNet neither the US nor the government in Kabul can afford to press the effort to wipe out the opium trade right now. "That would drive the peasants into the hands of the Taliban," he said. "What is really needed now is to stabilize Afghanistan, and to do that the best thing may be to achieve a degree of political stability without tackling the drug problem. If you undermine the Karzai administration by waging war on the opium crop, you will just create a chaotic situation like there was ten years ago, and that's what gave rise to the Taliban in the first place," Thompson argued. "Getting political stability, getting the refugees home, getting infrastructure repaired—all of that should be a bigger priority than wiping out opium."

And trying to wipe out the trade probably wouldn't work anyway, Carpenter said. "In reality, we have little choice but to ignore it. We are not going to stamp it out. Opium has been a major cash crop for Afghanistan as long as anyone wants to remember. As we see with prohibitionist strategies in general, suppression doesn't work. If there is demand, there will be suppliers. If we do try to crack down, we will provoke political instability and probably hostility from the warlords against the occupation, and that could get American soldiers killed," Carpenter argued. "Walters will be overruled, although no one will say so out loud."

Maybe so. But it would also be nice if the US government could have a drug policy that did not stink of hypocrisy and situational ethics.

Plan Columbia: The Pentagon's Shell Game

Peter Gorman

Stopping the hard drug trade, ending a 35 year-old civil war, eliminating human rights abuses and returning political stability to one of the oldest democracies in the Americas all sound like good ideas, but the bottom line in Plan Colombia has more to do with big business, and particularly the oil business, than any of the above.

"On the worst days, there are sometimes more than 30 of them," she says. "They come in with nothing but their *muchilas*, backpacks. They've left everything to get out of Colombia. Or even worse, they come from our own border here in Ecuador. They are sick. Some have sores and rashes. They can't breath, they complain their joints ache or that they can no longer see clearly. No one believes us but that doesn't mean it isn't true."

The woman paused. Her name is Sister Carmen Rosa Perez and she is a nun working at the Iglesia Miguel de Sucumbios in Lago Agria, the largest city in Sucumbios, one of the districts that fronts the Putumayo River. Across the river is

> THEY ARE SICK. SOME HAVE SORES AND RASHES. THEY CAN'T BREATH, THEY COMPLAIN THEIR JOINTS ACHE OR THAT THEY CAN NO LONGER SEE CLEARLY. NO ONE BELIEVES US BUT THAT DOESN'T MEAN IT ISN'T TRUE."

the Colombian department of Putumayo, a remote region in northwest Amazonia that has become the center of both Bill Clinton's Plan Colombia and George Bush's expanded Andean Initiative. Sister Carmen's job since October, 2000 has been to see to the refugees from Colombia's raging civil war and get them properly registered. In two years she and the other nuns at the church have registered 3,676 refugees of the combat. The vast majority has come from Colombia, to escape the violence of the right wing paramilitaries, the AUC, the leftist Revolutionary Armed Forces of Colombia, the FARC, or the Colombian military. But in the past several months, she says, there are more and more Ecuadorians passing through the church as well. They don't come to register as refugees of a foreign land, but because they have been brutalized, either by the conflict spilling across the river that separates the two countries, or by the loss of their crops to the defoliation that plays such a key part of Plan Colombia. The church, says Sister Carmen, makes sure that those with physical ailments who have made the roughly ten mile journey from the border are seen by someone with at least a rudimentary knowledge of medicine, which frequently is all they have to offer.

"At first they came to escape the violence, but now they mostly come to try to find work and food to feed their families. The spraying has killed all their crops, all their animals, even the animals of the forest are gone."

Sister Carmen speaks plainly. She is not new to this. She came from Colombia, in Putumayo, eight years ago, after she graduated from the religious University of Saint Thomas.

The Business of Plan Colombia

When Bill Clinton unveiled Plan Colombia in late 1999, its stated goals included eradicating the coca and opium poppy plants used to make cocaine and heroin, respectively, while helping the Colombian government end its civil war, reduce human rights abuses, and reestablish political stability through aid to its military and police forces. There was beauty in the Plan's simplicity: eliminating the plants which produced the drugs that generated black market funding for its civil war would almost solve all the problems facing Colombia simultaneously. While President Bush has expanded Plan Colombia's vision—along with renaming it the Andean Initiative—to include the deconstruction of all "terrorist groups" operating in Colombia, he's kept the other stated goals in place.

Yet Plan Colombia may not have been fueled by a sense of US good heartedness and justice nearly as much as it was by the push of big business. The war in Colombia had been raging for more than 30 years, after all, before the US decided to get involved. Cocaine use had already

> YET PLAN COLOMBIA MAY NOT HAVE BEEN FUELED BY A SENSE OF US GOOD HEARTEDNESS AND JUSTICE NEARLY AS MUCH AS IT WAS BY THE PUSH OF BIG BUSINESS.

peaked during the crack epidemic of the late 1980s and '90s that swept across the United States like a bad wind and was on the decline long before intervention in Colombia became a White House imperative, but in 1996, the US-Colombia Business Partnership was founded to represent US companies with interests in Colombia, and a well-financed lobbying effort for just such intervention began. The companies represented by the Business

Partnership included the Occidental Petroleum Corp, the Enron Corp, Texaco (now merged with Chevron) and BP Amoco among others. Each of those companies had huge stakes in Colombia and all had suffered financial losses because of the war.

As nearly all the funding for Plan Colombia was toward military ends, the early winners in the final $1.3 billion Plan Colombia sweepstakes that Congress approved as an emergency measure in 2000 were three military contractors: Sikorsky Helicopters, Bell Helicopter Textron Corp, and DynCorp. Sikorsky, of Stratford, Connecticut, secured a $360 million contract for 30 Black Hawk helicopters; the Ft. Worth-based Bell got a $66 million contract for 33 of its Huey helicopters, and DynCorp, a Reston, Virginia-based corporation, had an ongoing

THE BIGGEST POTENTIAL WINNERS IN THE PLAN COLOMBIA SWEEPSTAKES THOUGH, THE OIL COMPANIES, WOULD HAVE TO WAIT A WHILE FOR THEIR PAYOFF, BUT WHEN IT COMES IT WILL BE A GOOD ONE.

contract upgraded and renewed for two years for nearly $600 million. Thus DynCorp, a company which primarily utilizes former military personnel for its government contracts worldwide became the lynchpin of Plan Colombia. Their contract calls for them to help in drug interdiction, troop and supply transport, reconnaissance, search and rescue missions, aircraft maintenance, helicopter and crop-dusting pilot training and a host of other jobs. Most importantly, DynCorp was given the lucrative aerial fumigation contract to eliminate all the coca plants and poppy growing in Colombia. Monsanto, the pharmaceutical giant from St. Louis which had provided Agent Orange as a defoliant during the Viet Nam war was also a beneficiary as one of its products, Roundup—glyphosate—was chosen as the Plan Colombia herbicide.

The biggest potential winners in the Plan Colombia sweepstakes though, the oil companies, would have to wait a while for their payoff, but when it comes it will be a good one. The US Geological Survey Hollin-Napo Unit, part of the World Petroleum Resource Assessment 2000 was released just prior to the passage of Plan Colombia in April 2000. What it indicated was that there were between 130 and 300 commercially viable but undiscovered oil fields in the region covering Southern Colombia, northeastern Ecuador, and northwestern Peru. The heaviest concentration of those lay in Putumayo in Colombia and across the river in Sucumbios, Ecuador. Estimates as to the size of the fields began at a minimum of 1 million barrels—less is not considered commercially viable—and topped out at 750 million barrels. But those estimates may be low: One of the fields pinpointed in the Hollin-Napo Survey was discovered earlier this year—the Ishpingo-Tamococha-Tiputini, or ITT oil field—and has 1.41 billion barrels of proven reserves. Fifteen foreign companies are currently

WITH ORGANIZED CRIME IT IS THE SAME AS WITH AMERICAN COMMERCIAL GIANTS: THE BOTTOM LINE IS WHAT IS IMPORTANT."

bidding on the rights to develop it and extract the oil. The ITT field alone "doubles Ecuador's known oil reserves," according to Leslie Wirpsa, a graduate Fellow in Human Rights at Stanford, who is studying oil in the region.

There are problems standing in the way of most of the oil exploration in both Putumayo and Sucumbios, however. In Colombia there is the civil war and coca; in Ecuador there is indigenous ownership or the protected reserve status of much of the land and it, with its extraordinary biodiversity, is diligently protected by local and foreign environmentalists.

Another issue that exists in both Putumayo and Sucumbios is the difficulty of pinpointing oil reserves because of the thick jungle canopy that covers much of the region. Satellite photography, an invaluable tool in oil exploration, cannot see through forests. Geologists can read a lot just from the type of vegetation growing in an area, but not as much as they can seeing the surface itself.

Gordon Staples, Research and Product Developer for RADARSAT, a Canadian Satellite Imaging company that works extensively in oil and gas exploration, says that "it's an art to read these satellite images for oil exploration. In the dense forests of Central Canada geologists see variation in forest-type which implies geological formation—they can read the topology despite not seeing it. But in areas of dense tropical jungle the geology is that much more complex and there are fewer geologists who can do that. In other words, the differentiation between oil deposits and subsurface water deposits is considerably easier— cheaper—if there is no ground cover."

Coca in Colombia

There are more than 200 species in the Erythroxylaceae, or coca, family, but only two have a high enough alkaloid content to have any commercial value in the manufacture of cocaine: Erythroxylum coca v coca, or Bolivian coca and Erythroxylum novogranatense v novogranatense, or Colombian coca. Both species have been cultivated for at least 3,000 years—as evidenced on pottery dating to at least 500 BC—and the plant's leaves have traditionally been utilized for religious, social and medicinal reasons. When the cocaine alkaloid was isolated in the mid-19th century though, only Bolivian coca was used in its production. It grows well in the moist tropical forests on the eastern slopes of the Andes mountains in Bolivia and Peru at altitudes ranging from 1,500 to 6,500 feet and has an alkaloid content considerably higher than any of the others.

Then, during the mid-1990s, when Colombia overtook Peru as the world's number one producer of coca, Colombian coca was pressed into commercial use because Bolivian coca doesn't grow there. Colombian coca grew well on either mountain slopes or in the sweltering lowland jungle and was particularly drought resistant. According to botanist James Duke, Ph.D., an expert on Erythroxylum who formerly worked with the US Department of Agriculture on alternative crop issues in Amazonia, the switch to Colombian coca presented a problem, however, because it had a lower alkaloid content than Bolivian coca. "The poorer alkaloid content of the Colombian coca was the reason the Colombian Cartels never minded sharing their profits with Bolivia and Peru," says Duke. "If Colombian were as good or better than Bolivian or Peruvian coca, that's what the Colombian's would have used. With organized crime it is the same as with American commercial giants: the bottom line is what is important."

With a lesser alkaloid content, meeting 70-80% of the world's demand for cocaine necessitated growing considerably more acreage than formerly needed with Bolivian coca. Calls to both the Drug Enforcement Administration (DEA) and the State Department to compare the alkaloid content of the two coca species revealed that neither knew the answer. A DEA spokesman admitted they had never done such a test, and the US Dept. of State, through Rebecca Brown-Thompson, spokesperson for Rand Beers, Assistant Secretary of State for International Narcotics and Law Enforcement Affairs said "we've never bothered to check that" and questioned why it would be of interest.

The question that Brown-Thompson dismisses as unimportant goes straight to the heart of Plan Colombia, because the increase in the use of the lesser alkaloid-content Colombian coca over the potent Bolivian coca has led to major increases in acreage under cultivation in the last 10 years. [Editor's note—the US State Department released figures on March 22, 2004 in their annual report on coca cultivation in Colombia, stating that acreage devoted to growing coca in Colombia has decreased an incredible 21% in 2003, dropping from 355,347 acres in 2002 to 280,071 acres in 2003. Peru saw a drop of 15%, while Bolivia racked up a 17% increase. There was a total 15% drop in total production for the region. This has made no dent in availability in the US though, leading to speculation that production has simply moved yet again into surrounding regions or further into the jungles.] It seems that when it's the time of year for Congress to allocate more funding for spraying the numbers are always up, but when it's time to look at the success of the program they are always down.) Colombia, for instance, was estimated to be growing about 250,000 acres as late as 1998. But State Department numbers released on March 7, 2002, suggest that during 2001, Colombia had roughly 420,000 acres, close to 700 square miles of coca under

cultivation, an increase of 40% over four years. Despite the near-doubling of Colombia's crop, however, cocaine prices have not decreased: the standard law enforcement measuring stick being the price of a gram of cocaine in New York City, which dropped from $100-$120 in 1980 to $30-$50 in 1992 and has remained stable ever since. The stability of the price is the law enforcement indicator

DEPUTY ASSISTANT BROWNFIELD WAS EITHER MISINFORMED OR LYING.

that there is no increase in available product, which in turn reinforces the idea that it has taken a great deal of Colombian coca to simply replace the more potent but diminished supply of Bolivian coca from Bolivia and Peru.

That increase, much of which has taken place in the southern Colombian state of Putumayo, has been a perfect accident for generating numbers that justify Plan Colombia's key stated component of coca eradication in the media, and therefore the US public's eyes.

Coca Eradication

In the year prior to the implementation of Plan Colombia, a US-financed coca eradication project already in place— which utilized DynCorp's services under the direction of the Colombian police—saw more than 160,615 acres of coca fumigated by the Colombians, who claimed that 85% of the plants sprayed died. A US CIA assessment of their work stated that their numbers were unjustified, claiming that only 25% of the fumigated plants were actually killed. Colombian authorities were indignant, claiming that what the US, which relied exclusively on satellite images rather than ground checks, was seeing on their images were new shrubs and grass reclaiming the jungle floor, rather than coca.

The issue is important because coca takes a considerable time to reach an age when it can begin to be harvested commercially—three years from seed and more than a year from cuttings (see SIDEBAR). If the US assessment was correct, most of the plants would continue to produce cocaine alkaloid, as well as cuttings for new plantings. If the Colombian assessment was correct, not only would the area sprayed be almost devoid of coca for between one and three years, there might not even be enough healthy plants remaining to produce the cuttings necessary to regenerate the sprayed area.

But utilizing the numbers discrepancy, when Plan Colombia went into effect, the US made sure that DynCorp was firmly at the helm of the fumigation effort, rather than an adjunct to the Colombian police.

During 2001, the first year spraying was done under the banner of Plan Colombia, Anne Patterson, the US Ambassador to Colombia, estimated that 198,000 acres of Colombia's coca were fumigated, much of that in

Peter Gorman

Putumayo. With the onset of Plan Colombia came the onset of problems for the people in the regions being sprayed. Farmers who were told they could opt to be paid by the US for voluntary crop eradication complained they were sprayed despite having uprooted their coca and that few were ever paid. Others claimed that despite US assurances from the State Department that spraying would be pinpoint and only utilized on coca crops of more than seven acres, thousands of people with small family farms were sprayed as well, got sick and were ultimately displaced by the spraying. Additionally, there were complaints of animals dying and food crops poisoned.

The US denied the allegations, insisting that the product being used, a variant of Monsanto's household herbicide Roundup, was safe. On April 30, 2001, shortly after Plan Colombia's coca fumigation began, William R. Brownfield, Deputy Assistant Secretary of State for the Bureau of Western Hemisphere Affairs wrote in the *Philadelphia Inquirer* that "Some critics have claimed that aerial spraying of illegal drug crops is done indiscriminately and that it harms people, kills animals and damages the environment. Others charge that US policies exacerbate human rights problems and have resulted in large numbers of displaced persons. These claims are untrue....

"...Areas to be sprayed are carefully selected, and spraying is tightly controlled, not indiscriminate. Aerial eradication focuses on industrial-scale operations, not smaller-scale growers. The agent used in aerial eradication is the herbicide glyphosate....It is one of the least harmful herbicides to appear on the world market....Accounts claiming that glyphosate causes damage to humans, animals and the environment are unfounded."

Deputy Assistant Brownfield was either misinformed or lying. Four months before he opined in the *Inquirer*, Dutch journalist Marjon van Royen had elicited and published an admission by the State Department in the Dutch newspaper NRC *Handlesblad*, that it wasn't Roundup, but Roundup Ultra that was being utilized in the spraying in Colombia. Additionally, at that same time the State Department admitted that a Colombian product called Cosmoflux was added to the spray mixture as a surfactant to help keep the herbicide on the plant long enough to do its work. Along with their admissions, the State Department was quick to add that both Roundup Ultra and Cosmoflux were approved by the US Environmental Protection Agency.

That was nonsense. The EPA had never heard of Cosmoflux and according to a spokesperson even now they have not tested it: "We don't examine products made for use in a foreign country."

The question of whether it was Roundup or Roundup Ultra that was being used, and the presence of Cosmoflux is not a minor one in the context of the collateral damage spraying might do to food crops, animals and people.

Roundup Ultra is considerably stronger than the regular Roundup found in garden centers. It was only approved for use in the US in November 2001, and then only for certain commercial, non-agricultural applications. The handling instructions correspond to the highest Environmental Protection Agency toxicity rating, Class 1, while the Roundup used in yards and gardens falls into the lower, Class 3 EPA toxicity rating. Aside from the toxicity of Roundup Ultra, there is also the question of the chemical formulation of Cosmoflux. When environmentalists pointed out to the State Department that no toxicological tests had ever been performed on the mixture of Roundup Ultra with Cosmoflux, the British company ICI, makers of one of the key ingredients of Cosmoflux, decided to withdraw its component from the final product. According to a report published in the July 1, 2001 London *Observer*, "ICI does not want its name dragged into such a programme, particularly as there have been reports of children in Colombia who have inhaled the chemicals falling ill." When questioned about what replaced the withdrawn ICI component in Cosmoflux, the State Department's Rebecca Brown-Thompson said "We have found a Colombian company to make it," but would not reveal the manufacturer.

Scientists who have requested the Cosmoflux formula to conduct such testing have been told by the State Department that the information is "proprietary" and "classified."

Despite US denials that Roundup Ultra combined with Cosmoflux is hazardous to humans and animals, the warning label of common Roundup alone suggests otherwise. Regarding humans: "Do not allow workers into treated areas for a period of four hours." Regarding animals: "We recommend that grazing animals such as horses, cattle, sheep, goats, rabbits, tortoises, and fowl remain out of the treated area for two weeks." Regarding plant life: "Avoid contact of herbicide to foliage, green stems, exposed non-woody roots or fruit of crops, desirable plants, and trees because severe injury or destruction is likely to result."

The label makes particular note of drift as well, under a section boldly headlined "ATTENTION," in which it is stated in capital letters: "AVOID DRIFT. EXTREME CARE MUST BE USED WHEN APPLYING THIS PRODUCT TO PREVENT INJURY TO DESIRABLE PLANTS AND CROPS."

Those warnings were more accurate than Deputy Assistant Brownfield's assessment of the damage the fumigation campaign was doing. Two health and environmental studies were carried out after complaints from campesinos were made shortly after Plan Colombia spraying began: one in the southern Colombian department of Putumayo and the other in the northern Ecuador province of Sucumbios. The Colombian study, conducted by biologist Elsa Nivia between February and April of 2001 indicated that more than four thousand people in Putumayo were suffering from acute eye irritation, respiratory problems, heart arrhythmias, skin lesions and rashes, temporary paralysis, and temporary blindness among other health problems. Additionally, thousands of animals had died, and food crops were destroyed.

The Ecuadorian study, done by the environmental organization Ecological Action in May and June of the same year under the direction of Dr. Adolpho Mondonaldo was even more revealing, as Ecuador was not supposed to

FUMIGATION IS DEATH. FUMIGATION IS ETHNOCIDE. GLYPHOSATE KILLS. IT DESTROYS FOOD CROPS AND PASTURELAND AND CONTAMINATES THE WATER. IT CONDEMNS ENTIRE COMMUNITIES TO DEATH BY STARVATION.

be sprayed or affected by drift. Dr. Mondonaldo, studying villages at distances of two, five and ten kilometers from the Putumayo river on the Ecuadorian side found that 100% of those living within two and five kilometers of the river suffered the identical symptoms as those living in Putumayo, Colombia. Among those people living ten kilometers from the river 89% suffered identical symptoms. As in Colombia, damage to food crops was severe, reaching 85-90% reduction in production.

The US State Department did not officially respond to the studies, but had already shown a disregard for reports that people, animals and food crops were being affected by the spraying when it released a report in early December, 2000 that noted: "As their illegal lives have been affected by the spraying, these persons do not give objective information."

Dr. Maldonado responded to his critics by noting, "If we have a series of pathologies that occur with great frequency near a particular point and decrease as the distance from that point increases, it means there is—or was—something at that point. That's just common sense, especially if the symptoms differ completely from pathologies found in other areas with similar characteristics."

FIRST COME THE HELICOPTERS, THEN COME THE PLANES, THEN THE SMELL AND THE SPRAY FALLS AND KILLS EVERYTHING."

The complaints were not coming from those with what the US described as "commercial plantations"—more than seven acres—in its Plan Colombia literature. The vast majority came from farmers who, as a CIA 2002 bulletin titled "Coca Factsheet, A Primer" noted, had less than one hectare of coca under cultivation. (One of the reasons for having such small plots, according to the same fact sheet, is that "It can take up to almost 300 man days to harvest one hectare," about 2.5 acres.) The complaints were not coming only from what the Colombian government repeatedly called "environmental extremists." The German government complained in the Spring of 2001 that chemical drift had destroyed several fishponds they'd underwritten and Colombia's own Human Rights Ombudsman office contacted the State Department to

call for an end to the fumigation. Klaus Nyholm, chief of the United Nations drug control efforts in Colombia weighed in against crop fumigation as well, claiming that the spraying was driving coca farmers to clear new areas of virgin jungle in which to grow.

The indigenous peoples of Putumayo also complained bitterly about the spraying in an open letter to the Colombian and US governments. The letter, titled "SOS from the Indigenous Peoples of Putumayo" was dated July 2, 2002 and signed by members of thirteen distinct tribal groups. It reads, in part, "Today we are caught in the crossfire, menaced by killings and displacement, while the State manifests its presence in the air with planes that slowly kill our plants and animals, our subsistence crops, and our people....We hold the Colombian government responsible for the misery, hunger, destruction and violence that fumigation causes in our territories. Fumigation is death. Fumigation is ethnocide. Glyphosate kills. It destroys food crops and pastureland and contaminates the water. It condemns entire communities to death by starvation.... The indigenous people of Putumayo reject the cultivation of illicit crops. But we equally reject the violent methods with which it is combated."

For its part, the US has continued to deny the allegations of human illness from glyphosate use, dismissing them as either over-dramatized or the inventions of coca growers. The closest the US has officially come to accepting that there might be problems came on September 5, 2002, when the Bush Administration, presented a report on the health and environmental risks of glyphosate to Congress. In it, it was noted that aerial spraying of herbicide "may cause eye irritation to farmers on the ground" but poses no "unreasonable risks or adverse affects" to humans or the environment. According to a Bush Administration official the irritation felt "as if you had baby shampoo in your eyes. It goes away after 72 hours." (Johnson and Johnson, makers of Johnson's Baby Shampoo refused to respond to the allegation that their shampoo could cause 72-hours of painful eye irritation in babies.)

The report was made at the insistence of Congress, which tied more than $15 billion in foreign aid to the assessment of the health and environmental risks associated with coca fumigation program in Colombia. Environmentalists railed against the report's results, noting that the Administration was investigating its own program with no outside oversight.

One of the reasons that the US has been able to deny the allegations of human illness caused by the fumigation campaign is that many of the problems may not be caused directly by the glyphosate as sprayed, but according to the product's safety sheet, when burned "4% of the volume released into the air is acetonitrile." Acetonitrile is methyl cyanide (CH_3CN), which is metabolized into hydrogen cyanide (HCN) by the human body, the same ultra-toxic gas used in the Nazi death camps. It is so dangerous to humans that Monsanto's own safety instructions include a caution that "When burned, stay out of smoke," and goes on to note that "firefighters or others who may be exposed to vapors or products of combustion should wear full protective clothing and self-contained breathing apparatus."

The health problems related to inhaling burning glyphosate are far more dangerous than general exposure to non-burning glyphosate. Drug Enforcement Administration documents produced in connection with early glyphosate spraying of Colombian marijuana fields list some of the hazards of inhaling burning glyphosate

OIL CORPORATIONS SUCH AS TEXACO ARE DESPISED BY THE LOCAL POPULATION IN ECUADOR BECAUSE OF THE DEVASTATION THEY HAVE CAUSED TO THE RAINFOREST THROUGH YEARS OF OPERATIONS THERE....

as "chest pains, cough, abdominal cramps, dyspnea [difficulty breathing], nausea, headache, chills, lassitude, and fatigue." Other DEA documents conceded additional health problems include "pale to ashen-gray skin, shallow pulse, hypotension, transient paralysis, and tachynea."

The issue is important because the coca growers in Colombia, like the farmers throughout Amazonia, utilize the slash-and-burn method of agriculture: they cut a section of forest and burn the vegetation on it to produce potash, which enhances soil nutrients. After the fumigation of their crops has killed them, the coca farmers do the same thing to clear the dead plants before they replant. "All the people cut and burn the fields," says Sister Carmen of Sucumbios. "There are no tractors here. The people cut and burn their fields after spraying and we think they are suffering for breathing of those burning chemicals. But there are large interests here at work, political and economic interests."

When questioned about the possibility of hydrogen cyanide poisoning from inhaling burning glyphosate, Monsanto spokesperson Janice Armstrong said there were "only trace amounts of acetonitrile…in the burning glyphosate." When reminded that her company's product safety sheet said otherwise, she said she was "unaware" of the safety sheet information and referred all other questions to the State Department's Rebecca Brown-Thompson.

Rebecca Brown-Thompson was likewise unaware that 4% of the volume released in burning glyphosate would

metabolize into hydrogen cyanide. "But then why is that a problem?" Told that the farmers in the spray areas, as well as those exposed to drift were slash-and-burn agriculturalists, she pleaded ignorance. "I didn't know that. They really do that there?" When pressed to answer whether the State Department was aware of the acetonitrile component in burning glyphosate, Brown-Thompson said she didn't think so but couldn't answer any more questions on the issue.

Drift

As noted, the problems occurring in Colombia from the fumigation campaign have reached across the Putumayo river and deep into Ecuador. According to Sister Carmen the "frontier region has changed drastically since Plan Colombia's inception. The refugee's arrival is one element, but the people who live there who are Ecuadorians are abandoning their homes and fields to get away from the spraying."

Cesar Cerda, a Qichua Indian whose village in Sucumbios is near the Putumayo frontier says "the planes come to the river, sometimes they come to our side and spray. Even when they don't the spray comes across the river and kills our food. Our plantanos, our yucca, our coffee is all gone. No one has died in our community but others say there have been deaths in theirs. Even our animals are dead. And there are no animals to hunt in the forest because they have gone somewhere else. First come the helicopters, then come the planes, then the smell and the spray falls and kills everything."

Cerda was asked why the community didn't just move. "That is what they want. They want domination of the area so they can combat the rebels. They want economic domination of our land too. But we don't want to run away from our homes."

Asked if he or his representatives had complained to the government, Cerda said they had. "They won't come because they say there is no problem here. Why? Because they have made pacts with the United States. But the truth is that life on the river has changed since Plan Colombia started."

...THAT THE SPRAYING OF PLAINTIFFS' PERSONS, LANDS AND LIVESTOCK WITH TOXIC FUMIGANTS IS NOTHING LESS THAN AN ACT OF MERCENARY WAR CARRIED OUT SURREPTITIOUSLY BY THE DYNCORP DEFENDANTS..."

Sister Carmen says that both the church where she works and the indigenous groups have sent repeated requests to Quito, Ecuador's capital, asking for an investigation of the drift that has come into Ecuador. "They always promise they will send someone but they never have. Our government backs Plan Colombia, so why should they come? In whose interest would it be to investigate the complaints of the victims?"

When questioned about the allegations that DynCorp crop dusters were spraying right up to the river that marks the border between Colombia and Ecuador, Brown-Thompson of the State Department denied that planes ever came closer than 10 kilometers of the border. "It's a no-spray zone to protect against accidents."

Regardless of Brown-Thompson's claims, the drift of glyphosate affected so many people that a class-action lawsuit on behalf of the people of Sucumbios against DynCorp was filed by the International Labor Rights Fund in September, 2001. The suit alleges that the drift in Ecuador is purposeful, rather than the result of pilot error or an accident of wind. Among the allegations in the lawsuit are that "the American oil industry maintains a lobbying group in Washington D.C. under the name the US-Colombia Business Partnership that lobbies the Congress of the United States, and the Executive Offices and related agencies of the United States, for continuous funding and expansion of Plan Colombia.

"Plaintiffs further allege on good faith, information and belief that contributing members to the US-Colombia Business Partnership, include Texaco, Inc., Occidental Petroleum, and B.P. Amoco, which have or expect to have oil interests in the region of Ecuador where Plaintiffs reside. Oil corporations such as Texaco are despised by the local population in Ecuador because of the devastation they have caused to the rainforest through years of operations there....

"Plaintiffs allege...that it is cheaper for corporations such as Texaco to lobby for money designed to intimidate the local population rather than to take the necessary actions to repair the damage to the environment they created by their reckless practices...and that this lobbying is one of the causes of the creation of the fumigation program operated by the DynCorp Defendants.

"Plaintiffs allege...that the spraying of Plaintiffs' persons, lands and livestock with toxic fumigants is nothing less than an act of mercenary war carried out surreptitiously by the DynCorp Defendants..."

When asked about the lawsuit's allegations, the State Department's Brown-Thompson continued to adamantly deny that any herbicide is entering Ecuador or that any people or legal crops and farm animals have been harmed in Colombia. "We use satellite imagery to pinpoint areas to be sprayed, then send in planes to verify the presence of large areas of illegal crops," she says. "After that, the crops are sprayed, and subsequently those sprayed areas are checked to see that no additional crops were affected."

IN ADDITION U.S. SPECIAL FORCES WILL TRAIN TWO COLOMBIAN BRIGADES IN SPECIALIZED WARFARE TO PROTECT OIL PIPELINES.

Calls to several crop-dusting companies in the US southwest found that to limit drift, spraying is done at an altitude that was equal to the height of the plant being sprayed. But reports from Colombia and comments from the US State department indicate that the spraying in Plan Colombia is generally being done at heights of 50-100 feet. Crop-dusters, from whose ranks DynCorp recruits its pilots for dusting operations in Colombia, as a point of pride, like to touch the plants they are spraying. "The planes are never more than one-to-three feet from the ground when we're spraying cotton, maybe five feet when it's corn," said one pilot at Ballards Crop Dusting in Winter, Texas. "The only time you want to fly higher than that is when you want broad-swath spraying, drift."

Asked how much drift would occur with a plane flying at ten feet, the pilot said, "at least 50 feet on either side of the plane."

Corky Wilson, owners of Wilson Aerial Spray in Lockney, Texas, agreed. "Hell, if you're flying at ten feet you're not crop dusting. You're burning. The only time we do that in Texas is to kill mesquite trees."

Told that the US admits its planes frequently spray at altitudes of 50-100 feet, Wilson laughed. "You're burning the whole forest now. Hell, at 20 feet on a windless day you've got a 150 foot drift on either wing. At 100 feet you got a cloud that might travel miles."

When told what US crop dusters had explained about drift altitude, and asked for a response, the State Department continued to insist that there was no glyphosate drift either in Colombia or Ecuador. Asked if satellite photos were available to prove that, Brown-Thompson said they were not as the State Department considered them "classified." Representatives of DynCorp were even more tight-lipped about the issues, refusing to return both calls and emails requesting their response to these several issues.

One other element related to the fumigation must be considered to draw a clear picture of the health and environmental impact that glyphosate has on spray areas: While the US label for Monsanto's Roundup Ultra states that in most situations aerial application should not exceed 1 quart per acre of the product, in Colombia the use rate is nearly 4 1/2 quarts. That figure comes from a State Department written answer to a question from a US Representative on the quantity of glyphosate being used in Colombia. Brown-Thompson said she "didn't know" when asked why such a heavy concentration of herbicide was needed, but was sure it "has nothing to do" with trying to kill jungle growth through drift, or to displace locals by making life unbearable in the region.

An Allegation

While most of the problems related to Plan Colombia appear to be occurring along the border regions of both Colombia and Ecuador, startling new allegations have been made that spray planes are going deep into Ecuadorian Amazonia. Inez Sheguango Fonaqen, a

| WHERE DO THE NEW PLANTS COME FROM AND
| WHEN DO THEY HAVE TIME TO MATURE?

Quichua Indian and the Regent of the territory along the upper Rio Napo, claims that central Amazonia is also being fumigated. "Planes come into Ecuador regularly," she told this reporter. They are spraying the jungle here, killing the jungle and jungle animals here."

Asked how they could come in unnoticed, Sheguango says "they come at night. They come late with no lights and fly over the jungle. I have asked the government in Quito for a film camera because I can prove it, but the government says they won't give me one. They say our communities are inventing the problems and inventing the story, but we're not."

There are not many communities along the upper Napo where Ines Sheguango lives, so it is difficult to know if she's telling the truth. But two things do hint that she may not be off the mark. The first is that in July, 2001, US Ambassador to Colombia Anne Patterson told reporters "there are...plans to outfit some crop dusters with night-vision scopes to enable pilots to spray after dark, when they are less exposed to fire from guerrillas, paramilitaries or farmers who grow coca."

The second came from the State Department's Rebecca Brown-Thompson, who, when asked about the possibility of night incursions into Ecuador, said: "They cannot be our planes entering Ecuador. If it's true I would like to see proof of that. But I can only speak for the US Department of State's Bureau of International Narcotics and Law Enforcement Affairs. I cannot speak for other areas of government."

The US Department of Defense did not respond to calls on the question. If the allegation were true, of course, it would be proof that at least one key element of the Plan Colombia/Andean Initiative campaign really is to defoliate the region, and if that were true it could only be to get at the commodities the region has to offer. Oil is one known commodity. There may be others, minerals or something else just as valuable as oil that we don't even know of yet.

"The United States wants US companies here," says Inez Sheguango, "for the petroleum, the wood, the minerals and everything the jungle has, both here and in Colombia."

New Oil Leases in Putumayo

While the allegation made by Inez Sheguango may or may not finally be proven true, the presence of oil, and plenty of it, in both the Colombia department of Putumayo and the Ecuadorian province of Sucumbios is a reality. Aside from the ITT field and its 1.41 billion barrel reserve of oil in Ecuador, the Hollin-Napo survey suggests a great deal more. In Putumayo earlier this year, Colombia's state-owned oil company, Ecopetrol, signed contracts with two firms to explore for oil in blocks located in Putumayo. Canada's Petrobank Energy and Resources, through its Colombian subsidiary Petrominerales, has contracted to explore 30,000 hectares in Putumayo's Moqueta region, while the US Argosy Energy International, long a player in Colombia, has signed a contract to explore the 20,000 hectare Gayuyaco area. Ecopetrol has estimated that Putumayo has a minimum of 2.4 billion barrels of undiscovered oil reserves. Ecopetrol is hoping to sign several more contracts in Putumayo before the end of the year.

Endgame

It is difficult to imagine that half-a-dozen representatives of major corporations ever sat around a table with ranking members of the State Department and explained to them that if they would be so kind as to eliminate the rainforest in southern Colombia and northern Ecuador along with the rebels, the paramilitaries, the indigenous and the campesinos who lived there, those corporations would, in turn, deliver enough oil to at least act as a temporary cushion against any future problems in the Mideast.

| THE ELIMINATION OF COCA FROM SOUTHERN
| COLOMBIA HAS NO EFFECT ON WORLD SUPPLY.

Nevertheless, even if the intentions of Plan Colombia/the Andean Initiative were honestly to eliminate the cocaine and heroin scourge and thereby take the money out of Colombia's civil war, the fact is that Plan Colombia will finally be about oil.

The pursuit of rebels by the Colombian military in the south, along with the spraying of coca fields there, is forcing both the rebels, as well as the campesinos to cross into Ecuador for safety.

The pressure on the rebels is about to increase substantially. On September 27, 2002, Army Gen. Galen Jackman told reporters that President Bill Clinton's directive that the US share intelligence with the Colombian military only when it deals with drug trafficking is about to be scrapped. From now on, the US will alert the Colombian military to any and all intelligence it gathers not only on drug trafficking but on rebel and paramilitary movements, planned attacks, logistics and other military operations. In addition US Special Forces will train two Colombian

Brigades in specialized warfare to protect oil pipelines. The initial training will take place in an area where Los Angeles-based Occidental Petroleum has a pipeline that has been repeatedly attacked by rebels, but will be able to be adapted to the protection of other pipelines as well.

"We need to treat [the rebels and paramilitaries] as they are, which are terrorist organizations...and we need to help the Colombians deal with those organizations," said Jackman, the Director of Operations for the US Southern Command.

Pressure on the campesinos is about to increase as well, as the US has doubled the spray area in Colombia in 2002 to fumigate 90% of the coca crop, and in 2003 plans to fumigate 100%. Those campesinos, without a livelihood and with their food crops and livestock dead, will have to move, most of them to the south and Ecuador. With the drift in Ecuador already eliminating a large segment of the population on the border, with the added pressure of thousands of refugees cutting new fields from the jungle there, it shouldn't take long to have the entire region cleared of both people and rainforest.

At that point the oil fest can begin in earnest.

Where's the Cocaine Coming From?

Because the coca plant is very slow growing, the questions that come to mind when thinking about all the plants the US has paid to have eradicated in Colombia are: where do the new plants come from and when do they have time to mature?

According to US State Department documents, the Bolivian coca plant, the world standard for making cocaine until the mid-1990s, takes three years from seed to first harvest. Colombian coca, which replaced Bolivian coca as the world's standard in the late-1990s, grows considerably faster because it is planted from cuttings, not seed. A 2002 CIA bulletin titled "Coca Fact Sheet: A Primer" suggests it can be harvested in as little as 6-8 months. (Dr. James Duke, who has worked with the plant in Colombia suggests that a year is what's needed for harvest from cuttings.)

The same CIA Fact Sheet suggests there are between 14,000 and 45,000 plants per hectare (about 2.5 acres) of coca. If we average that out to 20,000 plants per hectare, there would be 8,000 plants per acre.

Last year, under the aegis of Plan Colombia, more than 250,000 acres of coca were destroyed in Colombia. This year that number will increase to nearly 400,000, or almost every acre of coca under cultivation in Colombia. At 8,000 plants per, that comes to 3,200,000,000 plants. That's three billion, two hundred million plants.

Where are the cuttings for next year's crop going to come from if we've wiped out their entire crop this year? Where did this year's three billion cuttings come from if we wiped out most of the crop last year?

Cuttings come from mother plants. If we assumed that a mother plant was capable of producing a startlingly high 1,000 cuttings per annum, there would still need to be 3,200,000 mother plants somewhere. Where are that many mother plants being kept? Has anyone bothered to look for such a large greenhouse?

Of course, even if there were such a greenhouse in Colombia, there would still be the question of distribution: How on earth would anyone distribute three billion cuttings without being noticed?

Those questions were posed to the State Department, which had no real answer. "I've never thought of that before," said Rebecca Brown-Thompson, spokesperson for Rand Beers, the Assistant Secretary of State for International Narcotics and Law Enforcement Affairs. "Why don't you ask the Drug Enforcement Administration?"

A DEA spokesman responded with: "I get what you're getting at, the numbers don't add up. But Plan Colombia has nothing to do with the DEA. That's State Department all the way."

The reason there is no answer is that there are no cuttings. There might be some, of course, but not three billion, not three million. Colombian coca growing, on the scale it's grown to during the last decade, is now done like it is done in Bolivia and Peru, from seed. Which means it takes three years to produce its first harvest. And since we've been wiping out more and more of the crop annually, there are fewer and fewer mature plants to harvest. Next year, if we're being told the truth, there won't be any. Which means there won't be a harvest in Colombia.

> ...THE ADMINISTRATIVE COURT RECOGNIZED THE HARM TO HEALTH AND BIODIVERSITY, SOIL AND WATER BODIES THAT THE AERIAL FUMIGATION IS DOING, BUT THOSE WITH VESTED INTERESTS CHOOSE TO IGNORE THAT."

That should wipe out the world's coca supply for at least three years, at a minimum, by which time any stored cocaine will have hit the streets and been used up. The world ought to be cocaine dry.

It won't be. The prices probably won't even fluctuate. And if they don't it will mean only one thing: that the elimination of coca from southern Colombia has no effect on world supply. Which will suggest that it never did, that the coca that produces the world's supply is grown elsewhere, maybe in unsprayed, protected valleys, or that Peru and Bolivia are still producing sufficient supplies, despite a reduction in their crops.

Of course, that would suggest that Plan Colombia is a sham. That the spraying of southern Colombia and the collateral damage it's causing—displacement of thousands of people, loss of legal crops and animals and rainforest defoliation—are being done for other ends.

What are those ends? Oil is an obvious answer. There may be others. We won't find out for a while, but keep your eyes on it. It'll become apparent soon enough.

Update: Fumigations Continue in Colombia Despite Court Ordered Suspensions

Despite two Colombian court rulings during the past year ordering the suspension of US-sponsored Plan Colombia aerial fumigation of coca and poppy crops until environmental and human impact studies can be carried out, Colombia continues to spray Monsanto's Roundup Ultra on fields and US officials continue to maintain an eerie and criminal silence on the issue. The most recent ruling came several months ago, on June 13, when Colombia's Administrative Tribunal of Cundinamarca, the second highest court in the country, responded to a Popular Action lawsuit brought by concerned citizens arguing that Plan Colombian spraying violates Colombian citizens' right to a healthy environment. The Court agreed and ordered the immediate suspension of all narco-crop fumigation nationwide. The verdict supplemented two earlier court decisions ordering the suspension of spraying on indigenous land and compliance with the Environmental Management Plan put in place for Plan Colombia fumigation. Colombia itself cheered the court victory when Yamile Salinas, then-of the Ombudsman's Office, in a statement released shortly after the verdict, noted: "This court order formally adopts many of the requirements for environmental and human protection that the Colombian Ombudsman and Comptroller General, along with both national and international non-government organizations have been demanding for years,"

"Unfortunately," says Astrid Puentes, a Colombian human rights attorney with Earthjustice, the legal branch of the Sierra Club, "while that decision should have been enough to protect the health and human rights of the environment and people of Colombia, the US and Colombian governments insist that that the spraying is not harmful, and so it continues. The Administrative Court recognized the harm to health and biodiversity, soil and water bodies that the aerial fumigation is doing, but those with vested interests choose to ignore that."

Among those with vested interests beyond the governments Puentes mentioned, are Texas' Bell Helicopter Textron and Connecticut's Sikorsky Helicopter,

which provide Huey helicopters used to move troops and supplies Blackhawk choppers used to protect spray planes, respectively, as well as Kansas' Monsanto, which provides the Roundup Ultra used in the spraying. DynCorp, of Reston, VA, is the most vested of all: As the State Department's primary outsourcing company in Colombia it has a roughly $600 million dollar contract to actually do the spraying and maintain the spray planes and helicopters utilized in the fumigation operation. At issue is the core of the supposed US assault on cocaine and heroin trafficking in the Western Hemisphere. When Plan Colombia was initiated by former President Bill Clinton in 2000, its stated aim was to eliminate the coca and poppy plants in Colombia used to make cocaine and heroin. If they were eliminated, the thinking went, not only would much of drug traffic in the US disappear, but the funds generated by that traffic in Colombia, which support both paramilitary and rebel groups involved in that country's brutal civil war would dry up as well.

While the plan as envisioned by Clinton and expanded into The Andean Initiative by President Bush looks good on paper (at least to the naive, who actually believe

TO MANY, IT CONTINUES TO LOOK LIKE THE SPRAYING IS MEANT MORE TO CLEAR THE LAND OF PEOPLE SO THAT OIL EXPLORATION CAN GET GOING FULL STEAM IN THE REGION THAN IT IS TO ELIMINATE COCA CROPS.

the US has a real interest in stopping the drug trade in Colombia or anywhere else), not only has there been enormous collateral damage from the spraying, the US, which entered into the plan with the stated intention of improving human rights in Colombia, has lost all pretense of credibility toward that end and is clearly active in contributing to the worsening human rights situation there, and we are breaking the law in both Colombia and here at home in doing so.

The Popular Action lawsuit hinged on the fact that in 2001, a binding environmental management plan was put into effect in Colombia by the Minister of the Environment. One of the stipulations of that plan was that a battery of impact studies would be conducted to determine whether or not the fumigation was harmful to the environment and humans. Those studies have never been done, and so the Colombian Administrative Tribunal's decision was made in favor of the plaintiffs. But Colombia's President, Alvaro Uribe Velez—who happened to be the mayor of Medellin during the Medellin cocaine Cartel's heyday and whose campaign manager looks to be up to his eyes in the cocaine trade—interpreted the law as permitting the spraying to continue while his administration's National Directorate of Narcotics appeals the decision to Colombia's highest court.

In the US, there are also laws connected with the monies being utilized to pay for the spraying. One of them states that all fumigation is done in compliance with Colombian law. What has covered the US legally has been a March, 2002 letter from the Colombian Minister of Exterior Relations to the US Department of State which reads in part: "the Government of Colombia hereby certifies that the aerial spraying program supported by the United States is being carried out in accordance with each and every applicable Colombian law on the matter."

But where that might have been close enough for government work a year ago, the continued spraying in light of the June Court decision and several recent events—which the State Department has not commented on—have to bring the legality of continued US support for the spraying before impact studies are done into question.

In October, under pressure, according to Earthjustice's Puentes, the Colombian Minister of the Environment modified the environmental management plan. "They eliminated and weakened environmental conditions of the plan." Among the changes were the height at which spray-planes could fly. Where the legal height had been 100 feet—absurd for crop dusting as spraying at that altitude can create drifts that extend for miles, according to several Texas crop dusters—the ceiling was raised even higher. Also changed on orders by Uribe was the prohibition against spraying in Colombia's national parks—"something," says Puentes, "which had been going on illegally but which overnight became legal."

Senator Patrick Leahy (D-VT), Ranking Member of the Appropriations Committee's Subcommittee on Foreign Operations who has long questioned the Plan Colombian fumigation, bristled at the thought of in-park spraying, and attached an amendment to the Fiscal 2004 Foreign Operations Bill, which would prohibit the use of US funding in the fumigation of Colombia's 25 million acres of National Parks, but didn't have the political clout to make it stick. It is estimated that about 15,000 acres of illegal cultivation is ongoing in the parks.

Colombia's national parks are among the world's most biodiverse areas, and environmentalists worldwide have fought their fumigation on the grounds that it will wreak havoc on their fragile ecosystems. Several Colombian politicians have also fought the park spraying on the grounds that it is constitutionally illegal, as the Colombian Constitution makes the parks completely off limits to both development and modification. They plan to challenge it in court on both that issue and the ground that the spraying will contravene several international treaties, including the Biodiversity Covenant, ratified in 1994, as well as the Rio De Janiero Summit Treaty of 1992. Moreover, Colombia's national treaties protect the lands of indigenous peoples, many of whom live within Colombia's national parks and whose lands are expected to be among the first areas to be sprayed there. Thousands of indigenous are expected to be forced to move if park spraying occurs on a large scale.

Uribe recently stacked the deck in his favor when he appointed Sandra Suarez, who formerly headed the office in charge of Plan Colombia, the office in charge of the aerial spraying, as Colombia's new Minister of the Environment. Suarez has made it clear that the chemicals used to process coca are already damaging the parks. Camilo Gonzalez Posso, former Minister of Health in Colombia agrees that those chemicals are having a "tremendously harmful" impact but adds "that is not an argument that justifies throwing gasoline on the fire." The Bush administration, however, has noted that spraying the parks is the only way to save them, and that not fumigating the parks will be "an invitation to the growers to destroy the forests and their natural resources," according to TIME magazine. [Editor's note—On March 24, 2004, the Colombian government announced a halt to plans to spray Colombia's National Parks. "There won't be any spraying in the parks until other alternatives are examined, such as manual eradication," said Colombian Environment Minister Sandra Suarez, as quoted by the Environmental News Network. The international outcry over this latest aspect of the US-backed Andean Initiative has derailed these plans for the immediate future.]

Uribe upped the ante on fumigation-protesting when he recently, on several occasions, announced that anyone objecting to fumigation in any part of Colombia or "working to protect human rights and the environment" would be viewed as a sympathizer with terrorists, according to Anna Cedarstav, a staff scientist with Earthjustice.

Perhaps the Uribe administration's most publicly astounding assault on human rights' sensibilities in connection with the Plan Colombia spraying—as purposeful spraying of indigenous lands, overt spraying onto farmland and so forth are not publicized—occurred on November 2, when an international environmental commission studying the effects of recent fumigation in the Colombian department of Arauca was stopped by a US-trained Colombian anti-narcotics battalion and had their film, cameras and notes confiscated. The commission, which included Colombians and representatives of France, the US, England and Spain, had previously met with Colombian Vice-President Carlos Frank about their work. That the Bush Administration has not commented on these recent developments—and that the State Department has ignored repeated requests both by phone and in writing to address them—is par for the course and absolutely shameful.

The continued backing of the fumigation while Uribe flaunts Colombian law is flat out illegal. That the coca produced in Colombia is making its way to the streets of the US is not in question. That the growing and processing of that coca into cocaine is ravaging the environment of Colombia as well as fueling a civil war there is also not in question. What is in question is the fumigation itself and the herbicide being used to eliminate it.

Every study but the two carried out by the US and Colombia has shown that the fumigation is having a major impact on both human life and the environment. (The sham US study, carried out by the Environmental Protection Agency, not only evaluated an incomplete chemical mix—it didn't have the full complement of chemicals as mixed being used to evaluate—but relied exclusively on data provided by the State Department. No member of the EPA spent even one hour of time on the ground in Colombia as they have no standing there, and even then the EPA had major questions about the fumigation.)

One recent study carried out by the respected Dr. Adolfo Mondonaldo of Ecological Action, shows the "presence of genetic damage in a population" of people exposed to the Plan Colombia fumigation. American toxicologist Mark Cherniak recently presented a paper to the Council of State of Colombia stating that "the exposure to glyfosate (the active ingredient in Round-up) represents a risk in expectant mothers."

The problems don't end there. Food crops have been destroyed, rainforests ravaged, tens of thousands of peasants have been displaced because their crops, livestock and water sources have been poisoned. The most humane solution would be a permanent cessation of the fumigation. Given that is not going to happen, there minimally needs to happen what was ordered by the Colombian courts: a temporary suspension of the fumigation until environmental and human impact studies can be made and safety guidelines put into place. Yet even that is not happening and is not going to happen. What would be harmed by a temporary suspension of the fumigation until environmental and human impact studies can be made? Nothing. Which suggests that both the US and Colombia know that if impact studies were made the fumigation would be permanently stopped.

If that turned out to be the case, since all the fumigation so far—for all the alleged success it's had in eliminating Colombia's coca crop—hasn't actually lessened the supply of coca in the US one iota, what would be the harm in stopping it permanently? Politically it would be embarrassing for the Bush Administration, of course, but his out would be that the whole plan was former President Clinton's cockeyed idea. So it must be more than that that's preventing those studies.

To many, it continues to look like the spraying is meant more to clear the land of people so that oil exploration can get going full steam in the region than it is to eliminate coca crops. "We know at least one element of Plan Colombia" says Astrid Puentes, "is the US training of Colombian soldiers to protect the Occidental Oil pipeline in Canon Limon from rebel attacks. Some people think the fumigation will clear the land for exploration as well." If indeed that's the case, it would explain why those pesky studies aren't being carried out.

Between Dyncorp and the A.U.C. - Glyphosate and Paramilitary Terror in Colombia's Cimitarra Valley

Bill Weinberg

Leaving Barrancabermeja in a canoe—a small launch with an outboard motor—the perilous patchwork of armed groups that vie for control of Colombia´s Medio Magdalena region becomes immediately obvious. Navy gunboats painted in camo line the shore along the huge oil refinery that looms over the Rio Magdalena. Just a few minutes later, a little past the edge of the city, paramilitary checkpoints on either bank survey the river traffic. They don't stop our boat because we are flying the flag of Peace Brigades International from the bow, and the paras like to give foreign human rights observers a wide berth. There are practically no suburbs—just past the para checkpoint we find ourselves in an endless expanse of wetlands and jungle broken only by the most primitive of campesino settlements. Herons laze on the green banks as we make our way north to the Rio Cimitarra—a tributary of the Magdalena where coca growers, paras and guerillas have all staked their turf.

WHEN THE CAMPESINOS TAKE US ON A TOUR OF THE VEREDA, SHOWING US THE PLOTS WHICH HAVE BEEN DESTROYED BY FUMIGATION FLIGHTS, THEY ALL TELL SAME STORY—LEGAL FOOD CROPS AND FOREST DESTROYED ALONG WITH THE COCA BUSHES.

I've come to this remote and conflicted region with a commission from the Colombian rights group Humanidades Vigentes, accompanied by two representatives of the Peace Brigades for our protection. We spend a mosquito-haunted night at Puerto Machete, the little riverside settlement where the canoa drops us off. Then it is a four-hour hike along an unimproved dirt road and jungle trails to our destination: the little campesino vereda (settlement) of La Floresta. The last hour on the trail seems endless. We wade streams, sink knee-deep into mud, crawl under barbed-wire fences, climb and descend hill after hill. When a campesino from La Floresta passes us on his mule, I ask hopefully "Falta mucho?" (Is it much further?) He nods gravely and answers "Si, siempre." Yes, always.

Poison from the Skies, Fear on the Land

There is no electricity in La Floresta, and no running water. The only sign of any government presence is in the form of destroyed land.

Our commission has come to document the impact of aerial glyphosate fumigation of the settlement's lands to wipe out coca crops. The impacts are obvious as soon as we arrive. Marina Salguero, the official health promoter for Floresta and nearby settlements, who is licensed by the local municipal government of Cantagallo, maintains an extremely makeshift clinic in a little hilltop hut. A thin old man with big rash on his leg sits in the hut with a penicillin IV in his arm. His skin irritation, a result of being caught in his fields when the fumigation overflight swooped down, has become infected, Salguero says.

"I get cases like this all the time," she says. "Children with head pain, vomiting, diarrhea, skin irritation. Every time the planes come." She points out a stretch of land on a nearby hill glaringly brown and dead in the green landscape—the result of the last fumigation, 15 days earlier. The brown stretch is right beside a house. "Their home, their kitchen was fumigated. Their crops all destroyed—maize, platano, yucca."

Salguero admits that coca is grown at La Floresta—"just to have a little money," she says. "You saw how bad the road is here." She notes that having to haul out legal crops on the road—followed by a river trip to the nearest town, with paras sometimes stealing whatever goods the campesinos carry—means the cost of getting crops to market eats virtually all profits. In contrast, men come to the vereda to buy the coca and carry it out themselves.

"We are completely abandoned by the government here—municipal, departmental, national," Salguero protests. "What alternative do we have? I'm responsible for three veredas, and I don't even have a thermometer."

On this recently-settled agricultural frontier, where land is cleared from the rainforest with no oversight, the campesinos have no ability to interact with the bureaucracy for credit or aid. "Here the land is not titled," says Salguero. "Everyone has his predio (plot) and works it."

When the campesinos take us on a tour of the vereda, showing us the plots which have been destroyed by fumigation flights, they all tell same story—legal food crops and forest destroyed along with the coca bushes. They pull up the dead stalks of yucca, killed before they could be harvested. They claim over 100 chickens have been killed by glyphosate spraying in the village since first fumigation flights in 2001. Sometimes it is clear that the legal crops were destroyed because they were planted amid coca crops. Sometimes it looks as if the glyphosate drifted, or was sprayed wildly wide of its target. Everywhere it is clear that the spraying is degrading these hard-won lands not only by direct poisoning, but by destroying the plant cover that holds down the soil, leading to erosion and muddy streams.

The fumigation flights, carried out by planes from the private firm Dyncorp under contract to the US State Department, are accompanied by up to seven helicopters from the Colombian army or National Police. They take off from the airport in Barrancabermeja. Army ground troops also come to burn down coca paste labs from time to time, or to search for guerillas. The campesinos complain that the troops demand mules for transport and chickens for food without compensation.

But it is the paramilitaries from the Central Bolivar Bloc (BCB) of the notorious Colombian United Self-Defense Forces (AUC) that have a far tighter grip on the community, and demand periodic payments of war taxes. The campesinos show us a document from the BCB`s local "Frente Conquistadors of Yondo" ordering the president of Floresta´s peasant council, the Junta de Accion Comunal, to show up in paramilitary-controlled Yondo town to make a "declaration" about production on their lands for taxes to the outlaw army. The campesinos also pay taxes to the guerillas—"Whoever has guns," says Uriel Nieto, a member of the peasant council.

La Floresta is one of several communities that make up the Cimitarra Valley Campesino Association (ACVC), which has been pressuring for a better deal for the marginal region since it was founded in 1996. Yondo's mayor Saul Rodriguez calls ACVC a front for the guerillas. "It's a lie," says Uriel. "We work as a community, not as an arm of the guerilla."

Government Targets Campesino Activists, Not Paras

In 1998, following a series of cross-country marches and other protest campaigns, the ACVC worked out plan for the "Integral Development and Protection of Human Rights in the Magdalena Medio." The plan was drawn up with the allied Federation of Agricultural Workers and Miners of Southern Bolivar (Fedeagromisbol), an alliance of campesinos and small-scale gold miners in the Sierra San Lucas who have been increasingly pushed out of the region by corporate gold interests in recent years. The plan was conceived as an alternative to government plans to forcibly eradicate coca in the region. The ACVC argued that with government investment in the region and a crackdown on paras, the campesinos could wean themselves off the coca economy.

Things have worked out differently. A special army unit called the Bloque de Busqueda, or Search Bloc, was formed specifically to target the paras, but never accomplished much. And since President Alvaro Uribe came to power, the paras have increased their hold on the region—while the ACVC itself has been the target of a crackdown.

Since March of this year, ACVC leaders Gilberto Guerra and Andres Gil have been wanted on "rebellion" charges related to past protest campaigns and alleged collaboration with the guerillas. They are currently in hiding. Says Miguel Cifuentes, secretary of the ACVC's governing junta: "There are paras and assassins in the prisons. They are worth more alive than dead."

Cifuentes denies that the ACVC has ever collaborated with the guerillas. "This is part of the Uribe government strategy to debilitate the movement," he says. "They use denunciations in the press, charges against us—and when that fails, they try to kill us."

HE WAS JUST 15 MINUTES PAST THE NAVY PRESENCE AT BARRANCABERMEJA WHEN PARAS OPENED FIRE ON HIS CANOA FROM THEIR SHORELINE CHECKPOINT.

Cifuentes speaks from experience. On March 4, days before charges brought against Guerra and Gil, Cifuentes was on the Rio Magdalena on his way to the Cimitarra Valley, when he was the target of an assassination attempt. He was just 15 minutes past the Navy presence at Barrancabermeja when paras opened fire on his canoa from their shoreline checkpoint. Cifuentes was only on the river because he had been given bad information that there was no para checkpoint up that day. "I knew if we stopped they'd kill me," he says. His finger was grazed by a bullet, and his cellular radio hit, but he managed to get away to a nearby island, where he hid for 12 hours—at one point, while paras searched the island for him with flashlights. Local human rights workers finally rescued him. He has not ventured back into the Cimitarra Valley since, but helps staff the ACVC's office in Barrancabermeja.

Laboratory of the Counter-Reform

The Medio Magdalena region, which includes the Cimitarra Valley and straddles the departments of Antioquia, Santander, Cesar and Bolivar, has ironically been dubbed by the Colombian government and foreign aid agencies a

"Laboratory of Peace." The program includes a European Union-backed proposal to promote African palm oil as an alternative crop and a spur to economic development in the region. Cifuentes opposes the African palm proposal as a technocratic pseudo-solution. "It is a monoculture, and it displaces traditional crops, worsening the food crisis in region and increasing campesino debt," he says.

Jorge Enrique Gomez is Medio Magdalena regional chief of the Defensoria del Pueblo, an official human rights watchdog created by Colombia's 1991 constitutional reform. He has been at his post since February 2002, when he returned to the Medio Magdalena after ten years in

GOMEZ BELIEVES THAT AS LONG AS FUMIGATION CONTINUES, NO ALTERNATIVE CROP PROGRAM WILL MAKE MUCH DIFFERENCE.

exile in El Salvador and Guatemala. He fled Colombia after receiving death threats for his work documenting local human rights abuses with CREDHOS, the Barrancabermeja-based non-governmental watchdog. Gomez believes that as long as fumigation continues, no alternative crop program will make much difference.

"To fumigate licit crops is a bad investment and a mixed message to the campesinos," he says. "Cultivation of illicit crops is a result of the lack of any government presence in the zone. Fumigations affect the poorest sector of the populace." He argues that the fumigations are not only counter-productive, but illegal.

"It's the position of the Defensoria del Pueblo that the fumigations are against international humanitarian law. Article 93 of the Colombian Constitution recognizes the Geneva Conventions and other international codes. So the fumigations are also illegal under Colombian law." He cites the Defensoria's Resolution 026-02, issued in response to fumigations in Putumayo department, which officially found the program illegal. He acknowledges that the Defensoria's resolutions are nonbinding, but says they have "moral power."

The ACVC's 1998 accord with the government was supposed to instate a more meaningful alternative development program. The accord, signed by Gil and Guerra with President Andres Pastrana, established the Cimitarra Valley as a "Campesino Reserve Zone," or ZRC, where small holdings are protected by law, and large holdings or latifundios are banned. The ZRC proposal set maximum holdings based on 72-hectare Family Agricultural Units, with no more than three allowed in a single private holding within the Zone. The Cimitarra ZRC, which covered the municipalities of Remedios and Yondo in Antioquia and San Pablo and Cantagallo in Bolivar, was officially declared in December 2002, in accordance with the 1998 accord. It was one of five declared throughout Colombia, with the other four in Meta and Guaviare departments. But in April 2003, the Cimitarra ZRC was eliminated by official

decree of the Colombian National Institute of Agrarian Reform (INCORA), on the grounds it was exacerbating conflict in the region.

The INCORA decree disbanding the zone, Resolution 046-03, was protested by dissident members of INCORA's governing junta, who sent a letter to the body arguing that overturning the ZRC was illegal. INCORA was a semi-democratic body, with junta members representing campesinos elected via the National Association of Campesino Land Users (ANUC) and the National Federation of Agriculture (FANAL); members representing Indians elected via the Colombian Indigenous Organization (ONIC); members representing Afro-Colombians elected via the Process of Black Communities (PCN); and members representing women elected via National Association of Campesino, Black and Indigenous Women (ANMUCIC). But the majority on the INCORA junta—representing government agricultural agencies and the landed elite (via the National Ranchers Federation, or FEDEGAN, and the Colombian Farmers Society, or SAC)—voted in favor of overturning the Cimitarra ZRC.

In May, shortly after the vote, INCORA, established in the 1960s, was officially dissolved by President Uribe. It has been replaced by the Colombian National Institute of Rural Development (INCODER), which is charged with titling colonized lands, rather than land redistribution. Campesino organizations charge that the bureaucratic change is the final nail in the coffin of Colombia's tentative agrarian reform measures.

Big ranches in Yondo municipality which existed before the ZRC was declared are still intact. Under the ZRC, they were supposed to be bought by the government and redistributed to campesinos—but they never were before the ZRC was overturned. ACVC's Miguel Cifuentes claims these ranches both launder narco profits and serve as a base of support for paramilitary activity.

"We developed our own plan for a sustainable economic alternative," says Cifuentes. "We called for roads, schools, hospitals, mills for sugar and rice, local cooperatives to exploit fish and timber, so the campesinos can take their product directly to the market without intermediaries. We called for rational exploitation of gold that doesn't pollute the water. These solutions could work. But there is no political will to provide the resources. The region means nothing to those in power."

Drug War Economics

U.S. Cocaine 'Lord' Faces Challenge; Monopoly Game

Cynthia Cotts

A buyer of medical cocaine wants the DEA to end a seller's longtime sales lock.

Since the early 1980s, the Drug Enforcement Administration has waged war on Colombian drug lords, a war you can read about every day in the newspaper. But you've probably never read about a partnership the DEA has forged with the kingpin of US cocaine.

For 13 years the US government has protected a cocaine-dealing company that boasts a plush headquarters, a distinguished board of directors, and a diverse portfolio of chemical products. Yet no one is clamoring for a police raid, and no company executive is likely to be arrested, for the firm operates in the bizarre, little-known world of legal cocaine.

The US coke dealers don't have to resort to violence to protect their turf. But these captains of industry can be just as greedy as their doppelgangers below the border. While the Americans sell less cocaine than the Colombians, they partly make up for it by charging more. A kilo of imported cocaine now costs a dealer about $25,000, while a kilo of domestic legal cocaine costs about $42,000.

The US cocaine kingpin goes by a respectable-sounding name: the Mallinckrodt Group. It's a St. Louis company that calls itself a "world leader in the production of medicinal narcotics." That's an industry term for drugs derived from opium or cocaine. All of the drugs known as "medicinal narcotics" are classified as Schedule II drugs under the federal Controlled Substances Act, 21 USC. 952. That means they are subject to the tightest regulatory control.

Mallinckrodt is unique in that it holds the exclusive US license to manufacture pharmaceutical cocaine for medical use. It also holds licenses to import raw opium for the manufacture of medicinal opium products, which it sells in bulk to other manufacturers.

Its main competitor is Johnson & Johnson, which is also licensed to import and manufacture opium products. With two dominant players, the US legal opium market is, at least arguably, competitive. But when it comes to cocaine, Mallinckrodt has a true monopoly. Mallinckrodt's involvement in narcotics dates back to the 19th century,

but markups have not always been so steep. As recently as the mid-1980s, the company was charging only $1,800 for a kilo of cocaine.

In 1986, however, Mallinckrodt was bought by International Minerals & Chemical Corp., a manufacturer of fertilizer and veterinary products. In 1994, the parent company changed its name to Mallinckrodt, relocated to St. Louis, and began making sales projections for the millennium. The price list was revised frequently, and today, in 1996, a kilo of cocaine sells for $42,000—20 times what it cost 10 years ago.

"Mallinckrodt would like to tell you the increases were based on costs and shortages," says Gerald Wojta, president of Roxane Laboratories of Columbus, Ohio,

> FOR 13 YEARS THE US GOVERNMENT HAS PROTECTED A COCAINE-DEALING COMPANY THAT BOASTS A PLUSH HEADQUARTERS, A DISTINGUISHED BOARD OF DIRECTORS AND A DIVERSE PORTFOLIO OF CHEMICAL PRODUCTS.

which has been manufacturing medicinal narcotics since 1981. "But I'm personally convinced that around 1990, the chairman of the board [of Mallinckrodt] leaned back with a big cigar in his mouth and said, 'What? You mean to tell me that you've got an exclusive and you're not getting the maximum selling price?' Then somebody told him what they're charging for cocaine on the street, and he said, 'Christ! You should at least be charging that!'" A spokesman for Mallinckrodt declined to comment.

End of the Monopoly?

Mr. Wojta is no impartial observer. Every year, Roxane buys 100 kilos of cocaine powder from Mallinckrodt and turns it into a solution that is used, ironically, as an anesthetic for nasal surgery. Moreover, in 1995, Roxane asked the DEA for its own license to import cocaine. If Roxane gets it, Mr. Wojta plans to buy pharmaceutical cocaine from a German company that has agreed to sell it for a mere $6,000 per kilo.

Think of Roxane's relation to Mallinckrodt as that of David to Goliath, an upstart to a Fortune 500 company. Last year, Roxane recorded $100million in legal narcotics sales. Mallinckrodt, with total sales of $2.2 billion, took in $260 million in pharmaceutical sales, including $10 million from cocaine.

While Mallinckrodt officials aren't talking about this dispute, the company has hired a lawyer to ward off Roxane's attack on their monopoly. It has filed an objection with the DEA, arguing that if Roxane gets a license to import cocaine, that will increase the risk of illegal diversion.

At a hearing last Feb. 5, lawyers for both companies appeared before a DEA administrative law judge. Roxane is represented by Mike Sandler, of Seattle's Foster, Pepper & Shefelman; Mallinckrodt, by Steve Poplawski, from the St. Louis office of Bryan Cave L.L.P.

The judge's decision must be in compliance with the Controlled Substances Act. Sec. 952 states that the DEA may consider granting additional import licenses if "competition among domestic manufacturers of [a] controlled substance is inadequate."

If competition were the only criterion, Roxane would be guaranteed to win. But under other provisions of the statute, the DEA must balance two distinct interests. The

> WHILE THE AMERICANS SELL LESS COCAINE THAN THE COLOMBIANS, THEY PARTLY MAKE UP FOR IT BY CHARGING MORE. A KILO OF IMPORTED COCAINE NOW COSTS A DEALER ABOUT $25,000, WHILE A KILO OF DOMESTIC LEGAL COCAINE COSTS ABOUT $42,000.

agency has a duty to prevent diversion, and it is compelled to serve the public interest, including the maintenance of an adequate supply under competitive conditions.

Mallinckrodt has seized on the diversion issue, which traditionally has been invoked to limit the number of companies allowed to enter the narcotics business. Mr. Wojta, on the other hand, is stressing the importance of public interest. He promises that if he gets the license, "Roxane will pass on as much of the savings to the customer as possible."

The DEA docket is moving slowly this year as a result of judicial attrition; the agency is down to a single administrative law judge, Mary Ellen Bittner. She is expected to rule on Roxane's application by September. After she does, the head of the DEA will make a final decision. Given the sometimes astronomical values attached to it, cocaine has surprisingly humble roots.

The story begins in the jungles of Bolivia and Peru, where peasants pick coca leaves destined for the US market. Government-approved brokers sell the leaves to Stepan Chemical Co., the only company in the United States authorized to import cocaine. Stepan ships bales of leaves to a factory in New Jersey, where the plant is processed into a paste. The paste is sent to Mallinckrodt labs, where it is refined into a powder, known as cocaine hydrochloride, which the street sellers get by other means. Mallinckrodt then sells the powder to three companies—Roxane, Astra, and Schein—which process it into gel and liquid form for sale to hospitals and HMOs.

Cocaine hydrochloride is the same white powder that dominated night life throughout the 1980s, but street cocaine is no match for Mallinckrodt's 99% purity. DEA officials insist there is still enough demand for cocaine to justify restricting the legal stuff to just one wholesale distributor. (The DEA permits several middlemen to operate because medical cocaine products—the gels and liquids—have no appeal on the black market.)

A Century-Old Tradition

The legal cocaine business is so hush-hush that Mallinckrodt doesn't advertise its monopoly or explain how it got it. The truth is, the company was founded by three brothers in 1867. In 1898 they began importing narcotics. Back then, anyone could. Raw opium and cocaine were freely traded on the world market.

By the 1930s, concerns about the spread of drug addiction had led the United States and other countries to sign a series of treaties restricting the drug trade. The new international laws drew a bright line between "ethical" narcotics, sold for medical and scientific uses, and "evil" opium and cocaine, sold unscrupulously on the black market.

For all the talk about preventing addiction, however, the Depression-era drug laws also served US economic interests. In the wake of the 1931 Geneva Narcotics Treaty, European manufacturers were temporarily prohibited from exporting medicinal narcotics to the United States. Meanwhile, the Federal Bureau of Narcotics was given the power to decide which American companies would be awarded the lucrative import and manufacturing licenses.

In the 1930s, Mallinckrodt directors began currying favor with the Bureau of Narcotics and petitioning President

> EVERY YEAR, ROXANE BUYS 100 KILOS OF COCAINE POWDER FROM MALLINCKRODT AND TURNS IT INTO A SOLUTION THAT IS USED, IRONICALLY, AS AN ANESTHETIC FOR NASAL SURGERY.

Franklin D. Roosevelt to help them gain "world control of narcotics," according to company correspondence. But for the next 50 years, it was Merck & Co. that held the exclusive license to manufacture cocaine. Mallinckrodt concentrated on opium products, such as morphine and codeine.

Atomic Sideline

During World War II, the St. Louis company won a contract to produce a ton of uranium a day for the Manhattan Project. Mallinckrodt continued to process uranium until

1966, dumping nuclear waste at various sites in the St. Louis suburbs. Only very recently, after the public was alerted to high levels of radioactivity at the downtown plant and dump sites, did the company announce a plan to reduce the contamination.

During the 30 years after World War II, Mallinckrodt kept its lock on opium imports and remained one of only three companies licensed to manufacture codeine.

Then the company got its big break. In 1980, against the objections of the existing cartel, Johnson & Johnson convinced the DEA to give it a license to import opium for the manufacture of codeine. Johnson & Johnson arrived with such a flourish in 1983, that Merck, its former supplier, stopped manufacturing opium and cocaine altogether.

When Merck closed down its lagging narcotics business, it was only natural that Mallinckrodt would be awarded the cocaine monopoly. After all, the St. Louis company was one of the oldest chemical manufacturers in the country, and it had been prepared for a long time to assume control of the market.

Johnson & Johnson was the last big player to break into the import business. But in recent years, the DEA has quietly been expanding the number of companies licensed to import and export Schedule II narcotics. If the trend toward freer trade sticks, Roxane has a good chance of winning. Indeed, a source close to the cases, who asked not to be identified, says DEA lawyers have already filed a brief recommending that Roxane get the green light.

Postscript 2004

Following publication of this article in 1996, the DEA granted Roxane a license to import pharmaceutical cocaine, but Wojta retired soon after, and the company has since divested itself of medicinal narcotics. Mallinckrodt, now owned by Tyco, continues to manufacture cocaine hydrochloride. Injectable lidocaine is still used for many kinds of surgery including circumcision, for which it is said to reduce crying.

The legal stuff goes by many names, including Xylocaine, an AstraZeneca product which comes in liquid, jelly and spray form and is touted as the most widely used local anaesthetic in the world; Cook-Waite Lidocaine, manufactured by Eastman Kodak's dental division, and the generic EMLA, a/k/a Eutectic Mixture of Local Anesthetics, a blend of lidocaine and prilocaine. Despite the proliferation of medicinal forms, one might say that cocaine by any other name lacks the kick.

"America's Heroin Crisis, Columbian Heroin, and How We Can Improve Plan Columbia": Government Reform Committee, US House of Representatives, Dec. 12, 2002

Transcribed by Sanho Tree

Editor's Note—Spectators at this full hearing of the House Government Reform Committee were treated to what was for the most part a typically boring retread of every other Congressional hearing on US anti-drug policies held for the last few decades. One Representative after another demanded to know why the US-backed Plan Colombia has not yet succeeded in decimating the crops and ending the flow of cocaine and heroin into the US from south of the border, with officials blaming the peasants of Colombia for the drugs that US consumers insist on buying by the boatload.

"I was at this recent hearing about the 'Colombian Heroin Crisis' when Rep. Burton (former uber-drug warrior) came within an inch of talking about ending drug prohibition," wrote Sanho Tree of the Institute for Policy Studies in an email correspondence. "The expressions on the drug warriors' faces was priceless when they slowly realized their formerly staunch ally was about to turn on them." Committee Chairman Representative Dan Burton asked witness Tom Carr—director of the Baltimore-Washington High Intensity Drug Trafficking Area—why all the anti-drug hearings he's attended over the previous 35 years sound the same, with the same questions asked by politicians and the same answers given by witnesses, yet nothing ever changes. As the US government every year spends billions more in US tax dollars assisting the Colombian government eradicate scattered drug crops and battle rebellious peasants' armies, the hectares and acres covered in coca and poppy

> "THE EXPRESSIONS ON THE DRUG WARRIORS' FACES WAS PRICELESS WHEN THEY SLOWLY REALIZED THEIR FORMERLY STAUNCH ALLY WAS ABOUT TO TURN ON THEM."

crops throughout war-torn Colombia exponentially grow in size and number. There has been exactly zero dent put into the flood of drugs heading into the US, as the peasants on the ground suffer the consequences of toxic poisons sprayed upon them, their food crops, livestock, and their environment. The obvious futility finally got to Rep. Burton, who went so far as to compare the current War On Some Drugs and Users to the failed US experiment with alcohol prohibition of decades past—but never was quite able to utter the word "legalization." Little was accomplished at the hearing itself, but seeing Rep. Burton questioning the effectiveness of Plan Colombia

and of drug prohibition itself may signal the beginning of seriously questioning the effects of the anti-drug laws by the politicians who create the laws themselves. The following exchange between Rep. Burton and Carr was carried out during public testimony, in front of television cameras and broadcast by the cable channel C-SPAN to the US public at large.

[An undercover narcotics detective from Howard County, Maryland, going by the name of "Matt" strictly for this hearing, ends his presentation, and Burton begins.]

CHAIRMAN DAN BURTON (R-IN): I've been in public life off and on for about 35 years, but I want to tell you something. I have been in probably a hundred or a hundred and fifty

> I DON'T THINK THAT AL CAPONE WOULD HAVE BEEN THE MENACE TO SOCIETY THAT HE WAS IF HE COULDN'T SELL ALCOHOL ON THE BLACK MARKET [BUT] HE DID AND WE HAD A HORRIBLE, HORRIBLE CRIME PROBLEM.

hearings like this at various times in my political career and the story is always the same. This goes all the way back to the sixties. You know—35-40 years ago. And every time I have a hearing, I hear that people who get hooked on heroin and cocaine become addicted and they very rarely get off of it. And the scourge expands and expands and expands. And we have very fine law enforcement officers like you go out and fight the fight. And you see it growing and growing, and you see these horrible tragedies occur. But there is no end to it.

And I see young guys driving around in tough areas of Indianapolis in cars that I know they can't afford and I know where they are getting their money. I mean that there is no question. A kid can't be driving a brand-new Corvette when he lives in the inner city of Indianapolis in a ghetto. You know that he has gotta be making that money in some way that is probably not legal and probably involves drugs.

Over 70% of all crime is drug-related. And you alluded to that today. We saw on television recently Pablo Escobar gunned down and everybody applauded and said "that's the end of the Medellín cartel." But it wasn't the end. There is still a cartel down there. They are still all over the place.

When you kill one, there's ten or twenty or fifty waiting to take his place. You know why? It's because of what you just said a minute ago, Mr. Carr, Mr. Marcocci. And that is that there is so much money to be made in it—there is always going to be another person in line to make that money.

And we go into drug eradication and we go into rehabilitation and we go into education, and we do all of these things. And the drug problem continues to increase. And it continues to cost us not billions, but trillions of dollars. Trillions! And we continue to build more and more prisons, and we put more and more people in jail, and we know that the crimes that they're committing are related most of the time to drugs.

So I have one question I would like to ask all of you, and I think this is a question that needs to be asked. I hate drugs. I hate people who succumb to drug addiction, and I hate what it does to our society. It has hit every one of us in our families or friends of ours. But I have one question that nobody ever asks, and that is this question: What would happen if there was no profit in drugs? If there was no profit in drugs, what would happen? And I'd like any of you to answer. If they couldn't make any money out of selling drugs, what would happen?

THOMAS CARR: I would like to comment. If we took away all the illegal drugs today, we're still going to have a problem.

BURTON: I understand that. I'm talking about new drugs.

CARR: What you are arguing then is complete legalization.

BURTON: No, I am not arguing anything. I am asking the question. Because we have been fighting this fight for thirty to forty years and the problem NEVER goes way. New generations—younger and younger people—get hooked on drugs. Kids in grade schools are getting hooked on drugs. Their lives are ruined. They're going to jail. They're become prostitutes and drug pushers because they have to make money to feed their habit. And these horrible drug dealers—many of whom aren't using drugs—they'll send free drugs into school and schoolyards to hook these kids and the problem increases and increases and increases. And nobody ever asks this question. And I'm not inferring anything because I hate drugs. I hate the use of it. I hate

DON'T JUST TALK ABOUT KILLING PEOPLE LIKE ESCOBAR, WHO IS GOING TO BE REPLACED BY SOMEBODY ELSE. LET'S TALK ABOUT WHAT WOULD HAPPEN IF WE STARTED ADDRESSING HOW TO GET THE PROFIT OUT OF DRUGS.

what it's done to our society. But the question needs to be addressed at some point: What would happen if they don't make any money out of it?

CARR: I don't think you can create a situation where no one makes any money out of it. There's always going to

be a black market. I don't think the American public is going to say, "OK, well drugs don't cost anything, but only eighteen year olds can have it?" Or eighteen and above? Then you have a black market for the minors. No one is going to say two year olds can have heroin. Or five year olds. Where do you make that demarcation? So I don't think you can get to that point where you have a laissez faire type of drug business without any profit in it. Even with that, that would reduce some form of crime, but you're still going to have other crimes there because we aren't addressing the social issues.

BURTON: How about the overall effect on our society? The long-term problem with our society—the number of people that are being addicted in our society? Would it go up or down if there was no profit?

CARR: Oh, I think it would go up if people were told that it was free. I think people would try it more and get addicted.

BECAUSE WE HAVE BEEN FIGHTING THIS FIGHT FOR THIRTY TO FORTY YEARS AND THE PROBLEM NEVER GOES WAY. NEW GENERATIONS—YOUNGER AND YOUNGER PEOPLE—GET HOOKED ON DRUGS.

BURTON: No, no. I didn't say free.

CARR: I think people would try it more if it was available.

BURTON: [VERY CYNICAL CHUCKLE]. Well I don't think that the people in Colombia would be planting coca if they couldn't make any money, and I don't think they would be refining coca and heroin in Colombia if they couldn't make any money. And I don't think that Al Capone would have been the menace to society that he was if he couldn't sell alcohol on the black market [but] he did and we had a horrible, horrible crime problem. Now the people that are producing drugs in Southeast Asia and Southwest Asia and Colombia and everyplace else, they don't do it because they like to do it. They don't fill those rooms full of money because they like to fill them full of money. They do it because they are making money.

CARR: Exactly.

BURTON: And the problem in my opinion is that at SOME point we to have to look at the OVERALL picture… and I am not saying that there are not going to be people who are addicted and that you're not going to have education and rehabilitation and all of those things that you are talking about. But one of the parts of the equation that has NEVER been talked about—because politicians are AFRAID to talk about it—this is my last committee hearing as Chairman. Last time. And I thought about this and thought about this, and thought about this. And one of the things that ought to be asked is: "What part of the equation are we leaving out?" And, "Is it an important part of the equation?" And that is: the profit in drugs. Don't just talk about education. Don't just talk about eradication. Don't just talk about killing people like Escobar, who is going to be replaced by somebody else. Let's talk about what would happen if we started addressing how to get the profit out of drugs.

CARR: I think that's something that needs to be looked at, but I still question the idea that if you're taking the profit out of drugs—that doesn't mean you're eliminating the demand for drugs. People are still going to want heroin. So someone is going to produce it and someone is going to sell it.

BURTON: But the new addictions? Would they be diminished if you didn't have somebody trying to make money? If you didn't have these people going from Philadelphia to New York or from Washington to New York? Why would they drive from here to New York to get these drugs to sell them if they couldn't make any money?

CARR: I think they're going to make money. I don't know how you're going to eliminate them not making money.

BURTON: That's part of the equation.

CARR: If they couldn't make money, certainly they wouldn't. They'd do something else.

BURTON: That's right. And that's part of the equation that ought to be looked at and we haven't been looking at it.

CARR: Oh, I think you're right.

BURTON: Thank you. Ms. Schakowsky? Do you have a question?

REP. JAN SCHAKOWSKY (D-IL): Mr. Chairman, I wanted to stay and hear your question because I want to thank you for raising it. I think we can't be afraid to raise these kinds of questions when we discuss this whole issue of addiction and substance abuse and the attendant crime and law enforcement issues that go with it. And I think going forward—I'd welcome, under your leadership, that we explore FULLY this issue and follow your line of questioning...

Panel 1 witnesses:

Felix J. Jimenez Retired Special Agent in Charge, DEA New York Field Division Special Agent in Charge, Transportation Security Administration, New York Field Division

Detective Tony Marcocci Westmoreland County, Pennsylvania, District Attorney's Office

Detective Sergeant Scott Pelletier, Portland, Maine, Police Department Head, Portland Police Department, Maine Drug Enforcement Administration Heroin Task Force Undercover narcotics detective Howard County, Maryland, Police Department

Tom Carr Director, Baltimore-Washington High Intensity Drug Trafficking Area (HIDTA) http://www.whitehousedrugpolicy.gov/hidta/

Narcodollars for Beginners: How the Money Works in the Illicit Drug Trade—Parts I and II

Catherine Austin Fitts

Part I

A simple framework: The Solari Index and the Dow Jones Index

"The Latin American drug cartels have stretched their tentacles much deeper into our lives than most people believe. It's possible they are calling the shots at all levels of government."—William Colby, former CIA Director, 1995

The Solari Index is my way of estimating how well a place is doing. It is based upon the percentage of people in a place who believe that a child can leave their home and go to the nearest place to buy a popsicle and come home alone safely.

When I was a child growing up in the 1950s at 48th and Larchwood in West Philadelphia, the Solari Index was 100%. It was unthinkable that a child was not safe running up to the stores on Spruce Street for a Popsicle and some pinball. The Dow Jones was about 500, the Solari Index was 100% and our debt per person was very low. Of course I did not think about it that way at the time. All I knew was that life on the street with my buddies was sweet.

Today, the Dow Jones is over 9,000, debt per person is over $100,000, and my favorite hairdresser in Philadelphia, Al at the Hair Hut in West Philadelphia, and I just had a debate yesterday afternoon while Al was cutting my hair about whether the Solari Index in my old neighborhood was 0% (my position) or 10% (Al's position). Men always think it is

> AMERICA IS ABOUT AS STONED ON ILLEGAL DRUGS AS IT CAN GET, AND GROWTH IN CONTROLLED "SCHEDULE II" SUBSTANCES HAS MOVED TO RITALIN AND OTHER COCAINE-LIKE DRUGS FOR KIDS THAT GOVERNMENT PROGRAMS AND HEALTH INSURANCE WILL NOW FINANCE.

higher than women. Despite the boy-girl spread between us, it is fair to say that Al and I agree that the Solari Index is in the tank—both in the streets of Philadelphia and throughout America.

Life on the street ain't sweet any more. I watched the slide of the Solari Index as a child. A lot of it had to do with narcotics trafficking and the people that narco dollars put in power on our streets—and in city hall, in the banks, in

Congress, and the corporations and investors downtown and that ring the city.

My mission is to see the Solari Index return to 100% and to do so in a manner that moves the Dow up and our debt per person down and makes me and my partners a whole pile of money.

A few years back when my efforts to improve the Solari Index were threatening to reduce narcotics profits in a few places, I discovered that I could not look to the enforcement or the judicial establishment funded with my tax dollars to protect me. Narco dollars had the upper hand throughout government and the legal establishment.

That's when I decided that I would have to learn how the money works in the drug trade.

Here is what I have learned that has been useful to me, and may help you have a better map of how narco dollars impact you, your business, your family and the Solari Index in your neighborhood.

The Economic of Production—Sam and Dave do Boatloads of White Agricultural Substances

Okay, let's start at ground zero. It is 1947, and World War II is over. America is ready to go back to work to build the corporate economy. We are in New Orleans on the docks.

Two boats pull into the docks. The first boat is full of a white agricultural product grown in Latin America called *sugar*. The owner of the cargo, lets call him Sam, sells his boat load of white agricultural substance to the sugar wholesaler on the docks for how much money?

Ok, so let's say that Sam sells his entire boatload of sugar to the sugar wholesaler on the docks for X dollars.

Now, after Sam pays his workers and all his costs of growing and transporting the sugar, and after he and his wife spend the weekend in New Orleans and he pays himself a bonus and buys some new harvest equipment and pays his taxes, how much cash does he have left to deposit into his bank account? Or, another way of saying this is: What is Sam's net cash margin on his sugar business?

Well, it depends on how lucky and hard working and smart Sam is, but let's say that Sam has worked his proverbial you know what off and he makes around 5-10%. Sam the sugar man has a 5-10% cash profit margin. Let's call Sam's margin S for Slim or Slim Percentage. Back on the docks, the second boat—an exact replica of the boat carrying Sam's sugar—is a boat carrying Dave's white agricultural product called *drugs*. In those days this was more likely to be heroin, these days more likely to be cocaine. Whatever the precise species, the planting, harvesting and production of this white agricultural substance, Dave's drugs, are remarkably like Sam's sugar.

Okay, so if Sam the sugar man sold his sugar to the sugar wholesaler for X dollars, how much will Dave the drug man sell his drugs to the drug wholesaler for? Well, where Sam is getting pennies, Dave is getting bills. If Sam had sales of X dollars, let say that Dave had sales of 50-100 times X. Dave may carry the same amount of white stuff in a boat but from a financial point of view, Dave the drug man has a lot more "sales per boat" than Sam the sugar man.

Now, after Dave pays his workers and all his costs of growing and transporting the drugs, and after he and his wife spend the weekend in New Orleans and he pays himself a bonus and buys some new harvest and radar equipment and spends what he needs on bribes and bonuses to a few enforcement and intelligence operatives and retainers to his several law firms, how much cash does he have left to deposit into his bank account? Or, another way of saying this is what is Dave's net cash margin on his drug business?

It's also going to be a multiple of Sam's margin, right? Maybe it will be 20% or 30% or more? Let's call it B for Big, or Big Percentage. Dave the drug man has a much bigger "cash profit per boat" than Sam the sugar man. Part of that is, of course, once Dave has set up his money laundering schemes, even after a 4-10% take for the money laundering fees, it's fair to say his tax rate of 0% is lower than Sam's tax rate. While it is expensive to set up all the many schemes Dave might use to launder his money, once you do it you can save a lot avoiding some or all of the IRS' take.

Look at your estimate of Sam and Dave's sales and profits Now answer for yourself the following questions.

Who is going to get paid more, Sam or Dave?

Who is going to be more popular with the local bankers, Sam or Dave?

Who is going to have a bigger stock market portfolio with a large investment house, Sam or Dave?

Who is going to donate more money to political campaigns, Sam or Dave?

Whose wife is going to be bigger in the local charities, Sam or Dave's?

Whose company will have more prestigious law firms on retainer, Sam or Dave's?

Who is going to buy the other's company first, Sam or Dave?

Is Dave the drug man going to buy Sam the sugar man's company, or is Sam the sugar man going to buy Dave the drug man's company?

When they want to buy the other's company, will the bankers, lawyers and investment houses and politicians back Sam the sugar man or Dave the drug man?

Whose son or grandson has a better chance of getting into Harvard or getting a job offer at Goldman Sachs, Sam or Dave's?

Don't listen to me. And don't listen to Peter Jennings, Dan Rather, or Tom Brokaw. Who do you think pays their salaries? Who owns the companies they work for? Sam or Dave? Don't listen to anyone else. Think about the numbers and listen to your heart. What do you believe?

There is very little about how the money works on the drug trade that you cannot know for yourself by coming to grips with the economics over a fifty year period of Sam and Dave and their boat loads of white agricultural substance. It is the magic of compound interest.

As one of my former partners used to say, "Cash flow is more important than your mother."

Many Boatloads Later

It's more than fifty years now since the boats transporting Sam and Dave's white agricultural products docked in New Orleans. I don't know what the Narco National Product (Solari's term for that portion of the GNP coming from narco dollars) was in 1947, but lets say it was a billion dollars or less. Today, the Narco National Product that number is estimated to be about $400 billion globally and about $150 billion plus in the United States.

It helps to look at the business globally as the United States is the world leader in global money laundering. According to the Department of Justice, the US launders between $500 billion-$1 trillion annually. I have little idea what percentage of that is narco dollars, but it is probably safe to assume that at least $100-200 billion relates to US drug import-exports and retail trade.

Ok, so let's think about how much Sam and Dave have in accumulated profits in their bank and brokerage accounts.

Let's assume that the US narco national product in 1947 was $1 billion and it has grown to about $150 billion today. Assume a straight line of growth from $1 billion to $150 billion, so the business grows about $3 billion a year and then tops out at $150 billion as the Solari Index has bottomed out at or near 0%. America is about as stoned on illegal drugs as it can get, and growth in controlled "Schedule II" substances has moved to Ritalin and other cocaine-like drugs for kids that government programs and health insurance will now finance.

Let's take the Big Percent margin that we estimated for Dave the drug man's net cash margin.

Let's say that every year from 1947 through 2001, that the cash flow sales available for reinvestment from drug profits grew by $3 billion a year, throwing off that number times Big Percent. Okay, assume that the reinvested profit grew at the compound growth rate of the Standard & Poor's 500 as it got reinvested along the way.

That amount is an estimate for the equity owned and controlled by those who have profited in the drug trade. Total narco dollars. How much money is that? I made an Excel spread-sheet once to estimate total narco capital in the economy.

> MY NUMBERS SHOWED THAT DAVE THE DRUG MAN HAD BOUGHT UP NOT ONLY SAM'S COMPANIES, BUT— IF YOU THROW IN OTHER ORGANIZED CRIME CASH FLOWS—A CONTROLLING POSITION IN ABOUT MOST EVERYTHING ON THE NEW YORK STOCK EXCHANGE.

My numbers showed that Dave the drug man had bought up not only Sam's companies, but—if you throw in other organized crime cash flows—a controlling position in about most everything on the New York Stock Exchange.

When you think about it, this analysis makes sense. The folks with the Big Percent—big cash margin—would end up rich and in power and the guys working their you-know-what off for Slim Percent—a low cash margin—would end up working for them.

A Real World Example— NYSE's Richard Grasso and the Ultimate New Business "Cold Call"

Lest you think that my comment about the New York Stock Exchange is too strong, let's look at one event that occurred before our War on Drugs went into high gear through Plan Colombia, banging heads over narco dollar market shares in Latin America.

In late June 1999, numerous news services, including the *Associated Press*, reported that Richard Grasso, Chairman of the New York Stock Exchange, flew to Colombia to meet with a spokesperson for Raul Reyes of the Revolutionary Armed Forces of Columbia (FARC), the supposed "narco terrorists" with whom we are now at war.

The purpose of the trip was "to bring a message of cooperation from US financial services" and to discuss foreign investment and the future role of US businesses in Colombia. Some reading in between the lines said to me that Grasso's mission related to the continued circulation of cocaine capital through the US financial system. FARC, the Colombian rebels, were circulating their profits back into local development without the assistance of the American banking and investment system. Worse yet for the outlook for the US stock market's strength from $500 billion-$1 trillion in annual money laundering—FARC was calling for the decriminalization of cocaine.

To understand the threat of decriminalization of the drug trade, just go back to your Sam and Dave estimate and recalculate the numbers given what decriminalization does to drive Big Percent back to Slim Percent and what that means to Wall Street and Washington's cash flows. No narco dollars, no reinvestment into the stock markets, no campaign contributions.

It was only a few days after Grasso's trip that BBC News reported a General Accounting Office (GAO) report to Congress as saying: "Colombia's cocaine and heroin production is set to rise by as much as 50% as the US backed drug war flounders, due largely to the growing strength of Marxist rebels"

I deduced from this incident that the liquidity of the NY Stock Exchange was sufficiently dependent on high margin cocaine profits (Big Percent) that the Chairman of the New York Stock Exchange was willing for *Associated Press* to acknowledge he is making "cold calls" in rebel controlled peace zones in Colombian villages. "Cold calls" is what we used to call new business visits we would pay to people we had not yet done business with when I was on Wall Street.

I presume Grasso's trip was not successful in turning the cash flow tide. Hence, Plan Colombia is proceeding apace to try to move narco deposits out of FARC's control and back to the control of our traditional allies and, even if that does not work, to move Citibank's market share and that of the other large US banks and financial institutions steadily up in Latin America.

Part II

Buy Banamex anyone?—the Narco Money Map

Narcodollars On Your Map

It helps to look at the drug markets by looking at a map of the United States.

What are the four states with the largest market share in illegal narcotics trafficking? Draw a map if you want and shade them in on your map.

Yup. You got it. New York, California, Texas, and Florida.

It makes sense. Those are the biggest states. They have big coastal areas and borders and big ports. It would make sense that the population would grow in the big states where the trade and business flow grows. If you check back to Part I of *Narco Dollars for Beginners*, we described two businesses. One was Sam's sugar business that had a Slim percentage profit. The other was Dave's drug business that had a Big Percentage profit. It would make sense that these four states would be real big in both Sam's sugar business and Dave's drug businesses.

> SO THE GOVERNORS OF TWO OF THE LARGEST NARCO DOLLAR MARKET SHARE STATES JUST HAPPEN TO BE THE SONS OF THE FORMER CHIEF OF THE SECRET POLICE.

OK. Now. What are the four states with the biggest business in money laundering of narco profits and other profits of organized crime?

Not surprising? Same four states. They are all known as banking power places. New York, California, Texas, and Florida.

What's next? What are the four states with the biggest business in taking the laundered narco profits and using them to deposit money in a bank, or to buy another company, or to start a new company, or just buy stock in the stock market? That's what I call the reinvestment business. Same four, right? New York, California, Texas, and Florida.

Who were the governors of these four states in 1996?

Well, let's see. Jeb Bush was the governor of Florida. Governor Jeb is the son of George H. W. Bush, the former head of an oil company in Texas and Mexico and the former head of the CIA and the former head of the various drug enforcement efforts as Vice President and President. Then George W. Bush, also the son of George

H. W. Bush, was the governor of Texas. So the governors of two of the largest narco dollar market share states just happen to be the sons of the former chief of the secret police.

Do you think it is possible to become the governor of a state with the support of the Slim Percentage profit businesses and the opposition of the Big Percentage profit businesses, particularly after the Big Percentage profits have bought up all the Slim Percentage profit businesses?

What about the President?

Of course, George W. is President today fueled by the single most successful campaign fundraising in the history of Western civilization. Now do you know why Hillary Clinton wanted to be a Senator from New York? Now do you know why Andrew Cuomo wants to be New York governor and is reported to be doing polls to see if people associate him with the Mafia and organized crime?

When you think about it, the President would need to win the majority of the people who donate from the Slim Percentage profit businesses but control the reinvestment of the Big Percentage profit industry cash flow to win. The competition for the support of the people who control the reinvestment from the Big Percentage profit business cash flow in the biggest states would be fierce.

According to the Center for Responsive Politics analysis of the 2000 elections, donors in California, New York, the District of Colombia Metro Area (which is full of lawyers and lobbyists who represent all the other states), Texas, and Florida contributed $666.8 million, or approximately 47% of a total of $1.427 billion in donations.

Getting out of Narcodollars HQ

In 1996, my company and I were targeted by a private informant and a group of investigators working for the Department of Justice and the Department of Housing and Urban Development (HUD). If you have ever seen the movie *Enemy of the State* with Will Smith and Gene Hackman, then you understand how the drill works.

> FOR MORE THAN TWO YEARS I LIVED THROUGH SERIOUS PHYSICAL HARASSMENT AND SURVEILLANCE. THIS INCLUDED BURGLARY, STALKING, HAVING HOUSEGUESTS FOLLOWED AND DEAD ANIMALS LEFT ON THE DOORMAT.

Will Smith plays a successful Washington lawyer who is targeted in a phony frame and smear by a US intelligence agency. The spooky types have high-speed access to every last piece of data on the information highway—from Will's bank account to his telephone conversations—and the wherewithal to engineer a smear campaign through the papers and the Council on Foreign Relations types.

The organizer of an investment conference once introduced me by saying, "Who here has seen the movie *Enemy of the State*? The woman I am about to introduce to you played Will Smith in real life."

One day I was a wealthy entrepreneur with a beautiful home, a successful business and money in the bank. I had been a partner and member of the board of directors of a Wall Street firm and then Assistant Secretary of Housing-Federal Housing Commissioner during the first Bush Administration. I had been invited to serve as a governor of the Federal Reserve Board and instead started my own company in Washington, The Hamilton Securities Group. Thanks to our leadership in digital technology, financial software and analytics, Hamilton was doing well and poised for significant financial growth. One of my software tool innovations, Community Wizard, helped communities access data about how all the money works in their place. Accessible through the World Wide Web, Community Wizard was illuminating an unusual

> THE POWER OF NARCO DOLLARS COMES WHEN YOU COMBINE DRUG TRAFFICKING WITH THE STOCK MARKET.

pattern of defaults on HUD mortgages and other government and homeowner losses in areas in which the CIA had admitted to facilitating cocaine trafficking by Iran Contra supporters. According to the CIA, we were paying our government to help the narco dollars make money in a way that—if you read Community Wizard's comic book-like money maps—was losing taxpayers and homeowners billions of dollars.

The next day I was hunted, living through eighteen audits and investigations and a smear campaign directed not just at me but also at members of my family, colleagues and friends who helped me. I believe that the smear campaign originated at the highest levels. For more than two years I lived through serious physical harassment and surveillance. This included burglary, stalking, having houseguests followed and dead animals left on the doormat. The hardest part was the necessity of keeping quiet about the physical danger lest it cost me more support or harm my credibility. Most people simply do not believe that such things are possible in America.

In 1999, I sold everything to pay what to date is approximately $6 million of legal and administrative costs. My estimate of equity destroyed, damages and opportunity costs is $250 million. I moved to a system of living in several places on an unpredictable schedule in the hope that this would push up the cost of surveillance and harassment and so dissuade my tormentors from following.

The places were chosen to move me as far away as possible from the corridors of power in Washington and on Wall Street filled with people benefiting from narco dollars and their reinvestment. That strategy—combined with excellent legal and administrative work by a first rate team of very courageous people—has been successful in besting the targeting. It made it possible for me to understand how our economic addiction to narco dollars worked and how it was draining our neighborhoods. I teamed up with the members of my family and friends and their neighbors who were getting drained.

Four days after *Insight* Magazine published a cover story on me on May 21, 2001, the head investigator targeting us resigned unexpectedly. Three weeks later the last of eighteen audits and investigations was suddenly closed down. A follow-up article by *Insight's* Paul Rodriguez described the closed investigation as something that "many inside both HUD and the Department of Justice regarded as a political vendetta against Fitts."

The miracle had happened. We have overcome a serious targeting. Like in the movie where Will Smith comes out fine, my story has a happy ending. It's a wonderful feeling. As Winston Churchill's once said, "Nothing is more exhilarating than being shot at without result."

I believe that one of the reasons for my happy ending was that our actions to deal with the investigation reflected the understanding of narco dollars that I acquired from living and traveling throughout America and talking with people from all walks of life about how narco dollars were impacting our lives and neighborhoods in many different places.

Understanding narco dollars is something I need to know to help entrepreneurs around the country build the profitable deals and businesses that will get the Solari Index and Dow Jones in our neighborhoods rising together.

Where I live, folks do not want to know about what is wrong on the *Titanic*. They do not want to know that a flood of narco dollars is rolling over us. They know these things. What they want to know is how to build arks.

Georgie, West Philadelphia, and the Stock Market

One of my new homes is in the city in Philadelphia, near where I grew up in West Philadelphia. Another is in a very beautiful and close knit farming community in Hickory Valley, Tennessee where my father's family has lived since the 1850s.

Once a month I drive to Philadelphia from my home in Hickory Valley to attend a board meeting. I stay in a lovely little apartment in the first floor of a row house owned by my friend Georgie.

Georgie is one of my favorite people in the world. She lives in the apartment on the second floor. Just about my favorite thing in the world is hanging out with Georgie. We watch Oprah, we talk, we go to movies, and we giggle over ice cream with long names and cookies. Georgie is an awesome cook and my little apartment fills up daily with the smells of something delicious that Georgie is making.

One day Forest, my dog, and I were up in Georgie's apartment to enjoy a fresh plate of scrapple that Georgie had fried up that morning. The conversation turned to narco dollars. Georgie said that looking at the big picture was simply too overwhelming. Couldn't I explain this without using the words millions or billions, just dollars and cents in terms of our neighborhood in West Philadelphia?

I always have this problem explaining international money flows to moms and grand moms. Most really great women want to know about the real world. The world of real people— her world full of her kids and grandkids and other kids she loves.

So we got out a blank piece of paper and started to estimate.

Every day there are two or three teenagers on the corner dealing drugs across from our home in Philadelphia. We figured that if they had a 50% deal with a supplier, did $300 a day of sales each, and worked 250 days a year, that their supplier could run his net profits of approximately $100,000 through a local fast food restaurant that was owned by a publicly traded company.

WELL, IF THE DEPARTMENT OF JUSTICE IS CORRECT ABOUT $500 BILLION-TO-1 TRILLION OF ANNUAL MONEY LAUNDERING IN THE US, THEN ABOUT $20-40 BILLION SHOULD MOVE ANNUALLY THROUGH THE PHILADELPHIA FEDERAL RESERVE DISTRICT.

Assuming that company has a stock market value that is a multiple of 20-30 times its profits, a handful of illiterate teenagers could generate approximately $2-3 million in stock market value for a major corporation, not to mention a nice flow of deposits and business for the Philadelphia banks and insurance companies.

The Narcodollar Double Bind: Dow Jones Index Up, Solari Index down

As described in Part I, the Solari Index is my way of estimating how well a place is doing. It is based upon the percentage of people in a place who believe that a child can leave their home and go to the nearest place to buy a Popsicle and come home alone safely. The Solari Index is about how safe you feel you and your neighbor's kids are.

When I was a child growing up in the 1950s at 48th and Larchwood in West Philadelphia, the Solari Index was 100%. It was unthinkable that a child was not safe running up to the stores on Spruce Street for a Popsicle and some pinball. The Dow Jones was about 500, the Solari Index was 100% and our debt per person was very low. Of course I did not think about it that way at the time. All I knew was that life on the street with my buddies was sweet.

Life on the street ain't sweet anymore. To understand how this works, we need to understand "pop."

It's Not Just About the Profit, It's About the Pop

Here is the part that is particularly hard for women. It took several times at our sheet of paper before Georgie understood what I was saying.

The power of narco dollars comes when you combine drug trafficking with the stock market.

The "pop" is a word I learned on Wall Street to describe the multiple of income at which a stock trades. So if a stock like PepsiCo trades at 20 times its income, that means for every $100,000 of income it makes, it's stock goes up $2 million. The company may make $100,000, but its "pop" is $2 million. Folks make money in the stock market from the stock going up. On Wall Street, it's all about "pop."

The people who own a corporation make money on the stock going up. So a company has investors, with the most powerful investors typically being large institutions who are typically represented on the board of the company. The board is the group of people who decides what goes. The senior management officials who run the company day to day are also on the board. Most of the money they make comes from stock options that they get to encourage them to get the stock to go up for the investors. That means that what everyone who runs the company wants is for the stock to go up. The way to do that is to increase net income or to increase the multiple at which the stock trades.

So in the case of PepsiCo described above, if the management increases soda pop sales in a way that net income goes up by $100,000, the stock goes up $2 million. Now let's say, the board and management do a whole series of things to attract new investors and improve the company's image and, as a result, the stock starts trading at 22 times profits. Then, the stock value goes up even more. Whether increasing net income or increasing the multiple at which the stock market values the company profits, the board and the management are focused on making the stock go up. That is how their money works.

The winner in the global corporate game is the guy who has the most income running through the highest multiple stocks. He is the winning pop player. Like the guy who wins at Monopoly because he buys up all the properties on the board, he can buy up all the other companies.

So if I have a company that has a $100,000 of income and a stock trading at 20 times earnings, if I can find a way to run $100,000 of narcotics sales by a few teenagers in West Philadelphia through my financial statements, I can get my stock market value to go up from $2 million to $4 million. I can double my "pop." That is a quick $2 million profit from putting a few teenagers to work driving the Solari Index down in their neighborhood. Bottom line, I can make a lot of quick money on the stock going up and the Solari Index going down

OK, now what does this all mean for the Solari Index in Philadelphia? If I am a group of mothers in my neighborhood who want the Solari Index to go back up to a 100%, what's stopping me?

Well, if the Department of Justice is correct about $500 billion-to-1 trillion of annual money laundering in the US, then about $20-40 billion should move annually through the Philadelphia Federal Reserve District.

Assuming a 20% margin for the Big Percentage profits and a 20 times multiple on the stock of the companies that Dave and his investors and banking partners were using to launder the money, let's look at how much of the stock market value would be "addicted" to the drug and money laundering profits flowing through the Philadelphia area.

The total stock market value generated in the Philadelphia area with $20-40 billion in narco retail sales would be about $80-160 billion. If you add all the things you could do with debt and other ways to increase the multiples, you could get that even higher, say $100-250 billion.

Assuming that there are 3 million people in the greater Philadelphia area, the total stock market value generated would average anywhere from $27,000-to-85,000 per person. Imagine what would happen to the economy in Philadelphia if this stock market value suddenly disappeared because all the teenagers in Philadelphia stopped dealing or buying drugs?

Imagine what happens to your stock multiple if you are a Philadelphia corporate chieftain and you don't run narco dollars or large purchases fueled by narco dollars through your financial statements and you don't attract narco dollars to reinvest in your stock? What happens to your corporate income and your stock profit if the ones who invest narco dollars—accumulated over the last fifty years compounding at their magical compound interest—don't like you? How is everyone in Philadelphia who loses money on your stock going down going to feel about you?

The Department of Justice says that we launder $500 billion-1 trillion. Multiply those times a Big Percentage cash flow profit margin. Now figure how much of that "income" gets run through the income statement of publicly traded banks and companies and multiply that number by the multiple of income at which their stocks trade. *Voila.* I don't know what your number is. All I know is that, as Ed Sullivan used to say, it is "really, really BIG."

Editor's note—to read the conclusion of Catherine Austin Fitts' series *Narco Dollars for Beginners*, "Drugs as Currency," visit NarcoNews.com.

Can you tell me how you are going to save the [poppy seed] bagel? *Hemp Industries Association v. the Drug Enforcement Administration*

Adam Eidinger and Zoe Mitchell

Judge Alex Kozinski of the Ninth Circuit Court of Appeals had already asked Drug Enforcement Administration (DEA) attorney Daniel Dormont about the poppy seed bagel during the final arguments in the *Hemp Industries Association v. the Drug Enforcement Administration* (*HIA v. DEA*). But Judge Kozinski hadn't gotten the answer he wanted. He asked again:

> JUDGE ALEX KOZINSKI: Before you sit down, can you tell me how you are going to save the bagel?
>
> ATTORNEY DANIEL DORMONT: How can—I'm sorry?
>
> JUDGE ALEX KOZINSKI: Save the bagel. You started to tell me about the language in the statute, and then Judge Fletcher then asked you to get back to policy. I'm less interested in policy than I am in the language of the statute, so you just very quickly tell me now what's stopping the agency from outlawing the poppy seed bagels tomorrow?[1]

Although the DEA wasn't requesting a ban on poppy seeds because they contain trace opiates,[2] Judge Kozinski's questioning illustrated the absurdity of the DEA's recent attempt to ban another food product, hemp seed, because of its association with marijuana, an "illicit substance."

Hemp is not Marijuana and the Government Already Knows It

Despite drug war propaganda from the DEA and other drug enforcement agencies, hemp is not marijuana. Eric Steenstra, the president of Vote Hemp, an industrial hemp advocacy group, comprehensively explains why: "It's really quite simple. The difference between hemp and marijuana is that it's two varieties of the same plant: one which contains a high amount of THC and is used for drugs and one which contains an extremely low amount of THC and has no potential to be used as a recreational drug."[3] In more scientific terms, both hemp and marijuana are part of the genus *Cannabis*; however, hemp contains only trace, insignificant amounts of Tetrahydrocannabinols—commonly known as THC—the psychoactive ingredient in marijuana.[4]

Because of this substantial difference between hemp and marijuana, the US Congress specifically excluded hemp from various anti-marijuana laws and when necessary, supported the industrial hemp industry. The 1937 Marihuana Tax Act, which effectively banned marijuana, did not ban industrial hemp. This Act, "defined marijuana as 'all parts of the plant *Cannabis sativa* L., whether growing or not; the seeds thereof; the resin extracted from any such plant; and every compound, manufacture, salt, derivative, mixture, or preparation of such plant, its seeds or resin; but shall not include the mature stalks of such plant, fiber produced from such stalks, oil or cake made from the seeds of such plant, any other compound, manufacture salt, derivative, mixture, or preparation of such mature stalks (except the resin extracted there from), fiber, oil, or cake, or the sterilized seed of such plant which is incapable of germination.'"[5]

Additionally, the US Government subsidized industrial hemp production during World War II through the War Hemp Industries.[6] Nearly one million acres of industrial hemp were cultivated for the war effort.[7] Industrial hemp cultivation in the United States remained legal until Congress passed the 1970 Controlled Substances Act (CSA).

The CSA retained the definition of marijuana from the Marihuana Tax Act; however, it effectively nullified the pre-existing dichotomous relationship between marijuana and hemp in two important ways. First, the CSA banned the cultivation of any cannabis plant, "except where the DEA issued a limited-use permit, by setting zero tolerance for THC."[8] Unfortunately, because the DEA's Drug War paranoia has confused non-psychoactive industrial hemp varieties of cannabis with psychoactive "marijuana" varieties, the US became (and remains) the only major industrialized nation to prohibit the growing of industrial

> "...TELL ME NOW WHAT'S STOPPING THE AGENCY FROM OUTLAWING THE POPPY SEED BAGELS TOMORROW?"

hemp. Thus, this section of the CSA is responsible for both decimating whatever was left of the domestic industrial hemp industry and creating a profitable market for hemp exporters abroad.

Second, the CSA "banned 'any material, compound, mixture, or preparation which contains any quantity of Tetrahydrocannabinols (THC)'"[9] This shift in the hemp/ marijuana discourse is what makes things difficult for hemp food proponents. As stated above, hemp food contains trace amounts of THC. While it is impossible to have a THC-free hemp food product, it is difficult to have a healthy diet without hemp food.

No, You Can't Get High But You Can Get Healthy and Harassed

While smoking or eating hemp—even in large quantities— will not get one "high," there are substantial benefits to consuming hemp food products or hemp oil. Hemp seed has a well-balanced protein content and the highest amount of essential fatty acids (EFAs) of any oil in nature: EFAs are the "good fats" that, like vitamins, the body does not produce and requires for good health. Dr. Udo Erasmus, an internationally recognized nutritional authority on fats and oils, writes in *Fats that Heal—Fats that Kill*: "Hemp seed oil may be nature's most perfectly balanced oil."[10] Not surprisingly, shelled hemp seed and oil are increasingly used in natural food products, such as corn chips, frozen waffles, nutrition bars, hummus, nondairy milks, breads, and cereals. In the last few years, despite the CSA and the requirement to import all industrial hemp, the hemp foods industry has grown from less than $1 million to over $6 million in annual retail sales. Namely, the DEA was concerned that people who tested positive for marijuana use in drug tests could blame the positive result on consumption of hemp food products. While much earlier versions of hemp food may have caused false positive results, "current seed-cleaning technology and the correspondingly low trace THC levels in hemp oil and hemp nut, producing a confirmed positive test result would require that unrealistically high amounts of hemp oil or hemp nut be eaten."[11]

Additionally, most North American hemp food companies voluntarily observe reasonable THC limits similar to those adopted by European nations as well as Canada and Australia. These limits, part of a program called *Test Pledge*, protect consumers with a wide margin of safety from any psychoactive effects or workplace drug-testing interference. However, for the erratic DEA agents, it's not enough; they continue to use "past drug-test interference problems as [the] pretext to harass the hemp industry. This irrational policy is especially puzzling as the DEA has quite sensibly not attacked poppy seed bagels and pastries for promoting opium use, despite the fact that poppy seeds come from the same species as the opium poppy…"[12]

THE 1937 MARIHUANA TAX ACT, WHICH EFFECTIVELY BANNED MARIJUANA, DID NOT BAN INDUSTRIAL HEMP.

The Precarious Legal Status of Hemp Food and Oil…and the DEA itself

As a part of the Executive Branch, the DEA's mission statement describes an agency committed to stamping out illicit drugs and enforcing the CSA.[13] It does not describe an agency that interprets the CSA for its own gain and disregards the concerns of the public. That is, however, exactly what the DEA did with the hemp food issue.

Although the CSA explicitly excluded hemp, the DEA attempted to ban it through administrative law.

Administrative law refers to how Rules are developed for existing laws. In other words, these Rules refer to how the law is enforced. There are two types of Rules: Interpretive and Final. An Interpretive Rule is issued and it immediately goes into effect, while the Rule is "promulgated." The DEA would want to issue an Interpretive Rule if a new "dangerous and illicit" drug appeared. Although this drug would not be scheduled under the CSA, the DEA could consider this drug "an emergency" and receive public comments while the Rule is in effect.

Final Rules are proposed first as a kind of "warning." The public can read the proposed Final Rule and comment. Before these Rules take effect, they must be published in the Federal Register and the public must be allowed to comment. Although certain changes require a Congressional hearing, administrative law allows Executive Branch agencies to both interpret the law, and create it.[14]

In late 2000, hemp advocates learned that the DEA was planning on banning hemp food within the next year.[15] By December 2000, the hemp industry immediately contacted Attorney Joseph E. Sandler, who sent a 29 page letter to then DEA Administrator Donnie Marshall two months later.[16] The letter asked for an open dialogue about the hemp food issue and requested that the DEA refrain from making any regulations that would damage the hemp food industry. The DEA never responded; however, on October 1, 2001 they published the first Rule banning hemp food.

After issuing the Interpretive Rule, the DEA gave the hemp food industry and grocery stores, like Whole Foods Market, a short grace period—until February 6, 2002— before hemp food products were to be removed from the shelves. During this time, the Hemp Industries Association (HIA) filed the first legal complaint against the DEA in the Ninth Circuit Court of Appeals. On January 7, 2002 the

Adam Eidinger and Zoe Mitchell

HIA and several major hemp food companies in the US and Canada filed their opening brief urging the court to throw out the DEA's Interpretive Rule. Additionally, the HIA filed a Motion to Stay in the same court so hemp food products would not be removed from the shelves before the court ruled on the Interpretive Rule.

The HIA was not the only organization to challenge the DEA on its Interpretive Rule. Days after the opening brief, Kenex, Ltd., a Canadian agro-firm that has been growing and processing hemp oil, seed and fiber products in Canada for distribution throughout the United States for the past five years, filed a notice of intent to sue the US Government for $20 million under the North American Free Trade Agreement (NAFTA). Kenex filed the NAFTA action

> "THE BLIND PREJUDICE AND BLOODYMINDEDNESS OF THE DEA TAKES MY BREATH AWAY, ESPECIALLY WHEN ITS ACTIONS ARE IN DIRECT CONTRADICTION TO CONGRESS."

because the DEA through its Interpretive Rule effectively prevented Kenex from accessing American markets for its hemp food products, on which the firm depends for over three-quarters of its business.[17] The Government of Canada, in response to the DEA's new rule, stated that, "In reviewing the interim rule there is no evidence that the effective ban on relevant Canadian food products on the US market is based on any risk assessment. Therefore, Canada objects to these measures."[18]

Jean Laprise, the president of Kenex stated that: "A few million dollars would not even begin to cover the cost of the financial hardships Kenex has suffered through DEA's harassment of our business and the hemp food marketplace in general. Since the DEA's new rule was announced, our US hemp seed and oil sales have virtually ceased. If the DEA is not stopped, we are finished. Tallying our current and future losses, we expect to be compensated at least $20 million under NAFTA."[19]

The DEA's ban of hemp food sales in the US conflicts with NAFTA for several reasons. The DEA did not provide any notice and opportunity to US trading partners or foreign companies to provide input into its ruling; the agency did not conduct a risk assessment or offer any other science-based rationale for issuance of the rule; the DEA did not seek to minimize impact on international trade; and it has not similarly regulated poppy seeds and their trace opiates. Anita Roddick, an investor in Kenex and founder of the *Body Shop*, which markets a highly successful line of hemp oil based cosmetics, stated in regard to the DEA's current attempt to sabotage the hemp industry: "The blind prejudice and bloodymindedness of the DEA takes my breath away, especially when its actions are in direct contradiction to Congress. This is one instance when we have to invoke NAFTA. Without its protection, the future is bleak for hemp companies like Kenex."[20]

In late January then DEA head Asa Hutchinson, who replaced Marshall, appeared on the National Public Radio program "Public Interest" with Steenstra to discuss the Interpretive Rule. Hutchinson stated that the Interpretive Rule was not necessarily final and could be changed following a complete review of the public comments: "The interpretive rule puts the public and companies on notice as to how we're going to apply and interpret the law... But we seek comments on it and we are obliged and should consider these comments and after we evaluate those comments we can issue a final rule that will discuss the comments from the public, make any adjustments that are reasonably justified and necessary, and then that final rule will be implemented."[21]

The NPR interview was particularly telling. Hutchinson wildly misinterpreted the CSA saying. "There is no such exemption for any part of the Cannabis plant that contains THC. We are bound by the law." Steenstra replied: "I don't know what law he is reading and he is simply wrong. The DEA doesn't want to admit that in the exact same section as the poppy seed exemption there is an exemption for hemp seeds and oil. This duplicity leaves hemp companies no choice but to look to the courts to invalidate DEA's rule."

During the program, Hutchinson admitted, "We have received thousands and thousands of comments on this... clearly the public and the industry has submitted their comments and (they) will be considered before any final rule is adopted." After receiving numerous hostile calls from listeners, Hutchinson said, "At the DEA we certainly are not against the hemp industry. We're against THC which is what we are concerned about under the law."[22]

At this point, however, the hemp industry had learned through a Freedom of Information Act request, that DEA had not acted with the approval of the US Department of Justice, of which the DEA is a part. In a March 2000 memo to then-DEA head Donnie Marshall, John Roth, the Chief of the Narcotic and Dangerous Drug Section of the Department of Justice wrote against any DEA attempt to restrict the import of hemp seed and oil: "Hemp products intended for human consumption have THC at levels too low to trigger a psychoactive effect and are not purchased, sold or marketed with the intent of having a psychoactive effect."[23] Given this letter, it is unclear why the DEA still moved forward with the hemp food ban.

> THE DEA DOESN'T WANT TO ADMIT THAT IN THE EXACT SAME SECTION AS THE POPPY SEED EXEMPTION THERE IS AN EXEMPTION FOR HEMP SEEDS AND OIL.

Even more unclear, however, is why the DEA handed the hemp industry its first court-related victory. On February 7, 2002 the DEA told the Ninth Circuit that they would extend the "grace period" for hemp food products that contain "any THC." The extension reassured retailers stocking and selling hemp food products that for an additional 40 days, the DEA will not commence enforcement action. In a letter to the court, Daniel Dormont, Senior Attorney for the DEA, wrote: "It is my understanding that the Court of Appeals wishes to know whether the Drug Enforcement Administration (DEA) was planning to commence enforcement action while the petitioners' motion for a

THE IRONY IS THAT IF THE DEA REALLY WANTED TO DAMAGE MARIJUANA CROPS AND CURTAIL MARIJUANA USE, THEY WOULD PLANT HEMP EVERYWHERE.

stay is pending, given that the grace period published in the interim rule ended yesterday (February 6). In the view of the Court's inquiry, DEA will extend the grace period for an additional 40 days, through March 18, 2002. As we discussed, this should allow the Court to rule on the motion prior to the expiration of the grace period."[24]

One month later, the Ninth Circuit granted the hemp industry its first Motion to Stay. Hemp foods would remain legal until the court ruled on the Interpretive Rule.

Meanwhile, the Kenex NAFTA suit was progressing through the official routes. On March 25, 2002, US federal agencies[25] at the US Department of State reviewed the company's notice of intent to sue the US government under the North American Free Trade Agreement (NAFTA). On August 2, 2002, Kenex filed a NAFTA Notice of Arbitration with the US State Department.

On March 21, 2003, while most Americans were captivated by the US led invasion of Iraq, the DEA published their final rules on hemp foods. Their "Final Rule" again attempted to ban the sale of all hemp food products on April 21, 2003. The "Final Rule" was virtually identical to the Interpretive Rule. The HIA and several hemp food and cosmetic manufactures returned to petition the Ninth Circuit to prevent the DEA from ending the legal sale of hemp seed and oil.

David Bronner, the Chairman of the HIA's Food and Oil Committee was positive that, "the DEA's charade of supposedly protecting the public from safe and nutritious hemp food is finally going to end. The hemp industry is optimistic that the Court will ultimately invalidate the DEA's rule, as one of the prime criteria in granting the Stay was whether the hemp industry is likely to ultimately prevail on the merits of the case."[26]

In response to the Final Rule, the HIA filed a new brief in the Ninth Circuit charging that the DEA's Final Rule should be invalidated because the agency exercised arbitrary and capricious authority by attempting to outlaw hemp seed and oil without holding formal hearings on the issue or finding any potential for abuse.[27] The brief also charged that the DEA acted in an arbitrary and capricious manner in exempting hemp seed mixed with animal feed, although Congress made no such distinction in the CSA.

Finally, the brief elucidated other major failures by the DEA—namely, the lack of hearings on the issue and the failure to comply with the Regulatory Flexibility Act, which requires assessing effects of the proposed change on small businesses. On April 17, 2003, the Ninth Circuit again granted the hemp industry's Motion to Stay the DEA's Final Rule banning hemp food.

2003 proved to be a positive year for the hemp industry's battle against the DEA. In addition to granting the Stay in April, the Ninth Circuit invalidated the DEA's Interpretive Rule. Writing for the majority opinion, Judge Betty Fletcher said, "Because the DEA rule is inconsistent with the THC regulation at the time of promulgation, it is a procedurally invalid legislative rule, not an interpretive rule. The petition requesting that we declare the rule to be invalid and unenforceable is granted."[28]

In late September 2003, the hemp industry faced off against the DEA in the final oral arguments in HIA v. DEA at the Ninth Circuit. While the Court challenged HIA attorney Joe Sandler over how the DEA could or could not control a hypothetical plant containing trace THC in the Amazon rainforest, the judges were completely unconvinced by DEA attorney Daniel Dormont's arguments that Congress did not exempt hemp seed from the CSA even if the seed contains tiny insignificant amounts of naturally-occurring THC.

According to the hearing transcript, Dormont was read back the section of the CSA dealing with the hemp seed exemption on three occasions by Judge Alex Kozinski. By the third occasion, a frustrated Kozinski stated "…I tried to say it once before. What this tells me is Congress knew full well that stalks and seeds and fiber could be carriers of some level of tetrahydrocannabinol (THC). They were aware of that. Nevertheless, it said unless you do the extracting part they are not marihuana under the definition. That is what it says to me."[29]

SOME DRUG POLICY REFORMERS HOPE THAT THE ABSURDITY OF THE HEMP FOOD BATTLE WILL ENCOURAGE THE MAINSTREAM PUBLIC TO TAKE A MORE CRITICAL LOOK AT THE DEA'S OTHER ACTIVITIES.

Near the end of the DEA's arguments, Judge Kozinski asked Dormont "Can you tell me how you are going to save the [poppy seed] bagel?" The question drew laughter from the packed courtroom, but it was a serious issue considering that the irrational logic behind the DEA's attempted hemp food ban could easily be applied to poppy seed bagels. Even the DEA acknowledged that hemp foods have no abuse potential, stating "The concern of the Drug Enforcement Administration isn't particularized to the particular products that these Petitioners make. The DEA has never said, has never focused on the particular products and said anyone can get high from them, or that they pose a harm to people." Chief Judge Mary Schroeder asked the DEA: "Did you take into account the objections of people who might say that this doesn't make a lot of sense?" Dormont admitted the rule "wasn't popular."[30]

Towards Drug Policy Reforms

The hemp food issue has garnered more support from mainstream Americans than any other "drug policy issue." Hemp food supporters held two "hemp food taste tests" at DEA offices around the country and encouraged DEA agents to try the tasty food. Steenstra commented: "We gave DEA employees a chance to taste what they would have been missing if their ban succeeded. They need to know there is nothing dangerous or deceptive about hemp food."[31] These taste tests in 2002 and 2003 were, collectively, the largest protests of the DEA in its history.

Additionally, hemp supporters sent a deluge of correspondence to the DEA after the "Interpretive Rule" became public. Over 115,000 public comments were submitted to the DEA against the rule. In 2002, 25 members of Congress wrote the DEA telling the agency that their "Interpretive Rule" that attempts to ban edible hemp seed or oil products containing "any THC" is "overly restrictive."

Unfortunately the swell of mainstream opposition to the DEA's Rules and the ban on industrial hemp hasn't quashed the drug warriors' rhetoric liking marijuana and hemp. A recent *Los Angeles Times* article quoted John Walters, "Drug Czar" and head of the ONDCP repeating the same tired and inaccurate language: "It is no coincidence that

HELLER IS CORRECT; IN RECENT YEARS THE DEA HAS TAKEN AN INCREASINGLY MEANDERING PATH AWAY FROM MERELY ENFORCING THE NATION'S DRUG LAWS AND TOWARD REINTERPRETING THE LAWS TO JUSTIFY THEIR INANE ACTIONS.

proponents of marijuana have invested a great deal of time and money in an effort to expand hemp cultivation. They do this not, one presumes, from any special interest in industrial fiber resources, but from an earnest belief that more widespread domestic hemp cultivation will make the cultivation and distribution of marijuana easier, and that a legal hemp industry would frustrate law enforcement efforts against marijuana trafficking."[32]

Marijuana reformers and growers easily dismiss Walters' argument. One outdoor marijuana grower from Mendocino County, California mentioned that if hemp were grown on the West Coast the outdoor female marijuana plants would be damaged by the hemp crops' cross pollination.[33] A Marijuana strain pollinated by hemp, obviously, does not yield the high THC content that marijuana users usually prefer. The irony is that if the DEA really wanted to damage marijuana crops and curtail marijuana use, they would plant hemp everywhere.

Marijuana growers, however, are not the only ones to dismiss Walters' reasoning; hemp and other drug policy reform advocates are equally dismissive because industrial hemp advocacy temporarily distracts from other pressing drug policy issues. While hemp food activists were busy fighting the DEA, medical marijuana patients and providers were being attacked and prosecuted and Tommy Chong and others were facing jail time for selling water pipes and other forms of "drug paraphernalia." Nonetheless, because the HIA is expected to win against the DEA in court, the hemp food issue has the potential to attract more people to drug policy reform for the long term. Some drug policy reformers hope that the absurdity of the hemp food battle will encourage the mainstream public to take a more critical look at the DEA's other activities.

In Conclusion: Just What is the DEA Doing Anyway?

In February 2003, the DEA received a damning report card from the White House. According to the White House's Performance and Management Assessments, the DEA "is unable to demonstrate its progress in reducing the availability of illegal drugs in the US" The White House blamed this on a lack of meaningful collaboration with other law enforcement agencies, misplaced budget priorities in the agency, lack of internal evaluation and accountability.[34]

Furthermore, the White House acknowledged that the DEA's explicit task of enforcing the nation's drug laws, overlaps with the tasks of other local, state and federal law enforcement agencies.[35] Although the White House was aware of the DEA's problems, they chose not to address them efficiently. Instead of cutting the DEA's budget and forcing them to reevaluate their priorities, the White House proposed a slight increase in the DEA budget for Fiscal Year 2004.

Upon learning of the negative evaluation, Shawn Heller, (now former) National Director of Students for Sensible Drug Policy said, "It is not surprising that the DEA is facing criticism from the Bush administration, the most stalwart supporters of the War on Drugs. Instead of working toward any meaningful goals, for the past few years the DEA has been focused on arresting medical marijuana patients who were not violating state laws and seeking to ban the lawful consumption and sale of hemp food..."[36]

Heller is correct; in recent years the DEA has taken an increasingly meandering path away from merely enforcing the nation's drug laws and toward reinterpreting the laws to justify their inane actions. While the attacks on medical marijuana patients and providers are particularly tragic, the battle to keep hemp food legal is comedic, bordering on absurd with dire implications.

In September 2003, the DEA received another damning report card. This time, the US Department of Justice's Office of the Inspector General (OIG) evaluated the DEA's implementation of the Government Performance and Results Act of 1993 (GPRA). GPRA "seeks to shift government performance and accountability away from a preoccupation with counting activities to focus instead on the results or outcomes of those activities." According to the OIG GPRA audit, "the DEA had failed to meet key aspects of GPRA as we identified deficiencies in each of the three areas reviewed."[37] Nonetheless, the DEA's final budget for Fiscal Year 2004 was $1.7 billion.[38]

At this point it is too early to tell if the DEA will spend any of that money attempting to ban hemp food. On February 6, 2004, the hemp food industry won the (likely) final battle against the DEA; the Ninth Circuit ruled against the DEA's arguments and permanently invalidated the DEA's attempted hemp food ban. Nutritious hemp foods such as waffles, bread, cereal, vegetarian burgers, protein powder, salad dressing and nutrition bars are unequivocally legal, unless the DEA appeals the case to the US Supreme Court. Additionally, if the DEA allows the Ninth Circuit ruling to stand, hemp seed and oil will remain legal to import; Kenex, the Canadian company, will drop their NAFTA suit because there will not be any potential for future financial loss.

Although it is unclear what will happen next, David Bronner, Chair of the HIA Food and Oil Committee, was ecstatic about the Ninth Circuit ruling: "...The court reasonably views trace insignificant amounts of THC in hemp seed in the same way as it sees trace amounts of opiates in poppy seeds."[39]

Endnotes

[1] Federal News Service, transcript of final oral arguments in *Hemp Industries Association et al v. Drug Enforcement Administration*, 17 September 2003.

[2] Opiates are active ingredients in heroin, opium, etc.

[3] Eric Steenstra, Interview with Adam Eidinger, December 2003.

[4] David P. West., "Hemp and Marijuana: Myths and Realities," (North American Industrial Hemp Council, Inc: Madison, Wisconsin), 3. Hereinafter referred to as "West."

[5] Pub. L. No 75-238, found in West, 9. Emphasis added.

[6] Hemp Industries Association, "History of Hemp."

[7] ibid.

[8] West, 11.

[9] Jacob Sullum, "Seeds of Discord," Creators Syndicate, October 30, 2001.

[10] Courtesy of Vote Hemp, found at http://votehemp.com/news.html, January 2004.

[11] Test Pledge, "Addressing the Trace THC Issue," Found at: http://testpledge.com/answers.htm on 5 January 2004.

[12] ibid.

[13] Mission Statement of the Drug Enforcement Administration, found at http://www.usdoj.gov/dea/, December 2003.

[14] A helpful guide to understanding the complexity of Administrative Law is http://www.lib.memphis.edu/govpubs/admin.htm. As a side note, Administrative Law is problematic because it restructures the division of powers elucidated in the US Constitution; the Legislative Branch (Congress) is supposed to make the laws, the Executive Branch (the DEA etc) is supposed to enforce the law, and the Judicial Branch (courts) is supposed to interpret the law.

[15] Eric Steenstra, interview by Zoe Mitchell, 21 January, 2004.

[16] Joseph E. Sandler, to Donnie Marshall, December 2000, found at http://votehemp.com, December 2003.

[17] Kenex had suffered previously at the hands of DEA's myopic and absurd refusal to distinguish between industrial hemp and drug varieties of cannabis. In 1999, US Customs at the behest of DEA impounded a Kenex shipment of hemp birdseed. Customs relinquished the shipment only after an experienced legal team demonstrated that the seizure was not justified by either the law or common sense and the *New York Times* published an embarrassing expose.

[18] Courtesy of Vote Hemp, found at http://votehemp.com/news.html, 21 January 2004.

[19] Jean Laprise, interview by Adam Eidinger. January 2002.

[20] Anita Roddick, interview by Adam Eidinger, January 2002.

[21] Asa Hutchinson, on NPR's "Public Interest," 30 January 2002.

[22] ibid.

[23] John Roth, memo to Donnie Marshall, March 2000.

[24] Daniel Dormont, letter to the US Court of Appeals for the Ninth Circuit, 7 February 2002.

[25] The following agencies attended: representatives from the Departments of State, Justice, Treasury, and Commerce, as well as from the Environmental Protection Agency, the Drug Enforcement Administration (DEA), the Office of National Drug Control Policy, the US Customs Service, and the Office of the United States Trade Representative.

[26] David Bronner, interview by Adam Eidinger. March 2003.

[27] ibid.

[28] US Court of Appeals for the Ninth Circuit opinion No. 01-71662 in *HIA v. DEA*, 30 June 2003, Found at: http://votehemp.com, January 2004.

[29] Federal News Service, transcript of final oral arguments in *Hemp Industries Association et al v. Drug Enforcement Administration*, 17 September 2003, found at: http://www.votehemp.com, December 2003.

[30] ibid.

[31] Eric Steenstra, interview by Zoe Mitchell, April 2003.

[32] Lee Grant, "The Demonized Seed." *Los Angeles Times Magazine* (18 January 2004).

[33] For obvious reasons, the marijuana grower wishes to remain anonymous.

[34] White House Performance and Management Assessment: Program: Drug Enforcement Administration. Found at: http://www.whitehouse.gov, 5 February 2003.

[35] ibid.

[36] Shawn Heller, interview by Zoe Mitchell, April 2003.

[37] Office of the Inspector General, "The Drug Enforcement Administration's Implementation of the Government Performance and Results Act Executive Summary." Found at: http://usdoj.gov, 30 December 2003.

[38] Department of Justice FY2004 Budget Summary, "Drug Enforcement Administration Budget Authority 1995-2004."

[39] David Bronner, interview by Adam Eidinger, February 2004.

Facts and Propaganda

Exaggerating MDMA's Risks to Justify A Prohibitionist Policy

Rick Doblin, Ph.D.

Reevaluation of the Risks of MDMA after the Ricaurte/McCann Retraction

The Ricaurte et al. retraction of their article claiming that MDMA causes Parkinson's, originally published in *Science* in September 2002 and retracted in September 2003, has created a unique opportunity for an interwoven series of challenges to the perception that any use of MDMA

ACCORDING TO THIS DOMINANT BUT MISLEADING VIEW, EVEN A SINGLE OR A FEW USES CAN CAUSE SIGNIFICANT LONG-TERM BRAIN DAMAGE WITH IMPORTANT DELETERIOUS FUNCTIONAL CONSEQUENCES.

(Ecstasy) is exceptionally risky and dangerous. This perception has been created in the minds of the general public, regulators and lawmakers by National Institute on Drug Abuse (NIDA), the Office of National Drug Control Policy (ONDCP), the Drug Enforcement Administration (DEA), and the Partnership for a Drug-Free America. According to this dominant but misleading view, even a single or a few uses can cause significant long-term brain damage with important deleterious functional consequences. From a scientific perspective however, claims about the negative effects of MDMA on dopamine, serotonin, and cerebral blood flow, by Drs. Ricaurte, McCann and Dr. Alan Leshner, ex-Director of the National Institute on Drug Abuse, respectively, have either been retracted, shown to contain major methodological flaws, or are clearly misleading.

The controversy surrounding the retraction provides some relatively easy ways to explain how scientific information has been misleadingly presented by grant-addicted scientists and prohibitionists and has facilitated the ramping up of the penalties against the non-medical use of MDMA, the efforts to shut down the rave movement, and

NO ACCOUNTING HAS YET BEEN MADE OF WHICH STUDIES USED THE MDMA FROM THE BOTTLE MISLABELED METHAMPHETAMINE.

the pressure to prevent research into the therapeutic uses of MDMA-assisted psychotherapy. Fortunately, the new NIDA Director, Dr. Nora Volkow, seems likely to live up to a statement she made in an August 19, 2003, *New York Times* interview, in which she said "If you want to be a scientist, you cannot allow politics to get in the way of your objectivity."

MDMA and Dopamine

Ricaurte/McCann now acknowledge that their evidence about MDMA damaging dopamine neurons was erroneous (Ricaurte et al. 2003) and was based on the mistaken administration to their primates of methamphetamine instead of MDMA, supposedly due to mislabeled ten gram bottles of MDMA and methamphetamine which arrived from the same provider in the same package.

A September 18, 2003 editorial in *Nature* asked NIDA Director Nora Volkow to conduct a "thorough public review of the circumstances and participant's roles in one of the more bizarre episodes in the history of drug research. The *Nature* editorial also accused former NIDA Director Leshner, now Executive Director of the American Association for the Advancement of Science (AAAS), which publishes *Science*, of "pander[ing] to the Bush administration's jihad against recreational drug use." The accusation was based in part on his hyperbolic statements in the press release that *Science* issued to draw attention to the original article, in which he said, "Using Ecstasy is like playing Russian roulette with your brain function." A September 18, 2003 news report in *The Scientist* mentions that Ricaurte/McCann have retracted a second paper and reports that two senior British scientists have demanded that *Science* investigate its review of the original article and release the comments of the peer reviewers. (All these news articles can be found online at: http://www.maps.org.)

An October 14, 2003 article in *Lancet Neurology* reports that the Multidisciplinary Association for Psychedelic Studies (MAPS) has filed a FOIA request with NIDA seeking more data on Ricaurte/McCann's other recent NIDA-funded research in order to determine whether additional studies need to be retracted. To date, Ricaurte et al. have accounted for less than 2 1/4 grams of the ten grams of methamphetamine that was contained in the original bottle mislabeled MDMA, all of which was used in research before the mislabeling was discovered. No accounting has yet been made of which studies used the MDMA from the bottle mislabeled methamphetamine.

Since MAPS is seeking to conduct FDA-approved research in which MDMA is administered to human subjects, our FOIA request also seeks the release of more details about

RICAURTE ET AL.'S RETRACTION LETTER ITSELF PROVIDES FURTHER EVIDENCE OF THEIR ANTI-ECSTASY BIAS.

the design and results of Dr. Ricaurte and McCann's subsequent studies that they mention in their retraction, in which they administered genuine MDMA to primates, both orally and by injection, and found no evidence of dopaminergic neurotoxicity. These studies can provide data that bears directly on the estimation of the risk of dopaminergic neurotoxicity to subjects in the human research that MAPS is seeking to conduct.

Ricaurte/McCann's anti-Ecstasy bias is now more clearly visible. In their original *Science* paper (Ricaurte et al. 2002) with its surprising results, the authors ignored three published human studies showing no effect of MDMA on dopamine (Kish 2000; Reneman et al. 2002; Semple et al. 1999), claimed that they administered the equivalent of a "common recreational dose regime" despite a reported 20% mortality rate in their primates (later modified to a 13.3% death rate when Ricaurte et al. admitted that they actually used five more animals than they reported to gather the data for their original Science article), and ignored their own research showing that oral administration of MDMA is less neurotoxic than the injection of MDMA (Ricaurte et al. 1988). These and other criticisms of the original study were published in *Science* in a letter written by the MAPS MDMA/PTSD (posttraumatic stress disorder) research team (Mithoefer et al. 2003).

Ricaurte et al.'s retraction letter itself provides further evidence of their anti-Ecstasy bias. In the retraction letter, Drs. Ricaurte and McCann still claim that doses of MDMA used by some humans could cause dopaminergic neurotoxicity and Parkinson's, based on exceedingly flimsy evidence.

Ironically, recent animal research has been published showing that MDMA, when administered in combination with L-Dopa, actually helps reduce dyskinesias, painful symptoms of Parkinson's (Iravani et al. 2003).

MDMA and Serotonin

McCann et al.'s evidence from their PET studies in Ecstasy users on which they based their claims that MDMA causes massive reductions in serotonin, published in the *Lancet* (McCann et al. 1998), are now generally considered to be based on methodologically flawed data. Basically, the

values for the serotonin transporter levels in McCann's control group are so spread out, with some control subjects having 35 times more serotonin transporters than others, as to be biologically implausible. To deal with this variation, McCann et al. log transformed their data, something no other PET researchers have needed to do (Kish 2002). Subsequent studies by other researchers using the same PET technique generated control values similar to McCann's Ecstasy users. A much larger and better controlled study, published in the *Journal of Nuclear Medicine* (Buchert et al. 2003), with 117 subjects as compared to McCann's 29, found that former users of Ecstasy, who had consumed an average of 799 doses and had abstained for about eighteen months, had serotonin levels identical to that of the control subjects. Buchert et al. found that current users of Ecstasy, with an average exposure of 827 doses, showed no reductions in some brain regions and only minimal reductions (4-6%) in two other brain regions, unlikely to be of even temporary clinical significance.

The data from McCann et al.'s *Lancet* paper formed the basis of NIDA's major anti-Ecstasy educational campaign, the Plain Brain/Brain After Ecstasy image. NIDA had this image printed on hundreds of thousands of cards distributed in bars and restaurants across the United States, used the image in NIDA publications and websites, and encouraged its use in media reports, all part of its now abandoned $42 million "club drugs" campaign. This image wasn't even an accurate representation of the data in the *Lancet* article if that data had actually been valid. NIDA used images chosen for dramatic effect comparing

IRONICALLY, RECENT ANIMAL RESEARCH HAS BEEN PUBLISHED SHOWING THAT MDMA, WHEN ADMINISTERED IN COMBINATION WITH L-DOPA, ACTUALLY HELPS REDUCE DYSKINESIAS, PAINFUL SYMPTOMS OF PARKINSON'S.

subjects from the extremes of the MDMA and control groups rather than from the subjects scoring closest to the median, using some normal individual variability to exaggerate the evidence of MDMA neurotoxicity. NIDA has now withdrawn this educational campaign and even told the Peter Jennings' Ecstasy documentary team that it couldn't locate a copy of the image!

From another perspective, NIDA's anti-Ecstasy educational campaign, and Dr. Leshner's other efforts to pander to the Bush and Clinton administration's jihad against recreational drug use, have been wildly successful. A simple chart showing the annual increases provided by Congress to NIDA's budget during the tenure of Dr. Leshner reveals the short-term dividends of exaggerating the risks of MDMA and other illicit drugs in support of prohibitionist policies.

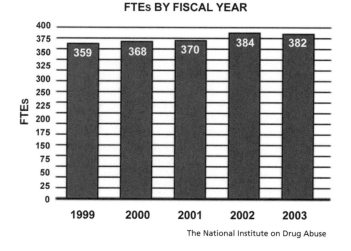

FTEs BY FISCAL YEAR

The National Institute on Drug Abuse

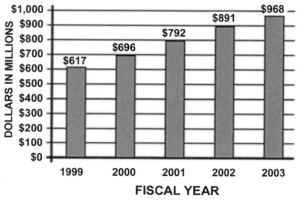

FUNDING LEVELS BY FISCAL YEAR

The National Institute on Drug Abuse

MDMA and Cerebral Blood Flow

Testimony that then-NIDA Director Alan Leshner gave on July 30, 2001 to the Senate Subcommittee on Government Affairs, illustrated with a large poster purporting to show

that MDMA negatively affects (reduces) cerebral blood flow, was clearly misleading. The poster showed a healthy-looking brain with what was represented as normal cerebral blood flow, with this image labeled "Baseline." For comparison purposes, the poster also contained a second brain scan image of the same subject with reduced cerebral blood flow. This image was labeled "Two weeks

post-MDMA." What Leshner didn't tell the Senators is that the scans were drawn from a study that showed no difference between Ecstasy users and controls in cerebral blood flow (Chang et al. 2000).

The images Leshner used in his Senate testimony came from one subset of the Ecstasy users in the larger study who participated in Dr. Grob's Phase I MDMA safety study. These ten subjects were scanned at baseline, like the other eleven Ecstasy-using subjects in Dr. Chang's research. They were then scanned again after receiving two doses of MDMA administered in the context of Dr. Grob's study, at time points ranging from two weeks to 2-3 months after the last dose of MDMA. Subjects scanned two weeks after MDMA showed a temporary reduction in cerebral blood flow while subjects scanned from 2-3 months after MDMA showed a return to baseline. The impression Leshner left the Senators was that MDMA caused permanent changes in cerebral blood flow when the changes were both temporary and of no clinical consequence. Transcripts of Leshner's testimony, as well as the images he used to illustrate his testimony, can be found on NIDA's website.

THESE IMAGES WERE GRAPHICALLY MANIPULATED TO REPRESENT AREAS OF LOWER CEREBRAL BLOOD FLOW AS HOLES AND ARE COMPLETELY FRAUDULENT.

Ironically, Leshner didn't realize that in order to participate in the Phase 1 study and receive MDMA, FDA required subjects to have already had substantial exposure to MDMA. On average, the subjects in Dr. Chang's study had an exposure to MDMA of 211 times. Thus, the healthy-looking brain that Leshner showed to the Senators to contrast with the image of the same brain two weeks post-MDMA was actually the brain of a heavy MDMA user at baseline! If he had fully understood the science underlying the images he showed to the Senator, Leshner should have reported that the baseline image dramatically illustrated that MDMA caused no persisting long-term differences in cerebral blood flow as compared to the non-MDMA using controls. Instead, he used the image to convey an impression of the dangers of MDMA at odds with what the study actually demonstrated.

Frightening and disturbing images of the brain of an MDMA user that showed explicit holes in the brain that were claimed to have been caused by MDMA have been shown on an MTV special documentary about Ecstasy, as well as on an Oprah Winfrey show. These images were graphically manipulated to represent areas of lower cerebral blood flow as holes and are completely fraudulent. According to a March 2001 educational program about drugs aimed at young people that NIDA helped create, Alan Leshner stated, "We've heard people talk about Ecstasy causing holes in the brain and of course that's a bit of an exaggeration, but there is a core truth to it." (PBS, In the Mix) We should be appalled, but not surprised, at the fact that the young woman whose brain scan image was manipulated has been working for several years at the Partnership for a Drug-Free America, miseducating other young people about the dangers of MDMA (her choice of employment, perhaps, reflecting the only *genuine* signs of brain damage).

MDMA and Research into Therapeutic Uses

Ever since MDMA was criminalized in the United States in 1985, exaggerated risk estimates have played an essential role in preventing research into the therapeutic uses of MDMA. In 1985, the FDA even refused to permit researchers to administer MDMA-assisted psychotherapy to a dying cancer patient who had experienced no significant side effects and had obtained relief from pain, both physical and emotional, through the use of such therapy that he had received prior to MDMA being made illegal. An FDA official wrote that even dying subjects deserved to be protected by US law from the potential damaging effects of MDMA neurotoxicity. In this case, it didn't matter that the damage was hypothetical, the benefits were real, and the patient was willing to accept the consequences of participating in the research.

In 1999, after human research with MDMA had begun in Switzerland, a group of Dutch researchers tried to stop Swiss researcher Dr. Franz Vollenweider from conducting basic safety studies by claiming in a letter to the journal *Neuropsychopharmacology* (Gijsman et al. 1999) that Dr. Vollenweider was engaging in unethical research. Their rationale was that Dr. Vollenweider was administering MDMA to MDMA-naive subjects, a design that Dr. Vollenweider considered useful to obtain the clearest evidence of the effects of MDMA but that Gijsman considered too risky due to the dangers of MDMA neurotoxicity. A debate took place in a series of letters published in *Neuropsychopharmacology*. Dr. Vollenweider defended his research and risk estimates (Vollenweider et al. 1999). Courageously, the editors disagreed with Gijsman and supported Dr. Vollenweider's research (Lieberman and Aghajanian 1999). Two years later, Drs. McCann and Ricaurte entered the discussion to raise the issue of the dangers of MDMA neurotoxicity from even a single dose (McCann et al. 2001) but were rebutted by Dr. Vollenweider (Vollenweider et al. 2001) and again by the editors (Aghajanian and Liberman 2001).

Sadly, the world's only fully-approveMDMA psychotherapy study was successfully halted for political reasons, with efforts to restart the study complicated by Dr. Ricaurte. In 2000, in Madrid, Spain, Jose Carlos Bouso (Ph.D. candidate), with the support of MAPS, was able to obtain all the necessary federal and local permissions to start the world's first legally-approved controlled study into any therapeutic use of MDMA. The study was designed as a double-blind, placebo-controlled, dose-response pilot study into the use of MDMA-assisted psychotherapy in the treatment of women survivors of sexual assault with chronic, treatment-resistant posttraumatic stress disorder (PTSD). By April 2002, six subjects had been enrolled in the study without any complications. On May 6, 2002, favorable media coverage of the study appeared in prominent Spanish media. On May 13, 2002, as a result of pressure from the Madrid Anti-Drug Authority, the Manager of the Hospital Psiquiatrico de Madrid sent a letter saying that he wouldn't let the experimenters use the facilities of the Hospital anymore. In October 2002, just one week after Ricaurte's paper in *Science* came out, the research team's struggles to resume the study were

IN 1985, THE FDA EVEN REFUSED TO PERMIT RESEARCHERS TO ADMINISTER MDMA-ASSISTED PSYCHOTHERAPY TO A DYING CANCER PATIENT WHO HAD EXPERIENCED NO SIGNIFICANT SIDE EFFECTS AND HAD OBTAINED RELIEF FROM PAIN, BOTH PHYSICAL AND EMOTIONAL, THROUGH THE USE OF SUCH THERAPY THAT HE HAD RECEIVED PRIOR TO MDMA BEING MADE ILLEGAL.

significantly complicated by the appearance in Madrid of Dr. Ricaurte, who give a highly-publicized talk about his MDMA/Parkinson's findings at the invitation of the Spanish Anti-Drug Agency. Additional talks by Dr. Ricaurte in Spain in April, June and July 2003, further reinforced both the scientific and popular perception in Spain of the dangerousness of even a few doses of MDMA.

(More information on the still-halted MDMA/PTSD study in Spain, including a timeline of events with dates of approval, Spanish media articles, withdrawal of approval, talks in Spain about the dangers of MDMA by Dr. George Ricaurte and media reports of the contents of his talks, is available online at http://www.maps.org.)

MAPS has now worked for 17 years, since it was founded in 1986, to sponsor FDA-approved research investigating the therapeutic uses of MDMA. From 1986 to 1992, concerns over the risks of MDMA neurotoxicity were used to justify FDA refusals to approve any research in which MDMA was to be administered to human subjects. Starting in 1992, after a change in personnel and policy, FDA approved three basic safety studies with MDMA. The evidence from these studies, as well as from research conducted abroad, eventually persuaded the FDA that the risk/benefit ratio of MDMA was favorable in certain patient populations. As a result, in November 2001, the FDA approved a MAPS-sponsored pilot study into the use of MDMA-assisted psychotherapy in treatment-resistant PTSD subjects.

The controversy over the neurotoxic risks of MDMA, and over its widespread recreational use, made it exceptionally difficult for MAPS to obtain Institutional Review Board (IRB) approval for our study of the use of MDMA-assisted psychotherapy in subjects with chronic, treatment-resistant posttraumatic stress disorder (PTSD). Once IRB approved the study, then two months later revoked approval after an IRB official who wasn't comfortable with the approval of MDMA psychotherapy research spoke to Dr. Una McCann and two other researchers. The other two researchers actually supported the study (one initially and the other after MAPS agreed to add some language to the informed consent form), but Dr. McCann and Dr. Ricaurte refrained from doing so. The IRB refused to review the scientific evidence and made a policy decision to return the fee that MAPS' paid for the review. Five other IRBs refused to even accept the protocol for review and one that did accept it finally tabled the review, after spending months formally reviewing the study before making it clear, through unreasonable demands, that the committee did not feel comfortable approving it. After diligent and persistent work, MAPS managed to obtain IRB approval in September 2003. (MAPS' interaction with various IRBs is discussed online at: http://www.maps.org.)

However, the study is still not fully approved. Research can start only after the principal investigator, Dr. Michael Mithoefer, receives a Schedule I license from the DEA so that he can legally possess and administer the total of 3 grams of MDMA that will be given to the subjects in the study (each MDMA subject in the MDMA group will receive two oral doses of 125 mgs each, three to five weeks apart). Dr. Mithoefer submitted his application to DEA for a Schedule I license over 17 months ago, with a decision from DEA still pending. On October 28, 2003, South Carolina DEA agents and officials from the South Carolina Department of Health and Environmental Control (DHEC) finally inspected Dr. Mithoefer's facility. They examined the DEA-required safe bolted to the concrete floor, the alarm system and the MDMA tracking procedures, in order to ensure that the 3.5 grams of MDAM will be protected from diversion to non-research uses. On November 12, 2003, Dr. Mithoefer received his Schedule I research registration (R1) from the DHEC. We expect that sometime soon DEA will issue Dr. Mithoefer his Schedule I license so that we can start MDMA psychotherapy research after more than 18 years of struggle. (MDMA was criminalized in 1985 on an emergency basis, justified in part based on Dr. Ricaurte's research in rats showing that MDA, a drug related to MDMA, caused reductions in serotonin at some doses.)

The above review isn't meant to build a case that MDMA is harmless, or completely benign. MDMA has its risks, some of which can be fatal, like hyperthermia, a very rare occurrence that results from overheating, most often due to prolonged exercise and inadequate fluid replacement. The effects of heavy Ecstasy use on neurocognitive functioning is still being researched, with some well-designed studies showing that heavy MDMA users perform worse on some neurocognitive tests. Whether this is due to MDMA remains to be determined. What the above review is trying to communicate is that the risks of MDMA-related brain damage have been exaggerated, in

yet another historical example of science being twisted to suit political ends. The risks that MDMA does present can be mitigated to a large extent by the wise use of harm reduction efforts. Unfortunately, the anti-rave legislation that Congress passed under the false assumption that MDMA caused unusually powerful brain damage after only a few doses perversely empowers police and prosecutors to use harm reduction efforts as a legal weapon against promoters and venue owners.

For almost two decades, MDMA research has been primarily focused on neurotoxicity research into the risks of MDMA, with MDMA psychotherapy research essentially forbidden. Perhaps the tide is turning and the next two decades will see a more balanced focus on research into both the potential risks and benefits of MDMA, with a variety of social, legal structures eventually to be created that will minimize the potential harms of MDMA and maximize its benefits. If we will it, it need not remain a dream.

Editor's note—On February 24, 2004, the DEA finally gave Dr. Mithoefer a Schedule 1 license. The first MDMA-assisted psychotherapy research project since MDMA was criminalized in 1985 is now moving forward. On March 12, 2004, four grams of MDMA arrived with all the appropriate DEA forms and procedures, and as noted at MAPS' website: "Patients are being scheduled for screening to see if they meet the inclusion and exclusion criteria...The tentative date for the first experimental session is April 16, completely coincidentally the same date that, in 1943, Albert Hofmann first accidentally discovered the psychedelic properties of LSD."

References

Aghajanian GK, Liebermann JA (2001) Caveat Emptor: Editors *Beware Neuropsychopharmacology.* 24,3:335-6.

Buchert R, Thomasius R, Nebeling B, Petersen K, Obrocki J, Jenicke L, Wilke F, Wartberg L, Zapletalova P, Clausen M. (2003) Long-term effects of "ecstasy" use on serotonin transporters of the brain investigated by PET. J *Nucl Med.* Mar;44(3):375-84.

Chang L, Grob CS, Ernst T, Itti L, Mishkin FS, Jose-Melchor R, Poland RE. (2000) Effect of ecstasy [3,4-methylenedio xymethamphetamine (MDMA)] on cerebral blood flow: a co-registered SPECT and MRI study. *Psychiatry Res.* Feb 28;98(1):15-28.

Gijsman HJ, Verkes RJ, van Gerven JM, Cohen AF. (1999) MDMA study. *Neuropsychopharmacology.* Oct;21(4):597.

Iravani MM, Jackson MJ, Kuoppamaki M, Smith LA, Jenner P. (2003) 3,4-methylenedioxymethamphetamine (ecstasy) inhibits dyskinesia expression and normalizes motor activity in 1-methyl-4-phenyl-1,2,3,6-tetrahydropyridine-treated primates. J Neurosci. Oct 8;23(27):9107-15.

Kish S.J. et al. (2000) Striatal serotonin is depleted in brain of a human MDMA (Ecstasy) user. *Neurology 55*: 294-296.

Kish S. (2002) How strong is the evidence that brain serotonin neurons are damaged in human users of ecstasy? *Pharmacol Biochem Behav*. Apr;71(4):845-55. Review.

Lieberman J and Aghajanian G. (1999) Editorial—Caveat Emptor: Researcher Beware. *Neuropsychopharmacology* 21 4:471-473.

McCann UD, Ricaurte G (2001) Caveat Emptor: Editors Beware. *Neuropsychopharmacology* 24: 333-334.

McCann UD, Szabo Z, Scheffel U, Dannals RF, Ricaurte GA (1998) Positron emission tomographic evidence of toxic effect of MDMA ("Ecstasy") on brain serotonin neurons in human beings. *Lancet* 352: 1433-7.

Mithoefer M, Jerome L, Doblin R (2003) MDMA ("Ecstasy") and Neurotoxicity. *Science, 300*: 1504.

Reneman L. et al. (2002A) Use of amphetamine by recreational users of ecstasy (MDMA) is associated with reduced striatal dopamine transporter densities: a [123I]beta-CIT SPECT study—preliminary report. *Psychopharmacology (Berl)* 159: 335-340.

Ricaurte GA, DeLanney LE, Irwin I, Langston JW (1988) Toxic effects of MDMA on central serotonergic neurons in the primate: importance of route and frequency of drug administration. *Brain Res* 446: 165-168.

Ricaurte GA, Yuan J, Hatzidimitriou G, Cord BJ, McCann UD (2002) Severe Dopaminergic Neurotoxicity in Primates After a Common Recreational Dose Regimen of MDMA ("Ecstasy"). *Science* 297: 2260-3.

Ricaurte GA, Yuan J, Hatzidimitriou G, Cord BJ, McCann UD (2003B) Retraction. *Science* 301: 1429.

Semple D.M. et al. (1999) Reduced in vivo binding to the serotonin transporter in the cerebral cortex of MDMA ('ecstasy') users. *Br J Psychiatry* 175: 63-69.

Vollenweider F, Gamma A, Liechti M, Huber T. (1999) Is A Single Dose of MDMA Harmless? *Neuropsychopharmacology* 21 (October) 4: 598-600.

Vollenweider FX, Jones RT, Baggott MJ. (2001) Caveat emptor: editors beware. *Neuropsychopharmacology*. Apr;24(4):461-3.

An Anatomy of Failure: The Drugs-and-Terror Ad Campaign

Paul Armentano

"Where do terrorists get their money? If you buy drugs, some of it might come from you." So claimed a prominent series of White House sponsored advertisements alleging that recreational drug use sponsors international terrorism. Nevertheless, despite spending tens of millions of dollars on the much-ballyhooed media campaign, the American public steadfastly refused to buy the federal government's message.

So pronounced was Americans' rejection of the campaign that the White House abruptly decided in 2003 to pull the plug on it altogether. The Feds' decision came after internal evaluations of the ads—that began pushing the specific drugs-fund-terror agenda shortly after September 11, 2001—determined that they had failed to discourage viewers from trying marijuana or other drugs and in some cases had fostered so-called "pro-drug beliefs" among teens.

Talk about a blowback.

For drug czar John Walters, the White House's decision to drop the controversial ads was no doubt particularly embarrassing. Walters inherited the $195 million-per-year program, dubbed the "National Youth Anti-Drug Media Campaign," after assuming office in late 2001. (Congress initially funded the program with a five-year $1.2 billion appropriation in 1998.) Almost immediately, he lobbied to shift the content of the campaign's public

WALTERS PROMISED THAT THIS CHANGE IN DIRECTION WOULD YIELD POSITIVE RESULTS AMONG TARGET AUDIENCES WITHIN SIX MONTHS.

service announcements from drug-abuse-associated health risks to the administration's questionable claim that recreational drug use aids terrorism.

Walters promised that this change in direction would yield positive results among target audiences within six months. "I can show you...by this fall that if I make the changes I want, you'll see the results you want," he told Congress in 2002, adding that he'd "live by the results," whatever they might be.

The results could not have been worse. According to a January 2003 evaluation of the ads completed by the firm Westat Inc. and the Annenberg Public Policy Center at the University of Pennsylvania, there were "no statistically significant...improvements in beliefs and attitudes" among viewers attributable to the Feds' multi-million-dollar ad campaign. In addition, reviewers discovered that teens who were more exposed to the campaign tended to "move more markedly in a 'pro-drug' direction as they aged than those who were exposed to less."

A follow up evaluation by Westat and Annenberg released later that year produced even more bad news for the administration, concluding, "There is little evidence

FOR DRUG CZAR JOHN WALTERS, THE WHITE HOUSE'S DECISION TO DROP THE CONTROVERSIAL ADS WAS NO DOUBT PARTICULARLY EMBARRASSING.

of direct favorable Campaign effects on youth, either for the Marijuana Initiative period or for the Campaign as whole....[Specifically,] youth who were more exposed to campaign messages are no more likely to hold favorable beliefs or intentions about marijuana than are youth less exposed to those messages, both during the Marijuana Initiative period and over the course of the Campaign."

The negative, though hardly surprising, findings proved not only to be the death knell for the drug czar's pet project, but also for Westat and Annenberg's tumultuous relationship with the White House. As part of the Bush administration's decision to deep-six the drugs-and-terror ads, the Feds also ceased funding the $8 million Westat and Annenberg evaluations, which had consistently been critical of the "National Youth Anti-Drug Media Campaign," at one point calling its results among the worst in the history of large-scale public communication campaigns.

(Curiously, however, the White House did not immediately choose to sever ties with the controversial advertising firm Ogilvy & Mather, who produced the drugs-and-terror ads and afterwards was accused in US District Court of engineering "an extensive scheme to defraud the United States government by falsely and fraudulently inflating the labor costs" of the Campaign.)

Nevertheless, despite the Campaign's abysmal performance (and associated accounting scandal), the White House and

Congress continue to enthusiastically back the anti-drug media program, recently voting to continue its funding to the tune of nearly $150 million per year for five years. Congress would be wise to scrap the program altogether.

Audiences rejected the White House's drugs-fund-terror premise because they saw it precisely for what it was: government propaganda. It's likely that future federal ad campaigns will be more of the same and elicit a similar negative reaction from the public.

| THE RESULTS COULD NOT HAVE BEEN WORSE.

While a small portion of black-market profits may theoretically fund certain terrorist groups around the globe, this fact is not the result of drugs per se, but the result of federal drug policies that keep them illegal—thus inflating their prices and relegating their production and trade exclusively to criminal entrepreneurs. Therefore, to break any supposed link between illicit drugs and terrorism, the solution is simply to decriminalize the drugs, thereby putting an end to the black-market effects of their criminalization.

Moreover, there exists no evidence that sales from the illicit cultivation and use of marijuana—by far Americans' illegal drug of choice—have ever been used to fund international terror campaigns. Much of the pot

| AUDIENCES REJECTED THE WHITE HOUSE'S DRUGS-FUND-TERROR PREMISE BECAUSE THEY SAW IT PRECISELY FOR WHAT IT WAS: GOVERNMENT PROPAGANDA.

consumed by Americans is grown domestically, and that which is imported comes primarily from Mexico, Jamaica, and Canada—none of which are known hotbeds for international terror organizations.

Of course, none of these facts matters to those in Washington, who seem content to simply exchange one lie about drugs—marijuana in particular—for another. Rather than proceed down this failed course, the US government ought to reassess and end its overall "do drugs; do time" mentality and recognize that drug abuse is a health issue that is best addressed by the private sector and not the criminal justice system. That's a message the public just might buy.

White Lines: Sugar, How Sweet it Ain't

Mickey Z.

"Everything is a dangerous drug except reality, which is unendurable."

—Cyril Connolly

One of the most convincing components of the anti-war-on-drugs argument revolves around which "drugs" are targeted... and why. From TV to phone sex to pharmaceuticals, addiction goes far beyond lurid headlines about drug-related crime and celebrities in rehab. Because it encompasses issues such as health, economics, exploitation, and the deception of public relations broader audience, I've chosen sugar to serve this purpose.

When observing the tenacity with which America's law enforcement agencies pursue those who allegedly partake in illegal drugs, one might wonder why so little attention is paid to more pervasive and often more dangerous "drugs" like alcohol, pharmaceuticals, food additives, television, computers, etc. For example, with all the focus on cocaine and its derivatives (i.e. crack), what about the most insidious white powder of all, sugar?

The United States Department of Agriculture reports that the average American consumes over 130 pounds of sugar (and sweeteners) each year. For those of you scoring at home, that's 10 pounds a month, more than 4 cups a week, and over 30 teaspoonfuls per day[1] of a substance the body would rather not ingest.

"The minerals needed to digest sugar—chromium, manganese, cobalt, copper, zinc, and magnesium—have been stripped away in the refining process," explains nutrition counselor Nancy Appleton, author of Lick the Sugar Habit. "The body has to deplete its own mineral reserves to use the refined sugar."[2]

Your body's troubles are only beginning at that point.

"The average person loses more than 90% of their immune function within 15 minutes of indulging in this poisonous substance," says Walt Stoll, M.D., a physician with a background in orthodox and complementary medicine. "This deficiency lasts for about two hours after the stress occurs."[3]

It also leaves you wanting more...a lot more.

"Sugar evokes a brain chemical called beta endorphin, the same chemical affected by morphine and heroin," explains Kathleen DesMaisons Ph.D., author of The Sugar Addict's Total Recovery Program. "The sugar creates a wonderful feeling of euphoria and well-being, but when it wears off, you feel edgy, irritable and cranky—this is actual withdrawal. If you use the drug [sugar] again, it relieves the symptoms, so you get caught in a cycle of needing it."[4]

In addition to the likely immune dysfunction and the potential cravings, the politics of sugar are woven into a bloody history of colonialism—and the marketing of the sweet stuff moves beyond mere advertising into the realm of mind control. As journalist/researcher, Anup Shah declares, "The consumption of sugar and its history gives a great insight into various inter-related issues, such as economics, human rights, slavery, environmental issues, health, consumerism issues and so on."[5]

"It did not require much political wisdom to see that America's concern was a matter of sugar and had nothing to do with humanitarian feelings," said Emma Goldman, at the beginning of the Spanish-American War.[6]

Sugar began as a luxury item but, as cross-Atlantic travel

> ...THE POLITICS OF SUGAR ARE WOVEN INTO A BLOODY HISTORY OF COLONIALISM—AND THE MARKETING OF THE SWEET STUFF MOVES BEYOND MERE ADVERTISING INTO THE REALM OF MIND CONTROL.

resulted in more expropriated land thus more sugar to go around, the price began to decrease. Predictably, consumption climbed and even more land and cheaper production methods were needed to meet the demand. This set off an inevitable cycle of conquest and exploitation.

"Modern economists like to talk about the spin-off effects of certain commodities, that is the extent to which their production results in the development of subsidiary industries," writes Richard Robbins in his book, Global Problems and the Culture of Capitalism. "Sugar production also produced subsidiary economic activities; these included slavery, the provisioning of the sugar producers, shipping, refining, storage, and wholesale and retail trade."[7] This appraisal runs contrary to the Sugar Association's decidedly romantic take on things: "Sugar has been on our tables and in our consciousness nearly 10,000 years before Romeo met Juliet or Columbus helped open a New World. Sugar has created empires, toppled careers, launched military campaigns, powered economies and been the ingredient for love around the world. So what is sugar; why is it so misunderstood and why

SUGAR HAS BEEN ON OUR TABLES AND IN OUR CONSCIOUSNESS NEARLY 10,000 YEARS BEFORE ROMEO MET JULIET OR COLUMBUS HELPED OPEN A NEW WORLD.

does it remain such an important part of our lives?"[8] While today's sugar industry may not be as overt in its quest for domination, it is no less aggressive. Its modern weapons of choice are propaganda and money.

According to the Center for Responsive Politics, the sugar industry made $3,141,254 in campaign contributions to Congress in 2002 (56% to Democrats, 44% to Republicans).[9] This money helps keep a system of government subsidy alive and well so sugar remains cheap and available to its potential addicts.

"Every time you add a teaspoon of sugar to your coffee, lick an ice cream cone, chow down a bag of cookies, or buy a bag of sugar, you're contributing to the profits earned by a very small group of sugar farmers—thanks to a US government price-support program," says John Morgenthaler, a journalist who specializes in medical nutrition. "Congress maintains a sugar-support program that guarantees domestic sugar producers a minimum price by restricting sugar imports and buying and storing excess production, as it does with other farm programs. According to the General Accounting Office (GAO), the program costs Americans $2 billion annually in inflated sugar prices, and storing excess sugar will cost another $2 billion over ten years.[10]

As reported in a November 2003 *New York Times* editorial, among the many dealers ready to pour taxpayer-funded sugar down taxpayer throats are the Fanjul brothers, "Florida's Cuban-American reigning sugar barons who preside over Palm Beach's yacht-owning society." The Fanjuls not only "harvest 180,000 acres in South Florida that send polluted water into the Everglades," they were responsible for generating nearly $1 million in "soft-money donations during the 2000 election cycle."[11]

Prior to Fidel Castro's takeover of Cuba, the Fanjuls had been "Cuba's leading sugar family for decades" and their Florida-based business "was aided by the embargo on Cuban sugar" and "an intricate system of import quotas that dates back to 1981."

Essentially, the government sweetens the pot for US growers by maintaining a quota. Only about 15% of American sugar is imported. As a result, the world price is about seven cents a pound, while "American businesses that need sugar to make their products must pay close to 21 cents."

For the folks who write the editorials at the *Times*, this issue provides the opportunity to take a gentle poke at the hand that feeds them: "The sugar situation hurts American businesses and consumers, but its worst impact is on the poor countries that try to compete in the global agricultural markets."

For anyone paying a little closer attention, corporate welfare is just the tip of the iceberg.

"Sugar is grown from the earth and nourished by the sun, soil and American family farmers who love the land and have tended crops for generations," notes the Sugar Association website.[12] "And, sugar is the same carbohydrate that is part of an apple, pear, a potato, or rice. While your taste buds and eyes may know the difference, your body does not and handles table sugar the same way it does the sucrose contained in any fruit or vegetable."

"Sugar dysfunction is the primary threat to human health today," says Majid Ali, M.D.[13] "The best way to preserve the integrity of carbohydrate metabolism is to protect it from large and sudden sugar overloads."

"To utilize refined carbohydrates, the body must rob healthy cells of nutrients they need to survive," explains health and nutrition journalist, Gary Null. "Indeed, the body leeches precious vitamins and minerals from itself in the process of digesting sugar, inducing a crisis state."[14]

The most important gland of the human immune system may be the thymus which, among many other things, is responsible for the production of T lymphocytes, a vital breed of white blood cell needed for cell-mediated immunity. Naturopathic doctors, Michael Murray and Joseph Pizzorno define cell-mediated immunity as "immune mechanisms not controlled or mediated by antibodies." The ingestion of just 75 grams of glucose has been shown to depress lymphocyte activity.[15]

WHILE TODAY'S SUGAR INDUSTRY MAY NOT BE AS OVERT IN ITS QUEST FOR DOMINATION, IT IS NO LESS AGGRESSIVE. ITS MODERN WEAPONS OF CHOICE ARE PROPAGANDA AND MONEY.

Also playing a crucial role in the immune system are neutrophils: white blood cells that phagocytise (engulf and destroy) bacteria, tumor cells, and dead particulate matter. This delicate dance of self-defense can be severely compromised by the introduction of sugar. According to Murray and Pizzorno, the ingestion of 100 grams of sugar "significantly reduced the ability of neutrophils to engulf and destroy bacteria...these effects started less than 30 minutes after ingestion and lasted for over five hours. Typically there was at least a 50% reduction in neutrophil activity two hours after ingestion."[16] Since neutrophils make up 60-70% of the total circulating white blood cells, impairment of their activity can lead to a severely compromised immune system and, eventually, chronic immune deficiency.

WITH OVERWHELMING EVIDENCE DOCUMENTING THE ADVERSE IMPACT OF REFINED SUGAR UPON THE HUMAN BODY, WHY ARE WE INGESTING 130 POUNDS OF SWEETENERS A YEAR?

The deleterious effect of sugar consumption upon our immune system also manifests itself in the presence of excess glucose in the bloodstream. Vitamin C and glucose compete for the same membrane transport sites into the white blood cells...and vitamin C and glucose have opposite effects on the body's immunity. Once the consumption of sugar has served to weaken our immune system, a wide variety of sugar-related illnesses can take advantage, e.g. diabetes, tooth decay, hypoglycemia, food allergies, cancer, heart disease, obesity, gastrointestinal disorders, and mycotoxicosis. While each is worthy of a book-length study, let's examine a few of these often life-threatening disorders.

Here's how Gary Null explains sugar's role in diabetes: "Exhausted by the constant demand of producing insulin to convert all that sugar into heat and energy, the pancreas will finally malfunction and the excess sugar then pollutes the bloodstream. Without sufficient insulin to covert the sugar into glucose, the body is deprived of an essential food, and the diabetic remains hungry, no matter how much he eats. Sugar accumulates in the bloodstream

"INFLUENCING ELEMENTARY SCHOOL STUDENTS IS VERY IMPORTANT TO SOFT DRINK MARKETERS BECAUSE CHILDREN ARE STILL ESTABLISHING THEIR TASTES AND HABITS."

faster than the body can excrete it through the kidneys in the urine, literally poisoning the victim."[17]

Another sugar-induced threat is obesity. Excess amounts of sugar, as mentioned, will eventually spill into the bloodstream where it is fed upon by fungi that, in turn, spew out poisons called mycotoxins. The liver is then forced to release low density lipoproteins (LDL cholesterol) to bind to these sugar-produced toxic acids. The result is obesity, a dangerously high cholesterol count, and potential heart disease. The nation's number one killer is clearly not just a fat and cholesterol problem. Excess amounts of sugar in the bloodstream may lead to an increase in a blood fat called triglycerides.

What about tooth decay? "Many clinicians believe that the first signs of the degenerative disease process are seen in the mouth," says Nancy Appleton.[18] Tooth enamel may be the strongest material in the human body, but it's no match for bacteria. The bacteria in your mouth, fed by the sugar you consume, bores holes in the enamel thus creating cavities. This occurs simultaneously with the depletion of the body's calcium supply as the body draws calcium from the bones to help restore an acid-alkaline balance after it is disrupted by the consumption of sugar...further weakening the integrity of your teeth.

With overwhelming evidence documenting the adverse impact of refined sugar upon the human body, why are we ingesting 130 pounds of sweeteners a year? The self-perpetuating cycle of consumption and dysfunction is made possible due to the addictive properties of the substance that sets the cycle in motion.

> "Since refined sugar is unnatural to the body and has a profound effect on body systems, it can properly be classified as a drug or toxin. In fact, sugar addiction is possible and is quite common."—William Randolph Kellas, Ph.D.[19]

The concept of food addiction is still the subject of much scientific debate but *Obesity Research*, the journal of the North American Association for the Study of Obesity, published a study in 2002 designed to "determine whether withdrawal from sugar can cause signs of opioid dependence."[20]

The study's authors believe that because "palatable food stimulates neural systems that are implicated in drug addiction...intermittent, excessive sugar intake might create dependency, as indicated by withdrawal signs."[21]

Since animal-based research is hardly reliable,[22] the study's conclusion must be taken with a grain of, uh, sugar: "Repeated, excessive intake of sugar created a state in which an opioid antagonist caused behavioral and neurochemical signs of opioid withdrawal. The indices of anxiety and DA/ACh imbalance were qualitatively similar to withdrawal from morphine or nicotine, suggesting that the rats had become sugar-dependent."[23]

Physicians operating on a more holistic plane have long understood the addictive powers of sugar and are not waiting around for the results of faulty and

"REPEATED, EXCESSIVE INTAKE OF SUGAR CREATED A STATE IN WHICH AN OPIOID ANTAGONIST CAUSED BEHAVIORAL AND NEUROCHEMICAL SIGNS OF OPIOID WITHDRAWAL..."

immoral animal tests to speak out. Majid Ali, M.D., is one such health professional. "Sudden rises in blood sugar evoke sudden insulin responses," he says. "Bursts of insulin drive the blood sugar down to hypoglycemic levels and trigger the release of adrenaline and related chemicals. This causes apprehension, light-headedness, mood swings, heart palpitations, and other signals that call out the body's need for more quick energy. The person reaches for more sugary snacks and repeats the whole cycle of the molecular roller coaster."[24]

> "In one of the most despicable marketing gambits, Pepsi, Dr. Pepper, and Seven-Up encourage feeding soft drinks to babies by licensing their logos to a major maker of baby bottles, Munchkin Bottling, Inc."
>
> —Michael Jacobson, the author of *Liquid Candy*, a 1999 study by the Center for Science in the Public Interest[25]

Whether or not you choose to label your sugar craving an addiction or a "molecular roller coaster" matters little to the hacks being paid to market it. One of the major sugar pushers is the beverage industry. A January 1999 trade magazine article stated baldly: "Influencing elementary school students is very important to soft drink marketers because children are still establishing their tastes and habits."[26]

In his book, *Fast Food Nation: The Dark Side of the All-American Meal*, author Eric Schlosser reports on the *Liquid Candy* study cited above:

> In 1978, the typical teenage boy in the United States drank about seven ounces of soda every day; today he drinks nearly three times that amount, deriving 9% of his daily caloric intake from soft drinks. Soda consumption among teenage girls has doubled within the same period, reaching an average of twelve ounces a day. A significant number of teenage boys are now drinking five or more cans of soda every day. Each can contains the equivalent of about ten teaspoons of sugar. Coke, Pepsi, Mountain Dew, and Dr. Pepper also contain caffeine. These sodas provide empty calories and have replaced far more nutritious beverages in the American diet. Excessive soda consumption in childhood can lead to calcium deficiencies and a greater likelihood of bone fractures. About twenty years ago, teenage boys in the United States drank twice as much milk as soda; now they drink twice as much soda as milk.[27]

"With the rise in consumerism, there has been a rise in sugar use," concludes Anup Shah. "With the increasing work demands, partly a result of rising consumerism, there has been a rise in convenience and fast foods. This implies more sugar! Exploitation has continued. From slavery, it has moved to consumers and children (albeit in another form), while the environment continues to suffer (and) an entire fast food industry has arisen due to consumerism."[28] As might be expected, this powerful and entrenched system of creating false needs, exploiting those false needs, and all the destruction involved on the production and consumption sides does not suffer opposition gladly.

In April 2003, the World Health Organization (WHO) released a report entitled, *Diet, Nutrition and the Prevention of Chronic Diseases*, stating what should be a truism: "Unbalanced consumption of foods high in energy (sugar, starch, and/or fat) and low in essential nutrients contributes to obesity."[29] As reported by John Morgenthaler, in the Health &

"WHAT YOU DON'T KNOW ABOUT SUGAR JUST MAY KILL YOU."

Wellness Update, the industry response came swiftly. "In an attempt to block the report, the Sugar Association—which includes sugar cane and corn farmers, and industry giants Coca-Cola, Pepsi-Cola and General Foods—threatened to lobby Congress to cut off $406 million," says Morgenthaler. "This amount is given annually by the United States to the WHO, and is nearly a quarter of the organization's budget."[30]

"We will exercise every avenue available to expose the dubious nature of the *Diet, Nutrition and the Prevention of Chronic Diseases* report," Sugar Association president, Andrew Briscoe, wrote to WHO director-general Dr. Gro Harlem Brundtland.[31]

"Cardiovascular disease, diabetes, cancers, obesity—these are no longer rich country problems," Brundtland countered. "The majority of chronic disease cases are occurring in the developing world. Our experience shows us that even modest, but population-wide interventions on diet and physical activity, can produce significant changes in the overall chronic disease burden in a surprisingly short time. The Report is significant because we will be using it as the critical science-based foundation for the WHO Global Strategy on Diet, Physical Activity and Health, which we are preparing to address this growing chronic disease burden."[32]

"What you don't know about sugar just may kill you," proclaims diet counselor, Mary Toscano.[33] Despite this gloomy reality, when faced with the frightening impact of sugar production, consumption, and marketing, it may be encouraging to note that the inclusion of sugar in the human diet pattern is quite new...in an evolutionary sense. Our ancestors survived without candy bars, soda pop, and chocolate (not to mention, hydrogenated oils, chemicals and additives, pesticides, hormones, and genetically modified food). The introduction of such harmful foodstuffs into our diet can and must be reversed. While having a "sweet tooth" is considered an endearing quality in contemporary America, our survival as a species just may depend on us moving forward past this era of gastronomical madness while at the same time rediscovering the "basics" that have gotten us this far.

I'm So Excited

For those of you smirking as you reach for that NutraSweet, you should know that artificial sweeteners aren't much better than the sugar they're replacing. Designed to reduce sugar intake, what these substances actually do is trick the brain into thinking a large amount of energy (sugar) is on the way. Thus, the brain instructs the liver to not produce glucose for a while and go into "storage mode." Within a half-hour, when the expected energy (sugar) hasn't arrived, the brain and liver panic and demand food. This, of course, results in overeating and obesity and explains why you see so many overweight people drinking diet sodas.

Besides the irony of promoting obesity, there are many health-related concerns about artificial sweeteners. For example, aspartame, found in more than 9,000 products, has been suspected in a wide range of medical problems—from migraines to joint pain to mood swings and behavioral issues in children. Neurosurgeon Russell L. Blaylock labels aspartame an "excitotoxin" because studies indicate it "can literally excite brain cells to death."[34]

Excitotoxins are a "class of substances that damage neurons through paroxysmal overactivity."[35] They can produce lesions similar to those of Huntingdon's chorea or Alzheimer's disease. "Glutamic acid (also called 'glutamate') is the chief excitatory neurotransmitter in the human and mammalian brain," explains researcher James South. "Glutamate and its biochemical 'cousin,' aspartic acid or aspartate, are the two most plentiful amino acids in the brain."[36] Aspartic acid makes up roughly 40% of the ubiquitous sweetener, aspartame. The rest is 50% phenylalanine, "an amino acid normally found in the brain but dangerous to humans when concentrated at high levels" and 10% methanol, a "wood alcohol known to be a deadly poison."[37]

Endnotes

[1] Nancy Appleton. *Lick the Sugar Habit* (Avery Publishing Group, 1988), p. 7; Conversely, the Sugar Association says: "Americans consume less sugar than reported. Of the total amount that is in the food supply, less than half is actually eaten" (www.sugar.org). But this is more semantics than science, as demonstrated by this Sugar Association statement: "There is virtually no sugar in soft drinks. Soft drinks and other fruit drinks are sweetened with high fructose corn syrup."

[2] Appleton, *Lick the Sugar Habit*, p. 9.

[3] http://askwaltstollmd.com

[4] http://www.bupa.co.uk/health_information

[5] http://www.globalissues.org/TradeRelated/Consumption/Sugar.asp

[6] Emma Goldman. *Living My Life* (New York: Dover Publications, Inc., 1931, 1970) p. 226.

[7] Richard Robbins. *Global Problems and the Culture of Capitalism*, (Allyn and Bacon, 1999), pp. 215-216.

[8] http://www.sugar.org

[9] http://www.opensecrets.org

[10] Smart Publications, Health & Wellness Update, John Morgenthaler, *How Sweet It Isn't: The political battle over sugar* http://www.smart-publications.com, July 29, 2003.

[11] "Harvesting Poverty: America's Sugar Daddies," *New York Times* editorial, November 29, 2003.

[12] http://www.sugar.org

[13] http://www.majidali.com

[14] Gary Null. *The 90s Healthy Body Book: How to overcome the effects of pollution and cleanse toxins from your body* (Health Communications, Inc., 1994), p. 74.

[15] Michael Murray and Joseph Pizzorno. *Encyclopedia of Natural Medicine* (Prima Publishing, 1991), p. 63.

[16] Murray and Pizzorno, *Encyclopedia of Natural Medicine*, p. 63.

[17] Null, *The 90s Healthy Body Book*, p. 78.

[18] Appleton, *Lick the Sugar Habit*, p. 68.

[19] William Randall Kellas and Andrea Sharon Dworkin. Thriving in a Toxic World: Today's Ultimate Solutions to Chronic Illness (Professional Preference, 1996) p. 239.

[20] Study: *Evidence That Intermittent, Excessive Sugar Intake Causes Endogenous Opioid Dependence*, Carlo Colantuoni, Pedro Rada, Joseph McCarthy, Caroline Patten, Nicole M. Avena, Andrew Chadeayne, and Bartley G. Hoebel: Obesity Research 10:478-488 (2002), http://www.obesityresearch.org

[21] http://www.obesityresearch.org

[22] http://www.animalresearch.org

[23] More specifically, this is what the study found: "Naloxone (20 mg/kg intraperitoneally) caused somatic signs, such as teeth chattering, forepaw tremor, and head shakes. Food deprivation for 24 hours caused spontaneous withdrawal signs, such as teeth chattering. Naloxone (3 mg/kg subcutaneously) caused reduced time on the exposed arm of an elevated plus maze, where again significant teeth chattering was recorded. The plus maze anxiety effect was replicated with four control groups for comparison. Accumbens microdialysis revealed that naloxone (10 and 20 mg/kg intraperitoneally) decreased extracellular dopamine (DA), while dose-dependently increasing acetylcholine (ACh). The naloxone-induced DA/ACh imbalance was replicated with 10% sucrose and 3 mg/kg naloxone subcutaneously."

[24] http://www.majidali.com/obesity.htm

[25] Eric Schlosser. *Fast Food Nation; The Dark Side of the All-American Meal*, (Houghton Mifflin Company, 2001), p.54.

[26] Schlosser, *Fast Food Nation*, p. 54.

[27] ibid.

[28] http://www.globalissues.org/TradeRelated/Consumption/Sugar.asp

[29] Morgenthaler, http://www.smart-publications.com

[30] ibid.

[31] ibid.

[32] ibid.

[33] http://www.santacruzsentinel.com/archive/

[34] http://www.additivesout.org.uk/

[35] http://www.books.md/E/dic/excitotoxin.php

[36] http://smart-drugs.net

[37] http://www.foodanddiet.com

Beyond Health and Safety—A hard look at *really* preventing drug abuse

Theo Rosenfeld

I remember only one thing from my early drug education. In eighth grade our counselor came to tell us about the dangers of drugs. He told the sorry tale of a teacher who found a strip of acid on the playground, grasped it firmly in her shaking hands, and immediately brought it to the principal, then collapsed. According to the story, she stayed in a coma for two weeks, the doctors pointing to an accidental ingestion of ten hits of LSD as the horrific culprit.

The counselor tried so hard to deliver this pessimistic urban myth as a true story and an earnest warning. (I can't imagine what he was trying to warn us about though—Don't pick up colored paper on the playground? Don't take ten hits of acid? Don't drop your stash?)

A quiet tension formed between the somber counselor, the kids who understood the story as a joke, and the naïve students trying to grasp a message in all this. Finally, at the point of the story when the doctors proclaim the

| "THIS IS BAD, BUT I LIKE IT. DOES THAT MEAN I AM BAD?"

amount of LSD consumed, the tension broke and humor won when somebody blurted out, "Holy shit! That's a LOT of acid." As I recovered from side-splitting laughter I saw on our counselor a look of total defeat, of someone who has just poured their passion into an exercise doomed from the get go.

Failing for lack of effort is one thing, but giving it all you've got and still failing sucks. Knowing that, I can't blame the current ranks of good people working in "prevention" for stubbornly persisting in the face of total failure. They have even more at stake than the passions of my eighth-grade counselor—although they certainly won't get any farther with their drug abuse prevention efforts.

Currently our culture defines drugs and health in a very narrow, polarized way. In this simple binary logic: No drug use = good / Drug use = bad. This logic pervades language and thought so much it structures many people's inner dialogues. For example, when a young person tries a drug and likes it, as often does happen, he or she faces a serious question of roles. "This is bad, but I like it. Does that mean I am bad?"

"Science-based" education and harm reduction have taken fantastic steps toward a more rational and honest understanding of drug use and drug abuse, but there are more steps to be taken. Often, harm reduction or science-based approaches get hung up on the mantra, "Neither condemn nor condone." They claim neutrality with a "non-judgmental attitude" while discouraging harmful behaviours, but fail to balance this with positive encouragement. Giving out straightforward health and safety information only differs from traditional scare tactics in that it does not *exaggerate* the dangers of drugs. Their overall tone is usually still foreboding.

The most innovative drug education and drug abuse prevention programs have taken extra steps to imbed their health and safety information within the cultural context of their target audience. The best of these come from peer-based initiatives originating within the culture they target. Unfortunately, peer-based programs suffer from chronic under-funding, and have a hard time getting the credit that they deserve.

So, if we just want to prevent drug *abuse* as best we can, what makes this so difficult?

Let's look at a few facts too often ignored by drug abuse prevention efforts: people tend to adapt behavioral change based on role-modelling; and a strong social support network strengthens one's capacity to avoid or diminish unwanted behaviour patterns, such as over-using drugs.

...THE CULTURE OF SILENCE THAT SURROUNDS OUR CRIMINAL BEHAVIOUR CONDEMNS EVERY NEW USER TO THE SAME DEADLY TRIAL AND ERROR PROCESS THAT THEY COULD EASILY AVOID IF THEY COULD LOOK TO THE PEOPLE WHO HAVE GONE BEFORE THEM.

We all fall into the same faulty binary logic when we advocate for honesty in drug education but stop at honestly explaining the dangers of drug use as well as fail

I CAN'T BLAME THE CURRENT RANKS OF GOOD PEOPLE WORKING IN "PREVENTION" FOR STUBBORNLY PERSISTING IN THE FACE OF TOTAL FAILURE.

to honestly speak of positive drug effects and experiences. Introducing the growth potential of drugs would allow us to contrast detrimental drug using behaviour with beneficial, or at least neutral, drug using behaviour. Talking openly about using drugs for possible benefit implicitly discourages reckless use. On the other hand, the culture of silence that surrounds our criminal behaviour condemns every new user to the same deadly trial and error process that they could easily avoid if they could look to the people who have gone before them. The challenge lies in offering role models and social contexts for positive drug use without proselytizing our personal favourite substances.

If we really do accept that drug use does happen, we must also accept that it happens *in context(s),* not as an isolated moment of "youthful indiscretion." If we look, we will always find it embedded in cultural fabrics, whether

> "GETTING HIGH" IS NOT THE SAME THING AS "GETTING FUCKED UP." SOME PEOPLE DO HURT THEMSELVES WITH DRUGS, WHILE OTHERS FIND GREAT BENEFIT IN THEIR USE.

talked about openly or not. Some cultures support the health and growth of individuals better than others. Does it not stand to reason that we could spare a great deal of drug abuse and ignorant mistakes if we weave more positive contexts for drug use?

By acknowledging and validating the positive experiences people have using drugs, we have a much more authentic stance from which to discourage the negative and more harmful or dangerous behaviours and experiences. This level of honesty allows us to access a powerful influential force in the lives of drug users—friends. Not only do friends *not* want to see each other get hurt, they get excited about introducing each other to *positive* new things. Positive information travels through informal networks much faster than information about health and safety. This approach also acknowledges and strengthens the social networks of drug users. Providing users with a language to assess the value of drug experiences increases the capacity of friends to help each other avoid pitfalls.

Drug abuse prevention could then focus on equipping individuals with tools for evaluating their own use, defining drug abuse relative to their own values, and avoiding harm. In doing this we could also restore trust and honesty in our relationships with young people—a big step toward preventing future drug abuse and harm. "Getting high" is *not* the same thing as "getting fucked up." Some people *do* hurt themselves with drugs, while others find great benefit in their use. We will find no simplistic answers to these complex issues of communication and behaviour. Using limited language, or ignoring any of the many dimensions of human drug use impairs any real effort at understanding the realities of drug use and health.

The time has come for drug abuse prevention to get real and cast aside both simplistic polarity and the overly cautious stance of current programs. The very personal decisions about drug use always come down to the individual in question—we can't make anybody's mind up about anything, least of all what they put in their body. We can however, develop in our culture a much deeper understanding of, and respect for, drugs.

Theo Rosenfeld

Marijuana vs. Cigarettes

Paul Krassner

I am most likely one of the very few who actually believed that former president Bill Clinton was telling the truth when he said that he had tried smoking marijuana but he didn't inhale because he wasn't a cigarette smoker and didn't really know how to inhale. That's exactly what happened with me, a non-cigarette-smoker, the first time I tried smoking pot, but of course I persisted until I got it right.

I'VE BEEN A POT SMOKER FOR AT LEAST 35 YEARS, BUT RECENTLY I STOPPED FOR A MONTH, JUST AS A CHANGE OF PACE, AND I HAD NO WITHDRAWAL SYMPTOMS.

I've been a pot smoker for at least 35 years, but recently I stopped for a month, just as a change of pace, and I had no withdrawal symptoms. I was simply aware at first of all the times I felt tempted, out of habit, whether it would occur before I ate, before I went to a movie, before making love, before listening to music, or before rolling a joint.

On the other hand, according to Dr. James West, outpatient medical director at the Betty Ford Center, "Smoking cigarettes is probably the most difficult addiction to break. Most recovering alcoholics who quit smoking will say that it was harder to quit smoking than to quit alcohol. About 70% of alcohol-dependent individuals are heavy smokers—more than one pack of cigarettes per day—compared with 10% of the population. Alcoholics eventually die from lung cancer more often than from alcohol-related causes."

Nearly 2,000 young people under the age of eighteen become smokers every day in America. And yet, although the World Health Organization (WHO) spent three years working out an agreement with 171 countries to prevent the spread of smoking-related diseases, particularly in the developing world, the United States opposed the treaty, including the minimum age of eighteen for sales to minors. Around the globe, tobacco now kills almost five million people a year. Within a generation, predicts WHO, the premature death toll will reach ten million a year.

Whereas, with marijuana, despite all the anti-pot propaganda, the worst that can happen is maybe you'll have a severe case of the munchies.

"Americans are fighting tobacco addiction at home while our government is supporting it abroad," writes *Boston Globe* columnist Ellen Goodman. "In fact, the administration thinks tobacco companies should be allowed to market overseas in ways that are prohibited here—with everything from free samples to sponsorship of youth events. When it comes to tobacco, we are standing outside the world community like a nicotine junkie on a city sidewalk, huffing and puffing away."

In October 2003, Health Canada released the results of a study which found that more teenagers smoke pot than cigarettes. Fifty-four percent of fifteen to nineteen year-olds said they had smoked marijuana more than once. Conversely, cigarette smoking has continued to decline among Canadian youths, with the latest national figures showing that only 22% of teens smoke regularly.

In the United States, on December 20, 2003, Associated Press reported on an annual survey known as *Monitoring*

"SMOKING CIGARETTES IS PROBABLY THE MOST DIFFICULT ADDICTION TO BREAK. MOST RECOVERING ALCOHOLICS WHO QUIT SMOKING WILL SAY THAT IT WAS HARDER TO QUIT SMOKING THAN TO QUIT ALCOHOL.

the Future (funded by the National Institute on Drug Abuse), which tracked drug use and attitudes among 48,500 students from 392 schools. The study concluded that marijuana remains by far the most widely used illegal drug. It has been tried at least once by 46% of 12th graders and used by more than a third in the past year.

John Walters, director of the White House Office of National Drug Control Policy, stated at a new conference that surveys in fifteen cities have found that more teens smoke marijuana than regular cigarettes. However, the drug czar added, "More kids are seeking treatment for marijuana dependency than all other drugs combined." He neglected to mention how many of them seek such treatment as their only option to prison time.

Interestingly enough, though, for those who are truly dedicated tobacco addicts, there is a porn Web site featuring Smokin' Hot Sluts—"the largest archive of gorgeous girls who love to smoke before, during, and after sex." Internet seekers are invited to "Tell our live babes your deepest, nastiest smoking fantasies, and they'll fulfill your dreams."

But what could such smoking fantasies possibly be? "Fuck my smoldering hot ass!" "Lesbian smoke orgies!" "Slide your filter tip deep inside me!" And, as if intended specifically for Bill Clinton and Monica Lewinsky, "Inhale and swallow!"

A Brief History on the War on Drugs

Valerie Vande Panne

Today in the United States, the inalienable rights Thomas Jefferson guaranteed in the Declaration of Independence, "life, liberty, and the pursuit of happiness," have been lost to the goal of a "drug-free America." People in the US are oppressed, incarcerated, and killed in the name of the War on Drugs, and nearly every nation on Earth has joined the battle.

The War on Drugs, while unquestionably a world war, is more American than baseball, apple pie, and McDonald's.

What follows is an exploration of the roots of War on Drugs in the United States. This story covers what you may not have learned in the US public school system: from the first measure passed democratically regarding tobacco and hemp at Jamestown, Virginia in 1619, to Ronald Reagan's declaration of war on drugs in 1982, it traces the roots of our drug war, grown like a weed

> THE WAR ON DRUGS, WHILE UNQUESTIONABLY A WORLD WAR, IS MORE AMERICAN THAN BASEBALL, APPLE PIE, AND MCDONALD'S.

out of the zealous ignorance of a frightened, greedy, puritanical people, who left their history elsewhere when they planted themselves in North America.

Kind reader, this is *our history,* and it must not be forgotten.

From Colonial America to Ronald Reagan

We find the first seeds of the War on Drugs planted with tobacco in colonial Virginia.

John Rolfe, an Englishman formerly shipwrecked in Bermuda, arrived in Jamestown early in the year 1614 on the *Elizabeth,* bringing with him high quality tobacco seeds. In Bermuda, the Spanish had outlawed the sale of tobacco seed to other nations under penalty of death, and Rolfe was seeking a new location to develop the tobacco trade.

Jamestown had been at war with the Paspagegh Indians for years, and the colonists took in (some historians say took hostage) Paspagegh Chief Powhatan's daughter, Pocahontas. The newly arrived Rolfe and the local leader Robert Sparkes negotiated a temporary truce with the tribe: Pocahontas took the Christian name Rebecca, she and Rolfe were married, and there was a short period of peace. Before the summer of 1614 ended, Rolfe sent the first shipment of Virginia tobacco to Great Britain. By 1616, he was lobbying for a monopoly on tobacco trade with England, but his pleas fell on deaf ears. King James I detested smoking, and wrote in his *A Counterblaste to Tobacco*:

> "[Tobacco is] a custome lothsome to the Eye, hatefull to the Nose, harmfull to the Braine, daungerous to the Lungs, and in the blacke stinking fume thereof, neerest resembling the horrible...smoke of the pit that is bottomless." [sic][77]

Though the settlers had problems with the Paspagegh, they managed to keep relations with the Chickahominy Indians amicable. This tribe supplied the colonists with food, enabling them to focus on tobacco cultivation. But when relations with the Chickahominy faltered, the colonists had to be provoked into growing their own food. In 1619, the first legislative assembly met and passed measures meant to restrict the cultivation of tobacco and encourage the production of a food supply, wine, hemp and flax. (They also passed measures addressing social behavior, idleness, and the wearing of clothing beyond one's social position.) Regardless, tobacco continued to be the crop of choice. The colonists took food from the Indians, sometimes by force, rather than grow a sufficient supply themselves.

For the next several decades, the Virginia colony suffered repeated food shortages, winters of starvation, and

> REGARDLESS, TOBACCO CONTINUED TO BE THE CROP OF CHOICE. THE COLONISTS TOOK FOOD FROM THE INDIANS, SOMETIMES BY FORCE, RATHER THAN GROW A SUFFICIENT SUPPLY THEMSELVES.

plagues of disease. Thousands died, only to be replaced by more immigrants. Merchants were encouraged to fortify connections with England by trading in indentured servants, slaves, and tobacco. Fifty acres of land was awarded to each individual responsible for bringing indentured servants or slaves to the colony. Around the same time, King Charles I ordered Virginia to limit its cultivation of tobacco. The General Assembly—made up primarily of plantation owners—opposed the order, their thirst for tobacco profits trumped their hunger pains.

More than twenty years after the official call for the cultivation of a food supply, the colony still didn't produce enough, and in 1640 Virginia colony Governor Sir Francis Wyatt issued a proclamation: tobacco cultivation could not exceed 1000 plants, and he insisted on the cultivation of corn.[78]

As the colonies began to produce more commodities, the British Parliament in 1659 demanded they ship their products—primarily tobacco, sugar, wool, and indigo—exclusively to England. Later, royal rulers William and Mary made further demands on the colonial shipping

THE ROOTS OF THE FUTURE WAR ON DRUGS WERE GROWING, WITH ALCOHOL AND THE SLAVE TRADE JOINING TOBACCO AS THE MAJOR ECONOMIC FORCES IN THE AMERICAN COLONIES.

industry, when they oversaw the *Act for the Encouraging of the Distillation of Brandy and Spirits from Corn*, in 1690. Within a few years, the triangular trade that encouraged alcohol production was flourishing: Sugar and molasses were brought from the West Indies to New England, where they were made into rum. The English took the rum to West Africa, where they traded it for slaves. Then they brought the slaves to the new world. Trade like this continued for over one hundred years.

The roots of the future War on Drugs were growing, with alcohol and the slave trade joining tobacco as the major economic forces in the American colonies.

But it wasn't all spirits, smoke, and slaves in colonial America. Hemp was also critical to the colonies, because it could be processed into any number of important items, including oil, cloth, paper, rope, and ship sails. The *Mayflower* arrived at Plymouth, Massachusetts, in 1620, and within ten years, hemp was being cultivated in Salem, and the first ropewalk (a place where fiber is woven into rope) was established in Boston. The colony of Massachusetts had, by the early 1700s, a measure "to encourage the sewing and well manufacturing of hemp,"[79] and England granted an award of six pounds for every ton of hemp produced. Hemp was accepted as payment for taxes. The monetary incentives from England existed through the mid-1700s and then the colonial governments offered bounties for local production. Most hemp was grown for domestic purposes, and in fact the colonies continued to import it. During the first six months of 1770, Boston imported nearly 500 tons of hemp from Great Britain. When the colonies began boycotting more and more British goods, they developed trade with Russia, and imported shipments of high-quality hemp from St. Petersburg.[80]

Hemp was so important at the time of the American Revolution that nearly all farmers grew at least a small amount of it. George Washington and Thomas Jefferson both grew hemp, and it became an important crop in the efforts to break ties with Britain and foster autonomy.

Yet, colonial Americans hadn't discovered hemp's potential for mind alteration, instead embracing alcohol. By the end of the Revolutionary War, the United States was considered to be the greatest consumer of "spirits" per capita in the world.[81] Employers gave alcohol to their workers, and colonial troops were supplied whiskey or New England rum. Benjamin Franklin, in his autobiography, described the custom of drinking at a printing-house where he worked:

> "We had an ale-house boy, who attended always in the house to supply the workmen. My companion at the press drank every day a pint before breakfast, a pint at breakfast with his bread and cheese, a pint between breakfast and dinner, a pint at dinner, a pint in the afternoon about six o'clock, and another pint when he had done his day's work…it was necessary, he supposed, to drink *strong* beer that he might be *strong* to labor."[82]

Despite this acceptance of spirited drink in the workplace, the temperance movement gained steam, growing out of the Puritan settlements. Dr. Benjamin Rush, a signer of the Declaration of Independence, wrote the first widely read pamphlet on the subject of alcohol, *Inquiry into the effects of ardent spirits on the human body and mind*, in 1785. He encouraged the removal of alcohol from the workplace, and the moderate use of beer, wine, and cider. The first temperance society was then formed in Litchfield, Connecticut in 1789. Its members pledged not to give liquor to farm hands, and the workers revolted in opposition.[83]

Within fifty years, the temperance movement would go from a movement of moderation and regulation, to demanding abstinence.

Ironically, financial issues rather than temperance inspired the first US conflict over alcohol. The young American government was in debt from its revolution, and decided in 1791 to impose a tax on distilled spirits. The small-time producer was taxed nine cents a gallon, the larger producer

BY THE END OF THE REVOLUTIONARY WAR, THE UNITED STATES WAS CONSIDERED TO BE THE GREATEST CONSUMER OF "SPIRITS" PER CAPITA IN THE WORLD.

six. The people of the "western" counties, the territory just west of the Appalachian Mountains, embarked on campaigns to refuse to pay the tax collectors. The protests eventually lead to a "Whiskey Rebellion" near Pittsburgh, Pennsylvania, and George Washington sent federal troops to stop it. This was the first time the federal government used troops to repress its own people. The leaders of the revolt were captured and convicted of treason; however, Washington later pardoned them, and under Thomas Jefferson's recommendation, the tax was repealed in 1801.[84]

The roots of the War on Drugs continued to grow through the turn of the century, and not only in the temperance

THE ART WORK OF THE DAY DEPICTED THE "FRUITS OF TEMPERANCE" AS A HAPPY, WELL-DRESSED FAMILY, WITH THE HUSBAND COMING HOME FROM A DAY OF WORK TO A JOLLY WIFE, A SON, A DAUGHTER, AND A BABY—SORT OF AN EARLY 19TH CENTURY *LEAVE IT TO BEAVER* LIFE STYLE.

movement: the practice of western medicine, capitalism and racism would become fertile ground for a war that was nearly 200 years away.

The medical industry underwent tremendous transformation during the 1800s. Early in the century, medicine was based upon the idea that illness was due to "bad blood" and treatments primarily consisted of purgatives or bleeding of the patient. Calomel (the poisonous chloride of mercury) was used to induce vomiting and had a violent laxative effect. Leeches and incisions were used to "bleed" the patient of bad blood. While these types of treatments were common, they did not do well for the reputation of those practicing medicine. One rhyme of the day went:

> "The man grows worse quite fast indeed, go call the doctor, ride with speed:The doctor comes like post with mail, doubling his dose of Calomel.

> The man in death begins to groan, The fatal job for him is done; He dies, alas! But sure to tell, A sacrifice to Calomel."[85]

The distrust of doctors grew, inspiring people to turn to the practice of homeopathy. Developed by German physician Samuel Hahnemann, homeopathy was based on the theory that "like is cured by like," and utilized small amounts of plant components that in a healthy person would produce the same symptoms that the sick person was suffering from. The system proved effective, and rapidly spread throughout the United States as a non-intrusive method of healing.

Homemade remedies or "vegetable compounds" also became popular. These types of treatments frequently combined traditional, sometimes Native American, herbal remedies in a tincture of alcohol to cure disease and illness.

The temperance movement during this time was growing. The American Society for the Promotion of Temperance was founded in Boston in 1826, and by 1833, there were more than 6,000 local temperance societies, with over one million members.[86] One exception was made as the movement became more and more abstinence-oriented: alcohol, for health purposes, was acceptable. There were some proponents of prohibition who were also manufacturers of alcohol-based vegetable compounds.

Outside of medicine, alcohol was depicted through propaganda as the single biggest threat to the new American family.

The art work of the day depicted the "Fruits of Temperance" as a happy, well-dressed family, with the husband coming home from a day of work to a jolly wife, a son, a daughter, and a baby—sort of an early 19th Century *Leave it to Beaver* life style. The artwork also showed the impoverished family destroyed by alcohol, the belligerent husband, and the grim hand of alcohol reaching for an innocent little girl. By 1845, New York State had passed the first prohibition law, forbidding the public sale of liquor; it was repealed in less than two years.[87]

Susan B. Anthony, famous for campaigning on behalf of women's rights, was forbidden to speak at a temperance rally, because she was a woman, and thus she was inspired to establish the "Women's State Temperance Society of New York" in 1852—the first society formed by and for women. Anthony worked relentlessly her entire life for the equal rights of women, the abolishment of slavery, and of the prohibition of alcohol.[88]

While the prohibitionists worked to gain power and vote in American society, the medical industry worked to ensure its own success. The American Medical Association was founded in 1847, and its first order of business was to discredit homeopathy. In its code of ethics, it prohibited members from consulting with homeopaths, hoping to taint the sect by considering them quacks.[89]

...OPIUM EATERS WERE ABLE TO CONTRIBUTE TO SOCIETY AS SUCCESSFULLY AS NON-OPIUM EATERS. IT WAS UNTHINKABLE THAT ONE WOULD LOSE THEIR JOB, HOME, OR CHILD OVER THE SUBSTANCE.

Regardless, homeopathy gained popularity, and so did the homemade, alcohol-based herbal remedies, which lead to the patent medicine industry. To combat this phenomenon, the American Pharmaceutical Association was founded in 1852, and by 1856 one of its main goals was "to as much as possible restrict the dispensing and sale of medicines to regularly educated druggests [sic] and apothecaries."[90]

Meanwhile, South American explorers were sending coca leaves to the US and Europe in bulk, insisting the plant had therapeutic powers: that it was conducive to health, longevity, and energy, and had numbing properties that might be explored for surgery. However, the shipments would take months to arrive, and when they did, the doctors found the leaves to have little benefit at all, leading many to assume the stories were mere travelers tales.[91]

Coca's heath benefits would be questioned through the 1860s. But there was little question surrounding the poppy plant, and its product, opium. In the 1760s, the Englishman Thomas Dover had introduced an opium compound, "Dover's Powder" for the treatment of gout, which opened the door to pain treatment never before experienced in western medicine. By 1781, poppy was being cultivated in Pennsylvania for medicinal use. By 1812, it was cultivated as far north as New Hampshire.[92] Many of the vegetable compounds popular over the next several decades, for everything from gout to headaches to "female troubles," contained opium. These remedies proudly advertised their merits and asserted they contained "no calomel."[93]

During the Civil War, opiates including laudanum and morphine made surgical procedures possible, and those with severe wounds, amputations, and pain survived in numbers unlike any previous war. Poppy was grown and opium produced in the Confederate states of Virginia, Tennessee, South Carolina, and Georgia.[94]

While it was recognized during the mid-1800s that habitual consumption of opium could create an addiction, the word "addict" was rarely used, and opium users (called "opium eaters") were unquestionably accepted by society—they worked, went to school and to church, and were active members of their communities. It was considered a godsend for those suffering from chronic pain, and opium eaters were able to contribute to society as successfully

as non-opium eaters. It was unthinkable that one would lose their job, home, or child over the substance. The most common class of people to use opium at this time was, in fact, the middle-American woman, who would sometimes share the "mother's little helper" with her children—especially for such ailments as teething. The 1878 *Annual Report of the Michigan State Board of Health* reported small numbers of opium eaters throughout towns and villages—as few as three in Huron (pop. 437) and as many as 20 in Hillsdale (pop. 4,189). Children were unashamedly included in the statistics.[95]

Coca, by this time, had its alkaloid cocaine isolated, and it was becoming popular for its own therapeutic value: Cocaine toothache drops were advertised, dentistry and eye surgery leapt forward, and recreationally 'Vin Mariani' was a popular French coca-laced wine, endorsed by Pope Leo XIII[96] and the well-known American inventor, Thomas Edison.[97] Peru and Bolivia were the primary sources of coca leaf, exporting between 20-30 million pounds of leaf during the 1880s to Europe and the US.[98]

"By 1878 coca was being promoted in advertisements in the United States for young persons suffering from shyness and as a stimulant," write Dr. Lester Grinspoon and James B. Bakalar in *Medical Uses of Illicit Drugs*. "In the same year, an American physician, W. H. Bentley, began to recommend coca as a cure for morphine addiction. Extract of coca was admitted to the United States Pharmacopoeia in 1882. In July, 1884, Sigmund Freud published a famous paper, *On Coca*, in which he recommended cocaine or coca extract for a variety of illnesses including the syndrome of fatigue, nervousness, and minor physical complaints then known

as neurasthenia. Referring to Freud's writings, the Parke-Davis Company declared in its pamphlet *Coca Erythroxylon and Its Derivatives*: 'If these claims are substantiated... [cocaine] will indeed be the most important therapeutic discovery of the age, the benefit of which to humanity will be incalculable.'"[99]

Indeed, coca was a breakthrough that continues to benefit humanity, and it wasn't just Parke-Davis singing its praises: The Woman's Christian Temperance Union was at the helm of the prohibitionist movement, and an Atlanta man named John Pemberton saw a market in the United States for an alcohol-free Vin Mariani. In 1886, he combined cola-nuts and coca-plants in a water-based tincture and sweetened it with sugar. Coca-Cola was born.[100]

During this time, America continued to enjoy its infatuation with tobacco. In the early 1800s the idea of taxing tobacco was presented in Congress, and though there was a long debate, it didn't manifest until after the Civil War. By 1880, tobacco tax accounted for 31% of federal tax receipts. Tax on tobacco has increased almost annually since then.[101]

Besides being able to purchase tobacco in general stores, and coca-based Coca-Cola over the soda fountain counter, opium could be obtained at pharmacies, in addition to local stores. In an 1883-1885 survey of the state of Iowa, which then had a population of less than two million, 3,000 stores reported they sold some form of opium.[102] In

1897, Bayer Pharmaceutical Products was touting heroin in its ads alongside aspirin.[103]

Just as the coca and opium businesses were taking off, the roots of the War on Drugs sprouted into a weed: In San Francisco, California the very first anti-drug law was passed in 1875. It was an ordinance that outlawed the smoking of opium in opium dens.[104] This law wasn't directed at the drug opium, (or any of its derivatives, like heroin, morphine, or laudanum) but at the specific racial group—the Chinese—and the way in which they consumed it.

The anti-smoking law was followed by a federal law in 1888 prohibiting the Chinese from participating in the opium trade, and it placed further restrictions on smoking opium.[105]

Within twenty years, opium control rolled into the patent medicine industry, and the Pure Food and Drug Act of 1906 was passed. It was meant to put an end to patent medicines and opium habits by forming the Food and Drug Administration. For the first time, food and drugs were regulated, and the manufacturer was required to disclose the contents of his or her product.[106]

By 1909, smoking opium was completely forbidden.[107] Anti-Chinese sentiment can be traced to the 1850s, when they first began immigrating to the US to work building the railroads. As their population grew, they took other work, at much lower wages than white American men.

In fact, the American Federation of Labor (AFL) played a huge roll in spreading anti-Chinese sentiment. "What other crimes were committed in those dark, fetid places, when these little innocent victims of the Chinamen's wiles were under the influence of the drug, are almost too horrible to imagine," wrote AFL leader (and president for nearly thirty years,) Samuel Gompers, in one of the first 'What about the children!' fear-mongering pieces. "There are hundreds, aye, thousands of our American girls and boys who have acquired this deathly habit and are doomed, hopelessly doomed, beyond the shadow of redemption."[108]

There was also the white, Christian fear that Chinese (or Black, or Mexican) men were luring white women into debauched activities. This racism against certain ethnicities in conjunction with the job market and fear of debauchery is a common theme throughout US history.

During the late 1800s, it was the Irish and the Germans who were arriving in vast numbers. Even though they shared the same color skin as the ruling American class, they were considered the scourge of the earth, and their drinking habits became a catalyst to further the temperance movement—the men were working for wages much lower than their native-born counterparts, and the women sold homemade alcohol from their kitchens to supplement the family income. When World War I began in Europe, anti-German sentiment in the US helped pass the Eighteenth Amendment, making prohibition a part of the US Constitution. A cartoon of the day depicted The Brewer and the Kaiser as two birds, and prohibition the stone that would kill them both. It became patriotic to support alcohol prohibition.[109]

Even hemp played its role in the ethnic racism of the nation. Throughout the century the hemp industry flourished and its products were manufactured and utilized by society with no qualms: Hemp rope was used in countless lynchings and hangings well into the 20th Century.

After the Civil War and through the early 1900s, alcohol was prohibited for sale to blacks in the south, and according to the New York Times, blacks sniffed cocaine instead. Reports of black men with super-human strength seducing white women became common in the media.[110]

These fears led to the Harrison Act in 1914, meant to impose a system of taxes on opium and coca products by controlling distribution.[111]

Surprisingly, during this time caffeine was considered a "poisonous" substance, and the US government took the Coca-Cola Company to court under the Pure Food and Drug Act. Coca-Cola Co. won, arguing caffeine was a naturally occurring substance. According to the lawsuit papers, by this time (1916), the cocaine alkaloids were removed from the formula.[112]

The battle for alcohol prohibition continued, and by 1920, the Eighteenth Amendment was in full effect. The black market exploded, violent crime skyrocketed, and jazz babies in the twenties roared on bathtub gin and the prohibition economy. For the first time in US history, American women frequented the places where alcohol was served; prior to prohibition, saloons were for men and prostitutes; Irish and Eastern European women were seen in family-oriented pubs. Now, the only option was the speak-easy, and adventurous young women of the jazz age couldn't help but check out its forbidden fruit.

As crime and violence spread and the Great Depression put the country in a strangle hold, the Women's Organization for National Prohibition Reform (WONPR) waged a vigorous campaign for the repeal of the Eighteenth Amendment. American-born Irish and German women, whose cultures tolerated alcohol in a way unfamiliar to puritanical American lineage, organized with the WONPR. They distributed propaganda declaring "Prohibition Failed!" and "For Your Children's Sake—Repeal Prohibition!" By December 1933, the failure was clear, and ratification of the repeal amendment passed in just 9 months and with more than 70% of the electoral vote—more quickly and by a larger margin than any other amendment.[113]

Alas, the weed of the War on Drugs continued to grow. In 1937, Congress passed the Marijuana Tax Act, which required anyone who possessed or sold marijuana to have a tax stamp. The government never issued any, refusing to do so.[114] This act was spearheaded by Harry Anslinger, and was preceded by decades of anti-marijuana and anti-Mexican propaganda. Fear of Mexicans taking jobs for

low wages and fear of them mingling with white women underscored much of the panic surrounding the plant.[115]

Previously, in the southwestern parts of the US, Mexicans were using marijuana recreationally, and by 1914, El Paso had an ordinance outlawing the possession or sale of marijuana.[116] Like the opium laws, the ordinance was not aimed at the plant, but at the class of people who used it—this time, Mexicans. A Texas policeman described the problem:

> "They [Mexicans] seem to have no fear, I have also noted that under the influence of this weed they have enormous strength and that it will take several men to handle one man while under ordinary circumstances one man could handle him with ease."[117]

About this time, Pancho Villa, the Mexican hero, was an aggravation to the US, and troops were sent into Mexico to capture him. Villa had failed to take US land when he launched attacks on the US, and the US failed to capture Villa. However, Villa's troops sang a battle song that lives in the US to this day:

> "La cucaracha, la cucaracha Ya no puede caminar Porque no tiene, porque no tiene Marihuana que fumar."[118]

Translated: "The cockroach, the cockroach, he can't walk, because he has no, because he has no, marijuana to smoke."

By 1915, California passed the first anti-marijuana law. Shortly thereafter, nearly every southwestern state followed suit by 1927: Utah, Wyoming, Texas, Iowa, Nevada, Oregon, Washington, Arkansas, and Nebraska.[119]

Though a very small portion of the US population used marijuana, fear of the plant spread with anti-Mexican sentiment. Thus began the series of laws made to control marijuana consumption.

However, hemp continued to be legal through World War II. The government needed hemp for rope, and the Department of Agriculture encouraged its cultivation.[120]

Fiorello LaGuardia, the great New York City politician, attempted to inject sanity in the spreading paranoia of the plant, with the 1944 LaGuardia Report. He commissioned the study, which to this day is considered one of the most thorough and accurate studies on marijuana. It found that "Smoking marihuana [sic] does not lead to addiction… does not lead to morphine, heroin, or cocaine addiction" and that "the publicity concerning the catastrophic effects of marihuana smoking in New York City is unfounded."[121] It gained little attention, as Harry Anslinger released his propaganda report days earlier, utilizing the same type-set, colors, and style as the LaGuardia Report.

Over the next several decades, the US government grew, and more and more laws were created dictating what drugs could be used and how, and mandating punishment for everyone from drug "criminals" to doctors writing prescriptions that the government didn't deem necessary. Laws were established prohibiting the cultivation of poppy with out a license (1942 Opium Poppy Control Act), setting mandatory sentences for drug law violations (the 1951 Boggs Amendment), and controlling synthetic drugs like LSD (Drug Abuse Control Amendments of 1965.) The 1970 Comprehensive Drug Abuse Control Act (the Controlled Substances Act) consolidated all previous laws, and eliminated the loop-holes in the law that were throw backs to the early 20th Century tax acts. Federal agencies were created, including the Bureau of Narcotics and Dangerous Drugs (later to become the Drug Enforcement Administration) and the Alcohol, Drug Abuse, and Mental Health Administration.

The weed of the War on Drugs was almost ready to bloom when Richard Nixon took office. President Nixon insisted more than 50% of all crime was caused by drugs and declared drug abuse public enemy number one.[122] During his administration, the Racketeering Influenced and Corrupt Organizations Act (RICO laws, the groundwork of asset forfeiture) was passed. DuPont Pharmaceuticals was granted $7.5 million a year for methadone maintenance programs.[123] All federal drug-enforcement authority finally lay entirely with the Justice Department—a feat that took years of manipulating checks and balances. Under the 1970 Controlled Substances Act, drugs began

to be "scheduled" by the Attorney General—not the doctors at the Food and Drug Administration. Nixon even experimented with practically closing the Mexican border to stop the influx of marijuana during "Operation Intercept."[124] Wiretap laws weakened personal liberties, and no-knock warrants were thoughtfully considered. Society was pepper-sprayed with more and more anti-drug propaganda, discretely presented in television shows like General Hospital[125] and advertised in anti-drug campaigns and literature. The War on Drugs was being fertilized.

However, the Carter administration temporarily stunted the war's growth, as eleven states decriminalized marijuana during his presidency, including New York and California. But then there was a scandal: His lead drug policy advisor, Dr. Peter Bourne, was publicly smeared for writing unnecessary prescriptions, and then for using cocaine.[126] Carter, suddenly, had to look tough on drugs, and the brief glimmer of hope that drug laws could be reformed was extinguished.

Nothing though, could compare with Ronald Reagan's fight against drugs. On June 24, 1982, Reagan appropriated federal monies for an umbrella department to oversee all drug control operations: the Drug Abuse Policy Office, later to become the Office of National Drug Control Policy. In his speech to the nation that day, he commended his wife Nancy for her work in regards to "treatment" of drug users, and promised that then-Vice President George Bush, via the South Florida Task Force, would "keep the pressure on that part of the country most vulnerable to drug smuggling." Reagan than announced:

> "We're rejecting the helpless attitude that drug use is so rampant that we're defenseless to do anything about it. We're taking down the surrender flag that has flown over so many drug efforts; we're running up a battle flag. We can fight the drug problem, and we can win. And that is exactly what we intend to do."[127]

While hardly a declaration of war, it preceded Reagan's radio address from Camp David, on October 2, 1982:

> "Now, for the very first time, the Federal Government is waging a planned, concerted campaign.
>
> Previous administrations had drug strategies, but they didn't have the structure to carry them out. We now have that structure.
>
> In addition to the enforcement element, our strategy will also focus on international cooperation, education, and prevention—which Nancy's very interested in—detoxification and treatment and research.
>
> The mood toward drugs is changing in this country, and the momentum is with us. We're making no excuses for drugs—hard, soft, or otherwise. Drugs are bad, and we're going after them. As I've said before, we've taken down the surrender flag and run up the battle flag. And we're going to win the war on drugs.
>
> Till next week, thanks for listening, and God bless you."

This was Reagan's first public declaration of War on Drugs. (Many experts contend Nixon declared the war on drugs; however, this writer did not find any evidence that he ever used the phrase publicly. He made drug abuse "public enemy number one," but he never said "war on drugs"—two very different statements. Nixon helped lay the foundation for the announcement that was to come from Reagan.) The weed blossomed into the poisonous plant we have today growing out of control across the globe.

Today, the US has a prison population exceeding 2.1 million people; the majority of people convicted of drug offenses are black or Hispanic men; racial profiling is a common practice among police departments; children are put into illicit-drug education programs, yet they're forced to take pharmaceutical drugs; teenagers are forced into "treatment"; those who suffer from chronic pain don't have access to proper pain medication; corruption and violence are rampant in our society; the economy is skewed by the illegal drug market and the legal industry established to keep it underground. Families are torn apart. Civil liberties no longer exist. The effects of the War go on and on, transcending what is presented here—piercing the heart of our nation.

I've written a brief history of the roots of the War on Drugs here; together, we must all write its ending.

End Notes

[1] King James I, 1604, *A Counterblaste to Tobacco;* David Moyer, *The Tobacco Reference Guide.*

[2] Library of Congress, *Thomas Jefferson Papers:* Virginia Records Timeline (information on Virginia and tobacco).

[3] Victor S. Clark, *History of Manufactures in the United States* Volume I: 1607-1860 W. Farnam. (New York, 1959).

[4] Alfred W. Crosby, Jr. *America, Russia, Hemp, and Napoleon - American Trade with Russia and the Baltic, 1783 – 1812* (Ohio State University Press, 1965).

[5] *New Advent Catholic Encyclopedia:* Temperance Movements (early Temperance information).

[6] Benjamin Franklin, 1791, *The Autobiography of Benjamin Franklin,* (Barnes and Noble Books, 1994).

[7] *New Advent Catholic Encyclopedia:* Temperance Movements.

[8] National Park Service, Friendship Hill.

[9] Sarah Stage, *Female Complaints: Lydia Pinkham and the Business of Women's Medicine,* (WW Norton and Company, Inc. 1979) (information on early medical practices, patent medicine, vegetable compounds, homeopathy, etc.)

[10] Schaffer Library of Drug Policy, Summary of Historical Events.

[11] Kenneth D. Rose, *American Women and the Repeal of Prohibition,* (New York University Press, 1996).

[12] Susan B. Anthony House, Biography of Susan B. Anthony.

[13] Sarah Stage, *Female Complaints: Lydia Pinkham and the Business of Women's Medicine,* (WW Norton and Company, Inc. 1979).

[14] Schaffer Library of Drug Policy, Summary of Historical Events.

[15] Joseph F. Spillane, *Modern Drug, Modern Menace: The Legal Use and Distribution of Cocaine in the United States, 1880-1920.*

[16] Edward M. Brecher and the Editors of Consumer Reports Magazine, *The Consumers Union Report on Licit and Illicit Drugs,* (1972).

[17] Sarah Stage, *Female Complaints: Lydia Pinkham and the Business of Women's Medicine*, (WW Norton and Company, Inc. 1979).

[18] Edward M. Brecher and the Editors of Consumer Reports Magazine, *The Consumers Union Report on Licit and Illicit Drugs*, (1972).

[19] ibid.

[20] ibid.

[21] *Life* magazine, May, 1984.

[22] Joseph F. Spillane, *Modern Drug, Modern Menace: The Legal Use and Distribution of Cocaine in the United States, 1880-1920*.

[23] Lester Grinspoon and James B. Bakalar, *Medical Uses of Illicit Drugs*, Schaffer Library of Drug Policy.

[24] Library of Congress: *Coca-Cola Television Advertising*.

[25] Schaffer Library of Drug Policy, History of Tobacco Regulation.

[26] Edward M. Brecher and the Editors of Consumer Reports Magazine, *The Consumers Union Report on Licit and Illicit Drugs*, 1972.

[27] ibid.

[28] ibid.

[29] Thomas Szasz, *Our Right To Drugs*, (Praeger Publishers, NY 1992).

[30] Edward M. Brecher and the Editors of Consumer Reports Magazine, *The Consumers Union Report on Licit and Illicit Drugs*, 1972.

[31] Schaffer Library of Drug Policy, The History of the Drug Laws.

[32] Kenneth D. Rose, *American Women and the Repeal of Prohibition*, (New York University Press, 1996).

[33] ibid.

[34] Edward M. Brecher and the Editors of Consumer Reports Magazine, *The Consumers Union Report on Licit and Illicit Drugs*, 1972.

[35] *United States v. Coca Cola Company of Atlanta*, Error to the Circuit Court of Appeals for the Sixth Circuit (courtesy Schaffer Library of Drug Policy).

[36] Kenneth D. Rose, *American Women and the Repeal of Prohibition*, (New York University Press, 1996).

[37] *The Marihuana Tax Act of 1937*, Schaffer Library of Drug Policy.

[38] ibid.

[39] Schaffer Library of Drug Policy.

[40] ibid.

[41] ibid.

[42] ibid.

[43] ibid.

[44] The La Guardia Committee Report, *The Marihuana Problem in the City of New York, Mayor's Committee on Marihuana* (New York Academy of Medicine, City of New York, 1944).

[45] Richard Reeves, *President Nixon Alone in the White House*, (Simon and Schuster, 2001).

[46] Painter, Plott, et al. *The National Drug Policies of the United States and the United Kingdom: A Study of Policy Process and Divergent National Perspectives*, April 28, 1998.

[47] Richard Reeves, *President Nixon Alone in the White House*, (Simon and Schuster, 2001).

[48] ibid.

[49] Dan Baum, *Smoke and Mirrors, The War on Drugs and the Politics of Failure*, (Little, Brown, and Company, Canada, 1996).

[50] *The Public Papers of Ronadl Reagan*, Ronald Reagan Presidential Library, University of Texas

[51] ibid.

Oliver North: Still in Denial

Preston Peet

Former US Marine Lieutenant Colonel Oliver North appeared on the FOX network's news program *Hannity and Colmes* on February 25, 2004 and boldly declared, "The fact is nobody in the government of the United States, going all the way back to the earliest days of this under Jimmy Carter, ever had anything to do with running drugs to support the Nicaraguan resistance. Nobody in the government of the United States. I will stand on that to my grave."

North was responding to statements by US Senator and Presidential candidate John Kerry (D-Massachusetts), published on his campaign website, that in the 1980s Sen. Kerry had helped hold Oliver North "accountable" for his

> NORTH WAS NEVER TRIED NOR EVEN CHARGED WITH DRUG TRAFFICKING, EVEN THOUGH HE ENABLED THE TRAFFICKING OF LITERALLY TONS OF DRUGS INTO THE UNITED STATES WHILE THE US WAS BUSY RATCHETING UP THE DOMESTIC WAR ON SOME DRUGS AND USERS.

actions while illegally assisting the Nicaraguan Contras wage their war. North told hosts Sean Hannity and Alan Colmes that Kerry was "wrong," that Kerry "makes this stuff up and then he can't justify it," specifically talking about the December, 1988 report titled *Drugs, Law Enforcement and Foreign Policy*, prepared and released by the Senate Subcommittee on Terrorism, Narcotics and International Operations, chaired by Sen. Kerry. The Kerry Committee investigated allegations that North, hired to work in President Ronald Reagan's National Security Council in 1981, and compatriots in the NSC had been funding, arming and training the Contras in contravention of the Boland Agreement, which banned military assistance to the Contras, in part by illegally selling missiles to Iran and using the proceeds to fund the Contra war, and in part by working with known drug traffickers in Contra supply operations.

"Oliver North was indicted in March 1988 on sixteen Iran-Contra charges," reported former DEA agent and decorated veteran Celerino Castillo in a March 8, 2003 article for ReconsiDer.org, protesting an appearance by North at a Salvation Army fundraising event near Castillo's home in Texas. "After deliberating for 64 hours over a twelve day period, the jury on May 6, 1989 returned a verdict of guilty on three counts which

included: (1) aiding and abetting obstruction of Congress, (2) shredding and altering official documents, and (3) accepting an illegal gratuity from General Richard V. Secord. Judge Gesell sentenced North on July 05, 1989 to two years probation, $150,000 in fines and 1,200 hours community service....North's convictions were vacated on July 20, 1990 after the appeals court found that witnesses in his trial might have been impermissibly affected by his immunized congressional testimony." In other words, North was convicted of some charges, such as shredding much of the evidence, but got off on a technicality. North was never tried nor even charged with drug trafficking, even though he enabled the trafficking of literally tons of drugs into the United States while the US was busy ratcheting up the domestic War on Some Drugs and Users (North is barred from ever entering Costa Rica due to drug trafficking charges, along with Gen. Secord, then-National Security Advisor Admiral John Poindexter, then-CIA Station Chief Joseph Fernandez, and former US Ambassador to Costa Rica Lewis Tambs, by order of the Noble Peace Prize Laureate and then-President of Costa Rica Oscar Arias.)

The actions Sen. Kerry is proud of investigating and subsequently holding North accountable for never included any allegations that North or anyone else in the US government was directly dealing or trafficking drugs (although there are numerous instances on public record of active CIA agents, not merely assets, trafficking drugs into the US, just not in the Kerry Report), or directly using drug proceeds to fund the Contra war, only that North and others had not reported allegations and knowledge of drug running by certain Contra supporters and US government and intelligence assets.

The Kerry Report describes one instance in which North directly intervened to help obtain a lenient prison sentence at Eglin Air Force Base federal prison camp in Florida for former Honduran general José Bueso Rosa,

> THE US JUSTICE DEPARTMENT CALLED THE BUESO ROSA CASE THE "MOST SIGNIFICANT CASE OF NARCO-TERRORISM YET DISCOVERED"

buying Bueso's silence about NSC-supported illegal covert Contra supply missions Bueso had been involved with.

The US Justice Department called the Bueso Rosa case the "most significant case of narco-terrorism yet discovered," as Bueso had been plotting to use the proceeds from a 345 pound cocaine shipment estimated by federal agents to be worth $40 million, intercepted on October 28, 1984 in Florida by the FBI, to assassinate Honduran President Roberto Suazo Córdoba.

North also claimed in an email message to Admiral John Poindexter on August 23, 1986, to have a "fairly good relationship" with Panamanian President and friend to drug traffickers Manual Noriega, when urging that the US government work to help repair Noriega's image in the US press. Poindexter wrote back, saying he had nothing against Noriega except for his "illegal activities." The *New York Times* had already at that point exposed Noriega's extensive ties to international drug trafficking. Unfazed by these reports, North still wanted to pay Noriega $1 million out of "Project Democracy" money, raised from the illegal sale of US arms to Iran, to enlist Noriega's help in sabotaging Sandinista facilities.

The Subcommittee report, also known as the Kerry Committee Report, lists on pages 146-147, fifteen entries from notebooks filled with Oliver North's own handwriting, detailing drug connections to operations which were supporting the Contras. These included references to arms in Honduras intended for the Contras which had initially been financed with $14 million in drug profits, according to a message from Secord to North, and direct knowledge of planes flying supplies south to the Contras that were returning to the US full of drugs. "Numerous other entries contain references to individuals or events which Subcommittee staff has determined have relevance to narcotics, terrorism or international operations," notes the Kerry Report, "but whose ambiguities cannot be resolved without the production of the deleted materials by North and his attorneys. Accordingly, the Subcommittee continues to believe that the production of the deleted material could shed important light on a number of issues in connections with foreign policy, law enforcement and narcotics and terrorism." The fifteen surviving entries taken directly from North's diaries and listed by the Kerry Report, as transcribed by the National Security Archive, an extensive online repository of declassified US government documents, are as follows:

> **May 12, 1984**...contract indicates that Gustavo is involved w/ drugs. (Q0266)
>
> **June 26, 1984**. DEA—(followed by two blocks of text deleted by North) (Q0349)
>
> **June 27, 1984**. Drug Case—DEA program on controlling cocaine—Ether cutoff—Colombians readjusting—possible negotiations to move on refining effort to Nicaragua—Pablo Escobar—Colombian drug czar—Informant (Pilot) is indicted criminal—Carlos Ledher—Freddy Vaughn (Q0354)

> **July 9, 1984**. [NOTE: Portions transcribed in Kerry Report but deleted from declassified version] Call from Clarridge—Call Michel re Narco Issue—RIG at 1000 Tomorrow (Q0384)—DEA Miami—Pilot went talked to Vaughn—wanted A/C to go to Bolivia to p/u paste—want A/C to p/u 1500 kilos—Bud to meet w/ Group (Q0385)
>
> **July 12, 1984**. [NOTE: Portions transcribed in Kerry Report but deleted from declassified version] Gen. Gorman-*Include Drug Case (Q0400) Call from Johnstone—(White House deletion) leak on Drug (0402)
>
> **July 17, 1984**. Call to Frank M- Bud Mullins Re—leak on DEA piece—Carlton Turner (Q0418) Call from Johnstone—McManus, LA Times—says/NSC source claims W.H. has pictures of Borge loading cocaine in Nic. (Q0416)
>
> **July 20, 1984**. Call from Clarridge:—Alfredo Cesar Re Drugs-Borge/Owen leave Hull alone (Deletions)/Los Brasiles Air Field—Owen off Hull (Q0426)
>
> **July 27, 1984**. Clarridge:—(Block of White House deleted text follows)-Arturo Cruz, Jr.—Get Alfredo Cesar on Drugs (Q0450)
>
> **July 31, 1984**.-Finance: Libya—Cuba/Bloc Countries - Drugs. . . Pablo Escobar/Federic Vaughn (Q0460)
>
> **July 31, 1984**. [NOTE: Portions transcribed in Kerry Report but deleted from declassified version] Staff queries re (White House deletion) role in DEA operations in Nicaragua (Q0461)
>
> **December 21, 1984**. Call from Clarridge: Ferch (White House deletion)—Tambs—Costa Rica—Felix Rodriguez close to (White House deletion)—not assoc. W/Villoldo- Bay of Pigs—No drugs (Q0922)
>
> **January 14, 1985**. $14 million to finance came from drugs (Q1039)
>
> **July 12, 1985**. $14 million to finance came from drugs
>
> **August 10, 1985**. Mtg w/A.C.—name of DEA person in New Orleans re Bust on Mario/ DC-6 (Q1140)
>
> **February 27, 1986**. Mtg w/ Lew Tambs- DEA Auction A/C seized as drug runners.—$250-260K fee (Q2027)

One might wonder what relevance these events of some twenty years ago and more have today, or why anyone who is against the whole idea of a War on Some Drugs and Users should be bothered in the first place by officially sanctioned drug trafficking. It isn't the officially sanctioned drug running itself that is particularly galling—it's the fact that millions of people's lives were turned into living hell for daring to buy and use the very drugs that the US

> "PEOPLE LIKE OLIVER NORTH THINK THEY CAN READILY GET AWAY WITH MAKING INACCURATE STATEMENTS BUT LUCKILY WE DO HAVE THE DOCUMENTATION WHICH IS WHY WE GET IT UP THERE, SO PEOPLE CAN SEE THE RECORD FOR THEMSELVES."

government, through it's assets, agents and officials like Oliver North, were busy assuring entered (and still enter as a result of other ongoing intelligence and military operations around the world) the US by the ton.

There's also the whole troubling aspect of the current War on Terror and the variety of ties North had to many bloodthirsty, murderous terrorists and countries that support them, including Iran. North wrote in an online column, February 20, 2004, again reacting to the Kerry Campaign website, that his detractors "may even cite some subcommittee hearings that Kerry held months after the close of the official investigation. His little witch hunt eventually did publish a report that was so incredibly biased as to give the word 'slander' an inadequate definition." It's a bit of a mystery that North can make this sort of comment when the Kerry Report is full of North's own diary notations, explicitly outlining a variety of drug connections to what he was doing, connections and allegations involving assets and supporters of the Contras of which he was aware yet never once reported to any proper US law enforcement authorities.

"A lot of people make a lot false statements and inaccurate statements, and statements full of BS on these shows," says Peter Kornbluh, a senior analyst at the National Security Archive and editor of *The Iran-Contra Scandal— the Declassified History*. "Oliver North is not known for his veracity, accuracy, or frankly his honesty. One of the reasons that my organization [National Security Archive] exists is that there isn't a lot of institutional memory in this town or in this country. There isn't a real clear focus on history. People like Oliver North think they can readily get away with making inaccurate statements but luckily we do have the documentation which is why we get it up there, so people can see the record for themselves." Kornbluh is very careful to point out that, in his opinion, the US government was not directly involved in trafficking drugs nor funding the Contra war with drug proceeds. "You have to be careful with your language. You don't want to be inaccurate like [North] is. The United States government was not itself involved in trafficking drugs. The Contra war was not a situation where drug smuggling

was financing the war. What was happening was that we were working with drug smugglers and knew that they were smuggling drugs but really didn't care in the grand scheme of things because what was more important was to kill lots of Sandinista and Nicaraguan peasants, and wage the paramilitary war in Central America." Kornbluh disputes that notion that the Contras needed or used drug funds to support their war, but says "it doesn't really make any difference. It doesn't make it any less reprehensible that the US government collaborated with drug smugglers because they had some contribution to make to the Contra war and allowed their drug smuggling to go forward. Oliver North tried to get a Honduran general [Bueso] off the hook and out of jail in the US because he was less worried about a very high level drug smuggler going to prison than he was about the guy actually turning around and spilling the beans about what was going on. That in my mind is just as criminal. A lot of people thought that there was some need to have drug smuggling money in the pot. There really never was a need."

Castillo, the only DEA officer on the ground in El Salvador while NSC and CIA-run hangers 4 and 5 at Illopango Airfield were being used in Contra supply operations and for drug smuggling, points out that the person sitting behind the wheel of the getaway car outside the bank is just as guilty and is charged the same as the people who

> YOU CAN BE HISTORICALLY ACCURATE AND STILL COME OUT WITH THE SAME DARK, UGLY PICTURE OF THE ACTIVITIES INVOLVING OLIVER NORTH AND RICHARD SECORD, AND ADMIRAL JOHN POINDEXTER AND OTHERS.

go inside with the guns. "It's not," Kornbluh says when it's pointed out that it seems a bit like semantics to assert that because North did not have his hands on the drugs, neither he nor any other US officials were involved in drug trafficking. "It's just being historically accurate. You can be historically accurate and still come out with the same dark, ugly picture of the activities involving Oliver North and Richard Secord, and Admiral John Poindexter and others. The drug smugglers thought they were gaining protection by being part of the CIA operation as well. You had one guy, the country's largest marijuana smuggler, Michael Palmer, a pilot for the humanitarian aid side [of the Contra support operations] in 1986, but who had already been indicted for smuggling huge quantities of marijuana, for distribution and trafficking, at the time he was still flying—and being paid with US government tax dollars I might add. If you just stick to the history you already have a dark enough picture."

"Our stories focused more on the elements of the Contras running drugs. I don't think we ever specifically alleged that US officials ran drugs," says Robert Parry, author of *Lost History—Contras, Cocaine, The Press and Project Truth*, who in the 1980s while writing for the *Associated*

Press wrote the first mainstream press articles about Oliver North's secret Contra-supply network and about Contra cocaine trafficking allegations. Parry thinks that North was perhaps setting up a straw man argument by stating that "Nobody in the government of the United States" was using drug money to support the Contras' war. "North may be making a fairly narrow point [in his comments on the *Hannity and Colmes* show], and I can't recall Kerry ever alleging that any specific US officials ran drugs. I think the issue was really that elements of the Contras were implicated and the strongest criticism of people in the US government was they didn't act as aggressively as they should have to stop it because of political and national security concerns. This was the point that hooked up the *San Jose Mercury News* [which published Gary Webb's *Dark Alliance* series in August 1996, outlining certain CIA assets' ties to the crack explosion in the United States, and got blasted in much of the US mainstream press for publishing it] for quite a while. The game often is to overstate what people have alleged then knock it down. I think that the allegations have been that the US government looked the other way as regards the evidence for whatever reasons or tried to discredit witnesses when someone came forward. In those kinds of instances I guess you could say they aided and abetted. I don't think the allegations were made that people in the US government brought the drugs in or sold them on the streets. This was the parody of Gary Webb's story, that the CIA was standing on street corners in Los Angeles slinging the crack cocaine. He never said that and no one did as far as I can tell, but this became the straw man that everyone knocked down. It does sound like he's [North] maybe somewhat exaggerating Kerry's position then giving a fairly narrow response to the exaggeration."

Despite these nuances, there is no denying that Oliver North knew that some of his assets were trafficking tons of drugs into the United States while there was a very

OLIVER NORTH IS "A CHRONIC LIAR."

"WHAT THE HELL WAS THIS GUY, THIS TERRORIST WHO BLEW UP A CUBAN CIVILIAN AIRLINER FULL OF CIVILIANS IN THE 1970S, DOING WORKING FOR THE US GOVERNMENT AT HANGERS 4 AND 5 AT ILLOPANGO AIRBASE?"

expensive and deadly serious War Against Some Drugs and Users going on and getting hotter. There's no two ways about it—by allowing his assets and associates to engage in such serious and widespread trafficking, North himself was involved in that drug trafficking, especially since there is no record anywhere of his reporting these allegations to any law enforcement agencies at all. There are plenty of people currently incarcerated inside US prisons on drug conspiracy charges, charges which stem solely from their not having informed law enforcement officials of their personal knowledge of ongoing drug trafficking. These people are no more guilty of explicitly trafficking in drugs than North is, in many cases much less.

Oliver North is "a chronic liar," Castillo emphatically states, hotly disagreeing with the notion that there was never any US government involvement in drug trafficking, especially during the Contra war. "It has been proven time and time again that several arms of the United States government were involved in sleeping with the cartels, specifically during the 1980s. The CIA's final Contra report [The Hitz Report, released in two volumes, in January and October, 1998] indicates and confirmed that assets for the CIA were in fact involved in drug trafficking. The Kerry Committee also confirmed that many of the assets were heavily involved. One thing very important to keep in mind is I have the case files. I have the names, and NADDIS numbers of all the traffickers that were involved in the Iran-Contra investigation, many of whom were documented as drug traffickers by other US government law enforcement agencies long before I documented them. These were all people who worked with Oliver North, mainly out of Illopango (the airbase in El Salvador out of which North and the CIA both ran Contra support operations)." Castillo is also bothered by North's connections to genuine terrorists working for the US government's Contra operations. "There's Luis Posada Carriles, the Cuban long-time CIA asset who was working for North at Illopango. He was working with ["former" CIA agent and assassin of Che Guevara] Felix Rodriguez. What the hell was this guy, this terrorist who blew up a Cuban civilian airliner full of civilians in the 1970s, doing working for the US government at Hangers 4 and 5 at Illopango Airbase?"

In a just world, Oliver North would be doing prison time (or rather, non-violent citizens doing time for drugs wouldn't be). It is disheartening that he is able to get away with statements such as he made on *Hannity and Colmes* and elsewhere when so many US citizens have served and are now serving time for using, buying and selling the very same drugs he helped insure made it into the US Whether or not Oliver North or anyone else in the US government ever sat down and plotted to sell drugs is almost irrelevant in this case. The fact remains that there were US officials, agents, politicians and assets who all knew the trafficking was happening but did nothing to stop it, or worse actively participated in the trade and protected the traffickers from law enforcement. The CIA went so far as to institute a Memorandum of Understanding in March 1982 with the US Department of Justice that explicitly allowed the CIA to NOT report drug trafficking by CIA agents and other US government assets and "non" agents. The MOU exempted them from an Executive Order (E.O. 12333) signed by President Reagan in 1981 requiring any US officials to report drug trafficking by US employees. By changing the classification of thousands of agents to non-agents, or asset status, the CIA and others, like North, are able to claim it wasn't actually US government employees who were trafficking, but rather merely private entrepreneurs who took advantage of their covert status to line their pockets while helping the Contras.

The disturbing fact is that certain US government, military and intelligence factions have and will continue working with drug traffickers around the globe, as is the situation today in Afghanistan. There US military and intelligence forces are on the ground working with Northern Alliance warlords, who have replanted poppies and are churning out record crop sizes since US forces went in to Afghanistan, completely reversing the Taliban's near complete extermination of Afghanistan's poppies. US Deputy Secretary of State Richard Armitage recently told the September 11 Commission that prior to September 11, the US could not openly work with the Northern Alliance due to certain pesky details, like their drug trafficking, but since September 11 the US government has been able to work around those details. This obviously doesn't mean the Northern Alliance has stopped growing poppies, just that political considerations allow the US government to once again turn a blind eye to massive drug trafficking by their allies. There's nothing inherently wrong with poppies nor any other currently illegal drugs, nor with the trafficking of these drugs, but so long as there is a US taxpayer-funded War on Some Drugs and Users underway, US officials, including the FOX-employed Oliver North, should not be allowed to ally themselves with, nor profit in any way from the illegal drug trade, since the drug using citizenry in the United States has to pay for those alliances and profits with their blood and their very lives.

Preston Peet

How Rock 'n' Roll fell out of Love with Drugs

Alan Travis and Sally James Gregory

Young musicians today are more likely than those of previous generations to decry the harm that drugs can cause, according to research in America.

The study, based on an analysis of drug lyrics in English-language popular music since the 1960s, was last week highlighted as one of the few pieces of good news in the annual survey by the European monitoring center for drugs and drug addiction, the EU's drugs agency.

The research, published by the University of Texas at Austin, explodes the conventional wisdom that popular music encourages teenagers to abuse drugs. The author, John Markert of Cumberland University, Tennessee, says that although there has always been a generally hostile

> SONGS DEALING WITH ILLEGAL DRUGS HAVE ALWAYS DOTTED POPULAR MUSIC. IN THE 1930S, FATS WALLER DREAMED ABOUT A FIVE-FOOT JOINT IN *VIPER'S DRAG*, AND HARRY "THE HIPSTER" GIBSON POSED THE QUESTION: "WHO PUT THE BENZEDRINE IN MRS. MURPHY'S OVALTINE?"

attitude towards heroin and other hard drugs, teenage listeners today "are being exposed to more negative images of marijuana and LSD than older listeners."

The research comes as MPs are preparing to vote to approve the reclassification of cannabis. Songs dealing with illegal drugs have always dotted popular music. In the 1930s, Fats Waller dreamed about a five foot joint in *Viper's Drag*, and Harry "the Hipster" Gibson posed the question: "Who put the benzedrine in Mrs. Murphy's Ovaltine?" But it was not until the 1960s that it became a constant theme.

Mr. Markert's study, *Sing a Song of Drug Use-Abuse*, is based on analysis of 784 songs since the 1960s that explicitly mention an illegal substance. It shows that while heroin and cocaine have largely been treated with hostility by musicians, their attitude towards cannabis and LSD has changed sharply over the years. Mr. Markert found 100 songs with lyrics about heroin, more than half from the 1990s. But whether it is Lou Reed's "It's my wife, it's my life" from the song *Heroin*, Neil Young's "I watched the needle take another man" from *The Needle and the Damage Done*, or Pearl Jam's "It's my blood" from *Blood*, they demonstrate an increasingly hostile attitude in the 1990s.

Nearly twice as many songs deal with cocaine and they are also generally negative. Some from the 1960s and 1970s such as "She don't lie, she don't lie, cocaine," from Eric Clapton's version of JJ Cale's *Cocaine*, and the Grateful Dead's "Drivin' that train, high on cocaine," are hardly negative. But by the 1990s the attitude is far more trenchant with rap music presenting cocaine, particularly crack, as a loser drug.

Prince's 1990 *New Power Generation* is typical: "Cocaine was the thing that I took on... I was headed 4 the kill, steal, destroy, and die." But the research argues that there has been a much bigger shift in attitudes towards marijuana and LSD, and musicians use their hostility to drugs to attack the older generation. Mr. Markert says that while Jimi Hendrix's *Purple Haze* personified 1960s acid rock, four-fifths of the songs that explicitly mention LSD are post 1980 and overwhelmingly hostile.

"Contemporary young people view LSD as the drug of older, screwed-up middle-aged people," he says. The majority of the songs in the sample are about cannabis and generally take a positive approach, although the more recent songs are more equivocal. Few 1960s songs explicitly mention marijuana, mainly because they would have been banned from radio. The veteran country singer Willie Nelson produced a platinum-selling album, *Hempilation*, in 1995 singing the praises of cannabis.

In the 90s, several over 30s musicians, such as JJ Cale, Tom Petty, and Sheryl Crow, released albums that lauded marijuana and were geared to an older, more marijuana accepting audience. They contrast sharply with the message from Biohazard's 1994 *Failed Territory*—"another neighborhood gets destroyed by the drug deal"—which

> THE RESEARCH ARGUES THAT THERE HAS BEEN A MUCH BIGGER SHIFT IN ATTITUDES TOWARDS MARIJUANA AND LSD, AND MUSICIANS USE THEIR HOSTILITY TO DRUGS TO ATTACK THE OLDER GENERATION.

attacks the systemic problem associated with drug use and is shared by nearly half of the 1990s songs analyzed by Mr. Markert.

"1990s music such as Biohazard's sees nothing good with dope. Drugs are bad; there is no equivocation, no okay drugs such as marijuana or LSD and many of them link cannabis to other drugs such as cocaine as a gateway drug."

"1990S MUSIC SUCH AS BIOHAZARD'S SEES NOTHING GOOD WITH DOPE. DRUGS ARE BAD; THERE IS NO EQUIVOCATION, NO OKAY DRUGS SUCH AS MARIJUANA OR LSD AND MANY OF THEM LINK CANNABIS TO OTHER DRUGS SUCH AS COCAINE AS A GATEWAY DRUG."

How rock'n'roll fell out of love with drugs

1960s

"Puff, the magic dragon, lived by the sea
And frolicked in the autumn mist in a land called Honalee."
Peter, Paul and Mary, *Puff The Magic Dragon*, 1963

"Everybody must get stoned."
Bob Dylan, *Rainy Day Women #13 & 35*, 1966

"One pill makes you larger
And one pill makes you small,
And the ones that mother gives you
Don't do anything at all.
Go ask Alice
When she's 10 feet tall."
Jefferson Airplane, *White Rabbit*, 1967

"Picture yourself in a boat on a river
With tangerine trees and marmalade skies
Somebody calls you, you answer quite slowly,
A girl with kaleidoscope eyes."
The Beatles, *Lucy in the Sky with Diamonds*, 1967

"When I put a spike into my vein
And I'll tell ya, things aren't quite the same
When I'm rushing on my run
And I feel just like Jesus' son
And I guess that I just don't know."
Velvet Underground and Nico, *Heroin*, 1967

1970s

"I hit the city and I lost my band
I watched the needle take another man
Gone. The damage done."
Neil Young, *The Needle and the Damage Done*, 1972

"If you wanna hang out, you gotta take her out, cocaine
If you wanna get down, get down on the ground, cocaine
"She's all right, She's all right, She's all right."
Eric Clapton, *Cocaine*, 1977

1980s

"Pass the dutchie from the left hand side."
Musical Youth, *Pass the Dutchie*, 1984

"Your daddy works in porno
Now that mommy's not around.
She used to love her Heroin
But now she's underground."
Guns N' Roses, *My Michelle*, 1987

1990s

"But that's okay 'cos we're all sorted out for E's & wizz
And tell me when the spaceship lands 'cos all this has just got to mean something."
Pulp, *Sorted for E's & Wizz*, 1995

"I'm on crack
I'm doing lines all the time
John Belushi was a friend of mine
Can't relate, I'm losin weight
Grinding my jaw, breaking the law
Stealing tens and twenties from my ma and pa."
Dickies, *I'm On Crack*, 1995

"Sun so bright that I'm nearly
Blind Cool cos I'm wired and I'm out of my mind
Warms the dope running down my spine
But I don't care 'bout you and I've got nothing to do."
Spiritualized, *Ladies and Gentlemen We Are Floating*, 1997

"You're living life fucked-up every single day
And now I can't remember the last time you were straight
You're a joke but no one's laughing any more."
White Town, *Peek and Poke*, 2000

For Medicinal Use

Does Treatment Work?

Lonny Shavelson

Editor's Note—At the end of the 1990s, physician, journalist, and photographer Lonny Shavelson spent just over two years following five addicts in California as they picked their way through a variety of drug treatment programs. The result was his phenomenal and disturbing book, *Hooked: Five Addicts Challenge Our Misguided Drug Rehab System.* The following wraps up his investigation into San Francisco's "treatment upon demand" policies, first implemented in 1996, which offer treatment to any addict who professes a need or finds themselves in drug court. At times harrowing, maddening, very often sad and on occasion inspiring, *Hooked* is an uncompromising look at occasional successes, but more often than not the drawbacks and failures inherent in modern drug treatment in the US.

When I began this book, the question *Does treatment work?* formed the tiniest seed of an inquiry. The closer I moved in to the smell of the flower of rehab, the more sharply I felt the thorns.

It is tempting to synthesize an answer by writing an updates on how Darlene, Mike, Darrell, and the others have fared since the final chapter. But the successes or failures of drug treatment cannot be gauged by a book's-end listing of how the characters are doing. Rehab is an ongoing process, not a moment in time.

This is not to say that I've come to no conclusions. A number of truths about rehab and addicts were hammered into me while I worked on this book. Those conclusions, either by seemingly endless repetition or blatantly obvious *truth*, reach beyond moment or person.

Relapse: *When an addict in rehab gets worse and heads back to drugs, the programs must increase treatment, not withdraw it.*

Relapse to drug use, I had thought, means that both addict and rehab have failed. I was wrong. I know now that relapse is one of the many ways in which an addict learns to stay off drugs. "Don't get me wrong, Ms. Holmes," Judge Lam told Crystal. "It's not that we encourage relapses. It would have been better if you had prevented it. But that's what you're going to rehab to learn."

If addicts already knew how to keep from relapsing, they wouldn't need treatment in the first place. Yet people who come to rehab asking for help with their compulsive drug use will get thrown out of treatment for using drugs. For two years I watched a variety of programs send dozens of clients back to the streets because they had relapsed. There are no acceptable excuses for such a practice.

Detox: *Each and every rehab programs must be required to have a formal, structured association with a drug detox center where is can send relapsed clients.*

"They'll contaminate the whole house," say many in the rehab programs about addicts who've returned to drugs. "We can't have them here." I agree. But there is nothing to keep programs from referring relapsed clients to detox centers, instead of kicking them out into the streets. We must require that every program be formally linked to a detox center that will work with the addicts to help them get clean again and, it is hoped, back to rehab. The rehab programs, too, must *encourage* their relapsed clients to return for more treatment.

Humiliation: *Abuses and humiliation in the name of therapy must cease. Cities must establish an ombudsman to monitor the rehab programs, and addicts must be allowed to access the ombudsman without repercussions.*

Relapsed Walden House Brothers or Sisters who want to come back into treatment are first confronted by an in-your-face screaming match at a House Meeting that debases them. The programs argue that this is a way to teach addicts that there are consequences to their actions, or that humiliation forces the addicts to look more deeply

> RELAPSE TO DRUG USE, I HAD THOUGHT, MEANS THAT BOTH ADDICT AND REHAB HAVE FAILED. I WAS WRONG.

into their emotions and behaviors. The fact is, humiliation most commonly leads to addicts being humiliated and little else.

While rehab organizations across the country now claim that less aggressive treatment has replaced the older Synanon-style "emotional surgery without anesthetic," my investigations following addicts through multiple programs over the past two years show that attack therapy is still commonplace.

There are many proven and effective ways to dole out consequences that will let addicts in treatment know, without thoroughly debasing them, when they have erred. Shaming and degradation induce no human being to come back for more.

Stick and stay and *keep coming back* are the most potent tools for the drug treatment industry. If there is a single

KICKING ADDICTS OUT OF PROGRAMS BECAUSE OF RELAPSES, OR HEAPING ABUSE ON THEM WHILE THEY ARE IN THE PROGRAMS, KEEPS THEM FROM COMING BACK.

consistent finding that has come out of rehab research it is that the longer clients can be maintained in the programs the more likely they are to emerge clean and sober, and stay that way. Kicking addicts out of programs because of relapses, or heaping abuse on them while they are in the programs, keeps them from coming back.

Psychological counseling: *All rehab counselors must be trained to recognize and treat the multitude of addicts who also have psychological disorders, and refer them to appropriately intensive additional care when needed.*

RECURRENT RELAPSES ARE CAUSED BY PSYCHOLOGICAL DYSFUNCTION, NOT MERE LACK OF WILLPOWER.

There is no benefit to our spending rehab funds to treat dually diagnosed addicts unless we have dually trained counselors. At least 40% of the people are so devastated by drugs that they hit rehab with a psychological disturbance, with depression and post-traumatic stress disorder heading the list. These dually diagnosed addicts uniformly receive inadequate care. "Many addiction counselors have had little or no training in diagnosing and treating mental disorders," reports the fed's Substance Abuse and Mental Health Services Administration. In addition, "Mental health professionals…have received little or no training about addictive disorders." Yet an astounding ten million citizens annually have drug disorders combined with psychological disturbances and "Their needs have not been addressed by the majority of mental health and substance abuse treatment programs."

I am certain of one thing: When an addict, no matter how together he or she seems (think of Mike), works vigorously to get into rehab, persists in the program with clear and sincere intentions of overcoming addiction, and yet still repeatedly relapses to drug use—there is invariably an additional psychological disturbance underlying that failure to stay clean. Recurrent relapses are caused by psychological dysfunction, not mere lack of willpower. Until proven otherwise, a recurrently relapsing addict should be assumed to have an underlying psychological disorder. Every willing addict who repeatedly relapses in spite of actively participating in rehab must be evaluated and treated by mental health professionals trained and

WITH HUNDREDS OF THOUSANDS OF ADDICTS RICOCHETING THROUGH REHAB EVERY YEAR, CITY AND STATE HEALTH DEPARTMENTS MUST TIGHTLY MONITOR AND REGULATE THE PROGRAMS.

experience in both addiction and psychiatric care. Addicts who have relapses again and again will continue to do so until their mental and emotional disturbances are dealt with by competent professionals.

Case Management: *Cities must establish a comprehensive case management system to guide addicts through the maze of programs and services. The case managers should not work for any particular rehab programs, but rather represent and advocate for the addicts in the overall system.*

Imagine that Glenda had been provided with a case manager to supervise her care after she'd graduated from Friendship House. She could have been referred to appropriate housing, provided with daily outpatient rehab, encouraged to keep in contact even when she'd resumed drinking—given a chance to head back toward sobriety. Had she been fortunate enough to have been arrested and sent to Drug Court, she would have received those services. There is no reason any city cannot establish an identical case management system, outside of the courts. Cities that do not set up such a system should not receive a penny of federal funding.

On April 21, 2000, Glenda's friends gathered around the benches in Hallidie Plaza for her memorial service. She had continued drinking until her liver failed and she died. Could a good case manager in an organized rehab system have prevented Glenda's death from alcoholism at age 38? Glenda never had the opportunity to find out.

When Mike left Walden, that program should have been required to notify his case manager (had he had one), who would have picked up from there. Instead of being ostracized, Mike would have been offered counseling and support, referred to detox and then, quite possibly, back to Walden or another rehab program.

Oversight: *Government agencies that provide funds to the programs must assure that addicts are receiving comprehensive and effective treatment.* In San Francisco alone, 135 drug treatment programs are run by forty independent organizations, which rely on government funding. San Francisco budgeted $49 million for drug abuse services in 1999, money that came from city, state, and federal sources. The government must assure that those millions of dollars are buying appropriate services.

According to Michael Siever, co-chair of San Francisco's Treatment on Demand Planning Council, "The Department of Public Health does not have the data to tell us what's going on." Or in Baltimore, another city attempting to provide rehab to all addicts who need it: "The money is well spent only if the city's treatment programs produce results," reported the Baltimore Sun. "Currently, there is no way to tell…Forty-four treatment contractors run their programs largely as they choose."

Every drug rehab program in the country must currently be licensed to operate and demonstrate its treatment capabilities and adequacy of care for the addicts. Yet with 135 such government-certified programs in San

THE NATIONAL DRUG CONTROL STRATEGY'S 282-PAGE FISCAL YEAR 2000 BUDGET SUMMARY USES THE TERM "CASE MANAGEMENT" ONLY FOUR TIMES, "RELAPSE PREVENTION" JUST ONCE. BUT "HELICOPTER" SHOWS UP FIFTEEN TIMES, AS IN, "THESE HELICOPTERS WILL AUGMENT EIGHTEEN UH-1NS ALREADY IN COLOMBIA…"

Francisco, Darlene bounced repeatedly from mental health to substance abuse services, until Dr. Pablo Stewart intervened; Mike was kicked out of Walden for using drugs and offered no resources to pick himself up and move on again; Darrell graduated from a three-month program and received no further support to maintain his sobriety; Glenda was tossed back to the streets after emerging clean and sober from her program. Crystal, with thorough and comprehensive oversight from Drug Court, repetitively relapsed, resisted treatment, and then finally achieved long-lasting sobriety.

These are anecdotes about a few addicts, whose stories are repeated hundreds of thousands of times across the country each year. It is time for all city governments and innumerable state and federal agencies to maintain a true vigilance over the rehab programs, and cut off funding to those programs that do not meet specific standards of care. It is no longer adequate for the fed's Center for Substance Abuse Treatment to issue yet another "Treatment Improvement Protocol" (they have now put out 36) without assuring, by funding-tied penalties and enforcement, that the programs actually enact and follow the carefully delineated and crucially needed treatment improvements.

Before investing a single additional dollar in drug treatment, or establishing one more rehab bed for an addicts in need, our government must first establish rigorous oversight of the programs, along with independent case management for the addicts. With hundreds of thousands of addicts ricocheting through rehab every year, city and state health departments must tightly monitor and regulate the programs.

Funding priorities: *Federal funds and efforts must be shifted from drug interdiction abroad to drug rehab at home.*

For fiscal year 2001, our Office of National Drug Control Policy has budgeted $17.7 billion to bring our drug problem under control. But only 19% of those dollars are aimed at treating addicts. While $50 million is set aside to support Drug Courts, $420 million will be spent to build new prisons, $1.3 billion to fight the drug war in Colombia. These treatment budgetary shortcomings are exacerbated by our lack of attentiveness to the details necessary for successful rehab: The National Drug Control Strategy's 282-page Fiscal Year 2000 Budget Summary uses the term "case management" only four times, "relapse prevention" just once. But "helicopter" shows up fifteen times, as in, "These helicopters will augment eighteen UH-1Ns already in Colombia…"

A 1994 RAND study, prepared under the auspices of the White House Office of National Drug Control Policy (and the United States Army), examined cocaine consumption in the United States. Here's how much money is needed to gain every 1% reduction in addicts' cocaine use: $34 million on rehab for drug addicts in the United States; or, $246 million for police to enforce drug laws in the United States; or, $366 million at the border to prevent the drugs from coming in the country; or, $783 million spent in the countries that produce the drugs. Every dollar spent on drug rehab at home, concluded the study, yields the same effect as twenty-three dollars spent abroad.

It's not difficult to read these numbers and be certain that increasing drug treatment dollars from 19% of the total drug budget to, say, 50% would have the overall effect of substantially decreasing drug abuse at home, which, when all is said and done, is the goal of our national drug policy. Looking at cocaine use alone, according to the RAND study, reallocating 25% of money spent abroad to money spent at home "would include a one-third reduction in annual cocaine consumption."

"The struggle against illegal drugs is not a war," claims drug czar General Barry McCaffrey. "Addicted individuals are to be helped," he explained, "not defeated." Yet the

DOES REHAB WORK FOR THOSE WHO ARE MOST DISASTROUSLY ADDICTED? I STILL DON'T KNOW. IN THE TWO YEARS OF THIS INVESTIGATION I RARELY SAW REHAB DONE WELL ENOUGH TO LEARN IF IT MIGHT WORK.

vast majority of our anti-drug dollars are still spent on battles abroad rather than on treatment at home.

Does rehab work for those who are most disastrously addicted? I still don't know. In the two years of this investigation I rarely saw rehab done well enough to learn if it might work.

What we today call drug rehab does not provide consistent and coherent help to the majority of addicts who come seeking it. It may well be that the nature of the beast of addiction makes effective treatment of addicts a pie-in-the-sky dream, even with the best that rehab could offer. Or it may be that the frustratingly unimpressive treatment results we see today with those most insanely addicted are merely what happens in a rehab system that is as ill as the addicts themselves.

Can rehab work? After two years of ricocheting through rehab with these addicts, I believe the answer is a resounding *Yes*.

Rehab can work—in a cohesive, coordinated system that links drug programs to mental health services, and joins both together to provide addicts with lifelong care and case managers who stick with them through thick and thin.

I present this conclusion not as an act of faith but as a reality backed up by the struggles and dreams of Mike, Darlene, Darrell, Crystal, Glenda, and all those whose lives have been overrun by tragic events *and* the tragedies of drug addiction.

On March 24, 2000, three years after beginning drug rehab, Mike stood in an orange jail jumpsuit, head bowed, in the Superior Court of the state of California, at the bench of Judge Kevin V. Ryan, for sentencing. He faced twenty-five years to life in the state penitentiary, but the district attorney had finally agreed to a plea bargain.

"The prosecution wants the defendant to plead guilty and be sentenced to eight years in state prison," announced the black-robed judge from the high bench at the front of the court. "It is alleged that the defendant, who had a substance abuse problem, entered the home of his sister-in-law and stole some material property, and tried to cash one of her checks for $118, and was unsuccessful."

Mike, silent, leaned forward over his clasped hands at the defense table, chewed on his lower lip, and then looked up as the judge ruffled the papers in front of him.

"Pursuant to Penal Code section 1385(a), the Court has considered specifically the nature and circumstances of this present felony or felonies, the nature and circumstances of his prior conviction, the history of drug addiction, the lack of history of violence, and the interests of society in general."

Then Judge Ryan slowly read Mike's sentence, item by item:

> Eight years in the state penitentiary. That sentence to be suspended, and instead the defendant will spend one year in the county jail, which time he has already served.

> The defendant is to be released from jail immediately, to a two-year residential drug rehab program in San Francisco, which he is ordered by the court to successfully complete.

> The defendant will remain on probation for five years, during which time any drug use or violation of the law will return him to this court, to fulfill the eight-year penitentiary sentence that has been suspended.

"The Court does not believe," announced the judge in a clear, loud voice, "that there is a prospect that this defendant can rehabilitate himself."

The next day, Mike was released to rehab. I wish him Godspeed, and pray that he receives the help he needs.

Political Update: December 2000

In the first year of the new century, California and New York initiated revolutionary plans for drug rehab. California voters overwhelmingly passed Proposition 36, the Substance Abuse and Crime Prevention Act, "to divert

| GOOD INTENTIONS DO NOT ASSURE QUALITY REHAB.

from incarceration into community-based substance abuse treatment programs non-violent defendants…charged with simple drug possession or drug use offenses." As of July 2001, some 36,000 additional addicts in California will head to rehab each year, under court order. Likewise, in New York, Chief Judge Judith S. Kaye ordered systemic changes in the courts so that nearly all non-violent drug addicts will be sent to rehab instead of prisons. The policy, which will propel some 10,000 arrested addicts annually to treatment, is to be in full effect by 2003.

The backers of Proposition 36 plan a cross-country campaign, with Michigan and Ohio next on the list for citizen initiatives modeled on the one just passed in California. This national paradigm shift from jails toward rehab is the inevitable result of public frustration with years of incarcerating hundreds of thousands of addicts while seeing little improvement in our nation's crisis of drug addiction.

Good intentions do not assure quality rehab. If Proposition 36 and the New York judicial mandate for treatment are to succeed, the officials putting the plans into action must establish detailed oversight of the treatment programs, provide for improved training and formal certification of rehab counselors, make skilled care readily available for addicts who have additional mental health problems, and aid recovering addicts in job training and housing procurement.

With the implementation of Proposition 36 in California, strict oversight and quality control of the rehab programs will be as important as tightly monitoring the addicts sent to those programs. Unfortunately, a RAND study found that Proposition 36 "…does not specify procedures for ensuring the quality of the treatment provided." On a national level, the Center of Substance Abuse Treatment announced (in the same month that Proposition 36 passed) that we still do not have "commonly accepted standards for what constitutes effective substance abuse treatment in the United States." Establishing such standards, and enforcing them, is essential to the success of the new push to rehab both in New York and in California.

Along with not supervising the programs, Proposition 36 fails to monitor the addicts. Frequent drug testing is a crucial component of any rehab program, both to rapidly discover relapses and as a deterrent to drug use. But no Proposition 36 money, says the statute, can be spent on drug testing, with the rationale that every dollar is needed for treatment. This limitation must immediately be changed by the California legislature, which is responsible for implementing the new proposition. As Drug Courts across the country have shown, a swift response to relapse is crucial to keeping addicts on track toward sobriety. A majority of those in rehab will, at some point in time, relapse. Without adequate drug testing, those relapses will be missed until users are again lost in their addiction.

The rehab methods employed by our Drug Courts provide an ideal model for successful drug treatment. Yet during the campaign for Proposition 36 an intense animosity evolved between California's Drug Court judges and the proposition advocates. Dave Fratello, who managed the Proposition 36 campaign, claimed that if Drug Courts were expanded, "the money would go to judges, staff, administrative costs, and monitoring expenses, with little

IN NEW YORK'S PILOT DRUG TREATMENT COURT STUDY, ONLY 14% OF THE OFFENDERS WHO PARTICIPATED WERE ARRESTED AGAIN. THE RE-ARREST RATE FOR ADDICTS WHO DID NOT PARTICIPATE IN THE SPECIAL COURTS WAS 35%.

left to pay for actual treatment services…Proposition 36 makes it a priority to invest in treatment programs, rather than Drug Courts…" Drug Court Judge Ronald P. Kreber fired back that that Proposition 36 would be a "death knell" for the Drug Courts. "Under the initiative," said Judge Kreber, "a defendant would have in incentive to accept the authority of the Drug Court. The personality of the addict is lacking self-discipline, and most would

opt for a program that has little or no sanctions." Judge Steven V. Manley, president of the California Associate of Drug Court Professionals, pointed out that Drug Courts work because of mandatory testing, immediate sanctions for drug use, frequent appearances in front of the same judge, and close supervision of rehab. The proposition will cripple and gut the heart of an effective treatment program," said Manley. "Treatment standing alone does not work."

Now that the campaign is over and millions of dollars are to be allocated, wisdom dictates that prior battle be set aside and funds got to rehab systems with the best track records: those established by the Drug Courts. Drug Courts need the funds, and Proposition 36 advocates need the experience and leadership of the Drug Court judges and case managers to guide an additional 36,000 arrested addicts successfully through rehab every year. In regard to the Drug Courts, California would do well to follow the example of New York. New York's Commission on Drugs and the Courts tracked the results of a number of pilot drug Treatment Court programs, then made detailed policy recommendations. This contrasts greatly with the indistinct plans for treatment in California.

In New York's new system, Drug Courts will provide "supervision and monitoring of addicted offenders by judges and others throughout the treatment process, continued drug testing and strict systems of sanctions and rewards to motivate defendants to succeed in treatment." California's Proposition 36 offers no more guidance than, "As a condition of probation the court shall require participation in and completion of an appropriate drug treatment program."

Recognizing that the drug rehab involves lifestyle changes as well as stopping drug use, the New York system will coordinate "education, job training, basic health care, or housing assistance…Drug Court case managers and judges will track the progress being made in these areas as well." California's Proposition 36 states only that the court *may* impose requirements such as vocational training. And instead of regular visits with a judge, an arrested addict in a rehab program in California will be monitored only by quarterly reports to the addicts' probation officer.

The California proposition limits rehab to one year; New York provides for more than one year if needed. In California, an arrested addict graduates from rehab when there is "reasonable cause to believe that the defendant will not abuse controlled substances in the future." In New York, the addict "must satisfy other requirements likely to encourage a drug-free lifestyle, such as having a job or obtaining a G.E.D. or vocational degree."

In New York's pilot Drug Treatment Court study, only 14% of the offenders who participated were arrested again. The re-arrest rate for addicts who did not participate in the special courts was 35%.

New York's comprehensive treatment plans have a fighting chance at success, while California's vaguely elaborated system will merely push dysfunctional addicts through poorly functioning rehab programs. But California could emulate its eastern cousin with ease; there are 109 Drug Courts in California with detailed and proven rehab practices, and outstanding success rates. The majority of the $120 million in annual Proposition 36 funds should go to expanding this Drug Court system.

"Now the battle is going to be over implementation," says drug policy reform expert Ethan Nadelmann. "The $120 million [a year] could do a lot of good, or it could be frittered away.

Lonny Shavelson

Ten Years of Therapy in One Night

Daniel Pinchbeck

In 1962, Howard Lotsof, a nineteen year-old heroin addict in New York, ordered from a chemist iboga, a plant used in West African rituals, and tried it for extra kicks. After consuming the bitter rootbark powder, he experienced a visionary tour of his early memories. Thirty hours later, when the effects had subsided, he found that he had lost all craving for heroin, without withdrawal symptoms of any kind. He said he then gave iboga to seven other addicts and five stopped taking drugs immediately afterwards.

In 1985, Lotsof patented the ibogaine molecule for the purposes of addiction treatment, but could not get his treatment approved. In the interim years, ibogaine had been declared, along with LSD and several other psychedelic molecules, an illegal "schedule one" substance, with potential for abuse and no medical value. Although it found dedicated support among a ragtag group of

IBOGA IS THE SACRED ESSENCE OF THE RELIGION OF THE BWITI TRIBE OF GABON AND CAMEROON.

countercultural activists and left-over Yippies, in 1995 the National Institutes of Health discontinued research into the substance, and pharmaceutical companies have since ignored it, perhaps due to low profit potential.

But now, interest in ibogaine is growing rapidly, passing a "tipping point" through a combination of anecdotal evidence, underground activism, journalism and scientific research. Articles have appeared in US publications ranging from the authoritative *Journal Of The American Medical Association* (*JAMA*) to the populist *Star*. The *JAMA* piece, "Addiction Treatment Strives For Legitimacy," described the drug's stalled and tortured path through the regulatory agencies, noting that the treatment's frustrated supporters in the US have set up an "underground railroad" to give addicts access to the drug: "While unknowable scores of addicts continue ingesting ibogaine hydrochloride purified powder—or iboga whole-plant extract containing a dozen or more active alkaloids—few trained researchers witness the events."

The *Star* took a more colorful approach: "Rare Root Has Celebs Buzzing" it said, trumpeting the treatment as the hot ticket for "the numerous celebs who look for relief from their tough lives in the bottom of a bottle of Jack Daniel's, a needle or prescription medicine." The article insinuates that "some of our favorite A-listers" not only

get cured but enjoy the hallucinations as an illicit "fringe benefit." Outside the US, new clinics have opened in Mexico, Canada, and Europe, offering reasonably priced, medically supervised opportunities to try ibogaine as a method of overcoming addiction. In fact, at one new clinic in Vancouver, the treatment is free.

Iboga is the sacred essence of the religion of the Bwiti tribe of Gabon and Cameroon. Most members of the tribe ingest it just once in their lives, during an initiation ceremony in which massive amounts of the powdered bark are consumed. Through this ritual, they become a baanzi, one who has seen the other world. "Iboga brings about the visual, tactile, and auditory certainty of the irrefutable existence of the beyond," wrote the French chemist Robert Goutarel, who studied the Bwiti. The iboga bark's visionary power is produced by a complicated cocktail of alkaloids that seems to affect many of the known neurotransmitters, including serotonin and dopamine. Its complex molecular key may lock into the addiction receptors in a way that resets patterns and blocks the feedback loops that reinforce dependency.

In an essay on ibogaine's anti-addictive properties, Dr. Carl Anderson of McLean Hospital, Virginia, speculated that addiction is related to a disrupted relationship between the brain's two hemispheres, and that ibogaine may cause "bihemispheric reintegration." Ibogaine also accesses REM sleep in a powerful way—many people need considerably less sleep for several months after an ibogaine trip.

Six years ago, I became a member of the Bwiti. I had heard about ibogaine from an assistant in an anarchist bookstore in New York. On a magazine assignment, I went to Gabon

AT ONE POINT, I HAD A VISION OF A WOODEN STATUE WALKING ACROSS THE ROOM AND SITTING IN FRONT OF ME—LATER, I WAS TOLD THIS WAS "THE SPIRIT OF IBOGA" COMING OUT TO COMMUNICATE WITH ME.

and took iboga in an initiation ceremony. It was one of the most difficult, yet rewarding, experiences of my life. I had heard the substance described as "10 years of psychoanalysis in a single night" but, of course, I did not believe it. As the tribesmen played drums and sang around me until dawn, I lay on a concrete floor and journeyed back through the course of my life up to that point, witnessing forgotten scenes from childhood. At one point,

I had a vision of a wooden statue walking across the room and sitting in front of me—later, I was told this was "the spirit of iboga" coming out to communicate with me. My Bwiti initiation was complicated by a belligerent, greedy shaman who called himself The King and demanded more money from us before, during and after the ceremony. The King was also dissatisfied with the visions I described, and threatened to keep feeding me more iboga until I reported more impressive sights. The initiation, which lasted more than 20 hours, was ultimately liberating. At one point, I was shown my habitual overuse of alcohol and the effect it was having on my relationships, my writing and my psyche. When I returned to the US, I steadily reduced my drinking to a fraction of its previous level—an adjustment that seems to be permanent.

"IBOGAINE STOPS THE PHYSICAL ADDICTION WITHOUT CAUSING WITHDRAWAL," HE SAYS, "AND IT DEALS WITH THE UNDERLYING PSYCHOLOGICAL ISSUES THAT LEAD TO DRUG USE."

Recently, I tried ibogaine for a second time. I took it at the Ibogaine Association, a clinic in Rosarito, Mexico. I had been contacted by a heroin addict who had been inspired to take ibogaine after reading the book I wrote about my experiences: three months after his first treatment in Mexico, he was still clean—after a twelve year dependency. He told me, "Your book saved my life." He had given Dr. Martin Polanco, the clinic's founder, a copy of my book, and he had offered me a free treatment. I was curious to see how the experience would differ away from its tribal context. My new friend wanted to take it again to reinforce the effect. We went down together.

Polanco estimates that his clinic has treated nearly 200 addicts in its first eighteen months. About one third of those patients have managed to stay clean—either permanently or for a considerable period; many have returned for a second treatment. "Ibogaine needs to be much more widely available," Polanco says. "We still have a lot to learn about how to administer it, how to work with it." He does not think iboga is a cure for addiction, but is convinced it is a powerful tool for treatment—and, in some cases, it is a cure. He plans to set up several non-profit clinics. "This is something that should be non-profit," he says. "After all, it is a plant. It came up from the earth. It does give you some guidance. It shows you how you really are." He chuckles. "That can be scary."

"Ibogaine stops the physical addiction without causing withdrawal," he says, "and it deals with the underlying psychological issues that lead to drug use."

The Ibogaine Therapy House in Vancouver, British Columbia, opened last November. "So far, we have treated fourteen people quite well," says Marc Emery, the clinic's founder and head of the BC Marijuana Party. "They all say that their life has improved." Emery, nicknamed the "Prince of Pot," is funding the free clinic with proceeds from his successful hemp seed business. "Ibogaine stops the physical addiction without causing withdrawal," he says, "and it deals with the underlying psychological issues that lead to drug use."

Emery estimates that treatment for each patient at the clinic costs around $1,500, which includes two administrations of the drug. "When I found out about ibogaine, I felt that someone should be researching this, but the drug companies aren't interested because there is no commercial potential in this type of cure." Neither he nor Polanco is too concerned about ambiguous studies on ibogaine's toxicity. As the *JAMA* article noted, "One reviewer wrote that the drug's toxicology profile was 'less than ideal,' with bradycardia [an abnormally slow heartbeat] leading the list of worrisome adverse effects."

"From the masses of reports I have studied, a total of six people have died around the time they took ibogaine," says Emery. "Some were in poor health, some took other drugs at the time of their treatment. That doesn't scare me off. I have a lot of confidence in ibogaine."

At this stage, with little scientific study, the true toxicology of ibogaine is impossible to determine—the treatment is unlicensed in other countries and illegal in the US. The decision whether or not to take such a risk is entirely personal. Emery notes that his clinic screens for heart problems and other medical conditions that might contraindicate the treatment. It also gives patients small daily doses of iboga for two weeks after their initial treatment. "Iboga tends to make anything bad for you taste really crappy. If possible, we want our patients to quit cigarettes at the same time. We think that cigarettes can lead people back to other addictions."

Emery notes that nobody has so far criticized the project, and he is seeking support from local government. "Iboga tells you to change your ways or else—it goes over all of your health and personal issues. It is like the ghost of Christmas past."

TWENTY MINUTES AFTER INGESTING THE TEST DOSE, I STARTED TO FEEL NERVOUS AND LIGHT-HEADED. AS I TOOK THE OTHER PILLS—A GEL-CAPPED EXTRACT OF THE ROOTBARK POWDER—I REALIZED I WAS IN FOR A SERIOUS TRIP.

Randy Hencken drove us from San Diego to the Ibogaine Association. A 25-year-old former heroin addict who had kicked the habit after two ibogaine treatments at the clinic, he was now working for the association, going to local methadone centers with flyers and keeping in contact with former patients. The first treatment costs $2,800, including an initial medical examination and several days' convalescence afterwards, but subsequent visits are only $600—and it seems most addicts need at least two doses of ibogaine to avoid relapsing.

The Ibogaine Association is in a quiet, dignified house overlooking the Pacific, decorated with Buddhist statues and yarn paintings from Mexico's Huichol people. I was given a medical examination by Polanco and a test dose of the drug. Twenty minutes after ingesting the test dose, I started to feel nervous and light-headed. As I took the other pills—a gel-capped extract of the rootbark powder—I realized I was in for a serious trip.

The nurse led me back to my room. My head already spinning, I lay back on the bed as she hooked me up to an electrocardiograph and headphones playing

AS SO OFTEN THESE DAYS, I PONDERED ON THE TERRIBLE STATE OF THE WORLD—WARS AND TERRORS AND ENVIRONMENTAL RUIN. I SAW SHEETS OF RADIOACTIVE FLAME DEVOURING CITIES, HUGE CROWDS REDUCED TO CINDERS.

ambient music. Why was I doing this again? Ibogaine is no pleasure trip. It not only causes violent nausea and vomiting, but many of the "visions" it induces amount to a painful parading of one's deepest faults and moral failings. I had a loud, unpleasant buzzing in my ears—the Bwiti probably pound on drums throughout the ceremony to overwhelm this noise. With my eyes closed, I watched as images began to emerge like patterns out of TV static. I saw a black man in a 1940s-looking suit. He was holding the hand of a five-year-old girl and leading her up some stairs. I understood that the girl in the vision was me and that the man represented the spirit of iboga. He was going to show me around his castle.

While startling at the time, such an encounter with a seeming "spirit of iboga" is a typical vision produced by the Bwiti sacrament. In many accounts, people describe meeting a primordial African couple in the jungle. Sometimes, the iboga spirit manifests itself as a "ball of light" that speaks to the baanzi, saying, "Do you know who I am? I am the chief of the world, I am the essential point!" Part of my trip took the form of an interview that was almost journalistic. I could ask direct questions of "Mr. Iboga" and receive answers that were like emphatic, telegraphed shouts inside my head—even in my deeply stoned state, I managed to scrawl down in my notebook many of the responses.

I asked Mr. Iboga what iboga was. I was told simply: "Primordial wisdom teacher of humanity!"

Later, my personal faults and lazy, decadent habits were replayed for me in detail. When I asked what I should do, the answer was stern and paternal: "Get it straight now!"

This ideal of straightness, uprightness, kept returning during the trip—a meaningful image for me, as I suffer from scoliosis, a curvature of the spine. When I was shown other faults that seemed rather petty and insignificant, I tried to protest that some of these things really didn't matter. Iboga would have none of it, insisting: "Everything matters!"

Iboga told me that I had no idea of the potential significance of even the smallest actions. I reviewed some events in my life and my friends' lives that seemed bitterly unfair. Yet, in this altered state, I felt I could sense a karmic pattern behind all of them, perhaps extending back to previous incarnations. Iboga affirmed this, dictating: "God is just!"

To many readers, these insights may sound trivial. They did not feel that way at the time. They were delivered with great force and minimalist precision. While they might have been manifestations of my own mind, they seemed like the voice of an "other." Generally, I never think in such direct terms about "God," and "primordial wisdom teacher" is not my syntax.

During the night, I had numerous visions and ponderous metaphysical insights. At one point, I seemed to fly through the solar system and into the sun, where winged beings were spinning around the core at a tremendous rate. Up close, they looked like the gold-tinged angels in early Renaissance paintings. Perhaps due to my recent reading of the Austrian visionary Rudolf Steiner, this whole trip had a kind of eco-Christian flavor to it. At one point, I thought of humans as an expression of the Gaian Mind, the earth's sensory organs and self-reflective capacities, at the planet's present state of development. If we are changing quickly right now, I considered, it is only because the earth has entered an accelerated phase of transformation, forcing a fast evolution in human consciousness.

The loud buzzing sound that ibogaine produced seemed to be something like a dial tone, as if the alkaloid were in itself a device for communicating on a different frequency

THE "GOOD AND EVIL" THAT IBOGA REVEALS IS NOT ABSTRACT BUT DEEPLY PERSONAL, AND ROOTED IN THE CHARACTER OF THE INDIVIDUAL!

than the usual one. Thinking of my girlfriend and our child, I realized that I was lucky—"You are lucky!" Mr. Iboga echoed. I felt tremendous, tearful gratitude that I had been given a chance to live and love, to explore and try to understand so many things.

As so often these days, I pondered on the terrible state of the world—wars and terrors and environmental ruin. I saw sheets of radioactive flame devouring cities, huge crowds reduced to cinders. I asked Mr. Iboga if this was going to be the tragic fate of humanity. The answer I received was startling—and reassuring: "Everything is safe in God's hands!"

As ludicrous as it may sound, this message has stayed with me and alleviated much paranoia and anxiety. While tripping, I decided that Mr. Iboga was a form of enlightened mind, like a buddha who had chosen a different form, as a plant spirit rather than human teacher, to work with humanity, imparting a cosmic message of "tough love." At one point I asked if he would consider incarnating as a person, and the answer I got was, basically, "Already did that!"—implying that, in some previous cycle, he had passed through the perilous stages of evolution we are now navigating. I also came away from this trip with the suspicion that iboga was the original inspiration for the tree of the knowledge of good and evil in the Biblical tale. The plant's placement in equatorial Africa, cradle of humanity, would support this idea, as well as its sobering moral rectitude. The "good and evil" that iboga reveals is not abstract but deeply personal, and rooted in the character of the individual!

Late in the night, I retched and vomited out bitter rootbark residue. I put on a CD of African drumming. Closing my eyes, I watched a group of smiling Bwiti women dance around a jungle bonfire. After that, the visions died down, although it was impossible to sleep until late the next night.

My friend in recovery had a less visionary experience. His faults were also paraded in front of him in repetitive loops that seemed endless. At one point, I heard him scream out, "No! No! No!" He saw a possible future for himself if he didn't kick heroin—becoming a dishwasher, sinking into dissolute old age with a bad back and a paunch. He asked what he could do to help save the world. He was told: "Clean up your room!" Meditating on his experience later, my friend quipped, "Ibogaine is God's way of saying, 'You're mine, bitch!'"

Reckless Disregard

Jay R. Cavanaugh, Ph.D.
Member, California State Board of Pharmacy 1980-90

There are several mass murderers loose in America. Collectively they kill more innocent men, women, and children than all the drunk drivers, illicit drug pushers, and gang bangers combined.

This collection of serial killers with reckless disregard of human life, extinguishes the hopes and lives of over 100,000 Americans every year. Another two million are seriously harmed or injured each year. In the past decade they are responsible for over one million innocent deaths yet not only have they not faced justice, they have enriched themselves with profits that would make Bill Gates envious.

These parasitic killers come not from some cave in Afghanistan, but from plush office suites. They don't have tattoos, assault rifles, or long hair. They dress well, they

THE DEPREDATIONS, SCOPE, AND CALLOUSNESS OF THESE MODERN KILLERS MAKE CHARLES MANSON AND JOHN WAYNE GACY PALE IN COMPARISON.

speak well, and they prey on the most common human weakness, hope. They claim their aim is to treat the sick, cure the ill, and enrich life while the reality is far more than brutal. Not only do many of their lethal and toxic products not help many of the people counting on them but even when they do help, such as the case with life sustaining AIDS drugs, they are withheld from all but those few who can afford to pay prices that are akin to blackmail. Millions in Africa, South America, and elsewhere are dying from their inability to pay for overpriced drugs and every effort to provide humanitarian supplies, even in the midst of epidemics, has been resisted in court.

The depredations, scope, and callousness of these modern killers make Charles Manson and John Wayne Gacy pale in comparison. These murderers in three-piece suits and designer dresses kill more Americans in an hour than any mass murderer could hope to kill in a lifetime.

Collectively these pitiless people have engaged in the longest running and most destructive continuing criminal enterprise in history. Who are they? They are nameless and faceless executives who hide behind the alleged respectability of names like Eli Lilly, GlaxoSmithKline, Merck and Co., Pfizer, and many more. At least the

psychotics Manson and Gacy were aware at some level that they were killers. Not the drug companies. To them, the deaths are nothing more than the unavoidable collateral damage in the war on disease and the pursuit of earnings.

While the suffering from hundreds of thousands of deaths, millions of adverse reactions, millions addicted, and economic havoc is damning, it is only one half of the coin. The other half is the active support and participation of the pharmaceutical industry in the so called war on drugs. Obviously they don't support war on their own drugs, only those of their competition. The biggest threat the pharmaceutical companies face today is medical cannabis. Patients who can grow their own at home for pennies instead of buying high priced pharmacy synthetics threatens the bottom line. This is why 80-90% of the war on drugs is against cannabis and why the drug companies are leaders in supporting both "community anti-drug groups" and drug warrior political candidates. Take a look at the campaign contributions from the drug industry and you see why both leading Democratic and Republican politicians have continued a war on medical cannabis despite the demonstrated futility and cruelty of the drug war.

The earnings gained from reckless disregard are astronomic. The entire "war on drugs" (in reality a culture war on cannabis) costs a futile $40 billion dollars a year of taxpayer money. Not one dime of this money goes to prevent the millions of prescription drug addicts or the millions who spend their Social Security on needless drugs instead of buying groceries. Author Alexandra Marks documents the steep rise in the non-medical abuse of prescription drugs. She points out that in 2003 some 9 million Americans secured prescription drugs through the Internet without ever seeing a physician. So much for regulation, when folks can buy thousands of doses of

THE FDA IS IN ESSENCE THE ENFORCEMENT ARM FOR DRUG COMPANY EXTORTIONISTS.

sedating drugs without question and have them delivered next day mail. Where is the FDA and DEA in regulating high priced Internet drugs? Be assured that the drug industry bosses have insured that prescription drug abuse is simply not a priority.

A recent review of the nations' outlay for high priced prescription remedies indicated: "Prescription drug spending rose 15.3% in 2002, with total spending for prescription drugs hitting $162.4 billion, compared with $140.8 billion in 2001. Drug costs are expected to exceed $180 billion for 2004. Medicare and the State Medicaid programs are collapsing under the weight of unfettered health care costs led by toxic prescription drugs. Nearly 20 million Americans remain uninsured and have no prescription drug coverage. President Bush's new drug

> WE HAVE A WAR ON THE WRONG DRUGS
> AND THE WRONG DRUG PUSHERS.

plan for seniors and the disabled is described by many experts as "cynical" and "utterly inadequate." These costs are the unavoidable result of advanced research and development according to the drug industry but their own statistics prove they spend far more for marketing than research.

Reckless disregard is recession proof, inflation proof, and immune from truth telling. The Dow Jones Industrial average may plummet but drug stocks do nothing but rise. Why shouldn't they rise? State and private programs to secure lower cost American drugs from Canada have been crushed by heavy handed Federal enforcement efforts claiming these drugs are "unsafe." So, you can't import your medicine and you can't grow it. Patients are forced to buy drug industry concoctions at monopolistic prices even though the industry itself admits that perhaps only 50% of patients receive any benefit despite the price and toxicity.

While the Federal Government wastes nearly a billion dollars each year to warn folks from using nontoxic cannabis it ignores scientific evidence of pharmaceutical drug dangers and provides the FDA stamp of approval that allow pharmaceutical drug pushers to reap record profits. *The FDA is in essence the enforcement arm for drug company extortionists.* The drug companies shell out nearly $20 billion dollars a year to prime the pump for useless and dangerous drugs. Drug companies spend more money on bribing doctors and politicians and on advertising drugs folks don't need and would be better off without than they do on finding all of the miracle cures that are always just around the corner.

We have a war on the wrong drugs and the wrong drug pushers. Our physicians who are supposed to be looking out for us seem blinded by the honorariums, free samples, and outright bribes offered by the pharmaceutical company representatives. Eli Lilly and Company pays cash bonuses to doctors to have their sales people sit in on patient consultations and give samples of its latest concoctions. Little does the patient realize that in drug culture only the first fix is free. Pfizer creates a whole new and utterly fabricated disease of wide spread female sexual dysfunction then promotes Viagra to treat it. Pfizer

also promotes its brain numbing drug Neurontin for every "off label" use imaginable and is willing to pay doctors to try out their product.

Our decision makers in Washington are influenced by huge campaign donations from the drug companies and not from any scientific proof, medical evidence, or the cries of anguish from the sick, disabled, and dying. Even universities and scientists have been co-opted by the drug cartel. Is research money tight? The answer is simple, just be willing to ignore ethics and take pharmaceutical company money for so called "independent" research. Then give the perverted "results" to the sales folks and harm some more patients. The *Observer* recently published reports that physicians and researchers no longer even have to write professional papers for publication. The drug companies have teams of ghost writers who know exactly how to spin the results for their newest products. With universities and medical centers dependent upon the drug companies for well over half of all their research money not a word of protest is heard about the perversion of science for profit. Where is the FDA in all of this? They are involved in what is called "fast track." The FDA exists today to get new and more profitable drugs to market. Today's "regulator" is tomorrow's high priced pharmaceutical executive or consultant.

Just as the small print warnings on a pack of cigarettes doesn't absolve the tobacco companies from helping to kill 500,000 Americans a year, neither does the small print

> IF THE GOVERNMENT AND THE AMA HAVE BEEN
> BOUGHT AND SOLD, THEN HOW ARE ORDINARY
> AMERICANS TO KNOW WHAT TO DO?

about "adverse reactions" absolve the pharmaceutical companies from their advertising fueled carnage. At least the tobacco companies never claimed that their poisonous products would treat illness. Tobacco can't be advertised in mass media anymore due to the harm but the latest drug products fill our television screens, websites, newspapers, and magazines. Over 50% of patients today come to the doctor with a new prescription in mind from this advertising blitz and most physicians are more than happy to comply.

How are folks to know the truth and make decisions in their own interest? How do patients protect themselves from the predatory practices of the drug makers? If the government and the AMA have been bought and sold, then how are ordinary Americans to know what to do?

Don't ask for the truth in the ads we all read and see ad nauseum. Don't ask for the truth on the Internet either. Ask a health question on nearly any major health website and you'll get information from experts that are consultants for the drug companies and the sites themselves are sponsored and censored by the same drug companies. Any mention of cheap, safe, and effective cannabis as medicine is banned as promoting illegal activities. This as pop-up ads tell us that we need Viagra to make a marriage work, Prozac for when times seem dark, and above all that little purple pill.

We are fighting the wrong drug war on the wrong people and we are paying for this terrible mistake through great suffering and loss of life. Intentional and reckless disregard for human life is the very definition of homicide. Why then are we punishing the sick growing medical marijuana while ignoring the real holocaust being perpetrated by supposedly responsible and humanitarian companies? In today's America greed is only rewarded and mass murder ignored.

References

"Our drugs don't Work" http://news.independent.co.uk

Iatrogenic Causes of Death, http://www.drugintel.com

Drug Intel Newsletter, http://www.drugintel.com/news/

Protecting Drug Company Profits, http://www.sptimes.com

Drug Company Profits Exceeded R&D Spending by 60%—The most profitable industry, http://www.tilrc.org, http://www.tac.org.za

Drug Industry Lobbying, http://www.commondreams.org

Congressional Campaign Contributions by drug industry spiral, http://www.house.gov

How our elected representatives are bought and paid for, http://www.motherjones.com

Clinton, Freud, and Clinical Cannabis

Ethan Russo, M.D.

I recently traveled from Montana to Washington, D.C. to speak at the National Organization for Reform of Marijuana Laws (NORML) Conference. I sampled local culture as well, with visits to the Sigmund Freud Exhibit at the Library of Congress, and the National Holocaust Museum. These seemingly disparate events seem in retrospect to hold some common themes.

Confronted by the statement attributed to Freud, it is sad commentary that contemporaneously a cigar can not easily be seen as merely a cigar. How did I come to be in this situation, pondering unusual juxtapositions? I am a clinical neurologist, who for some years has investigated herbal and ethnobotanical treatments for migraine. The herbal treatment par excellence for that disorder for some 4000 years is cannabis.

Let me be clear about something. I smoked marijuana in college. Unlike the man on Pennsylvania Avenue, [then-President Clinton] I did inhale—deeply, repetitively, and with malice aforethought. I daresay that I enjoyed it, and that I still miss it. That was many years ago, however, and due to prevailing attitudes, responsibilities, and the need for plausible deniability, I have given up my "vice," despite the fact that I have at least three medical conditions that could benefit from resumption of its usage.

I did not intend to be an activist when I began this research, but rather simply to examine the issue of cannabis in migraine treatment by modern scientific means. I filed an IND (Investigational New Drug) application to the FDA in 1996, but was informed that they could not approve a project without a legal supply of cannabis. That supply can only be obtained through NIDA (National Institute on Drug Abuse), which in turn required an application for funding by NIH (National Institutes of Health). I followed this Byzantine process in two successive years, but was twice rejected. Progress has occurred with a recent FDA approval, but NIDA still must evaluate the study before any cannabis would be released. Funding will need to be privately obtained.

To date, only one clinical study on cannabis has been approved in the last fifteen years, that after six years of efforts, and only when it was altered from an efficacy study (one that tests whether cannabis works), to a safety study (one that examines whether it is safe). I can not make a similar compromise. Every week the medical literature contains new studies that demonstrate protective and useful medical effects of cannabinoids on our physiology. The only scientific question for a given clinical condition treated with cannabis is now "Does it work?" not "Is it safe?"

The NORML audience greeted me as a hero and commiserated with my recent rejection by the powers that be. There were Democrats, Republicans, Libertarians, and Reformers, or as one observer astutely opined: "Ties and Tie-dyes." I appeared as the former, but identified with the latter.

I met some very interesting, fine people:

Lynnette Shaw is a social worker, who was under federal indictment in Marin County, California for distribution of Cannabis to AIDS patients. I would liken her to the heroic resistance fighters of World War II.

Tanya Kangas was Director of Litigation for NORML, despite the fact that she has never personally used marijuana. She is reminiscent of the "righteous gentiles" that harbored Jews in occupied countries under the Nazi yoke.

Irvin Rosenfeld is one of six surviving people in the USA who receive cannabis legally from the government under the "Compassionate Use Program." Because the grass is so

> I AM A CLINICAL NEUROLOGIST, WHO FOR SOME YEARS HAS INVESTIGATED HERBAL AND ETHNOBOTANICAL TREATMENTS FOR MIGRAINE. THE HERBAL TREATMENT PAR EXCELLENCE FOR THAT DISORDER FOR SOME 4000 YEARS IS CANNABIS.

low grade, treatment of the pain from his rare connective tissue disease requires him to smoke ten to twelve reefers a day. He is a successful stockbroker, contrary to propaganda mythology of shiftless marijuana users. His lungs are free of observed pathology, and an MRI has proven his brain to be free of shrinkage. I believe Irvin to be a modern Oskar Schindler. He could easily keep quiet, riding out the war in silence in his privileged position, but rather, he has become vocal in reminding others that our beneficent government shut down the Compassionate Use Program to new enrollees several years ago.

Finally, I met a very pleasant young woman who shall remain anonymous. She formerly was the chief of a campus police force, but now produces and distributes X-rated videos. Lest you scoff, and ponder marijuana stereotypes, I would submit that her work is no big deal when we all involuntarily paid $40 million for the overtly pornographic Starr Report.

It is time to stop the hypocrisy about medical marijuana. In the UK, the House of Lords has recommended that physicians be allowed to prescribe cannabis. Twenty percent of America has already voted on ballot initiatives, and overwhelmingly so, to approve this usage, and are thus demonstrating the type of good sense that eludes our federal politicians.

It is also high time to admit defeat in the "Drug War." As with other Holy Wars, it is hopelessly expensive, murders innocents, and displays ideological fervor without moral persuasiveness.

AS WITH OTHER HOLY WARS, IT IS HOPELESSLY EXPENSIVE, MURDERS INNOCENTS, AND DISPLAYS IDEOLOGICAL FERVOR WITHOUT MORAL PERSUASIVENESS.

The concept of probable cause must resume for drug testing. Currently, we're all suspects. I can understand testing after transportation accidents, but no correlation of negative tests to good job performance has ever been demonstrated. The concept of observation during urination is an obscenity. It could be that some of us are circumcised, and therefore subversives, communists, or Jews.

The D.A.R.E. program is a proven loser, of money and young minds. I have school age patients who need daily Ritalin to treat their ADHD, but sport the "drug free" slogan on their T-shirts. The hypocritical message of total abstinence is a cruel joke and lies to children, while legitimizing and reinforcing societal cynicism. Teenagers

THE CONCEPT OF OBSERVATION DURING URINATION IS AN OBSCENITY. IT COULD BE THAT SOME OF US ARE CIRCUMCISED, AND THEREFORE SUBVERSIVES, COMMUNISTS, OR JEWS.

will experiment whether it pertains to sex or drugs. A refreshingly honest approach to harm reduction would encourage responsible behavior in both spheres.

While we're at it, it is time to decriminalize or even outright legalize reasonable private use of marijuana by adults. It is inevitable that some prefer cannabis to Cabernet: Chaque à son goût! Go ahead and tax and regulate it, much as alcohol is presently. The profits can go to needle exchange programs, methadone maintenance, and to genuine treatment programs for addictive drugs.

Let's save our farmers by allowing them to grow hemp. Canada already has. We should also be making use of this versatile miracle crop that provides fabric and paper with the added bonus of a high quality protein and essential fatty acid seed.

Most of all, we need to stop demonizing our sick people and the doctors who are attempting to assist them. I would be a criminal for even discussing therapeutic values of cannabis to patients under legislation submitted by Lauch Faircloth in the Senate (R-NC) in 1998. Fortunately for me, he fell on his political sword.

As I came to learn in Washington, Shulamith Firestone said in 1970, "Freud was merely a diagnostician for what feminism purports to cure." To paraphrase her opinion, I have come to believe that cannabis is merely a therapeutic compass to what American medicine fails to cure. That shortcoming can be easily rectified. Marijuana is medicine. Let us liberate our patients. Let my people toke.

No Relief in Sight

Jacob Sullum

Editor's note—This article was originally published in 1997, but the war against pain relief continues unabated along with just about every other facet of the War on Some Drugs and Users. This article could be describing events that took place last week somewhere in the United States. While there has been some growing awareness and acceptance among the medical profession of using opiate medications as an effective and overall safe way of treating chronic, debilitating pain, federal agents are still bursting into doctors' offices and dragging out physicians in handcuffs in front of waiting patients, seizing records and files and bank accounts, forcing many physicians to shut down their practices.

There's the case of William Hurwitz, M.D., discussed in detail below, who announced in August, 2002 that he was phasing out his own practice treating patients for pain, due to overzealous police actions against those who prescribe opiate pain medications. Urging that the practice of medicine be brought back under the control of doctors, not the police, Dr. Hurwitz elaborated on his decision in an article published in the Spring, 2003 issue of the *Journal of American Physicians and Surgeons*, titled "Pain Control in the Police State." Dr. Hurwitz found himself under investigation, again, during which all his assets were seized by federal agents under federal asset forfeiture laws. In September, 2003 he was finally indicted and arrested for prescribing legal medications, including the controversial, powerful narcotic, OxyContin. He closed his office, and his patients were left stranded, trying to find someone else willing to treat their pain in a compassionate and adequate manner. Tragically, as you will see in this article, this was not Dr. Hurwitz's first confrontation with investigators nor the first time patients of his were forced to search for the relief they absolutely need to live a satisfactory life as they deal with their agonizing, oftentimes debilitating pain.

Torture, despair, agony, and death are the symptoms of "opiophobia," a well-documented medicalsyndrome fed by fear, superstition, and the war on drugs. Doctors suffer the syndrome. Patients suffer the consequences.

David Covillion finally got relief from his pain with the help of Jack Kevorkian. The pain came from neck and back injuries Covillion had suffered in April 1987, when his station wagon was broadsided by a school bus at an intersection in Hillside, New Jersey. The crash compounded damage already caused by an on-the-job injury and a bicycle accident. Covillion, a former police officer living in upstate New York, underwent surgery that fall, but it only made the pain worse. Along with a muscle relaxant and an anti-inflammatory drug, his doctor prescribed Percocet, a combination of acetaminophen and the narcotic oxycodone, for the pain.

The doctor was uneasy about the Percocet prescriptions. In New York, as in eight other states, physicians have to write prescriptions for Schedule II drugs—a category that includes most narcotics—on special multiple-copy forms.

> THE DAY HE CALLED HURWITZ, COVILLION WAS PLANNING HIS DEATH.

The doctor keeps one copy, the patient takes the original to the pharmacy, and another copy goes to the state. After a year or so, Covillion recalled in an interview, his doctor started saying, "I've got to get you off these drugs. It's raising red flags." Covillion continued to demand painkillers, and eventually the doctor accused him of harassment and terminated their relationship.

"Then the nightmare really began," Covillion said. "As I ran out of medication, I was confined to my bed totally, because it hurt to move....At times I'd have liked to just take an ax and chop my arm right off, because the pain got so bad, but I would have had to take half of my neck with it." He started going from doctor to doctor. Many said they did not write narcotic prescriptions. Others would initially prescribe pain medication for him, but soon they would get nervous. "I'd find a doctor who would treat me for a little while," he said. "Then he'd make up an excuse to get rid of me." Eventually, Covillion went through all the doctors in the phone book. That's when he decided to call Kevorkian.

The retired Michigan pathologist, who has helped more than 40 patients end their lives, was reluctant to add Covillion to the list. At Kevorkian's insistence, Covillion sought help from various pain treatment centers, without success. He called Kevorkian back and told him: "I'm done. I have no more energy now. I just don't have the fight. If you don't want to help me, then I'll do it here myself." Kevorkian urged him to try one more possibility: the National Chronic Pain Outreach Association, which referred him to Dr. William E. Hurwitz, an internist in Washington, D.C., who serves as the group's president.

The day he called Hurwitz, Covillion was planning his death. "I had everything laid out," he said. "I got a few hoses and made it so it would be a tight fit around the exhaust pipe of my car. I taped them up to one of those giant leaf bags, and I put a little hole in the end of the bag. All I had to do was start the car up, and it would have filled the bag right up, pushed whatever air was in there out, and it would have filled the bag up with carbon monoxide. Same thing as what Dr. Kevorkian uses. And then I had a snorkel, and I made it so I could run a hose from the bag full of gas and hook it up to that snorkel, and all I had to do was put it in my mouth, close my eyes, and go to sleep. And that would have been it. I would have been gone that Friday."

But on Thursday afternoon, Covillion talked to Hurwitz, who promised to help and asked him to send his medical records by Federal Express. After reviewing the records, Hurwitz saw Covillion at his office in Washington and began treating him. "The last three years I've been all right," he said in a July interview. "I have a life." Yet Covillion was worried that his life would be taken away once again. On May 14 the Virginia Board of Medicine had suspended Hurwitz's license, charging him with excessive prescribing and inadequate supervision of his patients. At the time Hurwitz was treating about 220 people for chronic pain. Some had been injured in accidents, failed surgery, or both; others had degenerative conditions or severe headaches. Most lived outside the Washington area and had come to Hurwitz because, like Covillion, they could not find anyone nearby to help them.

In July, after the case was covered by the *Washington Post* and *CBS News*, the Pennsylvania pharmaceutical warehouse that had been supplying Covillion with painkillers stopped filling Hurwitz's prescriptions, even though he was still licensed to practice in D.C. The pharmacist who informed Covillion of this decision (in a telephone conversation that Covillion recorded) suggested that Hurwitz had prescribed "excessively high amounts." At the same time, he recommended that Covillion "find another doctor" to continue the prescriptions. Covillion's reply was angry and anguished: "There is no other doctor!"

Hurwitz may not be the only physician in the country who is willing to prescribe narcotics for chronic pain, but there are few enough that patients travel hundreds of miles to see them. "I call it the Painful Underground Railroad," says Dr. Harvey L. Rose, a Carmichael, California, family practitioner who, like Hurwitz, once battled state regulators who accused him of excessive prescribing. "These are people who are hurting, who have to go out of state in order to find a doctor. We still get calls from all over the country: 'My doctor won't give me any pain medicine.' Or, 'My doctor died, and the new doctor won't touch me.' These people are desperate."

So desperate that, like Covillion, many contemplate or attempt suicide. In an unpublished paper, Rose tells the stories of several such patients. A 28-year-old man who underwent lumbar disk surgery after an accident at work was left with persistent pain in one leg. His doctor refused to prescribe a strong painkiller, giving him an antidepressant instead. After seeking relief from alcohol and street drugs, the man hanged himself in his garage. A 37-year-old woman who suffered from severe migraines and muscle pain unsuccessfully sought Percocet, the only drug that seemed to work, from several physicians. At one point the pain was so bad that she put a gun to her head and pulled the trigger, unaware that her husband had recently removed the bullets. A 78-year-old woman with degenerative cervical disk disease suffered from chronic back pain after undergoing surgery. A series of physicians gave her small amounts of narcotics, but not enough to relieve her pain. She tried to kill herself four times—slashing her wrists, taking overdoses of Valium and heart medication, and getting into a bathtub with an electric mixer—before she became one of Rose's patients and started getting sufficient doses of painkiller.

> "WE FREQUENTLY SEE PATIENTS REFERRED TO OUR PAIN CLINIC WHO HAVE CONSIDERED SUICIDE AS AN OPTION, OR WHO REQUEST PHYSICIAN-ASSISTED SUICIDE BECAUSE OF UNCONTROLLED PAIN."

> IN MEDICAL JOURNALS AND TEXTBOOKS, THE CAUSE OF THIS MISERY HAS A NAME: OPIOPHOBIA.

Patients who cannot manage suicide on their own often turn to others for help. "We frequently see patients referred to our Pain Clinic who have considered suicide as an option, or who request physician-assisted suicide because of uncontrolled pain," writes Dr. Kathleen M. Foley, chief of the pain service at Memorial Sloan-Kettering Cancer Center, in the *Journal of Pain and Symptom Management*. But as she recently told the *New York Times Magazine*, "those asking for assisted suicide almost always change their mind once we have their pain under control."

One thing that supporters and opponents of assisted suicide seem to agree on is the need for better pain management. Concern about pain was an important motivation for two 1996 decisions by federal appeals courts that overturned laws against assisted suicide in New York and Washington. In the New York case, the US Court of Appeals for the Second Circuit asked, "What business is it of the state to require the continuation of agony when the result is imminent and inevitable?" With the US Supreme Court scheduled to hear a combined appeal of those decisions during its current term, the persistent problem of inadequate pain treatment is sure to be cited once again.

In medical journals and textbooks, the cause of this misery has a name: *opiophobia*. Doctors are leery of the drugs derived from opium and the synthetics that resemble them, substances like morphine and codeine, hydromorphone (Dilaudid) and meperidine (Demerol). They are leery despite the fact that, compared to other pharmaceuticals, opioids are remarkably safe: The most serious side effect of long-term use is usually constipation, whereas over-the-counter analgesics can cause stomach, kidney, and liver damage. They are leery because opioids have a double identity: They can be used to get relief or to get high, to ease physical pain or to soothe emotional distress.

Doctors are afraid of the drugs themselves, of their potency and addictiveness. And they are afraid of what might happen if they prescribe opioids to the wrong people, for the wrong reasons, or in the wrong quantities. Attracting the attention of state regulators or the Drug Enforcement Administration could mean anything from inconvenience and embarrassment to loss of their licenses and livelihoods. In the legal and cultural climate created by what amounts to an eight-decades long war on drugs, these two fears reinforce each other: Beliefs about the hazards of narcotics justify efforts to prevent diversion of opioids, while those efforts help sustain the beliefs. The result is untold suffering. Dr. Sidney Schnoll, a pain and addiction specialist who chairs the Division of Substance Abuse Medicine at the Medical College of Virginia,

"THE UNDERTREATMENT OF PAIN IN HOSPITALS IS ABSOLUTELY MEDIEVAL.... THE PROBLEM PERSISTS BECAUSE PHYSICIANS SHARE THE WIDESPREAD SOCIAL ATTITUDES THAT THESE DRUGS ARE UNACCEPTABLE."

observes: "We will go to great lengths to stop addiction—which, though certainly a problem, is dwarfed by the number of people who do not get adequate pain relief. So we will cause countless people to suffer in an effort to stop a few cases of addiction. I find that appalling."

Because pain is hard to verify objectively, the conflict between drug control and pain relief is inevitable. It can be alleviated through regulatory reform, but it can never be eliminated. A system that completely prevented nonmedical use of prescription drugs would also leave millions of patients in agony. Conversely, a system that enabled every patient with treatable pain to get relief would also allow some fakers to obtain narcotics for their own use or for sale to others. In deciding how to resolve this dilemma, it's important to keep in mind that people who use prescription drugs to get high do so voluntarily, while patients who suffer because of inadequate pain treatment have no choice in the matter.

A woman who recently served as a chaplain at a New York City hospital encountered many patients in severe pain. "You let them squeeze your hand as hard as they want to, and cry, scream, express their frustration," she says. "It's horrible being in pain. It's really debilitating. It kills the spirit." She found that nurses were reluctant to give patients more medication. "If a patient seemed to really be in agony, I would go to a nurse," she says. "They were concerned about giving them too much." She recalls one patient who was in "terrible pain" following surgery. "They only had him on Tylenol," she says. "He complained about it, but then he said, 'Well I suppose they know best. They don't want me to get addicted to anything.'"

"IT'S HORRIBLE BEING IN PAIN. IT'S REALLY DEBILITATING. IT KILLS THE SPIRIT."

Clinicians and researchers have long remarked on the link between opiophobia and undertreatment of pain. In a 1966 pharmacology textbook, the psychiatrist Jerome H. Jaffe, who later became Richard Nixon's drug czar, noted that patients who take narcotics long enough develop tolerance (a need for larger doses to achieve the same effect) and physical dependence (resulting in withdrawal symptoms). But he cautioned that "such considerations should not in any way prevent the physician from fulfilling his primary obligation to ease the patient's discomfort. The physician should not wait until the pain becomes agonizing; *no patient should ever wish for death because of his physician's reluctance to use adequate amounts of potent narcotics.*"

Jaffe's admonition suggests that undertreatment of pain was common, an impression confirmed in the early 1970s by two psychiatrists at Montefiore Hospital and Medical Center in New York. Assigned to handle "difficult" patients, Richard M. Marks and Edward J. Sachar discovered a very good reason why so many continued to complain even after being treated with narcotics: They were still in pain. "To our surprise," they wrote in the February 1973 *Annals of Internal Medicine*, "instead of the primary issue being personality problems in the patient, in virtually every case it was found that the patient was not being adequately treated with analgesics and, further, the house staff for various reasons was hesitant to prescribe more."

Marks and Sachar's surveys of patients and doctors found "a general pattern of undertreatment of pain with narcotic analgesics, leading to widespread and significant distress." In part they blamed "excessive and unrealistic concern about the danger of addiction," which doctors erroneously equated with tolerance and physical dependence. Marks and Sachar emphasized the distinction between a patient who seeks a drug for pain relief and an addict who seeks a drug for its euphoric effects: The patient can readily give up the drug once the pain is gone, whereas the addict depends on it to deal with daily life. (The definition of addiction is fraught with social and political implications, but this distinction suffices for the purposes of this article.) Marks and Sachar estimated that less than 1% of patients treated with narcotics in a hospital become addicts. Although they urged better training in pain treatment, they concluded with a prescient warning: "For many physicians these drugs may have a special emotional significance that interferes with their rational use."

Subsequent studies confirmed that patients treated with narcotics rarely become addicts. In 1980 researchers at Boston University Medical Center reported that they had reviewed the records of 11,882 hospital patients treated

IT IS STARTLING TO REALIZE, AS THE END OF THE 20TH CENTURY APPROACHES, THAT THE IDEA OF GIVING PATIENTS ENOUGH MEDICATION TO RELIEVE THEIR PAIN IS JUST CATCHING ON.

with narcotics and found "only four cases of reasonably well documented addiction in patients who had no history of addiction." A 1982 study of 10,000 burn victims who had received narcotic injections, most of them for weeks or months, found no cases of drug abuse that could be attributed to pain treatment. In a 1986 study of 38 chronic pain patients who were treated with opioids for years, only two became addicted, and both had histories of drug abuse.

Despite such reassuring findings, many patients continued to suffer because of their doctors' opiophobia. In December 1987 the *New York Times* ran a story with the headline, "Physicians Said to Persist in Undertreating Pain and Ignoring the Evidence." Russell Portenoy, director of analgesic studies at Memorial Sloan-Kettering Cancer Center, told the *Times*, "The undertreatment of pain in hospitals is absolutely medieval....The problem persists because physicians share the widespread social attitudes that these drugs are unacceptable." He added that "many physicians fear sanctions against themselves if they prescribe the drugs more liberally." The article cited a recent survey in which 203 out of 353 patients at a Chicago hospital said they had experienced "unbearable" pain during their stay. More than half were in pain at the time of the survey, and 8% called the pain "excruciating" or "horrible." Most of the patients said nurses had not even asked them about their pain. The same study found that nurses were dispensing, on average, just one-fourth the amount of painkiller authorized by physicians.

The ordeal of Henry James, which began and ended the same year the *New York Times* article appeared, illustrates this stingier-than-thou tendency. James, a 74-year-old with prostate cancer that had spread to his leg and spine, was admitted to Guardian Care of Ahoskie, a North Carolina nursing home, in February 1987. Like many patients in the late stages of cancer, James was in severe pain, and his doctor had prescribed 150 milligrams of morphine every three or four hours, "as needed." The nursing staff thought that was far too much. They started cutting back his doses, substituting headache medicine and placebos. He received 240 doses in January but only 41 in February. The nursing supervisor, Rebecca Carter, told James and his family that she didn't want him to become an addict. She also said that if he took too much pain medication early on, it wouldn't work anymore when he really needed it.

James died after four months of agony. His family sued Guardian Care, and at the trial pain experts testified that the amount of medication Carter and her staff dispensed was grossly inadequate. They also noted that narcotic doses can be increased indefinitely to compensate for tolerance, so Carter's concern that the medicine would stop working was "ridiculous." In November 1990 the jury ordered the nursing home to pay James's estate $15 million, including $7.5 million in punitive damages. After the verdict, an unrepentant Carter told the *Los Angeles Times* "nothing whatsoever has changed....We still give drugs the way we always have."

Outside of Guardian Care, however, things were starting to change by the mid-1980s. As critics drew attention to the torture inflicted by undertreatment, the use of painkillers began rising substantially. Between 1979 and 1985, for example, consumption of oxycodone and hydromorphone rose 40% and 67%, respectively, according to DEA figures. The National Institute of Drug Abuse acknowledged the problem of opiophobia. In 1989 NIDA Director Charles Schuster confessed, "We have been so effective in warning

"THEY'RE AFRAID OF THE DRUGS, BECAUSE EVERY PARENT HAS HEARD NANCY REAGAN SAY, 'SAY NO TO DRUGS.' SO THEY'RE SAYING, 'MY GOD! DRUG ADDICTION COULD BE WORSE THAN MY CHILD'S CANCER.'"

the medical establishment and the public in general about the inappropriate use of opiates that we have endowed these drugs with a mysterious power to enslave that is overrated." A 1993 article in NIDA's newsletter said "these drugs are rarely abused when used for medical purposes" and lamented that "thousands of patients suffer needlessly." In 1992 and 1994 the US Department of Health and Human Services issued guidelines urging more aggressive treatment of postoperative pain and cancer pain, respectively. The 1994 guidelines said 90% of cancer pain could be controlled with available methods. On the same day that HHS released the guidelines, the *New England Journal of Medicine* published a national study estimating that 42% of cancer outpatients do not receive adequate pain treatment.

It is startling to realize, as the end of the 20th century approaches, that the idea of giving patients enough medication to relieve their pain is just catching on. One reason for the slow progress is that advocates of better pain treatment have been fighting deeply rooted prejudices. Americans have always had mixed feelings about psychoactive substances. To deal with our ambivalence, we tend to divide drugs into neat categories: good and bad, legal and illegal, therapeutic and recreational. We are not comfortable with drugs that straddle categories, as the opioids do. The discomfort is strengthened by historical experience, ranging from Civil War veterans hooked on morphine to middle-class housewives hooked on over-the-counter remedies in the years before the Harrison Narcotics Act of 1914. The nexus between medical treatment and opiate addiction was vividly portrayed in Eugene O'Neill's "Long Day's Journey Into Night," written in 1940 and set in 1912. Mary Tyrone, the wife of a stage actor, is a shaky, nervous woman who uses morphine to escape her troubles. She became addicted as a result of injections she received following the birth of her son. "I was so sick afterwards," she says, "and that ignorant quack of a cheap hotel doctor—all he knew was I was in pain. It was easy for him to stop the pain."

Patients still worry about getting hooked on painkillers. Schnoll, the Virginia pain and addiction specialist, cites the impact of anti-drug propaganda "telling us that there's an addict on every corner, under every stone. So of course people are fearful. I find that my own patients are often unwilling. I have to convince them to take the medications I'm prescribing them." Foley, the Sloan-Kettering pain specialist, says the problem is especially vexing in the case of children. "Parents are so afraid of addicting their kids that they do not want to treat them," she says. "They say, 'The pain's not so bad,' or, 'We don't want him to be sleepy,' or, 'We don't want to make him an addict.' They say to the kid, 'Be tough.' But they're very torn and confused. They're afraid of the drugs, because every parent has heard Nancy Reagan say, 'Say no to drugs.' So they're saying, 'My God! Drug addiction could be worse than my child's cancer.'"

By perpetuating such attitudes, the war on drugs obstructs pain relief. Through efforts to prevent narcotics from falling into the wrong hands, it has a more direct effect. A 1987 DEA report cites declines of 30% to 55% in the use of Schedule II drugs within two years after the adoption of multiple-copy prescription programs in various states during the 1960s and 1970s. "I think it's a testament to the percentage of misprescribing and criminal prescribing that goes on," says Gene Haislip, the DEA's director of diversion control. "I don't think there's any evidence that they're discouraging appropriate medical use. We think there's some evidence to suggest they're discouraging

inappropriate prescribing, but I don't have any reason to think they really have an impact on legitimate practitioners." Haislip likens compliance with a multiple-copy prescription program to filing an income tax return. "We don't decide not to make money because we have to report it," he says. "And I don't think doctors are deciding, 'Well, this patient isn't going to get medical treatment that's appropriate because somewhere somebody may read something and ask me some questions.'"

The tax code, of course, has a big impact on the way people make (or don't make) money. And despite Haislip's reassurances, there is substantial evidence that prescription monitoring has a chilling effect on the practice of medicine. To begin with, a large percentage of doctors in multiple-copy states—in California, almost half—do not even request the special forms, which suggests that "legitimate practitioners" are deterred by the hassle and scrutiny involved. "When I was in Illinois," says Sidney Schnoll, "there were physicians who just didn't want to carry triplicate forms. Sometimes they would call me up and say, 'You have triplicates, don't you? Can you write a prescription for so-and-so?' That's not good medicine."

Furthermore, it hardly seems plausible that frivolous or fraudulent prescriptions could account for a third to a half of a state's licit narcotic use, as Haislip suggests. The limited research on this question does not support that view. A 1984 study reported in the *American Journal of Hospital Pharmacy* found that Schedule II prescriptions at a major Texas hospital dropped more than 60% the year after the state began requiring triplicate forms for such drugs. At the same time, prescriptions of analgesics not covered by the program rose. A 1991 study reported in *The Journal of the American Medical Association* found a similar pattern in New York state, which added benzodiazepines, a class of sedatives that includes Valium, to the drugs covered by its monitoring program in 1989. Prescriptions for benzodiazepines dropped substantially in New York, while use of several other sedatives rose, even as consumption of those drugs fell in the rest of the country. The researchers noted that "[t]he alternative sedative-hypnotic medications are less effective, more likely to be abused, and more dangerous in overdose than benzodiazepines." These studies suggest that multiple-copy prescription programs lead physicians to replace monitored drugs with less appropriate alternatives.

This sort of behavior is reinforced every time a conscientious doctor gets hassled by the authorities because someone thought his prescriptions looked suspicious. In 1987 two state drug agents visited the office of Ronald Blum, associate director of New York University's Kaplan Comprehensive Cancer Center. "They showed me their badges and guns, and read me my

> "I BEGAN LOOKING AT WHY PHYSICIANS WERE RELUCTANT TO PRESCRIBE OPIOIDS IN APPROPRIATE AMOUNTS, AND I REALIZED THAT THE BOTTOM LINE WAS THAT THEY WERE AFRAID OF SANCTIONS BY REGULATORY AGENCIES."

rights," he told the *Journal of NIH Research*. It turned out that Blum had filled out some narcotic prescription forms incorrectly. The Department of Health charged him with three administrative violations, including failure to report his cancer patients to the state as habitual drug users. A year and a half later, after Blum had spent $10,000 in legal fees, the state finally dropped the charges. In 1987 the DEA investigated Portland, Oregon, oncologist Albert Brady because he was prescribing high doses of Dilaudid to a cancer patient in a nursing home. Although the DEA concluded that Brady was not supplying drugs to the black market, it notified the state Board of Medical Examiners, which fined him $5,000 for overprescribing and suspended his license for a month. It does not take many incidents like these to "have an impact on legitimate practitioners." Brady told the *Journal of NIH Research* that his two partners "changed their practice overnight and became reluctant to prescribe sufficient doses of painkillers."

As the Brady case illustrates, even in states that do not require special forms for certain drugs, physicians have to worry about attracting the attention of state licensing boards. A 1991 survey of 90 physicians reported in the *Wisconsin Medical Journal* found that most were concerned enough about regulatory scrutiny to prescribe lower doses, indicate smaller amounts, allow fewer refills, or select a different drug than they otherwise would have. Given the attitudes of many regulators, such caution is understandable. In 1992 the University of Wisconsin Pain Research Group surveyed state medical board members throughout the country. The results, as reported in the newsletter of the American Pain Society, were striking: "Only 75% of medical board members were confident that prescribing opioids for chronic cancer pain was both legal and acceptable medical practice....If the patient's chronic pain did not involve a malignancy, only 12% were confident that the practice was both legal and medically acceptable." Since these are the people who define the limits of appropriate medicine, their beliefs are bound to affect the treatment of pain.

Dr. C. Stratton Hill, a professor of medicine at the M.D. Anderson Cancer Center in Houston, became interested in the impact of regulatory expectations on medical practice about a decade and a half ago. "Patients with obvious cancer pain were given doses that were not adequate," he says. "So I began looking at why physicians were reluctant to prescribe opioids in appropriate amounts, and I realized that the bottom line was that they were afraid of sanctions by regulatory agencies."

Hill and other physicians lobbied for what came to be known as the Intractable Pain Treatment Act, which the Texas legislature approved in 1989. Essentially, the law said doctors would not be punished for prescribing narcotics to patients suffering from pain that could not be relieved through other means. But this assurance "did not make any difference in what the doctor did," Hill says, "because there was no commonly understood standard of practice. The doctor could still be charged and have to defend himself, and that cost money. Maybe the doctor would win, but that would be $25,000 later."

In 1995 Hill and his colleagues convinced the state Board of Medical Examiners to adopt rules clarifying the vague provisions of the state Medical Practice Act under which doctors were most commonly charged. Under the new rules, a doctor who prescribes a drug in good faith for a legitimate medical purpose (including pain relief) is not subject to sanctions, provided he observes certain safeguards and keeps careful records. Hill thinks the new policy may be having an impact. The year after the rules were issued, 17 doctors were charged under the relevant sections, compared to 37 the year before.

Hill's work in Texas helped inspire similar efforts in California, where Harvey Rose emerged from his battle with regulators—which took $140,000 in legal fees and five years to resolve—determined to help other doctors avoid similar conflicts. In 1990 the state legislature adopted an Intractable Pain Treatment Act modeled after the Texas statute, and in 1994 the Medical Board of California issued guidelines intended to reassure wary doctors. Although California's current approach is decidedly more enlightened than the policies of other states, Rose says "doctors are still fearful. They just don't want to deal with patients like this, because they're afraid it's too difficult. They're never sure if they're getting enough records and covering their butts enough. It's much easier just to say, 'No, I'm sorry. I don't take care of your kind.'"

That was essentially the response encountered by Cynthia A. Snyder, a nurse who recently described her own search for pain relief in *The Journal of Law, Medicine, and Ethics*. After a cerebral aneurysm and brain surgery in 1983, Snyder suffered from seizures, memory loss, and "terrible, unrelenting pain." But she soon learned that "I lacked the 'proper diagnosis' to control my pain. I did not have terminal cancer." Like many other patients in the same situation, Snyder found that her desperation for relief was viewed with suspicion. "Several times," she

"SEVERAL TIMES," SHE WRITES, "I WAS OPENLY ACCUSED OF BEING AN 'ADDICT' AND OF FALSELY REPORTING CHRONIC PAIN JUST TO OBTAIN PRESCRIPTION DRUGS....FINALLY, I FOUND MYSELF BEGGING, AS THOUGH I WERE A CRIMINAL."

NONE OF HIS CURRENT PATIENTS HAD ANYTHING BAD TO SAY ABOUT HIM. MANY TRAVELED LONG DISTANCES TO SHOW THEIR SUPPORT AT HIS HEARING BEFORE THE BOARD OF MEDICINE, AND MORE THAN 50 TESTIFIED ON HIS BEHALF.

writes, "I was openly accused of being an 'addict' and of falsely reporting chronic pain just to obtain prescription drugs....Finally, I found myself begging, as though I were a criminal." After five years of suffering, she found a physician willing to prescribe regular doses of codeine. "Within two weeks, I felt reborn!" she recalls. "I began writing again. My doctorate was completed, and once more I began to teach part-time. *My hope was restored, and my life was no longer crippled by constant severe pain.*"

Eventually, Snyder reports, "the precise neuropathology of the pain was discovered." But that was years after her brain surgery. When she was searching for a doctor to help her, she could not offer any definitive evidence of her pain. There were records of the aneurysm and the operation, but only her complaint testified to her ongoing suffering. This is often the case with intractable pain. How do you prove the existence of migraine headaches or back pain, not to mention poorly understood conditions such as fibromyalgia and chronic fatigue syndrome? A doctor can take a patient's history, inquire about symptoms, and perform an exam. He can consider the patient's character and reputation. But in the end, he is only surmising that the pain is real. Ultimately, he has to take the patient at his word, knowing that misplaced trust could mean professional ruin.

Ask William Hurwitz. The doctor who offered David Covillion an alternative to a Kevorkian-style death lost his license in August, as did Jerome A. Danoff, the pharmacist who filled prescriptions for many of Hurwitz's patients. The investigation began in May 1995, when agents of the DEA and the Virginia Department of Health Professions visited Danoff's store because a wholesaler had reported unusually large orders of narcotics. Hurwitz asked his patients to sign waivers of confidentiality and opened up his records to the investigators. A year later, when relatives of two patients who had died in January 1996 complained to the Virginia Board of Medicine, the board suspended Hurwitz's license, charging him with misprescribing not only for those patients but for 28 others.

It's doubtful that the deaths resulted from Hurwitz's negligence. One patient, a Tennessee man with a head injury that impaired his sense of smell, died after eating rotten chicken fajitas and vomiting all weekend. Hurwitz

"THE BOARD OF MEDICINE HAS TOLD MY PATIENTS, 'DROP DEAD.'"

believes he died of intestinal hemorrhaging caused by food poisoning, but the medical examiner, after finding a lot of empty Dilaudid bottles, concluded that the man had died of an overdose, a theory that was not supported by a blood test. On the other hand, needle tracks indicated that the man had been dissolving his painkiller and injecting it, contrary to Hurwitz's instructions, and his girlfriend said he had been taking excessive doses of a muscle relaxant. In the other case, which involved a Florida woman suffering

from facial pain after failed jaw surgery, toxicology tests showed that she had taken oxycodone and morphine in much higher doses than Hurwitz had prescribed. He believes her death was a suicide, and the patient's mother, who defends him, concurs. Her ex-husband thinks his daughter died of an accidental overdose and blames Hurwitz.

The investigators found one former patient who complained that Hurwitz had given him too many pills and too little information about their side effects. But none of his current patients had anything bad to say about him. Many traveled long distances to show their support at his hearing before the Board of Medicine, and more than 50 testified on his behalf. Hurwitz's motives were not in doubt, and the hearing focused largely on the amounts of medication he had prescribed. His patients were taking anywhere from 10 to 200 pills a day.

Hurwitz explained that some patients are especially resistant to narcotics to begin with, and all develop tolerance. He insisted that the number of pills is not the issue, since a patient who would otherwise be incapacitated by pain can function well on doses of narcotics that would kill the average person. In fact, Virginia has an Intractable Pain Treatment Act that allows doctors to prescribe narcotics "in excess of the recommended dosage upon certifying the medical necessity." Dr. Mitchell Max, director of the Pain Research Clinic at the National Institute of Health, testified: "I see nothing wrong with the doses, the amount, the number of pills per se....He is just taking regimens that work in cancer patients that everyone agrees on, and using them in people who had life-impairing, or even life-threatening, levels of pain.... We routinely give doses up to 10 times that size in patients with cancer."

The state questioned the thoroughness of Hurwitz's examinations, documentation, and monitoring. Hurwitz says most of his pain patients came to him with well-established problems, and "my main purpose in doing the diagnosis was to make sure that the patients were who they said they were. If they said they had back surgery, I wanted to see a back scar. If they said they had no leg, I wanted to look at the stump. So my physical exam was really limited to confirmatory findings that would illustrate the complaints and make sure they weren't conning me." As for monitoring, he saw patients who lived in the area once a month, but those who lived hundreds of miles away might visit his office only once or twice a year. The visits were supplemented by a monthly written report and telephone calls.

"The average practitioner does have reservations about prescribing long-term opiates," testified Dr. Stephen P. Long, director of acute pain services at the Medical College of Virginia Hospitals. "I would have performed a more thorough physical exam. I would like to have seen

Jacob Sullum

more detailed documentation." On the other hand, Dr. James Campbell, director of the Blaustein Pain Treatment Center at Johns Hopkins University, said Hurwitz "is doing heroic things for his patients. I think what he is doing involves enormous sacrifice. There are a lot of bad doctors out there, but he is not one of them."

On August 10, after the longest hearing in its history, the Virginia Board of Medicine found Hurwitz guilty of inadequate screening, excessive prescribing, and deficient monitoring. It revoked his license, saying it would be restored after three months if he agreed to take courses in narcotic prescription, pharmacology, psychiatry, addiction, medical record keeping, and pain management. Even then, he would be forbidden to prescribe narcotics for a year. Hurwitz has registered for the courses, but he has also filed an appeal in Arlington Circuit Court. After the Virginia ruling, the D.C. Board of Medicine suspended Hurwitz's license. Unable to practice, he had to give up his office. About the same time, the Virginia Board of Pharmacy revoked Jerome Danoff's license for two years and fined him $10,000. He also planned to appeal.

Meanwhile, Hurwitz's patients were left high and dry. "I'm flabbergasted," he told the *Washington Post* after his Virginia license was revoked. "The Board of Medicine has told my patients, 'Drop dead.'" Said Laura D. Cooper, a patient with multiple sclerosis: "The board has made no provision for the patients. If I can't get medicine, I'm going to die the next time I get sick, and that's not histrionics. Some of us are candidates for suicide right now." Cooper, an attorney, has filed a federal class-action suit against the Virginia Board of Medicine, the Department of Health Professions, and the DEA on behalf of herself and Hurwitz's other pain patients.

David Covillion is not a party to the suit. He killed himself on September 11.

For current information about this issue, readers can visit these extensive websites:

Dr. William Hurwitz— http://www.drhurwitz.com/

Pain Relief Network—http://www.painreliefnetwork.org/

Protecting Children—America's Real Drug Abuse Epidemic

Sharon L. Secor

The drug war rages on with our government's continued commitment to stamping out illegal drug use and production both domestically and internationally. Yet despite the aggressive prohibitionist posturing and persistently expressed concern for the well-being of our nation's children, our government finds it convenient to ignore the most dangerous drug abuse trend in the nation, taking place each day in institutions and agencies that it supports. This is not surprising, considering that those who ultimately profit from the sales of these abused drugs are among the nation's greatest political contributors and also fund the most powerful lobbying groups to grace the political system.

The child protective system is among the most egregious of those who practice the chemical restraint of children and medical abuse of children. While parents who use or

> THE CHILD PROTECTIVE SYSTEM IS AMONG THE MOST EGREGIOUS OF THOSE WHO PRACTICE THE CHEMICAL RESTRAINT OF CHILDREN AND MEDICAL ABUSE OF CHILDREN.

abuse drugs run the risk of never seeing their children again, drugs seem to rank high among the methods of choice for child control within the child protective system. What more efficient way is there to deal with a child's anguished cries for parents and home, a seized child's temper tantrums, withdrawal, depression, and general acting out?

The *Miami Herald* found that almost 600 Florida Medicaid recipients under the age of six were given powerful psychiatric drugs in 2000, drugs that are meant for the treatment of schizophrenia and other severe psychotic mental illnesses. Mental disorders such as these are almost never found in children so young.

"I'm starting to get scared here," said Jack Levine, president of the Tallahassee-based Center for Florida's Children, according to the May 7, 2001 *Miami Herald* report by Carol Marbin Miller.

The drugs, which include Clozaril, Zyprexa, and Risperdal, have serious side effects, even in adults. Yet, 46 two-year-olds, 67 three-year-olds, and 177 four-year-olds were "prescribed" anti-psychotics.

"According to records reviewed by the *Herald*, as well as several interviews, children in foster care administered anti-psychotics have experienced lethargy, agitation, tremors and even the development of unusually large breasts," wrote Miller. In addition, "one boy even began to produce breast milk."

After the *Miami Herald* made this information public, the Florida Statewide Advocacy Council, which is a part of the Department of Children and Families, did a two year investigation. They studied 1,180 foster children.

The results of the study, released in September of 2003, revealed that more than half of these children were taking psychotropic drugs that are not FDA cleared as being safe for children. Furthermore, 44% of the children were not even seen by a doctor and 59 of these children had no diagnosis, with 143 having a diagnosis that was termed "other."

Even "infants and toddlers were being administered the drugs," reported the *Miami Herald* on September 19, 2003.

City Agency's Psych Drugs Imperil Foster Kids, an April 16, 2001 article by Douglas Montero, described the "cocktail of psychiatric medications" that many New York City foster children are forced to take. Sometimes these are made up of four or more powerful drugs.

> PARENTS WHO RESIST SUCH TREATMENT FOR THEIR CHILDREN "FACE MEDICAL-NEGLECT CHARGES IN FAMILY COURT."

The Administration for Children's Services, according to the article, isn't sure how many of the 31,000 children in their care have been prescribed psychiatric drugs, but "a state audit of 401 randomly selected kids last year found that more than half were being treated for mental problems—and that most likely means medication."

Parents who resist such treatment for their children "face medical-neglect charges in Family Court," wrote Montero, pointing to the case of Tariq Mohammad, who was forced to take antipsychotic medication for years in foster care. The family was successful, however, in winning a civil suit against ACS. A court-appointed psychiatrist found that the boy did not need any medication at all.

Children die like this. Children like foster child Jimmy Wood, who was fourteen years old at the time of his prescription drug overdose. The *Denver Post*, reported on January 19, 2004, that "he was last heard crying alone in a closed bedroom."

Mollie Gonzalez died when she overdosed on the anti-seizure medicine that was kept, according to the *Denver Post*, in a small refrigerator in the bedroom in which she slept. In addition to the Tegratol, she was also taking Prozac and chloral hydrate, a powerful sedative used to sedate hospital patients. She was ten.

As though the dangerous chemical restraint of children in state custody isn't brutal enough, a recent story, also by Montero, reveals a breathtaking abuse of drugs, power and infants in state foster care.

Montero reported in a *New York Post* article, published February 29, 2004, that the New York State Health Department "has launched a probe into potentially dangerous drug research conducted on HIV-infected infants and children"—foster children at Incarnation Children's Center in Manhattan.

With money from "federal grants and, in some cases, pharmaceutical companies," approximately 36 different experiments were performed, including 13 that used about 50 children—some just three months old—to test the effects of high doses of AIDS medicines, according the information cited in Montero's report. Other experiments included studying the "safety," "tolerance" and "toxicity" of AIDS drugs, through methods that mixed up to six different medications. Yet another sought to determine the effects of double-dosing infants with measles vaccine.

"They are torturing these kids, and it is nothing short of murder," said Michael Ellner, quoted by Montero. Ellner is a minister and president of Health Education AIDS Liaison, which is an advocacy group for HIV parents.

Dr. David Rasnick, a biochemist and expert in the field of AIDS medicine, was "outraged," according to Montero, citing the "acute toxicity" and fatal potential of the medications, as well as the variety of severe side effects associated with the drugs.

Montero also noted that "the foster-care agency described the experiments on its own Web site, which was abruptly shut down after the *Post* began making inquiries."

It is not only the state and federally sponsored child protective systems that drug children with an astounding lack of concern for their well-being. The education system has become notorious for its participation in the pharmaceutical scam associated with the pseudo-disorders popularly known as Attention Deficit Disorder, and Attention Deficit Hyperactivity Disorder.

The symptoms associated with these "disorders" are vague and subjective, including such things as scholastic under-performance, difficulty in or inability to pay attention to a task or follow instructions, easy distractibility, forgetfulness, daydreaming, over-activity, impulsiveness, and aggressive behavior.

According to the Drug Enforcement Administration, between the years 1991 and 2000, the per year production of methylphenidate, which is the generic form of Ritalin and one of the primary medications prescribed for ADD and ADHD, rose by 740%. Other stimulants used in the treatment of ADD and ADHD have risen to 25 times previous levels. Interestingly, these disorders seem to be an American phenomenon, as the other Western industrialized nations—with the exception of Canada—use Ritalin at a mere one tenth of the rate of Americans, though through the miracles of modern pharmaceutical advertising, their rates are beginning to increase.

THE CITIZEN'S COMMISSION ON HUMAN RIGHTS REPORTS THAT IN THE UNITED STATES "AT LEAST SIX MILLION CHILDREN" ARE PRESCRIBED "MIND-ALTERING DRUGS," INCLUDING THE INFAMOUS RITALIN, FOR "EDUCATIONAL REASONS."

The Citizen's Commission on Human Rights reports that in the United States "at least six million children" are prescribed "mind-altering drugs," including the infamous Ritalin, for "educational reasons." In addition, according to their statistics, "Two million children take antidepressant and antipsychotic drugs." Because of the devastating side effects of some of these drugs, in December of 2003, Britain banned the use of anti-depressants, except for Prozac, in children under eighteen, due to links to increased suicide attempts discovered in clinical trials.

Dr. Joseph T. Coyle wrote in the February 23, 2000, issue of *The Journal of American Medical Association*, of the trend towards prescribing psychotropic medications to an increasing number of very young children, citing a study of Michigan Medicaid claims which found 223 children—three years old and younger—diagnosed as suffering ADD or ADHA. Only 25% of these children were receiving psychological services (no mention of how many of the parents were receiving psychological services). However, 60% of these children were prescribed psychotropic medications, with half of these taking two or more types.

"It should be emphasized that most of the drugs prescribed involve off-label use because efficacy of psychotropic drugs has not been demonstrated in very young children," Coyle pointed out, adding that methylphenidate, the generic form of Ritalin, "carries a warning against its use in children younger than six years." According to Coyle, "there is virtually no clinical research on the consequences of pharmacologic treatment of behavioral disturbances of very young children." In addition, noted Coyle, the diagnosing of such disorders in children so young has not yet been proven to be reliable or valid.

There's a lot of money involved. In 2001, pharmaceutical companies brought in $600 million in profit from just the drugs used to treat ADD, according to an April 18, 2003, report published by *CNSNews.com*. Data released by the Federal Election Commission on Monday, February 09, 2004, shows that pharmaceutical companies have given $107,595,713 to federal political candidates between 1990 and the present, with about two-thirds of these funds going to Republicans. Somehow, it seems doubtful that our corporate-friendly governmental drug war warriors will be rushing to do zero-tolerance battle against this drug abuse epidemic.

Czar Walters Stands on Methadone

Doug McVay

Sometimes, getting a federal official to take a good stand and get involved in a policy debate is simple. It can be about being at the right place, at the right time, to ask the right question.

On March 9, 2004, John Walters spoke to a group of students and concerned citizens at George Washington University. The event was to promote a student organization sponsored by the Drug Free America Foundation called Students Taking Action Not Drugs (STAND), an organization formerly known as International Students In Action.

(The DFAF STAND group's mission statement, on their website at www.standnow.org, makes clear that they exist in large part to work against the growing movements on US campuses to reform drug laws. This distinguishes them from other organizations called Students Taking Action Not Drugs or STAND, which have been in existence for more than a decade in middle schools and high schools and which are dedicated instead to mainly working against substance use by young people.)

Walters' presentation was relatively bland: Drug use is bad, sobriety is good, treatment and prevention are good, we (the feds) are making wise decisions and things are looking up. He's been much more politically careful since taking office, and has avoided making controversial comments—no more talk of youth as "super predators," for example. Instead, Walters sends assistants like Andrea Barthwell and Scott Burns into the trenches to make outrageous statements.

> DRUG USE IS BAD, SOBRIETY IS GOOD, TREATMENT AND PREVENTION ARE GOOD, WE (THE FEDS) ARE MAKING WISE DECISIONS AND THINGS ARE LOOKING UP.

During the Q&A following his presentation, I asked Mr. Walters about his failure to get involved in opposing an attempt to limit access to methadone treatment that is nearing success just across the Potomac from Washington DC, in Virginia. In that state, a bill to restrict access to methadone treatment had just passed both houses of the legislature and is on its way to the governor's desk.

The bill, SB607, was pushed by conservative Republican legislators. Media reports of increasing methadone diversion and overdose deaths helped generate public support for the measure. ONDCP and its director had been silent on the issue, until that evening.

He bristled at the suggestion that ONDCP had fallen down on the job. He said that it was unrealistic to expect that his office could possibly follow every piece of legislation, every bad bill, in every state. Yet the ONDCP does track, and get involved in working against, efforts at the state and even local levels to medicalize marijuana and to institute treatment alternatives to incarceration programs.

Walters has always expressed support for methadone treatment, and he repeated that support. The ONDCP also supports expansion of access to methadone treatment. He said flatly that attempts to restrict access to methadone were wrong-headed, and that he would oppose such efforts. (His statements, and those of other ONDCP officials contacted for comment, are the subject of a news article on March 12, 2004, in the *Roanoke Times*, a major newspaper in southern Virginia.)

According to the *Roanoke Times*, "Dr. Andrea Barthwell, deputy director for demand reduction in the drug czar's office, said a law restricting methadone treatment could have adverse effects for both drug addicts and the communities where they live. 'It may in fact be eliminating the possibility of offering a beacon of hope to some of society's most disenfranchised,' Barthwell said."

"Critics of the legislation say it is based on fears of clinic-related crime that have no factual basis," continued the *Times* report. "Police in every Virginia jurisdiction that has a methadone clinic have said the drug treatment centers do not cause major problems with crime. Studies have also shown that methadone treatment leads to reduced criminal activity among addicts. 'Methadone is probably the most-studied model of care to treat addiction,' Barthwell said. The drug czar's office, which coordinates all aspects of federal drug programs and spending, has long been in support of methadone maintenance programs. While there is a legitimate need to closely monitor methadone patients and be mindful of their presence in the surrounding neighborhood, Barthwell said, clinics that provide the medication have historically been responsive to community concerns."

Walters does still need to be educated on some aspects of methadone. Walters talked about the growing number of reported methadone overdoses, asserting that because of these it may be necessary to keep a closer eye on methadone treatment programs. A federal panel however has found that clinic methadone isn't the source of the problem.

In response to growing concerns and media reports regarding methadone overdoses, the US Substance Abuse and Mental Health Services Administration of the Dept. of Health and Human Services examined the issue of methadone-associated mortality. According to

"CRITICS OF THE LEGISLATION SAY IT IS BASED ON FEARS OF CLINIC-RELATED CRIME THAT HAVE NO FACTUAL BASIS."

their report, issued in February 2004, treatment clinics are not to blame. The consensus panel concluded: "the data confirm a correlation between increased methadone distribution through pharmacy channels and the rise in methadone-associated mortality. The data, thus, support the hypothesis that the growing use of oral methadone, prescribed and dispensed for the outpatient management of pain, explains the dramatic increases in methadone consumption and the growing availability of the drug for diversion to illicit use. Although the data remain incomplete, National Assessment meeting participants concurred that methadone tablets and/or diskettes distributed through channels other than OTPs [Opioid Treatment Programs] most likely are the central factor in methadone-associated mortality." (p. 24)

Some contend that the increase in methadone pain prescriptions is due to heightened federal and state scrutiny of doctors prescribing OxyContin. The increase in OxyContin use in rural areas such as conservative Republican southwest Virginia is blamed for the increased demand in these regions for opiate substitution (methadone) treatment. Because a patient may have to make a several hour-long round trip to get to treatment, some people in need drop out or don't even start.

Walters' comments on access to methadone treatment were timely. Though the legislation in Virginia is on its way to the governor's desk, it isn't law yet. The ONDCP director's statement may give the more-liberal Democratic governor of Virginia, Mark Warner, political cover to be able to veto the bill. Nearby in the state of West Virginia, a similar legislative effort to restrict methadone treatment hasn't gone quite as far. Methadone opponents in South Carolina have kept their opposition at the local level—so far. It's hard to say how much impact Walters can have on these anti-methadone legislative moves from his bully pulpit, but at least now he's speaking out.

Though the sponsors of that bill in Virginia didn't just say "Oh, never mind then," when contacted, Walters is a conservative drug warrior working for a conservative Republican president. By speaking out, he would have given members of the Republican majority in Virginia's legislature political cover to vote against the bill, possibly killing it. This issue is still playing out in other parts of the country, so we may yet get to see what good a drug czar can do.

Stanislav Grof interviewing Dr. Albert Hofmann at the Esalen Institute in Big Sur, California, 1984

Stanislav Grof, M.D.

Grof: It is a great pleasure and honor for me this morning to welcome and introduce Dr. Albert Hofmann, to the extent to which he needs introduction at all. As you all know, he became world famous for his discovery of a compound that is probably the most controversial substance ever developed by man, lysergic acid diethylamide, or LSD-25. When LSD made its entry into the world of science, it became overnight a sensation because of its remarkable effects and also unprecedented potency. It seemed to hold tremendous promise in the research of the nature and etiology of schizophrenia, as an extraordinary therapeutic agent, as a very unconventional tool for training of mental health professionals, and as a source of inspiration for artists.

Dr. Hofmann's discovery of LSD generated a powerful wave of interest in brain chemistry and, together with the development of tranquilizers, was directly responsible for what has been called the "golden age of psychopharmacology." And then his prodigious child became a "problem child." This extraordinarily promising chapter in psychology and psychiatry was drastically interrupted by unsupervised mass self-experimentation

WHETHER OR NOT LSD RESEARCH AND THERAPY AS SUCH WILL RETURN INTO MODERN SOCIETY, THE DISCOVERIES THAT PSYCHEDELICS MADE POSSIBLE HAVE PROFOUND REVOLUTIONARY IMPLICATIONS FOR OUR UNDERSTANDING OF THE PSYCHE, HUMAN NATURE, AND NATURE OF REALITY.

and the ensuing repressive administrative, legislative, and political measures, as well as the chromosome scare and the abuse by the military and secret police. But I firmly believe that this chapter is far from being closed. Whether or not LSD research and therapy as such will return into modern society, the discoveries that psychedelics made possible have profound revolutionary implications for our understanding of the psyche, human nature, and nature of reality. And these new insights are here to stay as an important part of the emerging scientific world-view of the future.

But before we start this interview, I would like to add a little personal note. Dr. Hofmann's discovery of LSD and his work, in general, have had a profound impact on my own professional and personal life, for which I am immensely grateful. My first LSD session in 1956, when I was a beginning psychiatrist, was a critical landmark and turning point for me and since then my life has never been the same. So this interview gives me the opportunity to express my deep appreciation and gratitude to Dr. Hofmann for the influence he has had on my life.

What I would like to ask you first has something to do with the way people tend to qualify your discovery of the psychedelic effects of LSD. It is usually referred to as a pure accident, implying that there was nothing more involved in this entire matter than your fortuitous intoxication. But I know from you that the history was somewhat more complex than. Can you clarify this for us?

Hofmann: Yes, it is true that my discovery of LSD was a chance discovery, but it was the outcome of planned experiments and these experiments took place in the framework of systematic pharmaceutical, chemical research. It could better be described as *serendipity*. (Dr. Hofmann is using here a word coined in the eighteenth century by Horace Walpole after his tale *Three Princes of Serendip*—which is another name for Ceylon—who made during their travels fortunate discoveries while pursuing other things). That means that you look for something, you have a certain plan, and then you find something else, different, that may nevertheless be useful.

And that is exactly what happened with LSD. I had developed a method for the synthesis of lysergic acid amides in the context of a systematic study, the purpose of which was to synthesize natural ergot alkaloids. At that time, in the 1930s, a new ergot alkaloid had been discovered which is named *ergometrine*, or *ergonovine*; it is the real active principle of ergot. The presence of this alkaloid in ergot is the reason why it has been used in obstetrics to stop uterine bleeding and as an oxytocic to stimulate the muscular activity of the uterus. And this substance turned out to be an amide of lysergic acid.

Until the late 1930s, it had not been possible to prepare such substances in the laboratory. I discovered a technical procedure that made it possible and was able to achieve partial synthesis of ergonovine; I then also used this procedure to prepare other lysergamides. First came the modifications of *ergonovine* and one of these modifications, *methergine*, a homologue of *ergonovine*, is today the leading medicament in obstetrics to stop *post partum* bleeding. I also used this procedure to prepare not so close derivatives of *ergonovine*, more different than *methergine*. And one of these compounds was LSD-*25, lysergic acid diethylamide*. The plan, the intention I had, was to prepare an analeptic, a circulatory and breathing stimulant.

Grof: Was there some indication in the early animal experiments that LSD could be an activating agent?

AT THE END OF THE SYNTHESIS, SOMETHING VERY STRANGE HAPPENED. I GOT INTO A DREAMLIKE CONDITION, IN WHICH ALL OF MY SURROUNDING WAS TRANSFORMING. MY EXPERIENCE OF REALITY HAD CHANGED AND IT WAS RATHER AGREEABLE.

Hofmann: No, I made LSD because it is an analog of *coramine*, which is *diethylamide of nicotinic acid*. Because of the structural relationship between LSD and the ring of the nicotinic acid, I hoped to get an analeptic. But our

MANY PEOPLE WHO HAVE TAKEN LSD, PARTICULARLY IN SUCH A HIGH DOSE, HAVE A LOT OF RESPECT FOR THAT RIDE. THEY REALIZE WHAT IT IS TO RIDE A BICYCLE IN THAT KIND OF A CONDITION.

pharmacologist concluded that *lysergic acid diethylamide* did not have any clinically interesting properties and suggested that it be dropped out of research. That happened in the year 1938. But all along, I had a strange feeling that we should again test this substance on a broader scale. Then, five years later, in 1943, I finally decided to synthetize another sample of LSD. At the end of the synthesis, something very strange happened. I got into a dreamlike condition, in which all of my surrounding was transforming. My experience of reality had changed and it was rather agreeable. In any case, I left the laboratory, went home, lay down and enjoyed a nice dreamlike state which then passed away.

Grof: Did you immediately suspect that this was an intoxication by the drug you were working with?

Hofmann: I had the suspicion that it was caused by something from the laboratory, but I believed that it could have been caused by the solvent I had used at that time. I had used *dichlorethylene*, something like chloroform, in the very final state of preparation. So, the next day in the laboratory, I tried the solvent and nothing happened. Then I considered the possibility that it might have been the substance I had prepared. But it did not make any sense. I knew I was very careful and my work was very clean. And, of course, I did not taste anything.

But I was open to the fact that, maybe, some trace of the substance had in some way passed into my body. That, maybe, a drop of the solution had come on my fingertips and, when

I rubbed my eyes, it got into the conjunctival sacs. But, if this compound was the reason of this strange experience I had, then it had to be very, very active. That was clear from the very beginning because I had not ingested anything. I was puzzled and decided to conduct some experiments to clear up this thing, to find out what was the reason for that extraordinary condition I had experienced.

Being a cautious man, I started this experiment with only 0.25 milligrams (the ergot alkaloids are usually administered in milligram dosages). That is an extremely low dose and I expected it would not have any activity. I thought I would increase very cautiously the quantity of LSD in subsequent experiments to see if any of the dosages were active. It turned out that when I ingested this quarter of a milligram, I had taken a very strong, a very high dosage of a very, very active compound. I got into a strange state of consciousness. Everything in my surroundings changed—the colors, the forms, and also the feeling of my ego had changed. It was very strange! And I became very anxious that I had taken too much and I asked my assistant to accompany me home. At that time we had no car available and we went home by bicycle.

Grof: Many people who have taken LSD, particularly in such a high dose, have a lot of respect for that ride. They realize what it is to ride a bicycle in that kind of a condition.

Hofmann: During this trip home on the bicycle—it was about four kilometers—I had the feeling that I could not move from the spot. I was cycling, cycling, but the time seemed to stand still. In my report afterward, I mentioned this trip on the bicycle to show that LSD affected the experience of time, as an example of the distortion of the sense of time. Then the bicycle trip became a characteristic aspect of the LSD discovery. As we arrived home, I was in a very, very bad condition. It was such a strange reality, such a strange new universe which I had entered, that I believed I had now become insane. I asked my assistant to call the doctor. When the doctor arrived, I told him that I was dying. I had the feeling that my body had absolutely no feeling any more. He tested me and shook his head, because everything was OK.

Then, nevertheless, my condition became worse and worse. When I was lying on my couch, I had the feeling that I had already died. I believed, I had a sense that I was out of my body. It was a terrifying experience! The doctor did not give me anything, but I drank a lot of milk, as an unspecific detoxicant. After about six hours, the

I HAD THE FEELING THAT I SAW THE EARTH AND THE BEAUTY OF NATURE AS IT HAD BEEN WHEN IT WAS CREATED, AT THE FIRST DAY OF CREATION. IT WAS A BEAUTIFUL EXPERIENCE! I WAS REBORN, SEEING NATURE IN QUITE A NEW LIGHT.

experience of the outer world started to change. I had the feeling of coming back from a very strange land, home to our everyday reality.

And it was a very, very happy feeling and a very beautiful experience. After some time, with my eyes closed, I began to enjoy this wonderful play of colors and forms, which it really was a pleasure to observe. Then I went to sleep and the next day I was fine. I felt quite fresh, like a newborn. It was an April day and I went out into the garden and it

FOR THE FIRST TEN YEARS, LSD WAS MY "WONDER CHILD;" WE HAD A POSITIVE REACTION FROM EVERYWHERE IN THE WORLD. ABOUT TWO THOUSAND PUBLICATIONS ABOUT IT APPEARED IN SCIENTIFIC JOURNALS AND EVERYTHING WAS FINE. THEN, AT THE BEGINNING OF THE 1960S, HERE IN THE UNITED STATES, LSD BECAME A DRUG OF ABUSE.

had been raining during the night. I had the feeling that I saw the earth and the beauty of nature as it had been when it was created, at the first day of creation. It was a beautiful experience! I was reborn, seeing nature in quite a new light.

Grof: We have seen this kind of sequence, the death-rebirth process, very regularly in psychedelic sessions. Many people link this experience to the memory of their biological birth. I wanted to ask you, if during the time when it was happening, it was just an encounter with death or if you also had the feeling that you were involved in a biological birthing process?

Hofmann: No, the first phase was a very terrifying experience, because I did not know if I would recover. First, I had the feeling that I was insane and then I had the feeling I was dying. But then, when I was coming back, I had of course the feeling of rebirth.

Grof: But there was no connection to actual memory of biological birth.

Hofmann: No.

Grof: When did you become aware that this drug could be of significance to psychiatry?

Hofmann: Immediately! I knew immediately that this drug would have importance for psychiatry but, at that time, I would never have believed that this substance could be used in the drug scene, just for pleasure. For me it was a deep and mystical experience and not just an everyday pleasurable one. I never had the idea that it could be used as a pleasure drug. And then, soon after my experience, LSD came into the hands of psychiatrists. The son of my boss at that time, Dr. Werner Stoll, who was working at the Burghoeltzli Psychiatric Institute in Zurich, conducted the initial experiments with LSD.

First, we checked it in our laboratory, because the head of the Chemical Department, Professor Stoll, and the head of the Pharmacology Department, Professor Rothlin, said that what I was telling them was not possible. They told me: "You must have made a mistake when you measured the dosage. It is impossible that such a low dosage could have an effect." And Professor Rothlin then made an experiment with two of his assistants. They took only one fifth of what I have taken, 50 micrograms, to check it out. And even then, they had a full-blown experience!

Then it was clear that LSD was a substance with the activity of a quite new dimension and the samples of LSD were sent to Dr. Stoll in Zurich. He conducted the first fundamental study exploring the use of LSD in clinical conditions. He first gave it to normal persons and he himself took also 50 micrograms. His classical description of the LSD experience appeared in his publication that was published in 1947. He used LSD also in schizophrenics and other categories of patients and he outlined most of the uses that LSD could have had in psychiatry. He also suggested, as one of the very important possibilities of the use of LSD, that psychiatrists should use the substance in self-experiments for training purposes. That they themselves should use the substance to enter and explore the world of changed consciousness, the world of their patients. He did it himself and he gave an example of such a procedure.

And it was also Doctor Stoll who described in his pioneering paper how LSD could be used as an adjunct to psychoanalysis. Not as a medicament, that would just be administered to the patient, but as a tool to intensify and deepen psychotherapy. This was based on the fact that LSD showed the potential to bring into consciousness forgotten or repressed memories. And if these were of a traumatic nature and had been the cause of mental disturbances, this had important therapeutic consequences. It also increased suggestibility and improved the contact between the patient and the psychiatrist. And based on these effects, Dr. Stoll suggested that LSD could be a very useful adjunct to psychoanalysis.

I TOOK A DOSAGE THAT WAS MENTIONED IN THE PRESCRIPTIONS IN THE OLD CHRONICLES—2.4 GRAMS OF DRIED MUSHROOMS—AND I HAD A FULL-BLOWN LSD EXPERIENCE.

Grof: He really outlined the three directions that became fundamental in the early psychedelic research. The first of these was the concept of "model psychosis"—using LSD as a means of creating a laboratory model for studying schizophrenia. The second one was the suggestion that LSD could be employed as a training tool for psychiatrists and psychologists. And the third direction was to explore the potential of LSD as an adjunct to psychotherapy or as a therapeutic tool.

So, this was, in a nutshell, the story of the discovery of LSD. And then we come to the next important chapter of your psychedelic research, the isolation and identification of the active principles of the magic mushrooms of the Mazatec Indians in Mexico. How long after the discovery of the psychedelic effects of LSD did Gordon Wasson contact you?

I TOOK IT IN THE LABORATORY AND I HAD TO GO HOME, BECAUSE I HAD AGAIN TAKEN A DOSAGE THAT WAS RATHER HIGH. AT HOME, EVERYTHING LOOKED MEXICAN—THE ROOMS AND SURROUNDINGS—ALTHOUGH I HAD NEVER BEEN IN MEXICO BEFORE.

Hofmann: For the first ten years, LSD was my "wonder child;" we had a positive reaction from everywhere in the world. About two thousand publications about it appeared in scientific journals and everything was fine. Then, at the beginning of the 1960s, here in the United States, LSD became a drug of abuse. In a short time, this wave of popular use swept the country and it became drug number one. It was then used incautiously and people were not prepared and informed about its deep effects. And then all kinds of things happened, which caused LSD to become an infamous drug. It was a troublesome time! Telephones, panic, and alarm! This had happened, that had happened….it was a breakdown. Instead of a "wonder child," LSD suddenly became my "problem child."

And then, one day in the 1960s, I saw in the newspaper a notice that an American amateur mycologist and ethnologist, Gordon Wasson, and his wife had discovered mushrooms, which were used in a ritual way by the Indians. These mushrooms seemed to contain a hallucinogen that produced an LSD-like effect. Of course, I did not know who these ethnologists were, but I certainly would have been interested in investigating these mushrooms. Then, I got a letter from professor Heim, a French mycologist from the Sorbonne in Paris. Mr. Wasson and his wife, who had discovered this very old Mexican mushroom cult and had published information about the ritual use of these mushrooms, had sent him some botanical samples of the plant. They had asked him if he could examine the mushrooms and make precise botanical investigation.

After Professor Heim completed the basic botanical work, he tried to isolate the active principle from the mushrooms, but he did not succeed. Gordon Wasson had also initiated chemical studies of the mushrooms in the United States, at the University of Delaware, but this work had not brought any positive results either. And so professor Heim, who knew about the work we had done with LSD in Basel, asked me in his letter if I would be interested to take on this research. So, in this way, LSD attracted the mushrooms to come into my laboratory.

At first, we had only 200 or 300 grams of these mushrooms. We tested them in animals, since we had some experience with LSD and we knew what kind of pharmacological activity could be expected from such psychoactive principles. We did not find anything and our pharmacologist suggested that the mushrooms probably were not active at all, that they were the wrong mushrooms, or that they had lost their activity when they had been dried in Paris. In any case, to clear the problem, I decided to make a self-experiment. I took a dosage that was mentioned in the prescriptions in the old chronicles—2.4 grams of dried mushrooms—and I had a full-blown LSD experience.

And it was very strange. I took it in the laboratory and I had to go home, because I had again taken a dosage that was rather high. At home, everything looked Mexican—the rooms and surroundings—although I had never been in Mexico before. I thought that I must have imagined all that, because I knew that the mushrooms had come from Mexico. For example, I had a colleague, a doctor who supervised me for this experiment. When he checked my blood pressure, I saw him as an Aztec. He had a German face, but for me he became an Aztec priest and I had the feeling he would open my chest and take out my heart. It was really an absolutely Mexican experience!

WE VISITED MARIA SABINA, THE CURANDERA OR THE SHAMAN WOMAN WHO HAD GIVEN THE MUSHROOMS TO THE WASSONS. THEY WERE PROBABLY THE FIRST WHITE PEOPLE WHO EVER INGESTED THE MUSHROOMS DURING THE SACRED CEREMONY.

After a few hours, I came back from the Mexican landscape and I knew that we had not used the right tests. The work with animals would not have taken us anywhere; we had to test the activity of all the fractions in humans. And from then on, my colleagues and myself tested personally all the extracts we made from the mushrooms. We extracted them with different solvents and used fractionating procedures to isolate the active principles.

Grof: How many steps did it take you from the beginning to the end to identify chemically the active principles?

Hofmann: We had about five or six steps. Finally, we ended up with a very small quantity, several milligrams of concentrated material that was still amorphous. And we could use it to make a paper chromatogram. It turned out that the substance was concentrated in four phases. We cut the paper chromatogram and four of my colleagues and myself ate these fractions. One of the fractions turned out to be active. Then we could make some tests with this fraction, crystallize it, get the color reaction specific for it, and so on. Finally, we were able to isolate the active principles and it turned out to be two substances, which I named *psilocybine* and *psilocine*, because they had been isolated from *Psilocybe mexicana*. Most of these magic mushrooms used by the Indians belong to the genus *Psilocybe*.

> I STARTED WITH THE LYSERGIC ACID AMIDES—METHERGINE AND LSD—AND LSD ATTRACTED THE MUSHROOMS. THE MUSHROOMS THEN BROUGHT THE OLOLIUQUI AND THE WORK WITH OLOLIUQUI TOOK ME BACK TO LYSERGIC ACID AMIDES. MY MAGIC CIRCLE!

Then, when we had these substances, we sent them for pharmacological testing. It turned out that they were about a hundred times less active than LSD, but still very active. It means that about five to ten milligrams is the active dose. Later I received a letter from Professor Moore in Delaware, who congratulated us for solving the problem of the mushrooms. He and his team had worked more than a year trying to isolate the active principles from these mushrooms and were not able to do it. They had tested all their extracts in animals, all kinds of animals, even fish, but were not able to find a lead. The reason for our success was that we used our own team for testing the fractions and did not rely on animal experiments. Professor Moore then sent me the rest of these mushrooms; after all this work, he still had about twelve kilograms left.

Grof: What was the overall time that it took you to identify the active alkaloids?

Hofmann: About half a year. And having chemically identified these substances, we were then able to synthetize them in the laboratory. And we were able to use for it the basic materials we had on hand from the LSD research, namely derivatives of tryptamine which could now be used for the synthesis of *psilocybine* and *psilocine*. Gordon Wasson, who was a banker by profession and an amateur mycologist, was very impressed by the results. He did not know what active principles meant; for him it was the mushrooms that were the active agent. And he came to Basel to visit us and I showed him these active principles in a pure crystalline form. It turned out that only about 0.5% of the mushrooms represents the active principles. Instead of 5 grams of the mushrooms you can take 25 milligrams of *psilocybine*. Gordon was quite fascinated to see these crystals and then he said: "Oh, by the way, there is another magic drug the Indians use which has not yet been studied scientifically. It is called *ololiuqui*.

Grof: And so began another important chapter of your research.

Hofmann: Yes. I went with Gordon Wasson to Mexico to study the other magic plant materials, *ololiuqui* (morning glory seeds) and *Salvia divinorum,* a new *Salvia* species that the Indians also used like the mushrooms. And we visited Maria Sabina, the *curandera* or the shaman woman who had given the mushrooms to the Wassons. They were probably the first white people who ever ingested the mushrooms during the sacred ceremony. It was already late summer or beginning of fall and there were no more mushrooms. We explained to Maria Sabina that we had isolated the spirit of the mushrooms and that it was now in these little pills. She was fascinated and agreed to make a ceremony for us.

And to participate in the ceremony, you always have to have a reason. The mushroom ceremony is a consultation, like going to a doctor or a psychiatrist if you have some problems. And Gordon told Maria Sabina: "I left New York three weeks ago and my daughter had to go to the hospital to have a child. I don't know what happened with her. Can the mushroom tell me what happened with my daughter?" So that was the reason they made a ceremony for us. It involved Maria Sabina, her daughters, and other shaman colleagues and it was a beautiful ceremony.

Grof: I understand that, on this occasion, Maria Sabina gave you the official "seal of approval," that after having taken the pills, she actually confirmed that their effects were identical to those of the magic mushrooms.

> IN MANY INSTANCES, IT ACTUALLY PRODUCED TERRIFYING AND DELETERIOUS EFFECTS INSTEAD OF BENEFICIAL EFFECTS. BECAUSE OF MISUSE, BECAUSE IT WAS A PROFANATION. IT SHOULD HAVE BEEN SUBJECTED TO THE SAME TABOOS AND THE SAME REVERENCE THE INDIANS HAD TOWARD THESE SUBSTANCES.

Hofmann: Yes. I gave her for the ceremony tablets of the synthetic psilocybine. I knew that she used a certain number of mushrooms and I assessed the corresponding quantity of tablets. We used them and it was really a full-blown wonderful ceremony which lasted till the morning. When we left, Maria Sabina told us that these tablets really contained the spirit of the mushrooms. I gave her quite a bottle of them and she said: "I can now also perform the ceremonies during the times when we have no more mushrooms."

Grof: And how did you now move from your mushroom research to the work with *ololiuqui*?

Hofmann: I got the supply of *ololiuqui*, seeds of a certain morning glory family, from Gordon Wasson. Gordon got them from a Zapotec Indian who had collected them for him. These seeds, like the mushrooms, were used in ceremonies for a kind of magic healing and for divination.

We were able to isolate the active principles responsible for the effect of these seeds and I was quite astonished to find out that these seeds contained as the active principles *monoamid* and *hydroxyethylamid of lysergic acid* and a bit of *ergonovine*. These were derivatives of lysergic acid which I had on my shelf through my studies with LSD. I initially could not believe that this was possible, because the lysergic acid derivatives I had worked with before were produced by a fungus.

Grof: And the morning seeds come from flowering plants that belong botanically to an entirely different category.

Hofmann: Yes, these plants belong to two very different stages of evolution in the plant kingdom, which are quite remote from each other. And it is absolutely unusual to find the same chemical products in quite different places of plant evolution.

Grof: I have heard that, at the beginning, your colleagues actually accused you that you must have contaminated your samples from the *ololiuqui* research by the products of your LSD work that you kept in your laboratory. Knowing how meticulous your work is, that was quite an outrageous accusation!

Hofmann: That is true. I gave the first report on this work in 1960, at the International Conference on Natural Products in Sydney. When I presented my results, my colleagues shook their heads and they said: "It is impossible that you find the same active principles in a quite different section of the plant kingdom. You are working with all kinds of lysergic acid derivatives; you must have mixed up something and that is the reason." But finally, of course, they checked it and confirmed our results.

That was the closing of a kind of magic circle. I started with the lysergic acid amides—*methergine* and LSD—and LSD attracted the mushrooms. The mushrooms then brought the *ololiuqui* and the work with *ololiuqui* took me back to lysergic acid amides. My magic circle!

I WAS NOT VERY HAPPY WITH THE NAME BECAUSE SALVIA DIVINORUM MEANS "SALVIA OF THE GHOSTS" WHEREAS SALVIA DIVINATORUM, THE CORRECT NAME, MEANS "SALVIA OF THE PRIESTS."

Grof: Have you actually tried the *ololiuqui*. yourself?

Hofmann: Yes, I did. But, of course, it is about ten times less active; to get a good effect, you need one to two milligrams.

Grof: And what was that experience like?

Hofmann: The experience had some strong narcotic effect, but at the same time there was a very strange sense of voidness. In this Void, everything looses the meaning. It is a very mystical experience.

Grof: Usually, when you read the psychedelic literature there is a distinction being made between the so-called natural psychedelics, such *psilocybine, psilocine, mescaline, harmaline,* or *ibogaine,* which are produced by various plants (and this applies even more to psychedelic plants themselves) and synthetic psychedelics that are artificially produced in the laboratory. And LSD, which is semisynthetic and thus a substance that was produced in the laboratory, is usually included among the latter. I understand that you have a very different feeling about it.

Hofmann: Yes. When I discovered lysergic acid amides in *ololiuqui*, I realized that LSD is really just a small chemical modification of a very old sacred drug of Mexico. LSD belongs, therefore, by its chemical structure and by its activity into the group of the magic plants of Mesoamerica. It does not occur in nature as such, but it represents just a small chemical variation of natural material. Therefore, it belongs to this group as a chemical and also, of course, because of its effect and its spiritual potential. The use of LSD in the drug scene can thus be seen as a profanation of a sacred substance.

And this profanation is the reason that LSD has not had beneficial effects in the drug scene. In many instances, it actually produced terrifying and deleterious effects instead of beneficial effects. because of misuse, because it was a profanation. It should have been subjected to the same taboos and the same reverence the Indians had toward these substances. If that approach had been transferred to LSD, LSD would never have had such a bad reputation.

Grof: Let me move to another subject. Can you tell us something about the attempts to isolate the active alkaloids from *Salvia divinorum*?

Hofmann: Yes. When I was in Mexico, we also encountered another plant that the Indians used ritually, like *ololiuqui* or like the mushrooms. It was a member of the *Salvia* species which had not been botanically identified. After a long trip into Sierra Mazateca, we finally found a *curandera* who conducted a ceremony with this plant and we had the opportunity to have an experience with it. Gordon Wasson, my wife, and myself ingested the juice of fresh leaves and experienced some effects, but it was very mild. It was a clear-cut effect, but different from the mushrooms.

Grof: Have you attempted the isolation and chemical identification of the active principle from *Salvia divinorum*?

Hofmann: I took the leaves and made extracts from them by pressing out the juice. I took this extract to Basel to my laboratory and wanted to chemically analyze it, but it was no longer active. It seems that the active principle is very easily destroyed and the problem of chemical analysis is not yet solved. But we were able to establish the botanical identity of this plant. It was determined at

the Botanical Department at Harvard that it was a new species of *Salvia* and it got the name *Salvia divinorum*. It is a wrong name, bad Latin; it should be actually *Salvia divinatorum*. They do not know very good Latin, these botanists. I was not very happy with the name because *Salvia divinorum* means "Salvia of the ghosts" whereas *Salvia divinatorum*, the correct name, means "Salvia of the priests." But it is now in the botanical literature under the name *Salvia divinorum*.

Grof: Was it Dr. Richard Schultes at Harvard who identified the plant?

Hofmann: No, it was done in the same Institute, but by two other botanists; they were the ones who gave it the name.

Grof: Was this the end of your research of psychedelic substances? Have you been since interested in any other psychedelic plants? And have you made any more attempts at identifying some of their active principles?

Hofmann: No. No more.

Grof: Was this work interrupted because of the political and administrative problems at Sandoz caused by the unsupervised use? Do you think you would have otherwise continued in this work? And would you have liked to carry on?

Hofmann: Yes, I have already said that the abuse and misuse in the drug scene brought many troubles to our company. Then came the legal restrictions from the health authorities in nearly all countries and, of course, management of our company was no longer interested in pursuing this avenue of research.

Grof: Did you yourself have any plans or interests in this regard?

Hofmann: I followed the literature and became interested at one point in the problems related to *Amanita muscaria*. I tried to get these mushrooms and to isolate the active principles from them, but then it turned out that Professor Reutz at the University of Zurich had already nearly solved the problem. In addition, the reports about the psychedelic effects of these mushrooms came from Siberian shamans. And the substances that had been isolated from the *Amanita* mushrooms which had been collected in our country have a narcotic effect but not a hallucinogenic or psychedelic effect.

It was my suggestion, and I still believe it, that the mushrooms grown in Siberia must be a different chemical race. It is known that, depending on where the mushrooms are grown, they might be botanically identical and not have the same chemical composition. I tried to get the mushrooms from my Russian colleagues, but the contacts I had were very unreliable. I got all kinds of evasive answers and excuses: "This year the mushrooms are already finished; maybe next season, next year." And the next year the story repeated itself. I did not get the mushrooms and finally I discarded the problem.

Grof: Was this interest inspired by Gordon Wasson's theory suggesting that the *Amanita muscaria* might have actually been the Vedic sacrament *Soma*?

Hofmann: Yes, Gordon believed that soma, the plant and sacrament which plays such an important role in the Vedic scriptures, was actually *Amanita muscaria*. But the Zurich studies showed that the active principles of *Amanita* are narcotics and not stimulants; they are not psychedelic substances. This was a major objection to the theory. I believed that I could solve this problem by studying the Siberian mushrooms but, as I said, it was not possible, because I could not get them.

Grof: There have been many controversial reports about the effects of *Amanita*. Many people who have tried it just got sick or experienced a trivial delirium. Others reported some variable experiences, but certainly nothing as consistent as the effect of the *Psilocybe* mushrooms.

Hofmann: It is definitely something different from the Mexican mushrooms, which have an unquestionable and clear-cut psychedelic effect.

Grof: Gordon has also published an article and later a book on the last meal of the Buddha, suggesting that Buddha's death, the *parinirvana*, occurred under the influence of psychedelic mushrooms. This issue involves a linguistic problem. The Pali canon describes that Buddha before his death feasted on pork. But Gordon Wasson and his team found that the term used, literally *"swine bits,"* is actually a folk name for a mushroom.

Hofmann: I cannot give you any informed judgment about this problem. He may be right but, as you said, it is mainly a problem of semantics. The description of Buddha's death is great; it certainly could be a psychedelic experience!

Grof: I would like to ask you now about another project, your work with Gordon Wasson concerning the Mysteries of Eleusis. In your book *The Road to Eleusis*, you suggest the possibility that it was a psychedelic cult that actually existed and practiced for almost 2000 years, since 1400 BC to 400 AD. And even then people did not just lose interest

> WHAT WAS IT THAT WAS BEING OFFERED AT ELEUSIS? WHAT COULD POSSIBLY HAVE BEEN SO POWERFUL AND INTERESTING THAT IT KEPT THE ATTENTION OF THE ANCIENT WORLD FOR ALMOST TWO THOUSAND YEARS WITHOUT INTERRUPTION?

in it, but it was terminated by an edict of the Christian emperor Theodosius who prohibited and suppressed all pagan ceremonies.

Hofmann: In professional circles of Greek scholars, it is absolutely clear that the ancient Greeks used some psychoactive substance in their cult. There exist many references to a sacred beverage, *kykeon*, that was administered to the initiates after preparations which took one week. After the adepts got this potion, they had, all together, powerful mystic experiences that they were not allowed to talk about and describe exactly. I had worked about twenty years ago with the Greek scholar, Professor Kerenyi, on this problem.

The interesting question is: what were really the ingredients of this *kykeon*, this sacred potion? We had studied many plants that Professor Kerenyi had suggested as possible candidates, but they were not at all psychedelic. Then came Gordon Wasson with his hypothesis; naturally, it involved mushrooms, because he saw mushrooms everywhere. He asked me, if the men in Greek antiquity had the possibility to prepare a psychedelic potion from ergot. He came to this idea, because the Mysteries of Eleusis were founded by the Goddess Demeter and Demeter is the goddess of grain and ergot (Mutterkorn). That gave him the idea that ergot could be involved in the preparation of *kykeon*.

I had all the materials at hand because, as part of our studies of ergot, we had collected all the literature and also many samples of ergot from all around the world. And this included the ergot that was growing in the Mediterranean basin, in Greece, and so on. And one or two of these wild ergots growing on grasses can also be found in rye fields or in barley fields. Rye did not exist in antiquity, but barley did, and in barley fields you can find certain wild ergots.

We had found and analyzed all this ergot before Gordon asked me his question and in one species growing on wild grass (*Paspalum*) we had found exactly the same components as in *ololiuqui*. Its main components were *lysergic acid amide*, *lysergic acid hydroxyethylamide*, and also *lysergic acid propanolamide (ergonovine)*. Therefore, I had no difficulty answering Gordon's question: Man

in antiquity had the possibility to prepare a psychedelic potion from ergot. He had to just collect the ergot, grind it, and put it into the *kykeon*.

Gordon, pursuing the problem of *kykeon*, addressed not only me, as a chemist, but also a Greek scholar Professor Carl Ruck at Harvard, who was a specialist on the role of medicinal plants in Greek mythology and Greek history. Professor Ruck was able to direct Gordon to some allusions in the *Hymn to Demeter* that provided support for his hypothesis. These passages mentioned that, indeed, there was some kind of ergot which was used to make this *kykeon* psychedelic. And the three of us then co-authored a book, which explored this evidence.

Grof: That was the book *The Road to Eleusis?*

Hofmann: Yes, that was *The Road to Eleusis*, which was published here in the United States and also came out in some other languages, such as Spanish and German.

Grof: You describe in this book that you actually did a self-experiment with one of the natural ergot alkaloids to test this hypothesis, to see if it was psychedelic. Was it *ergonovine?*

Hofmann: Yes, we had found active principles in this ergot which grows in Greece. It contained *lysergic acid amide* and *hydroxyethylamide*, about which it was already known that they were psychedelic. But it was not known if *ergonovine* had some psychedelic effects and I was interested to find out. *Ergonovine* had been used already for many decades in obstetrics without any reports that it had been psychedelic. But the dosage which is injected to women in childbirth, is only 0.5 mg and 0.25 mg. I tested it up to 2 mg and, in that dosage, it had clearly psychedelic effects. It had not been discovered earlier, because when it is administered, women are just at the end of the process of delivery. They are thus in a state in which they are not very good observers and, in addition, the dosage is too low to produce psychedelic effects. *Methergine* and *ergonovine* also produce psychedelic effects but in higher doses.

> THE ACTION OF LSD CAN BE UNDERSTOOD ONLY IN TERMS OF ITS INTERACTION WITH THE CHEMICAL PROCESSES IN THE BRAIN WHICH UNDERLIE THE PSYCHIC FUNCTIONS.

Grof: It is a very interesting hypothesis, because it gives a plausible answer to the intriguing question: What was it that was being offered at Eleusis? What could possibly have been so powerful and interesting that it kept the attention of the ancient world for almost two thousand years without interruption? And that it attracted so many exceptional and illustrious people? Also the fact that it was such a strongly guarded secret—the punishment for revealing the secret of the mysteries was death—suggests that something quite extraordinary, something extremely important was happening there.

Hofmann: It was a very important spiritual center for nearly 2000 years. All we have to do is to look at all the famous people, who for thousands of years in the world of antiquity, in the Roman and Greek world, were introduced to the Mysteries of Eleusis. For us it was a very interesting problem to find out what the initiates really got. There were two families in Eleusis who knew the secret of the *kykeon*, two generations of families who conserved the secret.

IT IS IMPORTANT TO REALIZE THAT THERE IS AN ENORMOUS LEAP FROM CHEMISTRY TO PSYCHOLOGICAL EXPERIENCE. THERE ARE LIMITS TO WHAT THIS BASIC CHEMICAL BACKGROUND CAN TELL US ABOUT CONSCIOUSNESS.

Grof: One often hears that the use of psychedelic materials is alien to the Western culture, that it is something that is practiced in pre-literate human groups, in "primitive" societies. The enormous effect that the death/rebirth mysteries of various kinds must have on the Greek culture, which is generally considered the cradle of European civilization, must be the best kept secret in human history. Many of the great figures of antiquity, such as philosophers Plato, Aristotle, and Epictetus, playwright Euripides, military leader Alkibiades, Roman statesman and lawyer Cicero, and others were initiates of these mysteries, whether it was the Eleusinian variety or some other forms—the Dionysian rites, the mysteries of Attis and Adonis, Mithraic or Korybantic mysteries, and the Orphic cult.

Hofmann: And it shows again that in old times, and also in our time among the Indian tribes, psychedelic substances were considered sacred and they were used with the right attitude and in a ritual and spiritual context. And what a difference if we compare it with the careless and irresponsible use of LSD in the streets and in the discotheques of New York City and everywhere in the West. It is a tragic misunderstanding of the nature and the meaning of these kinds of substances.

Grof: I would now like to move away from these cultural and historical explorations and go back to chemistry. Although pharmacology is not your primary interest, I would like to ask you a question about the mechanism of the action of LSD. There does not seem to be unanimity as to why LSD is psychoactive and there are several competing hypotheses about it. Do you have any ideas in this regard?

Hofmann: We have done some research that is related to this question. We labeled LSD with radioactive carbon, C^{14}. That makes it possible to follow its metabolic fate in the organism. Strangely enough, we found, of course in

animals, that 90% of the LSD is excreted very quickly and only 10% of it goes into the brain. And in the brain it goes into the hypothalamus and that is where the emotional functions are located. This corresponds also to the fact that it is primarily the emotional sphere that is stimulated by LSD. The rational spheres are rather inhibited.

UNDER THE INFLUENCE OF PSYCHEDELIC SUBSTANCES, THE VALVE IS OPENED AND AN ENORMOUS INPUT OF OUTER STIMULI CAN NOW COME IN AND STIMULATE OUR BRAIN.

And, of course, it is not LSD that produces these deep psychic changes. The action of LSD can be understood only in terms of its interaction with the chemical processes in the brain which underlie the psychic functions. Since LSD is a substance, its action can be described only in terms of interaction with other substances and with the structures in the brain, the receptors, and so on.

One of the popular hypotheses was, for example, the *serotonin hypothesis* of the British researchers Woolley and Shaw. It was found that LSD is a very specific and strong inhibitor of *serotonin* in some biological systems. And since *serotonin* plays a very important role in the chemistry of neurophysiological functions in the brain, this was seen as the mechanism underlying its psychological effects.

Since this antagonism between LSD and *serotonin* was very strong and specific, our pharmacologist was very interested to find out, if there are *serotonin* antagonists without hallucinogenic effect. This was not only an interesting theoretical question, but a matter of some practical interest, because *serotonin* is involved in the mechanism of migraine headaches and in certain information processes. A *serotonin* antagonist without psychedelic effects could be used as a medicament.

Grof: This was the reason why *2-brominated LSD,* a strong *serotonin* antagonist without psychedelic effects, was so important?

IT IS INTERESTING THAT ALDOUS HUXLEY ACTUALLY USED LSD TO EASE HIS TRANSITION AT THE TIME OF HIS DEATH.

Hofmann: We made all kinds of LSD derivatives. Also among them was the *2-brominated LSD*, which turned out to have strong antiserotonin effect, but without any psychedelic effects. After that finding, the *serotonin hypothesis* could not be sustained any more. Another problem was that the *serotonin* antagonism is not studied in the brain, but on peripheral biological preparations.

Grof: And then there is, of course, the complex question of the blood/brain barrier; which of the substances that show peripheral antagonism are actually allowed to enter the brain.

Hofmann: Yes. And LSD also has effects on other transmitters, such as *dopamine* and *adrenaline* and it is very complicated. For this reason, LSD was a very useful and influential tool in brain research and has remained that until this very day.

Grof: I am very interested in one particular hypothesis concerning the effects of LSD. It was formulated by Harold Abramson and his team in New York City. On the basis of some animal experiments, particularly with the *Siamese fighting fish (Betta splendens),* they came to the conclusion that the most relevant aspect of the LSD effect involves the enzymatic transfer of oxygen on the subcellular level. For me this was interesting, because it could account for the similarity between the LSD effects and the experiences associated with the process of dying. And there might also be connections to the effects of the holotropic breathwork that my wife Christina and I have developed. Unfortunately, it seems that this research remained limited to that one paper; I have not seen any additional supportive evidence for this hypothesis.

Hofmann: And there was another hypothesis, where the emphasis was, I believe, on the effect of LSD on the degradation of *adrenaline* and *noradrenaline* leading to abnormal oxidation products (Hoffer and Osmond's *adrenochrome* and *adrenolutine* hypothesis). But none of this has been confirmed and the question of the effective mechanisms of LSD is still open. And, in addition, it is important to realize that there is an enormous leap from

YES, THROUGH MY LSD EXPERIENCE AND MY NEW PICTURE OF REALITY, I BECAME AWARE OF THE WONDER OF CREATION, THE MAGNIFICENCE OF NATURE AND OF THE ANIMAL AND PLANT KINGDOM.

chemistry to psychological experience. There are limits to what this basic chemical background can tell us about consciousness.

Grof: If I understand you correctly, you feel, very much like I do myself, that even if we could explain all the biochemical and neurophysiological changes in the neurons, we are still confronted with this quantum leap from biochemical and electrical processes to consciousness that seems unbridgeable.

Hofmann: Yes, it is the basic problem of reality. We can study various psychic functions and also the more primitive sensory functions, such as seeing, hearing, and so on, which constitute our image of our every day world. They have a material side and the psychic side. And that is a gap which you cannot explain. We can follow the metabolism in the brain, we can measure the biochemical and neurophysiological changes, electric potentials, and so on. These are material and energetic processes. But matter and electric current are quite a different thing, quite a different level, than the psychic experience. Even our seeing and other sensory functions already involve the same problem. We must realize that there is a gap

which probably can never be overcome or be explained. We can study material processes and various processes at the energetic level, that is what we can do as natural scientists. And then there comes something quite different, the psychic experience, which remains a mystery.

THE TRUTH WILL FINALLY COME OUT AND THE TRUTH IS: IF LSD IS USED IN THE RIGHT WAY, IT IS A VERY IMPORTANT AND VERY USEFUL AGENT.

Grof: There seem to be two radically different approaches to the problem of brain/consciousness relationship as it manifests in psychedelic sessions. The first one is the traditional scientific approach that explains the spectrum of the LSD experience as release of information that is stored in the repositories of our brain. It suggests that the entire process is contained inside of our cranium and the experiences are created by combinations and interactions of engrams that have accumulated in our memory banks in this lifetime.

A radical alternative to this monistic materialistic view was suggested by Aldous Huxley. After some personal experiences with LSD and mescaline, he started seeing the brain more like a "reducing valve," that normally protects us against a vast cosmic input of information, which would otherwise flood and overload our everyday consciousness. In this view, the function of the brain is to reduce all the available information and lock us into a limited experience of the world. In this view, LSD frees us from this restriction and opens us to a much larger experience.

Hofmann: I agree with this model of Huxley's that in psychedelic sessions the function of the brain is opened. In general, we have limited capacity to transform all the stimuli which we receive from the outer world in the form of optical, acoustic, and tactile stimuli, and so on. We have a limited capacity to transfer this information so that it can come into consciousness. Under the influence of psychedelic substances, the valve is opened and an enormous input of outer stimuli can now come in and stimulate our brain. This then gives rise to this overwhelming experience.

Grof: Have you actually personally met Aldous Huxley?

Hofmann: Yes, I have met him two times and we had very good, very important discussions. And he gave me his book *Island*, which had come out just before he died. In it he describes an old culture on an island, which is trying to make a synthesis between its own spiritual tradition and modern technology brought in by an American. This culture used ritually something called *moksha* medicine and *moksha* was a mushroom that brought enlightenment. Moksha was given only three times in the lifetime of each individual. The first time it was during the initiation in a puberty rite, the second time in the middle of life, and the third time at death, in the final stage of life. And when Aldous gave me his book, he wrote: "To Dr. Albert Hofmann, the original discoverer of the *moksha* medicine." I am very proud to have this book, *Island*; it is a beautiful book.

Grof: It is interesting that Aldous Huxley actually used LSD to ease his transition at the time of his death.

Hofmann: Yes, after he had died, his widow sent me a copy of a paper. When he was in the process of dying (he was unable to talk because of his cancer of the tongue), he wrote on it: "0.1 milligrams of LSD, subcutaneously." So his wife gave him the injection of the *moksha* medicine.

Grof: There is a beautiful description of this situation in her book which is called *This Timeless Moment*.

Hofmann: Yes, *This Timeless Moment* by Laura Huxley.

Grof: I would like to ask you now something very personal. You must have been asked this question a number of times before, I am sure. You have had during your lifetime quite a few psychedelic experiences, some of which you described to us today. It began with the LSD experiences associated with the discovery of LSD, then the experiences during the work on the isolation of the active principles from the magic mushrooms and *ololiuqui*, the experience in the mushroom ritual with Maria Sabina, the sessions you described in *LSD, My Problem Child*, and some others. What influence have all these experiences had on you, on your way of being in the world, on your values, on your personal philosophy, on your scientific world view?

Hofmann: They have changed my life, insofar as they provided me with a new concept about what reality is. Reality became for me a problem after my experience with LSD. Before, I had believed there was only one reality, the reality of everyday life. Just one true reality and the rest was imagination and was not real. But under the influence of LSD I entered into realities which were as real and even more real than the one of everyday. And I thought about the nature of reality and I got some deeper insights.

> OUR VERY ESSENCE IS ABSOLUTE CONSCIOUSNESS; WITHOUT AN I, WITHOUT THE CONSCIOUSNESS OF EVERY INDIVIDUAL, NOTHING REALLY EXISTS. AND THIS VERY CENTER, THIS CORE OF THE HUMAN BEING IS INFLUENCED BY THESE KINDS OF SUBSTANCES.

I analyzed the mechanisms involved in the production of the normal world view that we call the "everyday reality." What are the factors that constitute it? What is inside and what is outside? What comes from the outside in and what is just inside. And I use for this process the metaphor of *the sender and the receiver*. The productive sender is the outer world, the external reality including our own body. And the receiver is our deep self, the conscious ego, which then transforms the outer stimuli into a psychological experience.

It was very helpful for me to see what is really, objectively, outside; something that you cannot change, something that is the same for everybody. And what is produced by me, homemade, what is myself, that which I can change. What is my spiritual inside that can be changed. And this possibility to change reality, which exists in everyone, represents the real freedom of every human individual. He has an enormous possibility to change his world view. It helped me enormously in my life to realize what really exists on the outside and what is homemade by me.

Grof: You have a tremendous awareness and sensitivity in regard to ecological issues, for example, the industrial pollution of water and air, the destruction of nature, the dying of the European forests, and so on. Would you attribute this to your psychedelic sessions, in which you experienced oneness with nature and the interconnectedness of creation? Do you think that these experiences somehow opened you to this greater ecological awareness, to a sharper sense of what we are doing to nature?

Hofmann: Yes, through my LSD experience and my new picture of reality, I became aware of the wonder of creation, the magnificence of nature and of the animal and plant kingdom. I became very sensitive to what will happen to all this and all of us. I have published and lectured about the main environmental problems we have in Europe and at home in this regard.

Grof: One often hears that in Europe one out of every three trees is dying. What do you think is happening to nature in Europe?

Hofmann: It is primarily the damage to the green particles of plants where photosynthesis takes place, in the small holes where the air has to pass through. People believe that the plants nourish themselves from the soil, but that is not true. They are nourished from the air and carbon dioxide is the main product used in this process. Only the water and minerals come from the earth. In order to filter out all the carbon dioxide that it needs as building material, the plant has to let pass through its leaves an enormous amount of air, because we have only 0.03% of carbon dioxide in the air.

In comparison with the plants, we use the air only as a source of oxygen that we need for oxidizing the substances we receive as food. The plants need about a thousand times more air than we do. That explains why the plants die first. And it is mainly the conifers that suffer, because their needles, where the photosynthesis takes place, remain in place for four to six years. Other plants have new leaves every year and the damaged leaves are put away, are disposed of. The conifers die first, but eventually, if this process continues, even the trees which change leaves follow.

Grof: The sun is the major source of energy supporting life. Do you feel there is a real danger that by interfering with photosynthesis, we might actually cut ourselves off from the supply of vital energy indispensable for continuation of life on this planet?

Hofmann: Yes, because only the green womb of Mother Earth is able to receive and utilize the stream of solar energy which comes to earth in the form of light and to transform it in chemical energy. This then makes it possible for the plants to build organic substances and pass them to other organisms. And if the receivers, the green plants, are damaged, this magic stream will be interrupted and life on earth will collapse and disappear. This is why I am active in the ecological field, trying to stimulate politicians to do something against this fundamental danger.

Grof: The discovery of LSD has been such an important part of your life and you have also personally experienced what positive impact this substance can have on us if it is properly used. I would like to ask you: what was your reaction to what happened in the 1960s in the United States.

Hofmann: Well, I was very sorry, really sorry. As I said, I would have never suspected LSD could be misused in such a way. Now I have the feeling that the situation has improved, because you never read in the newspapers about accidents with LSD any more, as it happened in the 1960s practically every day. People who use LSD today know how to use it. Therefore, I hope that the health authorities will get the insight that LSD, if it is used properly, is not a dangerous drug. We actually should not refer to it as drug; this word has a very bad connotation. We should use another name. Psychedelic substances, if they are used in proper ways, are very helpful for mankind.

Grof: You wrote a book entitled *LSD, My Problem Child.* I heard you say, at the conference, that you hope you might see the day when your problem child will become a desired child again.

Hofmann: I myself will not probably see this day, but it will definitely happen sometime in the future, I am sure. The truth will finally come out and the truth is: If LSD is used in the right way, it is a very important and very useful agent. LSD is no more playing a bad role in the drug scene and psychiatrists are again trying to submit their proposals for research with this substance to the health authorities. I hope that LSD will again become available in the normal way, for the medical profession. Then it could play the role it really should, a beneficial role.

Grof: Do you have a vision for the future concerning this, an idea how you would like LSD to be used?

Hofmann: We have a kind of model for it in Eleusis and also in the so-called primitive societies where psychedelic substances are used. LSD should be treated as a sacred drug and receive corresponding preparation, preparation of quite a different kind than other psychotropic agents. It is one kind of thing if you have a pain-relieving substance or some euphoriant and having an agent that engages the very essence of human beings, their consciousness. Our very essence is Absolute Consciousness; without an I, without the consciousness of every individual, nothing really exists. And this very center, this core of the human being is influenced by these kinds of substances. And therefore, excuse me for repeating myself, these are sacred substances. Because, what is sacred if not the consciousness of the human being, and something which attacks it must be handled with reverence and with extreme caution.

Grof: Many of us who have experienced psychedelics feel very much like you do, that they are sacred tools and that if they are properly used, they open spiritual awareness. They also engender ecological sensitivity, reverence for life, and capacity for peaceful cooperation with other people and other species. And, I think, in the kind of world we have today, transformation of humanity in this direction might well be our only real hope for survival. I believe that it is essential for planetary future to develop tools that can change the consciousness which has created the crisis that we are in.

Hofmann: That certainly would be a major step in the right direction. We need a new concept of reality and a new set of values for things to change in a positive direction. And LSD could help to generate such a new concept.

Appendix A—
Haircut: Trippin' Through a Day in the Life

Preston Peet

Editor's note— *Under the Influence* is a book full of hard journalism and social commentary. With what you glean from this book is it hoped that you will be able to see past the lies and propaganda driving the War on Some Drugs and Users and vote for those representative who will end the War. Now it's time to take a look at the War from a more personal viewpoint.

The following stories are from an unpublished manuscript of mine titled *Something in the Way*, relating my own experiences strung out on illegal street drugs, trying to make it day to day as a junkie living on the streets under prohibition policies. Dedicated to getting myself as far from my emotions and chronic pain as possible using lots of hard drugs for years, I'd first been introduced to opiates during extensive medical procedures after a serious car accident in my teens. It never helped to explain the reasons for getting high to police and prohibitionists though, because they did not want to know. To them, all illicit drug use is bad. While the way I used to get high was much of the time extremely self-destructive, things usually just got worse once the police got involved.

In the first story, *Haircut—Tripping Through a Day in the Life*, the police were trying to do what they thought was the right thing, but for me it was not the right thing, it

> WHILE THE WAY I USED TO GET HIGH WAS MUCH OF THE TIME EXTREMELY SELF-DESTRUCTIVE, THINGS USUALLY JUST GOT WORSE ONCE THE POLICE GOT INVOLVED.

merely gave me something else to feel guilty over and stress about when it did not work out. The way we treat most illicit drug use and users in this country does not differentiate between individual users and their circumstances. A treatment modality that works well for one person might and often does only make matters worse for the next. For that matter, not everyone who uses or even abuses drugs is best served by stopping altogether, which is the rational behind long-term methadone maintenance for instance. It's time to stop chasing after the people who find whatever it is they need in currently illicit drugs, and to start thinking of ways to reduce what harms can and do sometimes accrue from drug abuse to both the user and to society at large. In the end, without prohibition the following story simply wouldn't happen.

(On another note, there is some debate about the reality of the "coke bugs" mentioned in this story, with some cocaine abusers insisting, even years after stopping their use of cocaine, that the bugs were and are real, that they really aren't hallucinations at all. I myself reserve judgment, preferring these days to verbally debate the issue rather than conduct any more experiments.)

The second story, *Ketamine Dream—or Reality?*, relates a drug use experience that did not end in anyone being arrested or getting sick or with anything bad happening to anyone at all. The point being that not all drug use is abuse, even such drastic fashions as that related in this story.

Sitting on one of the benches at the entrance of Central Park West at 72nd Street, mid-November, I don't have anywhere to go to escape the drizzle and chill. I'm getting really tired of being strung out and on the street. I say this a lot, to myself and to others, but haven't made much effort to change my situation. Until just lately life had been relatively easy, what with it being warm and dry out. I've spent the Summer and the early part of Fall living in the park, sleeping in Strawberry Field, but the weather is no longer conducive to that. Now that the weather has turned against outside living, the cold and wet are taking their toll.

Though loosely reunited with my girlfiend, who's recently returned from New Orleans, I can't go and sleep with her. She's certifiably schizophrenic, and unstable is an understatement. Occasionally she will let me stay at her place for a few hours, insisting I sneak in at four in the morning, and leave by eight at the latest. Her roommate hates and mistrusts me, due to my being a junkie. If she spots me inside there's hell to pay. My girlfriend is strung out now as well, which has definite effects on her already crazy brain, making her a very dangerous woman. I prefer sleeping on the street to sleeping at her place, taking this all into consideration, but due to the weather being so lousy, I've put aside my fears and made a couple of requests to sleep over, but she'd said no anyway.

> THE RAIN, THOUGH LIGHT, IS STARTING TO REALLY BOTHER ME. I HAVE SOME PACKETS OF BOTH COKE AND DOPE WELL SHIELDED FROM THE DAMP IN ONE POCKET, BUT AM BEGINNING TO WORRY ABOUT THEM GETTING WET.

The night before I'd slept, as much as possible anyway, under the overhang at the entrance to the Museum of Natural History on Seventy-Ninth Street. It hadn't helped keep the rain off very well because the wind blew through there like in a wind tunnel. I'm shivering a lot today, with all my clothes either damp or full on wet and beginning to smell, a rather offensive, musty odor. My socks are disgusting, black with grime and putrid. I don't bother changing them, or buying new ones as my money goes mainly one place, and my feet are suffering because of it. I've discovered it's possible for there to be blisters, inside blisters, inside blisters, making me hobble like an old man when I walk. Not so bad as it was a month ago, I still walk with an ungainly step.

THERE'S NO WAY I'D PUT UP WITH THE LIVING CONDITIONS I DAILY CONTEND WITH WITHOUT THE DRUGS. NO HOME. NO JOB. DIRTY, HUNGRY, AND SICK ALL THE TIME. PEOPLE SNEERING AT ME AS THEY PASS, IF THEY DEIGN TO NOTICE ME AT ALL. EATING IN SOUP KITCHENS AND SLEEPING IN DOORWAYS. DODGING ANGRY COPS WITH SERIOUS ANTI-DRUGGIE ATTITUDES. WHY NOT DO RE-HAB?

A massive presence across the street, the Dakota building towers over the intersection. I often feel the ghost of John Lennon hovering when sitting here between the Imagine Circle, Strawberry Field, and the spot where Lennon, one of my heroes, was assassinated. With the sky gray and black behind it, the Dakota is an ominous presence. I'm sitting on the back of one of the benches lining the entrance to the park. The rain, though light, is starting to really bother me. I have some packets of both coke and dope well shielded from the damp in one pocket, but am beginning to worry about them getting wet. Debating on where I can go, and what I want to do for the evening, I see a blue and white police van, slowly pulling out of the trees and onto the drive in front of me.

It comes to a halt directly across the drive from me, parking alongside a pair of old street people sitting on one of the benches on that side. Lettered across the side of the van are the words "NYPD Outreach Program," so I relax. These guys drive around offering assistance getting street people help with an assortment of different problems they might have. Normally, I avoid them as I'm getting high constantly, but today an idea strikes me. They'd spoken to me late one night in the 72nd Street subway station across the street, asking if I'd wanted to go to a shelter while rousting me from the station. That night I'd refused, but now I suddenly think that might not be such a bad idea at all. I've got all the drugs I'll need to get me through the evening so I won't need to leave in the middle of the night to go make more money to score. The more I think about it, the more I think how nice it would be to be off the street for a night.

I cross the drive, approaching the driver's window.

"Excuse me officer, may I ask you something?" The cop whips his head around in surprise.

"Whoa kid, you scared the shit out of me." The cop laughs. He seems all right, not like most of the cops I've had experiences with. "Yeah, what'cha need kid?"

"I was wondering." I hesitate, not sure for a second if I want to ask after all, then plunge ahead. "Could you guys help me get into a shelter for the night? I'm homeless and don't have a lick of ID."

"Yeah, give us a minute. Don't go anywhere," the cop says. I walk back to my bag on the bench to wait. Now that I've asked I'm more enthusiastic about the idea of shelter. Especially if the cops are going to help me get into a place. After a couple minutes, the driver calls me back over.

"You interested in rehab, or just a shelter? We can do either."

"No, no re-hab, thanks." I don't think I'm up for going that far yet.

"OK, just wanted to check. Give us a few more minutes, we're calling around. See what we can do. You have no ID at all?"

"None."

"Alright, hang out. I'll let you know." I turn to walk away, but stop as a blinding explosion of an idea appears in my head. All my current troubles can be traced directly back to my drug use and trying to keep it going 24 hours a day while living on NYC streets. There's no way I'd put up with the living conditions I daily contend with without the drugs. No home. No job. Dirty, hungry, and sick all the time. People sneering at me as they pass, if they deign to notice me at all. Eating in soup kitchens and sleeping in doorways. Dodging angry cops with serious anti-druggie attitudes. Why not do re-hab? I'm ready, by god, so I turn back and once more approach the van.

"LISTEN. IF YOU'VE GOT ANYTHING, OH, I DON'T KNOW, THAT YOU SHOULDN'T HAVE, ANYTHING ILLEGAL, YOU SHOULD DUMP IT HERE, OK? I DON'T WANT TO HAVE TO ARREST YOU IF THEY FIND SOMETHING AT THE PROGRAM, AND THEY WILL SEARCH YOUR STUFF, VERY THOROUGHLY."

"Hey, 'scuse me again officer." I don't hesitate this time, blurting it right out. "Can you still get me into a re-hab? 'Cause if so, I'm ready. I want in!"

"Hold on, we'll call and see, give us another couple minutes. Sorry." As I sit back down I'm smiling, thinking about the cop apologizing to me. It's a first.

I'm also thinking about rehab. In my mind I'm picturing a warm, dry hospital setting, with nurses and drugs to help me through withdrawals, good, hearty food, nice beds and clean pajamas. This is too good an opportunity to pass up. Besides, I'm sick to death of the grind, the running around with no sleep for days, the sore, bruised arms and legs from shooting too much and missing often, and the cops, always more cops who often cause me more stress and grief than even my drug abusing does. It's a no win situation. I want out.

"Hey, come 'ere kid!" The officer tells me they've found a place, on Third Street in the Lower East Side. "Grab your bag and let's go. That is if you're still up for it. They'll take you with no ID. But I gotta tell you," the cop pauses, his eyes searching my face. "The thing is," the cop continues in a slightly slower, more heart-felt manner, like an older brother trying to sell his younger brother a bad idea, "it's a long-term residential treatment program. Six to twelve months. But it's a great place, with a killer program!" The policeman's words sink into my stoned, tired, and impressionable mind.

"Alright, what the hell, I'm game. Let's do it." I grab my bag and run back to the van's side door.

"Jump in, kid," says the cop on the passenger side. Slamming the door shut behind me, the cop jumps back in, and we begin to roll. I speak up.

"Excuse me. Do you guys mind if we stop at a bathroom somewhere so I can, uh, have a seat for a few minutes before we get there?" The two cops glance at one another for a second, then the driver suggests a park toilet, since we're still inside the 72nd Street entrance. The other cop agrees, so we drive over to the Sheep's Meadow toilets. Pulling to a stop outside the restroom, the cop opens the side door again. As I climb out, the cop stops me.

"Listen. If you've got anything, oh, I don't know, that you shouldn't have, anything illegal, you should dump it here, OK? I don't want to have to arrest you if they find something at the program, and they will search your stuff, very thoroughly." I stare at him for a moment, then smile.

"Alright. You got it." I walk into the bathroom.

As with most park toilets anywhere in the world, these are disgusting. It's hard to spend any time in here at all because of the stench, but I have a mission. I have to get rid of my drugs. I'm going clean, and don't want to do it in jail. Besides, I don't want to waste the stuff I have, and this will probably be my last chance to inject anything into myself. I enter one of the two stalls, hanging my overcoat over the stall door. I quickly dig from my pocket the cellophane, taken from a Marlboro pack, inside of which are a couple packets of both coke and dope, keeping dry. I set a cooker on the toilet paper dispenser, a silver rectangular box screwed onto the wall of the stall like a night table, a perfect platform for preparing

my poison. Opening the one new packet of coke, I dump the whole thing into the cooker, a fifteen-dollar bag, then wad up the yellow paper without licking it and toss it in the toilet. Some people like that taste, but not me, having grown tired over the years of that taste and numbness in my mouth. Only on the back of my sinuses after a shot, when I can more smell it in my head than taste it on my tongue do I like the taste at all. I fold up the other, partially filled packet of cocaine, containing only a tiny bit, deciding to smuggle it into the facility with me. It's the same with the dope. I save a little in the bottom of the bag I dump in the cooker with the coke, and fold up two packets of dope remnants for later. It's a risk, but getting sick is no fucking joke. To me it's worth it to try. I take one of the least used rigs I've got, draw up a little water from a small plastic bottle I carry, then squirt forty mills of water onto the brown and white powders sitting in the cooker. Already very high, I usually wouldn't be doing more so soon after the last shot, certainly not this much at one go. I hope the dope will help cut the effects of the coke and keep my heart from exploding. My hands move by rote, having performed this ritual hundreds of times before. Quickly tying off, I tap for a vein in my left wrist, getting one to stand out right away. I hit it fast, and once the rig is red with blood, quickly push the whole shot into my vein.

Before I can even get the needle out of my arm, I feel the rush of the shot. It slams into my head and heart, the pounding of my pulse quickly filling my ears with an overwhelming crescendo of sound. My skin is suddenly crawling with what feels like hundreds, thousands of nearly microscopic bugs, beginning at the corners of my mouth and nostrils and spreading, along with the drugs now in my system, right down to my toes. My fingertips come alive, and I lift them up to my face, trying to make out the little critters, but they're too small. I don't remember sitting down, but now I'm perched on the edge of the disgusting toilet. God only knows what kind of creatures

MY SKIN IS SUDDENLY CRAWLING WITH WHAT FEELS LIKE HUNDREDS, THOUSANDS OF NEARLY MICROSCOPIC BUGS, BEGINNING AT THE CORNERS OF MY MOUTH AND NOSTRILS AND SPREADING, ALONG WITH THE DRUGS NOW IN MY SYSTEM, RIGHT DOWN TO MY TOES.

COCAINE DIRECTLY INTO MY VEINS HITS ME LIKE A FREIGHT TRAIN, AND I'M A THOUSAND TIMES LARGER THAN THESE BUGS. MUST BE LIKE AN ATOMIC BLAST TO A CREATURE THIS SMALL.

are living in and on the grimy bowl. This thought only increases my consternation. I can literally feel the invasion of tiny monsters, swarming all over me, itching and tickling and biting.

"Hey! You almost done in there? We gotta be going, man! Hurry up now." One of the cops' voices cuts into my hallucinations, but does nothing to diminish the effects of the drugs. Close to panic, I'm sure the cops are going to notice all the bugs, how could they not? They must be visible on my face, it feels like there're so many, even if I'm having trouble making them out. I can see what might be some teeny mite-type bugs under my fingernails, and can feel them in my boots as well. My hands fly around my body and face, trying to catch and kill the bugs, but they're to small to see, much less catch. I think I feel them crunch like fleas between my nails a couple of times, but I'm really not sure, because when I move my fingernails apart, I still can't see anything, no bug guts, nothing.

TO ANYONE WITH THE SCANTEST EXPERIENCE WITH FUCKED-UP PEOPLE IT SHOULD BE BLATANTLY OBVIOUS I'M COMPLETELY OFF MY FACE, AND THESE TWO ARE COPS WITH EXPERIENCE WITH FUCKED-UP STREET PEOPLE. THEY'VE GOTTA KNOW I'M HIGH.

This has very recently started happening every time I do a shot of coke. Maybe they normally live under my skin, feeding on my blood, then when I shoot up, the bugs try to escape from the coke, or it gets them high too, and they all run to the surface of my skin in their own cocaine-induced frenzy. Thinking what shooting coke does to me, it doesn't seem that far-fetched. Cocaine directly into my veins hits me like a freight train, and I'm a thousand times larger than these bugs. Must be like an atomic blast to a creature this small.

I'm stuck in the toilet stall, thinking and feeling bugs. This is one of the reasons I hate using a public toilet. This always happens to me when I do. I get off, then wind up stuck in the stall, or locked in the whole bathroom if it's a small restaurant. I'll spend up to an hour in there, looking around on the floor to make sure I haven't dropped anything, or looking for anything some other druggie might have stashed or dropped getting high like I'm doing. Or as has been happening more and more lately, I'm attacked by these coke bugs that ravish me, causing me to pick at my skin and fingers until they're raw and bloody. Almost inevitably, someone will eventually come and begin banging on the door, yelling, "Come out of there you! We're going to call the Police!"

There is a small voice of rationality somewhere in my mind, that I can hear trying to talk to me, telling me it's the drugs, that I'm experiencing classic symptoms of cocaine psychosis, but all I can do is hear, and continue suffering out the trip. This time I'm running a bigger risk than usual, what with the cops themselves waiting for me right outside, so I struggle to get a grip. Somehow I

SOME PEOPLE ASSUME THAT CLEANING UP ONE'S ACT HAS TO ENTAIL A COMPLETE ALTERATION OF EXTERIOR AESTHETICS, AS IF IT'S THE PIERCINGS AND LONG HAIR THAT MAKE ME THE JUNKIE I AM.

manage to put everything away, and get my coat on. Skin going haywire underneath my coat, I pick up my bag and stumble outside. The cops are chatting up the young lady working the concession-stand around the corner from the toilets as they wait for me. I put my stuff into the van, and climb in.

"It's about time." The driver says, after the cops finish their conversation and get back in the van. Trying not to look him in the eye, I mumble, "Sorry," as they begin to drive.

Sitting behind them, I'm trying to discretely pick at the few reachable bugs I can still feel crawling frantically around, while simultaneously rummaging aimlessly through my bag, not looking for anything in particular. It's just another manifestation of the psychosis. Anytime one sees a street person sitting on the sidewalk somewhere digging maniacally through their belongings, rest assured that they are most probably tweaking. Tweaking is precisely what I'm doing now while voluntarily riding inside a police van. I begin to get paranoid, wondering what the police might be thinking. To anyone with the scantest experience with fucked-up people it should be blatantly obvious I'm completely off my face, and these two are cops with experience with fucked-up street people. They've gotta know I'm high. I lean forward, towards the cop riding shotgun, and begin babbling at him, trying to sooth his nerves.

JUAN IS SO COMPLETELY LACKADAISICAL ABOUT THE SEARCH, I IMMEDIATELY REGRET NOT BRINGING A RIG IN ALONG WITH THE DRUG REMNANTS. I'LL HAVE TO SNIFF ANYWAY, LIKE I'VE PLANNED. IT WOULD HAVE BEEN NICER TO HAVE A SET THOUGH.

"Do you like being a cop? Is this assignment something you chose, or was it given you as an order, to do this Outreach stuff?" I'm genuinely curious even if I am rambling. Rarely, if ever, have I an opportunity to talk to a cop as one human being to another. Usually any conversation with police is a question and answer session while I'm getting harassed or booked. I'm obviously wasted, having a lot of trouble coordinating my bag search and questioning, all the while trying to avoid eye contact. My pupils grow unbelievably huge when I'm on coke, and any cops worth their salt are going to be right on top of my condition.

Gradually the armies of coke mites recede, abandoning my skin, and I'm once again able to believe they were hallucinations and nothing more. Each time, just before booting, I tell myself there are no goddamned bugs, but once the coke hits me, I'm convinced they're real, and nothing can convince me otherwise until the cocaine wears off once more.

Now the heroin begins to assert itself, bringing me rapidly down to a manageable level, but this has the alternate effect on my pupils, shrinking them to mere pin pricks, my eyes glazing over. With the light hazel color of my eyes, it's immediately obvious I'm doped to the gills.

The two cops glance over at one another a number of times during the drive when I utter one especially off the wall comment or other. Rush hour, the drive takes a good while, which gives me time to come down quite a bit, so much so that by the time we reach the Project Renewal building, a former YMCA on Third Street, I'm close to nodding, a total porpoise head. The officers help me out of the van, lead me up the stairs and in through the front doors. Inside the building we approach a sign-in desk.

"This is the young man we called about," the cop next to me says. "He'd like to enter the program here and go straight." The cops step back, giving the guy behind the desk a clear view of me for the first time. He stands and walks around the desk, giving me a blatant once over.

"The first thing you're going to have to do is lose that hair." The guy's own hair is shorn to a half-inch afro, giving him the look of a marine. By this time I've really worked myself into a gung-ho attitude, convincing myself this is exactly what I want, that I'm willing to go to any lengths to get clean.

"OK, so be it. If that's what I have to do, that's what I'll do." Shoving doubt as deep into the furthest recesses of my mind as I can, outwardly I show an anything-you-say-facade, almost managing to believe I really am ready.

"Go with Juan here, he's a third level client. He'll take you downstairs, get you set up with something to eat, and search your stuff to make sure there's nothing you've forgotten, so we can check you in." The marine-type turns back to the cops, who both wish me luck as Juan leads me downstairs to the kitchen area.

"Are you hungry?" Juan asks.

"Well, to be honest, I've got some Capn' Crunch cereal I'd like to finish instead of throwing it away. I'm sure I won't be able to keep it, and you probably don't serve much of it here." Juan looks at me like I'm nuts, but says OK. While I eat almost an entire box of the sickly-sweet cereal, Juan gives a cursory search of my belongings, which don't consist of much more than what I'm wearing and what I have in the one beat up shoulder bag. Juan is so completely lackadaisical about the search, I immediately regret not bringing a rig in along with the drug remnants. I'll have to sniff anyway, like I've planned. It would have been nicer to have a set though.

After I eat, and all form signing is over, Juan takes me up to the top floor, and tells me I've got half an hour to take a shower. It's required that I do, because the other residents don't want to risk catching bugs from incoming street people. It's ironic to hear Juan say that, what with my major psychotic episode earlier, and I laugh to myself. Juan directs me to my bed, then to the showers. While

I get undressed, Juan stands just outside the bathroom door, ostensibly to keep an eye on me to make sure I don't get up to anything weird, like cutting my wrists. Sometimes people who come into this place are crashing hard from various substances, which can bring on a black kind of depression in some, thereby necessitating careful watching for the first few hours or even days. While Juan seems concerned about my possible depression, he doesn't seem to consider I might be getting high while out of sight in the shower.

As soon as I'm in the shower stall, I pull out the undiscovered packets of dope and coke. One after the other I sniff all contents up my nose, this time going ahead and licking each one to get it all, as this is supposed to be my final blast of sorts. It's not the same as banging it, not nearly as intense, leaving me more jonesing and anxious than anything else until the coke wears off again. Getting under a surprisingly hot, strong shower has a beneficial effect, so that by the time I'm done I'm feeling better, with the dope far outweighing the teeny bit of coke. When heavily doped, I'm able to act mostly human.

"It'll most probably be after the smoke break that you'll go see the barber. They'll have to shave it all off you know." Juan tells me I can leave my stuff on the bed, and asks if I've got any smokes. I don't, so he says he will get a hold of a couple for me.

I have really long hair, hanging down below my shoulder blades. It's been almost three years since the last cut. I start to think about what I'm getting myself into. Some people assume that cleaning up one's act has to entail a complete alteration of exterior aesthetics, as if it's the piercings and long hair that make me the junkie I am. Again I stuff doubt back down deep, telling myself they must know best here. It's their business to get people off drugs. So I blank my mind, and try to blindly follow directions. I've not been able to quit getting high on my own, so maybe it's time to hand over the choices to someone else.

NOW WITH MY HEAD SHAVED I IMMEDIATELY FEEL LIKE A PARIAH, MARKED WITH A STIGMA, ADVERTISING MY SUB-HUMAN STATUS. WHICH IS THE BASIC IDEA BEHIND THIS SORT OF THING.

Juan checks his watch, and says it's smoke time. On the way downstairs he explains to me that there are designated times throughout the day for smoking, for eating, for meetings, for everything. The system is strictly regimented, geared towards teaching addicts the concept of buckling under to authority and rule without questioning. Individuality is strongly discouraged here, with every aspect of the system accenting that conformity is the only way to get ahead, to become respectable and earn privileges.

Outside, there is a fenced-in concrete garden, with a couple of guys standing near the fence making sure no one comes by and drops anything through to anyone inside. Juan tells me to wait there for him and runs back inside. The longer one is in the program, and toes the line properly, they move downstairs floor to floor, obtaining more and more privileges as they descend, until finally they reach ground level where they act as monitors and disciplinarians, keeping the newer, fresher residents in line. I take a seat off by myself to smoke and think and wait for Juan to come back.

"I've just talked to the head guys. They said you don't have to shave your head, just cut it off your shoulders. Cool, huh?" Juan smiles at me. I shrug my shoulders, but really I'm relieved. I haven't been looking forward to being bald, not at all. Still quite down from the dope, my emotional responses are dulled, but I'm happy to hear this bit of news. Fifteen minutes later the smoke session is over, and everyone heads inside. Juan tells me to hold back as the rest file in, then to join the line forming against the wall in the hallway.

"That's the line for the barber," Juan says. I watch the barber as he works. While he seems to know what he's doing, all the guys before me are either Spanish or black, with hair types that are much different than mine. When it's finally my turn, I'm struggling to stay calm and not be nervous. I can tell this is going to be a disaster. Cutting off my hair might seem unimportant in the larger scheme of things, but mine means a lot to me. The barber sits me in the chair, and puts the sheet around my neck. Right away I pipe up.

"They said that it only has to come off my shoulders, OK? Leave as much of it as possible."

"OK, man." The barber sets to work with the scissors, cutting my hair into a short, jagged bob, kind of like Shaggy's from Scooby-Doo.

"Alright, I can live with this, it's not so bad," I think to myself. Then the barber picks up a set of electric clippers. "What the hell is he going to do with those, give me some sort of feathering job?" I wonder as the barber turns them on. While I'm occupied with this thought, the barber takes the clippers, buzzing away like a loud, angry bee, and placing them to the center of my forehead at my hairline, draws it back straight over the center of my head, mowing off a strip of hair two inches wide in a sort of reverse mohawk.

"Hey! What the Fuck are you doing, man!?" I yell, leaping half out of the chair. I stare at the damage in the mirror for a moment, not believing my eyes. "You don't speak English, you jerk!? Asshole!" I stare some more, then snap at him with a sigh of resignation. "Go ahead and finish it. Take it all off. Can't fucking save it now, can we." So the barber continues, shaving off the rest of my beautiful hair. Even though I'd initially said I'd go through with this chop job, when I'd been told I didn't have to shave it all,

I was ecstatic and relieved. Now with my head shaved I immediately feel like a pariah, marked with a stigma, advertising my sub-human status. Which is the basic idea behind this sort of thing.

These long-term residential drug treatment programs are most often geared towards breaking a person down, shredding them to a state of defenselessness and malleability, focusing on all their faults and their depravity. Once the person, already in a weakened state from the drug abuse, has been shattered, the program sets about putting them back together in its conception of a responsible, contributing, sane member of society. Re-programming them, if you will.

It's having an effect on me already. Allowed to spend the first night in bed and forgo attending the evening's meetings and activities, I take advantage of it, walking up the five flights of stairs as I'm not allowed to use the elevator yet. On the way up, one of the older residents on his way downstairs yells at me because my hands are in my pockets, which is also not allowed. By the time I get upstairs, I'm about to cry I'm so mad. The crash Juan was so concerned about earlier has arrived, dragging me down into a depression that's darker than the moonless night. What have I done? I lie down and quickly pass out, exhausted.

The next morning I wake up sick. I don't have a wake-up shot. The light hurts my eyes because my pupils are again extremely dilated, this time from lack of opiates. When Juan stops by my bed a few minutes later, I ask him how long it's going to be before I get some methadone or something to help with the withdrawals. Juan looks at me slack jawed.

"Oh, shit. What, you're not sick, are you?" Juan asks.

"Yeah I'm sick, and I'm going to be a hell of a lot sicker in a little while." I don't understand. What's the problem here?

"Listen man, you didn't know? This is a non-medical program. You kick here, you do it cold turkey. But hey, you got lots of support here. It'll be OK," Juan reassures me. Now it's me who regards Juan like he's got a screw loose, and laugh in his face.

"No way man. I'm not doing this cold, screw that. I'm outta here."

"No, stick it out a while. At least talk to someone who might be able to help you first." Juan implores, sounding almost like he really cares.

"OK, maybe." I sit back on the bed while Juan heads downstairs to find a counselor type to try and convince me to stay. When he's out of sight, I reach into my bag and pull out construction paper and a seam-tracer I'd swiped at Woolworth's. I don't know how Juan missed this bag of suspicious looking material during his search, but I'm glad he did. Putting the paper down on the book it had been stashed inside, I trace a grid pattern into the bright orange paper. After a few minutes, I put the seam tracer down, and tear out an almost perfect square of what looks just like a sheet of LSD, perforated lines and all. One hundred hits of completely blank, yet realistic-looking hits of acid. Just as I'm putting the sheet and the rest of the materials away back inside the book and picking up my bag, a counselor approaches my bed.

"LISTEN MAN, YOU DIDN'T KNOW? THIS IS A NON-MEDICAL PROGRAM. YOU KICK HERE, YOU DO IT COLD TURKEY. BUT HEY, YOU GOT LOTS OF SUPPORT HERE. IT'LL BE OK."

"I just spoke to Juan. Listen man, can we talk?" There's caring in his voice but his eyes are dead black holes, and I wave him away.

"Oh, I think not." I don't want to hear anything the man has to say. I'm beyond furious with myself for getting so fucked up the day before that I allowed the cops to entice me here, and for letting that idiot last night cut off all my hair. After the barber had finished shaving me bald, he'd gone to work on my goatee, taking that all off as well, leaving only a pencil thin mustache on my upper lip, which looked absolutely ridiculous. Then he turned off the clippers.

"What the hell are you doing?" I'd asked the barber.

"You allowed to have a mustache," he'd replied with a completely straight face.

"Screw that, take it off too. I don't want that ugly thing." Now I just want to go, to get back outside where I'm making my own choices, even if most of them are self-destructive and dangerous. I pick up my bag, and head for the stairs.

"Hey, you gotta sign some papers saying you're signing out against medical advice." The counselor sheds the kindly, concerned uncle stance and starts to berate me, but I'm having none of it.

"What medical advice? This is a non-medical program, remember? Fuck you. I'm gone." I head downstairs, ignoring the counselor's hollering, and walk out the front door. The first person I see is a young, long-haired metalhead, who buys $50 worth of blank paper from me. Then I go and get a fix. I'm not yet ready to go straight, preferring to fuck around over for a good while longer. I still have plenty of my youth to burn, and burn it I shall, back in the Lower East Side again.

Appendix B—
A Ketamine Dream—or Reality?

Preston Peet

I ring the bell, the door clicks open, and I bound up the stairs to the second floor. The apartment door opens as I reach the landing, letting me slip through into the welcoming warmth inside.

"Hey, you wanna get high?" I immediately ask, grinning at Kelly, the owner of the apartment, as soon as she shuts the door. It's a rhetorical question because Kelly is always ready to get high. Her roommate is out for the evening, doing a number on some rich gay white guy on the Upper West Side who's into getting tied up and beaten by a strapping young black man and paying lots of money for the pleasure. This means there's one less person I have to share my drugs with.

IT DOESN'T TAKE US LONG TO SHOOT OUR WAY THROUGH BOTH $20 BAGS OF COCAINE, AND FIVE OF THE SIX BAGS OF HEROIN. NEARLY ONE HUNDRED DOLLARS IN JUST OVER AN HOUR, DIRECTLY INTO OUR VEINS.

I break out my bags of coke and dope. We carefully set up our works on her bed. Outside the snow is coming down hard, with the wind howling at the windows, making the room feel even more comfortably warm and dry. Being homeless in the midst of one of the coldest winters New York City has experienced in decades, I love getting high here, enjoying the respite from ducking into the doorways and stairwells I usually have to hide in to shoot up my much needed and repeated fixes.

It doesn't take us long to shoot our way through both $20 bags of cocaine, and five of the six bags of heroin. Nearly one hundred dollars in just over an hour, directly into our veins. As I tweak out on the bedspread, the rush still overpowering and debilitating, I'm already thinking about having to go on a mission , back out into the freezing night air. I'm not at all relishing the prospect. But my jones for cocaine overrides almost all thought once I run dry. Despite the gnawing jones beginning to clamor in my mind, I don't jump up to go quite yet. Even if I wanted to go immediately I'm unable to because the ringing in my ears and the trembling of my knees from the massive influx of coke has me nailed to the bed.

Kelly is thinking along the same lines I am, knowing there isn't any more coke. She has a better plan than I do though, and asks a question I will always remember.

"Ever done Ketamine?" She asks me through her coke-clenched teeth.

"Nope, never." I might not ever have tried it, but I do know it can get us high, so I am interested.

Kelly climbs off the bed, goes to her closet, and reaching up onto the shelf, she pulls out a small white box.

"I got this yesterday from a friend. It's straight from the vet's office."

Sure enough, when she puts the box on the bed, I can see that it is full of little glass vials of pure liquid Ketamine. I've never seen Ketamine before, much less tried it, but it doesn't matter as the printing all over the box and on the vials themselves lets me know these are the real deal.

"Not like that, that'll totally dull the needle," Kelly says. I've been preparing to jam the tip of my rig through the rubber stopper on the top of a vial as I've seen done in the hospital and on tv countless times, but Kelly stops me. "Do it like this." She breaks off the top of the vial with a snap, then sticks the tip of the needle unimpeded into the solution inside. Drawing up 30 mils, she hands me the rig. "Here you go."

"EVER DONE KETAMINE?" SHE ASKS ME THROUGH HER COKE-CLENCHED TEETH.

Having exactly zero idea of what to expect, I lean back against the pillows and tie off. My veins are at this point in time still fairly cooperative, so I have no trouble registering a hit. I watch the thin red ribbon of blood spurt up inside the set, a sight which never ceases to thrill me, then loosen the tie, leaving the needle sticking out of my arm. Then I carefully, gently brace the needle as I push in the plunger, not wanting to push through my vein into the muscle. I'm totally unprepared for what comes next.

I WATCH THE THIN RED RIBBON OF BLOOD SPURT UP INSIDE THE SET, A SIGHT WHICH NEVER CEASES TO THRILL ME, THEN LOOSEN THE TIE, LEAVING THE NEEDLE STICKING OUT OF MY ARM.

I barely have time to pull the rig out of my arm before hearing an approaching roar, as though the wind outside has gotten into my head, filling my ears with the sound, completely overriding any sensation of the cocaine and heroin in me. The sound gets louder and louder, filling me up completely until I think I must be about to explode,

THERE'S A LOT MORE TO THE UNIVERSE THAT THESE TYPES DON'T WANT PEOPLE LIKE ME AND THE REST OF US TOO TO KNOW AND ACCESS, A LOT MORE KNOWLEDGE ACCESSED BY THE USE OF SUBSTANCES NATURAL AND SYNTHETIC BOTH, SUBSTANCES WHICH ARE DECREED SINFUL AND BANNED BUT THE USE OF WHICH CAN AND DOES OFTEN LEAD TO GNOSIS...

but before I can panic I hear a giant ripping sound and I'm out of my body, seeing myself and Kelly on the bed beneath me, both lying in a stupor. This is surprising to say the least, but I have no time to dwell on the weirdness. This view lasts but seconds before the air around me grows dark and the room is gone. Still floating, I'm suddenly surrounded by what look like giant amebas, gesturing with appendages that protrude larger and smaller from the writhing mass of colors that make up their core. I can distinctly hear them communicating with one another, but can't understand what they're saying. I'm not sure if they're talking about me or not but I'm not at all frightened. They aren't threatening as weird as they appear, with some seemingly aware and paying attention to me. I feel like I've returned somewhere I vaguely remember being before, but can't put my finger on when.

So enthralled am I with what I'm experiencing I don't at first consider the "where" of my situation but as though I'm lucid dreaming I'm able to consciously look around to take in some details of my surroundings. It looks a lot like far outer space, with millions of stars or light nodes of some kind glittering all around me as far as I can see in all directions with countless numbers of these creatures floating around me, undulating and waving gently as though underwater, moved by slow currents but going nowhere.

Finally blinking after what feels like hours in this space, I can see something new beneath me, some sort of design growing large, like it's rising to meet me or I'm descending towards it. I can't be sure which it is. As I, or it, draws closer, I realize I'm looking at a timeline, just like something in my old junior high school history books. It has my past, present, and future all marked out with different colored arrows signifying which is which. I can see where I've been, where I am now, and where I'm going, plain as day. An unsettled feeling comes over me as I see where I'm going according to this graphic display, but it is still an awe inspiring event. Who made this? Why am I being shown this? How long have I been here anyway? I've been locked into a total state of NOW, simply taking everything I was seeing in with no sense of actual time passing. But as I ask these questions, there's a definite shift in balance, a sense of vertigo flashes past and is gone.

Then I'm suddenly back in my body. One moment I'm in space with these bizarre creatures everywhere and a freakin' timeline of my life laid out before me, and the next I'm back inside my shell, still very high and unable to move but conscious of the skin between my bones and the bedspread beneath me. Kelly and I both slowly start to move at almost the same moment, gaining control over our limbs once again, sitting up in the bed and staring groggily at each another.

"What the fuck was that?" I gasp. I might sound upset, but it's excitement, not anxiety that forces my words out in an explosion of breath. Kelly shakes her head, still fogged by the drug. I on the other hand am only immobilized for a few minutes. As soon as I am able, I reach for the box of vials and set us each up another shot, and off we go again.

Three or four times in the span of about two hours we do this, mainlining 30 mils of pure liquid Ketamine each time, then rushing off to wherever it is that the drug takes us.

Because I am forever convinced that the drug definitely did take us somewhere, or at least showed us somewhere, as near as I can tell another dimension entirely. Whatever creatures I was seeing appeared to be aware of my being there, seemingly reacting to my presence. While I can remember these basic events, I know there is a lot more even that I cannot remember clearly but that I am still aware of, fleeting images which occasionally appear in my dreams.

That was the night I decided that there really is still magick in the world, magick that the Rush Limbaughs and the George W. Bushes and the Dick Cheneys and John Ashcrofts and Gen. Barry McCaffreys and Rand Beers and Mel and Betty Semblers and all the other prohibitionists and moralists and greed-headed fear-mongering warpigs of the world want to stamp out and deny to the rest of us. There's a lot more to the universe that these types don't want people like me and the rest of us too to know and access, a lot more knowledge accessed by the use of substances natural and synthetic both, substances which are decreed sinful and banned but the use of which can and does often lead to gnosis, or at least a new awareness and understanding of just how much we really don't know about the reality around us—and how false the reality the prohibitionists are pushing really is. Drugs might not be *the* way to attain or access this magick, but sometimes they sure as hell can do the trick.

Appendix C—
Drug War Online Resources

Education and Reform

http://www.drugwar.com
DrugWar.com

http://www.efsdp.org/
Educators For Sensible Drug Policy (EFSDP)

http://www.ssdp.org
Students for Sensible Drug Policy

http://www.druglibrary.org
DRCNet Online Library of Drug Policy

http://www.narcoterror.org/
Crime, Drug Prohibition and Terrorism: An Inevitable Convergence

http://www.csdp.org
Common Sense for Drug Policy

http://www.cjpf.org
Criminal Justice Policy Foundation

http://www.serendipity.li/wod.html
Prohibition: The So-Called War on Drugs

http://stopthedrugwar.org
Stop the Drug War

http://www.november.org
The November Coalition

http://www.norml.org
NORML—National Organization for the Reform of Marijuana Laws

http://www.mpp.org
Marijuana Policy Project

http://www.cannabisnews.com
Cannabis News

http://www.leap.cc/
Law Enforcement Against Prohibition

Prohibitionist Websites

http://www.whitehousedrugpolicy.gov/
Office of National Drug Control Policy

http://www.mediacampaign.org/
National Youth Anti-Drug Media Campaign

http://www.dea.gov
The Drug Enforcement Administration

http://www.drugfreeamerica.org
The Partnership for a Drug-Free America

http://www.druguse.com/
Drug Use

General Drug Information

http://www.druglibrary.org/schaffer/
Schaffer Library of Drug Policy

http://www.erowid.org/
The Vaults of Erowid
Documenting the complex relationship between humans and psychoactives

http://www.MAPS.org
Multidisciplinary Association of Psychedelic Studies

Drug Conspiracy

http://www.ciadrugs.com/
CIA Drugs

http://www.copvcia.com/
From the Wilderness Publications

Article Histories

I: Know You're Right

1— "Imagining a Post-Prohibition World" by Phil Smith was written especially for this volume.

2— "Chemical Bigotry" by Mary Jane Borden originally appeared in the *Columbus Free Press*, Wednesday, April 10, 2002.

3— "On Cognitive Liberty" by Richard Glen Boire was originally published in the *Journal of Cognitive Liberties*, a publication of the Center for Cognitive Liberty & Ethics, January, 2000.

4— "In the DEA's Line of Fire: Ayahuasca—Visionary Vine of the Amazon" by Peter Gorman was written especially for this volume.

5— "Is All Use Abuse" by Craig Morris was written especially for this volume.

6— "The Last Word on Drugs" by Jules Siegel was written especially for this volume.

II: The Incarceration of a Nation: Drug Enforcement and Prohibition

7— "Nixon Tapes Pot Shocker" by Mike Gray was originally published by United Press International (Wire), April 30, 2002.

8— "Prohibition is Treason" by Dan Russell is partly original work written especially for this volume, and partly culled, in abbreviated and revised form, from his book *Drug War: Covert Money, Power, and Policy* (Kalyx.com 1999/2000).

9— "Where Has All the Acid Gone" by Ryan Grim was originally published by *High Times* online at www.420.com, March 24, 2004.

10— "The Gang that Couldn't Grow Straight" by Michael Simmons originally appeared in *Penthouse*, October 2001, and has been updated for this volume.

11— "Tales of a Recovering Drug Warrior" by Eric Sterling was written especially for this volume.

12— "Kicking Out the Demons by Humanizing the Experience- an Interview with Anthony Papa" by Preston Peet was originally published online at DrugWar.com, May 1, 2002, and was reprinted in *Criminal Justice 03/04*, edited by Joseph L. Victor and Joanne Naughton, published by McGraw-Hill/Dushkin, 2003.

13— "Frying Pans and Fires: Forcible Medication, Medical Marijuana, and the Logic of Control" by Heidi Lypps was written especially for this volume.

14— "End Prohibition Now" by Jack Cole is a conglomeration of various speeches, including a presentation to European Parliament in Brussels, Belgium on October 16, 2002, and original writing. It is published in this form for the first time in this volume.

15— "Perceptions of Race, Class, and America's War on Drugs" by Clifford Wallace Thornton was written especially for this volume.

16— "An End to Marijuana Prohibition" by Ethan A. Nadelmann was originally published in the National Review, July 12, 2004.

III: Reform and Politics

17— "Rainbow Farm and Beyond: The Green Panthers Prepare for Civil War" by Cletus Nelson was written especially for this volume.

18— "A War on Sanity" by Paul Campos was originally published in the Naples *Daily News*, December 3, 2003.

19— "Marijuana Will Never Be Legal as Long as Most Pot-Smokers Are Apathetic Airheads" by Steven Wishnia was written especially for this volume.

20— "Seeking Peace in the War on Drugs" by Ethan Nadelmann was originally published in the *Utne Reader* on September 1, 2001, and is adapted from a talk given at the New York Open Center and reprinted in "Lapis: The Inner Meaning of Contemporary Life" (Spring 2001), published by the New York Open Center.

21— "The D.A.R.E. Generation vs. the H.E.A." by Abby Bair was written especially for this volume.

22— "Medical Marijuana Mom: A Maryland Patient Tells Her Story" by Erin Hildebrandt was originally published online by *High Times*, September 2, 2003.

23—"Strategizing to Beat State Drug-Reform Initiatives in the U.S. Capitol - Yeah, the One with the Dome" by Daniel Forbes was originally published in different form as a report entitled The Governor's Sub-Rosa Plot to Subvert an Election in Ohio, for the Washington DC based Institute for Policy Studies, May 30, 2002. It is published here in revised and updated form.

IV: War on Foreign Shores

24— "Who Takes Responsibility for Thailand's Bloody Drug War 'Victory'" by Preston Peet was originally published in *High Times* magazine, April 2004, with the update published in *High Times* magazine, August 2004.

25— "Drugs, Oil, and War: Preface" by Peter Dale Scott is the forward to his book, *Drugs, Oil, and War: The United States in Afghanistan, Colombia and Indochina*, published by Rowman & Littlefield in March, 2003.

26— "Hashish and the War on Terror—Drugs in Uniform" by Ron Jacobs was originally published at CounterPunch.org, January 6, 2004.

27— "Afghanistan: Drug War Yields to Terror War as Rumsfeld Glad-Hands Drug Dealing Warlords" by Phil Smith was originally published online in *Drug War Chronicle* (formerly the Drug Reform Coordination Network's *Week Online),* issue #316, December 19, 2003.

28— "Plan Colombia: The Pentagon's Shell Game" by Peter Gorman was originally published in different form in the *Fort Worth Weekly*, March 13-19, 2003," and has been extensively updated with the sidebar published here for the first time.

29—"Between Dyncorp and the A.U.C." by Bill Weinberg was originally published in Weinberg's WWIII Report (http://www.ww3report.com), August 27, 2003.

V: Drug War Economics

30— "US Cocaine 'Lord' Faces Challenge; Monopoly Game" by Cynthia Cotts originally appeared in the *National Law Journal* (New York Law Publishing Company, September 2, 1996). The 2004 postscript was added by the author especially for this volume.

31— "America's Heroin Crisis, Colombian Heroin and How We Can Improve Plan Colombia—Government Reform Committee, US House of Representatives, December 12, 2002" was witnessed and transcribed by Sanho Tree. A portion of Tree's transcription was first published in *Sojourners* magazine, May-June 2003, and Tree's entire transcription is published in this volume for the first time.

32— "Narco Dollars for Beginners" by Catherine Austin Fitts was originally edited and published at Narconews.com, October 24, 2001.

33— "Can you tell me how you are going to save the [poppy seed] bagel? *Hemp Industries Association v. the Drug Enforcement Administration*" by Adam Eidinger and Zoe Mitchell was written especially for this volume.

VI: Facts and Propaganda

34— "Exaggerating the Risks of MDMA to Justify a Prohibitionist Policy" by Rick Doblin was originally published in *Entheogen Review*, Autumnal Equinox 2003 issue, Vol. XII, Number 3, Pages 77-81.

35— "An Anatomy of Failure: The Drugs-and-Terror Ad Campaign," by Paul Armentano was originally published in *Freedom Daily*, a monthly journal published by the Future of Freedom Foundation in Fairfax, Virginia, in October 2003.

36— "White Lines: Sugar, How Sweet it Ain't" by Mickey Z. was written especially for this volume.

37— "Beyond Health and Safety – A hard look at *really* preventing drug abuse" by Theo Rosenfeld was written especially for this volume.

38— "Marijuana vs. Cigarettes" by Paul Krassner was written especially for this volume.

39— "A Brief History of the War on Drugs" by Valerie Vande Panne was written especially for this volume.

40— "Oliver North: Still in Denial" by Preston Peet was written especially for this volume.

41— "How Rock 'n' Roll Fell Out of Love With Drugs" by Alan Travis and Sally James Gregory was originally published in the *Guardian*, October 27, 2003.

VII: For Medicinal Use

42— "Does Treatment Work" by Lonny Shavelson was originally published as the afterward in *Hooked: Five Addicts Challenge Our Misguided Drug Rehab System*, published by The New Press, New York, 2001.

43— "Ten Years of Therapy in One Night" by Daniel Pinchbeck was originally published in the London *Guardian*, September 20, 2003.

44— "Reckless Disregard" by Jay Cavanaugh was originally published at the American Alliance for Medical Cannabis website, January 20, 2003, and was revised, updated and expanded especially for this volume.

45— "Clinton, Freud, and Clinical Cannabis" by Ethan Russo was originally published in *Medical Cannabis Quarterly*, Vol. 1, 1999.

46— "No Relief in Sight" by Jacob Sullum was originally published in *Reason*, January 1997.

47— "Protecting Children—America's Real Drug Abuse Epidemic" by Sharon Secor was written especially for this volume.

48— "Czar Walter's STAND on Methadone" by Doug McVay was written especially for this volume.

49— "Stanislav Grof interviewing Dr. Albert Hofmann at the Esalen Institute in Big Sur, California, 1984" by Stanislov Grof was originally published in the Multidisciplinary Association for Psychedelic Studies newsletter, February, 2001.

50— "Haircut: Trippin' Through the Day in a Life" by Preston Peet was originally written for the unpublished manuscript *Something in the Way*.

51— "Ketamine Dream—or Reality?" by Preston Peet was originally written for the unpublished manuscript *Something in the Way*.

Contributor Bios

Paul Armentano is the Senior Policy Analyst for NORML and the NORML Foundation in Washington, DC. His writing has appeared in dozens of magazines and newspapers, including the *Washington Post*, *Congressional Quarterly*, *Penthouse* magazine, and *Reason*, and several of his articles have been syndicated nationally by Universal Press International (UPI). Mr. Armentano has also contributed to numerous anthologies, including *Drug Abuse: Opposing Viewpoints* (Greenhaven Press, 1999), *You Are Being Lied To: The Disinformation Guide to Media Distortion, Historical Whitewashes and Cultural Myths* (The Disinformation Company, 2001), *Busted: Stone Cowboys, Narco-Lords and Washington's War on Drugs* (Thunder's Mouth Press/Nation Books, 2002), and *The New Prohibition: Voices of Dissent Challenge the Drug War* (Accurate Press, 2004).

Abby Bair earned a B.A. in Legal Communication from Ohio University in 2002. After graduation, she was awarded a fellowship through the Ohio Legislative Service Commission as a policy and communications assistant to the Ohio Senate Democratic Caucus. She has served Students for Sensible Drug Policy for more than four years, first leading Ohio University SSDP and later serving as the vice-chair of the Board of Directors. Ms. Bair currently works with SSDP as National Outreach Coordinator.

Richard Glen Boire, Esq. is a multimedia experimenter, best known for inventing truth decoys. He is also a director of the Center for Cognitive Liberty & Ethics and serves as its chief legal counsel. He received his Doctorate of Jurisprudence from the University of California, Berkeley in 1990.

Mary Jane Borden is a writer, artist, and activist in drug policy reform from Westerville, Ohio, the home of prohibition in the early part of the last century. She brings a unique perspective to the reform issue, one developed through thirty years of interest in the subject, nine years as a pharmaceutical company market research analyst, and three years as a full time drug policy reform activist. Borden holds a Bachelor of Arts degree from Otterbein College and a Masters in Business Administration from the University of Dayton. She is a past president of the Columbus Chapter of Women in Communications and its subsidiary, the Columbus Matrix Foundation. In 2000, she earned the Accredited in Public Relations (APR) certification from the Public Relations Society of America. Borden worked for nine years at Adria Laboratories, most in the capacity of Senior Analyst, before starting her graphic design business, which she has operated for ten years. She now serves as Director of Development for DrugSense, a non-profit Web-based organization that hosts many of the most popular drug policy Web sites in the world. She is also a co-founder of the Ohio Patient Network and currently serves as its Treasurer and Director of Public Relations.

Paul Campos is a law professor at the University of Colorado.

Jay R. Cavanaugh, Ph.D. served as a gubernatorial appointee to the California Board of Pharmacy from 1980-90. During his tenure he helped create and supervise the Board's enforcement program to stem the flood of pharmaceutical sedatives and narcotics to the black market. Cavanaugh received his baccalaureate degree in Biology from California State University, Northridge and his doctorate in Biological Chemistry from Tulane University.

Jack A. Cole is the executive director of Law Enforcement Against Prohibition, (LEAP). A retired New Jersey State Police detective lieutenant, Cole worked twelve years as an undercover narcotics officer. His investigations included international "billion-dollar" drug trafficking organizations. Cole ended his undercover career living nearly two years in Boston, posing as a fugitive murderer and drug dealer, while tracking members of a terrorist organization that robbed banks, planted bombs and ultimately murdered a New Jersey State Trooper. Cole dealt with the emotional residue left from his participation in the unjust war on drugs by working to reform current drug policy. He is writing his dissertation for the Public Policy Ph.D. Program at the University of Massachusetts. Cole focuses on issues of race and gender bias, brutality and corruption in law enforcement. He believes ending drug prohibition will go a long way toward correcting those problems. A sought after national and international lecturer, Cole has presented at over 250 venues around the world in just 18 months time.

Cynthia Cotts writes Press Clips, a weekly media column, for the *Village Voice*. Before joining the *Voice* in 1998, she was a staff reporter for the *National Law Journal* and a researcher for the *New Yorker* and *Vanity Fair*. She has also written for the *Nation*, *Rolling Stone*, *Lingua Franca*, *Salon*, *Slate*, *Feed*, the *New York Observer*, *Book Forum* and *Reason*. Cotts attended Yale Law School on a Knight Foundation fellowship for journalists and has a bachelors degree from Oberlin College.

Rick Doblin, Ph.D. is the founder (in 1986) and president of MAPS. Doblin's dissertation (Public Policy, Harvard's Kennedy School of Government) was on "The Regulation of the Medical Use of Psychedelics and Marijuana." His master's thesis at Harvard University focused on the attitudes and experiences of oncologists concerning the medical use of marijuana. His undergraduate thesis, at New College of Florida, was a twenty-five year follow-up to the classic Good Friday Experiment which evaluated the potential of psychedelic drugs to catalyze religious experiences. Doblin has also studied with Dr. Stan Grof and was in the first group to become certified as holotropic breathwork practitioners. His professional goal is to help develop legal contexts for the beneficial uses of psychedelics and marijuana, primarily as prescription medicines but also for personal growth for otherwise "healthy" people, and to also become a legally licensed psychedelic therapist. He currently resides in Boston with his wife and three young children.

Adam Eidinger is the Founder of the Mintwood Media Collective and is dedicated to ending the War on Drugs. Adam has organized campaigns to increase public awareness of the DEA ban on hemp food, including orchestrating two hemp food taste tests at DEA offices around the country. In 2002, he ran for the office of US "Shadow" Representative for DC on the DC Statehood Green Party ticket.

Catherine Austin Fitts is the President of Solari, Inc., a founding member of UnAnsweredQuestions.org and member of the Advisory Board of Sanders Research Associates. Ms. Fitts is former Assistant Secretary of Housing-Federal Housing Commissioner in Bush I and a former managing director and member of the board of directors of Dillon Read & Co. Inc.

Daniel Forbes has long covered drug policy and politics generally. He testified before both the U.S. Senate and the House of Representatives at two of the four congressional hearings his award-winning journalism caused and helped to curtail a covert federal propaganda program. He's published in *Slate*, *MSNBC*, *Salon*, the *Village Voice*, *Rolling Stone*, *Reason*, the *Nation.com*, *TomPaine.com*, *Newsday*, and *Alternet*. His disclosure in *Salon* proved that the White House Office of National Drug Control Policy provided hundreds of thousands of dollars of financial incentives per episode to the TV networks for government-dictated anti-drug scripts. The networks' total haul was over $22 million, and government consultants promulgated specific changes in specific shows. More than 100 articles and broadcasts followed, including

next-day, front-page coverage nationwide and editorials condemning the practice. His work has won awards from a chapter of the Society of Professional Journalists, the Columbia Graduate School of Journalism/Online News Association and the Lindesmith Center.

Peter Gorman is a former executive editor and Editor-in-Chief of *High Times* magazine, where he spent fifteen years investigating hard news related to the War on Drugs. In addition to his writing, which has also been featured in *Playboy*, *Geo*, *Omni* and a host of other major publications, Peter Gorman has spent a considerable amount of time in the jungles of Peru, studying ayahuasca with his old friend, the curandero Julio Jerena. He can be reached at peterg9@hotmail.com.

Mike Gray, like several other Hollywood realists, comes from a documentary film background. His Chicago-based Film Group chronicled the political violence of the 1960s, including the award-winning feature documentaries, *American Revolution II*, and *The Murder of Fred Hampton*. After moving to Hollywood in 1973, Gray began writing the screenplay that was to become the eerily prophetic *China Syndrome*. His years of research were confirmed less than two weeks after the movie's release by the accident at Three Mile Island. After six years of research and writing, Gray's seminal book, *Drug Crazy: How We Got Into This Mess and How We Can Get Out* (Random House, 1998) has already had a major impact on the drug war debate. The paperback was released in the spring of 2000. Gray's latest book, *The Death Game: Capital Punishment and the Luck of the Draw*, has just been released by Common Courage Press. Gray lives in Los Angeles with his wife, Carol, a reporter for public radio. Their son, Lucas, is an animator for *The Simpsons*.

Sally James Gregory is a contributor to the *Guardian*.

Ryan Grim is a regular contributor to the *Brooklyn Rail*, as well as a columnist for *SpinSheet* magazine. He is a resident poetry instructor for DC Writers Corps, and a self-avowed Phishhead. He has been unable to find any doses for a couple years now. He lives in Washington, DC, and has a Master's Degree in Public Policy, as does pretty much everyone else in the city.

Stanislav Grof, M.D. is a psychiatrist with almost fifty years of experience in research of non-ordinary states of consciousness. In the past, he was Principal Investigator in a psychedelic research program at the Psychiatric Research Institute in Prague, Czechoslovakia, Chief of Psychiatric Research at the Maryland Psychiatric Research Center, Assistant Professor of Psychiatry at the Johns Hopkins University in Baltimore, Maryland, and Scholar-in-Residence at the Esalen Institute in Big Sur, California. Among his publications are over 100 papers in professional journals and the books *Realms of the Human Unconscious*; *The Human Encounter with Death* (with Joan Halifax); *LSD Psychotherapy*; *The Adventure of Self-Discovery*; *Beyond the Brain*; *Books of the Dead*; *The*

Holotropic Mind; The Cosmic Game; The Transpersonal Vision; The Consciousness Revolution (with Ervin Laszlo and Peter Russell); *Psychology of the Future; Beyond Death*; and *The Stormy Search for the Self* (the last two with Christina Grof). He also edited the books *Ancient Wisdom and Modern Science; Consciousness Evolution and Human Survival*; and *Spiritual Emergency* (the last with Christina Grof).

Erin Hildebrandt is a small town wife and mom of five. In 2003 she began speaking out and writing about living with Crohn's Disease and needing medical marijuana. She testified before Maryland State House and Senate committees, has been featured in the *Baltimore Sun* and *Washington Post*, and has been quoted many times in local and national press. She has been interviewed on radio and TV news broadcasts, including NBC affiliate WBAL in Baltimore. In addition to an Op-ed in the *Baltimore Sun* and a web article in *High Times*, Erin has had numerous letters to editors published in papers like *Newsday*, the *Denver Post*, and Canada's *National Post*.

Ron Jacobs grew up as a military brat, following his father to colonial outposts around the globe. He became involved in antiwar and anti-imperialist activities in 1968 when his father went to Vietnam. He is the author of *The Way the Wind Blew: A History of the Weather Underground* and writes for a number of newspapers and periodicals. He now lives in Burlington, Vermont.

Paul Krassner is an award-winning political satirist. His latest album, *The Zen Bastard Rides Again*, will be released in September, 2004. When *People* magazine called him "Father of the underground press," he immediately demanded a paternity test. He published *The Realist* from 1958-1974, then reincarnated it as a newsletter from 1985-2001. "The taboos may have changed," he wrote, "but irreverence is still our only sacred cow." He is a columnist for *High Times* and *New York Press*, and the author of *Murder At the Conspiracy Convention and Other American Absurdities*, with an introduction by George Carlin. His Web site is at www.paulkrassner.com.

Heidi Lypps cut her teeth on drug policy and civil liberties issues at the Center for Cognitive Liberty & Ethics. An historian by training, she specializes in the history of the brain and thought, as well as crime and punishment. She knows that contemporary American drug policy is just a new version of the same old social control people have been fighting since, like, 1300 AD.

Doug McVay is a policy researcher and analyst living near Washington, DC. He is the editor of *Drug War Facts* and webmaster for DrugWarFacts.org and CommonSenseDrugPolicy.org. Doug has been active in drug policy reform efforts since the mid-1980s. He has worked for Common Sense for Drug Policy, NORML, and the Oregon Marijuana Initiative/Yes On 5 campaign, and is also a co-founder of the Cannabis Action Network.

Zoe Mitchell is best known for her intensive campaigns for social justice, media democracy, and liberty. She is a Partner at the Mintwood Media Collective, a worker-owned and operated public relations firm, and she is dedicated to ending the War on Drugs. With Adam Eidinger, she has worked with Vote Hemp, the International Anti-Prohibitionist League, the Drug Reform Coordination Network, Students for Sensible Drug Policy, Americans for Safe Access, and author Jacob Sullum. Zoe writes a blog called *A Ten, A Five and Five Ones* at http://zoemitchell.com.

Craig Morris is a lecturer in the Sociology Department at the University of Greenwich in London, England. He teaches numerous courses including Drugs and Drug Use in Society. His research interests are illicit drug use and language as a social practice. He came to contribute to this volume by way of an on-line acquaintance with editor Preston Peet, which has facilitated the discussion of many issues. They have yet to meet in the "real" world.

Ethan A. Nadelmann directs the Drug Policy Alliance (www.drugpolicy.org), the country's leading drug policy reform organization. He's the author of *Cops Across Borders: The Internationalization of US Criminal Law Enforcement.*

Cletus Nelson is a Los Angeles-based freelance writer who covers unconventional political movements, hidden history, conspiracy, and the war on drugs. His work has appeared in *EYE, Counterpunch, Signum, PANIK*, and several other publications. He is currently co-authoring a social history of the MC5.

Preston Peet is a New York City-based writer, editor, musician, actor, DJ, activist, and adventurer. Editor of *Under the Influence—the Disinformation Guide to Drugs*, Preston is a regular contributor to *High Times* magazine and website, the editor of the controversial website DrugWar.com and moderator of the DrugWar.com email list, a columnist for New York City's premier punk rock newspaper, The *New York Waste*, and has published in a variety of publications both in print and on-line, including *Media Bypass; Criminal Justice 03/04; 09/11 8:48AM—Documenting America's Greatest Disaster*; and *Alternet*. Besides publishing over 60 articles at the popular Disinformation website (www.disinfo.com), he has articles in The Disinformation Company's anthologies, *You Are Being Lied To* and *Everything You Know Is Wrong*. He lives in Manhattan with Vanessa (his other half) and ten rescued cats, and has been known to smoke the occasional joint or three. "It's time to end the War on Some Drugs and Users."

Theo Rosenfeld has developed a number of innovative peer–based health promotion and harm reduction programs with illicit drug users. Currently, through his company, Pala Community Development, he offers services as a trainer, researcher, and consultant. For more information, please see www.pala.ca.

Dan Russell, a 1970 graduate of the City University of New York, is the owner of Kalyx.com, a chain of internet retail stores. He is also the author of two well-reviewed books, *Shamanism and the Drug Propaganda* and *Drug War*, both available on Amazon.

Ethan Russo, M.D. is a clinical child/adult neurologist, and faculty member at University of Washington, and University of Montana. He is the author of *Handbook of Psychotropic Herbs*, editor-in-chief of *Journal of Cannabis Therapeutics*, and editor of three books, *Cannabis and Cannabinoids, Cannabis Therapeutics in HIV/AIDS*, and *Women and Cannabis*.

Sharon L. Secor is a freelance writer living in upstate New York. Her journey into freelance writing was inspired by Christine de Pisan (1364-1429), a widow and writer of social commentary who, in addition to being one of France's earliest well-known female authors, was able to support her children through her writing. Secor read her first college level psychology textbook in the fourth grade, along with the feminist literature of the era, beginning what has proved to be a lifelong passion for the humanities and social sciences. Ms. Secor is working towards completing a double major, in Journalism and Spanish—preparation for writing about social and economic issues in Latin America as influenced by increased industrialization and the expanding global marketplace. She plans to write for both English and Spanish language markets.

Lonny Shavelson is a writer, photojournalist, and physician whose articles and photographs have appeared in numerous publications: *New York Times, TIME, People, Family Circle, Hippocrates* (now *Health*), *Lear's, Mother Jones, Der Spiegel, Newsweek, Los Angeles Times*, and the Sunday newspaper magazines of the *San Francisco Examiner, San Francisco Chronicle, Baltimore Sun, Cleveland Plain Dealer*, and others. Shavelson has researched, written, and photographed stories about health care in the midst of war in Central America; needle exchange programs for drug addicts in Europe; people with mental illness in the US; sharecropping and child labor in the fields of California; Southeast Asian and Central American refugees in the US; the recruiting methods of young skinhead Nazis; TV evangelists vs. gays in San Francisco; towns where families have been made ill by the effects of hazardous wastes; people with terminal illnesses who are contemplating assisted suicide; drug addicts in rehab; and even about people who seek love through newspaper ads. Shavelson is the author of five books: *Personal Ad Portraits* (De Novo Press, 1983), *I'm Not Crazy, I Just Lost My Glasses* (De Novo Press, 1986), *Toxic Nation: The Fight To Save Our Communities From Chemical Contamination*, co-authored with Fred Setterberg (John Wiley & Sons, 1993), *A Chosen Death: The Dying Confront Assisted Suicide* (Simon & Schuster, 1995), and *Hooked: Five Addicts Challenge Our Misguided Drug Rehab System* (The New Press, 2001).

Jules Siegel is a writer and graphic designer whose work has appeared over the years in *Playboy, Best American Short Stories* and many other publications, most recently in Library of America's *Writing Los Angeles*. He contributes book reviews to the *San Francisco Chronicle*, and administers *Newsroom-l*, an email discussion list for journalists.

Michael Simmons is a longtime feature writer for the *L.A. Weekly*, Chief Left Coast Correspondent for *High Times*, former editor of *National Lampoon* and contributor to the *L.A. Times, Rolling Stone, Penthouse*, the *Progressive, Crawdaddy*, and many others. Also a working musician, he was named "The Father of Country Punk" by *Creem* magazine.

Phillip S. Smith is editor of the *Drug War Chronicle*, the weekly web-based drug policy newsletter published by the Drug Reform Coordination Network (www.drcnet.org). He has had an interest in drug policy since his first arrest on drug charges in 1974. He beat that rap, but later spent almost three years in prison for a half-pound of marijuana. Holder of a post-graduate degree from the Institute of Latin American Studies at the University of Texas at Austin, Smith has been writing about Latin America, US drug policy, and criminal justice matters for the past twenty years, usually in obscure left-wing publications. He currently resides in Nelson, British Columbia.

Eric E. Sterling, President of the Criminal Justice Policy Foundation since 1989, was counsel to the US House of Representatives from 1979 to 1989. He is on the boards of Families Against Mandatory Minimums, the Voluntary Committee of Lawyers, the Partnership for Responsible Drug Information, the Marijuana Policy Project, the Interfaith Drug Policy Initiative, Students for Sensible Drug Policy, and is an advisor to the Alliance of Reform Organizations, Drug Reform Coordination Network, Law Enforcement Against Prohibition, and the Flex Your Rights Foundation.

Clifford Wallace Thornton, called "America's foremost anti-Drug War African American activist" by the Amherst College online newspaper (Feb 2003), is founder of Efficacy, a non-profit organization that has been concentrating efforts on drug policy reform for five years. In the last three years Mr. Thornton has spoken to over 150,000 people in some 450 venues all over the US and in Canada. Mr. Thornton has completed over 400 radio shows on the topic of drug policy reform. Efficacy journeyed to New Zealand for eleven weeks in early 2004 on a speaking and organizing tour. Mr. Thornton's *Race, Class and the Drug War* presentations receive rave reviews from every corner of the US, New Zealand, and Canada.

Alan Travis is a contributor to the *Guardian*.

Sanho Tree is a Fellow and Director of the Drug Policy Project at the Institute for Policy Studies. A former military and diplomatic historian, his current work focuses on US involvement in the conflict in Colombia. He was recently featured in the ABC/John Stossel documentary on the drug war, which aired in July 2002, and appeared on *Politically Incorrect* in April of that year. He collaborated with Dr. Gar Alperovitz on *The Decision to Use the Atomic Bomb and the Architecture of an American Myth* (Knopf, 1995). Mr. Tree was associate editor of *Covert Action Quarterly*, an award-winning magazine of investigative journalism and worked at the International Human Rights Law Group in the 1980s.

Valerie Vande Panne's forefathers fought the British in the Revolutionary War, and each other in the Civil War. Her mother Charisse is a writer; her father David taught high school US history and government. Valerie Vande Panne spent her childhood in Greenville, Michigan. She left school early, motivated by miseducation and fluorescent lights. At the time of this writing, she lives in the City of New York, with her pit bull, Wax.

Bill Weinberg is an award-winning journalist and editor of the on-line weekly *World War 3 Report* (WW3Report.com). He is the author of *Homage to Chiapas: The New Indigenous Struggles in Mexico* (Verso 2000) and *War on the Land: Ecology and Politics in Central America* (Zed 1991). He also co-hosts the anarchist-oriented Moorish Orthodox Radio Crusade (Tuesdays at midnight on WBAI-NY, 99.5 FM). He is currently working on a book about Plan Colombia and indigenous resistance movements in the Andes.

Steven Wishnia is author of *The Cannabis Companion* (The Running Press); the short-story set *Exit 25 Utopia* (The Imaginary Press); and the forthcoming *Invincible Coney Island*, a travel-essay collection. He was formerly news editor at *High Times*, and his work has appeared in the *Village Voice*, the *Nation*, the *Progressive*, *Punk Planet*, and *In These Times*. He was also the bassist in the False Prophets, New York's leading leftist-punk band of the 1980s, whose music is collected on *Blind Roaches and Fat Vultures: Phantasmagoric Beasts of the Reagan Era* (Alternative Tentacles). He now plays with Gateria, as well as composing and performing music for slide shows by artists Mac McGill and Seth Tobocman. He lives in New York City.

Mickey Z. is a self-educated author and social commentator. His books include *Saving Private Power: The Hidden History of "The Good War," The Murdering of My Years: Artists and Activists Making Ends Meet* (both from Soft Skull Press), *Seven Deadly Spins: Exposing the Lies Behind US War Propaganda* (Common Courage Press), and *A Gigantic Mistake: Articles and Essays for Your Intellectual Self-Defense* (Library Empyreal). In addition, he has articles in three other anthologies: *You Are Being Lied To, Everything You Know is Wrong*, and *Abuse Your Illusions*. Mickey is a vegan, a poet, and a martial artist, and lives in Astoria, NY with his wife, Michele. He can be found on the Web at www.mickeyz.net.